TOURISM

TOURISM ▸ PRINCIPLES
Eighth Edition
PRACTICES
PHILOSOPHIES

Charles R. Goeldner
University of Colorado

J. R. Brent Ritchie
University of Calgary

Robert W. McIntosh
Emeritus, Michigan State University

John Wiley & Sons, Inc.
New York / Chichester / Weinheim / Brisbane / Singapore / Toronto

Copyright © 2000 by John Wiley & Sons, Inc. All rights reserved.

Published simultaneously in Canada.

This publication is designed to provide accurate and authoritative information in regard to the subject matter covered. It is sold with the understanding that the publisher is not engaged in rendering professional services. If professional advice or other expert assistance is required, the services of a competent professional person should be sought.

Library of Congress Cataloging-in-Publication Data:

Goeldner, Charles R.
  Tourism: principles, practices, philosophies / Charles R. Goeldner, J. R. Brent Ritchie, Robert W. McIntosh. —8th ed.
    p.   cm.
  Robert W. McIntosh's name appeared first on the 7th ed.
  Includes bibliographical references.
  ISBN 0-471-32210-5 (cloth : alk. paper)
  1. Tourism.   I. Ritchie, J. R. Brent.   II. McIntosh, Robert Woodrow, 1917– .   III. Title.
  G155.A1G6   1999
  338.4′791—dc21   99-24944

Printed in the United States of America.

10 9 8 7 6 5 4 3 2 1

DEDICATION

This book is dedicated to Robert W. McIntosh, Distinguished Professor of Tourism Emeritus, Michigan State University (MSU)—a pioneer in tourism education. To our knowledge, he was the first person in the United States to hold the title Professor of Tourism. Bob is retired, but he is still active and provides guidance and input on critical issues. He continues to remain an inspiration to all of us.

McIntosh's distinguished career at Michigan State University began in January 1946 as an extension specialist in the Tourist and Resort Service. He went on to develop the travel and tourism curriculum in the School of Hotel Restaurant and Institutional Management.

Bob served as a consultant to the School of Travel Industry Management at the University of Hawaii and was the school's first professor of hotel management and tourism (on a visiting basis).

Professor McIntosh was the author of the first introductory college textbook on tourism (*Tourism: Principles, Practices, Philosophies*), which was published in 1971. This text is the eighth edition of that pioneering work. Bob has written many other books, including *Uniform Classification of Accounts for Motels and Motor Hotels, Motel Management Training, Management Manual for Motor Hotels, Motel Planning and Business Management, Travel Agency Business Management, Passenger Traffic Management, Marketing and Sales Management, International Travel and Tourism, Travel Agency Business Management, Up With Profits, Tourism and the Hospitality Industry,* and *Employee Management Standards*. In addition, he has published 9 book chapters, 65 journal articles, 38 bulletins for the MSU Extension Service, and 4 special reports.

Bob has received many richly deserved honors. He was the 1962 recipient of the MSU Hotel Association Faculty Award and has been presented with distinguished service awards by the American Hotel and Motel Association, the Motel Association of America, Superior Motels, Inc., the Institute of Certified Travel Agents, the West Michigan Tourist Association, and the U.S. Travel Service of the Department of Commerce. He is a fellow of the Institute of Certified Travel Agents, an honorary life member of the Michigan Motel and Resort Association, and winner of the Life Achievement Award of the Society of Travel and Tourism Educators.

Robert McIntosh provided a role model for many people who have passed through his sphere of influence. Both of the undersigned have been blessed by his influence. We thank you for your influence and guidance.

Charles R. Goeldner
J. R. Brent Ritchie

PREFACE

Tourism can be defined as the science, art, and business of attracting visitors, transporting them, accommodating them, and graciously catering to their needs and wants.

In recent years, virtually every country throughout the world has taken steps to increase its number of visitors. The decrease in the cost of air travel and the development of technological resources such as the Internet have provided new opportunities for countries and individual tourism firms to promote tourism, both within and outside their borders. Political and industrial leaders have almost universally recognized the economic advantages that tourism can bring. However, what these countries have done to make tourism a viable, growing segment of their economy varies widely—from virtually nothing to the creation of superbly organized, highly productive tourism facilities. While the economic benefits of tourism have long been recognized, today greater attention is being paid to its social impact, which can be positive or negative, depending on how tourism is planned and managed.

This book is intended to be used primarily as a textbook for college and university courses in tourism. However, the book also provides valuable information and guidance for chambers of commerce, tourism planning and development organizations, tourism promoters, tourist accommodations and other businesses, transportation carriers, oil and automotive companies, and any other organization that is interested or involved in the movement of people from their homes to vacation or business destinations.

ORGANIZATION AND CONTENT

This book explores major concepts in tourism, what makes tourism possible, and how tourism can become an important factor in the wealth of any nation. It is written in broad, global terms, discussing the principles, practices, and philosophies of tourism that have been found to bring about success. In this eighth edition of *Tourism,* even greater attention has been paid to the global impact of tourism, both economically and socially.

For tourism to be successful, a great variety of components must work together seamlessly to create a positive travel experience. This book is divided into six parts, which examine the various components of tourism, their function, and their significance.

Part 1 provides a broad overview of tourism, with chapters devoted specifically to the global impact of tourism, a history of travel, and career opportunities.

Part 2 looks at the governmental and private-sector organizations that provide services, products, and destinations for travelers. Individual chapters discuss tourist organizations, passenger transportation, lodging and food service providers, travel agents and wholesalers, and tourism attractions.

In Part 3, students learn about travel motivation, travel behavior, and the sociology of tourism.

Part 4 is devoted to tourism planning and a further examination of the components of tourism. A new chapter on formulating tourism policy has been added to this part. Other chapters cover topics such as tourism supply, forecasting demand, the economic impact of tourism, tourism planning, and environmental issues. In light of the growing importance of the environment, a particular effort has been made to explore fully the managerial issues at the tourism/environment interface—a point at which there is much potential for conflict.

Part 5 examines the important fields of tourism research and tourism marketing.

Part 6 looks at projections for tourism into the twenty-first century and suggests how today's industry can prepare itself to accommodate future growth and meet tomorrow's challenges.

FEATURES

To help students better understand and process the information presented, a number of pedagogical features have been integrated into this textbook.

The **Learning Objectives** at the beginning of each chapter alert students to the important concepts that will be covered. The chapter **Introduction** sets the scene and provides some context for what students are about to read. When appropriate, boxes, tables, illustrations, photos, and Internet sites have been included to help illustrate important topics and ideas. The chapter discussion concludes with a written **Summary** to help students reinforce what they have read.

The authors have expanded the number and scope of the **Readings** that follow most chapters. Excerpted from journals, government reports, and industry publications, the readings provide concrete examples of how the concepts discussed in the chapter are being put into practice. The list of **Key Concepts** serves as a valuable checkpoint for understanding the chapter topics. A new directory of **Internet Sites** lists any web sites referred to in the chapter, as well as additional sites to which students can turn for more information.

Three types of exercises have been provided to gauge student understanding of the subject matter. The questions **For Review and Discussion** test student recall of important chapter concepts and include some critical thinking questions. The **Case Problems** present hypothetical situations that require students to apply what they have learned. They can be used for written assignments or as the catalyst for class discussions. New to this edition are a series of **Internet Exercises,** designed to increase students' familiarity with technology by having them visit important travel industry web sites and answer questions based on their investigation.

An *Instructor's Manual* (0-471-35671-9) is available to professors who have adopted this textbook. The *Instructor's Manual* contains teaching suggestions, sample syllabi, test questions and answers, and transparency masters of the artwork.

Powerpoint slides are also available from the publisher's Web site at **http://www.wiley. com/goeldner** for those who have adopted the book.

Instructors also have the option of adopting a package that combines *Tourism,* eighth edition, with **Microsoft™ Encarta™ Virtual Globe '99** (0-471-37964-6). This updated version of Virtual Globe comes on two CD's containing articles, videos, music, photos, and textual information on cultures from around the world, as well as maps, virtual flights, an illustrated glossary, and a place name game.

ACKNOWLEDGMENTS

As this eighth edition goes to press, we celebrate the thousands of students who have already begun their education in travel and tourism with previous editions of this book. We acknowledge their participation through their letters to us and to our publisher.

We are grateful for the help of all of the educators who have contributed to this edition through their constructive comments. They include:

Denis Auger, University of Ottawa

David Baker, Eastern Illinois University

John Bullaro, California Polytechnic State University

Liping Cai, Purdue University

Joseph Chen, Virginia Polytechnic Institute

Larkin Franks, Mount Hood Community College

M. J. Linney, El Paso Community College

Tony Psyck, State University of New York-Morrisville

Robert Robertson, University of New Hampshire

Cheryl Robinson, Miami-Dade Community College

Roberta Sebo, Johnson & Wales University

Patty Silfies, Western Kentucky University

We especially wish to thank Philip L. Pearce, Department of Tourism, James Cook University, Townsville, Queensland, Australia, for his contribution of Chapter 9, "Pleasure Travel Motivation." A special word of thanks must also go to Dr. Richard F. Patterson, Associate Professor of Hotel, Restaurant, and Tourism Management, Western Kentucky University, who developed the Internet Exercises for this textbook.

We also acknowledge the support of the staff at John Wiley & Sons, especially JoAnna Turtletaub, Matt Van Hattem, and Donna Conte. Special recognition must go to Deb Angus at the University of Calgary, who tirelessly prepared the manuscript, artwork, and the Instructor's Manual.

Charles R. Goeldner
University of Colorado

J. R. Brent Ritchie
University of Calgary

CONTENTS

PART THREE
▶ **UNDERSTANDING TRAVEL BEHAVIOR 251**

PART FOUR
▶ TOURISM SUPPLY, DEMAND, POLICY, PLANNING, AND DEVELOPMENT   361

CHAPTER 12 • Tourism Components and Supply   363

CHAPTER 13 • Measuring and Forecasting Demand   395

CHAPTER 14 • Tourism's Economic Impact   411

CHAPTER 15 • Tourism Policy: Structure, Content, and Process   443

CHAPTER 16 • Tourism Planning, Development, and Social Considerations   513

CHAPTER 17 • Tourism and the Environment   543

PART SIX
▶ TOURISM PROSPECTS   675

CHAPTER 20 • Tourism's Future   677

APPENDIX A • Key Travel Industry Contacts   707

APPENDIX B • Some Suggested Information Sources 715

Tourism

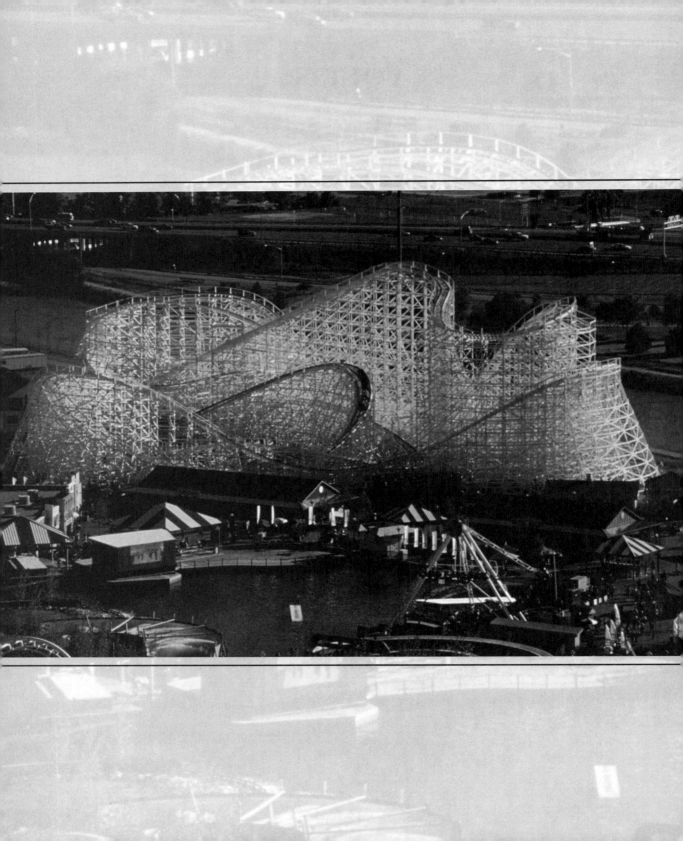

PART 1

TOURISM
OVERVIEW

◀ *At Six Flags Elitch Gardens, families can enjoy music, shows, and exciting roller coaster rides. (Photo courtesy of the Denver Metro Convention and Visitors Bureau.)*

CHAPTER 1

TOURISM IN PERSPECTIVE

- Appreciate how important this industry is to the economy of the world and of many countries.

- Understand what tourism is and its many definitions.

- Examine the various approaches to studying tourism and determine which is of greatest interest to you.

- Learn the components of tourism and tourism management.

- Know the benefits and costs of tourism.

◀ **LEARNING OBJECTIVES**

◀ *A cruise ship navigates the Geirangerfjord in Norway. (Photo courtesy of the Norwegian Tourist Board.)*

5

INTRODUCTION

Bon Voyage!

You are setting off on a voyage to learn about the subject of **tourism.** Assuming that the forecasters and futurists are correct, you are studying the world's largest industry. Tourism is alive with dynamic growth, new activities, new destinations, new technology, new markets, and rapid changes. Record numbers of tourists are traveling the globe, attracted by an increased variety of tour packages, cruises, adventure experiences, and independent itineraries. All of these visitors and the activities they generate change local communities. They have an economic and social impact that cannot be ignored. In today's society, attention must be paid to environmental issues, cultural issues, the way landscapes are created to appeal to tourists, economic issues, and how tourists behave.

The tourism industry is global. It is big business and will continue to grow. Meeting this growth with well-planned environmentally sound development is a challenge for planning all over the world whether it is Bali, Nepal, United States, Australia, Thailand, or Europe. The goal of this chapter and the book is to raise issues, provide frameworks, and generate your thoughtful consideration of the issues and changes facing this complex field as it prepares for the new millennium.

THE STUDY OF TOURISM

Human beings are innately curious concerning the world in which we live. We yearn to know what other places look like—what the people, their culture, the animals and plant life, and landforms may be elsewhere. Today, higher levels of education and the influence of television and other communication media have combined to create in us a much greater awareness of our entire world. We are now in a global economy and our industries must be globally competitive. We must think globally. Material prosperity in many developed countries, with accompanying higher standards of living, has made travel attainable for hundreds of millions of us. Although travel can be undertaken for many reasons, the most common are pleasure, business, and study. In this book we explore the multiplicity of social and economic phenomena that bring about and are created by this vast worldwide industry.

The subject of **travel** is exciting and fascinating. Humanlike beings have been moving from place to place for about 1 million years. Our early ancestors, *Homo erectus*, originated in eastern and southern Africa. But remains of these same forms of early humankind have also been found in China and Java (Indonesia). It has been estimated that migrations of this type took about 15,000 years, but this is a brief span of time in the long history of humanity. Various theories have been proposed regarding the motivation for such amazing journeys. Foremost is that these wanderings were in search of food and to escape from danger. Another theory is that people observed the migrations of birds and wanted to know where the birds came from and where they were going. Recently, in the most dramatic discovery of its kind ever made, the preserved body of a man dubbed the "iceman," who died 5000 years ago, was found in the ice in mountainous northern Italy. Some of the scientists studying his body and accoutrements have concluded that he was returning to his home in what is now Switzerland from a journey to the south of what is now Italy.

Since the times of the wanderings of ancient peoples, we have been traveling in ever-widening patterns about the earth. From the days of such early explorers as Marco Polo, Ibn Battuta, Christopher Columbus, Ferdinand Magellan, and James Cook to the present, there has been a steady growth in travel. In the twentieth century, the invention of the automobile and all-weather roads has brought about unprecedented growth. Following World War II, the invention of the jet airplane, especially the wide-bodied type, and the establishment of global air routes has made possible rapid travel for many millions. Thus national and international travel by air has experienced explosive growth. Luxurious cruise ships, comfortable motor coaches, streamlined passenger trains, and fine hotels, resorts, and motels have provided pleasant transportation and accommodations to visit the many attractions that entice visitors to travel around the globe. The study of tourism covers all these topics and how to handle this growth to achieve sustainable tourism.

ECONOMIC IMPORTANCE

The World Travel and Tourism Council (WTTC) has been measuring the economic impact of travel and tourism since 1991. In 1992 they released their first estimates of the impact of travel and tourism for the world, regions, and OECD countries indicating that travel and tourism is one of the world's largest industries and a generator of quality jobs. They continue their measurement efforts, and Table 1.1 shows their most recent world estimates for 1998 and 2010. In 1998 the global travel and tourism industry is expected to generate $3.6 trillion of economic activity and 231 million jobs (direct and indirect). Travel and tourism is projected to grow to $8.0 trillion of economic activity and 328 million jobs by 2010.

The travel and tourism industry will account for 8.2 percent of worldwide gross domestic product (GDP) in 1998, and this will grow to 8.7 percent by 2010. The broader travel and tourism economy, including industry demand, is expected to contribute

TABLE 1.1
World Economic Impact: Estimates and Forecasts

	1998		2010		
Factor	US$ Billion	% of Total	US$ Billion	% of Total	Real Annual Growth (%) 1998–2010
Personal consumption	2026.3	10.5	4477.0	11.2	3.7
Business travel	398.1	—	897.9	—	4.1
Government expenditures	252.8	6.8	542.1	7.4	3.2
Capital investment	778.6	11.8	1769.3	12.0	4.5
Exports	917.2	12.7	2276.5	12.3	5.4
GDP	3564.3	11.6	8008.4	12.5	4.0
Imports	808.7	11.5	1954.4	10.9	5.2
Employment (millions)	230.8	9.4	328.4	10.9	3.0

Source: World Travel and Tourism Council.

11.6 percent to GDP in 1998 and 12.5 percent in 2010. Travel and tourism is a catalyst for construction and manufacturing. In 1998, the private and public sectors combined are expected to spend $779 billion in new travel and tourism capital investment worldwide (11.8 percent of total), $1.8 trillion by 2010 (12.0 percent of total).

Travel and tourism is both a generator and receiver of government funds. Globally in 1998, travel and tourism is expected to generate $802 billion of taxes (10.6 percent of total) while channeling $253 billion to government expenditures (6.8 percent of total). By 2010, taxes should increase to $1.8 trillion (11.4 percent of total) and government spending to $542 billion (7.4 percent of total).

The economic figures cited show that tourism has grown to be an activity of worldwide **importance and significance.** For a number of countries, tourism is the largest commodity in international trade. In many others, it ranks among the top three industries. Tourism has grown rapidly to become a major social and economic force in the world.

In 1998, WTTC and the WEFA Group undertook major enhancements to their research methodology to reflect the satellite accounting standard (see Chapter 14) evolving under World Tourism Organization (WTO) auspices. Their estimates also use improved data sources and closer incorporation of WEFA global macroeconomic data. All WTTC/WEFA economic research has been restructured in line with the international standard for travel and tourism satellite accounting. This provides greater insight into the economic makeup of the "travel and tourism industry" and the linkages into the broader travel and tourism economy. The former shows the narrow production-side equivalent while the latter captures the economy-side impact, including capital formation, collective government expenditures, and trade exports.

WTTC is updating information on a quarterly basis. You are encouraged to examine their latest information on their web site (**http://www.wttc.org**).

As tourism has grown, it has moved from being the province of the rich to accessibility to the masses, involving millions of people. The WTO attempts to document tourism's growth in their annual publications entitled *Tourism Highlights* and *Compendium of Tourism Statistics*. Table 1.2 shows WTO international tourist arrival data up to 1998 and the strong rates of growth for the last several decades. Growth in international tourist arrivals slowed to 3 percent in 1997 and 2.4 percent in 1998, due primarily to the Asian financial crisis. WTO states that tourism is the world's largest growth industry with no signs of slowing down in the twenty-first century. Their study, *Tourism 2020 Vision*, forecasts that international arrivals will exceed 700 million in the year 2000, 1 billion by 2010, and 1.6 billion by 2020. Whether it is WTO or WTTC, dramatic growth appears to be in the future forecasts.

WTO's 1998 estimate of 625 million tourist arrivals was a result of good tourism growth in all regions except East Asia and the Pacific. Africa, the Middle East, and South Asia were the world's fastest growing tourism regions in 1998. Among the countries with the biggest gains were Portugal, Malaysia, Tunisia, South Africa, Brazil, Spain, Greece, Croatia, Ireland, and Korea.

Top 20

The world's top 20 tourism destinations are shown in Table 1.3; France ranks number one in tourism arrivals, with 70.0 million. France is followed by Spain, the United States, Italy, and the United Kingdom. These five leading destinations account for 36.0

TABLE 1.2
International Tourist Arrivals: 1950, 1960, 1970, and 1980–1998

Year	Arrivals (millions)	Percent of Growth
1950	25	—
1960	69	176
1970	166	141
1980	288	73
1981	290	1
1982	290	1
1983	293	1
1984	320	9
1985	330	3
1986	341	3
1987	367	8
1988	394	7
1989	425	8
1990	457	8
1991	463	1
1992	503	9
1993	520	3
1994	551	6
1995	565	3
1996	596	6
1997	613	3
1998	625	2

Source: World Tourism Organization (WTO).

percent of the world volume of tourism flows. The top 10 countries account for 51.7 percent of the flows. While this is a heavy geographical concentration, the trend is toward a gradual diversification with the emergence of new destinations in the Asia Pacific regions. China, Poland, and the Czech Republic have all made sizable gains in their world ranking.

A similar concentration pattern emerges if countries are classified according to their tourism receipts. These 10 leading countries account for 55 percent of the world

STATISTICAL DATA AVAILABILITY
▼

One of the problems in collecting and reporting statistical data for a book is the data lag. As this book was being revised, 1997 data and some 1998 data were just becoming available. Unfortunately, data lags are increasing rather than decreasing. This disturbing reality is especially upsetting when one considers that travel is a dynamic and changing industry. The data in this book provide a perspective on the size and importance of the industry and its sectors. Users are encouraged to access the sources provided to update the information and determine if trends are continuing or changing. One of the best ways to do that is to get on the Internet. Web site addresses are provided in many cases to enable you to locate the latest information available.

The United States ranks third in the number of international tourism arrivals, but earns the most revenue from international tourism receipts. *(Photo courtesy of the Office of Public Information/The Pentagon.)*

TABLE 1.3
World's Top 20 Tourism Destinations

Rank, 1998	Country	International Tourist Arrivals (thousands) 1998	% Change, 1998/97	Market Share % of World Total, 1998
1	France	70,000	4.7	11.2
2	Spain	47,743	10.0	7.6
3	United States	47,127	−1.3	7.5
4	Italy	34,829	2.2	5.6
5	United Kingdom	25,475	−0.2	4.1
6	China	24,000	1.0	3.8
7	Mexico	19,300	−0.3	3.1
8	Poland	18,820	−3.6	3.0
9	Canada	18,659	7.9	3.0
10	Austria	17,282	3.8	2.8
11	Germany	16,504	4.2	2.6
12	Czech Republic	16,325	−3.0	2.6
13	Russian Federation	15,810	3.0	2.5
14	Hungary	14,660	−15.0	2.3
15	Portugal	11,800	16.0	1.9
16	Greece	11,077	10.0	1.8
17	Switzerland	11,025	4.0	1.8
18	China, Hong Kong-SAR	9,600	−7.7	1.5
19	Turkey	9,200	1.8	1.5
20	Thailand	7,720	6.9	1.2
Total 1–20		446,956		71.5
World Total		625,236		100.00

Source: World Tourism Organization (WTO).

total and the top 20 countries account for 71 percent (see Table 1.4). Here, the United States leads, followed by Italy, France, Spain, United Kingdom, Germany, China, Austria, Canada, and Australia. For world tourism statistics, a visit to the World Tourism Organization's web site is a must: **http://www.world-tourism.org.**

Canada

Canada became the world's ninth most popular tourism destination in 1997, with 17.6 million international visitors, and held that rank in 1998 with 18.7 million, according to the WTO. Provisional estimates show that Canada had a 2.9 percent share of the world total, an increase of 1.7 percent from 1996, when it was in tenth place.

Results from Canada National Tourism Indicators (NTI) show that tourism spending in Canada for 1997 reached a record $44 billion, a 5.3 percent increase over 1996. Foreign visitors spent nearly $13 billion in spite of the Asian financial problems and economic conditions in France and Germany. The increase reflects United States travelers taking advantage of the lower priced Canadian dollar.

The NTI numbers also show Canadian domestic tourism spending at more than a 5 percent increase in 1997, or $31 billion, indicating Canadians vacationed less in the United States. Total tourism employment increased to 503,200. This marked a 2.3 per-

TABLE 1.4
World's Top 20 Tourism Earners

Rank, 1998	Country	Revised Estimates		
		International Tourism Receipts (US$ million), 1998	% Change, 1998/97	Market Share % of World Total, 1998
1	United States	74,240	1.3	16.7
2	Italy	30,427	2.4	6.8
3	France	29,700	6.0	6.7
4	Spain	29,585	11.0	6.7
5	United Kingdom	21,295	6.3	4.8
6	Germany	16,840	2.0	3.8
7	China	12,500	3.5	2.8
8	Austria	12,164	−1.8	2.7
9	Canada	9,133	4.1	2.1
10	Australia	8,575	−5.0	1.9
11	Poland	8,400	−3.2	1.9
12	Turkey	8,300	2.6	1.9
13	Switzerland	8,208	3.9	1.8
14	Mexico	7,850	3.4	1.8
15	China, Hong Kong-SAR	7,114	−23.0	1.6
16	Russian Federation	7,107	3.0	1.6
17	Singapore	6,501	−5.0	1.5
18	Thailand	6,392	−9.3	1.4
19	Netherlands	5,749	−7.6	1.3
20	Korea Republic	5,700	11.4	1.3
Total 1–20		315,780		71.0
World Total		444,741	2.0	100.00

Source: World Tourism Organization (WTO).

cent increase over the 1996 level, with employment gains strongest in air transportation and in vehicle rental and leasing.

Canada also ranked high in earnings from tourism in 1998 according to the WTO estimates. With U.S. $9.13 billion in receipts (excluding transport) from international tourists—2.1 percent of the world total—Canada came in as the ninth largest earner of international tourism receipts, up from eleventh place in 1997.

United States

In the United States, tourism is ranked as the third largest retail industry behind automobile and food sales. In employment, it is second to health services. Although tourism is often thought of as leisure travel, it also encompasses business and convention travel, meetings, seminars, recreation, student travel (if less than a year), transportation services, and accommodations. According to the Travel Industry Association of America (TIA) research department, travel and tourism generated $502.4 billion in domestic spending in 1997 and international airline payments. This total included expenditures by foreign travelers, as well as domestic travelers. The U.S. travel industry, already a leading employer, will continue its rapid rise into the twenty-first century as a job creator for Americans. Employment directly generated by travel has grown 33.3 percent in the last decade, outperforming total U.S. nonagricultural employment (20.4 percent).

Traveler spending in the United States is projected to total $529.8 billion in 1999 and $588.3 billion in 2000, according to TIA's *The Economic Review of Travel in America.* Readers are encouraged to examine the *TIA Travel Forecast,* which is based on TIA's domestic forecasting models, developed in conjunction with DRI/McGraw-Hill. It also includes inbound travel data from the U.S. Commerce Department's International Trade Administration. It is the opinion of the authors that TIA is the most authoritative source of information on the U.S. travel industry, and you should visit their extensive web site (**http://www.tia.org**).

Directly or indirectly, tourism is part of the fabric of most of the world's industries, including transportation, retailing, advertising, sports, sporting goods and equipment, clothing, the food industry, and health care. Tourism also plays a part in most communication media, particularly in the travel sections of newspapers. There are many print and visual media of direct interest to tourism suppliers and students of this subject, in addition to those engaged in marketing tourism, especially those of interest to airlines, cruise lines, motor coach and rail lines, tour companies, travel agencies, auto rental companies, accommodations, attractions including theme parks, and tourism educational organizations.

Politicians at all levels are typically very concerned with tourism. They look increasingly at tourism as a tool for economic development. In development, they have enacted laws requiring land-use plans with subsequent zoning and building codes to control location, number, and manner of construction of tourist facilities. Parks and recreation programs are enjoyed by tourists as well as local residents. Many governments impose taxes, all or part of which are paid directly or indirectly by tourists and their suppliers. The power of tourism politically is sometimes manifested in unusual ways. An example was the threat of a travel boycott of Alaska by environmental groups protesting the state's planned aerial shooting of 300 wolves. The plan was canceled.

Many industry analysts project a doubling of tourism by the year 2010, with constructive government policies. We believe that such policies will indeed be forthcom-

---

TOURISM: WHAT IT MEANS TO THE U.S. ECONOMY

▼

- Domestic and international travel and tourism in the United States generated an estimated $502.4 billion in expenditures in 1997. Travel and tourism is the nation's third largest retail industry. Largest is automotive and second largest is food stores.

- Travel and tourism was once again the nation's largest service export in 1997. The estimated 47.8 million international travelers to the United States generated an estimated $94 billion in expenditures, while the estimated 54.1 million Americans who traveled to international destinations only spent an estimated $72 billion. As a result, a travel trade surplus of $22 billion was generated because international travelers spent more money here than Americans spent abroad.

- In 1997, spending by domestic and international travelers generated $71.7 billion in tax revenue for federal, state, and local governments.

- Americans took nearly 1.3 billion person-trips (one person traveling 100+ miles, one way, away from home) in 1997, an increase of 8 percent.

- The favorite mode of transportation used by U.S. residents when traveling in 1997 was: auto/truck/RV (79%), plane (18%), bus (1%), and train (1%).

- In 1997, the top three activities participated in by U.S. resident travelers remained: (1) shopping, (2) outdoor activities, and (3) visiting museums and/or historical sites.

- States and territories plan to spend $524 million on tourism promotion during fiscal year 1998–1999, a 6.5 percent increase over fiscal year 1997–1998.

- Travel and tourism is the first-, second-, or third-largest employer in 32 states.

- In 1997 (latest year for which data are available), over 7.0 million jobs were directly supported through travel and tourism, resulting in $128 billion in payroll. Over 9 million jobs were supported indirectly, for a grand total of 16.0 million jobs.

- Approximately one out of every 17 Americans is employed due to the patronage of travelers to and within the United States.

- Travel and tourism provides more than 684,000 executive level positions each year.

Source: Travel Industry Association of America (TIA).

ing if tourism leaders will convey their message effectively. It is in all our interests to achieve this growth, provided that it is accomplished in an intelligent, planned, and thoughtful manner by developers and the public alike. There is an unequivocal responsibility to review the social and environmental factors vigilantly in order to preserve and enhance those qualities that give any destination its special appeal and character. These comprise its culture, natural resources, host population, and the spirit of the place. We hope that you will strive to assist in the achievement of these ultimate worthy goals.

WHAT IS TOURISM?

When we think of tourism, we think primarily of people who are visiting a particular place for sightseeing, visiting friends and relatives, taking a vacation, and having a good time. They may spend their leisure time engaging in various sports, sunbathing, talking, singing, taking rides, touring, reading, or simply enjoying the environment. If we consider the subject further, we may include in our definition of tourism people who are participating in a convention, a business conference, or some other kind of business or professional activity, as well as those who are taking a study tour under an expert guide or doing some kind of scientific research or study.

These visitors use all forms of transportation, from hiking in a wilderness park to flying in a jet to an exciting city. Transportation can include taking a chair lift up a Colorado mountainside or standing at the rail of a cruise ship looking across the blue Caribbean. Whether people travel by one of these means or by car, motor coach, camper, train, taxi, motorbike, or bicycle, they are taking a trip and thus are engaging in tourism. That is what this book is all about—why people travel (and why some don't) and the socioeconomic effects that their presence and expenditures have on a society.

Any attempt to define tourism and to describe its scope fully must consider the various groups that participate in and are affected by this industry. Their perspectives are vital to the development of a comprehensive definition. Four different perspectives of tourism can be identified:

1. **The tourist.** The tourist seeks various psychic and physical experiences and satisfactions. The nature of these will largely determine the destinations chosen and the activities enjoyed.

2. **The businesses providing tourist goods and services.** Businesspeople see tourism as an opportunity to make a profit by supplying the goods and services that the tourist market demands.

3. **The government of the host community or area.** Politicians view tourism as a wealth factor in the economy of their jurisdictions. Their perspective is related to the incomes their citizens can earn from this business. Politicians also consider the foreign exchange receipts from international tourism as well as the tax receipts collected from tourist expenditures, either directly or indirectly.

4. **The host community.** Local people usually see tourism as a cultural and employment factor. Of importance to this group, for example, is the effect of the interaction between large numbers of international visitors and residents. This effect may be beneficial or harmful, or both.

Thus, tourism may be defined as the sum of the phenomena and relationships arising from the interaction of tourists, business suppliers, host governments, and host communities in the process of attracting and hosting these tourists and other visitors. (See the Glossary for definitions of **tourist** and **excursionist**.)

Tourism is a composite of activities, services, and industries that delivers a travel experience: transportation, accommodations, eating and drinking establishments, shops, entertainment, activity facilities, and other hospitality services available for individuals or groups that are traveling away from home. It encompasses all providers of visitor and visitor-related services. Tourism is the entire world industry of travel, hotels, transportation, and all other components, including promotion, that serves the needs and wants of travelers. Finally, tourism is the sum total of tourist **expenditures** within the borders of a nation or a political subdivision or a transportation-centered economic area of contiguous states or nations. This economic concept also

Airlines are one of the many businesses providing tourism services. Here, airport counter personnel are providing efficient service to departing air travelers, making their vacation and business travel a more enjoyable experience. *(Photo courtesy of Southwest Airlines.)*

considers the income multiplier of these tourist expenditures (discussed in Chapter 14).

One has only to consider the multidimensional aspects of tourism and its interactions with other activities to understand why it is difficult to come up with a meaningful definition that will be universally accepted. Each of the many definitions that have arisen is aimed at fitting a special situation and solving an immediate problem, and the lack of uniform definitions has hampered study of tourism as a discipline. Development of a field depends on (1) uniform definitions, (2) description, (3) analysis, (4) prediction, and (5) control.

Modern tourism is a discipline that has only recently attracted the attention of scholars from many fields. The majority of studies have been conducted for special purposes and have used narrow operational definitions to suit particular needs of researchers or government officials; these studies have not encompassed a systems approach. Consequently, many definitions of "tourism" and "the tourist" are based on distance traveled, the length of time spent, and the purpose of the trip. This makes it difficult to gather statistical information that scholars can use to develop a database, describe the tourism phenomenon, and do analyses.

The problem is not trivial. It has been tackled by a number of august bodies over the years, including the League of Nations, the United Nations, the World Tourism Organization (WTO), the Organization for Economic Cooperation and Development (OECD), the National Tourism Resources Review Commission, and the U.S. Senate's National Tourism Policy Study.

The following review of various definitions illustrates the problems of arriving at a consensus. We examine the concept of the movement of people and the terminology and definitions applied by the World Tourism Organization and those of the United States, Canada, the United Kingdom, and Australia. Later, a comprehensive classification of travelers is provided that endeavors to reflect a consensus of current thought and practice.

World Tourism Organization Definitions

The International Conference on Travel and Tourism Statistics convened by the World Tourism Organization (WTO) in Ottawa, Canada, in 1991 reviewed, updated, and expanded on the work of earlier international groups. The Ottawa Conference made some fundamental recommendations on definitions of *tourism, travelers,* and *tourists.* The United Nations Statistical Commission adopted WTO's recommendations on tourism statistics on March 4, 1993.

Tourism

WTO has taken the concept of *tourism* beyond a stereotypical image of "holiday-making." The officially accepted definition is: "Tourism comprises the activities of persons traveling to and staying in places outside their usual environment for not more than one consecutive year for leisure, business and other purposes." The term **usual environment** is intended to exclude trips within the area of usual residence and frequent and regular trips between the domicile and the workplace and other community trips of a routine character.

1. **International tourism**
   a. **Inbound tourism**: visits to a country by nonresidents
   b. **Outbound tourism**: visits by residents of a country to another country
2. **Internal tourism**: visits by residents of a country to their own country
3. **Domestic tourism**: internal tourism plus inbound tourism (the tourism market of accommodation facilities and attractions within a country)
4. **National tourism**: internal tourism plus outbound tourism (the resident tourism market for travel agents and airlines)

Traveler Terminology for International Tourism

Underlying the foregoing conceptualization of tourism is the overall concept of **traveler,** defined as "any person on a trip between two or more countries or between two or more localities within his/her country of usual residence." All types of travelers engaged in tourism are described as **visitors,** a term that constitutes the basic concept of the entire system of tourism statistics. Visitors are persons who travel to a country other than the one in which they generally reside for a period not exceeding 12 months, whose main purpose is other than the exercise of an activity remunerated from within the place visited. Visitors are subdivided into two categories:

1. **Same-day visitors**: visitors who do not spend the night in a collective or private accommodation in the country visited—for example, a cruise ship passenger spending four hours in a port
2. **Tourists**: visitors who stay in the country visited for at least one night— for example, a visitor on a two-week vacation

There are many purposes for a visit—notably pleasure, business, and other purposes, such as family reasons, health, and transit.

United States

The Western Council for Travel Research in 1963 employed the term **visitor** and defined a **visit** as occurring every time a visitor entered an area under study. The definition of **tourist** used by the National Tourism Resources Review Commission in 1973 was: "A tourist is one who travels away from home for a distance of at least 50 miles (one way) for business, pleasure, personal affairs, or any other purpose except to commute to work, whether he stays overnight or returns the same day."

The *National Travel Survey* of TIA's research department, the U.S. Travel Data Center, reported in 1998 on all round-trips with a one-way route mileage of 100 miles or more, and it reported since 1984 on all **trips** involving one or more nights away from home, regardless of distance. Trips are included regardless of purpose, excluding only crews, students, military personnel on active duty, and commuters.

In the United States, the definition of a trip typically requires travel of at least 100 miles away from home or an overnight stay. Many trips in the United States are taken on the nation's highways. *(Photo courtesy of South Dakota Tourism.)*

Canada

In a series of quarterly household sample surveys known as the Canadian Travel Survey that began in 1978, trips qualifying for inclusion are similar to those covered in the *National Travel Survey* in the United States. The main difference is that in the Canadian survey, the lower limit for the one-way distance is 50 miles (80 kilometers) rather than 100 miles. The 50-mile figure was a compromise to satisfy concerns regarding the accuracy of recall for shorter trips and the possibility of the inclusion of trips completed entirely within the boundaries of a large metropolitan area such as Toronto.

The determination of which length of trip to include in surveys of domestic travel has varied according to the purpose of the survey methodology employed. Whereas there is general agreement that commuting journeys and one-way trips should be excluded, qualifying distances vary. The province of Ontario favors 25 miles.

In Canada's international travel surveys, the primary groups of travelers identified are nonresident travelers, resident travelers, and other travelers. Both nonresident and resident travelers include both same-day and business travelers. Other travelers consist of immigrants, former residents, military personnel, and crews.

United Kingdom

The National Tourist Boards of England, Scotland, and Northern Ireland sponsor a continuous survey of internal tourism, the United Kingdom Tourism Survey (UKTS). It measures all trips away from home lasting one night or more; these include (a) trips, taken by residents for holidays, (b) visits to friends and relatives (nonholiday), or (c) trips taken for business, conferences, and most other purposes. In its findings, the UKTS distinguishes between short (1 to 3 nights)- and long (4+ nights)-duration holiday trips.

The International Passenger Survey collects information on both overseas visitors to the United Kingdom and travel abroad by U.K. residents. It distinguishes five different types of visits: holiday independent, holiday inclusive, business, visits to friends and relatives, and miscellaneous.

Australia

The Australian Bureau of Industry Economics in 1979 placed length of stay and distance traveled constraints in its definition of *tourist* as follows: "A person visiting a location at least 40 km from his usual place of residence, for a period of at least 24 hours and not exceeding 12 months."

In supporting the use of the WTO definitions, the Australian Bureau of Statistics notes that the term "usual environment is somewhat vague." It states that "visits to tourist attractions by local residents should not be included" and that visits to second homes should be included only "where they are clearly for temporary recreational purposes."

Comprehensive Classification of Travelers

The main types of travelers are indicated in Figure 1.1. Shown is the fundamental distinction between residents and visitors and the interest of travel and tourism practi-

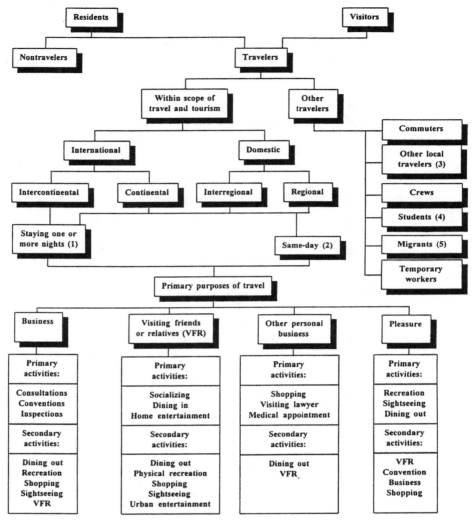

(1) *Tourists* in international technical definitions.
(2) *Excursionists* in international technical definitions.
(3) Travelers whose trips are shorter than those that qualify for travel and tourism; e.g., under 50 miles (80 km) from home.
(4) Students traveling between home and school only—other travel of students is within scope of travel and tourism.
(5) All persons moving to a new place of residence including all one-way travelers, such as emigrants, immigrants, refugees, domestic migrants, and nomads.

FIGURE 1.1 Classification of travelers.

tioners in the characteristics of nontravelers as well as travelers. It also reflects the apparent consensus that business and same-day travel both fall within the scope of travel and tourism.

Placed to one side are some other types of travelers generally regarded as being outside the area of interest, although included in some travel surveys. Foremost among these exclusions are commuters, who seem to fall outside the area of interest to all in the travel and tourism community. Other travelers generally excluded from studies on travel and tourism are those who undertake trips within the community, which for convenience are described arbitrarily as trips involving less than a specific one-way distance, such as 100 miles. These "other travelers" have been focused on in the Nationwide Personal Transportation Surveys conducted by the U.S. Department of Transportation. The broad class of travelers categorized as migrants, both international and domestic, is also commonly excluded from tourism or travel research. They are excluded on the grounds that their movement is not temporary, although they use the same facilities as other travelers, albeit in one direction, and frequently require temporary accommodation on reaching their destination. The real significance of migration to travel and tourism, however, is not in the one-way trip in itself, but in the long-run implications of a transplanted demand for travel and the creation of new travel destination for separated friends and relatives.

Other groups of travelers are commonly excluded from travel and tourism studies because their travel is not affected by travel promotion, although they tend to compete for the same types of facilities and services. Students and temporary workers traveling purely for reasons of education or temporary employment are two leading examples. Another frequently excluded group consists of crews, although they can be regarded as special subsets of tourists and **excursionists.**

Of those travelers directly within the scope of travel and tourism, basic distinctions are made among those whose trips are completed within one day. An additional meaningful division may also be made between those international travelers whose travel is between continents and those whose international travel is confined to countries within the same continent. In the case of the United States, the distinction is between (a) trips to or from the neighboring countries of Canada and Mexico or elsewhere in the Americas and (b) trips made to or from countries in Europe or on other continents.

The same type of distinction may be made between interregional and regional domestic travel. In the United States, there are eight travel regions. Travel between them would be regarded as interregional and within them as regional. In Canada, five major regions may be identified: Atlantic, Central, Prairies, West, and North. In practice, travel studies in Canada tend to show interprovincial data because of the large size of some provinces and the research and planning needs of each provincial department of tourism.

The purposes of travel identified in Figure 1.1 go beyond those traditionally accepted because of the growing evidence that "visits to friends and relatives" (VFR) is a basic travel motivation and a distinctive factor in marketing, accounting for a major proportion of travel. In any event, "primary purpose" is an arbitrary concept because many journeys are undertaken for a combination of reasons, such as "business and vacation" as recognized in the U.S. National Travel Survey conducted by the TIA's research department, the U.S. Travel Data Center.

Travel, Tourism, and Recreation

For the purposes of this book, the terms **travel** and **tourism** will be synonymous. Tourism may also be defined as people taking trips away from home, and it embraces the entire range of transportation, lodging, food service, and other activities relating to and serving the traveler. Consequently, a **tourist** is someone who travels away from home. The term **tourist industry** is used to describe the economic sectors (transportation, lodging, etc.) supplying the tourist, who is the consumer of the industry's products. The term **visitor,** which is common in international travel, will be synonymous with **tourist.** These definitions of *tourism, travel,* and *tourist* admittedly are very broad, but they permit the development of additional subcategories to define market segments, such as *out-of-state visitors, recreationists, conventioneers, the sports-minded,* and others. The definitions are also in keeping with those used by the *National Tourism Policy Study,* which construed the three terms **travel, tourism,** and **recreation** as follows:

1. *Travel:* the action and activities of people taking trips to a place or places outside their home communities for any purpose except daily commuting to and from work.

2. *Tourism:* a term that is synonymous with *travel.*

3. *Recreation:* the action and activities of people engaging in constructive and personally pleasurable use of leisure time. Recreation may include passive or active participation in individual or group sports, cultural functions, natural and human history appreciation, nonformal education, pleasure travel, sightseeing, and entertainment.[1]

BASIC APPROACHES TO THE STUDY OF TOURISM

Tourism commonly is approached through a variety of methods. However, there is little or no agreement on how the study of tourism should be undertaken. The following are several methods that have been used.

Institutional Approach

The institutional **approach to the study of tourism** considers the various intermediaries and institutions that perform tourism activities. It emphasizes institutions such as the travel agency. This approach requires an investigation of the organization, operating methods, problems, costs, and economic place of travel agents who act on behalf of the customer, purchasing services from airlines, rental car companies, hotels, and so on. An advantage of this approach is that the U.S. Census Bureau conducts a survey every five years on selected services that includes travel agents and lodging places, thus providing a database for further study.

Product Approach

The product approach involves the study of various tourism products and how they are produced, marketed, and consumed. For example, one might study an airline seat—

---

[1] *National Tourism Policy Study Final Report* (Washington, D.C.: U.S. Government Printing Office, 1978), p. 5.

how it is created, the people who are engaged in buying and selling it, how it is financed, how it is advertised, and so on. Repeating this procedure for rental cars, hotel rooms, meals, and other tourist services gives a full picture of the field. Unfortunately, the product approach tends to be too time-consuming; it does not allow the student to grasp the fundamentals of tourism quickly.

Historical Approach

The historical approach is not widely used. It involves an analysis of tourism activities and institutions from an evolutionary angle. It searches for the cause of innovations, their growth or decline, and shifts in interest. Because mass tourism is a fairly recent phenomenon, this approach has limited usefulness.

Managerial Approach

The managerial approach is firm-oriented (microeconomic), focusing on the management activities necessary to operate a tourist enterprise, such as planning, research, pricing, advertising, control, and the like. It is a popular approach, using insights gleaned from other approaches and disciplines. Although a major focus of this book is managerial, readers will recognize that other perspectives are also being used. Regardless of which approach is used to study tourism, it is important to know the managerial approach. Products change, institutions change, and society changes; this means that managerial objectives and procedures must be geared to change to meet shifts in the tourism environment. The *Journal of Travel Research* and *Tourism Management*, leading journals in the field, both feature this approach.

Economic Approach

Because of its importance to both domestic and world economies, tourism has been examined closely by economists, who focus on supply, demand, balance of payments, foreign exchange, employment, expenditures, development, multipliers, and other economic factors. This approach is useful in providing a framework for analyzing tourism and its contributions to a country's economy and economic development. The disadvantage of the economic approach is that whereas tourism is an important economic phenomenon, it has noneconomic impacts as well. The economic approach does not usually pay adequate attention to the environmental, cultural, psychological, sociological, and anthropological approaches. *Tourism Economics* is a journal utilizing the economic approach.

Sociological Approach

Tourism tends to be a social activity. Consequently, it has attracted the attention of sociologists, who have studied the tourism behavior of individuals and groups of people and the impact of tourism on society. This approach examines social classes, habits, and customs of both hosts and guests. The sociology of leisure is a relatively undeveloped field, but it shows promise of progressing rapidly and becoming more widely used. As tourism continues to make a massive impact on society, it will be studied more and more from a social point of view.

A prime reference in this area is *The Tourist, A New Theory of the Leisure Class*, by Dean MacCannel (Schocken Books, New York, 1976). Erik Cohen, of the Hebrew University of Jerusalem, has made many contributions in this area (see Chapter 11). Graham M. S. Dann, University of Luton, United Kingdom, has been a major contributor to the tourism sociology literature as well.

Geographical Approach

Geography is a wide-ranging discipline, so it is natural that geographers should be interested in tourism and its spatial aspects. The geographer specializes in the study of location, environment, climate, landscape, and economic aspects. The geographer's approach to tourism sheds light on the location of tourist areas, the movements of people created by tourism locales, the changes that tourism brings to the landscape in the form of tourism facilities, dispersion of tourism development physical planning, and economic, social, and cultural problems. Because tourism touches geography at so many points, geographers have investigated the area more thoroughly than have scholars in many other disciplines. Because the geographers' approach is so encompassing—dealing with land use, economic aspects, demographic impacts, and cultural problems—a study of their contributions is highly recommended. Recreational geography is a common course title used by geographers studying this specialty. Because tourism, leisure, and recreation are so closely related, it is necessary to search for literature under all these titles to discover the contributions of various fields. Geographers were instrumental in starting both the *Journal of Leisure Research* and *Leisure Sciences*. Another journal, *Tourism Geographies*, was launched in February 1999 with the aim of providing a forum for the presentation and discussion of geographic perspectives on tourism and tourism-related areas of recreation and leisure studies.

Interdisciplinary Approaches

Tourism embraces virtually all aspects of our society. We have cultural and heritage tourism, which calls for an anthropological approach. Because people behave in different ways and travel for different reasons, it is necessary to use a psychological approach to determine the best way to promote and market tourism products. Because tourists cross borders and require passports and visas from government offices, and because most countries have government-operated tourism development departments, we find that political institutions are involved and are calling for a political science approach. Any industry that becomes an economic giant affecting the lives of many people attracts the attention of legislative bodies (along with that of the sociologists, geographers, economists, and anthropologists), which create the laws, regulations, and legal environment in which the tourist industry must operate; so we also have a legal approach. The great importance of transportation suggests passenger transportation as another approach. The fact simply is that tourism is so vast, so complex, and so multifaceted that it is necessary to have a number of approaches to studying the field, each geared to a somewhat different task or objective. Figure 1.2 illustrates the interdisciplinary nature of tourism studies and their reciprocity and mutuality. *The Annals of Tourism Research,* an interdisciplinary social sciences journal, is another publication that should be on the serious tourism student's reading list.

The Systems Approach

What is really needed to study tourism is a systems approach. A system is a set of interrelated groups coordinated to form a unified whole and organized to accomplish a

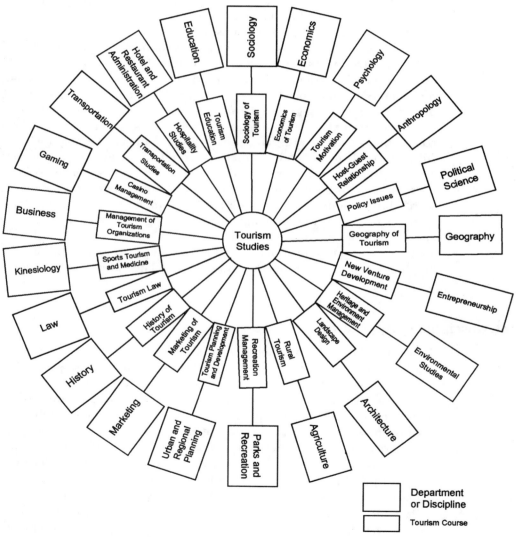

FIGURE 1.2 Disciplinary inputs to the tourism field. *(Adapted from Jafar Jafari, University of Wisconsin—Stout, Study of Tourism: Choices of Discipline and Approach.)*

set of goals. It integrates the other approaches into a comprehensive method dealing with both micro and macro issues. It can examine the tourist firm's competitive environment, its market, its results, its linkages with other institutions, the consumer, and the interaction of the firm with the consumer. In addition, a system can take a macro viewpoint and examine the entire tourism system of a country, state, or area and how it operates within and relates to other systems, such as legal, political, economic, and social systems.

COMPONENTS OF TOURISM AND TOURISM MANAGEMENT

Tourism is a complex phenomenon—one that is extremely difficult to describe succinctly. Any "model" of tourism must "capture" the composition—or components—of the tourism system, as well as the key processes and outcomes that occur within tourism. These processes and outcomes include the very essence of tourism, the travel experience, and the supporting means by which tourism is made possible. Figure 1.3 attempts to describe the complexity of the relationships among the many components of the tourism phenomenon.

Natural Resources and Environment

The most fundamental dimension of the model—indeed, the very basis of tourism—is the **Natural Resources and Environment** component. Any given destination is primarily and unchangeably characterized by its physiography (the nature and appearance of its landscape) and its climate (the kind of weather it has over a period of years; i.e., the conditions of heat and cold, moisture and dryness, and wind). Finally, the third component of the natural environment is people. In the case of people, we must distinguish between two very important categories of individuals: (1) those who "belong" to the destination (its residents) and (2) those who are current or potential visitors to the destination (the tourism market).

The Built Environment

Another dimension of the tourism phenomenon is the **built environment** that has been created by humans. This built environment first includes the **culture** of the residents of the host region. As discussed in Chapter 10, the culture of a people reflects many dimensions of its past development and its current way of life. Culture is relatively a very permanent characteristic of a destination, and one that cannot (and should not) be changed simply to enhance tourism development.

The infrastructure of a tourism destination is yet another dimension that has not been put in place mainly to serve tourism. Such basic things as roads, sewage systems, communication networks, and many commercial facilities (supermarkets and retail stores) have been put in place to meet the needs of local residents. While these components of the infrastructure can also be important to visitors, their primary functions are related to the ongoing daily needs of residents. In contrast, a destination's tourism superstructure includes those facilities that have been developed especially to respond to the demands of visitors. The most obvious examples include hotels, restaurants,

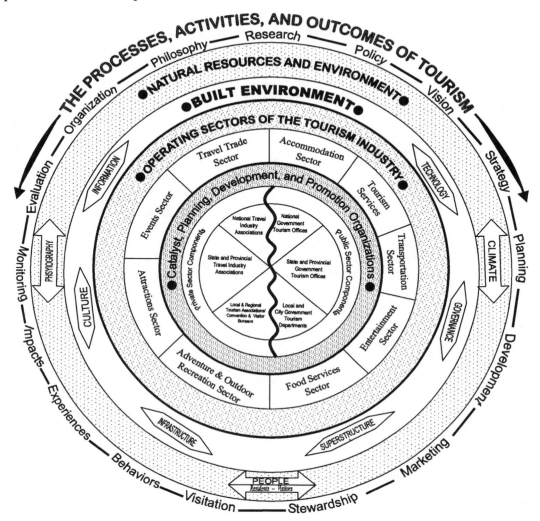

FIGURE 1.3 The tourism phenomenon: Components of tourism and tourism management.

conference centers, car rentals, and major attractions. Because of their special tourism orientation, the characteristics of components of the superstructure are essentially determined by visitor wishes rather than resident desires even though residents often desire many benefits from certain elements of the tourism superstructure.

Technology is one of the most recent, and still increasingly influential, dimensions of the built environment that is shaping the nature of both tourism products/services and travel experiences. In many ways, technology can be viewed as one of the most distinctive and most powerful characteristics of the built environment since the dawn of modern tourism following World War II.

The advent of jet aircraft and the massive invasion of telecommunications technology, linked closely with computer technology, have had a dramatic impact on the very essence of the tourism phenomenon. Indeed, each of these aspects of technology

Using natural resources for a white-water rafting trip is an exciting and memorable experience. *(Photo courtesy of West Virginia Department of Commerce.)*

has become so pervasive and so important that they, in fact, represent very specialized elements of both the tourism infrastructure and superstructure. However, because of their unique identification with the modern era of the built environment, each merits specific identification.

A recent addition to the built environment of a destination is that of information. Increasingly, the success of a destination is determined by its ability to assemble, interpret, and utilize information in an effective manner. Information is of several types: information concerning the potential tourism market, which is essential for destination design and development; information on the level of satisfaction of current visitors regarding the quality, or enjoyment, of their visitation experience; information regarding competitors and their activities; information concerning the functioning or performance of the destination in its efforts to profitably provide attractive experiences to visitors; and information concerning the extent to which residents of the host region understand and support tourism as a long-term component of the socioeconomic system.

Finally, a dimension of tourism that often receives inadequate attention is the overall system of governance within which the tourism system functions. This topic is discussed in greater detail in Chapter 15. For present purposes, it should be noted that the system of governance surrounding tourism (the legal, political, and fiscal systems regulating its functioning) has a profound impact on the ability of a destination to compete in the international marketplace and subsequently plays a major role in determining the profitability of individual firms. While the system of governance of a country or region may be viewed as an evolutionary dimension of overall culture, it is subject to influence and change within an observable timeframe. Sometimes these changes can be quite dramatic and can occur in a relatively short period of time in cul-

Airports are an important part of the built environment because they provide essential travel services. Shown here is the Denver International Airport. *(Photo courtesy of Denver Metro Convention and Visitors Bureau.)*

tural terms. Recent/current high-profile examples include the worldwide phenomenon of deregulation and privatization and the more focused process of economic (and eventually social) integration brought about by the formation of regional trade blocs such as the European Union (EU) and the North American Free Trade Association (NAFTA)—with a parallel initiative that will undoubtedly soon emerge in South East Asia.

Operating Sectors of the Tourism Industry

The **operating sectors** of the tourism industry represent what many of the general public perceive as "tourism." First and foremost, the **transportation** sector (see Figure 1.3) comprised of airlines, bus companies, and so on, tends to typify the movement of people and travel (see Chapter 5). The **accommodation** sector, which includes many well-known "brands" such as Hilton, Marriott, Howard Johnson, Best Western, and so on, is highly visible to the public. Similarly, the food services sector also contains a broad spectrum of brands and logos that have become part of everyday life in many communities. Examples include the world-famous chains of fast foods (McDonald's, Pizza Hut, Burger King, KFC) and internationally known gourmet restaurants such as Maxim's in Paris and Alfredo's, in Rome. The accommodations and food service sectors are covered in Chapter 6.

The **attractions** sector also contains many well-known icons in the tourism industry. The undisputed leader of the attraction world is Disneyland/Disney World. Other world famous attractions include the upscale Louvre museum in Paris, France; the Hermitage in St. Petersburg, Russia; Marineland and Knott's Berry Farm in the United States; the Pyramids in Egypt; Stonehenge in the United Kingdom; the

An icon known around the world is Disneyland's Sleeping Beauty Castle. It is one of the many attractions enjoyed by visitors to the theme park. *(Photo by Robert Holmes; courtesy of the California Division of Tourism.)*

Acropolis in Athens, Greece; and Niagara Falls, Canada. The primary focus of Chapter 8 is attractions.

Closely related to attractions is the events sector. Its icons include the Oktoberfest in Munich, Germany, the Calgary Stampede (Canada), the Mardi Gras of New Orleans and Rio de Janeiro, Brazil, the Boston Marathon, and the Super Bowl (USA), as well as such transient events as the World Cup of Soccer and the International Summer and Winter Olympic Games.

The adventure and outdoor recreation sector is one of the most rapidly growing components of modern tourism. Changes in demographics, values, and lifestyles are creating increasing demand for activities such as golfing, skiing, snowboarding, white-water rafting, para-sailing, hang-gliding, mountain biking, and mountaineering. Most of these activities are characterized by both an element of thrill seeking and an element of being outdoors. A closely related desire for closeness to nature has given rise to the phenomenon of ecotourism, an ill-defined and often abused term for any type of travel activity in a natural setting (see Chapters 8 and 17).

At the other end of the "natural-manufactured" spectrum is the equally fast growing component of entertainment. Certain destinations, most notably Las Vegas, Nashville, and Branson, Missouri have grown up on a heavy diet of world famous entertainers. More traditionally, New York/Broadway and Los Angeles/Hollywood have used various aspects of the entertainment industry to consolidate their worldwide reputations as "must see" destinations.

Less glamorous, but still essential to the success and well-being of the tourism industry, are the travel trade sector and tourism services (see Chapter 7). The travel trade is composed of the retail travel agent and the wholesale tour operator. Both of these entities are critical to linking "experience suppliers" and the tourist. The multifaceted travel industry services sector provides yet another type of critical support for successful tourism. Computer support service, retail services, financial services, specialized consulting services and tourism educators all make an important and usually unique contribution to the effective and efficient functioning of the complex tourism system. While the public (and even many firms themselves) do not identify themselves as part of the tourism juggernaut, the fact remains that, as soon as any one of these services becomes deficient, tourism suffers.

Planning, Development, Promotion, and Catalyst Organizations

It is widely acknowledged that the success of tourism ultimately depends on the competence and ability of all of the operating sectors discussed above (i.e., the front-line of tourism), to deliver a quality experience to each tourist—"one person at a time." There is another hidden component of tourism that is equally important in determining the success of a tourism destination. It is known by the unwieldy name of **Planning, Development, Promotion, and Catalyst Organizations** (PDPCO). It is the visionaries, policy makers, strategic planners, and individuals and groups who "make the right things happen" that are increasingly a determinant of successful tourism. In effect, in tourism it is as critical that we "do the right things" as that we "do things right." This means simply that policy makers need to ensure that their destination offers the kinds of travel experiences that are most appropriate to the visitor, always keeping in mind any limitations imposed by the resources of the destination.

Once the appropriate experiences have been identified through effective planning, it is essential to ensure that plans are translated into the facilities, events, and programs that are necessary to provide the visitor with the given experience "on the ground."

The organization responsible for providing the insight and leadership necessary to envisage and bring policies and plans into reality is increasingly referred to as the Destination Management Organization (DMO). The specific identity of this organization depends on the "level" of the destination. In most countries, it also involves two very important categories of stakeholders, namely, the public sector (governments) and the private sector (see Figure 1.3). At the national level, governments are usually represented by a National Government Tourism Office (such as a Department of Tourism, or a National Tourism Corporation). A National Travel/Tourism Industry Association typically represents the private sector.

At the state/provincial level, the public/private sector organizations are usually known respectively as the State/Provincial Government Tourism Office and the State/Provincial Travel Industry Association. The parallel equivalent at the city/municipal or regional level are Local and City Government Tourism Departments and Local and City Tourism Associations or, more commonly, a Convention and Visitor Bureau (CVB) (see Chapter 4).

The Importance of Integrated/Collaborative Planning and Development

One dimension of Figure 1.3 that is essential to note is the "wavy line" that forms the interface between the public and private sectors at all levels. This line is intended to convey the importance of integrated or collaborative planning and development efforts. Because both the public and private sectors each control (and often operate) an important percentage of tourism facilities, events, and programs, it is critical that policy, planning, and development efforts be continuously carried out within a joint, cooperative, collaborative organizational framework. Failure to acknowledge the importance of this reality leads only to antagonism, strife, and disjointed strategic planning and development. As such, each destination must strive to create DMOs where collaboration is built into the design. The actual name of the organization (be it a Tourism Authority, a Tourism Council, or a Tourism Partnership) matters little. What is important is the quality of the collaboration that occurs.

The Processes, Activities, and Outcomes of Tourism

The final dimension of Figure 1.3 which needs to be understood is the nature of the processes and activities that both surround and occur within the tourism system and that in the end, create the outcomes which are the essence of the phenomenon we call tourism.

We have previously addressed the issue of organizing the components of tourism so that they work together effectively. As indicated, a common result of these organizational efforts is the creation of a DMO.

For successful tourism, the DMO, in collaboration with all stakeholders, must define the tourism philosophy of the destination and formulate a supportive policy, vision, and strategy (see Chapter 15). These, in turn, provide direction and guidance for the detailed planning and development initiatives that will ultimately determine the nature and quality of the experiences the destination is capable of offering (see Chapter 16).

The availability of these "experience offerings" must be made known to potential visitors through effective marketing, defined in the broadest sense (see Chapter 19). Such marketing includes highly visible promotional efforts as well as the less glamorous dimensions of pricing and distribution of the travel products/experiences.

Successful **marketing** will attract a broad range of visitors whose behaviors provide them with enjoyment and the memorable experiences associated with these behaviors. These behaviors can give rise to both positive and negative impacts. The positive impacts pertain largely to the economic benefits (income and employment) that tourism provides. The negative impacts largely concern the ecological, social, cultural, and commemorative integrity of the destination.

The success of marketing efforts requires two subsequent activities. The first is a systematic monitoring of the levels and quality of visitation as well as visitor satisfaction regarding experiences and the destination (see Chapter 18—research). The second is a comprehensive program of stewardship to ensure that the success of tourism does not destroy the natural resources on which tourism depends so heavily (see Chapter 17).

The final activity that is essential to long-term success of tourism is an ongoing process of evaluation. Evaluation is simply an attempt to carefully assess the appropriateness, the effectiveness, the efficiency, and the overall performance of all components and processes in the tourism system. The results of the evaluation provide a critical source of information for the next ongoing stages of policy formulation, visioning, and strategic planning and development.

BENEFITS AND COSTS OF TOURISM

Tourism brings both economic and noneconomic **benefits and costs** to host communities. Some of the considerable economic impact and benefits were described in the preceding section. There are additional areas of benefit that have not received much research attention. These relate to the benefits occurring to the traveler, such as the contribution of pleasure travel to rest and relaxation, the educational benefit, the understanding of other people and cultures, and the physical and mental well-being of the traveler.

There is no question that tourism delivers benefits, but tourism is not perfect. Even advocates for tourism such as your authors (we have been accused of being cheerleaders for tourism) acknowledge that tourism is not an unqualified blessing. There are costs and benefits, and they do not accrue equally. Many of the social costs incurred are difficult or impossible to measure. Books such as *The Golden Hordes, Tourism: Blessing or Blight,* and *The Holiday Makers* (see the Selected References) point out some of the unpleasant aspects of tourism. Improperly planned and developed tourism can create problems. The demands of tourism may come into conflict with the needs and wishes of local residents. Thoughtless development, inappropriate development, overdevelopment, or unfinished development can easily damage the environment.

Tourism has been blamed for polluting beaches; raising the price of labor, land, goods, and so on; spoiling the countryside; contaminating the values of native people; crowding; congestion; noise; litter; crime; loss of privacy; creating social tensions; environmental deterioration; lack of control over a destination's future; and low-paid seasonal employment. These problems are common to many forms of development and in many cases represent dissatisfaction with the status quo or overdevelopment. They emphasize the need for a coordinated overall economic development plan of which tourism will be one part.

We must accept that tourism is neither a blessing nor a blight, neither poison nor panacea. Tourism can bring great benefits, but it can also bring social problems. The world has experience in how to increase the benefits of tourism, and at least some experience in how to lessen social problems. What has to be done is to balance the benefits and costs to come up with the best cost/benefit result.

Tourism students and executives must have a clear understanding of both the positive and negative impacts of tourism on the quality of life of a nation, a province or state, or a community. What are the positive aspects? The negative aspects? We need a balance sheet. First we look at the plus side of the ledger:

- Provides employment opportunities, both skilled and unskilled, because it is a labor-intensive industry
- Generates a supply of needed foreign exchange
- Increases incomes
- Creates increased gross national product
- Can be built on existing infrastructure
- Develops an infrastructure that will also help stimulate local commerce and industry
- Can be developed with local products and resources
- Helps to diversify the economy
- Tends to be one of the most compatible economic development activities available to an area, complementing other economic activities
- Spreads development
- Has a high multiplier impact
- Increases governmental revenues
- Broadens educational and cultural horizons and improves feelings of self-worth
- Improves the quality of life related to a higher level of income and improved standards of living
- Reinforces preservation of heritage and tradition
- Justifies environmental protection and improvement
- Visitor interest in local culture provides employment for artists, musicians, and other performing artists, thereby enhancing the cultural heritage
- Provides tourist and recreational facilities that may be used by a local population
- Breaks down language barriers, sociocultural barriers, class barriers, racial barriers, political barriers, and religious barriers
- Creates a favorable worldwide image for a destination
- Promotes a global community
- Promotes international understanding and peace

On the minus side of the ledger we find a number of problems that can be created by tourism, especially by its overdevelopment:

- Develops excess demand for resources
- Creates the difficulties of seasonality

- Causes inflation
- Can result in unbalanced economic development
- Creates social problems
- Degrades the natural physical environment and creates pollution
- Degrades the cultural environment
- Increases the incidence of crime, prostitution, and gambling
- Increases vulnerability to economic and political changes
- Threatens family structure
- Commercializes culture, religion, and the arts
- Creates misunderstanding
- Creates conflicts in the host society
- Contributes to disease, economic fluctuation, and transportation problems

Like all change, tourism exacts a price. However, it is here, it is huge, and it needs to be planned and managed. The challenge is to get the right balance, which is to have the benefits outweigh the costs and take steps to lessen the unfavorable impacts that are a part of change. Tourism development must be a part of overall economic development and must be done in a manner that is sustainable.

THE AGE OF TRAVEL

We close the chapter with a message that was delivered by David J. Humpreys, national chairman of the Travel Industry Association of America (TIA), in May 1991 at its international meeting in Denver. Mr. Humpreys provides a vision that we should all think about. Excerpts from his opening remarks deal with **"The Age of Travel."**

I want to take the opportunity to leave us with a thought we should keep with us as we help our industry march along on its determined path to become the largest in this nation and in this world. We should contemplate and think aloud about the special role and responsibility of being the most significant economic force in our global society. Because all of history—especially recent history—has an economic signature to it: The Agricultural Age; The Industrial Age; The Post Industrial Age; The Age of the Automobile; The Electronic Age; and The Computer Age. Some are, or have been, separate and distinct. Some have overlapped. But all have signified and continue to signify. All have left with us their special language, idiomatic expression, dress, and their culture.

The Agricultural Age left us in the United States with a nine-month school year, land-grant state colleges that first focused on agricultural training, research and development, and with an almost singular form-related meaning to the English word, "commodity."

The Industrial Age here left us with row housing, clustered urban areas with the factory as community hub, lunch buckets, mass production, and the assembly line.

The Computer Age has provided our language with new verbs such as "to access," "to network," "to download," and all of them are already in use outside of the medium that spawned them. So it has been, so it is, and so it shall be with The Age of Travel.

As delegates and as messengers, we have an obligation that goes along with our commercial obligations as business and professional people. And that is to think ahead. To have vision. To look forward to that time and that age that will be known as The Age of Travel.

How will our global society grow and change when the economic, cultural, and sociological impact of travel and tourism is fully felt?

And when we achieve our full presence in the political economy of the world, will we use our position widely and responsibly?

As business people and educators, we will have to face this and other challenges in the next century. As delegates and messengers, we should start to think about these challenges now.

SUMMARY

In this chapter we have examined the subject of tourism. The rapid growth in the movement of people, both domestically and internationally, has brought about an industry of vast proportions and diversity. Also, it is universal—found in all countries of the world, but in greatly varied qualities and proportions.

The economic importance and future prospects are also worthy of careful study. These considerations lead to the ways in which the study of tourism can be undertaken. There are a number of basic approaches to the study of tourism, and in this book we include all of them in the various chapters. By the time you complete the book you will know a great deal about the social and economic implications of tourism, and you will have developed a keen interest in our world and the fascinating panorama of places, peoples, cultures, beauty, and learning that travel provides in such abundance.

ABOUT THE READING

There is one reading in this chapter featuring quotes on tourism by past and present world leaders. It was prepared by the World Travel and Tourism Council.

READING 1.1

WHAT WORLD LEADERS HAVE TO SAY[2]

"Tourism is big business in Canada with a unique ability to create jobs nationwide. It is a people-intensive industry with a demonstrated ability to create jobs at a faster rate, more economically, than the economy as a whole."

Prime Minister Jean Chretien
Canada

"We, on our part, are consolidating and supporting the industry of tourism in Egypt, not only for its many advantages as a national and interna-

---

[2] This list of "Quotable Quotes" has been compiled by the World Travel & Tourism Council.

tional economic activity of utmost importance, and a field for provision of new working opportunities for our manpower, but also because it represents an effective tool in strengthening the changes of stability and peace."

President Mohamed Hosni Moubarak
Egypt

"I share your views on the need for more research into the relationship between tourism and employment and I am informed of Mr. Papoutsis' intention that the work programme of Directorate General XXIII for 1997 should give special attention to the aspect."

President Jacques Santer
European Union

"The economic importance of tourism in Germany is increasing steadily and is one of the leading sectors. Last year, two million people were employed in the industry and about 75,000 young people have received vocational training in the field. The importance of tourism for growth and employment should be safeguarded for the future."

Federal Chancellor Dr. Helmut Kohl
Germany

"Tourism is the perfect tool to build a just and prosperous society because it can not only create jobs needed to absorb Indonesia's abundant human resources but also instill new pride in Indonesian culture and spirituality."

President H. Muhammad Soeharto
Republic of Indonesia

"Tourism is important for Israel and its neighbours and for the enhancement of peace. I can't think of a better package than a trip to Israel and Jordan."

Prime Minister Benjamin Netanyahu
Israel

"Tourism has exerted enormous impact on the economic development of the Caribbean region as a whole. It accounts for a much as 25% of the total value of exports or goods and services, making the Caribbean the world's most tourist dependent region."

Prime Minister Percival J. Patterson
Jamaica

"I have always believed that as we get to know one another, we come to realize that those things which bring us together are far greater than those which separate us. Travel & Tourism give us the change to make friends from cultures different from ours and from countries distant from our own."

His Majesty King Hussein
Jordan

"The Asia-Pacific region, as one of the fastest growing regions in world tourism, is in urgent need of creating a vision for sustainable development for tourism. How we deal with our potential for growth will have a crucial impact on our future prosperity."

His Excellency Mr. Maumoon Abdul Cayoom
President of the Republic of Maldives

"The multi-billion-peso industry that we call, collectively, tourism is a critical component of our economic recovery. Earlier this week, I had a fruitful meeting with the President of the World Travel & Tourism Council, (WTTC), Geoffrey Lipman—and we both agreed that tourism is the driving force that will move Asia-Pacific well ahead of the other regions into the next century and beyond."

President H. E. Fidel V. Ramos
Philippines

"Tourism brings us a large revenue in foreign exchange earnings, but more importantly still, it makes a significant impact on the reconstruction and development programme. Tourism can contribute substantially to developing the people of our country as it is a highly labour intensive industry accommodating a wide spectrum of skilled and semi-skilled labour."

President Nelson Mandela
South Africa

"The Travel & Tourism industry in this country has performed excellently, gaining world market share, increasing its contribution to GDP and creating 1 in 5 of all new jobs."

Ex-Prime Minister John Major
United Kingdom

"Partnership is key to the Travel & Tourism industry's future success. Government, the tourism boards and the industry must unite to realize our common goal. Our future aim is clear. We want Britain to enjoy the benefits of a thriving, competitive and above all profitable industry."

Virginia Bottomley, Ex-Minister of National Heritage
United Kingdom

"The Travel & Tourism industry is essential to providing opportunity for all Americans in the 21st century. It is our largest business service export and the second largest employer in the nation."

"The Travel & Tourism industry is a powerhouse in the global economy, generating more than four hundred billion dollars in revenue and providing more than 10% of the world's income and employment."

President Bill Clinton
United States

KEY CONCEPTS

accommodations
Age of Travel
benefits of tourism
built environment
catalyst organizations
costs of tourism
culture
domestic tourism
economic impact
excursionist
expenditures
host community

host community government
importance of tourism
inbound tourism
internal tourism
international tourism
marketing
national resources
national tourism
operating sectors
outbound tourism
recreation
same-day visitors

study approaches to tourism
tourism
the tourist
tourist attractions
tourist industry
transportation
travel
trip
traveler
usual environment
visit
visitor

INTERNET SITES

The Internet sites mentioned in this chapter are repeated here for convenience plus some selected additional sites. For more information, visit these sites. Be aware that Internet addresses change frequently, so if a site cannot be accessed, use a search engine. Also use a search engine to locate many additional sites that are available.

American Society of Travel Agents
http://www.asta.net.com

Annals of Tourism Research
http://www.elsevier.com

Australia Tourist Commission
http://www.tourism.gov.au/welcome.html

CAB International
http://www.cabi.org

Canadian Tourism Commission
http://www.canadatourism.com

International Air Transport Association
http://www.iata.org

International Association of Amusement Parks and Attractions
http://www.iaapa.org

International Association of Convention and Visitor Bureaus
http://www.iacvb.org

International Festival and Events Association
http://www.ifea.com

International Hotel and Restaurant Association
http://www.ih-ra.com

Journal of Travel Research
http://www.sagepub.com

Tourism Industries
http://tinet.ita.doc.gov

Tourism Management
http://www.elsevier.com

Travel Industry Association of America
www.tia.org

Travel Trade
http://www.traveltrade.com

Travel Web Sites
http://www.yahoo.com/recreation/travel

Travel Weekly
http://www.twcrossroads.com

World Travel and Tourism Council
http://www.wttc.org

World Travel Organization
http://www.world-tourism.org

INTERNET EXERCISE

Site Name: World Travel and Tourism Council

URL: http://www.wttc.org/

Background Information: The World Travel & Tourism Council (WTTC) is the global business leaders' forum for travel and tourism. Its members are chief executives from all sectors of the travel and tourism industry, including accommodations, catering, cruises, entertainment, recreation, transportation, and travel-related services. Its central goal is to work with governments to realize the full economic impact of the world's largest generator of wealth and jobs, namely, travel and tourism.

Exercise

1. The WTTC's millennium vision identifies the potential for Travel and Tourism to generate more than 100 million new jobs across the global economy over the next decade, via public/private sector cooperation. It has four components. Explore the WTTC web site and describe the four components of WTTC's vision.

QUESTIONS FOR REVIEW AND DISCUSSION

1. Identify and describe the four perspectives contained in the definition of tourism, in terms of your home community.

2. Why do bodies such as the United States need specific tourism definitions? Why does a state or country need them? A county? A city?

3. What approach to tourism study does this course take? Which approach interests you most?

4. What are the components of tourism?

5. How important are tourist attractions?

6. Why are geographers, sociologists, anthropologists, and economists interested in tourism?

7. What will the tourism industry be like in the year 2010?

8. What are the benefits of tourism?

9. What are some negative aspects of tourism?

10. Why is tourism so popular?

11. Identify the principal factors creating The Age of Travel.

CASE PROBLEMS

1. Suppose that you are a high-school economics teacher. You plan to visit your principal's office and convince her that tourism should be included as part of one of your courses. What arguments would you use?

2. You are the minister of tourism of Jamaica, an island country. Identify the instructions you would issue to your statistics department concerning collecting data on tourist arrivals and expenditures.

SELECTED REFERENCES

Ap, John, and John L. Crompton. "Developing and Testing a Tourism Impact Scale." *Journal of Travel Research,* Vol. 37, No. 2, pp. 120–130, November 1998.

Boniface, Brian, G., and Christopher Cooper. *The Geography of Travel and Tourism.* London: Butterworth-Heinemann, 1994.

Brown, F. *Tourism: Blight or Blessing?* Oxford: Butterworth-Heinemann, 1998.

Buhalis, Dimitrois, A. Min Tjoa, and Jafar Jafari. *Information and Communication Technologies in Tourism 1998.* New York: Springer, 1998.

Burns, Peter M., and Andrew Holden. *Tourism: A New Perspective.* Upper Saddle River, NJ: Prentice-Hall, 1995.

Clements, Christine, et al. *Tourism Business Entrepreneurial Handbook: A Guide for People Interested in Starting a Tourism Business.* Denver, CO: Western Entrepreneurial Network, Colorado Center for Community Development, March 1995.

Cook, Roy, Laura Yale, and Joseph Marqua. *Tourism: The Business of Travel.* Upper Saddle River, NJ: Prentice-Hall, 1999.

Cook, Suzanne, and William Evans. *A Portrait of Travel Industry Employment in the U.S. Economy.* Washington, D.C.: TIA Foundation, 1996.

Cooper, C., et al. *Tourism: Principles and Practice.* Essex, UK: Longman, 1998.

Davidson, Rob, and Robert Maitland. *Tourism Destinations.* London: Hodder and Stoughton, 1997.

Degg, Richard, ed. *Leisure, Recreation, and Tourism Abstracts.* Wallingford, Oxon, England: CAB International, quarterly.

Feder, Anthony, J. "Are Leisure, Recreation, and Tourism Interrelated?" *Annals of Tourism Research,* Vol. 14, No. 3, pp. 311–313, 1987.

Frechtling, Douglas C.; *Annotated Bibliography on Health and Tourism Issues.* Washington, D.C.: Pan American Health Organization, 1992.

Fridgen, Joseph D., *Dimensions of Tourism.* East Lansing, MI: Educational Institute of the American Hotel and Motel Association, 1991.

Gee, Chuck, James Makens, and Dexter Choy. *The Travel Industry.* New York: John Wiley & Sons, 1997.

Getz, Donald, et al. "Roles, Issues, and Strategies for Convention and Visitors' Bureaux in Destination Planning and Product Development: A Survey of Canadian Bureaux." *Tourism Management,* Vol. 19, No 4, pp. 331–340, 1998.

Goeldner, C.R., and Karen Dicke. *Bibliography of Tourism and Travel Research Studies, Reports and Articles.* 9 Vols. Boulder, CO.: Business Research Division, University of Colorado, 1980.

Gunn, Clare A. *Tourism Planning.* New York: Taylor & Francis, 1994.

Harris, Robert, and Joy Howard. *Dictionary of Travel, Tourism and Hospitality Terms.* Victoria, Australia: Hospitality Press, 1996.

Hawkins, Donald E., and J. R. Brent Ritchie. *World Travel and Tourism Review: Indicators, Trends, and Forecasts.* Tucson, AZ.: CAB International, Vol. 1, 1991, Vol. 2, 1992, Vol. 3, 1993.

Holloway, J. Christopher. *The Business of Tourism.* London: Longman, 1998.

Howell, David W. *Passport: An Introduction to the Travel and Tourism Industry.* Cincinnati, OH: South-Western Publishing Company, 1993.

Hudman, Lloyd E., and Donald E. Hawkins. *Tourism in Contemporary Society.* Upper Saddle River, NJ: Prentice-Hall, 1989.

Hunt, John, and Donlynne Layne. "Evaluation of Travel and Tourism Terminology and Definitions." *Journal of Travel Research,* Vol. 29, No. 4, pp. 7–11, Spring 1991.

Inkpen, G. *Information Technology for Travel and Tourism.* Essex: Longman, 1998.

Jackson, Ian. *An Introduction to Tourism.* Victoria, Australia: Hospitality Press, 1997.

Jafari, Jafar. "Anatomy of the Travel Industry." *Cornell Hotel and Restaurant Administration Quarterly,* Vol. 24, No. 1, pp. 71–77, May 1983.

Jansen-Verbeke, Myriam, and Adri Dietvorst. "Leisure, Recreation, Tourism: A Geographic View on Integration." *Annals of Tourism Research,* Vol. 14, No. 3, pp. 361–375, 1987.

Khan, Mahmood, Michael Olsen, and Turgut Var. *VNR's Encyclopedia of Hospitality and Tourism.* New York: Van Nostrand Reinhold, 1993.

Krippendorf, Jost. *The Holiday Makers.* London: Butterworth-Heinemann, 1989.

Lavery, Patrick. *Travel and Tourism.* Huntingdon, England: Elm Publications, 1996.

Lavery, Patrick, and Carlton S. Van Doren, *Travel and Tourism: A North-American–European Perspective.* Huntingdon, England: Elm Publications, 1990.

Laws, Eric, ed. *The ATTT Tourism Education Handbook.* London: The Tourism Society, 1997.

Leiper, Neil. "The Framework of Tourism: Towards a Definition of Tourism, Tourist and the Tourism Industry." *Annals of Tourism Research,* Vol. 6, No. 4, pp. 390–407, October–December 1979.

Leiper, Neil. *Tourism Management.* Victoria, Australia: TAFE Publications, 1995.

Lickorish, Leonard J., and Carson L. Jenkins. *An Introduction to Tourism,* Oxford, UK: Butterworth-Heinemann, 1997.

Masberg, Barbara A. "Defining the Tourist: Is It Possible? A View from the Convention and Visitors Bureau." *Journal of Travel Research,* Vol. 37, No. 1, pp. 67–70, August 1998.

McDowall, Nerida. *An Introduction to the Hospitality Industry in Australia.* Victoria, Australia: RMIT Publishing, 1996.

Medik, S. *Understanding Tourism.* Oxford, England: Butterworth-Heinemann, 1997.

Medlik, S. *Dictionary of Travel, Tourism and Hospitality.* Oxford, England: Butterworth-Heinemann, 1996.

Mill, Robert Christie, and Alastair M. Morrison. *The Tourism System.* Dubuque, IA: Kendall/Hunt, 1998.

Morley, Clive L. "What Is Tourism" Definitions, Concepts and Characteristics." *Journal of Tourism Studies,* Vol. 1, No. 1, May 1990.

Nickerson, Norma P. *Foundations of Tourism.* Upper Saddle River, NJ: Prentice-Hall, 1996.

Pearce, Douglas. *Tourism Today: A Geographical Analysis.* Essex, UK: Longman Scientific and Technical, 1995.

Pearce, Philip L., Gianna Moscardo, and F. Ross. *Tourism and Community Relationships.* Tarrytown, NY: Elsevier Science, 1997.

Pompl, W. and P. Lavery, eds. *Tourism in Europe: Structures and Developments.* Tucson, AZ: University of Arizona Press, 1993.

Poon, Auliana. *Tourism, Technology and Competitive Strategies.* Port-of-Spain, Trinidad: Caribbean Futures Limited, 1994.

Powers, Tom. *Introduction to Management in the Hospitality Industry.* New York: Wiley, 1999.

Remington, Joan, and Marcel Escoffier. "Tourism: Who Needs It?" *Florida International University Hospitality Review,* Vol. 14, No. 1, pp. 19–25, Spring 1996.

Sebo, Roberto L. *The Traveler's World-Destination Geography.* Cincinnati, Ohio: South-Western Publishing Company, 1990.

Smith, Stephen L. J. "Defining Tourism: A Supply-Side View." *Annals of Tourism Research,* Vol. 15, No. 2, pp. 179–190, 1998.

Smith, Valene L., and William R. Eadington. *Tourism Alternatives: Potentials and Problems in the Development of Tourism.* Philadelphia: University of Pennsylvania Press, 1992.

Starr, Nona. *Viewpoint: An Introduction to Travel, Tourism and Hospitality.* Upper Saddle River, NJ: Prentice-Hall, 1997.

Theobald, William, ed. *Global Tourism: The Next Decade.* Oxford, England Butterworth-Heinemann, 1994.

Timmons, Veronica. *Travel and Tourism: Focus Canada.* Vancouver, British Columbia, Canada: Timmons and Associates, 1991.

Travel Industry Association of America. The White House Conferences on Travel and Tourism. Washington, D.C.: TIA, 1994.

Travel Industry Association of America. Tourism Works for America. Washington, D.C.: TIA, annual.

Turner, Louis, and John Ash. *The Golden Hordes.* London: Constable, 1975.

University of Colorado Business Research Division. *Tourism's Top Twenty.* Boulder, CO: University of Colorado, 1996. Published in cooperation with the Travel Industry Association of America.

Van Doren, Carlton S., and Sam A. Lollar. "The Consequences of Forty Years of Tourism Growth." *Annals of Tourism Research,* Vol. 12, No. 3, pp. 467–489, 1985.

Van Harssel, Jan. *Tourism: An Exploration.* Upper Saddle River, NJ: Prentice-Hall, 1994.

Walker, John. *Introduction to Hospitality.* Upper Saddle River, NJ: Prentice-Hall, 1999.

Waters, Somerset R. "The U.S. Travel Industry: Where We're Going." *Cornell Hotel and Restaurant Administration Quarterly,* Vol. 30, No. 4, pp. 26–33, February 1990.

Waters, Somerset R. *Travel Industry World Yearbook: The Big Picture.* New York: Child & Waters, annual.

Weiler, Betty, and Colin Michael Hall. *Special Interest Tourism.* New York: Wiley, 1992.

Weissman, Arnie. *Travel Around the World.* Austin, TX: Weissmann Travel Reports, 1997.

Witt, Stephen F., and Luiz Moutinho. *Tourism Marketing and Management Handbook.* London: Prentice-hall, 1994.

World Tourism Organization. *Concepts, Definitions, and*

Classifications for Tourism Statistics. Madrid: WTO, 1995.

World Tourism Organization. *Implications of the WTO/UN Tourism Definitions.* Madrid: WTO, 1995.

World Tourism Organization. *Recommendations on Tourism Statistics.* Madrid: WTO, 1996.

World Tourism Organization. *Yearbook of Tourism Statistics.* Madrid: WTO, 1997.

World Travel and Tourism Council. *The WTTC Report.* Brussels: WTTC, 1995.

World Travel Organization. *Tourism Compendium.* Madrid: WTO, 1998.

Youell, R. *Tourism: An Introduction.* Essex, England: Longman, 1998.

Young, George. *Tourism: Blessing or Blight?* Baltimore: Penguin Books, 1973.

CHAPTER 2

TOURISM THROUGH THE AGES

- Recognize the antiquity of human travel over vast distances on both sea and land.

- Understand how these journeys have evolved from trips that were difficult and often dangerous, to mass travel for millions today.

- Learn the names of some of the great travelers in history who wrote astonishing accounts of exotic places they had visited.

- Discover the many similarities in travel motivations, economic conditions, political situations, attractions, and tourist facilities during the period of the Roman Empire and today.

◄ *For generations, travelers have flocked to the Great Wall of China. It is some 3946 miles long and at least 2600 years old. It is the only man-made structure on earth visible to the naked eye from the moon. (Photo courtesy of the China National Tourist Office.)*

INTRODUCTION

> We travel long roads and cross the water to see what we disregard when it is under our eyes. This is either because nature has so arranged things that we go after what is far off and remain indifferent to what is nearby, or because any desire loses its intensity by being easily satisfied, or because we postpone whatever we can see whenever we want, feeling sure we will often get around to it. Whatever the reason, there are numbers of things in this city of ours and its environs which we have not even heard of, much less seen; yet, if they were in Greece or Egypt or Asia . . . we would have heard all about them, read all about them, looked over all there was to see.
>
> The younger Pliny, second century C.E.[1]

Twentieth-century travelers, tiredly pulling their carry-on bags from the overhead bin and waiting to walk down the jetway to a foreign destination, may think their experience is uniquely modern. But they are the latest in a long line of travelers reaching back to antiquity. From earliest times, "all modes of carriage (from animal to the sonic jet) and accommodations (from the meanest hovel to the five-star luxury hotel) have given a livelihood to countless legions."[2] Like today's travelers, these travelers did not do it alone. "Guiding, counseling, and harboring the traveler is among the world's earliest vocations."[3]

Typically, modern travelers enlist a travel agent to make plane reservations, book some hotels, and make recommendations for special tours upon arrival in Athens or Madrid. Despite specialized help, they typically arrive feeling dirty and tired, complain about the crowded flight, and hope to clear customs without waiting in a long line. A middle-aged couple ruefully recall that the travel agent was not able to book a hotel that she could recommend. (An automobile festival or a visit by the Pope had filled major hotels, and there was little choice.) Also, the local bank was out of pesatas or zylotis or won—or whatever the name of the destination country's currency. So the couple has to exchange money before getting a cab to that unpromising hotel and are sure that the driver won't speak English, will spot them as greenhorns, and will drive them all over—with the meter running on and on.

EARLY BEGINNINGS

The invention of money by the **Sumerians** (Babylonians) and the development of trade beginning about 4000 B.C.E. mark the beginning of the modern era of travel. Not only were the Sumerians the first to grasp the idea of money and use it in business transactions, but they were also the first to invent cuneiform writing and the wheel, so

---

[1] Lionel Casson, *Travel in the Ancient World* (London: George Allen & Unwin, 1974), p. 253. A note on style: B.C.E. (Before the Common Era) and C.E. (Common Era), used by some authors and often used in scholarly literature, are the alternative designations corresponding to B.C. and A.D.

[2] Eric Friedheim, *Travel Agents: From Caravans and Clippers to the Concorde* (New York: Travel Agent Magazine Books, 1992), pp. 27–28.

[3] Ibid., p. 5.

Ancient Egyptian pyramids and the Sphinx were some of the world's first tourist attractions. *(Photo courtesy of Air France.)*

they should be credited as the founders of the travel business. People could now pay for transportation and accommodations with money or by barter.

Five thousand years ago, cruises were organized and conducted from Egypt. Probably the first journey ever made for purposes of peace and tourism was made by Queen Hatshepsut to the lands of Punt (believed to be on the east coast of Africa) in 1480 B.C.E. Descriptions of this tour have been recorded on the walls of the Temple of Deit El Bahari at Luxor. These texts and bas reliefs are among the world's rarest artworks and are universally admired for their wondrous beauty and artistic qualities. The Colossi of Memnon at Thebes have on their pedestals the names of Greek tourists of the fifth century B.C.E.

Beginning in 2700 B.C.E. the pharaohs began to take advantage of the abundance of good building stone in the Nile valley to build their elaborate burial tombs. They included the step pyramid of Djoser, the Sphinx, the three great pyramids at Gizeh, and the pyramid complex at Abusir.[4] These great outdoor wonders began attracting large numbers as early as the New Kingdom from 1600 to 1200 B.C.E. "Each monument

---

[4] Casson, *Travel in the Ancient World*, p. 32.

was a hallowed spot, so the visitors always spent some moments in prayer, yet their prime motivation was curiosity or disinterested enjoyment, not religion."

They left evidence of their visit in inscriptions such as the following: "Hadnakhte, scribe of the treasury, came to make an excursion and amuse himself on the west of Memphis together with his brother, Panakhti, scribe of the Vizier."[5] Like tourists through the ages, they felt the need to leave evidence of their visit. Some hastily painted their names; others scratched their names in the soft stone with a sharp point. The latter method was so common that the technical term we give to such scribblings is graffiti, Italian for "scratching."

A second recognizable tourist trait was the urge to acquire souvenirs. Harkhuf, an envoy of the pharaoh to the Sudan, brought home a pygmy trained in native dances to present his ruler! Early **Egyptians** also purchased bargains or specialties abroad for their friends and relatives. In 1800 B.C.E. young Uzalum received this request: "I have never before written to you for something precious I wanted. But if you want to be like a father to me, get me a fine string full of beads, to be worn around the head."[6]

Herodotus reported:

> The Egyptians meet to celebrate festivals not once a year but a number of times. The biggest and most popular is at Bubastis . . . , the next at Busiris . . . , the third at Said . . . , the fourth at Heliopolis . . . , the fifth at Buto . . . , the six at Papremis. . . . They go there on the river, men and women together, a big crowd of each in each boat. As they sail, some of the women keep clicking castanets and some of the men playing on the pipes, and the rest, both men and women, sing and beat time with their hands. . . . And when they arrive at Bubastis, they celebrate the occasion with great sacrifices, and more wine is consumed at this one festival than during the whole rest of the year.[7]

When this holiday throng arrived at its sites, there were no commercial facilities offering food and lodging. Like modern attendees at a Grateful Dead concert, they had to sleep in the open and feed themselves as best they could.[8] In contrast, government officials such as Harkhuf, the provider of the dancing pygmy, enjoyed the comforts of temples and government depots in their travels.

Early Roads

The wheel led to the development of a heavy wagon that could be drawn by teams of oxen or onagers, a type of wild ass. "A walker or animal needs only a track,"[9] but a vehicle needs a road. There were not many **early roads** that could take wheeled traffic. A king of Ur bragged that he went from Nippur to Ur, a distance of some 100 miles, and back in a day. This boast, sometime around 2050 B.C.E., implies the existence of a

---

[5] Ibid., p. 32.
[6] Ibid., p. 34.
[7] Ibid., p. 31.
[8] Ibid., p. 35.
[9] Ibid., p. 25.

carriage road.[10] Even the best of the highways, however, were minimal. Paving was almost nonexistent until the time of the Hittites, who paved a mile and a third of road between their capital and a nearby sanctuary to carry heavily loaded wagons on festal days. Even then their war chariots, light horse-drawn carts invented for war, rolled over the countryside on dirt roads. Also, bridges were rare in a land that experienced frequent flooding. A hymn tells of King Shulgi exulting, " 'I enlarged the footpaths, straightened the highways of the land.' . . . but not every Mesopotamian monarch was a Shulgi, and there must have been long periods with nobody to 'straighten' the roads."[11]

Roads were better on the island of Crete, where the Minoans flourished from 2000 to 1500 B.C.E., and on the Greek peninsula of the Myceneans, who flourished from 1600 to 1200 B.C.E.[12] A two-lane road, $13\frac{1}{2}$ feet wide, ran from the coast of Crete of the capital at Cnossus. In Greece, roads were usually one-lane, although some were as much as $11\frac{1}{2}$ feet wide, making two-way traffic possible. Bridges and culverts kept them passable.

Who traveled? Mainly three groups: the military, government officials, and caravans. The warlike Assyrians, like the Romans after them, realized that roads were basic to moving their war chariots efficiently. As their empire expanded from the Mediterranean in the west to the Persian Gulf in the east, they [the Assyrians] improved roads, largely for military use.

The Epic of Gilgamesh (ca. 2000 B.C.E.) recounts the travels of a Sumerian king who is given directions by a deity. By only a slight stretch of the imagination, Gilgamesh's deity might be regarded as the first travel guide! This adds a fourth reason to credit the Sumerians with the beginnings of the travel industry.

The history of roads is thus related to the centralizing of populations in powerful cities. Alexander the Great found well-developed roads in India in 326 B.C.E. In Persia (now Iran) all the cities and provinces were connected by roads to the capital, Susa. These roads were built between 500 and 400 B.C.E. One of these roads was 1500 miles long.

The **Romans** started building roads in about 150 B.C.E. These were quite elaborate in construction. The roadway was surveyed using a cross-staff hung with plumb bobs. Soldiers and laborers dug the roadbed, and then stones and concrete were evenly placed. Paving stones were then laid on top, and the highway was edged with curbstones and contoured to a sloping crown to shed the rain. Some of these roads are still in use.

By the time of emperor Trajan (ruled from C.E. 98 to 117), the Roman roads comprised a network of some 50,000 miles. They girdled the Roman Empire, extending from near Scotland and Germany in the north to the south well within Egypt and along the southern shores of the Mediterranean Sea. To the east, roads extended to the Persian Gulf in what is now Iraq and Kuwait.

The Romans could travel as much as 100 miles a day using relays of horses furnished from rest posts 5 to 6 miles apart. Romans also journeyed to see famous tem-

---

[10] Ibid., p. 25.

[11] Ibid., p. 27.

[12] Ibid., p. 27.

ples in the Mediterranean area, particularly the pyramids and monuments of Egypt. Greece and Asia Minor were popular destinations, offering the Olympic Games, medicinal baths and seaside resorts, theatrical productions, festivals, athletic competitions, and other forms of amusement and entertainment. The Roman combination of empire, roads, the need for overseeing the empire, wealth, leisure, tourist attractions, and the desire for travel created a demand for accommodations and other tourist services that came into being as an early form of tourism.

Roman tourists went about sightseeing much as we do today. They used guidebooks, employed guides, left graffiti everywhere, and bought souvenirs. The examples are diverse and often amusing. A **Greek** named Pausanias wrote a *Guidebook of Greece*, which is the only guidebook to survive from ancient times. Written between C.E. 160 and 180 (during the reigns of emperors Hadrian, Antoninus Pius, and Marcus Aurelius), it "marks a milestone in the history of tourism. He [Pausanias] is the direct ancestor of the equally sober and unimaginative, painstakingly comprehensive and scrupulously accurate Karl Baedeker."[13]

The Silk Road

In 1889, Rudyard Kipling penned the oft-quoted line, "East is East and West is West and never the twain shall meet." Actually, East and West had already met more than 2000 years earlier on the now-fabled **Silk Road.**

Indeed, it is a misnomer to even call it a road. From the beginning, some silk route sections were mere directions across trackless steppe or desert rather than visible paths: ". . . the majority of states on the Silk Routes traded with their nearer neighbors, and travellers were like participants in a relay race stretching a third of the way around the world."[14]

Marco Polo, who traveled to China from Italy in the 13th century, became the first western explorer to compose a popular and lasting account. Though his chronicle is probably more fiction than history, since it draws from the tales of many traders, his observations often ring true. In spite of omissions and exaggerations, his book has remained an international best seller.[15]

Just as the Silk Road was not a road, so silk was but a part of the trade. Westbound caravans carried furs, ceramics, spices, the day lily for its medicinal uses, peach, apricot, and even rhubarb.[16] Eastbound ones carried precious metals and gems, ivory, glass, perfumes, dyes, textiles, as well as the grape vine, alfalfa, chives, coriander, sesame, cucumber, fig, and safflower.[17]

For protection against marauders, merchants formed caravans of up to 1000 camels, protected by armed escorts. Each two-humped Bactrian camel could carry 400–500 pounds of merchandise. The long route was divided into areas of political and economic influence. "The Chinese traders escorted their merchandise as far as Dunhuang or beyond the Great Wall to Loulan where it was sold or bartered to Cen-

---

[13] Ibid., p. 299.
[14] Peter Neville-Hadley, *China: The Silk Routes* (Old Saybrook, CT: Globe Pequot Press, 1997).
[15] J. D. Brown, *Frommer's China: The 50 Most Memorable Trips* (New York: Simon & Schuster, 1998), p. 371.
[16] Neville-Hadley, p. 61.
[17] Stephen G. Haw, *A Traveller's History of China*, 2nd ed. (New York: N.W. Publishing Group, 1998), pp. 84–85.

tral Asian middlemen—Parthians, Sogdians, Indians, and Kushans—who carried the trade on to the cities of the Persian, Syrian, and Greek merchants. Each transaction increased the cost of the end product, which reached the Roman Empire in the hands of Greek and Jewish entrepreneurs."[18]

The Classical World

The lands of the Mediterranean Sea (2000 B.C.E. to C.E. 500) produced a remarkable evolution in travel. In the cradle of Western civilization, travel for trade, commerce, religious purposes, festivals, medical treatment, or education developed at an early date. There are numerous references to caravans and traders in the Old Testament.

Beginning in 776 B.C.E., citizens of the city states came together every four years to honor Zeus through athletic competition. Eventually, four of these national festivals emerged: the **Olympic Games,** Pythian Games, Isthmian Games, and Nemean Games. Each festival included sacrifice and prayer to a single god. They honored the deity by offering up a superlative athletic or artistic performance.

Thus

the festivals furnished in one unique package the spectrum of **attractions** that have drawn tourists in all times and places: the feeling of being part of a great event and of enjoying a special experience; a gay festive mood punctu-ated by exalted religious moments; elaborate pageantry; the excitement of contests between performers of the highest calibre—and, on top of all this, a chance to wander among famous buildings and works of art. Imagine the modern Olympics taking place at Easter in Rome, with the religious services held at St. Peter's. . . .[19]

Greek inns provided little more than a night's shelter. A guest who wanted to wash had to carry his own towel down the street to the nearest public bath. Once there, he took off his clothes in a dressing room and put his clothes in someone's care, lest they be stolen while he bathed. "The bath itself . . . was a big basin over which he leaned while an attendant sloshed water over him."[20]

Everyday folk could also be found wending their way to the sanctuaries of the heal-ing gods, especially Aesclepius. Such places were usually located in a beautiful setting that included pure air and water (often with mineral springs). The sanctuary at Epi-daurus also included facilities for rest and diversion, including the temple with ad-mired sculptures, colonnades for shaded walks, a stadium for athletic events, and the second-largest theater in Greece. The Greeks recognized rest and diversion as impor-tant elements in treatment of the sick.

People also traveled to seek advice of the oracles, especially those at Dodona and Delphi. Statesmen, generals, and other powerful figures sought advice before taking an important action. Socrates' disciple inquired about his master's wisdom at the tem-ple of Delphi.[21]

---

[18] Judy Bonavia, *The Silk Road from Xi' an to Kashgar,* revised by William Lindesay and Wa Qi, 2nd ed. (New York: W. W. Norton & Co., 1999).
[19] Casson, *Travel in the Ancient World,* pp. 76–77.
[20] Ibid., p. 89.
[21] Ibid., pp. 84–85.

The Parthenon, temple of the goddess Athena, dates from the fifth century B.C.E. It sits atop the rocky plateau of the Acropolis, overlooking the modern city of Athens, Greece. *(Photo courtesy of the Greek National Tourist Organization.)*

While visitors to festivals, businessmen, the sick, and advice seekers comprised the bulk of travelers in the fifth and fourth centuries B.C.E., there was also another small category, the tourist. Greece's "Father of History," Herodotus, would undoubtedly have qualified for the top category of frequent traveler miles if such awards had been given. In addition to traveling all over Greece and the Aegean Islands, he sailed to Cyrene in north Africa, explored southern Italy and Sicily, and sailed from Ephesus on the west coast of Asia Minor to Sardis. He got as far east as Babylon by sailing to Syria, then striking east to the Euphrates and following a caravan track for weeks. There he looked upon the ancient city of Babylon:

> . . . square in shape, with each side 14 miles long, a total of 56 miles. Babylon is not only of enormous size; it has a splendour such as no other city of all we have seen. . . . The city wall is $85\frac{1}{2}$ feet wide and 342 high. . . . Its circuit is pierced by one hundred entrances, with gates, jambs, and lintels of bronze . . . The town is full of three- and four-storey houses and is cut through with streets that are absolutely straight, not only the main ones but also the sidestreets going down to the river.[22]

His figures are inflated, probably because he got them from his guides. He loved doing the sights and, like most modern tourists, was dependent on guides for information. A Greek entering Asia minor would encounter strange tongues and Oriental

---

[22] Ibid., p. 99.

ways. It would not be until Alexander conquered the Persian empire that the Greek ways would spread into the ancient east.

Herodotus writes of many Greeks going to Egypt: "some, as might be expected, for business, some to serve in the army, but also some just to see the country itself." Possibly, Herodotus's travel combined business and pleasure, as did that of Solon, who led Athens through a crisis, then took a trip abroad. Athens developed into a tourist attraction from the second half of the fifth century on, as people went to see the Parthenon and other new buildings atop the Acropolis.

Today's traveler who gets into trouble in a foreign city usually turns to his country's consul. The ancient Greek turned to his proxenos (Gr. pro, before or for; and xenos, foreigner). The primary duty of the proxenos was to aid and assist in all ways possible any of his compatriots who turned up in the place of his residence, particularly those who had come in some official capacity.[23] His more mundane duties might include extending hospitality, obtaining theater tickets, or extending a loan for someone who had run short of funds while visiting. More complex duties included negotiating ransom for relatives of someone taken as a prisoner of war. The heirs of someone who died in the city might ask the proxenos to wind up essential financial matters there.[24]

As the fourth century B.C.E. came to a close in Greece, people traveled despite its discomfort and dangers. Traveling by sea, they worried about storms and pirates; by land, about bad roads, dismal inns, and highwaymen. Only the wealthy described by Homer could escape the worst pitfalls.

Those who traveled for business, healing, or entertainment at festivals represented the majority. A small minority traveled for the sheer love of it—like Herodotus, the world's first great travel writer.

The museum, born in the ancient Near East, came of age with the Greeks. Sanctuaries such as Apollo's at Delphi and that of Zeus at Olympia gradually accumulated valuable objects donated either as thank-you offerings for services rendered or as bribes for acts the supplicant hoped would be rendered. Herodotus describes six gold mixing bowls dedicated by Gyges of Lydia and weighing some 1730 pounds and a gold lion from Crosesus weighing 375 pounds. While Herodotus singled these out because of their cost, others were notable for their aesthetic qualities. The Greeks had few precious metals, but hewed the plentiful marble with consummate skill. The temple of Hera exemplifies the scope and quality of sculpture acquired from the seventh through the third centuries B.C.E.:

> All over the Greek world through generous gifts of statues and paintings from the hopeful or the satisfied, temples became art galleries as well as houses of worship—exactly as Europe's cathedrals and churches were destined to become. . . . And they drew visitors the same way that art-laden churches to today to see the treasures and only incidentally, to say a prayer.[25]

In Asia Minor, beginning with the installation of a democratic government in Ephesus by Alexander the Great in 334 B.C., some 700,000 tourists would crowd in Ephesus

---

[23] Ibid., p. 93.
[24] Ibid., pp. 240–241.
[25] Ibid., pp. 240–241.

(in what is now Turkey) in a single season to be entertained by the acrobats, animal acts, jugglers, magicians, and prostitutes who filled the streets. Ephesus also became an important trading center and, under Alexander, was one of the most important cities in the ancient world.

Early Ships

The Phoenicians were master shipwrights, building tubby wooden craft with a single square sail. By 800 B.C.E. they had built a network of trading posts around the Mediterranean emanating from their own thriving cities along the coast in what is now Lebanon. Acting as middlemen for their neighbors, they purveyed raw materials and also finished goods, such as linen and papyrus from Egypt, ivory and gold from Nubia, grain and copper from Sardinia, olive oil and wine from Sicily, cedar timbers from their homeland, and perfume and spices from the East. Presumably, they also occasionally carried a few passengers. They were the first creators of a maritime empire.

The Greeks followed the **Phoenicians** in becoming great sea traders. Improved ships accelerated a flourishing Mediterranean trade. Merchant ships also carried paying passengers (although Noah with his ark probably deserves credit for being the first cruise operator, even though his passengers were primarily animals). Unlike Noah's passengers, those sailing on Greek ships had to bring their own servants, food, and wine. Widely varying accommodations aboard, stormy seas, and pirate attacks were worrisome realities.

Polynesians

Among early voyages, those in Oceania were amazing. Small dugout canoes not over 40 feet in length were used for voyages from Southeast Asia southward and eastward through what is now called Micronesia across the Pacific to the Marquesas Islands, the Tuamotu Archipelago, and the Society Islands. About C.E. 500, **Polynesians** from the Society Islands traveled to Hawaii, a distance of over 2000 miles. Navigation was accomplished by observing the position of the sun and stars, ocean swells, clouds, and bird flights. Considering the problems of fresh water and food supplies, such sea travel was astonishing. Later, navigation by the early explorers was facilitated by using a sandglass to measure time, a "log" line trailed behind the ship to measure distance, and a compass to gauge direction.

Europeans

The collapse of the Roman Empire in the fourth and fifth centuries spelled disaster for pleasure travel and tourism in Europe. During the Dark Ages (from the fall of the Western Roman Empire, C.E. 476, to the beginning of the modern era, C.E. 1450), only the most adventurous persons would travel. A trip during this period in history was dangerous; no one associated travel with pleasure. The most notable exception to this in Europe during the period was the Crusades.

By the end of the Dark Ages, large numbers of pilgrims were traveling to such popular shrines as Canterbury in England (immortalized in Chaucer's Canterbury Tales) and St. James of Compostella. Fewer made the long, expensive, and often dangerous journey to the Holy Land. Beginning in 1388, King Richard II required pilgrims to carry permits, the forerunner of the modern passport. Despite hardship and dangers, they went by the thousands to pay reverence to hallowed sites, to atone for sins, or to fulfill promises they had made while ill.

A fourteenth-century travelers' guide gave pilgrims detailed directions about the regions through which they would pass and the types of inns they would encounter along the often inhospitable routes. Innkeeping had nearly disappeared except for local taverns, and a few inns were scattered throughout Europe. They typically were filthy, vermin-infested warrens. In Germany and other areas, guests commonly had to share beds. At the other end of the spectrum lay an inn of quality, such as the one described in Mandeville's guide. He quotes the mistress of the inn: "Jenette lyghte the candell, and lede them ther above in the solere (upper room), and bere them hoot watre for to wasshe their feet, and covere them with uysshons." Inns in Spain and Italy provided a bed for each guest.

Travelers of any social distinction were, however, generally entertained in castles or private houses. Church monasteries or hospices offered accommodations for the majority. They offered services well beyond bed and board. They could provide a doctor and furnish medicines, replace worn garments, provide guides to show a visitor around the sights, or even grant a loan of money. They also offered opportunities for meditation and prayer.

The most famous stopover was the French Alpine hospice of the Great Saint Bernard, established in 962. (The Saint Bernard dogs that were sent to find and rescue travelers have been made famous by ads showing a little flask of wine appended to the dogs' collars.) St. Catherine's Monastery at the foot of Mt. Sinai still flourishes. Those who could afford to pay were expected to leave a generous donation.

Eventually, providing hospitality services for increasing numbers became burdensome to the religious houses. They could not turn the poor away, because Christian charity was an important element in the Church's mission; nor could they turn away the nobles, who made generous financial contributions. But they could, and increasingly did, refer the middle classes to taverns, inns, and wine shops. Thus, the church played an important role in the development of the hospitality industry during this period.

The Grand Tour

The **"Grand Tour"** of the seventeenth and eighteenth centuries was made by diplomats, businesspeople, and scholars who traveled to Europe, mainly to the cities of France and Italy. It became fashionable for scholars to study in Paris, Rome, Florence, and other cultural centers. While making the Grand Tour began as an educational experience, it has been criticized as eventually degenerating into the simple pursuit of pleasure. The following description from *A Geography of Tourism* describes the Grand Tour.

One of the interesting aspects of the Grand Tour was its conventional and regular form. As early as 1678, John Gailhard, in his *Compleat Gentlemen,* had prescribed a three-year tour as customary. A generally accepted itinerary was also laid down which involved a long stay in France, especially in Paris, almost a year in Italy visiting Genoa, Milan, Florence, Rome, and Venice, and then a return by way of Germany and the Low

Nowhere else in the United States can visitors experience so extensively life in the eighteenth century as in Colonial Williamsburg, with its mile-long Duke of Gloucester Street, horse-drawn carriages, and hundreds of restored colonial homes and gardens. *(Photo courtesy of Virginia Tourism Corporation.)*

Countries via Switzerland. Of course, there were variations to this itinerary, but this was the most popular route: It was generally believed that "there was little more to be seen in the rest of the civil world after Italy, France, and the Low Countries, but plain and prodigious barbarism."[26]

The term Grand Tour persists today, and the trip to Europe—the Continent—can be traced back to the early Grand Tour. Today's concept is far different, however: The tour is more likely to be three weeks, not three years.

Americans

The vast continent of North America, principally in what is now Florida and in the Southwest, was originally explored by the Spanish in the sixteenth century. Remarkably long journeys were made, often under severe conditions. The Spanish used horses, which were unknown to the American Indians until that time. In the East, Cape Cod was discovered by Gosnold in 1602 and the Plymouth Colony was established in 1620.

Early travel was on foot or on horseback, but travel by small boat or canoe provided access to the interior of the country. Generally, travel was from east to west. As roads were built, stagecoach travel became widespread, and "ordinaries" (small hotels) came into common use. Among the most remarkable journeys were those by cov-

---

[26] H. Robinson, *A Geography of Tourism* (London: Macdonald and Evans, 1976), p. 13.

ered wagon to the West across the Great Plains. This movement followed the Civil War (1861–1865). Construction of railroads across the country (the first transcontinental link was at Promontory, Utah, in 1869) popularized rail travel. The Wells Fargo Company organized the **American Express** Company in 1850. This pioneer company issued the first traveler's checks in 1891 and began other travel services, later becoming travel agents and arranging tours. Today, American Express is known throughout the world for its traveler's checks, credit cards, and various travel and financial services.

One of the most significant events in America's travel history is the amount of travel done by service men and women during World War II. Over 12 million Americans served in the armed forces from 1941 to 1945. Most were assigned to duty at places far removed from their homes, such as the European and Pacific theaters of war. Extensive domestic travel was commonplace, introducing the military traveler to different and often exotic places and bringing a broader perspective of what the North American continent and foreign countries had to offer visitors. Travel thus became a part of their experience. Following the war, a large increase in travel occurred when gasoline rationing was removed and automobiles were again being manufactured. Air, rail, and bus travel also expanded.

EARLY (AND LATER) TOURIST ATTRACTIONS

Sightseeing has always been a major activity of tourists; this has been true since ancient times. Most of us have heard of the seven wonders of the ancient world, but few could win a trivia contest by naming them:

1. The Great Pyramids of Egypt, including the Sphinx
2. The Hanging Gardens of Babylon, sometimes including the Walls of Babylon and the Palace, in what is now Iraq.
3. The Tomb of Mausolus at Halicarnassus, in what is now Turkey
4. The Statue of Zeus at Olympia in Greece
5. The Colossus Rhodes in the Harbor at Rhodes, an island belonging to Greece.
6. The Great Lighthouse (Pharos) in Alexandria, Egypt
7. The Temple Artemis (also called the Temple of Diana) at Ephesus, at the time part of Greece, now in Turkey

The Great Pyramids of Egypt are the sole remaining wonder.

Just as tourists in ancient times traveled to see these wonders, modern tourists travel to see such natural wonders as the Grand Canyon, Yosemite National Park, Yellowstone, Niagara Falls, the oceans, the Great Lakes, and human-built wonders such as great cities, museums, dams, and monuments.

Spas, Baths, Seaside Resorts

Another interesting aspect in the history of tourism was the development of spas, after their original use by the Romans, which took place in Britain and on the continent. In the eighteenth century, spas became very fashionable among members of high so-

The Great Pyramids of Egypt are the sole remaining wonder of the seven wonders of the ancient world. *(Photo courtesy of the United Nations.)*

ciety, not only for their curative aspects but also for the social events, games, dancing, and gambling that they offered. The spa at Bath, England, was one such successful health and social resort.

Sea bathing also became popular, and some believed that saltwater treatment was more beneficial than that at the inland spas. Well known in Britain were Brighton, Margate, Ramsgate, Worthing, Hastings, Weymouth, Blackpool, and Scarborough. By 1861 these successful seaside resorts indicated that there was a pent-up demand for vacation travel. Most visitors did not stay overnight but made one-day excursions to the seaside. Patronage of the hotels at these resorts was still limited to those with considerable means.

Thus, tourism owes a debt to medical practitioners who advocated the medicinal value of mineral waters and sent their patients to places where mineral springs were known to exist. Later, physicians also recommended sea bathing for its therapeutic value. While spas and seaside resorts were first visited for reasons of health, they soon became centers of entertainment, recreation, and gambling, attracting the rich and fashionable with or without ailments. This era of tourism illustrates that it is usually a combination of factors rather than one element that spells the success or failure of an enterprise. Today, one finds that hot springs, although they are not high on travelers' priority lists, are still tourist attractions. Examples in the United States are Hot Springs, Arkansas; French Lick, Indiana; and Glenwood Springs, Colorado. The sea, particularly in the Sunbelt, continues to have a powerful attraction and is one of the leading forces in tourism development, which is evident by the number of travelers to Hawaii, Florida, the Caribbean, and Mexico.

EARLY ECONOMIC REFERENCES

As tourists traveled to see pyramids, visit seaside resorts, and attend festivals and athletic events, they needed food and lodging, and they spent money for these services. Traders did the same. Then as now, the economic impact of these expenditures was difficult to measure, as evidenced by the following quotation from Thomas Mun, who in 1620 wrote in England's *Treasure by Foreign Trade:* "There are yet some other petty things which seem to have a reference to this balance of which the said officers of His Majesty's Customs can take no notice to bring them into the account; as mainly, the expenses of the travelers."[27]

THE FIRST TRAVEL AGENTS

In 1822, **Robert Smart** of Bristol, England, announced himself as the first steamship agent. He began booking passengers on steamers to various Bristol Channel ports and to Dublin, Ireland.

In 1841, **Thomas Cook** began running a special excursion train from Leicester to Loughborough (in England), a trip of 12 miles. On July 5 of that year, Cook's train carried 570 passengers at a round-trip price of 1 shilling per passenger. This is believed to be the first publicly advertised excursion train. Thus, Cook can rightfully be recognized as the first rail excursion agent; his pioneering efforts were eventually copied widely in all parts of the world. Cook's company grew rapidly, providing escorted tours to the Continent and later to the United States and around the world. The company continues to be one of the world's largest travel organizations.

The first specialist in individual inclusive travel (the basic function of **travel agents**) was probably **Thomas Bennett** (1814–1898), an Englishman who served as secretary to the British consul general in Oslo, Norway. In this position, Bennett frequently arranged individual scenic tours in Norway for visiting British notables. Finally, in 1850 he set up a business as a "trip organizer" and provided individual tourists with itineraries, carriages, provisions, and a "traveling kit." He routinely made advance arrangements for horses and hotel rooms for his clients.

HISTORIC TRANSPORTATION

Another element in the tourism equation is transportation. The early tourists traveled on foot, on beasts of burden, by boat, and on wheeled vehicles.

Stagecoach Travel

Coaches were invented in Hungary in the fifteenth century and provided regular service there on prescribed routes. By the nineteenth century, stagecoach travel had become quite popular, especially in Great Britain. The development of the famous En-

---

[27] George Young, *Tourism: Blessing or Blight?* (Middlesex, England: Pelican Books, 1973), p. 1.

glish tavern was brought about by the need for overnight lodging by stagecoach passengers.

Water Travel

Market boats picked up passengers as well as goods on ship canals in England as early as 1772. The Duke of Bridgewater began such service between Manchester and London Bridge (near Warrington). Each boat had a coffee room from which refreshments were sold by the captain's wife. By 1815, steamboats were plying the Clyde, the Avon, and the Thames. A poster in 1833 announced steamboat excursion trips from London. By 1841, steamship excursions on the Thames were so well established that a publisher was bringing out a weekly *Steamboat Excursion Guide.*

Rail Travel

Railways were first built in England in 1825 and carried passengers beginning in 1830. The newly completed railway between Liverpool and Manchester featured special provisions for passengers. The railroad's directors did not expect much passenger business, but time proved them wrong. The typical charge of only 1 penny per mile created a sizable demand for rail travel—much to the delight of the rail companies. Because these fares were much lower than stagecoach fares, rail travel became widely accepted even for those with low incomes.

Early rail travel in Britain was not without its detractors, however. Writers in the most powerful organs of public opinion of that day seemed to consider the new form of rail locomotion a device of Satan. When a rail line was proposed from London to Woolrich to carry passengers at a speed of 18 miles per hour, one aghast contributor to the *Quarterly Review* wrote, "We should as soon expect the people of Woolrich to be

Older-style rail travel is still available in many places across the United States, so that tourists can experience this memorable mode of transportation. The steam train shown here carries visitors to the Grand Canyon National Park in Arizona. *(Photo by James B. Winters.)*

Automobiles dominate travel today, but visiting the William F. Harrah Automobile Museum in Reno, Nevada provides an appreciation of the old days, when cars were not quite so comfortable. *(Photo courtesy of the Reno News Bureau.)*

fired off upon one of Congreve's ricochet rockets as trust themselves to the mercy of such a machine going at such a rate." Another writer deemed the railroads for passenger transportation as "visionary schemes unworthy of notice." Between 1826 and 1840 the first railroads were built in the United States.

Automobile and Motorcoach Travel

Automobiles entered the travel scene in the United States when Henry Ford introduced his famous Model T in 1908. The relatively cheap "tin lizzie" revolutionized travel in the country, creating a demand for better roads. By 1920 a road network became available, leading to the automobile's current dominance of the travel industry. Today, the automobile accounts for about 84 percent of intercity miles traveled and is the mode of travel for approximately 80 percent of all trips. The auto traveler brought about the early tourist courts in the 1920s and 1930s, which have evolved into the motels and motor hotels of today. Motorcoaches also came into use soon after the popularization of the automobile and remain a major mode of transportation.

Air Travel

Nearly 16 years after the airplane's first flight at Kitty Hawk, North Carolina in 1903, regularly scheduled air service began in Germany. This was a Berlin–Leipzig–Weimar route, and the carrier later became known as Deutsche Lufthansa. Today, Lufthansa is a major international airline. The first transatlantic passenger was Charles A. Levine, who flew with Clarence Chamberlin nonstop from New York to Germany. The plane

Full-scale reproductions of the Wright Brothers' 1902 glider and 1903 flying machine are on display at the Wright Brothers National Memorial in Kill Devil Hills, North Carolina. The world's first powered aircraft flight took place here on December 17, 1903. *(Photo courtesy of North Carolina Travel and Tourism Division; photo by Clay Nolen.)*

made a forced landing 118 miles from Berlin, their destination, which they reached on June 7, 1927. This was shortly after Charles Lindbergh's historic solo flight from New York to Paris.

The first U.S. airline, Varney Airlines, was launched in 1926 and provided scheduled airmail service. However, this airline was formed only 11 days before Western Airlines; which began service on April 17, 1926. Varney Airlines later merged with three other lines to form United Airlines. On April 1, 1987, Western merged with Delta Airlines. At first, only one passenger was carried in addition to the mail, if the weight limitations permitted. The first international mail route was flown by **Pan American Airways** from Key West, Florida to Havana, Cuba on October 28, 1927. Pan Am flew the first passengers on the same route on January 16, 1928. The trip took 1 hour 10 minutes, and the fare was $50 each way.

The various U.S. airlines gradually expanded their services to more cities and international destinations. During World War II their equipment and most staff were devoted to war service. Development of the DC-3 and the Boeing 314A transoceanic Clipper in the early 1940s established paying passenger traffic and brought about much wider acceptance of air travel. The jet engine, invented in England by Frank Whittle, was used on such military planes as the B-52. The first American commerical jet was the Boeing 707. The first U.S. transcontinental jet flight was operated by American Airlines on January 25, 1959, from Los Angeles to New York City, and the jumbo jet era began in January 1970 when Pan American World Airways flew 352 passengers from New York to London using the new Boeing 747 equipment.

Because of its speed, comfort, and safety, air travel is the leading mode of public transportation today, as measured in revenue passenger miles (one fare-paying passenger transported one mile).

ACCOMMODATIONS

The earliest guest rooms were parts of private dwellings, and travelers were hosted almost like members of the family. In the Middle East and in the Orient, caravansaries and inns go back into antiquity. In more modern times, first the stagecoach and then railroads, steamships, the automobile, motorcoach, and airplane expanded the need for adequate accommodations. The railroad brought the downtown city hotel, the automobile and motorcoach brought the motel, and the airplane led to the boom in accommodations within or near airports. Housing, feeding, and entertaining travelers is one of the world's most important industries.

CHRONOLOGIES OF TRAVEL

Herein are two chronologies of travel: (1) a chronology of ancient migrations, early explorers, and great travelers and (2) a chronology of travel arrangers of their business and their suppliers. The selected travelers and explorers not only made remarkably long and arduous journeys to little known (and often mistaken) places, but also wrote vivid descriptions or had scribes write for them. Their hardships were sometimes unbelievably difficult, often dangerous, and occasionally fatal.

The comfortable and pleasant (even inspiring, sometimes) traveling facilities of today are truly a tribute to the development of modern technology, design, and engineering.

CHRONOLOGY OF ANCIENT MIGRATIONS, EARLY EXPLORERS, AND GREAT TRAVELERS

1 million years ago	*Homo erectus* originates in eastern and southern Africa; makes extensive migrations north to the Middle East and to Asia.
350,000 years ago	Early *Homo sapiens* evolves from *H. erectus;* dwells in Africa, Europe, and Asia.
50,000–30,000 years ago	Anatomically modern man, *H. sapiens,* evolves and expands into Australia from southeastern Asia and into northeastern Asia.
15,000 years ago	Upper Palaeolithic people cross into northern latitudes of the New World from northeast Asia on a land bridge.
B.C.E.	
4000	Sumerians (Mesopotamia–Babylonia) invent money, cuneiform writing, and the wheel; also, the concept of a tour guide.
2000–332	Phoenicians begin maritime trading and navigating over the entire Mediterranean Sea area. They may possibly have sailed as far as the

	British Isles and probably along the coast of western Africa and to the Azores.
1501–1481	Queen Hatshepsut makes the journey from Egypt to the lands of Punt—believed to an area along the eastern coast of Africa.
336–323	Alexander the Great leads his army from Greece into Asia, crossing the Indu Kush mountains (Afghanistan–Kashmir area), and to the Indus River.

C.E.

500	Polynesians from the Society Islands sail to Hawaii, a distance of over 2000 miles.
800–1100	Vikings establish trade and explore Iceland, Greenland, and the coast of North America.
1271–1295	Marco Polo, a Venetian merchant, travels to Persia, Tibet, Gobi desert, Burma, Siam, Java, Sumatra, India, Ceylon, the Siberian arctic, and other places.
1325–1354	Ibn Battuta, the "Marco Polo of Islam," a Moroccan, makes six pilgrimages to Mecca; also visits India, China, Spain, and Timbuktu in Africa.
1492–1502	Christopher Columbus explores the New World, including the Bahamas, Cuba, Jamaica, Central America, and the northern coast of South America.
1497	John Cabot, an Italian navigator, sailing from Bristol, England, discovers North America at a point now known as Nova Scotia.
1513	Vasco Núñez de Balboa, a Spanish explorer, discovers the Pacific Ocean.
1519	Ferdinand Magellan sails west from Spain to circumnavigate the globe. He was killed in the Philippines, but some of his crew completed the circumnavigation.
1540–1541	Francisco Vasquez de Coronado, a Spanish explorer, seeks gold, silver, and precious jewels (without success) in what is now Arizona, New Mexico, Texas, Oklahoma, and other areas of the American Southwest.
1602	Bartholomew Gosnold, English explorer and colonizer, navigates the eastern coast of the (now) United States from Maine to Narragansett Bay; discovers and names Cape Cod. In 1606 his ship carried some of the first settlers to Virginia.
1768–1780	James Cook, an English naval officer, explores the northeastern coast of North America, and in the Pacific he discovers New Caledonia, New Zealand, Australia, and Hawaii. He was killed in Hawaii.
1784–1808	Alexander Mackenzie, a Scot, made the first overland exploration across North America north of Mexico; discovers the river now named for him which flows into the Arctic Ocean and the Fraser River, which discharges into the Pacific.
1804–1806	Meriwether Lewis and William Clark, Americans, lead an expedition that opened the American West, discovering the Columbia River and traveling to the Pacific coast.
1860–1863	John H. Speke, an Englishman, discovers the source of the Nile River to

be the Victorian Nile flowing out of Ripon Falls, issuing from the north shore of Lake Victoria.

1925–1934	William Beebe, American underwater explorer and inventor, develops the "bathysphere" and dives to 3034 feet offshore Bermuda.
1951–1955	Elizabeth Marshall Thomas, an American, explores the Kalahari desert in central Africa.
1969	Neil Armstrong, Edwin Aldrin, Jr., and Michael Collins, American astronauts, make pioneer journey to the moon in the Saturn V space vehicle. First Armstrong and then Aldrin step out of the lunar module onto the moon's surface. Collins continues to pilot the command and service module, which later joins with the lunar module for their return to earth.

CHRONOLOGY OF TRAVEL ARRANGERS, THEIR BUSINESSES, FACILITIES, EQUIPMENT, AND SUPPLIERS

B.C.E.

2000	Caravansaries (inns) established in the Near East and the Orient in ancient times. Located on caravan routes, they provided overnight rest needs for travelers and traders and for their donkeys and camels. These people traveled in groups for mutual assistance and defense.
776	Greeks begin travels to the Olympic Games. Subsequently, the games were held every four years.

C.E.

500–1450	During Europe's Middle Ages, a royal party in unfamiliar territory sends out a "harbinger" to scout the best route, find accommodations and food, then return to the group as a guide.
1605	The hackney coach introduced in London.
1801	Richard Trevithick, in England, perfects a steam locomotive capable of pulling heavy railcars.
1815	John L. McAdam and Thomas Telford, Britishers, invent all-weather roads, subsequently with a bituminous top.
1822	Robert Smart of Bristol, England starts booking passengers on steamships sailing to Ireland.
1826–1840	Railroads begin service in the United States, first hauling minerals (such as coal) and, later, passengers.
1829	The Tremont House, the first "modern" hotel, opens in Boston.
1830	First passengers carried by rail in England.
1838	Stendhal, the pseudonym of Henri-Marie Boyle of France, authors *Les Mémoires d'un touriste,* believed to be the first disseminated printed use of the French word tourist.
1841	Thomas Cook organizes a special excursion train carrying 570 passengers from Leicester to Loughborough, England, a trip of 12 miles.
1850	Thomas Bennett, secretary to the British consul general in Oslo, Norway, sets up a "trip organizer" business as a sideline. He provides individual pleasure travel itineraries and other services.

1869	The first transcontinental railroad across the United States is completed.
1873	American Express Company created by joining the original American Express Company formed in 1850 with the Wells Fargo Company, founded in 1852.
1902	The American Automobile Association (AAA) founded in Chicago.
1903	Wilbur and Orville Wright make the first successful gasoline-powered airplane flight at Kitty Hawk, North Carolina.
1908	Henry Ford introduces the famous Model T automobile.
1918	Deutsche Lufthansa provides the first scheduled air passenger service from Berlin to Leipzig and Weimer.
1920	U.S. road system begins great improvement.
1926	Varney Airlines and Western Airlines become the first airlines in the United States.
1927	Charles A. Lindbergh flies solo from New York to Paris nonstop.
1927	Charles A. Levine becomes the first transatlantic passenger, flying from New York to within 118 miles of Berlin, his destination, because of a forced landing.
1927	Pan American Airways flies first international commercial mail flight from Key West, Florida to Havana, Cuba.
1928	Pan Am flies first passenger flight on the same route.
1931	American Society of Steamship Agents founded in New York.
1936	Air Transport Association (ATA) formed in Chicago.
1939	Frank Whittle, an Englishman, develops the first jet engine capable of powering a fullsized airplane.
1944	The American Society of Travel Agents (ASTA) founded from the American Society of Steamship Agents.
1951	Founding of Pacific Asia Travel Association (PATA) in Honolulu, Hawaii.
1952	The U.S. Congress creates the National System of Interstate Highways.
1954	Great Britain produces the Comet, the first passenger jet plane.
1958	Boeing Commercial Airplane Company produces the B-707, the first commercial jet plane built in the United States.
1959	American Airlines flies the first transcontinental B-707 flight from Los Angeles to New York.
1961	The U.S. Congress creates the U.S. Travel Service.
1964	American Airlines inaugurates the SABRE computerized reservation system (CRS).
1970	Pan American World Airways flies the first Boeing 747 "jumbo jet" plane with 352 passengers from New York to London.
1971	Amtrak assumes responsibility for all long-distance and intercity passenger rail service in the United States.
1978	British Airways and Air France begin passenger service on the supersonic Concorde airplane.
1981	France's high-speed train the TGV, sets a world speed record and begins carrying passengers.
1990	The Fall of the Berlin Wall.
1994	The "age of travel," wherein the most complex trip can be planned and arranged

by a single phone call from the traveler, might involve numerous airlines, a cruise ship, sightseeing tours, a local rental car, other ground services, and entertainment—all reserved by amazing computerized reservation systems worldwide; the entire trip, except for incidentals, is paid for by a single credit card.

1994	The "Chunnel" undersea railway opens, providing rail travel under the English Channel between England and France.
1995	Delta Airlines introduced commission caps putting a ceiling on payments to travel agents for domestic tickets.
	Denver International Airport (DIA) opened as the first new U.S. airport in 20 years.
	The first White House Conference on Travel and Tourism was held.
1996	Alaska Airlines became the first carrier to accept on-line bookings and take payment through a web site on the Internet.
1998	Hong Kong opened new $20 billion airport.

SUMMARY

Early explorers, traders, and shippers laid the groundwork upon which our modern age of travel is based. Human needs to arrange trips and facilitate movements have not changed over the ages: Building roads, vehicles, and ships and providing overnight rest accommodations go back into antiquity. The brave explorers who went into the unknown made available to their contemporaries knowledge of what the world was really like.

Over the centuries, inventions such as the sandglass to measure time, the "log" line to measure distance, and the compass to gauge direction made possible successful sea exploration. The roads of early Persia and those of the Roman Empire were used for exploration, for military purposes, for transporting tribute, and for pleasure trips and recreation.

Subsequent inventions of better roads, stagecoaches, passenger railroads, passenger ships, automobiles, motorcoaches, and airplanes created an ever-speedier and more pleasant means of travel. Hotels and inns became more commodious and comfortable, with the added convenience of location, services, and appointments.

However, the conditions for an ever-expanding tourism market are little different now from Roman times. Tourism will flourish if prospective travelers are convinced that they will be safe and comfortable and well-rewarded by their trip. When the Roman Empire declined, tourism declined. The wealthy class was reduced, roads deteriorated, and the countryside was plagued by bandits and scoundrels. Today, wars, unrest, and terrorism are similarly detrimental to tourism. Peace, prosperity, effective marketing, and reasonable travel costs remain the essential ingredients needed for the universal growth of travel.

ABOUT THE READING

This reading presents information about Newport, Rhode Island, which claims to be America's first resort. The article explores the history of Newport and finds that this claim is valid.

READING 2.1

NEWPORT, RHODE ISLAND—AMERICA'S FIRST RESORT

by Michael R. Evans
Appalachian State University

Reprinted from *Journal of Travel Research*, Vol. 36, No. 2, Fall 1997, pp 63–67, copyright © 1997 by Sage Publications. Reprinted by permission of Sage Publications, Inc.

Many communities around the world are looking for sustainable economic development. Sustainable tourism development is a management strategy that asks how a community can meet its immediate economic requirements without compromising the opportunity of future generations to have an equally viable and prosperous life (MacGregor, 1993). In the long term, the success of any tourism destination may depend on the quality of the natural and cultural environment (Manning and Dougherty, 1995). Many authors, including Cohen and Richardson (1995), suggest the need to work against incompatible industries that might harm the cultural and natural resources of a tourism destination. Wigle (1994) has suggested strategies for success in heritage tourism, and Mak and Moncur (1995) have offered success strategies in nature tourism.

Purpose of the Research

Newport, Rhode Island, claims to have learned the basic lessons in sustainable tourism development. The current slogan for the Newport County Convention and Visitors Bureau (NC-CVB) is "Newport: America's First Resort." The NC-CVB also refers to Newport as "Legendary Newport/Queen of Resorts." The purpose of this article is two-fold. First, Newport's declaration as "America's First Resort" is investigated. Second, the question, How has Newport been able to position, sustain, and thus manage itself as a fashionable tourism destination for over 300 years? is explored.

A Brief Introduction

Newport claims to have been a well-known New England seaside tourism destination for approximately 300 years. Today, the resort city of Newport, Rhode Island's premier tourism magnet, is used to shape a positive image of Rhode Island and, accordingly, at-tract people to other parts of the state. The city and Newport County are surrounded by the Narragansett Bay and the Atlantic Ocean. Newport is now known for sailing races, Gilded Age mansions, and music festivals (i.e., jazz, folk, and chamber music). However, many visitors come to Newport for natural seaside beauty, including beaches and nature parks. The city also has tradition of tennis and golf and is one of the best places in the eastern United States to view more than 350 historic colonial homes and gardens dating from the early 1700s.

Colonial Period to the Civil War

The first travel destination of North America was most likely the summer gathering places of the various New England Native American tribes. Stafford Springs, Connecticut, may be America's first travel destination according to historical records (Amory, 1952). The Native Americans introduced the Pilgrims to the mineral springs in this New England town in the early 1600s. According to Amory (1952) the history of America's first, real resort indicates the ups and downs of tourism development. Stafford Springs may hold the distinction of being the first resort, but today it is a quiet New England village that hardly would be considered a tourism mecca.

It seems that America's first tourism products were all health related. Health improvement was the primary motivation to visit any resort destination in the 1600s and 1700s. Travelers sought the benefits of the mineral and sulphur springs for gout, fevers, and so forth. Since there were many areas in the United States that had healing springs that could be thought of as tourism products, it is quite hard to determine the actual sequence of early American resort development. Most of the early resort areas were explored (by the English, French, or Spanish) in the 1700s and then settled at later dates, with taverns and hotels added much later. Established in 1639, Newport became the "first settled" destination among today's contemporary U.S. resort cities. Newport may also be home to one of the first taverns in America, the White Horse Tavern. It opened in 1673 and still operates today. It is important to note that almost all of the travel during this period was for commercial business or for health, but not for pleasure as we know it today.

Other than Newport (see Exhibit 1), some of the early American resort destinations were places like White Sulphur Springs, West Virginia (settled in 1770); Saratoga Springs, New York (settled in 1771); and Hot Springs, Arkansas (settled in 1807). Newport would later compete for national attention with these and other seaside destinations such as Bar Harbor, Maine (settled in 1763) and Cape May, New Jersey (settled in 1775). Much later, southern areas such as Palm Beach, Florida (settled in 1880) and Sarasota, Florida (settled in 1885) would become well-known resort destinations. In the late 1800s many wealthy American families would visit many of these destinations on a grand tour of the eastern United States. For example, they would visit Newport in the summer, Saratoga Springs in the fall, and Palm Beach in the winter.

In the 1730s (Jefferys, 1992) Newport become a nationally known summer destination for health-related reasons. Escaping the southern heat, yellow fever, and other related heat and health problems of the Deep South, affluent plantation owners from the West Indies and southern states would come by sailing ship (from Charleston and Savannah) to various New England coastal ports in late spring to buy fertilizers and farming supplies. They would drop off their families in Newport for the summer and return in September, with plantation crops for the northern mills and to pick up their families for the voyage back home. These southern visitors stayed in rooms or houses rented for the season and enjoyed Newport's wonderful summer climate without insects. During the later colonial period Newport developed a reputation for culture, arts, and crafts. Leisure-time activities such as fishing, horseback riding, and hunting were also popular with the wealthy who could travel for pleasure during the late 1700s.

The pre- and post-American Revolution period was

an economic disaster (1770 to 1830) for Newport. The entire trading economy suffered under British occupation and considerable maritime warfare. Many military confrontations between the English, French, and Colonial troops had an adverse effect on the Newport seaport. However, after the American Revolution, Newport witnessed the return of business activity and a slowly expanding summer resort industry.

During the 1830s tourism rebounded strongly. Large hotels started to be built (e.g., the Ocean House and the Atlantic House, which had 125 rooms), and visitors came by trains and large steamboats from New York, Philadelphia, Baltimore, and Boston. Thus, an era of great hotels (1830 to 1860) had a positive influence on Newport's tourism future. Amory (1952) concludes that during this period "social resorts" like Newport would attract "solid people" desiring long vacations filled with good scenery and solitude. Newport now attracted some of America's leading writers and artists (e.g., Henry Wadsworth Longfellow and Edith Wharton), who shaped a positive social image of Newport. Other U.S. resort destination areas, however, grew quickly during this period, and Newport had competitors like Cape May, Bar Harbor, and Saratoga Springs.

The Civil War era in the 1860s had a profound effect on Newport tourism. The war period was a disaster for summer tourism because the historic and beneficial link with the southern states was destroyed. Southern families failed to return after the war and tourism activity was thereby limited. During the Civil War, Newport inherited the U.S. Navy and Naval Academy. Newport's deep and safe harbor thrust the city into a new form of economic activity. For the next 100 years Newport would remain a major military installation that manufactured weapons, housed war ships, and trained navy seamen.

Exhibit 1
Early American Resort Destinations

Destination	Settled
Newport, Rhode Island	1639
White Sulphur Springs, West Virginia	1770
Saratoga Springs, New York	1771
Bar Harbor, Maine	1763
Cape May, New Jersey	1775
Hot Springs, Arkansas	1807
Palm Beach, Florida	1880
Sarasota, Florida	1885

The Gilded Age

During the mid- and late 1800s, Newport had the reputation for being "where the action was." This positive image was used effectively to sell many of the most influential Americans on the benefit of being seen at the right social event in Newport. At the turn of the century, many of New York's high society citizens were attracted to Newport because of the cool summer climate and Newport's growing reputation as the place to be seen (Boss 1981).

The so-called Gilded Age (1880 to 1913) was a time to forget the simple life and focus on meeting the right people in American high society. Also during this time, the factories of the Industrial Revolution turned cities into crowded, dirty places that were inappropriate for socializing in summer. The Gilded Age was a time of anxious competition among the wealthiest families in the United States. This period was known for the lavish parties of the 400 most famous American families, including the Belmonts and Astors, and, of course, the famous Vanderbilts. It became fashionable to build a summer "cottage," thereby avoiding a stay in Newport hotels. The ambition of those in the high society of this period was to be and look as much like European aristocracy as possible by living in America's only palaces, castles, and country estates.

Today, the finest collection of mansions in the United States can be seen in Newport. Most were designed by the leading architects of the era (for example, Richard Morris Hunt, who designed the Breakers, Marble House, and Ochre Court) and were influenced by the great buildings of Europe. High-society films like *The Great Gatsby* portray the images of extravagant homes and the lifestyles of the rich and famous. The mansion owners designed and built these summer cottages for the rituals of conspicuous consumption. A positive aspect of the Newport mansion era is that it facilitated an American school of architecture that would later become Newport's main heritage tourism product, annually attracting more than one million visitors.

The business of leisure also flourished during the Gilded Age. The wealth and sense of adventure and innovation of high society families in Newport fostered the development of new recreational activities. For example, yachting and sailing grew in popularity during this period. In fact, the New York Yacht Club held its first annual regatta in 1883. Later, in 1930 the America's Cup races were first held in Newport, and, in 1936, the Bermuda Yacht races became a Newport tradition. The cool steady summer ocean breezes and numerous sailing races helped establish Newport's early claim of being the "sailing capital of the world."

In 1881 the nation's first tennis match was held in Newport. Today, visitors still play tennis on nine grass courts at the Newport casino complex that houses the Tennis Hall of Fame. Other lawn sports like croquet and polo were also popular during this period. The World Croquet Association is still headquartered in Newport. In 1893 golf became an established sport in the area with the founding of the Newport Golf Club. This group organized the first U.S. amateur golf tournament in 1895. Since then Newport has had many

professional tournaments. Newport has had a long tradition of recreational sports, including sport fishing, coaching (horse-drawn carriages), car racing, cliff walking, biking, and most recently (in 1976), gaming (jai alai, keno, and slot games in one facility). Nonetheless, gaming has remained a low-key activity that is not strongly promoted.

It has been said that "mass" tourism always follows "class" tourism. Destinations made popular by the wealthy become magnets for middle-class visitors. It is interesting to note that during the Gilded Age thousands of middle-class visitors from New England came to Newport for short weekend trips during the summer. Steamers transported working people who labored in the New England textile mills, factories, and machine shops from all over New England. Most of these middle-class visitors gathered at public beaches that had boardwalks with festive retailing. Their recreational activities included walking along the beach, attending band concerts, New England clam bakes, visiting dance halls, and riding on carousels (Panaggio, 1994).

Post-Gilded Age, the Great Depression, and Two World Wars

The Gilded Age ended with the imposition of a federal income tax in 1914. Many of the families who owned Newport summer mansions could not afford the expense of having several homes and/or the staff to maintain these facilities. In addition, mansion owners like the Vanderbilts made their wealth in shipping and railroads, and these industries became much less profitable during this era. World War I, the Great Depression in the 1930s, plus a major hurricane in 1938 that damaged Newport, forced city officials to rethink, change, rebuild, and position the resort area once again.

The city and the tourism industry were on hard times during this period. For the wealthy of the late 1940s, the introduction of air conditioning and jet planes provided other options for taking a long summer vacation in one destination. Starting in the 1940s, the high cost of maintaining the Gilded Age summer homes prompted many mansion owners to donate their homes to colleges (mainly to Newport's Salve Regina University) and/or civic groups in order to gain tax credits from the federal government. In years to come many of these mansions would be operated as public museums that would encourage tourism development.

Finally, from 1914 through World War II, Newport

became a major military facility that clashed with tourism development efforts. During the 1940s, Newport's main economic activity became the navy and not the tourism industry.

1950s to the Present

During this period, Newport looked to the future through its past and the heritage tourism movement got underway. The Newport Historical Society (started in 1854) and the Newport Preservation Society (established in 1945) became crucial to Newport's economic and tourism future. Today, both groups continue to pioneer in preserving, restoring, and marketing heritage tourism. Combined, these organizations now own and manage 13 historical buildings that can be viewed by the public. These heritage attractions provide a core tourism product that most visitors want to see. Currently, approximately 25% of visitors indicate that they visit Newport for the purpose of seeing the historical architecture.

In 1973 the navy announced that all navy installations (mostly cruisers and destroyers) would be moved (except the Naval War College). The navy's long-standing presence in Newport, which started during the Civil War and continued during World War II, contributed greatly to the region's economy; therefore, the pull-out was a serious blow. Once again Newport turned to tourism to develop a new economy. Up until the move, basic navy operations had a very negative impact on tourism. The navy's presence encouraged the establishment of bars, brothels, tattoo parlors, and other businesses that discouraged other visitors. Many of these problems disappeared in the 1970s when the navy left and Newport city officials encouraged more preferable types of tourists.

During this same period, state conservation groups (for example, Save the Narragansett Bay) pushed hard to guard against industrial pollution and to protect the state's ocean coastline. Other local environmental groups were formed to protect Newport's waterfront development and demanded public access to the waterfront and beaches. Environmental groups were formed to protect local trees, parks, and areas that would later be developed as bird and animal sanctuaries. These groups prevented off-shore oil drilling (by big oil companies like Shell Oil) as an economic option during the navy's exodus in the 1970s. Because of those early efforts in heritage tourism and nature tourism, or ecotourism, Newport has remained an attractive city that harmoniously combines business, nature, and a historical past.

Just as Newport's historic preservation movement was getting underway, major downtown redevelopment activity supported by federal funds changed the Newport waterfront area from an untidy commercial area to a retail and residential area more appropriate for major tourism growth. In 1969 a new access bridge and highway road construction allowed for the development of a year-round motoring tourist economy and moved Newport away from a one-season summer resort area. Finally, in 1988, an $8 million gateway transportation center was built; the center currently houses the Newport County Convention and Visitors Bureau (NC-CVB) and the Visitor Welcome Center. The project also provided much-needed downtown parking. For a small city of 28,000 residents, this facility may be one of the best visitor complexes in the United States. During the late 1980s, Marriott and Doubletree hotels were added to the downtown area to attract the convention and meeting markets.

The NC-CVB was organized in 1988 to promote tourism, and today it has three principal departments: a department of tourism (for pleasure and tour markets), a department for meetings and conventions, and a department of special events. Recently, this combined marketing effort generated approximately $680 million in tourism revenue and 3.5 million visitors. The total NC-CVB annual budget is approximately $1.25 million. Today, Newport houses 200 major (50 or more visitors) conventions and meetings a year and attracts 7,000 motor coach tour groups. Special events have been a major thrust of Newport's recent tourism development efforts, and the NC-CVB is unique in that it has established a department to specifically direct these efforts. Newport may be best known for the Newport Jazz Festival, but the city also lures visitors with 23 other major festivals and events (500 people or more). Finally, Newport continues to look for new markets, including international visitors. The city works closely with other New England states to attract international visitors (now 7% of total visitation). Newport attracts new visitors (44% are first-time visitors) but continues to draw repeat visitors (56%). The city lodging industry has a year-round average daily rate of about $90 and a year-round hotel occupancy of 64%.

Despite the recent good health of the tourism industry, there have been some tourism-related problems. Tourism growth has brought much heavier auto traffic in the summer. Streets are very congested during major festivals and events and on weekends. Also, while real estate development has expanded the tax base, property taxes continue to rise and year-round homeowners are concerned that taxes might be out of control. Many property owners resent these high property taxes and blame them on tourism. In their minds, high taxes are due to huge summer crowds that need government services. Many locals resent the regional-day-trippers (53% of total visitation) who enjoy Newport's charm but leave without paying the true cost to maintain a beautiful city. For example, large numbers of college students and/or young adults come to Newport to bar-hop on weekends, and most stay in private homes. This group has no effect on hotel, fine dining restaurants, local attractions, and retail or arts and crafts establishment revenues.

Analysis of Newport's Historical Data

After reviewing the written history and interviewing local tourism professionals, community business leaders, and general citizens of Newport, the following basic lessons in sustainable tourism emerge:

- For 300 years Newport has enjoyed a pleasant climate that has made the area a very desirable summer destination for recreation and good health.

- For 200 years the military/navy presence has had a negative impact on the tourism industry. Throughout Newport's history, basic military operations clashed with pleasure tourism. However, the Newport Naval War College now seems to have a positive effect on the tourism industry. This professional college coexists with tourism in a period of peace.

- For 200 years Newport has had a strong image as a cultural center for arts, crafts, furniture design, and Yankee food and drink that has attracted many famous people. Today, music festivals, fine-dining establishments, antique shops, and arts and crafts businesses reinforce the image of Newport's cultural tourism product.

- For 200 years Newport has attracted well-known writers, artists, and other VIP tourists. Newport attracts distinguished visitors from Hollywood, heads of state, business leaders, and U.S. presidents. This list has included Queen Elizabeth, Presidents Nixon and Bush, and the celebrated Kennedys, who were married and spent summers in Newport. Visiting VIPs help develop a positive "pop culture" image for the destination.

- It has been stated that "mass" tourism follows "class" tourism, but for at least 100 years class (or society) tourism and mass tourism have coexisted and even prospered together at the same destination.

- For 100 years Newport has been on the cutting edge of new sports, gaming, and recreational activities, (i.e., golf, tennis, sailing, car racing, biking, polo, etc.). Many of these games were made popular in Newport over a 100-year period. Most recently, ESPN's 1995–96 X (Extreme) Games brought a young and new market to Newport for extreme recreation (adventure tourism). Today, approximately 40% of the visitors indicate that they visit Newport for various recreational activities.

- For 100 years Newport has had strong community support for historic preservation that later developed into a nationally known heritage tourism product. In the past 50 years many important projects have been completed. In 1995 approximately 25% of the visitors indicated that they planned to only see the historical architecture.

- For 25 years Newport has had strong leadership to protect the ocean coast that evolved into a nature or ecotourism product. For example, citizens turned down the option of drilling for off-shore oil in the bay, which would have hurt tourism but would have brought quick and big money. Another example of an ecotourism project is the federal funding of the reconstruction of the famed Three Mile Cliff Walk, which demonstrates commitment to protecting the ocean's natural beauty. Recently, several national and state parks have been developed that include a great deal of public access to the ocean coast, beaches, and natural areas.

- For 25 years special events and festivals have been used effectively to develop a positive national image for quality entertainment. The fact that the NC-CVB has a full-time coordinator for events demonstrates its commitment to this key tourism development effort.

- For 25 years Newport has kept gaming a low-key tourism activity. Newport has not permitted gaming to become the area's major tourism product but allows it to prosper in the current recreational mix.

- For 25 years the development of excellent infrastructure has made Newport a four-season resort destination. Newport sought state and federal funding for county highways, a visitor welcome center, and downtown parking that has made Newport accessible to many large urban areas, including Boston and New York.

Summary and Conclusions

Newport's Historical Claims

The historical record and data in Exhibit 1 indicate that the current slogan used by the NC-CVB ("Newport: America's First Resort") is valid. Also, considering the many important events that have taken place and the numerous VIPs who have spent time in Newport, it does seem that the area has earned the name "Legendary Newport/Queen of Resorts."

The Issue of Newport's Sustainable Tourism Product

Travel and tourism may well be the top level of human consumption. The tourism industry must be sensitive to the actions of all other economic sectors that influence the availability and quality of the tourism product. Newport has met its economic development needs without compromising the opportunity of future generations to have an equally viable and prosperous life. In reality, Newport has had periods of strong tourism growth followed by decline, but city officials have always turned to tourism for major economic focus. Over the years the citizens of Newport have learned the limits of economic development and the fragile capacities of both the cultural and unique seaside environment. Combined community efforts by various civic groups in heritage tourism, cultural tourism, nature tourism, and adventure tourism, mixed with special events and festivals, have produced a unique destination that prides itself on a variety of tourism experiences.

Despite examples of general degradation caused by tourism around the world, Newport is a clear success story in sustainable tourism development. Newport's tourism product is unique, multifaceted, and well-positioned for continued success beyond 2000.

Finally, from management perspective, success has come from much hard work and cooperation from various civic groups and effective leadership with logical decision making about the tourism product and the type of visitor Newport wants to attract in the future.

References

Amory, Cleveland (1952). *The Last Resorts.* New York: Harper and Brothers.

Boss, Judith A. (1981). *Newport's Pictorial History.* Norfolk, VA: Donning Company.

Cohen, Judy, and John Richardson (1995). "Nature Tourism vs. Incompatible Industries: Megamarketing the Ecological Environment to Ensure the Economic Future of Nature Tourism." *Journal of Travel and Tourism Marketing,* 4 (2): 107–16.

Jefferys, C. P. B. (1992). *Newport: A Short History.* Newport, RI: Newport Historical Society.

MacGregor, James R. (1993). "Sustainable Tourism Development." *VNR's Encyclopedia of Hospitality and Tourism,* edited by Mahmood Khan, Michael Olsen, and Turgut Var. New York: Van Nostrand Reinhold.

Mak, James, and James Moncur (1995). "Sustainable Tourism Development: Managing Hawaii's Unique Touristic Resource—Hanauma Bay." *Journal of Travel Research,* 33 (Spring): 51–56.

Manning, E., and D. Dougherty (1995). "Sustainable Tourism: Preserving the Golden Goose." *The Cornell Hotel and Restaurant Administration Quarterly,* April.

Panaggio, Leonard J. (1994). *Portrait of Newport II.* Newport, RI Bank of Newport.

Wigle, Ray (1994). "Making History Seem Tempting: Marketing an Historic Site as a Visitor Attraction." *Journal of Travel and Tourism Marketing,* 3 (2): 95–102.

KEY CONCEPTS

accommodations	early beginnings	Olympic Games	Silk road
air travel	early roads	Pan American Airways	stagecoaches
American Express	early ships	Phoenicians	Sumerians
Americans	Egyptian	Polynesians	Thomas Bennett
attractions	European	rail travel	Thomas Cook
automotive travel	Grand Tour	Robert Smart	travel agents
classical world	Greeks	Romans	water travel

INTERNET SITES

National Amusement Park Historical Association
http://www.napha.org

National Geographic
http://www.nationalgeographic.com

National Trust for Historical Preservation
http://www.nthp.org

Smithsonian Institute Museums
http://www.si.edu

INTERNET EXERCISES

Site Name: The National Amusement Park Historical Association

URL: http://www.napha.org/

Background Information: The National Amusement Park Historical Association (NAPHA) is an international organization dedicated to the preservation and enjoyment of the amusement and theme park industry—past, present, and future.

Exercises

1. Trace the evolution of the amusement park from medieval Europe to the present day.

2. What is the prognosis for the amusement park industry in the United States today?

QUESTIONS FOR REVIEW AND DISCUSSION

1. Of what value is learning the fundamentals of tourism's long history?

2. Do today's travelers have motivations and concerns similar to those of travelers who lived during the Classical Era?

3. What were the principal travel impulses of such early sea explorers as Columbus, Cabot, Balboa, Magellan, and Gosnold?

4. Give some examples of how guides operated in early tourism. Why were they so important? Are their functions the same today? Their ethics? (When discussing, include tour escorts.)

5. Describe the parallels that exist between tourism in Roman times and those of today.

6. Why have the Olympic Games survived since 776 B.C.E.?

7. In the 1990s how consequential for the international traveler is an ability in foreign languages?

8. Can one's money be converted to that of any other country?

9. Are museums, cathedrals, and art galleries really important to most visitors? Provide some outstanding examples.

10. How significant were religious motivations in early travel? Do these still exist? Examples?

11. Early religious houses such as churches and monasteries often accommodated travelers. Give reasons for this.

12. What, if any, were the impacts of Marco Polo's writings on the growth of travel by Europeans during the Renaissance (fourteenth through sixteenth centuries)?

13. Specifically, why did travel by rail supersede that by stagecoach?

14. Are medical and health travel motivations still important?

15. Describe ancient tourist attractions. How significant are they now?

16. Why has air travel become the primary mode for middle- and long-distance trips?

17. Who was the first travel agent, and what services did he provide? The first rail passenger agent? Tour operator? Steamship agent?

18. How have computerized reservations systems (CRSs) aided travel agencies and the traveler?

19. What will travel be like 20 years from now?

SELECTED REFERENCES

Belasco, Warren James. *Americans on the Road: From Autocamp to Motel, 1920–1945.* Cambridge, MA: MIT Press, 1979.

Burkart, A. J., and S. Medlik. *Historical Development of Tourism.* Aix-en-Provence, France: Centre des Hautes Études Touristiques, 1990.

Casson, Lionel. *Travel in the Ancient World.* London: George Allen & Unwin, 1974.

Douglas, Ngaire, and Norman Douglas. "P&O's Pacific." *Journal of Tourism Studies,* Vol. 7, No. 2, pp. 2–14, December 1996.

Evans, Michael R. "Newport, Rhode Island—America's First Resort: Lessons in Sustainable Tourism." *Journal of Travel Research,* Vol. 36, No. 2, pp. 63–67, Fall 1997.

Fagan, Brian M. *The Great Journey: The Peopling of Ancient America.* New York: Thames and Hudson, 1987.

Friedhiem, Eric. *Travel Agents: From Caravans and Clippers to the Concorde.* New York: Travel Agent Magazine Books, 1992.

Gee, Chuck Y., and Matt Lurie, eds. *The Story of the Pacific Asia Travel Association.* San Francisco: Pacific Asia Travel Association, 1993.

Jakle, John A. *The Tourist: Travel in the Twentieth Century North America.* Lincoln, NE: University of Nebraska Press, 1985.

Kreck, Lothar A. "Tourism in Former Eastern European Societies: Ideology in Conflict with Requisites." *Journal of Travel Research,* Vol. 36, No. 4, pp. 62–67, Spring 1998.

Lerner, Judith. "Traveling When the World Was Flat." *The Travel Agent Magazine,* pp. 26–29, March 8, 1982.

Lewin, Roger. *In the Age of Mankind: A Smithsonian Book of Human Evolution.* Washington, D. C.: Smithsonian Books, 1988.

McIntosh, Robert W. "Early Tourism Education in the United States." *Journal of Tourism Studies,* Vol. 3, No. 1, pp. 2–7, May 1992.

Murray, Michael, and Brian Graham. "Exploring the Dialectics of Route-Based Tourism: The Camino de Santiago." *Tourism Management,* Vol. 18, No. 8, pp. 513–524, December 1997.

National Geographic. *Into the Unknown: The Story of Exploration.* Washington, D.C.: The National Geographic Society, 1987.

National Geographic. *Peoples and Places of the Past: The National Geographic Illustrated Cultural Atlas of the Ancient World.* Washington, D.C.: National Geographic Society, 1983.

Rae, W. Fraser. *The Business of Travel: Fifty Years' Record of Progress.* London: Thomas Cook & Son, 1891.

Rinschede, Gisbert. "Form of Religious Tourism." *Annals of Tourism Research,* Vol. 19, No. 1, pp. 57–67, 1992.

Robinson, H. A. *A Geography of Tourism.* London: Macdonald and Evans, 1976.

Rugoff, Milton. *The Great Travelers.* New York: Simon and Schuster, 1960.

Smeral, Egan, and Stephen F. Witt. "The Impacts of Eastern Europe and 1992 on International Tourism Demand." *Tourism Management,* Vol. 13, No. 4, pp. 368–376, December 1992.

Strand, Curt R. "Lessons of a Lifetime: The Development of Hilton International." *Cornell Quarterly,* Vol. 37, No. 3, pp. 83–95, June 1996.

Towner, John. "Approaches to Tourism History." *Annals of Tourism Research,* Vol. 15, No. 1, pp. 47–62, 1988.

Towner, John. "The Grand Tour: A Key Phase in the History of Tourism." *Annals of Tourism Research,* Vol. 12, No. 3, pp. 297–333, 1985.

Towner, John. "The Grand Tour: Sources and a Methodology for an Historical Study of Tourism." *Tourism Management,* Vol. 5, No. 3, pp. 215–222, September 1984.

Towner, John, and Geoffrey Wall. "History and Tourism." *Annals of Tourism Research,* Vol. 18, No. 1, pp. 71–84, 1991.

Towner, John. "What is Tourism's History?" *Tourism Management,* Vol. 16, No. 5, pp. 339–344, August 1995.

Van Doren, Carlton S. "Pan Am's Legacy to World Tourism." *Journal of Travel Research,* Vol. 32, No. 1, pp. 3–12, Summer 1993.

CAREER OPPORTUNITIES

- Evaluate future job opportunities in the tourism field.

- Learn about the careers available.

- Discover which careers might match your interests and abilities.

- Know additional sources of information on careers.

◀ **LEARNING OBJECTIVES**

◀ *A flight attendant checking in air travelers. (Photo courtesy of United Airlines.)*

INTRODUCTION

Every student eventually must leave the college or university campus and seek a career-oriented job. This is a difficult decision-making time, often filled with doubt as to what goals or ambitions should be pursued. Coming face to face with the problem of getting a first major career-oriented job is a challenging task. You are marketing a product—yourself—and you will have to do a good job of communicating to convince a prospective employer that you have the abilities needed and that you will be an asset to the firm.

JOB FORECASTS

The World Travel and Tourism Council (WTTC) estimates that today there are 231 million people worldwide, some 10 percent of the total workforce, employed in jobs that exist because of the demand generated by tourism. While tourism contributes to gross domestic product (GDP), capital investment, employment, foreign exchange, and export earnings, it is the job creation capacity of tourism that is its most significant feature. By 2010, WTTC forecasts that there will be 328 million people around the globe having jobs created by tourism. Job growth and GDP growth usually go hand in hand, so WTTC projections on both GDP and jobs growth in regions of the world are shown in Table 3.1.

TABLE 3.1
Travel and Tourism GDP and Jobs Estimates

	GDP US$ Billion		Jobs (Millions)	
	1998	**2010**	**1998**	**2010**
World	3564.3	8008.4	230.8	328.4
Africa	48.0	137.7	16.3	23.1
North Africa	23.5	72.1	3.0	4.2
Sub-Saharan Africa	24.5	65.6	13.3	18.9
Americas	1236.5	2345.0	33.7	45.4
North America	1078.8	1986.5	20.8	26.3
Latin America	129.0	290.0	9.9	15.3
Caribbean	28.8	68.5	2.9	3.7
Asia/Pacific	797.7	2252.5	136.2	200.3
Oceania	72.0	146.0	2.7	3.4
Northeast Asia	607.6	1588.7	77.6	98.5
Southeast Asia	77.2	361.4	22.2	40.6
South Asia	40.9	156.4	33.7	57.8
Europe	1439.3	3164.9	41.6	55.0
European Union	1178.1	2393.5	22.0	25.2
Other Western Europe	101.3	233.6	4.4	6.6
Eastern Europe	159.9	537.8	15.2	23.2
Middle East	42.7	108.2	3.1	4.6

Source: World Travel and Tourism Council.

JOB REQUIREMENTS

Are you suited to work in the tourism field? Do you like working with people? Would you be genuinely concerned for a customer's comfort, needs, and well-being even if the customer might be rude and obnoxious? If you can answer in the affirmative, you can find a place in this industry. You have to like to do things for other people and work helpfully with them. If not, this is not the industry for you. Courtesy comes easily when customers are pleasant and gracious. But a great deal of self-discipline is required to serve every type of person—especially demanding and indecisive ones. In tourism, the customer might often change his or her mind. This requires patience and an unfailing cheerful personality.

You must also ask if you have the physical stamina required to carry out many of the jobs available. It is difficult to work long hours on your feet or to work in a hot, humid, or cold environment. You might be involved in the pressure of a crush of people, such as at an airline ticket counter. A travel agency counselor must have keen vision, excellent hearing, and well-endowed nerves. Try to evaluate your physical attributes and skills to determine if you can perform.

To enhance your chances of getting a job and deciding if you would like it, visit several types of tourist-related organizations. Watch the activities being performed. Talk to managers, supervisors, and employees. Try to obtain an internship. Work experience means a great deal. Once you have had that, these skills can be utilized in a wide variety of tourism enterprises in any number of locations.

A customer service representative is one of the many jobs available in the rental car field. *(Photo courtesy of the Hertz Corporation © Hertz System, Inc. Hertz is the registered service mark and trademark of Hertz System, Inc.)*

CAREER POSSIBILITIES

Tourism today is one of the world's largest industries. It is made up of many segments, the principal ones being transportation, accommodations, food service, shopping, travel arrangement, and activities for tourists, such as history, culture, adventure, sports, recreation, entertainment, and other similar activities. The businesses that provide these services require knowledgeable business managers.

Hotels offer a wide range of managerial job opportunities. The Radisson Plaza Hotel at Mark Center in Alexandria, Virginia is just one of thousands of properties that offer job opportunities. *(Photo courtesy of Radisson Hotels International, Inc.)*

Familiarity with tourism, recreation, business, and leisure equips one to pursue a career in a number of tourism-related fields. Even during times of severe economic downturn, tourism has performed well. Tourism skills are critically needed, and there are many opportunities available in a multitude of fields.

Because tourism is diverse and complex and each sector has many job opportunities and **career paths,** it is virtually impossible to list and describe all the jobs one might consider in this large field. However, as a student interested in tourism, you could examine the following areas, many of which are discussed in more detail in Chapters 5 to 8.

Airlines

The airlines are a major travel industry employer, offering a host of jobs at many levels, ranging from entry level to top management. Illustrative jobs are reservation agents, flight attendants, pilots, flight engineers, aircraft mechanics, maintenance staff, baggage handlers, airline food service jobs, sales representatives, sales jobs, computer specialists, training staff, office jobs, clerical positions, ticket agents, and research jobs. Because airlines have to meet safety and other requirements, opportunities also exist with the Federal Aviation Administration (FAA). The FAA hires air traffic controllers and various other specialists. Airports also use a wide range of personnel from parking attendants to managers. Other air-related jobs are available with associations such as the Air Transport Association.

Tourists traveling create many jobs where employees do not come into contact with the public, such as this airplane refueling job. *(Photo courtesy of Southwest Airlines.)*

Bus Companies

Bus companies require management personnel, ticket agents, sales representatives, tour representatives, hostesses, information clerks, clerical positions, bus drivers, personnel people, and training employees.

Cruise Companies

The cruise industry is the fastest-growing segment of the tourism industry today. Job opportunities include those for sales representatives, clerical workers, market researchers, and recreation directors. Because of its similarity in operations, the cruise industry has many of the same jobs as the lodging industry.

Railroads

Passenger rail service is currently dominated by Amtrak, which hires passenger service representatives, sales representatives, reservation clerks and other types of clerks, conductors, engineers, coach and lounge car attendants, and station agents.

Rental Car Companies

With increased pleasure air travel and the growth of fly/drive programs, rental car companies are becoming an even more important segment of the travel industry. This sector of tourism employs reservation agents, rental sales agents, clerks of various kinds, service agents, mechanics, and district and regional managers.

Hotels, Motels, and Resorts

The range of jobs in hotels and motels is extremely broad. The following list is representative: general manager, resident manager, comptroller, accountants, management trainees, director of sales, director of convention sales, director of personnel, director of research, mail clerks, room clerks, reservation clerks, front office manager, housekeepers, superintendent of service, bellhops, lobby porters, doormen, maids, chefs, cooks, kitchen helpers, storeroom employees, dishwashers, waiters, bartenders, apprentice waiters, heating and air conditioning personnel, maintenance workers, engineers, electricians, plumbers, carpenters, painters, and laundry workers.

Resorts tend to have the same jobs as those mentioned for hotels and motels; however, larger resorts will have greater job opportunities and require more assistants in all areas. Resorts also have a number of additional job opportunities in the areas of social events, entertainment, and recreation, such as for tennis and golf pros. At ski resorts there will be ski instructors, members of a safety patrol, and so on. The American Hotel and Motel Association estimates that the lodging industry employs approximately 1.64 million people; and by the year 2005, lodging industry labor demands will increase 25 percent.

Travel Agencies

Travel agencies range from very small to very large businesses. The smaller businesses are very much like any other small business. Very few people carry out all the business operations, and jobs include secretarial, travel counseling, and managerial activities. In large offices, job opportunities are more varied and include commercial account specialists, domestic travel counselors, international travel counselors, research directors, and advertising managers. Trainee group sales consultants, accountants, file clerks, sales personnel, tour planners, tour guides, reservationists, group coordinators, trainees, operations employees, administrative assistants, advertising specialists, and computer specialists are other possibilities.

Tour Companies

Tour companies offer employment opportunities in such positions as tour manager or escort, tour coordinator, tour planner, publicist, reservations specialist, accountant, sales representative, group tour specialist, incentive tour coordinator, costing specialist, hotel coordinator, office supervisor, and managerial positions. Often, a graduate will begin employment as a management trainee, working in all the departments of the company before a permanent assignment is made.

Food Service

Many job opportunities are available in the rapidly growing food service industry, such as head waiters, captains, waiters, waitresses, bus persons, chefs, cooks, bartenders, restaurant managers, assistant managers, personnel directors, dieticians, menu planners, cashiers, food service supervisors, purchasing agents, butchers, beverage workers, hostesses, kitchen helpers, and dishwashers.

Tourism Education

As tourism continues to grow, the need for training and education grows. In recent years many colleges and universities have added travel and tourism programs, existing programs have expanded, vocational schools have launched programs, trade associations have introduced education and certification programs, and private firms have opened travel schools. There are job opportunities for administrators, teachers, professors, researchers, and support staff.

Tourism Research

Tourism research consists of the collection and analysis of data from both primary and secondary sources. The tourism researcher plans market studies, consumer surveys, and the implementation of research projects. Research jobs are available in tourism with airlines, cruise lines, management consulting firms, state travel offices, and so on.

Professional chefs find great satisfaction in creating tasty, nutritious, and virtually irresistible food items. *(Photo courtesy of Doral Golf Resort and Spa.)*

Travel Communications

There are a number of opportunities available in travel writing as editors, staff writers, and freelance writers. Most major travel firms have a need for public relations people who write and edit, disseminate information, develop communication vehicles, obtain publicity, arrange special events, do public speaking, plan public relations campaigns, and so on. A travel photographer could find employment in either public relations or travel writing. Television is a medium with increasing opportunities.

Recreation and Leisure

Jobs in recreation and leisure are enormous. Some examples are activity director, aquatics specialist, ski instructor, park ranger, naturalist, museum guide, handicapped program planner, forester, camping director, concert promoter, lifeguards, tennis and golf instructors, coaches for various athletic teams, and drama directors. Many recreation workers teach handicrafts. Resorts, parks, and recreation departments often employ recreation directors who hire specialists to work with senior citizens or youth groups, to serve as camp counselors, or to teach such skills as boating and sailing. Management, supervisory, and administrative positions are also available.

Attractions

Attractions such as amusement parks and theme parks are a major source of tourism employment. Large organizations such as Disney World, Disneyland, Six Flags, Worlds of Fun, and Sea World provide job opportunities ranging from top management jobs to clerical and maintenance jobs.

Festivals and Events

Festivals and events are one of the fastest growing segments of the tourism industry. Event management is emerging as a field, is becoming more professional, and is providing a new source of job opportunities. Events are creating offices and moving them to year-round operation. A study of the International Special Events Society showed that event managers earned between $25,000 and $75,000 per year and that the majority held baccalaureate degrees.

Sports Tourism

Sports are popular throughout the world, with many sports teams and enterprises becoming big businesses offering job opportunities in the management and marketing areas.

The Black American West Museum is an example of one of the many museums and attractions that provide job opportunities in tourism. *(Photo courtesy of Denver Metro Convention and Visitors Bureau.)*

Tourist Offices and Information Centers

Numerous jobs are available in tourist offices and information centers. Many chambers of commerce function as information centers and hire employees to provide this information. Many states operate welcome centers. Job titles found in state tourism offices are: director, assistant director, deputy director, travel representative, economic development specialist, assistant director for travel promotion, statistical analyst, public information officer, assistant director for public relations, marketing coordinator, communications specialist, travel editor, media liaison, media specialist, photographer, administrative assistant, information specialist, media coordinator, manager of travel literature, writer, chief of news and information, marketing coordinator, market analyst, research analyst, economist, reference coordinator, secretary, package tour coordinator, and information clerk.

Convention and Visitors Bureaus

As more and more cities enter the convention and visitor industry, employment opportunities in this segment grow. Many cities are devoting public funds to build convention centers to compete in this growing market. Convention and visitors bureaus require managers, assistant managers, research directors, information specialists, marketing managers, public relations staff, sales personnel, secretaries, and clerks.

Meeting Planners

A growing profession is meeting planning. Many associations and corporations are hiring people whose job responsibilities are to arrange, plan, and conduct meetings.

Gaming

One of the fastest-growing sectors is gaming. Today, one is hard-pressed to find a state where gambling is not allowed or a gaming proposal is in front of the state legislature. From riverboats to Indian reservations to land-based casinos, new destinations are being created. Casinos provide job opportunities ranging from managers to marketers to mechanics to clerical and maintenance jobs.

Other Opportunities

A fairly comprehensive list of career opportunities has been presented. Others that do not fit the general categories listed are club management, corporate travel departments, hotel representative companies, in-flight and trade magazines, and trade and professional associations.

CAREER PATHS IN TOURISM

In addition to considering one of the foregoing kinds of positions within a particular segment of the tourism sector, it is also useful to examine the various **career paths** that might be pursued. Because the tourism industry is so large and so diverse, it offers a

Gaming provides employment opportunities at casinos in hotels, resorts, and aboard ships. *(Photo courtesy of Merv Griffin's Resorts Casino Hotel, Atlantic City, New Jersey.)*

One of the best jobs in tourism is to serve as the head of a city convention and visitors bureau. Shown here is Eugene Dilbeck, President of the Denver Metro Convention and Visitors Bureau. *(Photo courtesy of Denver Metro Convention and Visitors Bureau.)*

broad range of challenging positions. While each of these positions offers its own unique opportunities and demands, people will find that the experience gained from working in a range of jobs in different subsectors of tourism can strengthen their understanding of the industry as a whole. Depending on one's career objectives, this broader understanding of tourism can be especially valuable when applying for certain types of positions. Examples include those in destination management organizations and national or provincial/state tourism offices.

To offer employees opportunities for growth and development, educators and personnel managers attempt continually to develop the concept of career paths in tourism. A schematic model illustrating the concept is shown in Figure 3.1. The fundamental premise of this general model is that people can pursue a variety of reasonably well-defined alternative routes, first through the educational system and subsequently through the industry itself. Based on the training and experience gained, combined with high-quality performance, a person can pursue a career path starting at different levels, with the ultimate-goal of achieving the position of senior executive. While not everyone will have the ability or will necessarily want to pass through all levels of the model, it does provide defined career paths for those who are interested. It also indicates what combination of training and experience is normally required to achieve various positions.

Although clearly an oversimplification, the career path model demonstrates that people may take a variety of routes in pursuing their careers at different levels within and across the various subsectors of tourism. The specific positions that will appeal to different people will, of course, vary according to their particular educational background and their occupational skills. The chosen career path will also reflect a person's values and interests. Just how the chosen occupation might reflect individual values and interest is shown in Figure 3.2. As indicated, front-line staff (entry level

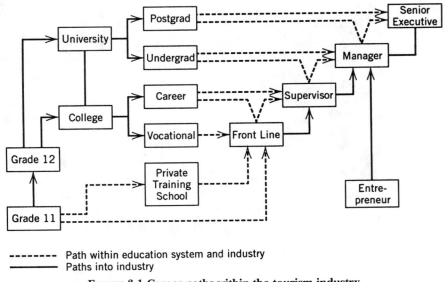

- - - - - - - -   Path within education system and industry
————————   Paths into industry

FIGURE 3.1 Career paths within the tourism industry.

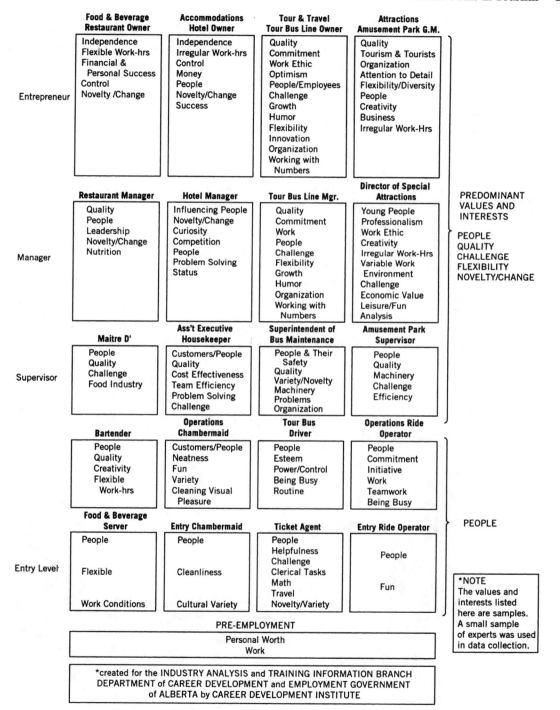

	Food & Beverage Restaurant Owner	Accommodations Hotel Owner	Tour & Travel Tour Bus Line Owner	Attractions Amusement Park G.M.	

Entrepreneur	Independence
	Flexible Work-hrs
	Financial &
	  Personal Success
	Control
	Novelty /Change
		Independence
		Irregular Work-hrs
		Control
		Money
		People
		Novelty/Change
		Success
			Quality
			Commitment
			Work Ethic
			Optimism
			People/Employees
			Challenge
			Growth
			Humor
			Flexibility
			Innovation
			Organization
			Working with
			  Numbers
				Quality
				Tourism & Tourists
				Organization
				Attention to Detail
				Flexibility/Diversity
				People
				Creativity
				Business
				Irregular Work-Hrs	

	Restaurant Manager	**Hotel Manager**	**Tour Bus Line Mgr.**	**Director of Special Attractions**	PREDOMINANT VALUES AND INTERESTS

Manager	Quality
	People
	Leadership
	Novelty/Change
	Nutrition
		Influencing People
		Novelty/Change
		Curiosity
		Competition
		People
		Problem Solving
		Status
			Quality
			Commitment
			Work
			People
			Challenge
			Flexibility
			Growth
			Humor
			Organization
			Working with
			  Numbers
				Young People
				Professionalism
				Work Ethic
				Creativity
				Irregular Work-Hrs
				Variable Work
				  Environment
				Challenge
				Economic Value
				Leisure/Fun
				Analysis
					PEOPLE
					QUALITY
					CHALLENGE
					FLEXIBILITY
					NOVELTY/CHANGE

	Maitre D'	**Ass't Executive Housekeeper**	**Superintendent of Bus Maintenance**	**Amusement Park Supervisor**	
Supervisor	People Quality Challenge Food Industry	Customers/People Quality Cost Effectiveness Team Efficiency Problem Solving Challenge	People & Their Safety Quality Variety/Novelty Machinery Problems Organization	People Quality Machinery Challenge Efficiency	
	Bartender	**Operations Chambermaid**	**Tour Bus Driver**	**Operations Ride Operator**	

	People
	Quality
	Creativity
	Flexible
	  Work-hrs
		Customers/People
		Neatness
		Fun
		Variety
		Cleaning Visual
		  Pleasure
			People
			Esteem
			Power/Control
			Being Busy
			Routine
				People
				Commitment
				Initiative
				Work
				Teamwork
				Being Busy	

	Food & Beverage Server	**Entry Chambermaid**	**Ticket Agent**	**Entry Ride Operator**	PEOPLE
Entry Level	People Flexible Work Conditions	People Cleanliness Cultural Variety	People Helpfulness Challenge Clerical Tasks Math Travel Novelty/Variety	People Fun	

PRE-EMPLOYMENT

Personal Worth
Work

*NOTE
The values and
interests listed
here are samples.
A small sample
of experts was used
in data collection.

*created for the INDUSTRY ANALYSIS and TRAINING INFORMATION BRANCH
DEPARTMENT of CAREER DEVELOPMENT and EMPLOYMENT GOVERNMENT
of ALBERTA by CAREER DEVELOPMENT INSTITUTE

FIGURE 3.2 Career paths in tourism, sample occupations, values, and interests.

and operations) must like dealing with people and possess a strong interest in providing them with high-quality service. Supervisors, managers, and entrepreneurs must possess additional values and interests that enable them to face the challenges of change as they attempt to meet the needs of a demanding and ever-shifting marketplace.

INTERNSHIPS

One of the best ways to get the job you want is to have internship (cooperative education) experience. Internship opportunities abound in the tourism area. Most internship programs are designed to provide students the opportunity to: (1) acquire valuable, hands-on experience to supplement their academic learning; (2) learn potential practical skills; (3) develop professionalism; (4) interact with segments of the local business community, develop an appreciation for the daily operation and long-term strategic direction of a corporate or small business environment; and (5) develop a further understanding of their chosen field.

Some examples of internship programs and sources of internships are Marriott, Hyatt, Universal Studios, the National Tourism Foundation, and Resort Recreation and Tourism Management. The Marriott Lodging Internship Program is designed to stimulate student interest in Hotel Management and a career with Marriott International. Through the program, students gain practical work experience necessary to

Campus career fairs are places where students can learn about jobs, internships, and career paths. Here college recruiters for Disney Worldwide Services, Inc., visit with students from the University of Colorado. *(Photo by the author.)*

pursue a management career in the hospitality industry. In addition, it provides Marriott with an opportunity to make sound evaluations of potential management candidates. Internship opportunities are available in their Marriott Hotels, Resorts and Suites; Renaissance; Residence Inn; Courtyard; and TownePlace Suites brands; and their timeshare business, Marriott Vacation Club International.

The Hyatt Hotels and Resorts Internship Program was created to generate student interest in hotel management and spark a desire to join a hospitality leader after graduation. Internships also give Hyatt the opportunity to recognize potential managers and continue developing relationships throughout the academic year. Structured internship opportunities are available in over 10 of their hotel and resort locations.

Universal Studios Florida has internships in advertising, convention sales, food services, human resources, information systems, marketing, merchandise, park operations, production, public relations, technical entertainment, and technical services. Active juniors, seniors, and graduate students are eligible for the program.

The National Tourism Foundation, located in Lexington, Kentucky, publishes an annual internship list that covers tour operator internships, tour suppliers internships, and destination marketing organization internships. The publication lists over 220 internships.

Resort Recreation and Tourism Management (RR&TM), located in Hilton Head, South Carolina, has an internship program designed for college students pursuing a career in the hospitality industry. RR&TM provides hands-on experience through a training site. They place interns in lodging, food and beverage, commercial recreation and tourism positions.

Other Sources of Career Information

Most of the career opportunities available in the travel field have been listed. It is hoped that this overview will provide you with a guide and point out that industries are so large that they are worthy of much further study by themselves. In considering career opportunities, it is important to gather information before you invest a great deal of time looking for a job. The following are good references:

Riegel, Carl and Melissa Dallas. *Hospitality and Tourism Careers.* Upper Saddle River, NJ: Prentice-Hall, 1998.

Rubin, Karen. *Flying High in Travel, A Complete Guide to Careers in the Travel Industry.* New York: John Wiley & Sons, 1993.

These books discuss tourism jobs. One book on how to get a job is particularly recommended:

Bolles, Richard. *What Color Is Your Parachute? Practical Manual for Job Hunters and Career Changes.* Berkeley, CA: Ten Speed Press, 1998.

The information provided in this section should be an important starting point for you. However, it is really just the tip of the iceberg. It is up to you to explore the subject further and to gain additional information. You need to learn not only about careers in tourism and travel-related fields, but also about the task of marketing your-

A major resort complex such as this provides a wide range of job opportunities. These include maintenance, lift operators, food and beverage service, accommodations, ski, golf and tennis professionals and instructors, department heads, supervisors, and management. *(Photo courtesy of Vermont Department of Tourism and Marketing.)*

self—how to work up resumés and how to conduct yourself during interviews. General books on getting a job will help you in this task.

SUMMARY

A career in tourism offers many exciting and challenging employment opportunities. As indicated in Chapter 1, tourism is the largest industry in the world today. In the United States over the past decade, travel industry employment has grown at a rate more than twice the growth rate for all U.S. industries. This growth is expected to continue in the United States and throughout the rest of the world. The labor–intensive tourism industry has a need for motivated people of all ages and backgrounds. Those who prepare themselves, maintain high energy, have a talent for working with people, and have a dedication to high-quality service will find themselves climbing the career ladder to success.

ABOUT THE READINGS

There are two readings in this chapter. The first was prepared by TIA and indicates how some famous tourism professionals started their careers and where they are today.

The second reading comes from the CHRIE publication *Hosteur* and provides information on getting a job.

READING 3.1

FROM HUMBLE BEGINNINGS TO MAJOR SUCCESS

George Snyder and Noel Irwin-Hentschel started out as unknowns in the travel and tourism industry. He worked as a baggage clerk for Greyhound bus lines while she, on a $5-a-day trek through Europe and the Middle East at 17, became a tour guide at a resort in Eilat, Israel. He went on to spend 30 years climbing the corporate ladder at Greyhound and eventually left and became president and chief executive officer of the American Bus Association. She returned to the United States two years later to immerse herself in the tourism industry through schooling and a number of tourism related jobs before starting American Tours International (ATI) at age 24 with partner, Michael Fitzpatrick, president of ATI. Today Irwin-Hentschel, mother of seven, is the chair and CEO of ATI, a $150 million enterprise that provides travel services to more than 800,000 international visitors a year.

The success stories of these two individuals, as well as those of thousands of others, epitomize the tremendous professional growth opportunities within the travel and tourism industry.

"Everyone has to start somewhere," said Greg Farmer, former Under Secretary of Commerce for Travel and Tourism, who himself spent more than a year as a busboy and waiter at a restaurant in Miami, Florida. "Travel and tourism is one of the only industries left with a built-in apprenticeship program. You can start at the bottom and work your way to the top. It's the recipe of the American dream."

Following is a compilation of travel leaders who were asked the question: "What was your first tourism-related job and where are you today?"

Now	Then

Ronald Allen
Past Chairman of the
  Board, President &
  CEO
Delta Air Line, Inc.
Atlanta, GA
	1963 Part-time Methods
	  Analyst in Delta's
	  Methods and
	  Training Department.

Roger Ballou
President & CEO
Global Vacation Group
  and Senior Advisor
Thayer Capital Partners
Washington, D.C.
	1979 Regional Vice
	  President, AMEX
	  Destination Services
	  Marketing.

Edward Book
Past President
  (1978–1995)
Travel Industry
  Association of America
Washington, D.C.
	1951 Worked as a
	  counter person,
	  dishwasher, and cook
	  at Howard Johnson
	  restaurant, Harris-
	  burg, PA.

Robert Darbelnet
President & CEO
American Automobile
  Association
Heathrow, FL
	1973 Emergency Road
	  Service Drive,
	  Quebec Automobile
	  Club.

Robert Dickinson
President
Carnival Cruise Lines
Miami, FL
	1972 Assistant to the
	  President, American
	  International Travel
	  Service, Boston, MA.
	  Part of his job was to
	  give shipboard tours.

Leslie Doggett
Deputy Assistant
  Secretary of
  Commerce for Tourism
  Industries
Washington, D.C.
	1981 Front Desk
	  Attendant, Resorts
	  International,
	  Atlantic City, NJ.

Now	Then	Now	Then
Richard Fain Chairman & CEO Royal Caribbean Cruises, Ltd. Miami, FL	During his college years, he worked as a computer programmer.	Richard Nunis Chairman Walt Disney World Attractions Lake Buena Vista, FL	1955 Part-time summer orientation instructor for new hires at Disneyland, CA.
Noel Irwin-Hentschel Chairman & CEO American Tours International Inc. Los Angeles, CA	At 17, she was tour guide at a resort in Israel. At 24, she opened ATI.	Gary Paxton CEO Dollar Rent A Car Tulsa, OK	1968 Worked for Dollar Rent A Car first office in Seattle, WA, "Jack- of-all-trades"—washed cars, wrote rental agreements, shuttled customers.
Steven Lew Consultant, Civic Affairs Universal Studios, Inc. Universal City, CA	At 10, he worked as a stockboy at the Town House Hotel, Kansas City, KS. He con- tinued to work there through his teenage years.	Caletha Powell Executive Director New Orleans Black Tourism Network, Inc. and Co-Founder and Executive Director African American Travel and Tourism Assoc. New Orleans, LA	Account Executive, Dollar Rent A Car.
George Kirkland President Los Angeles Convention & Visitors Bureau Los Angeles, CA	1970 Sales Manager, Convention & Tourism Department, Oakland Chamber of Commerce, CA.		
William S. Norman President Travel Industry Associa- tion of America Washington, D.C.	During his high school, he was a bellman for the Breakers Hotel, Virginia Beach, VA.	George Snyder, Jr. President & CEO American Bus Association Washington, D.C.	1957 Baggage Clerk for Greyhound Bus Company, loading and unloading luggage.

READING 3.2

LAUNCHING YOUR CAREER: EXPERIENCE REFLECTS DESIRE

by Charlie Adams & Lynn Huffman
Texas Tech University

Reprinted from the *Hosteur*, Publisher: International CHRIE, Vol. 7, No. 2, Spring 1998.

Some jobs at the entry level require no experience and no particular preparation. A strong work ethic and a desire to learn are all that are needed. However, employment in technical, supervisory, and managerial positions typically require more experience and an academic background. Two-year and four-year hospitality degree programs have been designed to provide the preparation needed to enter these higher level careers.

What To Do Now So You Can Be Ready Then

Getting Started

Upon entering college it is important to decide what directions your career could take within the hospitality field. Career positions are available in restaurants, lodging, casinos, cruise lines, and sales. America's "service economy" also means employers outside the field are looking to hospitality graduates to fill entry-level management positions. The question that you must answer is, "What do I want to do with my career?" Talking to hospitality professionals, college students, and professors is a good way to answer your questions about possible career paths.

Another important step is to write a resume early, preferably during the first year in the hospitality program. Writing a resume forces you to evaluate your experiences and set goals for your future. A resume serves to outline your education, work history, activities, and accomplishments. You may be asking yourself, "How am I going to write a resume when I don't have any experience?" Everyone has done something that can be put into a resume, and everybody has to start somewhere. The resume also serves as a self-evaluation tool, illustrating where you have been and what you need to do to become more marketable. As you develop your hospitality skills, your resume will develop right along with you.

There are few rules for writing a resume, but following these rules is critical to your success. The most important rule is to do your own resume so that you don't have to pay someone else every time your resume is updated. Paying someone is expensive and inconvenient. Chances for employment, scholarships, and internships often arise at some of the strangest times. By doing your own resume you can make changes in a timely manner and always be prepared to take advantage of new other opportunities. Secondly, there can be no mistakes in a resume. It is the one document that has to be perfect! Recruiters and prospective employers will often discard resumes that have mistakes. Thirdly, it should be concise, one page long. People who read resumes usually read many of them, and they tend to only spend about 30 seconds looking at a resume the first time. A resume should be well organized, easy to read, and contain specific information that helps sell you to the reader. Last, and most important, is to remember that this is your resume. Teachers, college placement services, and the library are good sources of advice. Each may have their favorite style and their contributions are important, but you are still the person who decides what belongs in your resume.

Filling the Gaps

It is significant to remember that part of your hospitality education involves working in the hospitality field while you are in college. Your work experience is far more important than simply a means of earning money. It is vitally important to have work experience in the area in which you hope to start your career. Hospitality has a variety of "foundation skills" in which a person needs to be competent. Restaurateurs have all had to tend bar, cook, wait tables, wash dishes, expedite, or bus tables as the result of someone quitting

or not reporting to work. Lodging professionals perform a wide variety of management duties including front desk, housekeeping, banquets and catering, accounting, food and beverage, and sales. Your college work experience should result in acquiring a working knowledge of positions relevant to your career area and developing an appreciation for each position's importance. Recruiters look for managers whose experience reflects their desires. Getting experience during college in one area of hospitality and then suddenly wanting to do something different upon graduation raises a red flag with recruiters. Having career goals that are consistent with your work experience demonstrates your understanding, commitment, and maturity in facing the opportunities and challenges that await you in a hospitality career. It is especially important to experience others areas of our industry. This broadens your knowledge and may introduce you to a career path that you had not anticipated. At the very least, you may decide that some areas of our industry are not for you. Ideally, you will find your heart's desire.

Getting the Job

When beginning the interview process, one of the first items of business is to make sure that you understand the importance of a conservative appearance and in investing in clothes for the interview. Often the interview process itself includes attending dinners, presentations, and meeting industry professionals in an informal setting. A conservative and well-manicured look will give you a great deal of added confidence.

Hospitality professionals are judged based upon their appearance by customers and employers who are acutely aware of the role appearance plays in customers' perceptions. Recruiters will spend only about a half-hour to an hour interviewing you, but they will start forming an opinion from the moment they meet you. Your appearance and behavior will determine how other people view you. Conveying a proper appearance is something that you need to work on, particularly in your last year. It is not something that you simply decide to do overnight. Grooming and appearance are something that you have to work at and develop.

Being focused is critically important to the job search process and interviewing. Focusing involves being dedicated to and patient with the job search, having realistic expectations, researching companies, and customizing your resume to target different employers. You must realize that your job search is going to take time. It requires that you take a course load your last semester that will allow you to research companies, attend presentations, career fairs, and interview. A common mistake of graduating seniors is to take a heavy load in order to graduate. Though this may be necessary, these students simply cheat themselves. Selecting the right company is hard work and requires thought, preparation, and time. Getting a job is a job in itself. It is never easy but is critical to your success.

You must know what you want from your career. Ask yourself, "What is the one nonnegotiable item upon which I will base my first career choice?" Your nonnegotiable item is the one thing that you must have in a job. Examples of nonnegotiable items might include money, quality of life, where you want to live, number of hours you want to work, or even your spouse's career. Identifying the one thing that is really important to you will help match yourself with compatible companies.

Determining which organizations match your interests requires researching companies. Research can be done by using the Internet, library, placement office, or visiting the business and talking with industry professionals. Researching companies will provide you with information about how to approach the company for an interview and prompt you to ask intelligent questions during the interview.

Remember to take one final hard look at your resume before you start to interview. Ask yourself if your resume matches your skills and abilities with the needs of companies with which you will be interviewing. An important consideration would be to have two or three versions of your resume that are tailored to fit a particular company or segment of the industry. Be assured, no work history is perfect. It is important to look for weak spots in your resume. There may be a job that you left after a short period of time or your experience may not directly apply to the job you want. Be prepared to explain questionable areas on your resume. It is important to be honest, so think about answers to possible questions that may be asked in the interview

Students are usually frightened about the first interview largely because they don't know what to expect. Improving interviewing skills requires that you interview early and often. Part of your job search strategy should be to pick two or three companies with which to interview for practice. As you interview with different companies your skills will improve as you will be more familiar with the process and know what to

expect. Recruiters use the first interview to determine if you are a possible candidate for employment. Their intent is to determine your level of desire and potential compatibility with their organization. Interviewers will focus on your experience, flexibility, and enthusiasm. Experience is important, but it is not the only element for success. Being flexible about relocation and conveying a genuine desire to work with the company is vital. If a choice must be made between experience and enthusiasm most recruiters will take enthusiasm. It is the single most important quality in selling yourself!

Upon completion of a successful first interview, you will usually be invited back for a second interview. This is where things get more serious. Interviewers may have you talk to several people, take a personality profile test, or even work for a day (job preview). Personality profile tests are usually designed to see how closely your traits match those of successful managers in the company. A job preview allows you to work with a manager and have your performance evaluated. This is the part of the interview process where you have the opportunity to really sell yourself by showing the company what you can do.

Thank you letters are very important, yet are frequently neglected. Make sure that you get the interviewer's business card and write a thank you letter the same day. Most recruiters enjoy getting a personalized handwritten card that simply thanks them for their time and emphasizes your interest in the company. The card is another opportunity to get you name in front of the recruiter.

No period of time is more uncertain or nerve wracking for a graduating senior than when the interviews are over. Companies will generally respond within two weeks of the final interview. If a company is going to extend you an offer they will usually do it verbally, but they should always follow up the offer in writing. The written formal offer will discuss the position, salary, location, and starting date. It will also include a date of acceptance. (If you need a time extension, you should contact the company and explain to them why you need more time to consider the offer.) When you accept or decline an offer, do it in writing. It should be remembered that if you turn a company down, don't expect them to make the offer again. Your decision is important and should be final. A big mistake made by graduating seniors is to accept an offer as insurance with the plan to turn it down if something better comes along. Imagine what kind of an impression this leaves with recruiters about you and your school. Your actions reflect on all the graduates who follow you, so always be professional.

Conclusion

The hospitality industry offers dynamic and exciting careers. While many students work in more than one area of hospitality while they explore their career in- terests, you should try to focus eventually on the area for which you feel best suited. You need to think about what you want to do after graduation so that your work experience can give you foundation skills that will make you marketable as a manager. Your work experience should reflect you career desire.

KEY CONCEPTS

airlines
accommodations
attractions
bus companies
career path
convention and visitors bureaus
cruise lines
employment forecasts
food service
meeting planning

railroads
recreation
rental car companies
tour companies
tourism education
tourism job requirements
tourism research
tourist offices and information centers
travel agencies
travel communications

INTERNET SITES

AH&MA Educational Institute
http://www.ei.ahma.org

American Hotel and Motel Association
http://www.ahma.com

Cooker Restaurant Corporation
http://www.cookers.com

Hilton Hotels
http://www.hilton.com

Hospitality Net Virtual Job Exchange
http://www.hospitalitynet.nl/job

Hyatt Hotels and Resorts
http://www.hyatt.com

Marriott International
http://www.careers.marriott.com

MGM Grand Hotel Casino
http://www.mgmtgrand.com

National Restaurant Association Educational Foundation
http://www.edfound.org

National Tour Association
http://www.ntaonline.com

Resort Recreation & Tourism Management
http://www.rrtm.com

Sodexho Marriott
http://www.sodexmarriott.com

Travel Industry Association of America
http://www.tia.org

World Travel and Tourism Council
http://www.wttc.org

INTERNET EXERCISES

Activity 1

Site Name: Hospitality Net

URL: http://www.hospitalitynet.org/

Background Information: Hospitality Net is the leading hospitality industry resource on the Internet with information on employment opportunities, events, industry news, links to other sites, and so on.

Exercises

1. What are the categories for the job opportunities listed on this web site?

2. Choose a category and find a job that would be of interest to you. Describe the job, where it is located, and why it appeals to you.

Activity 2

Site Name: World Travel & Tourism Council

URL: http://www.wttc.org/

Background Information: The World Travel & Tourism Council (WTTC) is the global business leaders' forum for travel and tourism. Its members are chief executives from all sectors of the travel and tourism industry, including accommodations, catering, cruises, entertainment, recreation, transportation, and travel-related services. Its central goal is to work with governments to realize the full economic impact of the world's largest generator of wealth and jobs—travel and tourism.

Exercise

1. What is the WTTC's vision on jobs in the travel and tourism industry for the next decade?

QUESTIONS FOR REVIEW AND DISCUSSION

1. What is the growth potential for tourism jobs?

2. As a career in tourism, what position appeals to you at present?

3. What preparation will be needed for that position?

4. What are its probable rewards?

5. Identify the position's advancement opportunities.

6. Are your writing and speaking skills good enough to land a job?

7. What criteria would you use to choose a company for an interview?

8. How important is salary in your job choice?

9. Evaluate the job satisfaction in your chosen career.

10. What will tourism be like in the year 2010? What position might you visualize yourself to be in by that date?

CASE PROBLEMS

1. Donnell C. is graduating from a four-year travel and tourism curriculum. She has had several job offers. What type of organization would afford her the broadest range of experiences? How important is her beginning salary?

2. Jim B. is a successful local travel agency manager. He is visited one day by a very bright high-school senior who is most interested in becoming a travel agent. What educational preparation advice would you offer?

SELECTED REFERENCES

Altman, Lois A., and Linda R. Brothers. "Career Longevity of Hospitality Graduates." *FIU Hospitality Review*, Vol. 13, No. 2, pp. 77–83, Fall 1995.

Antil, Frederick H. "Career Planning in the Hospitality Industry." *The Cornell Hotel and Restaurant Administration Quarterly*, Vol. 25, No. 1, pp. 46–52, May 1984.

Antil, Frederick H. "Learning Hospitality Management Through a Rigorous Work–Study Experience." *Hospitality and Tourism Educator,* Vol. 1, No. 2, pp. 24–29, Summer/Fall 1988.

Brownell, Judi. "Addressing Career Challenges Faced by Women in Hospitality Management." *Hospitality & Tourism Educator,* Vol. 5, No. 4, pp. 11–16, Fall 1993.

Brownell, Judi. "Women in Hospitality Management: General Managers' Perception of Factors Related to Career Development." *International Journal of Hospitality Management,* Vol. 13, No. 2, pp. 101–118, June 1994.

BTN. *Travel Manager Salary and Attitudes Survey,* Skokie, IL: Business Travel News—North America, No. 379, 1997.

Burns, Peter M. "Tourism's Workforce: Characteristics and Inter-Cultural Perspectives." *Tourism Recreation Research,* Vol. 22, No. 1, pp. 49–54, 1997.

Charles, Kwame R. "Career Influences, Expectations, and Perceptions of Caribbean Hospitality and Tourism Studies: A Third World Perspective." *Hospitality and Tourism Educator,* Vol. 4, No. 3, pp. 9–14, May 1992.

Choy, Dexter J.L. "The Quality of Tourism Employment." *Tourism Management,* Vol. 16, No. 2, pp. 129–138, March 1995.

Cook, Suzanne, and William Evans. *A Portrait of Travel Industry Employment in the U.S. Economy.* Washington, D.C.: TIA Foundation, 1996.

Educational Institute. *Hotel/Motel Careers.* East Lansing, MI: Educational Institute, no date.

Gagnon, Patricia J., and Bruno Ociepka. *Travel Career Development,* 6th Edition. Wellesley, MA: Institute of Certified Travel Agents, 1998.

LaLopa, Joseph M. "Commitment and Turnover in Resort Jobs." *Journal of Hospitality and Tourism Research,* Vol. 21, No. 2, pp. 11–26, 1997.

Langton, Bryan D. "High Quality Travel and Tourism Jobs." *Viewpoint,* Vol. 1, No. 2, pp. 26–33, no date.

National Recreation and Parks Association. *Careers in Parks, Recreation and Leisure Services.* Alexandria, VA: NRPA, no date.

Nebel, Eddystone C. III, Ju-Soon Lee, and Brani Vidakovic. "Hotel General Manager Career Paths in the United States." *International Journal of Hospitality Management,* Vol. 14, No. 3/4, pp. 239–243, December 1995.

Rice, Kate. "The Professional Prospects for Women in Travel." *Travel Counselor,* No. 29, pp. 20–22, October 28, 1996.

Riegel, Carl, and Melissa Dallas. *Hospitality and Tourism Careers.* Upper Saddle River, NJ: Prentice-Hall, 1998.

Ross, Glenn. F. "Tour Guide Employment Motivation." *The Tourist Review,* Vol. 52, No. 2, pp. 32–40, 1997.

Rubin, Karen. *Flying High in Travel: A Complete Guide to Careers in the Travel Industry.* New York: John Wiley & Sons, 1993.

Samuels, Jack, and Reginald Foucar-Szocki. *Guiding Your Entry into the Hospitality, Recreation, and Tourism Mega-Profession.* Upper Saddle River, NJ: Prentice-Hall, 1999.

Sciarini, Michael P., et al. "College Freshmen Perceptions of Hospitality Careers: Gender and Ethnic Interest." *Journal of Hospitality and Tourism Education,* Vol. 19, No. 3, pp. 18–28, 1997.

Timmons, Veronica. *Career Exploration in Tourism: A Guide to Finding and Getting a Job in the Tourism Industry.* Vancouver, British Columbia, Canada: Timmons and Associates, 1991.

Tourism Canada. *Career Guide to the Tourism & Hospitality/Recreation Industry.* Ottawa: Tourism Canada, 1986.

U.S. Department of Labor. *Occupational Outlook Handbook.* Washington, D.C.: U.S. Government Printing Office, 1998.

Williams, Anna Graf, and Karen J. Hall. *Creating Your Career Portfolio: At a Glance Guide.* Upper Saddle River, NJ: Prentice-Hall, 1997.

Woods, Robert H. and Michael P. Sciarini. "Where Hospitality Students Want to Work: 1995–96." *Journal of Hospitality and Tourism Education,* Vol. 9, No. 2, pp. 6–9, 1997.

WTTHRC, *Steps to Success Global Good Practices in Travel and Tourism Human Resource Development.* Vancouver: World Travel and Tourism Human Resource Centre, 1998.

Zedlitz, Robert H. *Getting a Job in the Travel Industry.* Cincinnati, OH: South-Western Publishing Company, 1990.

PART 2

HOW TOURISM IS ORGANIZED

◄ *The Dallas/Fort Worth International Airport covers 17,500 acres. Parking facilities and an airport hotel can be seen in the center of the photograph. An automated shuttle train provides transportation to other terminals.*

CHAPTER 4

WORLD, NATIONAL, REGIONAL, AND OTHER ORGANIZATIONS

- Understand the magnitude of world tourism in terms of the vast numbers of organizations that serve the needs of their diverse memberships.

- Recognize the variety of types and functions of tourism organizations.

- Know why states support official offices of tourism.

- Learn how national, regional, and trade organizations are structured and operated.

◀ **LEARNING OBJECTIVES**

◀ *The Taj Mahal in Agra, India is a favorite travel destination along the Asian Highway. The Asian Highway was initiated in 1958 and funded by the national governments in Asia. (Photo courtesy of the United Nations.)*

INTRODUCTION

The complex organization of tourism involves literally hundreds of thousands of units. Tourism organizations can be reviewed as follows: (1) geographically with the following breakdowns: international, regional within world, national, regional within nation, state or provincial, regional within state or province, and local categories; (2) by ownership, such as government, quasi-government, or private; (3) by function or type of activity, such as regulators, suppliers, marketers, developers, consultants, researchers, educators, publishers, professional associations, trade organizations, and consumer organizations; (4) by industry, such as transportation (air, bus, rail, auto, cruise), travel agents, tour wholesalers, lodging, attractions, and recreation; and (5) by motive, profit or nonprofit.

The purpose of Chapters 4 through 8 is to discuss the major types of tourist organizations and how they interrelate and operate, focusing on illustrative examples. The discussion begins with official international tourism groups in this chapter and ends with the private organizations and firms that make up the tourism industry covered in Chapters 5, 6, 7, and 8. Additional important supplemental areas that facilitate the tourism process, such as education, publishing, and marketing and publicity, are also included in Chapter 8.

INTERNATIONAL ORGANIZATIONS

World Tourism Organization

The **World Tourism Organization** (WTO) is the most widely recognized and leading international organization in the field of travel and tourism today. It serves as a global forum for tourism policy issues and a practical source of tourism know-how. Its membership includes 138 countries and territories and more than 350 Affiliate Members representing local government, tourism associations, educational institutions, and private sector companies, including airlines, hotel groups, and tour operators. With its headquarters in Madrid, WTO is an intergovernmental body entrusted by the United Nations with the promotion and development of tourism. Through tourism, WTO aims to stimulate economic growth and job creation, provide incentives for protecting the environment and heritage of destinations, and promote peace and understanding among all the nations of the world.

The World Tourism Organization had its beginnings as the International Union of Official Tourist Publicity Organizations set up in 1925 in The Hague. It was renamed the International Union for Official Tourism Organizations (IUOTO) after World War II and moved to Geneva. IUOTO was renamed the World Tourism Organization (WTO), and its first General Assembly was held in Madrid in May 1975. The Secretariat was installed in Madrid early the following year at the invitation of the Spanish government, which provides a building for the headquarters. In 1976, WTO became an executing agency of the United Nations Development Programme (UNDP); in 1977, a formal cooperation agreement was signed with the United Nations itself.

The World Tourism Organization is an official consultative organization to the United Nations and has the objective of promoting and developing tourism worldwide. *(Photo by Ron Nelson.)*

WTO is engaged in many activities. The transfer of tourism know-how to developing countries is a major task. Here WTO contributes decades of experience in tourism to the sustainable development goals of nations throughout the world. WTO projects are based on the policy of sustainability, ensuring that the economic benefits of tourism development are not offset by damage to the environment or to local cultures.

WTO is well known for its statistics and market research. Research has been one of WTO's most important contributions. Their work here has set international standards for tourism measurement and reporting, measured the impact of tourism on national economies, produced forecasts, examined trends, and made the results available in publications.

Human resource development is another WTO goal. In cooperation with its network of 14 Education and Training Centers throughout the world, WTO sets standards for tourism education. The newly developed Graduate Tourism Aptitude Test (GTAT) is an example of their efforts to encourage standardization of curricula and to make degrees in tourism more internationally comparable. WTO also offers seminars, distance learning courses, and practicum courses for tourism officials from member countries.

WTO attempts to facilitate world travel through elimination or reduction of governmental measures for international travel as well as standardization of requirements for passports, visas, and so forth. They work to improve the quality of tourism through trade liberalization, access for travelers with disabilities, safety and security, and technical standards. They also work to improve the promotional efforts of member governments through effective media relations and serve as a clearinghouse for international tourism information.

In addition to these global activities, WTO engages in regional activities. Each region of the world—Africa, Americas, East Asia and the Pacific, Europe, Middle East and South Asia—receives special attention from that region's representative as the WTO Representatives meet with top tourism officials from each of the countries in their region to analyze problems and help seek solutions, act as a liaison between tourism authorities and the UNDP to create specific development projects, organize national seminars of topics of particular relevance to an individual country, such as Tourism Promotion in Mexico or Ecotourism in Kyrgyzstan, and hold regional conferences on problems that are shared by many countries so that members can exchange experiences and work toward common goals, such as Safety and Security in Eastern Europe or Aviation and Tourism Policy in the Caribbean.

They are also involved in regional promotion projects. The Silk Road and the Slave Route are two projects, being implemented in cooperation with the United Nations Scientific and Cultural Organization (UNESCO). Launched in 1994, WTO's Silk Road project aims to revitalize through tourism the ancient highways used by Marco Polo and the caravan traders who came after him. The Silk Road stretches 12,000 km from Asia to Europe. Sixteen Silk Road countries have joined forces for this project: Japan, Republic of

The WTO works with the UNDP, which finances tourism planning projects and infrastructure improvements, such as this project to improve transportation in Southern Africa. *(Photo courtesy of the United Nations.)*

Korea, DPR Korea, China, Kazakstan, Kyrgyzstan, Pakistan, Uzbekistan, Tajikistan, Turkmenistan, Iran, Azerbaijan, Turkey, Georgia, Greece, and Egypt. Joint promotional activities include a brochure and video, familiarization trips, and special events at major tourism trade fairs. The Slave Route, initiated in 1995 as part of the United Nations' International Year of Tolerance, aims to boost cultural tourism to western African nations. Its immediate goals are to restore monuments, enhance history museums, and launch joint promotional campaigns in selected tourism generating markets, which will motivate foreign visitors to learn about the history of these countries and to discover their roots. The project is expected to be expanded in the future to include other nations in southern and eastern Africa, as well as countries in the Caribbean.

WTO is primarily financed by members' contributions. Full members pay an annual quota calculated according to the level of economic development and the importance of tourism in each country. Associate members pay a fixed annual contribution of U.S. $20,000 and affiliate members pay U.S. $1700 a year. WTO's budget for the two-year period 1996–1997 totaled U.S. $18,099,000. Membership dues accounted for about 90 percent of the budget, with the remainder coming from UNDP support costs, investment income, and sales of publications and electronic products. Visit the WTO web site at **http://www.world-tourism.org.**

World Travel and Tourism Council

This council is a global coalition of the top 100 chief executive officers from all sectors of the industry. These include accommodation, catering, cruises, entertainment, recreation, transportation, and travel-related services. Established in 1990, WTTC is led by a 15-member executive committee, which meets twice a year and reports to an annual meeting of all members. Day-to-day operations are carried out by the President and a small staff based in London, Brussels, and Washington, D.C.

The council's goals have been restated in their "Millennium Vision," and they are to work with governments to make tourism a strategic economic development and employment priority, move toward open and competitive markets, pursue sustainable development, and eliminate barriers to growth to realize the full economic potential of tourism and its job generating ability. WTTC has done more to create awareness of the economic importance of tourism than any other organization.

The WEFA Group undertakes extensive research on behalf of the WTTC to determine travel and tourism's total size and contribution to world, regional, and national economies. The WTTC report, *Travel and Tourism in the World Economy,* prepared by WEFA, is their primary vehicle used to convey the message that this is the world's largest industry, that it has been growing faster than most other industries, that it will continue to grow strongly, and that it can create jobs and increase gross domestic product (GDP). WTTC plans to continue publishing this report and enhance its methodology. In fact, they continue to increase the number of economic impact reports, and under the auspices of the WTO they have developed proposals for an international standard Satellite Accounting System.

International Air Transport Association

The **International Air Transport Association** (IATA) is the global organization for virtually all the international air carriers. The principal function of IATA is to safely facilitate the movement of persons and goods from any point on the world air network to any other by any combination of routes. This can be accomplished by a single ticket bought at a single price in one currency and valid everywhere for the same amount and quality of service. The same principles apply to the movement of freight and mail.

Resolutions of IATA standardize not only tickets but waybills, baggage checks, and other similar documents. These resolutions coordinate and unify handling and accounting procedures to permit rapid interline bookings and connections. They also create and maintain a stable pattern of international fares and rates. In effect, they permit the linking of many individual international airline routes into a single public service system.

While developing standards and procedures for the international airline industry to support interlining and enhancing customer service continues to be a principal aim, IATA is involved in many other areas such as industry support, the environment, consumer issues, regulatory monitoring, legal support, corporate communications, scheduling, facilitation, safety, security, and services.

IATA is a valuable information source on the world airline industry. Their Airline Product Database provides a comparison of the product across 30 major carriers. Their annual publication, *World Air Transport Statistics*, is an authoritative source of international airline data. In addition, IATA makes passenger and freight forecasts. Their market research helps the industry develop its strategic and tactical marketing plans.

In summary, IATA's mission is to represent and serve the world airline industry. They serve four groups interested in the smooth operation of the world air transport system: (1) airlines, (2) the public, (3) governments, and (4) third parties such as suppliers and travel and cargo agents. IATA works closely with the International Civil Aviation Organization. IATA's head office is in Montreal, its executive office is in Geneva, Switzerland, and it has regional offices around the world. The IATA web site is at **http://www.iata.org.**

International Civil Aviation Organization

The International Civil Aviation Organization (ICAO) is an organization of governments joined to promote civil aviation on a worldwide scale. This organization, established in 1944, has adopted a plan, "Guiding Civil Aviation Into the 21st Century," to deal more effectively with the constantly evolving challenges facing civil aviation, particularly in the area of flight safety. The strategic action plan focuses on eight major objectives to further the safety, security, and efficiency of international civil aviation and identifies 43 related activities. The eight objectives are as follows:

1. Foster the implementation of ICAO Safety Standards and Recommended Practices to the greatest extent possible worldwide.

2. Develop and adopt new or amended Standards, Recommended Practices, and associated documents in a timely manner to meet changing needs.

3. Strengthen the legal framework governing international civil aviation by the development of new international air law instruments as required and by encouraging the ratification by states of existing instruments.

4. Ensure the currency, coordination, and implementation of Regional Air Navigation Plans and provide the framework for the efficient implementation of new air navigation systems.

5. Respond on a timely basis to major challenges to the safe and efficient development and operation of civil aviation.

6. Ensure that guidance and information on the economic regulation of international air transport is current and effective.

7. Assist in the mobilization of human, technical, and financial resources for civil aviation facilities and services.

8. Ensure the greatest possible efficiency and effectiveness in the operations of the organization.

Visit the ICAO web site at **http://www.ca.org/ICAO.**

DEVELOPMENTAL ORGANIZATIONS (INTERNATIONAL AND NATIONAL)

Financing is always a major problem in tourism development. Large financial organizations are willing to make developmental loans. Examples include the **World Bank** (U.S.), International Finance Corporation (U.S.), the OPEC Fund for International Development (Austria), African Development Bank (Côte d'Ivoire), East African Development Bank (Uganda), Inter-American Development Bank (United States), Caribbean Development Bank (Barbados), Asian Development Bank (Philippines), European Investment Bank (Luxembourg), European Development Fund (Belgium), European Bank for Reconstruction and Development (United Kingdom), Islamic Development Bank (Saudi Arabia), and the Arab Fund for Economic and Social Development (Kuwait). Examples of national organizations are FONATUR (Mexico) and EMBRATUR (Brazil). Further sources include governments of countries that want additional hotel development or other supply components and are willing to make low-interest loans or grants or offer other financial inducements for such types of development.

REGIONAL INTERNATIONAL ORGANIZATIONS

Organization for Economic Cooperation and Development

The **Organization for Economic Cooperation and Development** (OECD) was set up under a convention, signed in Paris on December 14, 1960, that provides that the OECD shall promote policies designed to (1) achieve the highest sustainable economic growth and employment and a rising standard of living in member countries while maintaining financial stability, and thus to contribute to the development of the world economy; (2) contribute to sound economic expansion in member as well as nonmember countries in the process of economic development; and (3) contribute to the expansion of world trade on a multilateral, nondiscriminatory basis in accordance with international obligations.

Members of OECD are Australia, Austria, Belgium, Canada, Czech Republic, Denmark, Finland, France, Germany, Greece, Hungary, Iceland, Ireland, Italy, Japan, Korea, Poland, Portugal, Spain, Sweden, Switzerland, Turkey, the United Kingdom, and the United States. OECD's Tourism Committee fosters development of tourism in member countries by studying the tourism problems confronting the governments and sectors of the economy in view of the large development of transit traffic in recent years and by making recommendations based on its findings. The Tourism Committee actively seeks standard definitions and methods for compiling tourism statistics and issues a report entitled *Tourism Policy and International Tourism in OECD Member Countries.* The 1997 report is available on diskette only. Visit the OECD web site at **http://www.oecd.org.**

Asia is one of the fastest growing travel destinations in the world. Kuala Lumpur, the capital of Malaysia, is one of many locations in Asia that can provide rewarding travel experiences for visitors from Western cultures. (*Photo courtesy of the Malaysia Tourism Promotion Board.*)

Pacific Asia Travel Association

The **Pacific Asia Travel Association** (PATA) represents countries in the Pacific and Asia that have united to achieve a common goal, namely, excellence in travel and tourism growth in this vast region. Its work has been to promote tourism through programs of research, development, education, and marketing. PATA has gained a reputation for outstanding accomplishment among similar world organizations. For this reason a more detailed look at this association's organization and activities is presented as a reading at the end of this chapter. Visit the PATA web site at **http://www.pata.org.**

European Travel Commission

The **European Travel Commission** (ETC) is the strategic alliance, which provides for the collaboration between 28 European National Tourism Organizations (NTOs). Founded in 1948, the ETC fills a unique role functioning as a "National Tourism Office of Europe." Its goal is to attract millions of potential and existing overseas customers from the major overseas markets to come to Europe. This is done through promotional campaigns and industry trade shows. The headquarters of the ETC is located in Brussels, Belgium.

NATIONAL ORGANIZATIONS

Tourism Industries

The United States is an example of how not to develop tourism. In April 1996 the United States Travel and Tourism Administration (USTTA), which served as the nation's official government tourist office charged with developing tourism policy, promoting inbound tourism from abroad, and stimulating travel within the United States, was eliminated. Congress has made clear its intention that the federal government rely on the private industry to market the United States as a destination, a primary function of the former USTTA. This responsibility to market the United States to potential international visitors and increase the number of international travelers to the United States is now in the hands of the interim U.S. National Tourism Organization (US-NTO). The USNTO was created through legislation passed by Congress in October 1996. Its mission is to brand, position, and promote the U.S. travel product abroad. The organization is looking for a long-term funding solution; however, the chances of a funded USNTO are dim.

While USTTA was eliminated, some of its functions and people were transferred to the International Trade Administration and a **Tourism Industries** (TI) office was established. The mission of this office is to foster an environment in which the U.S. travel and tourism industry can generate jobs through tourism exports.

The Tourism Industries initiative is operated by a Deputy Assistant Secretary, Department of Commerce and 12 employees. Tourism Industries is organized into three groups: (1) Deputy Assistant Secretary for Tourism Industries, (2) Tourism Development, and (3) Tourism Policy Coordination, including the Tourism Policy Council. The organization structure of Tourism Industries is shown in Figure 4.1.

The office of the Deputy Assistant Secretary is responsible for the following: fostering economic development through tourism trade development; representing the United States in tourism-related meetings with foreign government officials; serving as the principal point-of-contact in the U.S. government for the U.S. tourism industry on policy, international commercial diplomacy and tourism trade development issues; furthering the recommendations of the national tourism strategy from the White House Conference on Travel and Tourism (WHCTT); and interacting with the Foreign Commercial Service to advise and assist the tourism trade development officers on matters of policy, technical assistance, and research.

The Tourism Development group is formed to (1) collect and disseminate baseline data for international travel, to and from the United States, incorporating six comprehensive research programs and databases; (2) lead in the development of a satellite account for travel and tourism; (3) forecast and report the economic impact of international travel markets on the U.S. economy; (4) develop and manage a customer response and information service system (CRISS), eventually providing an interactive data retrieval system on the Internet; and (5) provide technical assistance to communities and businesses to help match their tourism strengths with the most promising international markets and to help them bring their tourism products to the market.

The Tourism Policy Coordination group is formed to (1) reinvigorate the Tourism Policy Council (TPC) dedicated to federal agency coordination for all tourism-related activities; (2) enhance communication with the industry, Congress, and state and local governments through the establishment of an electronic network (TPCNet) for travel and tourism information, data, and technical assistance available throughout the federal government; (3) coordinate interagency federal programs that affect tourism development, including facilitation issues such as support of the Visa Waiver Pilot Program; and (4) represent tourism industry needs and issue areas

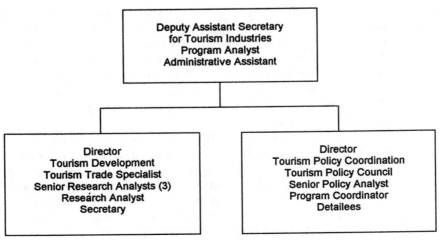

FIGURE 4.1 Organizational structure of the U.S. tourism industries.

for international commercial diplomacy and in intergovernmental organizations and other relevant forums.

The Tourism Policy Council is composed of nine Federal agencies and the President of the U.S. National Tourism Organization. The composition of the Tourism Policy Council is shown in Figure 4.2.

A reading at the end of the chapter presents the Tourism Industries 1998 Fiscal Year Business Plan and provides information on their objectives and tactics. Visit Tourism Industries web site at **http://tinet.ita.doc.gov.**

Canadian Tourism Commission

The **Canadian Tourism Commission** (CTC) is a working partnership between tourism industry businesses and associations, provincial and territorial governments, and the Government of Canada. CTC was one of the first public–private partnerships to be established. It is responsible for promoting and maintaining the orderly growth of tourism in Canada. CTC has one of the best and most comprehensive tourism programs in the world and serves as a model that many other nations strive to equal. For this reason a detailed look at the scope, structure, and operations of the CTC is presented as a reading at the end of this chapter.

Federal Aviation Administration

Numerous responsibilities for efficient and safe air travel are assigned to the **Federal Aviation Administration** (FAA). This U.S. government organization in the **Department of Transportation** formulates regulations and supervises or controls various aspects of airline and airport operations. Examples of these functions are air traffic control, air

FIGURE 4.2 Composition of the Tourism Policy Council.

The U.S. Federal Aviation Administration (FAA) provides air traffic control, air safety, and other vital aviation regulation and services. Shown here is the FAA control tower and Concourse C at the new Denver International Airport. *(Photo courtesy of Denver International Airport.)*

safety, flight standards, aviation engineering, airport administration districts, airways facilities, and certification of new aircraft. The FAA also examines and licenses pilots and flight engineers. The FAA is illustrative of governmental regulating bodies.

Department of Transportation

The Department of Transportation has the federal authority to protect air travelers and to police industry practices. It has responsibility for in-flight smoking rules, charters, denied boarding compensation, baggage liability, handicapped traveler rules, passenger notices, computer reservations bias, and antitrust authority.

Other Government Agencies

Numerous other government agencies play an active role in tourism. The Department of State issues passports, the Customs Service monitors international travel, Statistics Canada and the U.S. Bureau of Census compile travel statistics and data, the Interstate Commerce Commission regulates bus transportation, the National Maritime Commission deals with ships, the National Park Service and the Forest Service provide and administer many scenic attractions and facilities, the Bureau of Land Management is involved in several tourism initiatives (such as Back Country Byways, Adventures in the Past, and Watchable Wildlife), the Bureau of Reclamation administers over 300 recreation areas in 17 western states, and the Federal Highway Administration is involved in the National Scenic Byways program, with the objective of increasing tourism while preserving the environment. Others are the National Trust for Historic Preservation, National Marine Sanctuary Program, Tennessee Valley Authority, Army Corps of Engineers, Fish and Wildlife Service, and the Immigration and Naturalization Service.

Travel Industry Association of America

The Washington, D.C.-based **Travel Industry Association of America** (TIA) is the leading private tourism organization in the United States. The nonprofit association serves as the unifying organization for all components of the U.S. travel industry. The business of travel and tourism in America is served by more than one-half million different organizations that offer a wide range of services to the traveler.

Originally founded in 1941, TIA has grown from a small association of travel officials into a national nonprofit organization with a membership that now represents all components of the travel industry: airlines, attractions, hotels and motels, travel agents, tour operators and brokers, convention and visitors bureaus, state government travel offices, area and regional tourism organizations, food service establishments, auto rental companies, intercity bus and rail lines, cruise lines, and other segments of what is known today as the travel industry.

TIA serves the U.S. travel and tourism industry through a number of programs that market and promote the U.S. travel experience, both abroad and at home; by furnishing research, publications, and reports for and about the industry as well as U.S. and international travelers; by providing strategic leadership for the industry in the U.S. business community and in matters of government at all levels; through its councils and committees that represent specific components of the industry; with its foundation, which finances research and scholarships in the area of travel and tourism; and through its nearly half-century old awards program that honors achievements by both individuals and organizations within the travel and tourism industry.

The current mission of the TIA is to represent the whole of the U.S. travel industry to promote and facilitate increased travel to and within the United States.

TIA fulfills this mission by accomplishing these objectives to (1) promote a wider understanding of travel and tourism as a major U.S. industry that contributes substantially to the economic and social well-being of the nation, (2) bring cohesion to the travel industry and provide communications forums for industry leaders, (3) serve as the authoritative source for travel industry research, analysis and forecasting, (4) initiate and cooperate with governmental entities in the development and implementation of programs, policies, and legislation that are responsive to the needs of the industry, as well as intervene in those issues and initiatives that would directly affect the facilitation and promotion of travel to and within the United States; and (5) to develop and implement programs beneficial to the travel supplier and consumer.

TIA has also taken a leadership role in organizing industry councils to provide a unified voice for segments of the industry that enables them to address legislative issues of mutual concern, carry out educational programs unique to their industry components, and offer guidance in the development of TIA policies and programs. Each of the councils is described briefly.

The National Council of State Tourism Directors (NCSTD), formed in 1969, was the first of the national councils to be established under the umbrella of TIA. Its purpose is to provide a forum for state tourism directors to exchange ideas and information on matters common to state and territorial tourism offices and to develop unified positions on industry issues at the national level. While there is great diversity among the states and territories in terms of specific needs and priorities, there are a number of common concerns in such areas as education, communication, marketing, research, and public affairs where NCSTD serves as a catalyst for developing programs that benefit all states and territories and, therefore, the entire U.S. travel industry. All 50 states, the five U.S. territories, and the District of Columbia are represented in NCSTD.

The State Travel Information Center Directors' Alliance (STICDA) was created in 1986 as an affiliate organization of the National Council of State Tourism Directors. Representing 45 states, its members are dedicated to providing quality, courteous, and beneficial visitor and information services to motorists. STICDA provides its members with a national forum for identifying common problems, defining needs, and pursuing opportunities that include the areas of communications, education, research, legislation, cooperation, technology, standards, and other common issues.

Established in 1976, the National Council of Area and Regional Tourism Organizations (CARTO) represents nearly 200 TIA member destination marketing organizations that comprise areas larger than an urban center—for example, county-wide, multicounty within state, statewide, or multistate organizations whose concern is the promotion and facilitation of travel to and within that specific area or region. CARTO provides a forum and communications network for professionals from these organizations to address matters common to their specific areas of interest and to develop consensus positions on national issues.

The National Council of Attractions (NCA) was formed in 1976 to unify the widely diverse travel attractions segment within TIA, which includes historic, cultural, scientific, scenic, natural, themed, and entertainment attractions, as well as attraction-related service organizations. NCA has over 200 members.

Also established in 1976, the National Council of Urban Tourism Organizations (NCUTO) ensures that urban destination promotion organizations are represented in tourism promotion and policy development activities at the national level. NCUTO represents over 160 convention and visitors bureaus and chambers of commerce that are members of TIA.

In the fall of 1997, TIA launched a new government affairs department consisting of four people. The mission of TIA's government affairs function is to pursue appropriate actions to achieve the adoption and implementation of legislation and public policies, which have a favorable impact on the travel and tourism industry.

In 1998, TIA focused on three policy issues: securing long-term funding for the U.S. National Tourism Organization, Inc.; making permanent and expanding the Visa Waiver Pilot Program; and ensuring that the reauthorization of the Intermodal Surface Transportation and Efficiency Act (ISTEA). Success was achieved with a two-year extension of the Visa Waiver Pilot Program to April 30, 2000, and work continues to make it a permanent program. The effect of the extension measure extends the program for the current 26 participating countries and adds two new countries: Greece and Portugal. The 10-year-old program already includes the nations of Andorra, Argentina, Australia, Austria, Belgium, Brunei Darussalam, Denmark, Finland, France, Germany, Iceland, Ireland, Italy, Japan, Liechtenstein, Luxembourg, Monaco, Netherlands, New Zealand, Norway, San Marino, Slovenia, Spain, Sweden, Switzerland, and the United Kingdom.

The federal TEA-21 bill permits state governments to use their highway funds to finance other types of transportation improvements. New York State is contributing money to the rebuilding of several sleek-looking Turboliner trains for Amtrak, as part of an initiative to improve passenger rail service in the New York City–Albany–Buffalo corridor. *(Photo by Matt Van Hattem.)*

The Intermodal Surface Transportation Efficiency Act of 1991 (ISTEA) was reapproved under a new name, the Transportation Equity Act for the 21st Century (TEA-21). Beyond providing for safe and efficient highway travel, there are three important programs that will be continued in the reauthorization plan with substantial funding increases. These programs are (1) Scenic Byways, (2) Transportation Enhancements, and (3) Federal Lands Highways.

TIA supports three major marketing programs: (1) the internationally acclaimed Discover America International Pow Wow®, which brings together international tour operators and journalists from over 65 nations with U.S. travel suppliers, yielding the sale of over $3.0 billion worth of the U.S. travel product and invaluable media promotion of travel and tourism in America; (2) the Marketing Outlook Forum, an annual educational event that provides travel industry leaders in an intensive two-day series of seminars and prepares these leaders to understand and deal with the issues while providing detailed projections concerning future travel patterns; and (3) The Discover American National Domestic Travel Marketing Program, an ongoing, multifaceted, nationwide campaign that provides the industry with the opportunity to tie into the national promotional campaigns that use the "Discover America" theme and logo. The campaign is designed to encourage U.S. consumers to see more of their country through themed promotions, electronic travel information, and widespread use of the title logo, which reinforces the urge to "Discover America."

REGIONAL ORGANIZATIONS

Regional tourism organizations have the goal of attracting tourists to their specific geographic region. There are several types of regional associations, such as multicountry, multistate, and multicounty. Examples range from PATA, which covers the Pacific region of the world, to groups such as Travel South, USA, which promotes travel in the southern states, to the West Michigan Tourist Association, which promotes only a region in Michigan—the northwestern section. Another multistate organization is Foremost West, which promotes tourism in Colorado, Utah, Arizona, New Mexico, Nevada, and Wyoming. Pennsylvania probably has more regional tourism organizations within its boundaries than any other state—59 tourist promotion agencies represent Pennsylvania's 67 counties.

STATE AND CITY ORGANIZATIONS

State

Traditionally, states have promoted tourism as a tool for economic development. In most states, a tourism office has been established by statute and charged with the orderly growth and development of the travel and tourism industry in the state. These offices conduct programs of information, advertising, publicity, and research relating to the recreational, scenic, historic, highway, and tourist attractions in the state at large.

Each of the 50 states has a government agency responsible for travel development and promotion. Three states—Alaska, Hawaii, and Texas—have two entities devoting funds and resources to tourism development. In Hawaii, responsibility for travel development rests primarily with a privately operated nonprofit organization, the Hawaii Visitors and Convention Bureau, which receives money from the state. The services performed and programs administered by the Hawaii Visitors Bureau are similar to those of the official state travel offices; thus all states are supporting tourism activity. The majority of states house their tourism offices in a Department of Economic Development (or Commerce).

Any review of **state travel offices** must start with the U.S. Travel Data Center's annual *Survey of State Tourism Offices*. Their report covering the fiscal year 1998–1999, published in January 1999, is the twenty-sixth annual report in the series and includes responses from 50 states. It shows that state travel offices are expected to spend more than $524 million on tourism development in fiscal year 1998–1999, about 7.5 percent higher than the $487.8 million spent by states in fiscal year 1997–1998. The $524 million figure for fiscal year 1999 averages out to over $10.7 million per state.

Illinois was the industry leader in tourism spending, with a state tourism budget of $40.1 million. Hawaii was second with a $37.9 million budget, and Texas was third with $29.5 million. Rounding out the top 10 were Florida with $27.3 million, Pennsylvania with $23.1 million, Massachusetts with $21.4 million, New York with $18.7 million, Virginia with $17.3 million, Louisiana with $16.5 million, and Michigan with $15.2 million. According to the report, the average state tourism budget has increased 30 percent in the past five years. State general revenues are the sole source for state travel offices in 21 states, while other states use lodging and other tourism dedicated

State governments have enacted many laws and regulations affecting tourism. Examples are organizations for promotion, transportation, food products, restaurant inspection, licensing boats, and many others. *(Photo courtesy of Montana Travel Promotion Division.)*

tax revenues, membership fees, lottery revenues, highway funds, motor vehicle funds, and other sources of funding.

Domestic advertising is the largest portion of most state travel office budgets, followed by personnel and administrative costs. Tourism office staff ranged from 4 to 150 employees, but the average office size was 36 employees.

States plan to spend more than $160 million on domestic advertising, an average of $3.3 million per state. The figure is 8.3 percent higher than the previous period.

Auto tourists are provided with timely travel information and free phone reservation services at a state highway welcome center. *(Photo courtesy of Michigan Department of Transportation.)*

Besides advertising, states use a number of other means to promote travel to their destinations. Forty-nine states use toll-free phone numbers for visitor inquiries (average 13 lines), 36 states have international visitor centers, 47 states hold annual governors conferences on tourism, and 32 states have some form of matching-based tourism development fund. Most states also conduct travel-related research.

Other types of programs engaged in by state travel offices are product development, cultural heritage, rural development, transportation, sports authority development, regulatory, and environmental. A list of official state travel offices is provided in Appendix A.

City

Most major cities have also recognized the importance of tourism and have established convention and visitors bureaus. In many smaller communities, the **chambers of commerce** perform this function. Larger cities now own the central convention facilities. A great deal of promotion and sales effort is then devoted to backing these facilities.

Convention and Visitors Bureaus

A **convention and visitors bureau** is a not-for-profit umbrella organization that represents a city or urban area in the solicitation and servicing of all types of travelers to that city or area, whether they visit for business, pleasure, or both. It is the single en-

---

STATE TOURISM OFFICES EMBRACE NEW TECHNOLOGY
▼

- Internet web sites have become the technology of choice for state tourism offices, according to a report published by the National Council of State Tourism Directors (NCSTD), an industry council of the Travel Industry Association of America (TIA).

- The report, *1997 Survey on Technology Uses,* found that state tourism offices will spend more than $1.7 million this year just developing and maintaining their Internet web sites, and the average state will invest $59,900 this year developing and maintaining their site.

- While states are using their web sites for traditional purposes such as listing calendars of events (100 percent), linking to related sites (96 percent), and displaying state and local tourist maps (92 percent), they are getting bolder in the way they use their sites. According to the survey, 42 percent of state tourism offices plan to offer online shopping through their sites, 38 percent plan to offer discussion forums, 37 percent plan to offer online reservation services, and 35 percent plan to offer trip itineraries.

- The states with the web sites getting the highest number of "hits" per week were Colorado (206,000), California (200,000), North Carolina (175,000), Texas (120,000), and Ohio (100,000).

- Besides web sites, a growing number of tourism offices are using interactive kiosks, fax-on-demand services, and CD ROM products to promote their states. Thirty-six percent of states say they use information kiosks today, and 19 percent plan to do so in the future. Thirty-six percent of states use fax-on-demand services, 17 percent use CD ROM products, and 14 percent and 15 percent, respectively, plan to use these technologies in the future.

Source: Travel Industry Association of America.

---

tity that brings together the interests of city government, trade and civic associations, and individual "travel suppliers"—hotels, motels, restaurants, attractions, local transportation—in building outside visitor traffic to the area.

Urban tourism is an increasingly important source of income and employment in most metropolitan areas, and therefore it warrants a coordinated and concerted effort to make it grow. This growth is best nurtured by the role a convention and visitors bureau can play in continually improving the scope and caliber of services the city provides to corporate and association meeting planners, to individual business travelers, and to leisure travelers.

The bureau is the city's liaison between potential visitors to the area and the businesses that will host them when they come. It acts as an information clearinghouse, convention management consultant, and promotional agency for the city and often as a catalyst for urban development and renewal.

Typical services offered to meeting planners include orientation to the city, liaison between suppliers and meeting planners, and meeting management. The meetings and conventions market is huge. The Convention Liaison Council estimates that meetings and conventions are an $82 billion-per-year industry (see Chapter 6).

International Association of Convention and Visitors Bureaus

Most of the city convention and visitors bureaus belong to the **International Association of Convention and Visitors Bureaus** (IACVB), Suite 702, 2000 L Street NW, Washington, D.C. 20036. This group was founded in 1914 as the International Association of Convention Bureaus to promote sound professional practices in the solicitation and servicing of meetings and conventions. In 1974, the words "and Visitors" were added to IACB's name to reflect most bureaus' increasing involvement in the promotion of tourism. Since its inception, the association has taken a strong position of leadership in the travel industry. The organization has over 400 members in 30 countries. IACVB provides its members with numerous opportunities for professional dialogue and exchange of industry data on convention-holding organizations.

The IACVB Convention Industry Network (CINET) is the world's leading meetings and convention database, tracking historical and future records on more than 20,000 meeting profiles of associations and corporations. The database provides marketing and sales direction to thousands of conventions and visitor bureaus, hotels and motels, and other convention industry suppliers.

To encourage exchange between its members, IACVB holds an annual convention, organizes annual educational seminars leading to certificates in sales or bureau operations, organizes topical workshops and seminars, makes regular studies of convention industry trends, maintains a consulting service, and provides its members with government and industry liaison. Visit their web site at **http://www.iacvb.org.**

SUMMARY

The World Tourism Organization represents governmental tourist interests and aids in world tourism development. Individual countries, states, and provinces have their own tourist promotion and development organizations that work to promote tourism in their area and coordinate tourism promotion with other groups. Most governments play a regulatory as well as developmental role in tourism through such agencies as civil aeronautics boards, federal aviation administrations, customs offices, passport bureaus, and so on. Government agencies typically compile research statistics and gather data. Governments also operate tourist enterprises such as airlines, national parks, and sometimes hotels and campgrounds.

ABOUT THE READINGS

There are four readings in this chapter. The first three deal with national tourism organizations: U.S. Tourism Industries, Canadian Tourism Commission, and Australia Office of National Tourism. The fourth covers the Pacific Asic Travel Association (PATA).

The U.S. Tourism Industries reading presents their 1998 business plan to provide a feel for their activities and what an abbreviated business plan looks like.

Over the years, one of the world's best national tourism organizations has been Canada. Still at the cutting edge, Canada now has a public/private partnership with the Canadian Tourism Commission. Its basic functions and structure serve as a model for any country aspiring to improve tourism.

Another exceptional national tourism office is Australia. Currently the world leader in tourism promotion expenditures, the Australian National Tourism Office is another model that other countries might wish to emulate as they are active in aiding all facets of Australia's tourism.

Similarly recognized is the PATA. This is a regional association within the world group. It is unique in having a worldwide network of PATA chapters. It is also respected for its outstanding conferences and travel marts that are highly successful and valuable for the attendees.

READING 4.1

UNITED STATES TOURISM INDUSTRIES 1998 FISCAL YEAR BUSINESS PLAN

Mission

To foster an environment in which the U.S. travel and tourism industry can generate jobs through tourism exports.

Goal

To assist travel and tourism exporters by providing research data and services and by advocating policies that strengthen economic development opportunities for tourism.

Customers

In providing research information, technical assistance, and policy coordination, Tourism Industries serves the needs of a diverse base of customers.

Public Sector	Private	Internal
State/local economic	Regional tourism	ITA (e.g., FCS, MAC)
Development offices/ mayors	Organizations	Other DOC agencies (e.g., BEA, ESA, MBDA)
State/local tourism offices	Associations	Federal agencies (e.g., DOT, Interior, State, USTR)
Convention and visitor bureaus (CVBs)	Hotel chains	
Congress	Car rental companies	
Universities	Airlines	
Airport authorities	Route planners	
Governments of other countries	Media	

National tourist offices	Consultants
International organizations (OECD/ WTO/APEC)	Investment advisors
Federal agencies	Attractions Small businesses Entrepreneurs

With the minimal staff in TI, our priority customers are considered to be:

Industry associations

State/local economic development offices/mayors/governors

State/local tourism-offices

Regional tourism organizations

Convention and visitor bureaus (CVBs)
- Airport authorities
- ITA (e.g., FCS, MAC)
- Other DOC agencies (e.g., BEA, ESA, MBDA)

Objectives

Objective 1. To expand tourism development export opportunities, particularly for medium-sized businesses and second tier destinations.

Tactics

1. Provide reports and interpretation/analytical services on research developed through the following research programs:
   - Summary of International Travel to the United States (based on I-94 forms)
   - U.S. International Air Travel Statistics (based on I-92 forms)
   - Survey of International Air Travelers (In-Flight Survey)
   - Canadian Travel to the United States
   - Pleasure Travel Markets to North America
   - Forecast of International Travel to the United States

- Receipts and Payments Analysis of International Travel

2. Coordinate federal tourism-related policy through the Tourism Policy Council (TPC). Examples of programs, activities, and policies include the following:
   - Making the Visa Waiver Pilot Program (VWPP) permanent
   - Encouraging the use of technology by the public and private sectors to make the United States a "user-friendly" destination
   - Developing products attractive to international visitors that will also further community development, such as multicultural tourism, scenic byways, and national heritage areas
   - Spotlighting and expanding export financing programs for tourism exports and business development
   - Conducting TPC meetings and policy committee work that further presidential initiatives of community development, economic empowerment, and people-to-work, as well as improving U.S. competitiveness globally
3. Offer technical assistance in helping industry members enter or expand their presence in the international marketplace.
4. Distribute a manual for the Commercial Service (CS) officers (both domestic and foreign) designed to familiarize them with tourism as an export and how to develop services to facilitate growth in tourism exports.

Measurement

1. Number of reports and services provided to industry
2. Track customer use and satisfaction
3. Assess impact of policy coordination through TPC
4. Work with CS to identify new products in the marketplace

Objective 2.   To provide timely and accurate international tourism statistics.

Tactics

1. Use the Tourism Policy Council Research Committee to address impediments to producing the baseline data, in particular, in a timely and accurate manner (Summary of International Travelers to the United States).
2. Expand airline participation in In-Flight Survey, particularly the foreign flag carriers, through direct sales calls to enhance traveler representation and overall respondent base (sample size).

3. Implement the Sample Enhancement Program (SEP) which is designed to increase the overall respondent base of the In-Flight Survey and allow more expansive subgroup analyses through partnership investment, generally by states and cities.

Measurement

1. Reach workable agreement on resolving impasse for producing accurate and timely baseline date within five months, with an agreement initially with INS and Department of Commerce (TI and BEA) to be drawn up by August 30.
2. Track implementation of the agreement, with focus on benefits gained.
3. Account for the number and nature of participating airlines in the In-Flight Survey.
4. Account for the increase in respondent base directly related to SEP.

Objective 3.   To expand outreach efforts to private industry, governmental agencies, and other entities in order to educate them on the programs and services offered by the federal government that will benefit U.S. tourism development.

Tactics

1. Establish and communicate 1998 TPC priorities, and communicate the status on implementing the TPC strategy recommendations and the National Tourism Strategy recommendations from the 1995 White House Conference on Travel and Tourism (WHCTT).
2. Attend and/or speak at conferences and seminars throughout the world.
3. Hold monthly roundtables with industry, press, and customers attending. See attached listed of potential topics.
4. Enhance the office's Customer Response Inquiry Service System (CRISS), including the Internet site for availability.
5. Develop and distribute an explanatory brochure on the development of a Travel and Tourism Satellite Account (TTSA).
6. Create and distribute White Papers on the challenges of improving and maintaining the U.S. Statistical System for Travel and Tourism.

Measurement

1. Account for the number and nature of conferences and seminars in which an office member spoke.

2. Account for number and nature of roundtables held.

3. Detail number, nature, and method of customer inquiries, along with a survey of customer satisfaction on fulfillment of request and/or counseling.

Objective 4. **To provide the tools for improved economic policy decision-making as it relates to tourism development.**

Tactics

1. Develop a Travel and Tourism Satellite Account (TTSA).

2. Report on the economic impact of international travel on state economies.

3. Maintain close alliance with producers of data (Census, Bureau of Labor Statistics) using the revised Standard Industrial Classification System called NAICS.

4. Produce and distribute the economic impact of travel and tourism on the United States as analyzed by the geographic information system (GIS), initially by Congressional district.

5. Contribute to efforts to improve services data in the federal government.

Measurement

1. Report on the status of the TTSA, how much has been accomplished.

2. Assess use of economic impact data according to industry members.

For further information contact:
Tourism Industries
International Trade Administration
U.S. Department of Commerce
Washington, D.C.
Telephone: (202) 482-0140
Internet: **http://tinet.ita.doc.gov**

READING 4.2

CANADIAN TOURISM COMMISSION

Introduction

The Canadian Tourism Commission (CTC) is a working partnership between tourism industry businesses and associations, provincial and territorial governments, and the Government of Canada. It plays an important strategic role in bringing people to Canada and growth to the country's economy.

The CTC has authority to plan, direct, manage, and implement programs to generate and promote tourism in Canada. It is made up of industry representatives from across Canada acting to ensure that the tourism industry remains a vibrant and profitable part of the Canadian economy. The main thrusts of the Commission are to position Canada as a desirable destination to both international and domestic travelers, as well as to provide timely and accurate information to the tourism industry to assist in decision-making.

The Commission coordinates the efforts of the many players in the tourism sector, among them hoteliers, attractions, tour operators, airlines, local and provincial associations, and government agencies. This partnership arrangement provides a unique opportunity to develop coordinated programs that will benefit the industry, governments, and the country as a whole. For the federal government, establishing and funding the Commission represents an increased commitment to tourism in Canada.

Both private and public sectors join forces with the CTC in designing and implementing effective marketing strategies and programs that increase tourism revenues to Canada. Some of these activities include: gathering and maintaining data on potential markets; analyses of international and domestic marketplace opportunities and issues; market research and analysis; advertising; public relations; promotional projects; and travel trade activities.

The Commission also provides services to the tourism industry to help it remain internationally competitive. With its partners, the CTC identifies and implements programs and services to satisfy the industry's evolving need for information. These services include: assessments of the structure and performance of the industry and its subsectors; study and interpretation of developments on international and domestic markets; gathering and maintenance of data on tourism economic impact; and other issues such as revenues, capacity, and tourist consumption of specific products and services.

The CTC actively pursues partnership opportunities for its marketing, research, and industry and product development programs; interested organizations or individuals are invited to contact the Commission. It should be noted, however, that the CTC does not provide grants or subsidies, nor does it act as a lobby group on behalf of the industry.

Organization

Dedicated tourism industry leaders volunteer their time and talent to act as members of the Canadian Tourism Commission's Board of Directors. Collectively, they represent—and must sometimes reconcile—the diverse issues and views that reflect the Canadian tourism industry's sectoral, geographic, private, and public sector interests.

The industry-based, decision-making body is composed of 26 members with a wide variety of skills and knowledge. Board members represent all regions of the country and all sectors of the tourism industry. Seventeen members are from the private sector, including the Chairperson; seven represent provincial and territorial governments; one acts on behalf of the federal government, as does the CTC's President.

The CTC staff is made up of experienced professionals who fulfill two roles: They provide up-to-date information to facilitate decision-making by the CTC Board, its partners, and the industry, and they carry out the programs which are developed by the Working Committees and approved by the Board of Directors. See Figure 1.

Research

The CTC research program is world class. Canada is the first country in the world to publish a tourism satellite account that accurately measures the economic significance of tourism on an equal footing with other industries. Following the creation of the Tourism Satellite Account, Canada was also the first country to develop and publish national tourism indicators anchored to solid, thorough statistical analysis, permitting timely monitoring that was never before possible.

Through these measurement tools, certain trends have emerged. The CTC Research team has identified that different parts of the tourism industry respond differently to changes in the economy. Some commodities and segments of the industry, such as air

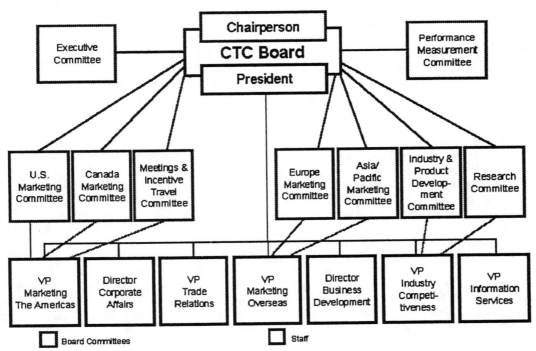

FIGURE 1 **Organizational structure of the Canadian Tourism Commission.**

transport, are economic bellwethers that track the Canadian and world economy. Accommodation and food services, on the other hand, are not as volatile. In addition, some segments respond more to variations in domestic tourism markets, whereas others respond more to international ones.

The research program focuses on updating and improving information on tourism in order to provide a sound basis for industry and financial decision-making. It concentrates on four main objectives: improving the definition and understanding of the tourism industry; assessing the performance of the tourism industry in Canada; developing methods of measuring the benefits of marketing; and sustaining and improving the scope and use of the national databases by developing new sources of information and communicating these findings effectively.

The Tourism Reference and Documentation Centre (TRDC)

The Tourism Reference and Documentation Centre (TRDC) was established in 1974 in response to the requirements of governments and businesses for a central clearinghouse of information on the tourism industry. Material for the Centre is provided by businesses and governments, national and international, to support the information requirements of the industry. Today, the Centre comprises the world's largest collection of documents on tourism. Two professional information specialists and a library assistant are available to help the industry locate the information it needs.

Industry and Product Development

In accord with the CTC's mission, which is to sustain a vibrant and profitable Canadian tourism industry, the Industry and Product Development Program objective is to assist the Canadian tourism industry to develop and sustain Canadian tourism products that match global demand.

This program does the following: (1) It takes a partnering approach to ensure a match between customer requirements and Canada's tourism products and services, provide quality support services and programs to partners in a timely, efficient, and effective manner, represent the interests of the Canadian tourism industry to governments and the private sector, and ensure that tourism is taken into account in policy and program development; (2) it ensures open and full communication of the CTC's planning process, priorities, and programs to all interested parties;

and (3) it measures program performance. Initiatives have been a product club program and expanding the winter tourism product.

The Canadian Tourism Exchange (CTX) is a major technology initiative being undertaken by the CTC to link Canadian tourism businesses and related organizations in order to enhance their competitiveness in the marketplace. CTX is being developed as a business-to-business Internet-based network that will mobilize the industry to a higher level of overall performance. Businesses will be able to access and share information on a timely basis and collaborate with one another on initiatives to improve business performance.

Marketing

Marketing is considered to be an investment that will be returned many times over in tax revenue from a growing and thriving Canadian tourism industry. Major marketing programs focus on the U.S. leisure travel market, the meetings and incentive travel market, and the Asia/Pacific, Europe, Canada, and the aboriginal tourism markets.

The United States, is Canada's most important international market, but it is also Canada's most formidable competitor in that same marketplace. Americans outperform Canadians in tour packaging and marketing, so it is easier for Americans to find an attractive package to visit some other part of the United States than to visit Canada, especially off-season. However, Canada enjoys a certain mystique in the American market. Among the most noteworthy of its advantages is the loyalty of U.S. visitors. Nine of ten Americans who visit Canada have been here before. A survey of Americans who had visited Canada recently showed that they rated Canada much better than the United States in terms of safety, cleanliness, beauty of its landscape, unspoiled wilderness, and friendliness of its people. Also, Canada's cities are considered more inviting than most large American cities.

The meetings and incentive travel program's strategy is to put Canada on buyers' competitive lists of destinations and to follow through with relationship-building, direct selling, and the opportunity to close the sale. It targets meeting and incentive travel decision-makers—a relatively small group—with an integrated approach that includes building awareness of Canada, direct mail, relationship marketing, promotions, sales calls, and referrals. The CTC's objective for the Asia-Pacific market is to increase revenue from the region to $2.7 billion by the year 2000—an increase of $1 billion from 1996. Greater attention will be focused on the Asia-Pacific market. Between 70 and 75 percent of the CTC's marketing investment in the Asia-Pacific region will be made in Japan.

In Taiwan, South Korea, and Australia the focus will be on consolidating the distribution network and triggering consumer interest in specific Canadian products and experiences. Also, efforts will be made to establish Canada's presence in the emerging Southeast Asia markets of Thailand, Malaysia, and the Philippines, where funds will be allocated for market research, promotional material, and special events.

The five-year strategy for the European market developed by the tourism industry in 1995 remains valid. In the United Kingdom, Germany, and France, emphasis will continue to be on building consumer awareness and selling thematic packages. These packages include outdoor, city, touring, cultural, and winter experiences. In developing markets, equal weight will be given to consumers and the travel trade. The main messages will be that Canada offers good value, quality, and diversity.

The Rediscover Canada theme, initiated to persuade Canadians to travel in Canada, continues. Efforts focused on increasing awareness of what Canada has to offer and on providing opportunities for the tourism industry to join with the CTC to stimulate the purchase of specific products and services. This program focused attention on increasing travel by Canadians during the low season and targeted particular market segments that expressed interest in various travel themes, such as history or culture. The aboriginal marketing program has focused on developing partnerships with stakeholders, initiating basic research and testing market response with highly targeted promotional activities.

More than 120 export-ready aboriginal cultural products have been identified in Canada which vary widely in terms of cultural distinctiveness. A major challenge in realizing the benefits of tourism lies in the increasing of business and marketing knowledge among aboriginal owner-operators. Also, there is little aboriginal product to be found in the existing distribution sales network. Although some inroads have been made toward improving these deficiencies, more effort will be required to take full advantage of the opportunities that had been identified.

Contacts:
Canadian Tourism Commission
235 Queen Street
Ottawa, Ontario
K1A 0H6
Canada
Telephone: (613) 954-3830
Fax: (613) 954-3964
Email: ctc_feedback@businteractive.com
Internet address:
http://www.canadatourism.com

READING 4.3

AUSTRALIA OFFICE OF NATIONAL TOURISM

The Office of National Tourism has been established within the Department of Industry, Science, and Tourism in recognition of the tourism industry's importance to the Australian economy. The Office of National Tourism works to maximise the contribution tourism makes to the well-being of Australians. It develops, implements, and delivers federal government policies and programs that:

• Encourage the development of tourism in Australia

• Identify opportunities in tourism

• Reduce barriers to industry development

• Provide information to assist industry decision-making

The Tourism Industry

Tourism is one of the fastest growing and economically important industries in Australia.

In 1995–1996, a record 4 million people visited Australia, generating $14.1 billion in export earnings.

By the year 2000, tourist expenditure in Australia is projected to rise to around $57 billion annually, with export earnings of around $21 billion.

Tourism also creates jobs: The industry accounts

for nearly 7 percent of the workforce and is helping to diversify the employment base of regional
economies. In the ten years to 2003, the tourism industry is expected to generate directly around
160,000 new jobs.

Tourism Portfolio

How the Office of National Tourism Works

The Office of National Tourism works with the
tourism industry, the Australian Tourist Commission
(ATC), and state and territory governments to facilitate the growth of tourism in Australia and to ensure
that this growth benefits all Australians. As part of this
role, it does the following:

- Encourages the development of an efficient
  tourism industry consistent with broader national
  economic objectives
- Encourages planning and management practices
  that promote ecologically sustainable tourism development and respect Australia's cultural diversity
- Encourages positive social outcomes from tourism

   The Office of National Tourism advises the federal
government on issues relevant to tourism. In particular, it does the following:

- Provides strategic direction and leadership to facilitate the achievement of the government's tourism
  objectives
- Provides tourism policy advice and support to the
  Minister for Industry, Science, and Tourism
- Ensures that program delivery is undertaken in an
  efficient and effective manner, and monitors and
  reviews program performance
- Monitors the performance of the Australian
  tourism industry and seeks to mitigate impediments
  affecting the achievement of objectives
- Fosters effective working relationships with commonwealth, state, territory, and international tourism agencies and with industry organizations

   The Office of National Tourism works to achieve
an efficient and effective operation that meets accountability requirements.

   It works with its portfolio partner, the Bureau
of Tourism Research, to provide the tourism industry with research, analysis, advice, and information to assist in the planning and growth of the industry.

The Office of National Tourism and the Tourism Portfolio

The Federal Government's Tourism portfolio comprises the Office of National Tourism, the Bureau of
Tourism Research, and the Australian Tourist Commission

   The Bureau of Tourism Research is responsible
for the major research activities undertaken by
the portfolio. It reports to the Minister for Industry,
Science, and Tourism and the Tourism Ministers'
Council.

   The Australian Tourist Commission, the commonwealth agency responsible for the promotion of Australian tourism overseas, is a statutory authority separate from the Department of Industry, Science, and
Tourism.

   The department and the Australian Tourist Commission report directly to the Minister for Industry,
Science, and Tourism.

Areas of the Office of National Tourism

Regional and environmental tourism supports the development of a competitive tourism industry that is ecologically sustainable and draws on Australia's regional
and cultural diversity and heritage. This area:

- Promotes the development of ecologically sustainable tourism
- Contributes to the diversification of regional
  economies through tourism development
- Contributes to the development of self-determination, self-management, and self-sufficiency of aboriginal peoples and Torres Strait Islanders through
  involvement in the tourism industry.

International and Industry Development works to enhance the international competitiveness of Australia's
tourism industry and to strengthen international relations in the tourism area. This area:

- Participates in bilateral and multilateral tourism activities
- Encourages the development of tourism businesses
  providing high-quality products and experiences
- Seeks to ensure the efficiency and effectiveness of
  the ATC's operations and marketing activities
- Promotes Australia at selected international expositions
- Facilitates the development of a skilled, flexible
  tourism workforce

- Maintains and enhances effective working relationships between the commonwealth, state, and territory tourism agencies and industry
- Contributes to the effectiveness of current and proposed arrangements for safeguarding consumer interests

Tourism transport and business development works to develop an economic environment in which tourism can most benefit the economy. This area:

- Coordinates the effective development and implementation of federal government tourism policies in consultation with other stakeholders
- Enhances understanding of the economic role and significance of the tourism industry
- Seeks to ensure that industry assistance measures and economic, taxation, and other regulatory instruments are appropriate to, and do not disadvantage, tourism relative to other industries
- Facilitates the availability and distribution of information on federal government initiatives to assist the development of tourism enterprises
- Encourages the adoption of efficient workplace practices to improve the quality and competitiveness of tourism services
- Contributes to the development of a greater capacity to provide relevant and realistic forecasts of tourism demand, infrastructure, and labour force needs
- Encourages appropriate investment in the tourism industry and seeks to reduce impediments to investment in, and inefficiencies in the operation of, tourism infrastructure
- Encourages greater efficiency and competition in aviation and surface transport operations
- Seeks a reduction in impediments to the efficient provision of transport infrastructure and the processing of inbound passengers.

Bureau of Tourism Research

The Bureau of Tourism Research is a nonstatutory body administered by the Department of Industry, Science, and Tourism and jointly funded by the commonwealth government and state/territory governments.

The bureau is responsible for providing accurate, timely and comprehensive statistics and analyses on tourism to aid industry and government decision-making. It also forecasts and assesses the economic impacts of tourism.

The bureau collects tourism statistics and undertakes strategic research to monitor tourism trends and developments. This information is made available to the industry in detailed reports. It is also used by federal and state territory governments to assist in developing effective policies.

The bureau has two information lines:

- For statistical information on tourism, phone (06) 279 7176
- To order any of the wide range of publications produced by the bureau, phone (06) 279 7183.

Tourism Forecasting Council

The Tourism Forecasting Council was established by the federal government in 1993 to provide tourism-related industries with credible and relevant forecasts. Its main source of technical forecasting data is the Bureau of Tourism Research.

The council comprises (1) a high-profile reporting body consisting of heads of tourism industry, finance, and building sector organizations and (2) a similarly structured, technically oriented advisory body.

The council's priority has been to develop forecasts covering inbound, domestic, and outbound tourism movements so that a better picture of future tourism activity can be developed. Visitor nights and expenditure have also been identified across these sectors.

Australian Tourist Commission

The Australian Tourist Commission plays a vital role in increasing the number of overseas visitors to Australia. It is responsible for promoting Australia overseas to the general public and to specialist groups such as the incentive market.

The commission works to maximize the benefits to Australia of overseas visitors, while reducing the potential adverse environmental and social impacts of international tourism.

Its operations are conducted through nine overseas offices, and its head office in Sydney.

Further Information

To find out more about the Office of National Tourism and to receive any of its wide range of publications; contact:

The Information Officer
Office of National Tourism
Department of Industry, Science and Tourism
GPO Box 1545
CANBERRA ACT 2601

Telephone (06) 279 7222
(toll free) 008 804 465
Fax: (06) 248 0734
Internet address:
http://tourism.gov.au/welcome.html

READING 4.4

PACIFIC ASIA TRAVEL ASSOCIATION

Founded in Hawaii in 1951 to develop, promote, and facilitate travel to and among the destination areas in and bordering the Pacific Ocean, the Pacific Asia Travel Association (PATA) brings together governments, airline and steamship companies, hoteliers, tour operators, travel agents, and a wide range of other tourism-related organizations.

Members exchange ideas, seek solutions to problems, and participate in shaping the future of travel in Asia and the Pacific Area. Membership totals over 2200 organizations worldwide. Since its founding, the Association has become an important source of accurate, up-to-date information for its members in the fields of marketing, development, research, education, and other travel-related activities. PATA's activities and long-range plans are examined and adjusted each year at the Association's Annual Conference. PATANET, the Association's web site, is at **www.pata.org**.

Committees

Standing committees on management, marketing, development, education, and research carry out the Association's ongoing program. PATA publishes a variety of reports, studies, publicity materials, directories, and periodicals. The principal periodical is *PATA Travel News* (PTN), a monthly journal with a circulation of about 58,000 copies. The main objective of PTN is to promote travel to and within the Pacific-Asia region. Eighty percent of the editorial content is feature material based on research and photographs obtained by the editors in the field.

PATA'S marketing efforts are directed to influencing more individuals to travel to and within the Pacific area. The committee also strives to improve marketing skills at the point of sale and in destination areas.

Development activities are geared to improving and advancing facilities and services in new destinations, increasing the handling capacity of existing destinations, and preserving their heritage and quality.

In research, PATA concentrates on the operation of numerous travel research seminars, the publication of an annual Pacific Asia statistical report, and the conduct of cooperative research studies.

PATA Conferences and Marts

Two of the more visible activities are the PATA Annual Conference and the PATA Travel Mart. The Conference, held in a member country each year, brings together up to 2000 people who join in discussions of the current needs and problems of Pacific tourism and participate in the Association's annual business meeting. Sessions of the Conference offer selected themes to assist members in gaining a better working knowledge of tourism. The PATA Travel Marts bring to a single location the buyers and sellers of travel who meet to negotiate contracts for future business. An example would be a tour operator who meets with travel agents in countries which might supply travelers to participate in that company's tour offerings. Specifically, a tour operator in Australia would meet with travel agents from the United States who might be sending clients to Australia; or a tour operator in the United States who is operating tours to Australia would be meeting with a ground operator (such as a local tour company) from Australia, who would supply a local tour for this tour group when it arrived in Sydney.

The work of the official PATA organization is greatly augmented by an international network of PATA chapters. They comprise over 17,000 individual members worldwide. Chapter members meet regularly to learn about the various PATA destinations through educational presentations and out-of-country familiarization trips.

PATA moved its operational headquarters to

Bangkok, Thailand, in September 1998; the association's administrative headquarters is located in San Francisco, California. Division offices are located in Singapore to serve the Asia Region, in Sydney to serve the Pacific Region, in San Francisco for the Americas Division, and in Monaco for Europe. PATA also maintains an Office of Environment and Culture in Monaco and a Northeast Asia representative in Tokyo, Japan.

KEY CONCEPTS

Canadian Tourism Commission
chambers of commerce
convention and visitors bureaus
Department of Transportation
European Travel Commission
Federal Aviation Administration
International Air Transport Association
International Association of Convention and
    Visitors Bureaus
Organization for Economic Cooperation and Development
Pacific Asia Travel Association
state tourism offices
Travel Industry Association of America
tourism industries
World Bank
World Tourism Organization
World Travel and Tourism Council

INTERNET SITES

The Internet sites mentioned in this chapter are repeated here for convenience plus some selected additional sites. For more information, visit these sites. Be aware that Internet addresses change frequently; so if a site cannot be accessed, use a search engine. Also use a search engine to locate many additional sites that are available.

Asia-Pacific Economic Cooperation
http://www.apecsec.org.sg/

Australia Tourist Commission
http://tourism.gov.au/welcome.html

British Tourism Authority
http://www.bta.org.uk

Canadian Tourism Commission
http://www.canada tourism.com

Caribbean Tourism Organization
http://www.caribtourism.com

European Travel Commission
http://www.visiteurope.com

International Air Transport Association
http://www.iata.org

International Association of Convention and Visitor Bureaus
http://www.iacvb.org

International Civil Aviation Organization
http://www.ca.org/ICAO

Irish Tourist Board
http://www.Ireland.travel.ie

Organization for Economic Cooperation and Development
http://www.oecd.org

Organization of American States
http://www.oas.org

Pacific Asia Travel Association
http://www.pata.org

Tourism Industries
http://tinet.ita.doc.gov

Travel Industry Association of America
http://www.tia.org

United Nations
http://www.un.org

World Tourism Organization
http://www.world-tourism.org

World Travel and Tourism Council
http://www.wttc.org

INTERNET EXERCISES

Site Name: World Tourism Organization

URL: http://www.world-tourism.org

Background Information: The World Tourism Organization is the leading international organization in the field of travel and tourism. It serves as a global forum for tourism policy issues and a practical source of tourism know-how.

Exercises

Explore the WTO web site and find the following information:

1. How does the WTO communicate with its members and nonmembers?

2. As global competition in tourism becomes more intense, quality is the factor that can make the difference between success and failure. WTO's section for Quality of Tourism Development aims to help member destinations improve quality to become more competitive and ensure sustainable development. What are the basic components of WTO's quality program?

3. What is the "Child Prostitution and Tourism Watch?"

4. List five publications produced by the WTO and why they might be beneficial to a tourism professional.

QUESTIONS FOR REVIEW AND DISCUSSION

1. If you were minister of tourism for American Samoa, what types of assistance might you request from WTO?

2. Referring to question 1, what aid would probably be forthcoming from the Pacific Asia Travel Association?

3. Tourism is the largest export industry in American Samoa. How might its minister of tourism's office be organized?

4. Do you feel that education should be one of the principal functions of any tourism organization? Why or why not?

5. If you were the president of a large international development bank such as FONATUR, what interest would you have in the World Travel and Tourism Council (WTTC)?

6. Speaking philosophically, why should a national government transportation department have any authority to regulate or control passenger fares or cargo rates?

7. Referring to question 6, should a private international organization such as the International Air Transport Association (IATA) have any authority to govern passenger airfares? If so, why?

8. Explain how the OECD, headquartered in Paris, could help develop tourism in its European member countries.

9. What main points would you expound if you were supporting next year's Tourism Industries (TI) budget on the floor of the U.S. House of Representatives?

10. Is there any need for a private national organization such as the Travel Industry Association of America (TIA)?

11. A state senator strongly opposes the budget for tourism promotion. "Let the hotels and transportation companies promote our state," he exclaims, "we need this money for better schools." As a member of the senate's tourism committee, what would your rebuttal be?

12. If you are a Canadian citizen, how do you feel about your tax dollars being spent on research jointly with the Tourism Industries?

13. Is there a relationship between the work of the Tourism Industries and the U.S. trade deficit?

14. In what ways does a city's convention and visitors bureau function? How is this organization usually financed?

15. As the manager of a fine resort lodge, what arguments would you use with your board of directors to obtain financial support for your local and regional tourism promotion organization?

16. If you, as manager of a motor hotel, had joined a

tourist association and placed an ad in their publication, how would you ascertain if such investments were paying off?

17. What attributes of the Canadian Tourism Commission make it an outstanding national tourism organization?

CASE PROBLEMS

1. A quite popular tourist state has fallen on hard times. The state government can no longer provide adequate funds for their state park system. The governor has proposed a "group maintenance" policy for the parks. This means that all the parks in a given part of the state would be managed on a "group" basis. Eliminated would be all of the individual local park managers. Several million people visit these parks each year—an important part of the state's tourism. What might be some feasible solutions to this unfortunate situation?

2. Two city council members are having an argument. A proposed budget item for tourist promotion for the coming fiscal year is being considered. One member endorses this item enthusiastically. The other states: "We don't benefit much for tourists' spending here because of the high leakage. I won't vote for this item; let's forget it." You are attending this meeting as a representative of the C&VB. How would you respond? If you felt that your declarations were not very convincing, what research should be conducted immediately to strengthen your pro-tourism position?

SELECTED REFERENCES

Bonham, Carl, and James Mak. "Private versus Public Financing of State Destination Promotion." *Journal of Travel Research*, Vol. 35, No. 2, pp. 3–10, Fall 1996.

Bramwell, Bill, and Liz Rawding. "Tourism Marketing Organizations in Industrial Cities: Organizations, Objectives and Urban Governance." *Tourism Management*, Vol. 15, No. 6, pp. 425–434, 1994.

Gartner, William C. "State Level Research: Typology and Direction." *Visions in Leisure and Business*, Vol. 10, No. 1, pp. 50–62, Spring 1991.

Gartell, Richard B. *Destination Marketing for Convention and Visitor Bureaus*. Dubuque, IA: Kendall/Hunt, 1988.

Hawes, Douglas K., David T. Taylor, and Gary D. Hampe. "Destination Marketing by States." *Journal of Travel Research*, Vol. 30, No. 1, pp. 11–17, Summer 1991.

HVRF, *Local Government and Tourism: Facilitators for Growth*. Hunter Valley Research Foundation, Canberra: Australian Government Publishing Service, 1995.

McKercher, Bob, and Megan Ritchie. "The Third Tier of Public Sector Tourism: A Profile of Local Government Tourism Officers in Australia." *Journal of Travel Research*, Vol. 36, No. 1, pp. 66–72, Summer 1997.

National Tourism Policy Study: Ascertainment Phase. Washington, D.C.: U.S. Government Printing Office, 1977.

National Tourism Policy Study: Final Report. Washington, D.C.: U.S. Government Printing Office, 1978.

Organization for Economic Cooperation and Development. *Tourism Policy and International Tourism in OECD Member Countries*. Paris: OECD, 1996.

Owen, Charles. "Building a Relationship Between Government and Tourism." *Tourism Management*, Vol. 13, No. 4, pp. 358–362, December 1992.

Pearce, D. *Tourist Organizations*. Essex: Longman, 1992.

Pearce, Douglas G. "Regional Tourist Organizations in Spain: Emergence, Policies and Consequences." *Tourism Economics*, Vol. 2, No. 2, pp. 119–136, June 1996.

Pearce, Douglas G. "Tourist Organizations in Sweden." *Tourism Management*, Vol. 17, No. 6, pp. 413–424, September 1996.

Sims, Steven L. "Educational Needs and Opportunities for Personnel in Convention and Visitor Bureaus." *Visions in Leisure and Business*, Vol. 9, No. 3, pp. 27–32, Fall 1990.

Soteriou, Evi C., and Chris Roberts. "The Strategic Planning Process in National Tourism Organizations." *Journal of Travel Research*, Vol. 37, No. 1, pp. 21–29, August 1998.

STB. *Planning for the Digital Economy: An Implementation Plan for Scotland's Tourism Industry*. Edinburgh:

Scottish Tourist Board, 1996.

Sussmann, Silvia, and Michael Baker. "Responding to the Electronic Marketplace: Lessons from Destination Management Systems." *International Journal of Hospitality Management*, Vol. 15, No. 2, pp. 99–112, June 1996.

U.S. Travel Data Center. *Survey of State Travel Offices: 1997–1998*. Washington, D.C.: Travel Industry Association of America, 1998.

Wanhill, Stephen. "Encompassing the Social and Environmental Aspects of Tourism within an Institutional Context: A National Tourist Board Perspective." *Progress in Tourism and Hospitality Research*, Vol. 2, No. 3 and 4, pp. 321–335, September/December 1996.

WTO, *Investments and Financing in the Tourism Industry*. Madrid: World Tourism Organization, 1993.

WTO, *Budgets of National Tourism Administration*. Madrid: World Tourism Organization, 1996.

CHAPTER 5

PASSENGER TRANSPORTATION

- Comprehend the importance of transportation in tourism.
- Understand the airline industry and its role in travel.
- Examine the domination of the automobile in travel.
- Learn about the role of rail and motorcoach travel.
- Study the cruise industry.

◀ **LEARNING OBJECTIVES**

◀ *An Amtrak intercity passenger train glides overhead, as vacationers fish and relax at Powells Creek, Virginia. (Photo by Matt Van Hattem.)*

INTRODUCTION

Since the beginning of time, people have been traveling by various modes—from on foot to riding in a supersonic aircraft. Tourism and **transportation** are inexorably linked. As world tourism increases, additional demands will be placed on the transportation sectors (see Figure 5.1). Looking at the position occupied by the various modes of passenger transportation, one finds that air travel dominates long-distance and middle-distance tourism. The private automobile dominates for shorter trips and is the most popular means of travel for most domestic journeys. The automobile is also very important in regional and international tourism. Rail travel now plays a more limited role than it did in the past. However, this mode could increase its market share, especially in Europe. The development of high-speed trains and the opening of the Channel Tunnel will increase rail traffic. Motorcoach transportation reaches many communities that are not served by any other public mode; but quantitatively, motorcoaches account for a very small percentage of vehicle miles. Cruises are becoming more popular and are the fastest-growing segment of tourism. However, this segment is still small quantitatively.

An increase in traffic due to world tourism growth puts pressure on transportation facilities, and this can have adverse effects. Situations in the world vary widely within regions, countries, states, and provinces. Also, variations exist between such areas. Even so, the problems seem to be the same all over the world. Those needing urgent attention of policymakers are as follows:

1. *Congestion.* Serious congestion affects most passenger transportation modes, particularly on roads and at airports during peak periods. In major cities there is the danger of reaching gridlock. Congestion means delays that are a serious waste of time and energy.

2. *Safety and security.* Ensuring safety and security in transportation is a basic requirement for tourism.

3. *Environment.* An increase in traffic may harm the environment if an area does not have the carrying capacity for additional tourists. Transportation planning must take economic, social, cultural, and natural resources costs into account when designing expanded facilities.

4. *Seasonality.* Seasonal patterns of travel demand create overcrowding at certain times. Conversely, low occupancies and load factors will occur at other periods. At peak travel periods the problems of congestion, security, and the environment become much more severe.

All of these problems are challenges facing transportation planners. They have had and will continue to have an unfavorable impact on the perception that tourists have of their vacation experiences. Transportation problems have the potential of creating an unfavorable image of a tourist destination. As the modes of transportation are reviewed in this chapter, think about how they can be developed and integrated to serve the tourist in the best possible manner.

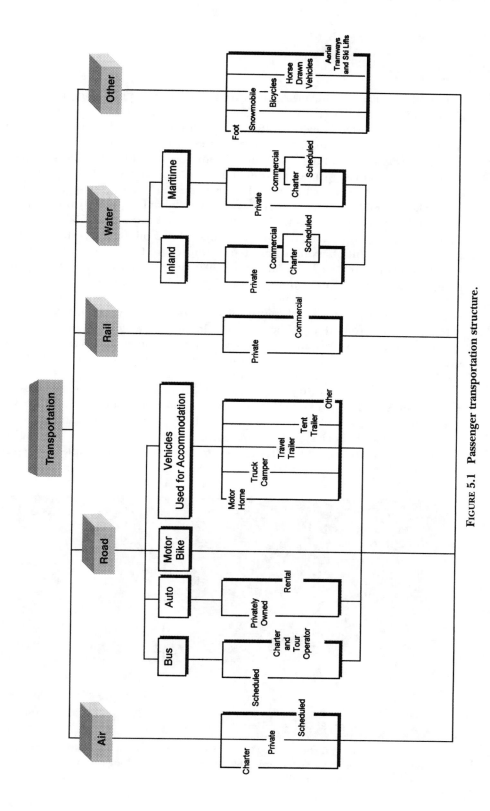

FIGURE 5.1 Passenger transportation structure.

137

THE AIRLINE INDUSTRY

In the span of 50 years the airline industry has grown from infant to giant. The world's **airline industry** now carries over 1 billion passengers per year. There are about 800 air carriers in the world. They range from huge companies such as British Airways with hundreds of planes to small one-plane airlines. According to Somerset Waters in *The Travel Industry Yearbook*, the world's airlines employ more than 3 million people and fly from 14,000 airports. Airlines all over the world are currently showing strong growth in both traffic and profits because of a passenger boom, low fuel prices, lower distribution costs, and increased cooperation through alliances. In 1997 the U.S. airline industry launched over 22,348 flights a day, employed more than 586,509 people, carried 1.6 million people each day, and recorded $109.5 billion in revenues. Fortunately, these impressive numbers have resulted in impressive financial results as the airlines achieved record profits of $5.2 billion in 1997. However, airlines are still repairing the damage caused by the enormous losses of the early 1990s. Over the four-year period 1990–1993, U.S. carriers lost more than $12.8 billion. The nation's economy and the tourism industry need a healthy air transportation system. Without airline passengers, rental cars go unrented, hotel beds go unsold, and attractions go unvisited.

The airlines have revolutionized travel, and the range and speed of jet travel has greatly expanded what tourists or business travelers could once accomplish with the equivalent time and funds at their disposal. Today, for example, it is possible to fly around the globe in less time than it takes to drive across the United States. The system is also incredibly efficient: You need only make one call to an airline or a travel agent and purchase a ticket to your desired destination; then all you have to do is go to the airport and check your bags through to the final destination. The logistics that make it happen are complex, but the system works well. For example, United Airlines

A late-model jet aircraft can carry hundreds of passengers in a minimum amount of time. Air travel is the most comfortable mode for mid- to long-distance trips. *(Photo courtesy of Southwest Airlines.)*

offers over 2200 flights a day to 139 destinations in 30 countries, and two U.S. Territories around the world. Other airlines have similar structures and combine to make a total system that blankets the country.

Although the major advantage of air travel is speed, which results in more time for other activities, there are negative aspects for those who wish to travel by air. These include some people's fear of flying and lack of geographic accessibility—many communities in the country are not served by air transportation. An additional problem is the length of time spent getting to and from the airport. Frequently, this time exceeds that spent en route.

The $109.5 billion air transportation industry in the United States is dominated by a small number of large firms; the major carriers—Alaska, American West, American, Continental, Delta, Northwest, Southwest, TWA, United, and US Airways—all record over $1 billion in revenue annually. Those air carriers recording annual revenues of $100 million to $1 billion include Air Transport International, Air Wisconsin, AirTran, Aloha, American International, American Trans Air, Arrow, Atlantic Southeast, Atlas Air, Business Express, Carnival, Challenge, Continental Express, Continental Micronesia, Emery Worldwide, Evergreen International, Executive Airlines, Hawaiian, Horizon Air, Kiwi, Mesa, Midway, Midwest Express, Polar Air Cargo, Rich, Simmons, Southern Air, Sun Country, Tower, Trans States, US Airways Shuttle, and World. There are about 52 regional airlines with annual revenues under $100 million. The top 10 airlines by revenue passenger miles are shown in Table 5.1. Despite the domination by the large carriers, there are a number of smaller firms in the market.

A 1997 survey of air travelers by the Gallup organization revealed that a record 80 percent of the entire adult population in the United States had flown. Two out of every five U.S. citizens flew during 1997. The survey found that 53 percent of airline trips during 1997 were for pleasure or other personal reasons, and 47 percent were for business.

One of the best sources of data on the airline industry is an annual report published by the Air Transport Association of America, 1301 Pennsylvania Avenue N.W., Washington, D.C. 20004. The International Air Transport Association (see Chapter 4)

TABLE 5.1

Top Ten Airlines by Revenue Passenger Miles

	Airline	Revenue Passenger Miles (millions)
1	United	121,350
2	American	106,936
3	Delta	99,624
4	Northwest	71,998
5	Continental	44,072
6	US Airways	41,578
7	Southwest	25,099
8	Trans World	28,359
9	America West	16,171
10	Alaska	10,362

Source: Air Transport Association, 1998.

makes forecasts and publishes financial and traffic statistics on the world airline industry. Their *World Air Transport Statistics* is in its 42nd year of publication and is reported to be the single most timely and authoritative source of international airline data.

Air Transport World (ATW) publishes an annual World Airline Report that typically appears in their July issue. The report is available from ATW at (202) 659-8500 or (**http://www.atonline.com**). The comprehensive report covers the world's top 25 airlines, world airline financial statistics, Africa, Asia/Pacific, Canada, Europe, Latin America/Caribbean, Middle East, U.S. Majors, U.S. Nationals, U.S. Cargo Carriers, U.S. Regional/Specialty Carriers, and World Airline Fleets. *Air Transport World* is published monthly by Penton Publishing Inc.

Another useful source of information on the airline industry is the U.S. Federal Aviation Administration. Consumer protection is the responsibility of the Department of Transportation.

Deregulation and Alliances

Under deregulation, the airline industry has undergone dramatic change. It is hard to believe that the 20th anniversary of U.S. airline deregulation has come and gone (October 1998). Looking back we can see that it has led to significant consolidation, hub systems, low airfares in competitive situations, and high airfares where competition is lacking.

The future holds more concentration as a wave of **alliances** have taken place and more are proposed. Alliances that would involve the largest six carriers in the United States are being discussed and range from equity positions, to code sharing, to frequent flyer programs reciprocity and other joint marketing arrangements. These are United–Delta, American–US Airways, and Continental–Northwest. While international alliances have been debated since KLM and Northwest linked in 1992, domestic alliance agreements are a recent phenomenon. United has the Star Alliance (created in May 1997), which included Lufthansa, Air Canada, Thai Airways, and SAS. Since then, United has added Brazil's Varig and they are considering additional partners. American and British Airways have launched a global alliance with Canadian Airlines, Qantas, and Cathay Pacific Airways, called "oneworld." They also plan to expand the grouping. There are other alliances and partners too numerous to mention, but the above alliances indicate the high level of concentration present.

Are alliances the wave of the future of the aviation industry? Will alliances benefit the consumer through greater choice, more seamless travel, lower fares, greater convenience, and frequent flyer miles? Or will alliances create oligopoly and monopoly, higher fares, and a noncompetitive situation? Only time and government action will answer these questions. The expectation is that the alliance trend will continue for several years unless regulatory agencies stop it. Authorities in both the United States and the European Union are analyzing how to deal with major airline alliances. The decisions made will shape the future of airlines around the world.

Safety

U.S. air carriers providing scheduled service have an enviable **safety** record. Table 5.2 shows accident statistics and indicates that being in the air is one of the safest places

TABLE 5.2

Safety: U.S. Air Carriers, Scheduled Service (aircraft with 10 seats or more)

Year	Departures (millions)	Fatal Accidents	Fatalities	Fatal Accidents Per 100,000 Departures
1987	6.6	4	231	0.046[a]
1988	6.7	3	285	0.030[a]
1989	6.6	8	131	0.121
1990	6.9	6	39	0.087
1991	6.8	4	62	0.059
1992	7.1	4	33	0.057
1993	7.2	1	1	0.014
1994	7.5	4	239	0.053
1995	8.1	2	166	0.025
1996	8.2	3	342	0.036
1997	8.2	3	3	0.037

[a] Sabotage-caused accidents are included in *Accidents and Fatalities,* but not in the *Accident Rates.*
Source: National Transportation Safety Board and the Air Transport Association.

you can be. The U.S. airline industry completed a perfect year in 1998, with no fatal accidents.

Growth

World and U.S. air transportation is expected to grow at a steady rate in the future. The stronger the world economy, the greater will be the rate of growth. An example of how the FAA expects U.S. carriers to grow is shown in Table 5.3, where forecasts are

TABLE 5.3

FAA Aviation Forecasts: Commercial Air Carriers, 1998–2009

Year	Passengers (millions)	RPMs (billions)	Jet Aircraft	Departures (millions)
1998	615.8	626.2	5,092	7.2
1999	635.4	650.9	5,224	7.3
2000	656.5	678.1	5,444	7.4
2001	680.3	709.3	5,698	7.6
2002	706.8	743.5	5,913	7.8
2003	734.3	779.2	6,149	7.9
2004	762.9	816.5	6,361	8.1
2005	792.6	855.6	6,574	8.3
2006	823.5	896.7	6,778	8.5
2007	855.8	939.8	6,983	8.7
2008	889.4	985.2	7,203	8.9
2009	924.3	1,032.5	7,419	9.2

Source: Air Transport Association.

given to the year 2009. Air transport growth is an essential ingredient in tourism's future because the growth of tourism is linked to air transport performance. Without growth in airline passengers, there are no new customers to rent cars, stay in accommodations, and visit attractions.

Air Transport Association of America

The airline industry is supported by three major organizations. IATA and ICAO have already been discussed under international organizations; they are two key associations controlling air travel. The major U.S. organization is the **Air Transport Association of America.**

In 1936, fourteen fledgling airlines met in Chicago to form the Air Transport Association (ATA) "to do all things tending to promote the betterment of airline business, and in general, to do everything in its power to best serve the interest and welfare of the members of this association and the public at large."

Today, from its headquarters in Washington, D.C., the ATA is the nation's oldest and largest airline trade association. Its membership of 23 U.S. and five associate (non-U.S.) airlines carried nearly 600 million passengers and more than 25 billion ton-miles of cargo in 1997. U.S. members account for more than 95 percent of the passenger and cargo traffic carried by scheduled U.S. airlines.

ATA is the meeting place where the airlines cooperate in noncompetitive areas to improve airline service, safety, and efficiency. The mission of the ATA is to support and assist its member carriers by promoting aviation safety, advocating industry positions, conducting designated industry-wide programs, and ensuring public understanding.

Thus, while the carriers are intensely competitive among themselves and with other forms of transportation in their individual promotion of airline service for the traveling and shipping public, they are equally intense in their mutual cooperation on matters of industry-wide importance, such as safety, technological progress, and passenger service improvement.

While ATA's agenda of issues continuously changes, its major priorities remain unchanged. They include:

- Assisting the airline industry in continuing to provide the world's safest system of transportation
- Advocating the modernization of the Federal Aviation Administration's air traffic control system, in order to improve service for airline customers and to benefit the environment
- Increasing the security of airline passengers and cargo against threats directed at the United States
- Seeking to prevent legislative and regulatory actions that would penalize airlines and their customers by imposing rate, route, service, or schedule controls on the industry
- Endeavoring to reduce the disproportionate share of taxes and fees paid by airlines and their customers at the federal, state, and local levels
- Improving the industry's ability to attract capital
- Helping to shape international aviation policy, to ensure that U.S. and foreign carriers can compete on equal terms

During its more than 60 years of existence, the ATA has seen the airline industry grow from the small, pioneering companies of the 1930s into key players in the world's economy. ATA members continue to play a major role in shaping the future of air transportation.

The ATA headquarters is located at 1301 Pennsylvania Avenue NW, Washington, D.C. 20004. Telephone (202) 626-4000. Web site: **www.air-transport.org.**

THE RAIL INDUSTRY

Rail passenger transportation, once the major mode of travel in the United States, reached its peak volume in 1920. Major railroads wished to rid themselves of the passenger business, and today the survival of service (other than commuter service) depends largely on **Amtrak.** In Canada the situation has been similar and future rail travel depends on VIA Rail.

Outside North America, where passenger rail service is less limited, **rail transportation** assumes a more important role. Ultramodern railway systems with high-speed trains operate in many countries, handling passenger traffic in an economical and efficient manner and providing an alternative to air travel. France and Japan are well known for their high-speed trains. France has been willing to subsidize its rail system. The French government has taken responsibility for rail infrastructure of the state-owned SNCF rail company. Japan continues to improve and expand its famous "bullet train." Some of the largest railways in the world are found in the former Soviet Union, India, and China.

Amtrak

Amtrak is the marketing name for the National Railroad Passenger Corporation, an operating railroad corporation, the controlling stock of which is owned by the U.S. government through the U.S. Department of Transportation. Amtrak's business is providing rail passenger transportation in the major intercity markets of the United States. The National Railroad Passenger Corporation was established by the Rail Passenger Service Act of 1970.

Although it receives financial support from the federal government, Amtrak is not a government agency. It is a corporation structured and managed like other large businesses in the United States and competes with all other modes in the transportation marketplace.

Serving 44 states and 500 destinations on its 23,000-mile route system, Amtrak carried more than 20 million intercity passengers in 1997. In addition, Amtrak carried more than 48 million commuters on trains operated under contract. Amtrak employs 23,000 people. Amtrak generated a record-making revenue of $1.67 billion in fiscal year 1997. Approximately 22,000 of its employees are represented by 14 different labor organizations.

Amtrak was launched as an experiment to identify the importance of rail passenger service to a balanced national transportation system. A key for continued support of Amtrak in the mid-1970s was the dramatic impact of the oil embargo and recognition of the need for alternative forms of transportation.

A modern long-distance Amtrak train crossing the southern Allegheny mountains in Pennsylvania. Rail travel is preferred by many because passengers are able to see the countryside and because of rail's impressive safety record. *(Photo by Matt Van Hattem.)*

In various transportation corridors, Amtrak is the dominant public carrier. Amtrak provides energy-efficient and environmentally benign service in some of the nation's most densely populated, congested, and polluted rail corridors including the Washington, D.C.–Boston Northeast Corridor and between San Diego and Los Angeles, San Francisco and Sacramento, St. Louis and Chicago, and Chicago and Detroit. In the Northeast Corridor alone, annual Amtrak ridership between New York and Washington, D.C., is the equivalent of 7500 fully booked 757s or 10,000 fully booked DC-9s. Amtrak currently serves almost half of the combined air-rail market between the endpoints of New York and Washington, D.C.; when intermediate cities (such as Baltimore and Philadelphia) are included, Amtrak's share of the air-rail market rises to 70 percent.

To preserve passenger rail service in America, Congress, the Administration, and Amtrak agreed on a plan for Amtrak to modernize service and make it operationally self-sufficient by 2002. Consequently, Amtrak has begun an aggressive capital investment program funded by $2.2 billion in legislation passed in 1997 by the U.S. Congress. This money will supplement annual capital appropriations that Amtrak receives from the federal government. These improvements will further improve service to customers while also helping to reduce expenses to gradually end the need for federal operating assistance, as mandated by Congress.

Amtrak has put into service 50 new Amtrak Viewliners, the first single-level sleeping cars designed in the United States in 40 years. These cars feature an extra row of windows to provide more light during the day and give upper birth customers their own window at night. Viewliner bedrooms also have high-tech amenities (such as television monitors) to give customers maximum comfort and enjoyment.

Amtrak now has 195 new Superliner II passenger rail cars, which operate exclusively on the *Coast Starlight* between Seattle and LA, *Auto Train* to Florida, and many of Amtrak's long-distance overnight trains in service. These two-level cars offer spacious accommodations for coach and first-class sleeping car patrons and include lounge and dining car service.

Amtrak has successfully introduced over 180 new Genesis Series diesel locomotives that operate on many of Amtrak's trains throughout the United States. These lightweight, aerodynamic passenger locomotives are designed to meet the needs of Amtrak's long-distance passenger service.

A number of new business initiatives are underway, the most exciting of which is the introduction of high-speed rail travel between Boston, New York, and Washington, D.C. Linking major cities from Boston to Washington, D.C., along the densely populated Northeast Corridor is expected to generate more than $150 million in revenue.

Northeast Corridor operations already account for more than half of Amtrak's total ridership and revenue, due primarily to Amtrak's ability to compete with the airlines in the lucrative business travel market between New York and Washington, D.C., by offering three-hour service. By reducing travel times between New York and Boston from the current four-and-a-half-hour trip to three hours with the onset of high-speed rail, Amtrak similarly will be able to compete with the air shuttles for business travel in the New England market.

A consortium of GEC Alsthom and Bombardier won the bid to build the new train which Amtrak is marketing under the name Acela Express. They proposed a new train utilizing French TGV propulsion systems and equipped with tilt technology to negotiate the many curves of the Northeast Corridor at relatively high speed.

Amtrak has ordered 18 Acela Express trains that will each operate as a set with locomotives at the front and rear and six cars in between, including four coaches, a first-class car, and an upscale bistro car. Each Acela Express train will carry 304 customers. Each seat will be equipped with 120-volt outlets for laptop computers, three audio channels, extra-large tray tables, and attendant call buttons. Business travelers will have a choice of 32 tables dispersed throughout the trains to hold impromptu meetings or spread out paperwork. Video entertainment or live news programming will be aired over monitors in the dining car.

Amtrak's commitment to the project extends beyond the trains; all aspects of service, from ticketing to stations to on-board service, are being revamped in order to create a world class experience. A successful launch will not only spark the development of high-speed rail projects in other densely populated corridors in the United States, but will also position Amtrak's Northeast Corridor service among the world's elite passenger rail operations.

By the time all of the high-speed Acela Express train sets are operational in the year 2000, Amtrak expects to be earning a significant profit from the service that will advance the railroad's goal of operational self-sufficiency. Travelers will enjoy a more relaxing and productive travel experience, and American passenger rail service will enter the new millennium with bright prospects for dramatic expansion.

Because Amtrak is subsidized, suppliers of the other modes of transportation (especially bus) feel that Amtrak is attracting its customers with taxpayer assistance. However, even with the controversy, Congress is likely to see that Amtrak remains in business for the foreseeable future.

THE MOTORCOACH INDUSTRY

The American Bus Association (ABA) reports that there are between 26,000 and 28,000 commercial buses in use for charters, tours, regular route service, and special operations in North America. Carriers involved in the regular-route part of the industry operate approximately 8000 to 10,000 over-the-road intercity coaches. The amount of time that motorcoach fleet buses spend in charters is 66.6 percent, in tours 22.5 percent, and in regular route scheduled service 10.9 percent. The average cost of a new 45-foot motorcoach is approximately $365,000. Average operating cost for a motorcoach is $1.46 per mile (includes driver, fuel, normal equipment usage).

As reported at the 1993 White House Conference on Global Climate Change, intercity bus service is the most energy-efficient passenger transportation mode. In 1991, it was twice as efficient as Amtrak service, three times as efficient as automobiles and mass transit, and four times as efficient as commercial aviation. In comparing data from large bus companies, the carriers consume 997 BTU per passenger-mile, compared to 1995 for Amtrak, 3325 for passenger cars, and 4457 for certificated air carriers' domestic operations.

Regular/Route/Scheduled Bus Service

There are about 100 privately owned companies in the United States that offer regular route bus service. Greyhound Lines Inc. is the only nationwide bus carrier for regular route service. The Trailways National Bus System, a federation of independently owned bus companies that market intercity service under the Trailways name, covers a large portion of the United States. Other independent companies provide service on a regional basis and feed passengers into the Greyhound or Trailways systems, into the Amtrak rail system, and into airports. The approximate number of places in the United States served by intercity buses is 4200. This compares to about 750 airports with scheduled airline service, and to about 600 Amtrak stations (108 of which are served only by contract bus service).

According to the U.S. Department of Transportation, the top 17 carriers in the United States reported 33.7 million revenue passengers in 1996. The previous year, 20 carriers reported 43.2 million revenue passengers. Overall operating revenue for the 17 carriers was $835.8 million in 1996. Revenue for the top 20 carriers in 1995 was $917.3 million.

Charters and Tours

Both domestic and international travelers are heavy users of **motorcoaches** because coach travel gives them time to see and experience sights with a group of friends without having to deal with traffic and road maps. About one-third of U.S. motorcoach and tour operators polled by ABA report an increase in overseas visitors. Sales of tours and charters are expected to grow in the 3 to 5 percent range. Because of the increasing

The motorcoach industry is the most pervasive form of intercity public transportation in the world. Motorcoaches provide both scheduled and charter service. This motorcoach carried passengers from Alice Springs, Australia to Ayers Rock. *(Photo by the author.)*

popularity of motorcoach tours, tour operators nationwide now conduct trips to myriad destinations and drive you there safely in state-of-the-art equipped vehicles at an economical price.

Trends

The motorcoach company acquisition trend continued strongly in 1997 and 1998. Since its initial public offering in 1996, Coach USA has acquired 53 U.S. and Canadian transportation companies and is the largest provider of motorcoach tour and charter services in the United States. Other major industry consolidators are Laidlaw and Global Passenger Services, which has a subsidiary, Travelways, providing tour and sightseeing services. Greyhound Lines, the only U.S. nationwide carrier, closed several deals from North Carolina to Mexico City to firm up its position in the regular route side of the market. Some mid- and small-sized companies not interested in being acquired by the Coach, Laidlaw, or Global are finding mergers with similar sized carriers to be advantageous, or they are joining cooperatives or consortiums to enhance their market position. Experts predict that the merger and acquisition trend is likely to be a force in the industry for some time.

Do you expect to enjoy a full-length feature film on your next trip? Or relax in a comfortable seat? If you think you can do these traveling only on an airline, think again. Leisure motorcoach travel is a popular way to see North America. The modern trip by motorcoach is nothing like you remember from your childhood days. Forget your preconceived ideas of crowded, stuffy buses. Today's luxury vehicles have reclining seats and air conditioning and are among the safest and cleanest modes of transportation available.

In a United Motorcoach Association (UMA) consumer profile, the profile of motorcoach riders was determined to be younger, better educated, and more affluent than many believed. The "baby boomer" generation, ages 35 to 54, is the largest segment of motorcoach travelers. The "boomer" group has more bus users, 36 percent, than those 55 and older or 18 to 34 year olds, 32 percent respectively. Nearly half of motorcoach users, 46 percent, have a college degree or more. Motorcoach users are also fairly well off financially: 36 percent have a household income of $50,000 or more, and 33 percent have a household income of $25,000 to $49,000.

Issues

A major issue facing motorcoach company owners today is a proposed rule from the U.S. Department of Transportation (DOT) on wheelchair accessibility for motorcoaches, which is part of the Americans with Disabilities Act. ABA and the industry have proposed and support a service-based system as opposed to the equipment-based approach from the Transportation Department. The DOT proposal requires wheelchair lifts and securement locations installed on over-the-road buses on a phased-in schedule up through the year 2012. For charter and tour companies, accessible buses would have to make up 10 percent of their fleets by 2002, and charter and tour operators would have to make accessible bus service available on 48 hours' advance notice. All new buses obtained for fixed-route services would have to be accessible beginning in 2000. Large carriers would have to make sure that half of their buses were accessible by 2006 and that all were accessible by 2012. Until then, carriers would have to make accessible buses available on 48 hours' advance notice.

Motorcoach Organizations

The **American Bus Association** (ABA) is the national organization of the intercity bus industry and serves as the prime source of industry statistics. ABA represents approximately 700 motorcoach and tour companies in the United States and Canada. Its members operate charter, tour, regular route, airport express, special operations, and contract services (commuter, school, transit). Another 2300 member organizations represent the travel and tourism industry and suppliers of bus products and services who work in partnership with the North American motorcoach industry. ABA has a total membership of about 3000.

ABA's headquarters in downtown Washington, D.C., is located in a building that incorporates the restored 1940 art deco Greyhound bus terminal. Address: American Bus Association, 1100 New York Ave., NW, Suite 1050, Washington, DC 20005-3934, (202) 842-1645, (800) 283-2877 (U.S. & Canada), FAX: (202) 842-0850, e-mail:abainfo@buses.org. Their web site is **http://www.buses.org.**

The **United Motorcoach Association** (UMA), founded as the United Bus Owners of America in 1971, is a trade association with nearly 1000 motorcoach company members and motorcoach industry manufacturers, suppliers, and vendors spread across North America. UMA member companies provide a broad variety of charter motorcoach services, much of it for preformed groups. Other member services include tours, schools, intercity transit, and shuttle or commuter lines. UMA serves the informational, legislative, regulatory, and business needs of its member companies. Within the membership, companies range from one and two vehicles to those with many hundreds of coaches; from small tour-specific companies to those performing intercity route service, charter operations, and tour operations on a coast-to-coast scale.

UMA's offices are located at 113 S. West Street, Alexandria, VA 22314-2824. Telephone (800) 424-8262 or (703) 838-2929, e-mail: info@uma.org. Web site address: **http://www.uma.org**.

THE AUTOMOBILE

Most of the travel in the world takes place in the **automobile.** In the United States the U.S. Travel Data Center, in its 1996 *Travel Market Report,* using full-year results from the National Travel Survey, reports that 80 percent of the person-trips are made by auto (includes rental cars, trucks, and RVs) compared to 17 percent by air, 1 percent by bus, and 1 percent by train. Affordability, flexibility, and convenience make auto travel the most popular mode of transportation all over the world. Because passenger car registrations continue to increase worldwide, motor vehicles will continue to be the dominant mode of transportation for decades to come.

All studies show the automobile's dominance, whether the study is from the Air Transport Association, the Highway Administration, the Census Bureau, or the *National Travel Survey* of TIA's research department the U.S. Travel Data Center. There is no doubt that the great bulk of intercity transportation of passengers is by automobile. Data also indicate that this has been constant for several decades. The energy crisis that many have forgotten made some inroads into auto travel, causing some shifts to common carriers, but these inroads have been small. However, because of the great dominance of the automobile in travel, only a small shift in automobile travel to the common carriers can result in enormous increases in the carriers' business.

The interstate highway system significantly encouraged vacation travel and especially encouraged long-distance travel. It made automobile travel much faster and more comfortable. A major concern of tourism groups today is the maintenance of the highway network. There is growing evidence that the highway system is in need of substantial repair to prevent it from suffering further deterioration. A poor road system costs the individual driver, the bus operator, and other users additional funds in terms of increased fuel use and vehicle maintenance, and the knowledge that a highway is in poor condition may cause the traveler to select another destination to avoid the problem.

On the whole, people's attitudes are very favorable toward travel by automobile. The key feature of the automobile is immediate accessibility and convenience. The automobile owner can leave from his or her own doorstep at any hour of the day or night and travel to a chosen destination. When two or more persons travel by automobile, the per-person cost of travel is more favorable than it is with the other transportation modes. Air is the primary competitor to the automobile when it comes to travel, especially for long trips. The advantages of air travel—the quality of service, speed, and comfort—must be weighed by travelers against the automobile's advantages of price and accessibility.

Recreation Vehicles

The **recreation vehicle** (RV) segment deserves special mention because, according to the Recreation Vehicle Industry Association (RVIA), there are currently 9.3 million RVs on the road in the United States, enjoyed by some 30 million enthusiasts. One in ten vehicle-owning households has an RV, with ownership predicted to increase 21 percent by the year 2010. RVers travel an average of 5900 miles per year spending some 23 days in their vehicle. In Canada, estimates put privately owned RVs at 500,000 to 850,000. While the RV market has had its ups and downs because of events such as the energy crisis, the recession, and the Gulf War, the market for recreation vehicles in 1997 closed out its best five-year period since 1978, with sales at $11.9 billion.

Slideout technology, introduced during the mid-1990s, has now advanced to become available in living rooms, dining rooms, bedrooms, and kitchens. It is a mechanism that, at the touch of a button, lets a portion of the room and the objects in it, such as a couch, table, or refrigerator, slide outward up to about three and one-half feet. Slideouts are available in a wide variety of RVs: motorhomes, mini-motorhomes, travel trailers, fifth-wheel trailers, and even folding camping trailers. Electronics have also come to RV travel, with direct broadcast satellite systems, computer hook-ups, onboard global positioning systems (GPS), and rear-view monitors now popular options.

The typical U.S. RV owner is 48 years old, is married, owns their home, and has an annual income of $47,000. The University of Michigan study indicates that intentions to purchase an RV are strongest among 35 to 54 year olds, 24 percent of whom plan to purchase an RV in the future.

Of increasing economic significance is the steady rise in RV rentals. The Recreation Vehicle Rental Association (RVRA) reports that its members experienced significant growth during 1997 and projects that RV rentals will increase by 30 percent during 1998. Such demand has encouraged hundreds of businesses to enter the rental market, while others have expanded their operations. RVRA members reported adding an average of 16 units to their fleets during 1998. More than 400 national RV rental chain outlets and local RV dealerships offer state-of-the-art, late-model-year vehicles for rent.

Travel agencies around the world are responding to the demand by including RV rental information in their customer brochures. Also available from some rental dealers are comprehensive tour packages that include services such as airline and railway connections for fly-drive and rail-drive plans, one-way packages, off-season rates, vacation planning, guided escort tours, and campground discounts. The recent surge of foreign visitors has helped increase the RV rental market. Arrivals from Japan, Australia, New Zealand, and the United Kingdom are major customers. An estimated half million overseas visitors a year rent RVs.

Visit the Recreation Vehicle Industry web site: **http://www.rvamerica.com/rvia.**

Highways and Scenic Byways

Automobile travel in the United States will receive a boost from the **Highways and Scenic Byways program.** The Intermodal Surface Transportation Efficiency Act of 1991 (ISTEA) established the Scenic Byways program, which provided $80 million over six years for carrying out eligible programs on designated scenic byways. According to the Federal Highway Administration, the United States has 4 million miles of roads and approximately 51,500 have been designated or are potential scenic byways. All 50 states have existing byways, with an average of nine routes per state. An ISTEA reauthorization bill, The Transportation Equity Act for the 21st Century (TEA-21), became law on June 9, 1998 and will ensure continuation of the National Scenic Byways program. The act calls for $148 million for improvements to roads of scenic or historic value. TEA-21 provides 40 percent more funding for transportation than the 1991 law it replaced authorizing a six-year expenditure of $216 billion.

Rental Cars

An important aspect of automobile travel is the **rental car industry,** whose growth has been paralleling or exceeding the growth in air travel. While there is no question about the rental car business having heavy use by businesses, it also has substantial vacation use and frequent combination trip use.

According to *Business Travel News* in their *1998 Business Travel Survey,* the rental car industry grosses around $14 billion. The major companies are Hertz, Enterprise, Avis, Budget, National, Alamo, Dollar, Thrifty, and Advantage. Table 5.4 shows them ranked by their 1997 total revenue.

Recent years have witnessed a vast change in the ownership of the major rental car companies. The major automobile companies that bought up most of the major rental

A customer-oriented transportation system requires that the interface between different modes of travel be facilitated. Technology is increasingly used to ensure fast and convenient service. *(Photo courtesy of Budget Rent-A-Car Company.)*

TABLE 5.4
U.S. Rental Car Companies Ranked by Revenue

Car Company	Revenue $000
Hertz	3,891,320
Enterprise	3,680,000
Avis	3,034,400
Budget	2,700,000
National	1,750,000
Alamo	1,300,000
Dollar	1,056,051
Thrifty	541,000
Advantage	89,640

Source: Business Travel News.

companies in the late 1980s have been shedding them. General Motors sold National and their stake in Avis, Ford sold Budget, and Chrysler sold Thrifty and Dollar. Hertz, the industry leader, is the only car rental company to remain in the hands of an automobile manufacturer as Ford Motor Company retained 80 percent of its stock.

Enterprise Rent-A-Car is one of the surprises in the rental car business. The privately held rental car firm has the largest fleet of rental cars in the United States, with 355,000. It was launched as an insurance replacement firm that supplies rental cars to people whose vehicles have been damaged or stolen or are undergoing mechanical repairs. They have now gone global and serve all rental markets today; however, they are not in airport locations dominated by the big four: Hertz, Avis, Budget and National. Enterprise delivers its cars to customers who phone for service.

Computerized navigation systems have come to rental cars and are predicted to be a growing attraction.

Many of the auto rental systems are international and have services in virtually every tourist destination area in the world. These companies arrange for the purchase, lease, or rental of automobiles domestically and abroad. Companies representative of this type of organization are American Rental Systems; Auto-Europe, Inc.; Europcar; Hertz International, Ltd.; The Kemwell Group, Inc.; Inter Rent; and Open Road International, Inc.

Taxi and Limousine Service

Taxi and limousine companies play an exceedingly important part in tourism. Local transportation companies perform vital services for bus, rail, and shipping lines. Businesspersons and tourists alike would have a difficult time getting from place to place if these services were not available. Inclines and aerial trams serve as a form of taxi service and are of a special interest to visitors in scenic tourist destination areas as a form of recreation and sightseeing.

The International Taxicab and Livery Association (ITLA) in Kensington, Maryland is the major taxicab association. It was formed in 1966 by a merger of the National Association of Taxicab Owners, the Cab Research Bureau, and the American Taxicab Association. ITLA has 900 members who are fleet owners operating 70,000 passenger vehicles including taxicabs, limousines, liveries, vans, and minibuses. The association sponsors an annual convention and trade show, is involved with political action, and publishes *Taxi and Livery Management*, quarterly.

The National Limousine Association is located in Alexandria, Virginia. The association was founded in 1985, has 800 members, and is made up of (a) limousine owners and operators and (b) limousine manufacturers and suppliers to the industry. It seeks to promote and advance industry professionalism, the common interests of members, and the use of limousines. It monitors legislation, sponsors seminars on safety, regulatory issues, and management, compiles statistics, and offers insurance plans.

Oil Companies

Oil companies the world over have a very important stake in automobile tourism and thus are organized in many ways to serve the wants and needs of travelers. In the

Trams and cable cars can greatly enhance visitors' abilities to enjoy many different views of a destination. Here, the halfway point on the Palm Springs tram's journey from the 2643-foot Valley Station to the 8516-foot Mountain Station is reached when the two cars pass between towers two and three. At this point, the two cars are 34 feet apart. *(Photo courtesy of Palm Springs Aerial Tramway.)*

United States, many of the major oil companies publish road maps as a touring service. Some companies have organized motor clubs, such as the American Oil Motor Club, which provides travel information and routing services for its members, among other services. An example of special travel services is the *Mobil Travel Guide,* which has eight regional editions and lists over 22,000 hotels, motels, and restaurants. They also cover more than 3000 cities and towns and describe 11,000 points of interest. The accommodations are rated from one to five stars in quality and indicate the prices of typical meals and accommodations to suit every budget. Each *Guide* also contains a variety of special sightseeing tours with easy-to-follow maps.

Automobile Clubs and Organizations

The **American Automobile Association** (AAA) is the world's largest single-membership travel group, with a membership of over 41 million in the United States and Canada. This organization promotes travel in several different forms among its members, including auto travel as a primary form of transportation. It also operates worldwide travel services similar to those provided by a travel agency or tour company. The AAA Travel Department also provides travel services for nonmembers and is thus competitive with other tour companies and retail travel agencies. This additional service gives the club a certain glamour and status in the community, and nonmembers who are brought into the club office through the travel service become prospects for new members in the automobile club.

The AAA provides emergency road service to members. It also provides insurance protection to motorists through its various state and city affiliate organizations (such as the Automobile Club of Michigan), publishes travel maps and *Tour Books,* and has a national touring board as well as a national touring bureau staff. The principal function of the *Tour Books* is to describe the history, attractions, points of interest, and accommodations in hotels, resorts, motels, and restaurants that have been inspected and approved by AAA field representatives. All accommodations listed have been selected on the basis of a satisfactory report submitted by the AAA field representative.

An organization of wider geographic membership is the World Touring and Automobile Organization, with headquarters in London, England. Other organizations of a similar nature are the International Road Federation of Washington, D.C.; the Pan American Highway Congress, Washington, D.C.; Inter-American Federation of the Automobile Clubs, Buenos Aires; and the International Automobile Federation, with headquarters in Paris.

THE CRUISE INDUSTRY

Cruise Lines International Association (CLIA) states that cruising is currently the fastest-growing segment of the travel industry. It is experiencing a surge of growth in passengers, ships, and ship passenger capacity. **Cruise lines** are expanding their fleets, adding new amenities and new ports of call. As with other sectors of travel suppliers, a great deal of consolidation is taking place.

Since 1980, the industry has had an average annual growth rate of 7.6 percent. In 1980, 1.43 million passengers cruised; in 1996, this total was 4.66 million. In 1997, a

TABLE 5.5
Number of North American Passengers

Year	Passengers (millions)
1980	1.43
1985	2.15
1990	3.64
1991	3.98
1992	4.14
1993	4.48
1994	4.45
1995	4.38
1996	4.66
1997	5.05

Source: Cruise Lines International Association.

new record was set with 5.05 million passengers and growth of 8.6 percent (see Table 5.5). Capacity utilization for the industry was a record 90.8 percent, and growth was experienced in all categories of cruises, from short cruises of one to five days to cruises of 18-plus days. The average length of a cruise increased from 6.4 days in 1996 to 6.5 days in 1997.

Although ships have been a means of transportation since early times, the cruise industry is young. Its purpose is really to provide a resort experience rather than point-to-point transportation. Though the modern-day cruise industry is barely 20 years old, it has established itself as an important component of the United States

The cruise industry is one of the most rapidly growing sectors of tourism. Its growth is expected to continue, and many new ships are scheduled to come on line in the next few years. *(Photo by Andy Newman; courtesy of Carnival Cruise Lines.)*

travel and tourism industry. A study in 1993 by the highly respected U.S. accounting firm Price Waterhouse indicated that the cruise industry has an estimated economic impact on the United States of approximately $14.5 billion annually. It is indirectly responsible for the employment of 450,000 Americans and directly responsible for the employment of 134,000.

Historically, most of the cruise companies have focused their marketing efforts on North American clientele. However, with a marked increase in recent years of European, South American, and Asian vacationers taking American-style cruises, those companies have begun to pay more attention to the international markets. Additionally, some of these cruise companies have positioned ships in Europe for seasonal operations, thereby creating greater awareness among European clientele.

The cruise industry's performance and satisfaction are the pacesetter for the rest of the travel industry. No other vacation category can touch a cruise for product satisfaction and repeat business. Of those who have cruised in the last five years, the average number of cruises per person is 2.4, or one cruise every two years.

Growth has affected not only passenger and ship capacity, but the ports of embarkation as well.

Embarkation Ports

Ports within the state of Florida serve as home for the majority of the U.S.-based cruise industry. This is primarily due to the state's close proximity to the prime cruising waters of the Caribbean. Most of these cruises are of three, four, and seven days in length, though there are some voyages of 10 and 14 days. Miami currently claims the title "Cruise Capital of the World." Ports in Ft. Lauderdale, Tampa, and Port Canaveral also play host to a number of cruise ships. Several ships operating Caribbean cruises are also based in New Orleans, Louisiana.

CLIA MEMBER LINES
▼

American Hawaii Cruises	Mediterranean Shipping Cruises
Bergen Line, Inc.	Norwegian Cruise Lines
Carnival Cruise Lines	Orient Cruises
Celebrity Cruises	Premier Cruises
Commodore Cruise Lines	Princess Cruises
Costa Cruises	Radisson Seven Seas Cruise Line
Crystal Cruises	Regal Cruises
Cunard Ltd.	Royal Caribbean International
Delta Queen Steamboat Co.	Royal Olympic
Disney Cruise Line	Seabourn Cruise Line
First European Cruises	Silversea Cruises
Holland America Line	Windstar Cruises

New York City and Boston are popular embarkation points for cruises to New England, Bermuda, and Canada's maritime provinces.

On the West Coast of the United States, both Los Angeles and San Diego are home ports for cruises of three, four, and seven days to Mexico.

San Juan, Puerto Rico, a U.S. territory, has also become a popular port of embarkation for seven-day cruises to the Southern Caribbean.

One of the most popular summertime cruising areas in recent years is Alaska's Inside Passage. These cruises are frequently combined with land excursions into Alaska's interior and the Yukon Territory. Most of these cruises depart from Vancouver, British Columbia (Canada).

One company, Delta Queen Steamboat Company, offers cruises on some of America's most famous rivers, including the Mississippi and Ohio, on riverboats styled after turn-of-the-century paddlewheel steamers.

Cruise Itineraries Cover the Globe

Though the islands of the Caribbean continue to be the leading year-round destination, CLIA member cruise lines service cruising areas around the world. The Mediterranean Sea plays host to an increasing number of cruise ships during the summer season, and CLIA reports that the industry continues to show an increased emphasis on European and Southeast Asia itineraries. In 1998 the Caribbean share was over 46 percent, the Mediterranean over 11 percent, Alaska and Northern Europe over 8 percent, the Bahamas over 6 percent, and trans-canal and Western Mexico over 5 percent. African destinations are increasing sharply while Southeast Asia is declining.

And one of the world's greatest adventures—a transit of the Panama Canal—remains one of the industry's big attractions. These cruises usually either begin or end in San Francisco, Los Angeles, or Ft. Lauderdale, Florida.

New Ships and New Markets

The North American cruise industry has enjoyed tremendous success in the last decade and has continued to reinvest profits in new, modern cruise ships. Approximately 71 new ships have been introduced since 1990. Another 28 are expected to be introduced by 2002. Berths have been expanding at an average annual rate of 6.9 percent. CLIA reported 83,533 berths in 1990, and they predict that there will be 158,685 in 2001. As the cruise industry continues to expand, industry observers predict that new markets outside North America will become of greater importance in the coming years.

Consolidation

Consolidation that has been taking place in the travel industry is rampant in the cruise sector as well. Carnival Corporation is the world's largest cruise company and recently acquired Cunard and Costa Cruise Lines. They already own Holland America, Windstar, and Seabourn. Royal Caribbean International (RCI) is the second largest player and recently acquired Celebrity Cruises. Princess Cruises is the third largest company. These top three control 71 percent of all cruise berths. Competition is fierce, with these three companies adding new 2000 passenger ships and Disney launching its new cruise line. Carnival is building eight new ships, RCI four, and Princess five, all proposed to be launched between 1998 and 2001.

While CLIA members (see the box) represent 97 percent of the North American cruise market and 90 percent of the ships, the world cruise fleet is supplemented by freighter cruises, river cruises, yachts, ferries, and charters. There are about 80 freighters that provide accommodations for a limited number of passengers, such as 6 to 12. Freighter cruises tend to last a long time, go to unknown parts, have schedules that can change rapidly, and be moderately priced. They appeal to the more adventurous traveler. River cruises are popular in the United States on the Mississippi River on the *Delta Queen* and *Mississippi Queen,* in Egypt on the Nile, in Brazil on the Amazon, and in Europe on the Danube and Rhine, just to mention a few. Riverboat gambling is a recent addition on the Mississippi. Barge and canal trips are also popular in many places.

Cruise Lines International Association

Cruise Lines International Association (CLIA) is a marketing and promotional trade organization comprised of 24 of the major cruise lines serving North America, representing over 110 ships (see the box). CLIA was formed in 1975 out of a need for the cruise industry to develop a vehicle to promote the general concept of cruising. CLIA exists to educate, train, promote, and explain the value, desirability, and profitability of the cruise product.

When, in mid-1984, the Federal Maritime Commission consolidated other industry organizations into CLIA, it became the sole marketing organization of the cruise industry. CLIA represents almost 97 percent of the cruise industry, and more than 21,000 travel agents are affiliated with CLIA and display the CLIA seal, which identifies them as authorities on cruise vacations. The CLIA headquarters is located at 500 Fifth Avenue, Suite 1407, New York, NY 10110. Telephone (212) 921-4711, FAX (212) 921-0549, web site: **http://www.cruising.org.**

SUMMARY

Transportation services and facilities are an integral component of tourism. In fact, the success of practically all forms of travel depends on adequate transportation. Transportation services and facilities are the arteries through which the life blood of the travel industry flows. Travel by air dominates long- and middle-distance travel in the United States. But private automobiles carry the bulk (about 80 percent) of all travelers on short trips. Automobiles are also very important on long and international trips. Rental cars are popular, because they supplement air travel. Rail travel in the United States has declined substantially since the 1950s but is still important in commuting and longer-haul traffic. Motorcoach transportation is available at far more places than either air or rail, but it constitutes a rather small percentage of total vehicle miles. Vacationing on cruise ships has become the fastest-growing segment of the U.S. travel industry. New and refurbished cruise ships are appearing regularly.

Associations and groups of passenger carriers are important to their well-being and growth. Some of the most important are Air Transport Association of America, American Bus Association, United Motorcoach Association, American Automobile Association (affiliated with the Canadian Automobile Association), World Touring and Automobile Association, Recreation Vehicle Industry Association, International Taxicab and Livery Association, National Limousine Association, and the Cruise Lines International Association.

Increases in almost all forms of tourism automatically boost passenger traffic, sometimes creating problems. Congestion can be especially bad on streets and roads and at airport terminals. Safety and security are basic requirements, and successful tourism depends on these factors. The environment will be affected by any form of transportation. Careful planning and increased awareness and preventative measures are needed to minimize such undesirable effects.

Long-term projections show increases in the demand for transportation. Increased taxes on this industry are having an adverse effect. It is hoped that these can be mitigated in time. Rail travel is increasing in Europe and Asia, where high-speed trains are being used.

ABOUT THE READING

There is one reading in this chapter that discusses the Sydney, Australia Olympic Park Station and rail link. This ground transportation facility will not only serve the crowds at the Olympics, but will also transport visitors to this sporting and cultural center in the future because it has been designed as an integral part of the Sydney metropolitan rail system.

READING 5.1

AUSTRALIA'S OLYMPIC PARK STATION AND RAIL LINK

When it was decided to develop Homebush Bay into Sydney's premier sporting and cultural facility, it was clear that to be a success, it had to be serviced by the best available public transport network.

The NSW government decided the key to that network was a heavy rail link right into the heart of the Olympic and Showground facilities. As a result, the Olympic Co-ordination Authority has overseen the development of the Olympic Park Station and rail link, which opened on March 8, 1998.

The new 5.3-kilometer rail link will transport visitors to within a short walk of all the major facilities at Homebush Bay.

The $95 million project will move tens of thousands of people an hour to and from Homebush Bay for concerts, exhibitions, and sports matches as well as major events such as the Royal Easter Show and the Olympic and Paralympic Games.

It will be an important supplement to Sydney's metropolitan rail service and will provide an easy, fast, and comfortable alternative to driving.

Major Main Line Link

The Homebush Bay rail link is designed as an integral part of the Sydney metropolitan rail system. Trains traveling in either direction on the Main Western Line are able to enter the Homebush Bay loop. For major events the Olympic Park Station will be serviced by eight-car double-deck suburban trains, which are designed for rapid embarking and disembarking of passengers. Country trains from places like the Blue Mountains and Newcastle will also be able to drop off passengers directly into the heart of Homebush Bay.

The line is mostly above ground but goes below for one kilometer, allowing people to move freely around areas adjacent to the Olympic Park Station. Construction of the rail link began in August 1996, and track laying started in June 1997.

Capacity

The Homebush Bay rail link is designed for big crowds. During the Olympic and Paralympic Games, trains will run every two minutes. That's a total of 50,000 people an hour, or about three times the number that use Sydney's busy Town Hall interchange in any morning peak period.

Design

Olympic Park Station and its surrounding public spaces are designed to reflect the excitement of the Olympic and Paralympic Games and to capture the atmosphere of the world's great transport terminals. The station's design dramatically achieves this aim. The station is an imposing vaulted building that presents an exciting gateway to Homebush Bay and is a natural meeting place. It is situated next to the Showground and just 400 meters from the Olympic Stadium. The soaring 20-meter-high vaulted roof offers protection from the sun and the rain and creates a comfortable light and airy atmosphere for travelers.

Access

During the design of Olympic Park Station, OCA consulted with groups representing a wide range of people with disabilities and special needs to ensure that it would be accessible for everyone. The ground-level concourse is connected to the platforms below by a series of lifts, stairs, ramps, and escalators which provide easy access into and out of the station.

Environment

The Homebush Bay rail link is a major environmental feature in its own right. A train load of passengers can remove up to a thousand cars from the roads, helping improve Sydney's air quality. The design maximizes natural light and ventilation, thereby lowering energy consumption and reducing NSW's contribution to greenhouse gas emissions.

For More Information:
Visit our Information Centre at Australia Avenue, Homebush Bay
or telephone (02) 9735-4800
Produced by Olympic Co-ordination Authority
6 Australia Avenue, Homebush Bay NSW 2127
February 1998

Key Concepts

airline industry
Air Transport Association
alliances
American Automobile Association
American Bus Association
Amtrak
automobile
cruise lines
highways and scenic byways program

motorcoaches
oil companies
rail travel
recreational vehicles
rental cars
safety and security
taxi and limousine service
transportation (importance of)
United Motorcoach Association

Internet Sites

The Internet sites mentioned in this chapter are repeated here for convenience plus some additional sites. For more information visit these sites. Be aware that Internet addresses change frequently; so if a site cannot be accessed, use a search engine.

Air Transportaion Association of America
http://www.air-transport.org

Airports Council International— North America
http://www.aci-na.org

American Automobile Association
http://www.aaa.com

American Bus Association
http://www.buses.org

American Highway Users Alliance
http://www.highways.org

American Public Transit Association
http://www.apta.com

Civil Aviation Authority, UK
http://www.open.gov.uk.dot

Cruise Lines International
http://www.cruising.org

Europe by Eurail
http://www.railpass.com

Federal Aviation Administration
http://www.faa.gov

International Air Transport Association
http://www.iata.org

National Association of Railroad Passengers
http://www.narprail.org

Recreation Vehicle Industry
http://www.rvamerica.com/rvia

Regional Airline Association
http://www.raa.org

Travel Industry Association
http://www.tia.org

United Motorcoach Association
http://www.uma.org

INTERNET EXERCISES

Site Name: Cruise Lines International Association (CLIA)

URL: http://www.cruising.org/

Background Information: CLIA's primary objective is to help the over 22,000 CLIA-affiliated agencies become more successful at capitalizing on the booming and profitable cruise market. CLIA has 24 member lines who represent virtually 100% of the cruise industry.

Exercises

1. You are working for a travel agency and have a family in your office. You realize early in the conversation that the wife is very interested in a cruise but the husband has some definite reservations. After probing for several minutes, the husband identifies the following concerns and questions he has about cruises: (1) I will get bored and feel confined. (2) I am afraid I will get sea sick. (3) Cruises are only for rich people. (4) What can you do with kids on a ship? (5) What is there to do at night? How would you address these concerns/questions in order to sell this family a cruise?

2. Choose a cruise line and develop a summary of entertainment features the cruise line offers.

3. Choose a cruise line and identify what packages they offer for honeymooners and families with children.

QUESTIONS FOR REVIEW AND DISCUSSION

1. Explain why air travel now dominates long- and middle-distance travel.

2. What were the main reasons that rail passenger transportation declined in the United States after 1950?

3. Identify the social and economic factors that would bring about a resurgence in motorcoach travel.

4. Describe the principal appeals of cruising.

5. Why is the cruise market expected to continue its extraordinary growth pattern?

6. What might be at least a partial solution to the

problem of automobile congestion at major airports?

7. Similarly, make clear your ideas for alleviating flight arrival and departure congestion.

8. If you knew in advance that you would have a long drive through heavy traffic to reach the airport, followed by a wait in line for 20 minutes at the airline departure desk, and that your plane would be remaining on the runway for 30 minutes before taking off, would you still make the pleasure trip?

9. Evaluate the importance of safety and security in all forms of travel. What is the safest mode of passenger transportation?

10. Taking each mode of transportation, what specifically can be done to minimize damage to the environment?

11. If you were vice-president for marketing of an airline, what programs would you undertake to even out peaks and valleys in demand?

CASE PROBLEMS

1. The Rotary Club program chairman has asked you to give a talk on the advantages of cruises. He has also hinted that the club might be interested in taking a group cruise with their wives and children. What would you include in your talk?

2. Air transportation is truly a global industry. However, future growth in world demand is being impeded by many nations that have enacted various air regulations and restrictive laws. A beginning toward a "new world order" of global competition and interconnectedness has appeared. The first "open skies" agreement has now been established between the United States and the Netherlands. This agreement, dubbed "Open Skies I," signals the beginning of what could become global. The agreement abolishes all legal and diplomatic environments as well as all other trade barriers that impede airline efficiency. It also encourages competition. The Open Skies I accord completely deregulates air services between the two countries. If such pacts were to become a reality on a much wider scale, how would this affect demand for travel on the world's airlines? Explain and give several examples.

SELECTED REFERENCES

Air Transportation Association of America. *Air Transport 1997: The Annual Report of the U.S. Scheduled Airline Industry.* Washington, D.C.: ATA, 1998.

Air Transportation Association of America. *Air Travel Survey: 1990.* Washington, D.C.: ATA, 1990.

Beaver, Allan. "Frequent Flyer Programmes: The Beginning of the End?" *Tourism Economics,* Vol. 2, No. 1, pp. 43–60, March 1996.

Bennett, M. M. "Strategic Alliances in the World Airline Industry." *Progress in Tourism and Hospitality Research,* Vol. 3, No. 3, pp. 213–224, 1997.

Bull, Adrian O. "The Economics of Cruising: An Application to the Short Ocean Cruise Market." *Journal of Tourism Studies,* Vol. 7, No. 2, pp. 28–35, December 1996.

Dean, Christopher J. "Travel by Excursion Coach in the United Kingdom." *Journal of Travel Research,* Vol. 31, No. 4, pp. 59–65, Spring 1993.

Dennis, Nigel. "The North American Air Travel Market." *Travel and Tourism Analyst,* No. 1, pp. 5–22, 1991.

Dickinson, Robert, and Andrew Vladimir. *Selling the Sea.* New York: Wiley, 1996.

Dwyer, Larry, and Peter Forsyth. "Economic Significance of Cruise Tourism." *Annals of Tourism Research,* Vol. 25, No. 2, pp. 393–415, 1998.

Fockler, Shirley. "The U.S. Domestic Airline Industry." *Travel and Tourism Analyst,* No. 3, pp. 5–21, 1991.

Fujii, Edwin, Eric Im, and James Mak. "Airport Expansion, Direct Flights, and Consumers Choice of Travel Destinations: The Case of Hawaii's Neighbor Islands." *Journal of Travel Research,* Vol. 30, No. 3, pp. 38–43, Winter 1992.

Graham, B. *Geography and Air Transport.* London: Wiley, 1995.

Hall, J. Anthony, and Ron Braithwaite. "Caribbean Cruise Tourism: A Business of Transnational Partnerships." *Tourism Management,* Vol. 11, No. 4, pp. 339–347, December 1990.

Hanlon, J. P. "Hub Operations and Airline Competition." *Tourism Management,* Vol. 10, No. 2, pp. 111–124, June 1989.

Hanlon, J. P. "Regional Air Services and Airline Competition." *Tourism Management,* Vol. 13, No. 2, pp. 181–195, June 1992.

Hanlon, P. *Global Airline: Competition in a Transnational Industry.* London: Butterworth Heinemann, 1996.

Heraty, Margaret J. "Tourism Transport: Implications for Developing Countries." *Tourism Management,* Vol. 10, No. 4, pp. 288–292, December 1989.

Hunt, Jill. "Airlines in Asia." *Travel and Tourism Analyst,* No. 5, pp. 5–25, 1985.

Kristian Jens, and Steen Jacobsen. "Segmenting the Use of a Scenic Highway." *The Tourist Review,* Vol. 3, pp. 32–38, 1996.

Lowing, Graham. "The European Coach/Bus Holiday Market." *Travel and Tourism Analyst,* No. 6, pp. 5–16, 1990.

Marti, Bruce E. "The Cruise Ship Vessel Sanitation Program." *Journal of Travel Research,* Vol. 33, No. 4, pp. 29–38, Spring 1995.

McGee, William J. "Issues and Answers: International Airlines and U.S. Travel Agents." *Travel Counselor,* No. 29, pp. 28–32, October 28, 1996.

Miller, Laurence. "Carnival's Fantasy Class Cruise Ship: Ticket to Success." *FIU Hospitality Review,* Vol. 14, No. 2, pp. 45–52, Fall 1996.

Morrison, Alastair M., et al. "Comparative Profiles of Travelers on Cruises and Land-Based Resort Vacations." *Journal of Tourism Studies,* Vol. 7, No. 2, pp. 15–27, December 1996.

Moscardo, Gianna, et al. "Tourist Perspectives on Cruising: Multidimensional Scaling Analyses of Cruising and Other Holiday Types." *Journal of Tourism Studies,* Vol. 7, No. 2, pp. 54–63, December 1996.

National Technical Information Service. *Airport System Capacity: Strategic Choice.* Springfield, VA: NTIS, 1990.

National Technical Information Service. *Secretary's Task Force on Competition in the U.S. Domestic Airline Industry: Industry and Route Structures, Volumes I and II.* Springfield, VA: NTIS, 1990.

National Technical Information Service. *Secretary's Task Force on Competition in the U.S. Domestic Airline Industry: International Air Service.* Springfield, VA: NTIS, 1990.

OIA. *U.S. International Air Passenger and Freight Statistics.* Office of International Aviation, Washington, D.C.: Secretary for Aviation and International Affairs, 1996.

Page, S. *Transport for Tourism.* London: ITBP, 1994.

Pisarski, Alan. *Nationwide Personal Transportation Survey: Travel Behavior Issues in the 90's.* Washington, D.C.: U.S. Department of Transportation, 1992.

Semer-Purzycki, Jeanne, and Robert Purzycki. *Sails for Profit: A Complete Guide to Selling and Booking Cruise Travel.* Upper Saddle River, NJ: Prentice-Hall, 1999.

Teye, Victor B. "Land Transportation and Tourism in Bermuda." *Tourism Management,* Vol. 13, No. 4, pp. 395–405, December 1992.

Tourism Industries. *In-Flight Survey of International Air Travelers.* Washington, D.C.: International Trade Administration, 1997.

Vladimir, Andrew N. "Seabourn Cruise Line: A Case Study in Achieving Quality." *FIU Hospitality Review,* Vol. 13, No. 1, pp. 7–22, Spring 1995.

Yunis, Eugenio. "Airlines in South America." *Travel and Tourism Analyst,* No. 3, pp. 5–18, 1990.

CHAPTER 6

HOSPITALITY AND RELATED SERVICES

- Study the lodging industry, its ancient origins, its associations, names of leading companies, and its vital role in the economy.

- Appreciate the immensity of the restaurant-food service industry.

- Learn the current trends in resorts and timesharing mode of operation.

- Discover why meetings and conventions, as well as meeting planners, are so important to tourism.

◀ **LEARNING OBJECTIVES**

◀ *The Westin Alyeska Prince Hotel in Girdwood, Alaska. (Photo courtesy of Westin Hotels & Resorts.®)*

INTRODUCTION

As noted in Chapter 2, providing overnight accommodations for travelers goes back into antiquity—it is the world's oldest commercial business. Guestrooms were first part of private dwellings. Then came caravansaries and guest quarters provided in monasteries. Today, lodging and food service activities are enormous in economic importance. Many lodging places provide meeting rooms, convention facilities and services, restaurants, bars, entertainment, gift shops, gaming, health clubs, and other activities and facilities. See Figure 6.1 for the structure of the accommodations industry. In this chapter we examine this industry as well as the even larger food service business, meetings and conventions, and related services.

THE LODGING INDUSTRY

The World Tourism Organization (WTO) estimates that the world hotel room inventory grows by about 2.5 percent a year. In 1994 the WTO estimated that there were about 12.2 million rooms worldwide. Occupancy rates vary, but they average about 65 percent overall. Such places as London, Beijing, New York, San Francisco, Hawaii, the Caribbean area, and the city of Las Vegas are noted for higher occupancy rates. During the 1980s there was a great deal of overbuilding, especially in North America. The supply of rooms outstripped demand. This resulted in low occupancy and low room rates. For example, in the United States between 1986 and 1992 the hotel industry lost about $14 billion. Much of the problem was the result of overbuilding caused by tax laws that encouraged construction as a tax shelter. The law was changed in 1986, ending the tax shelter, but construction could not be ended in midstream. Currently, in most tourist destinations the creation of new lodging facilities is striking a better balance. After difficult years in the early 1990s, the remainder of the decade has been extremely profitable.

In Eastern Europe and the former Soviet Union there is now a considerable amount of new hotel construction to serve an anticipated growing demand.

Hotel accommodations are heavily concentrated in Europe and North America, with Europe accounting for 44.7 percent of the world's room supply and the United States accounting for 27 percent, for a total of over 71 percent. East Asia and the Pacific region account for 12.7 percent, Africa 3.1 percent, Middle East 1.5 percent, and South Asia 1.2 percent.

According to the **American Hotel and Motel Association** (AH&MA), the **lodging industry** (which includes hotels, motels, suites, and resort properties) enjoyed its most successful and profitable year in 1997, and expectations are that performance will be strong through the remainder of the decade. The industry numbered 49,000 properties, 3.8 million rooms, and $85.6 billion in sales in 1997.

Who is the typical lodging customer? According to the AH&MA, 23 percent are on vacation, 30 percent are transient business travelers, 26 percent are attending a conference or meeting, and 20 percent are traveling for other reasons such as a special event, family, or personal. The typical room night is generated by two adults (50 percent), over age 50 (38 percent), earning an average yearly household income of $51,300. They travel by auto (73 percent), make reservations (81 percent), and pay $67.60 per room night.

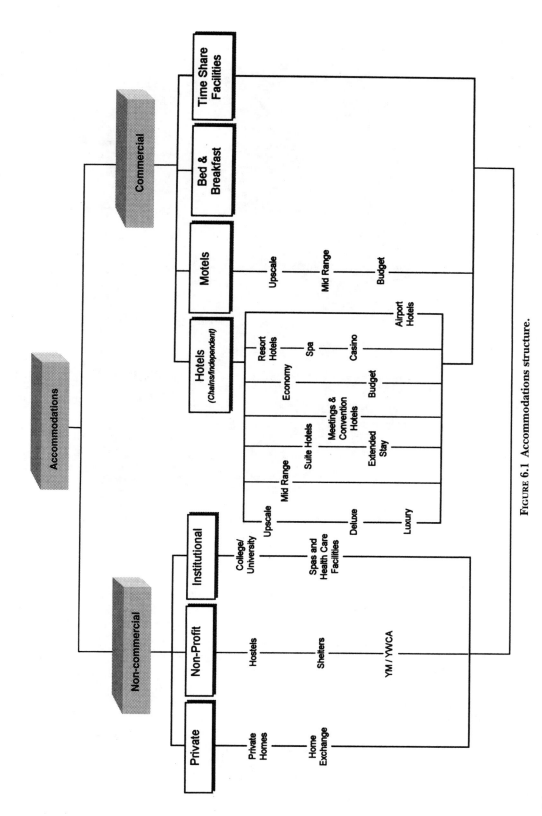

FIGURE 6.1 Accommodations structure.

Hotels throughout the world offer hospitality services to travelers of all ages. *(Photo courtesy of Radisson Hotels International, Inc.)*

For leisure travelers, 46 percent spend one night, 26 percent spend two nights, and 29 percent spend three or more nights. The typical business room night is generated by a male (76 percent), age 25–34 (35 percent), employed in a professional or managerial position (52 percent), earning an average yearly household income of $58,500. He travels alone (80 percent), makes reservations (91 percent), and pays $73.00 per room night. For a hotel stay, 37 percent of all business travelers spend one night, 23 percent spend two nights, and 39 percent spend three or more nights.

According to Smith Travel Research, 1997 surpassed 1996 as the most profitable year in the history of the U.S. lodging industry. Total industry pretax profits were $17.0 billion, nearly 40 percent more than the industry's $12.5 billion in 1996 and double the amount earned in 1995. Total industry revenues increased from an estimated $71 billion in 1995 to over $85 billion in 1997. The industry experienced its second year of declining occupancies in 1997. Also, the trend in the increases in room revenue per available room (RevPAR) slowed from an annual rate of over 6 percent to

Elegance and comfort meet in this spacious double guest room at The Phoenician Resort in Scottsdale, Arizona, which also offers scenic views of the desert. *(Photo courtesy of the Phoenician.)*

nearly 5 percent in 1997. In addition, for the first time since 1991, the rate of growth in supply in 1997 (3.4 percent) exceeded the corresponding increases in demand (2.5 percent). Industry occupancy fell 0.8 percent to 64.5 percent, and the average room rate grew over 6 percent to $75.16. This trend was worldwide as room rates continue to rise. RevPAR gained 5 percent, to $48.50.

The lodging industry has practiced market segmentation in recent years. Many of the big chains offer products at almost every price level: full-service luxury hotels, luxury all-suite hotels, resort hotels, moderately priced full-service hotels, moderately priced all-suites, moderately priced limited service, and economy or budget motels (see the box). Hotels and motels are classified in a variety of ways. One of the most common is by location, such as resort, city center, airport, suburban, or highway.

Consolidation

Mergers and acquisitions have been going on in the lodging industry for some time, but nothing like the current merger mania. One expects to see a gradual process of consolidation in the entire tourism industry, which includes lodging; however, the pattern of ownership in lodging is undergoing dramatic change. Consolidation is taking place at a mind-numbing rate. One of the catalysts driving the changes in ownership are **REITs (real estate investment trusts).** REITs emerged in the early 1980s and had a special tax status. The paired-share REIT, the structure that drove much of the mergers and acquisition activity, has been changed by legislation passed in July 1998. This

GLOSSARY

▼

- *Revenues per available room (REVPAR).* Total guestroom revenue for a given period divided by the total number of occupied rooms during the same period (excluding public rooms). A simple way to calculate is to multiply your occupancy times your room rate.

- *Average daily room rate per guest.* Total guestroom revenue for a given period divided by the total number of guests accommodated for the same time period.

- *Percentage of occupancy.* The percentage of available rooms occupied for a given period. It is computed by dividing the number of rooms occupied for a period by the number of rooms available for the same period.

- *Income before other fixed charges.* Income after management fees, property taxes, and insurance does not include deductions for depreciation, rent, interest, amortization, and income taxes. Comparisons beyond income after property taxes and insurance are virtually meaningless due to wide variances in ownership, depreciation methods, financing bases, applicable income taxes, and so on.

- *Full-service hotel.* A hotel that provides a wide variety of facilities and amenities, including food and beverage outlets, meeting rooms, and recreational activities.

- *Limited-service hotel.* A hotel that provides only some of the facilities and amenities of a full-service property. This category includes properties commonly referred to as motels or motor hotels.

- *Resort hotel.* A hotel in which all rooms have "separate," but not necessarily physically divided, "sleeping and living areas."

- *Convention hotel.* A hotel that provides facilities and services geared to meet the needs of large group and association meetings and trade shows. Typically, these hotels have in excess of 400 guest rooms and contain substantial amounts of function and banquet space flexibly designed for use by large meeting groups. They often work in concert with other convention hotels and convention centers to provide facilities for citywide conventions and trade shows.

legislation precludes paired-share REITs from further growth through asset acquisitions. Consequently, new structures can be expected to emerge.

The market capitalization of America's hotel real estate investments trusts rose to $19.4 billion in the first quarter of 1998 from just $142.4 million in 1993, according to the Lodging Research Network (**http://www.lodgingresearch.com**), the comprehensive Internet-based resource for lodging industry data and information from PricewaterhouseCoopers. At the same time, REITs boosted their number of owned hotels to 970 in 1998 from 39 in 1993. The total number of hotel rooms in REITs' hands was 183,784 in the first quarter of 1998, up from 6643 in 1993. Today there are 15 lodging REITs, and they are powerful industry players compared to only two in 1993. The recent flurry of mergers and acquisitions has created new mega companies that didn't exist five years ago. Starwood is hardly a household word, but it now controls Westin, Sheraton, and Caesar's organizations. Patriot American Hospitality has acquired Wyndham and Interstate Hotels Corporation. These examples are the tip of the iceberg. Consolidation will continue to take place both domestically and internationally, so one can expect more rooms but fewer recognizable ownership names.

Rank

There are a number of very **large companies** in the lodging industry, and many of the big chains are getting bigger. *Hotels*, published by Cahners Publishing Company, 1350 East Touhy Avenue, Des Plaines, Illinois 60018, compiles an annual listing of the world's 300 largest corporate hotel chains. The July 1998 issue reports the 28th annual listing of lodgings giant companies. The 1998 list is formatted so it places corporate chains, REITs, and management companies on the same footing. The concentration of the lodging industry is clearly demonstrated by the ranking of the top 25, which appears in Table 6.1. The survey covers slightly more than 5 million rooms and the 10 largest companies in the world have 2.7 million of these rooms, or 54 percent. In July 1998, the largest hotel company was the Cendant Corporation, Parsippany, New Jersey, with 499,056 rooms and 5566 hotels. Bass Hotels and Resorts bought Holiday Inn Worldwide, which put them in second place. While most of the international franchised hotel chains are headquartered in the United States; France has its Accor Group, ranked sixth, Club Med, ranked 17th, and Societe du Louvre, ranked 18th; England has Hilton International, ranked 13th; and Spain has Sol Melia, ranked 14th.

Trends

The **trend in the lodging industry** has been away from independently owned and operated properties toward chain and franchise affiliations, which get larger and larger.

Remodeling outstanding older hotel properties has become an important trend. The Ritz-Carlton Huntington Hotel & Spa in Pasadena, California, originally opened in 1907, has been beautifully restored. *(Photo courtesy of Wimberly, Allison, Tong, and Goo, Architects, Honolulu, Hawaii.)*

TABLE 6.1

Top 25 Hotel Chains

Rank, 1997[a]	Company Headquarters	Rooms, 1997	Hotels, 1997
1	**Cendant Corp.** Parsippany, NJ USA	499,056	5,566
2	**Bass Hotels & Resorts** Atlanta, GA USA	465,643	2,621
3	**Best Western International** Phoenix, AZ USA	300,000	3,800
4	**Choice Hotels International** Silver Spring, MD USA	292,289	3,474
5	**Marriott International** Washington, DC USA	289,357	1,477
6	**Accor** Evry, France	288,269	2,577
7	**Starwood Hotels & Resorts/Starwood Hotels & Resorts Worldwide Inc.** Phoenix, AZ USA	213,238	653
8	**Promus Hotel Corporation** Memphis, TN USA	178,802	1,119
9	**Hilton Hotel Corporation** Beverly Hills, CA USA	101,891	255
10	**Carlson Hospitality Worldwide** Minneapolis, MN USA	98,404	482
11	**Hyatt Hotels/Hyatt International** Chicago, IL USA	80,311	179
12	**Patriot American Hosp, Inc/ Wyndham International Inc.** Dallas, TX USA	7,220	241
13	**Hilton International** Walford, Herts, England	54,052	165
14	**Sol Melia** Palma de Mallorca, Spain	52,359	224
15	**Forte Hotels** London, England	47,814	260
16	**Interstate Hotels Corp.** Pittsburgh, PA USA	45,329	223
17	**Club Méditerranée SA** Paris, France	38,077	134
18	**Société du Louvre** Paris, France	37,732	591
19	**Richfield Hospitality Services Inc.** Englewood, CO USA	35,120	120
20	**La Quinta Inns** San Antonio, TX USA	34,772	271
21	**Red Roof Inns** Hilliard, OH USA	29,661	259
22	**Bristol Hotels & Resorts** Dallas, TX USA	28,800	101
23	**Prince Hotels Inc.** Tokyo, Japan	26,304	80

TABLE 6.1 (*Continued*)

Rank, 1997[a]	Company Headquarters	Rooms, 1997	Hotels, 1997
24	**Tokyu Hotel Group** Tokyo, Japan	24,877	115
25	**CapStar Hotel Company** Washington, DC USA	24,297	120

[a] Rankings are based on total rooms.

Source: Hotels, July 1998, p. 56.

There are also referral groups or voluntary membership associations. Both independents and chains have found it profitable to join together to market their properties.

The trend toward consolidation and acquisition will continue into the millennium because chains have the potential for improvement in productivity and the advantages that accrue to large size. Chains can most effectively use training programs, employee selection programs, major equipment with different layouts, prices, advertising, equipment, technology, marketing, and so on, and what works well in one property can be employed chainwide. One reason for the popularity of the referral groups is that members who are independent operators achieve the marketing benefits of chains without chain membership.

Franchising is also well known in the lodging industry and has made a rapid penetration into the marketplace. However, franchising generates mixed reports. Many managements believe that it is difficult to control the franchises and maintain the quality that the chain advertises and the standards that are supposed to be met. Thus, many chains are buying back franchises to ensure that management maintains the quality level desired. In other cases, firms are moving ahead rapidly with franchising because they can conserve cash and expand more rapidly by franchising. In addition, the franchisee, having invested his or her own capital, has great motivation to succeed.

Franchisees have the advantage that they receive a known "name," the knowledge, advice, and assistance of a proven operator. Franchising also spreads the costs of promotion, advertising, and reservation systems over all outlets, making the unit cost much lower. If the franchiser has an excellent reputation and image, the franchisee benefits greatly. Most of the companies with franchise operations also operate company-owned units. Industry predictions are that as the industry grows and matures, there will be less franchising, which will give the chains more control over their properties and operations so that they can maintain the desired quality control. Increased competitiveness and improved properties will necessitate having the ability to make these improvements.

A trend in the lodging industry appears to be that more large properties will be operated under management contracts. Investors, such as insurance companies, frequently purchase hotel properties and turn them over to chains or independents to manage—a process that has advantages to both parties. The owner has the financial resources and the manager has the reputation and experience to manage the property profitably. Other trends are the increased use of central reservation systems, emphasis on service, and the use of yield management techniques.

One of the increasingly popular amenities offered by modern hotels is a fitness facility. These facilities are provided in response to the changing lifestyles and demands of customers. *(Photo courtesy of the Sheraton Russell Hotel.)*

Bed and Breakfasts

Moving from the mega corporate chain to the **bed and breakfast** establishment demonstrates the diversity in lodging accommodations and the fact that many small businesses make up much of the tourism industry.

The growing bed and breakfast (B and B) segment is made up of over 20,000 privately owned homes, inns, and reservation services. B and Bs provide both luxury and economy accommodations and are found in resort areas as well as in many areas where major hotel and motel chains do not build. This brings tourism dollars into communities often neglected by most tourists.

Insight into the characteristics and operation of B and Bs is provided by their trade association, the Professional Association of Innkeepers International (web site: **www.paii.org**), who hired PKF Consulting to study the operations, marketing, and finances of B and Bs. Their study shows that in 1996 the average B and B had 7.4 rooms, total annual revenue of $146,045, average occupancy at 53 percent, and an average daily room rate of $107.55. Tourists and guests celebrating a special occasion such as a honeymoon, anniversary, birthday, and so on, make up the largest segment of customers (67 percent). Business travelers and meeting attendees accounted for 24 percent. The image of a B and B is a quaint home, hospitality from a gracious host, good food, and the domain of the leisure traveler. B and Bs are reaching out to some business and convention travelers by offering services such as fax machines, in-room coffee makers, and dedicated meeting facilities. The most used marketing techniques are travel guides and word-of-mouth referrals. However, in the last two years, bookings through the Internet have grown from 1 percent to 6 percent.

B and Bs provide the best possible avenue for travelers of all ages and locations to experience firsthand the lifestyles in areas of the country previously unknown to guests. The B and B host can become an area's best ambassador. For many single and retired people, B and Bs provide additional income. In many cases around the nation, the institution of a B and B has saved a historic property that might otherwise have been destroyed.

B and B reservation services inspect and approve B and B homes and inns, maintain ongoing quality control, and provide one-stop shopping for the traveler. They can provide the traveler with a chain of recourse in case of a problem. Reservation services are privately owned corporations, partnerships, or single proprietorships, each representing from 35 to 100 host homes and inns.

Timeshare Resorts

The World Tourism Organization (WTO) has named **timeshare** as one of the fastest growing sectors of the travel and tourism industry in its book *Timeshare: The New Force in Tourism*. WTO states that timeshare has grown at an annual rate of more than 15 percent since the 1980s, compared to a growth rate of slightly over 2 percent for hotel accommodations and 4 percent for tourism overall. Timeshare or vacation ownership, as it is also called, is worldwide.

Interval International reports that timeshare resorts are located in more than 81 countries and that owners reside in more than 174 countries. The United States is the leader in the timeshare market, with 37.3 percent of timeshare resorts and 52.4 percent of timeshare owners. Europe is second, with 28.7 percent of the resorts and 21.3 percent of timeshare owners. Since 1979, demand studies of the U.S. timeshare characteristics, motivations, satisfaction, and use patterns have been prepared by Ragatz Associates, for the American Resort Development Association (ARDA). Other analyses were conducted in 1980, 1982, 1983, 1989, 1992, and 1993. These frequent studies have provided a good picture of the demand side. The ARDA is a prime source of timeshare information. Visit their web site: **http://www.arda.org.**

The first national study on the supply side of the U.S. timeshare industry was conducted in 1993 by Ragatz Associates and provides an important benchmark to measure the industry. In the United States, there are 870 viable timeshare projects that are affiliated with one of the two major exchange companies. The projects contain 45,633 units, for an average of 52 units per project. Florida has the most projects (230), followed by California (68), South Carolina (62), Colorado (49), Hawaii (39), Texas (37), and North Carolina (35). These seven states account for 59.8 percent of the projects. Characteristics of the 870 projects show that 47.9 percent were built for timeshare, 89.5 percent sell a deed in perpetuity, 53.7 percent are located at a seashore or ocean beach area, 23.9 percent sell some form of floating time, 75 percent are controlled by a Home Owners Association, the average interval price is about $7800, 51.8 percent of the units are two bedroom, and 35.9 percent are one bedroom. A similar Ragatz study for Resort Condominiums International (RCI) found that U.S. timeshare volume was $2.3 billion in 1996, the average value of a week was $10,325, average maintenance fee per timeshare was $360, average occupancy was 80 percent, and the average project contained 82 units.

The timeshare industry contributes significantly to the U.S. economy. During a 10-year period, the average timeshare owner will return 4.5 times whereas the non-owner will return only 1.8 times. Timeshare occupancy rates during the 1990s have been over 80 percent compared to about 65 percent for hotels. The average timeshare vacationing party number is 3.6, spends 8.1 nights, and spends over $1400. They generate 60 million visitor-days. It is estimated that the resort timeshare industry contributes about $8.6 billion annually to the U.S. economy.

The ARDA has also conducted a study on worldwide vacation ownership which shows that the worldwide vacation ownership industry has experienced close to 900 percent growth from 1980 to 1995, with the number of households worldwide owning a timeshare surpassing 3 million.

Timesharing is expected to increase in the United States because major companies such as Disney, Marriott, Hyatt, Four Seasons, Ramada, and Hilton have become involved in bringing more respectability to the industry. Once considered to be a sleazy real estate proposition, with unfulfilled promises, high pressure, and marketing hype, timesharing has evolved into a mainstream option. Today, timeshares are being sold by some of the best names in the hotel industry. Vacation ownership or internal ownership is the terminology being used.

An example is Marriott. They entered the Vacation Ownership industry in 1984 and began redefining the timeshare industry. Incorporating the signature quality, service, and hospitality expertise of Marriott, a new product was created that offered the ownership of a first-class luxury villa and the flexibility to experience great vacation destinations around the world. Marriott Vacation Club International has successfully combined the benefits of property ownership, Marriott quality management, and fixed costs for a lifetime of vacations. Marriott has about 2000 villas at beach and ski resorts across the country. Over the past 10 years, Marriott has refined a low-key approach and sold "vacation ownership intervals" to more than 60,000 people.

Lodging Organizations

There are a large number of accommodation organizations: international, regional, state, and local. Of these, the American Hotel and Motel Association (AH&MA) is the largest and most prominent in the United States. AH&MA now represents over 11,000 members. AH&MA works on programs such as guest and employee communications, information processing and related technology, international travel, external and internal marketing, quality assurance programs, industry research, safety and fire protection, and so on.

AH&MA has one of the best information centers in the United States. Their information center provides a collection of resources covering the lodging, hospitality, and travel and tourism fields; a professional staff of librarians/researchers; a wealth of industry-specific and related knowledge; a resource center of over 70,000 current articles on more than 2,500 topics, reference materials, books, reports and surveys; and an access point to major domestic and international bibliographic and statistical data bases. AH&MA has a commitment to technology and is dedicated to providing members and the media with up-to-date information, industry trends, and association news via the World Wide Web. Visit their web site: **http://www.ahma.com.**

The International Hotel and Restaurant Association (IH&RA), located in Paris, France, is a global network for the hotel and restaurant industry in over 150 countries. It represents, protects, promotes, and informs its members. IH&RA research reports provide members with valuable information on the global hospitality industry, careers, taxes, and technology (web site is **http://www.ihra.com**).

Lodging Information Sources

Data on the lodging industry can be obtained from Smith Travel Research, Hendersonville, Tennessee. Smith is the leader in lodging industry tracking and analysis providing regular industry reporting to all major U.S. hotel chains, many independent hotels, and a variety of management companies and hotel owners. The company also tracks lodging industry performance in Canada, Mexico, and other major world destinations. Web site address is **http://www.str-online.com.**

PricewaterhouseCoopers, LLP (1301 Avenue of the Americas, New York, NY 10019), has Lodging Research Network (**www.lodgingresearch.com**), which contains econometric forecasts for the lodging industry, breaking lodging industry news, and exclusive database of lodging industry real estate acquisitions, financial data of publicly traded lodging companies, hotel construction data, lodging census data from Smith Travel Research, and an extensive research library.

In late 1998, the PricewaterhouseCoopers lodging and gaming groups and Smith Travel Research signed an agreement to form a worldwide alliance for lodging industry research. The organizations will cooperate to collect and report hotel operating data in over 20 countries outside of North America.

In addition, PFK consulting, San Francisco, Arthur Andersen Real Estate Services Group, Los Angeles, and U.S. Census Bureau, Washington, D.C., provide lodging information.

THE FOOD SERVICE INDUSTRY

Early Food Services

Like the lodging industry, the **food service industry** is a very old business. Such service came out of the early inns and monasteries. In cities, small restaurants began serving simple dishes such as soups and breads. One such restaurant, *le restaurant divin*—the divine restorative—opened in Paris in 1765. (Like *tourist, restaurant* is a French word.) The famous English taverns provided food, drink, and lodging.

In the United States the early ordinaries, taverns, and inns typically provided food and lodging. Good examples of these can be found in Colonial Williamsburg, Virginia. Politics and other concerns of the day were often discussed in such taverns.

With the development of stagecoaches, taverns began providing food and lodging along the early roads and in small communities. Some believe that these roadside taverns were really the beginnings of the American hotel industry. As cities grew, so did eating establishments. Some names of historic restaurants in the 1820s in New York City were Niblo's Garden, the San Souci, and Delmonico's.

French service was often used in these early restaurants. In French service, some kinds of entrées are prepared by the dining room captain right at the guests' table, sometimes using heat from a small burner, then serving from larger dishes onto the guest's plate. The kinds and amounts of each food item are chosen individually. By contrast, in Russian service the entire plate, with predetermined portions, is served to each guest.

Menus can be of two types, á la carte and table d'hôte. The á la carte menu consists of a complete list of all the food items being offered on that day. The patron then chooses items desired. In table d'hôte, a combination of items is chosen.

Eating and drinking places are big business. Although much of this activity is local, eating and drinking are favorite pastimes of travelers, and the food service industry would face difficult times without the tourist market. See Figure 6.2 for the structure of the food service industry. In 1998, the **National Restaurant Association** projected that food industry sales for the year would total $336.4 billion, 4.7 percent over 1997. The industry currently employees more than 9 million people. By the year 2005, eating and drinking places are expected to employ 2 million more people, generating the largest number of new jobs in any industry. Nearly 60 percent of all those in food service occupations are women, 13 percent are Hispanic, and 11 percent are African-American. The food service industry employs more minority managers than any other retail industry. Travelers contribute about $112 billion to food service sales each year, whether for a coffee shop breakfast, a dinner on an airline, a sandwich from

An unusual waiter indeed! This special breakfast dining experience at Disneyland delights children and can be the highlight of a family vacation. *(Photo courtesy of the Disneyland Hotel.)*

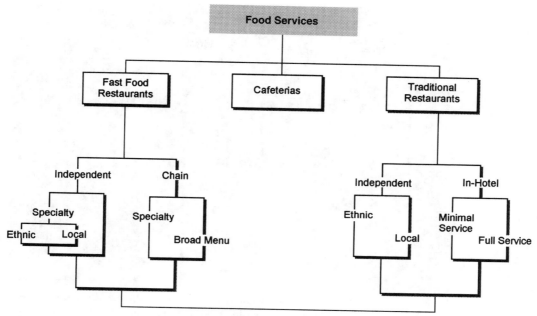

FIGURE 6.2 Food services structure.

a bus station vending machine, or a 10-course dinner on a cruise ship. Travelers, including foreign visitors, spend more money on food than anything else except transportation, and travelers account for about one-third of the total sales in the food service industry.

The food service industry consists of restaurants, travel food service, and vending and contract institutional food service. Local restaurants are made up of establishments that include fast-food units, coffee shops, specialty restaurants, family restaurants, cafeterias, and full-service restaurants with carefully orchestrated "atmosphere." Travel food service consists of food operations in hotels and motels, roadside service to automobile travelers, and all food service on airplanes, trains, and ships. Institutional food service in companies, hospitals, nursing homes, and so on, is not considered part of the tourism industry.

Over the past two decades, the food and beverage business has grown at a phenomenal rate. This has been especially true for the **fast-food** segment, with the franchising portion in the fast-food segment becoming the dominant growth sector. This remarkable increase has been gained at the expense of other food service operators and supermarkets. Franchisees control approximately three-fourths of the fast-food outlets, whose hamburgers, chickens, steaks, and pizzas dominate the fast-food business.

Fast-food chains have enjoyed great success in part because they limit their menus, which gives them greater purchasing power, less waste, more portion control, and, of importance to the consumer, lower operating costs. They are leaders in labor productivity in the restaurant industry. Most fast-food operations use dispos-

Theme restaurants that feature good food in a unique atmosphere, such as this western-themed restaurant, have become increasingly popular with tourists. *(Photo courtesy of Denver Metro Convention and Visitors Bureau.)*

able paper and plastic; the expense for these materials is more than offset by the savings resulting from not providing regular service and from not employing the personnel required to wash the dinner service. Fast-food operations also enjoy the advantages of specialization; they have become specialists in menu items, job simplification, and operating systems. Franchising has been used extensively in both the restaurant field and the lodging field as a means of achieving rapid growth. Using the franchisee's capital, the entrepreneur can get much more rapid penetration of the marketplace.

As noted earlier, franchise units account for approximately three-fourths of the growing fast-food portion of the industry. Advantages of franchising accrue to both sides. The franchisee gets the start-up help, advice from experienced management, buying power, advertising, and low unit costs from spreading fixed costs over large numbers of units. The franchisor has the advantage of a lower capital investment, rapid growth, and royalty income. The fast-food franchise operators have a great deal of concentration in their segment of the industry. The seven largest account for almost half of the fast-food units and almost half of the sales. Franchise firms are household words: McDonald's, Kentucky Fried Chicken, A&W Root Beer, Wendy's, Dairy Queen, Burger King, Pizza Hut, Arby's, and Taco Bell.

Although the fast-food segment is the most rapidly growing segment, the high-quality segment of the restaurant industry must not be overlooked. Much of this business is based on customers seeking a special or different experience in dining out. Local entrepreneurs who emphasize special menus, varying atmospheres, and high-quality food and service have most effectively satisfied this demand. New con-

These tourists never met a beer they didn't like! They are enjoying soup and beverages in a Dublin, Ireland microbrewery. *(Photo by the author.)*

cepts or trends include ethnic restaurants, especially those with an oriental or Mexican flavor; increased demand for health foods, fish, local produce, and regional dishes; and variety in portion sizes.

Restaurant Organizations

The National Restaurant Association (NRA), a full-service trade association with over 20,000 members, is the most important trade association in the food service field. Membership is diverse, running the gamut from the New Jersey prison system to Club 21 and including white tablecloth and fast-food members, institutional feeders, and vending machine operators.

The goals and objectives of NRA are channeled in three directions: (1) political action, (2) information, and (3) promotion. Through their Political Action and Political Education Committees, NRA promotes the political and legislative concerns of the industry and combats any potentially harmful attempts by government to regulate the operational aspects of the industry. Their Educational Foundation contributes to the current and future training and educational/informational needs of the food service industry.

NRA works to position the industry and its services before the public in a favorable light. The association regularly publishes surveys and reports on a wide variety of topics, ranging from employee management to consumer attitudes toward smoking in restaurants. Through its library's information service, NRA responds to thousands of requests for information. NRA is located at 1200 Seventeenth Street NW, Washington, D.C. 20036, phone (202) 331-5900, web site **http://www.restaurant.org.**

MEETING PLANNERS

Because of the growth in the meeting and conventions area, it is an area of interest to students of tourism. With the growth of more corporate and association meetings, there is a need for more meeting planners, meeting consultants, and suppliers of goods and services to meeting planners. Professional **meeting planners** are involved with such tasks as negotiating hotel contracts, negotiating with airlines, writing contracts, planning educational meetings and seminars, developing incentive meetings, negotiating with foreign countries and hotels for incentive travel, budgeting, promotion, public relations, and planning special events and post-meeting tours. Meeting planners are found in corporations, special-interest associations, educational institutions, trade shows, and government.

MEETINGS AND CONVENTIONS

The **conventions and meeting business** is huge and booming fueled by the robust economy. The Convention Liaison Council states that meetings and conventions are an $82 billion-a-year industry. The American Society of Association Executives estimates that the number of conventions, expositions, and meetings held each year rose by 11 percent from 1992 to 1995, for an annual total of over 200,000. For a city, the financial benefits of hosting a convention are substantial. The average convention at-

The meetings and conventions business is expanding internationally. In Singapore, a hub of international commerce, the Westin Stamford Hotel, Raffles City, has 80,000 square feet of meeting space. *(Photo courtesy of Westin Hotels and Resorts.®)*

tendee spent $218 per day in 1996, according to the International Association of Convention and Visitor Bureaus.

With an average stay of 4.1 days, delegates spent over $895 per event. Total expenditures include money spent on hotel rooms, restaurants, retail stores, taxis, car rentals, and other expenses. Exhibitors attending these conventions spent $1185.65 each per day, totaling $4007.53 for an average 3.38-day stay. Although smaller in size, the economic impact of a state and local convention is also great, with delegates to these conventions spending $362.09 during a 2.42-day stay. Spending per exhibitor at a state and local convention totaled $966.53 in 1996, with an average stay of just over 2.5 days.

There will probably be an oversupply of convention meeting facilities in the United States as the number of convention centers continues to grow. There are many U.S. cities building new convention centers or expanding their existing centers. Even though the United States leads the world in conventions, in terms of both numbers of attendees and the amount of exhibit and meeting space, the growth in facilities in outpacing the demand. There are more than 330 convention centers in the United States, 50 percent more than in 1980.

SUMMARY

Lodging and food services are major essential supply components of tourism. These services go back into antiquity. World hotel room inventory is growing about 2.5 percent yearly. Room occupancy averages about 65 percent. But such data vary considerably. The 1980s saw considerable overbuilding and losses, especially in North America. However, for the remainder of the 1990s, forecasters see a record profitability. About 75 percent of the world's lodging establishments are located in Europe and North America. There is a trend toward more franchising, chain or system ownership, and growth in bed and breakfast lodging.

Resort and timesharing arrangements are also increasing worldwide. The United States dominates this market, with 37.3 percent of the properties, and 52.4 percent of the timeshares. About 3.0 million households worldwide own time-share intervals. The American Hotel and Motel Association is the leading lodging trade association in the United States, but many others are active in North America and elsewhere. Eating and drinking places are big business. In the United States this industry grossed $336.4 billion in 1998, employed over 9 million persons, and is expected to add 2.0 million more people by the year 2005. The National Restaurant Association is the industry's most important trade association.

Meetings and conventions constitute a major reason for business travel. Expenditure on these stimulates all segments of tourism. In the United States there will probably be an oversupply of convention centers within a few years, because many cities are currently building new centers or expanding existing ones.

The profession of meeting planner is an important and growing one. Those attending meetings and conventions expect a rewarding experience. Thus, expert planning is critical to the success of such events. Meeting planners provide all arrangements necessary for a successful meeting, from transportation services to special events. They are particularly adept at negotiating elements needed for the meeting. Some corporations, associations, government agencies, and others have created their own meeting-planning department, with their own employees handling this important function.

KEY CONCEPTS

American Hotel and Motel Association
bed and breakfast
fast-food companies
food service industry
franchising
largest hotel companies
lodging industry

meeting planners
meetings and conventions
National Restaurant Association
REITs
timesharing resorts
trends in lodging industry

INTERNET SITES

The Internet sites mentioned in this chapter are repeated here for convenience plus some selected additional sites. For more information, visit these sites. Be aware that Internet addresses change frequently, so if a site cannot be accessed, use a search engine. Also use a search engine to locate many additional sites that are available.

American Culinary Federation
http://www.ocfchefs.org

American Hotel and Motel Association
http://www.ahma.com

American Resort and Development Association
http://www.arda.org

Canadian Pacific Hotels
http://www.cphotels.ca

Club Managers Association of America
http://www.cmaa.org

Council on Hotel, Restaurant and Institutional Education (CHRIE)
http://www.chrie.org

Disney Vacation Club
http://www.disney.com/Disney VacationClub/index.html

The Educational Foundation of NRA
http://www.restaurant.org/educate/educate.htm

The Educational Institute of AH&MA
http://www.ei-ahma.org

Hilton Grand Vacations Company
http://www.hgvc.com

Hilton Hotels
http://www.hilton.com

Hospitality Information Technology Association
http://www.hita.co.uk

Hyatt Hotels and Resorts
http://www.hyatt.com

Hyatt Vacation Club
http://www.hyatt.com/athyatt/vacation/index.html

International Association of Convention and Visitor Bureaus
http://www.iacvb.org

International Food Service Executives Association
http://ifsea.org

International Franchise Association
http://www.franchise.org

International Hotel and Restaurant Association
http://www.ih-ra.com

Interval International
http://www.interval-intl.com

Marriott International
http://www.marriott.com

Marriott Vacation Club
http://www.marriott.com/vacationclub

McDonald's Restaurants
http://www.mcdonalds.com

Meeting Professionals International
http://www.mpiweb.org

Meetings and Conventions
http://www.meetings-conventions.com

National Restaurant Association
http://www.restaurant.org

Patriot American Hospitality
http://www.patriotamerican.com

Professional Association of Innkeepers International
http://www/paii.org

Professional Convention Management Association
http://www.pcma.org

Raddison Hotels Worldwide
http://www.radisson.com

Resort Condominiums International, Inc.
http://www.rci.com/index.html

Smith Travel Research
http://www.str-online.com

Starwood Hotels and Resorts
http://www.starwoodhotels.com

Travel Bed and Breakfast Inns
http://www.innandtravel.com

INTERNET EXERCISES

Activity 1

Site Name: The National Restaurant Association (NRA)

URL: http://www.restaurant.org/

Background Information: The NRA provides information on consumer studies, trends in restaurants, and press releases that identify trends and issues confronting the industry.

Exercises

1. Choose a state or region in the United States and describe the potential for growth in the restaurant industry for that state/region.

2. What impact do you think travel has on the growth of the restaurant industry in the state/region selected? Why?

Activity 2

Site Name: Directory of Hotel and Restaurant Homepages

URL: http://www.wku.edu/~hrtm/hotlrest.htm

Background Information: This is a directory of the major hotel and restaurant chains with a link to their home pages.

Exercise

1. Choose a hotel chain and determine their projected growth rate. How does this compare with the growth figures identified in the textbook?

QUESTIONS FOR REVIEW AND DISCUSSION

1. Why are the world's lodging businesses growing at the rate of 2.5 percent per year?

2. Identify the reasons why Las Vegas has a high hotel occupancy.

3. Explain the current trend in the United States for slow expansion in the construction of new lodging places.

4. How successful do you think future tourism will be

in the countries of Eastern Europe and the former Soviet Union?

5. What reasons have brought about the concentration of lodging businesses in Europe and North America?

6. Why have chain and brand identification hotels and motels continued to expand worldwide versus independent properties?

7. Define franchising. What are the trends and benefits of such groupings? Give examples.

8. List services provided to its members by the American Hotel and Motel Association. Are state hotel and motel associations affiliated?

9. Similarly, what services do members obtain from the National Restaurant Association?

10. Are profit percentages on sales higher in fast-food places than in table service types? If so, why?

11. Explain timesharing. Describe its advantages over owning one's own resort property.

12. What characteristics of lifestyles of contemporary American and Canadian citizens are responsible for the growing attendance at meetings and conventions?

13. Would you be interested in a career as a professional meeting planner? If so, where would you find out more about this field?

CASE PROBLEMS

1. You are the food and beverage manager of a resort hotel located in an interesting historical destination similar to Colonial Williamsburg, Virginia. Recently, you decided that all the guest servers in the dining room should wear authentic costumes typical of those when the area was at its peak as an early trading center. Some of the staff object to this plan, saying that it is a silly idea and also that the costumes look like they might be uncomfortable. What would your reaction be?

2. Angelo V. and his son Leonard are co-owners of a fine-quality 150-seat table service restaurant. Leonard has been gradually acquiring more authority and responsibility for management. However, recently he and his father have had some sharp disagreements relating to becoming members of their state's restaurant association and the National Restaurant Association. Angelo feels that membership would be a waste of money. If you were Leonard, what would your arguments in favor be?

SELECTED REFERENCES

Angelo, Rocco M., and Andrew N. Vladimir. *Hospitality Today: An Introduction.* East Lansing, MI: Educational Institute of the American Hotel and Motel Association, 1998.

Astroff, Milton T., and James R. Abbey. *Convention Sales and Services.* Cranbury, NJ: Waterbury Press, 1991.

Breiter, Deborah, and Priscilla Bloomquist. "TQM in American Hotels: An Analysis of Application." *Cornell Quarterly: Hotel Restaurant and Administration,* Vol. 39, No. 1, pp. 26–33, February 1998.

Brotherton, Bob, and Sean Mooney. "Yield Management: Progress and Prospects." *International Journal of Hospitality Management,* Vol. 11, No. 1, pp. 23–32, 1992.

Brown, James R., and Chekitan S. Dev. "The Franchisor–Franchisee Relationship: A Key to Franchise Performance." *Cornell Quarterly: Hotel and Restaurant Administration,* Vol. 38, No. 6, pp. 30–38, 1997.

Cahners Travel Group, *The Meeting Market.* Secaucus, NJ: Reed, 1998.

Callan, Roger J. "Attributional Analysis of Customers' Hotel Selection Criteria by U.K. Grading Scheme Categories." *Journal of Travel Research,* Vol. 36, No. 3, pp. 20–34, Winter 1998.

Collins, Galen R. *Hospitality Information Technology: Learning How to Use It.* Dubuque, IA: Kendall/Hunt Publishing Company, 1994.

Crouch, Geoffrey I., and J.R. Brent Ritchie. "Convention Site Selection Research: A Review, Conceptual Model, and Propositional Framework." *Journal of Convention and Exhibition Management*, Vol. 1, No. 1, pp. 45–65, 1998.

CTC. *A Window on Canada's Accommodation Industry.* Ottawa: Canadian Tourism Commission, February 1996.

Davies, Brian, and Paul Downward. "The Structure, Conduct, Performance Paradigm as Applied to the U.K. Hotel Industry." *Tourism Economics*, Vol. 2, No. 2, pp. 150–158, June 1996.

Dwyer, Larry, and Peter Forsyth. "Impacts and Benefits of MICE Tourism: A Framework for Analysis." *Tourism Economics: The Business and Finance of Tourism and Recreation*, Vol. 3, No. 1, pp. 21–38, March 1997.

Educational Institute. *Case Studies in Hospitality Management.* East Lansing, MI: Educational Institute of the American Hotel and Motel Association, 1997.

Emerick, Robert E., and Carol A. Emerick. "Profiling American Bed and Breakfast Accommodations." *Journal of Travel Research*, Vol. 32, No. 4, pp. 20–25, Spring 1994.

Eyster, James J. "Hotel Management Contracts in the U.S.: The Revolution Continues." *Cornell Quarterly*, Vol. 38, No. 3, pp. 14–20, June 1997.

Fenich, George. "Convention Centre Development: Pros, Cons and Unanswered Questions." *International Journal of Hospitality Management*, Vol. 11, No. 3, pp. 183–196, August 1992.

Fiorention, Allessandro. "Budget Hotels: Not Just Minor Hospitality Products." *Tourism Management*, Vol. 16, No. 6, pp. 455–462, September 1995.

Gee, Chuck Y. *International Hotel Development and Management.* East Lansing, MI: Educational Institute of the American Hotel and Motel Association, 1994.

Getz, Donald, Don Anderson, and Lorn Sheehan. "Roles, Issues, and Strategies for Convention and Visitors' Bureaux in Destination Planning and Product Development: A Survey of Canadian Bureaux." *Tourism Management*, Vol. 19, No. 4, pp. 331–340, 1998.

Gilbert, David, and Andrew Lockwood. "Budget Hotels: The USA, France and UK Compared." *Travel and Tourism Analyst*, No. 3, pp. 19–36, 1990.

Go, Frank M., and Ray Pine. *Globalization Strategy in the Hotel Industry.* New York: Routledge, 1995.

Griffin, Robert K. "Factors of Successful Lodging Yield Management Systems." *Hospitality Research Journal*, Vol. 19, No. 4, pp. 17-30, 1996.

Gustin, Mary Elizabeth, and Pamela A. Weaver. "Are Hotels Prepared for the Environmental Consumer?" *Hospitality Research Journal*, Vol. 20, No. 2, pp. 1–14, 1996.

Hall, Stephen. *Ethics in Hospitality Management.* East Lansing, MI: Educational Institute of the American Hotel and Motel Association, 1992.

Haylock, Ron. "The European Timeshare Market: The Growth, Development, Regulation and Economic Benefits of One of Tourism's Most Successful Sectors." *Tourism Management*, Vol. 15, No. 5, pp. 333–342, October 1994.

Hiemstra, Stephen J., and Joseph A. Ismail. "Analysis of Room Taxes Levied on the Lodging Industry." *Journal of Travel Research*, Vol. 31, No. 1, pp. 42–49, Summer 1992.

Hiemstra, Stephen J., and Joseph A. Ismail. "Incidence of the Impacts of Room Taxes on the Lodging Industry." *Journal of Travel Research*, Vol. 31, No. 4, pp. 22–26, Spring 1993.

Hoyle, Leonard, H., David C. Dorf, and Thomas J.A. Jones. *Managing Conventions and Group Business.* East Lansing, MI: Educational Institute of the American Hotel and Motel Association, 1989.

Jakle, John, Keith A. Sculle, and Jefferson S. Rogers. *The Motel in America.* Baltimore, MD: The John Hopkins University Press, 1996.

Jones, Peter, and Abraham Pizam. *The International Hospitality Industry.* New York: John Wiley & Sons, 1993.

Kasavana L., and John J. Cahill. *Managing Computers in the Hospitality Industry.* East Lansing, MI.: Educational Institute of the American Hotel and Motel Association, 1997.

Katz, Jeff B. *Restaurant Planning, Design and Construction.* New York: Wiley, 1996.

Kaufman, Tammie J., Pamela A. Weaver, and Julia Poynter. "Success Attributes of B&B Operators." *Cornell Quarterly*, Vol. 37, No. 4, pp. 29–33, August 1996.

Kavanaugh, Raphael, and Jack D. Ninemeier. *Supervision in the Hospitality Industry.* East Lansing, MI: Educational Institute of the American Hotel and Motel Association, 1991.

Kimes, Sheryl E., et al. "Restaurant Revenue Management: Applying Yield Management to the Restaurant Industry." *Cornell Hotel and Restaurant Administration Quarterly*, Vol. 39, No. 3, pp. 32–39, June 1998.

Lattin, Gerald W. *The Lodging and Food Service Industry,*

3rd edition. East Lansing, MI: Educational Institute of the American Hotel and Motel Association, 1998.

Lawson, Fred. *Hotels and Resorts: Planning, Design and Refurbishment.* Worburn, MA: Butterworth-Heinemann, 1995.

Lawton, Laura J., David Weaver, and Bill Faulkner. "Customer Satisfaction in the Australian Timeshare Industry." *Journal of Travel Research,* Vol. 37, No. 1, pp. 30–38, August, 1998.

Luchars, James Y., and Timothy R. Hinkin. "The Service-Quality Audit: A Hotel Case Study." *Cornell Quarterly,* Vol. 37, No. 1, pp. 34–41, February 1996.

Manickas, Peter A., and Linda J. Shea. "Hotel Complaint Behavior and Resolution: A Content Analysis." *Journal of Travel Research,* Vol. 36, No. 2, pp. 68–73, Fall 1997.

Marvin, Bill. *Restaurant Basics: Why Guests Don't Come Back . . . and What You Can Do About It.* New York: Wiley, 1992.

Miller, James J., Cynthia S. McCahon, and Judy L. Miller. "Foodservice Forecasting Using Simple Mathematical Models." *Hospitality Research Journal,* Vol. 15, No. 1, pp. 43–58, 1991.

Mok, Connie, and Terry Lam. "Hotel and Tourism Development in Vietnam." *Journal of Travel and Tourism Marketing,* Vol. 7, No. 1, pp. 85–92, 1998.

Morrison, Alastair M., Stacey M. Bruen, and Donald J. Anderson. "Convention and Visitor Bureaus in the United States: A Profile of Bureaus, Bureau Executives, and Budgets." *Journal of Travel and Tourism Marketing,* Vol. 7, No. 1, pp. 1–20, 1998.

National Restaurant Association. "1998 Food Industry Forecast." *Restaurants USA,* Vol. 17, No. 11, pp. F1–F28, December 1997.

Nixon, Judith M. *The Hotel and Restaurant Industries: An Information Sourcebook.* Phoenix, AZ: Oryx Press, 1988.

Olsen, Michael, Eliza Ching-Yick Tse, and Joseph West. *Strategic Management in the Hospitality Industry.* New York: Wiley, 1998.

Oppermann, Martin. "Convention Cities—Images and Changing Fortunes." *Journal of Tourism Studies,* Vol. 7, No. 1, pp. 10–19, May 1996.

Oppermann, Martin and Key-Sung Chon. "Convention Participation Decision-Making Process." *Annals of Tourism Research,* Vol. 24, No. 1, pp. 178–191, 1997.

Patel, Dipan and John B. Corgel. "An Analysis of Hotel Impact Studies." *Cornell Hotel and Restaurant Ad-*

ministration Quarterly, Vol. 36, No. 4, pp. 27–37, 1995.

Poorani, Ali A., and David R. Smith. "Financial Characteristics of Bed-and-Breakfast Inns." *Cornell Hotel and Restaurant Administration Quarterly,* Vol. 36, No. 5, pp. 57–63, October 1995.

RCI, *The Public Image of Resort Timesharing.* Indianapolis, IN: Resort Condominiums International, 1998.

RCI, *The Resort Timeshare Industry in the United States.* Indianapolis, IN: Resort Condominiums International, 1998.

Roper, Angela, Anne Hampton, and Maureen Brookes. "The Multi-Cultural Management of International Hotel Groups." *International Journal of Hospitality Management,* Vol. 16, No. 2, pp. 147–160, June 1997.

Sadi, Muhammad A. "Adaptability of American Fast-Food Franchise Systems in International Markets." *Journal of Restaurant and Foodservice Marketing,* Vol. 2, No. 1, pp. 23–44, 1997.

Salmen, John. *Accommodating All Guests: The Americans with Disabilities Act and the Lodging Industry.* Washington, D.C.: American Hotel and Motel Association, 1992.

Scanlon, Nancy Loman. *Quality Restaurant Service.* New York: Wiley, 1998.

Spies, Rupert and Gretel Weiss. "Is Germany's Traditional Restaurant a Dying Breed?" *Cornell Hotel and Restaurant Administration Quarterly,* Vol. 39, No. 3, pp. 82–89, June 1998.

Steadman, Charles E., and Michael L. Kasavana. *Managing Front Office Operations.* East Lansing, MI: Educational Institute of the American Hotel and Motel Association, 1996.

Stipanuk, David M., and Jack D. Ninemeier. "The Future of the U.S. Lodging Industry and the Environment." *Cornell Hotel and Restaurant Administration Quarterly,* Vol. 37, No. 6, pp. 74–83, December 1996.

Talbot, Randy. *Meeting Management.* McLean, VA: EPM Publishing 1990.

Vallen, Gary and Jerry Vallen. *Check-In—Check-out.* Upper Saddle River, NJ: Prentice-Hall, 1996.

Van Hoof, Hubert B., and Thomas E. Combrink. "U.S. Lodging Managers and the Internet: Perceptions from the Industry." *Cornell Hotel and Restaurant Administration Quarterly,* Vol. 39, No. 2, pp. 46–54, April 1998.

Van Hoof, Hubert B., Marja J. Verbeeten, and Thomas E. Combrink. "Information Technology

Revisited—International Lodging-Industry Technology Needs and Perceptions: A Comparative Study." *Cornell Hotel and Restaurant Administration Quarterly*, Vol. 37, No. 6, pp. 86–91, December 1996.

Warnich, Rodney B., and Lawrence R. Klar, Jr. "The Bed and Breakfast and Small Inn Industry of the Commonwealth of Massachusetts." *Journal of Travel Research*, Vol. 29, No. 3, pp. 17–25, Winter 1991.

Woods, Robert H. *Managing Hospitality Human Resources*. East Lansing, MI: Educational Institute of the American Hotel and Motel Association, 1992.

WTO, *Timeshare: The New Force in Tourism*, Madrid: World Tourism Organization, 1996.

ORGANIZATIONS IN THE DISTRIBUTION PROCESS

- Become familiar with tourism distribution system organizations and their functions.

- Understand the role of travel agents and their dominance in the distribution system.

- Consider the impact of the Internet on the distribution system.

- Examine the role of the tour wholesaler.

- Recognize that travel suppliers can use a combination of all channels of distribution.

◀ LEARNING OBJECTIVES

◀ *Technology is changing the way tourism is planned and experienced. (Photo courtesy of United Airlines.)*

INTRODUCTION

The tourism **channel of distribution** is an operating structure, system, or linkage of various combinations of organizations through which a producer of travel products describes, sells, or confirms travel arrangements to the buyer. For example, it would be impractical for a cruise line trying to market cruises to have a sales office in every market city of 5000 or more people. The most efficient method is to market through over 30,000 retail travel agencies in the United States and pay them a commission for every cruise sold. The cruises could also be sold through such intermediaries as tour wholesalers (who would include a cruise in a package vacation), through corporate travel offices, or by an association such as an automobile club and others. Thus the cruise line uses a combination of distribution channel organizations to sell cruises.

Tourism distribution channels are similar to those of other basic industries such as agriculture or manufacturing (see Figure 7.1). Their products flow to the ultimate consumer through wholesalers, distributors, and middlemen. While there are similarities with other industries, the tourism distribution system is unique. Tourism produces mainly services that are intangible. There is no physical product that can be held in inventory and flows from one sales intermediary to another. Instead, the "product," for example, is a hotel room that is available on a certain day, which is very temporal. If the room is not sold, the revenue is lost forever.

TRAVEL AGENTS

Travel, whether for business or pleasure, requires arrangements. The traveler usually faces a variety of choices regarding transportation and accommodations; and

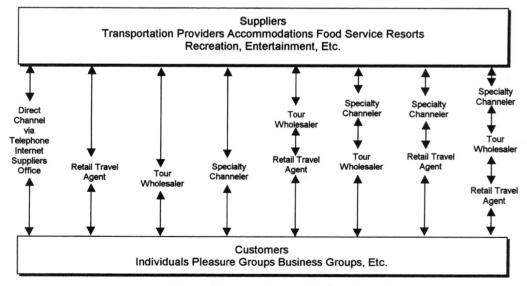

FIGURE 7.1. Tourism distribution channels.

if the trip is for pleasure, there are a variety of choices regarding destinations, attractions, and activities. The traveler may gather information on prices, value, schedules, characteristics of the destination, and available activities directly, investing a considerable amount of time on the Internet or possibly money on long-distance telephone calls to complete the trip arrangements. Alternatively, the traveler may use the services of a travel agency, obtaining all these arrangements at no cost or for a small fee.

What is a Travel Agent?

A **travel agency** is a middleman—a business or person selling the travel industry's individual parts or a combination of the parts to the consumer. In marketing terms a travel agent is an agent middleman, acting on behalf of the client, making arrangements with suppliers of travel (airlines, hotels, tour operators), and receiving a commission from the suppliers.

In legal terms, a travel agency is an agent of the principal—specifically, transportation companies. The agency operates as a legally appointed agent, representing the principal in a certain geographic area. The agency functions as a broker (bringing buyer and seller together) for the other suppliers, such as hotels, car rentals, ground operators, and tour companies.

A travel agent is thus an expert, knowledgeable in schedules, routing, lodging, currency, prices, regulations, destinations, and all other aspects of travel and travel opportunities. In short, the travel agent is a specialist and counselor.

Travel agents work with clients, saving them time and money. Using the latest computer reservation technologies, travel agents are able to access the most up-to-date information. *(Photo by the author.)*

Thanks to the reports sponsored by *Travel Weekly* magazine and couducted by Louis Harris and Associates, excellent data are available on the travel agency business. Started in 1970, these studies, conducted every two years, are regarded as the benchmark research in the retail travel industry. The latest *Travel Weekly—Louis Harris Study* was published in August 27, 1998 and represents the fourteenth in a series of studies on the character and volume of the U.S. travel agency market. Even though growth has now plateaued, the increase of the travel agency business over the last 30 years has been remarkable.

In 1970, the *Travel Weekly* study conducted by Louis Harris and Associates defined the travel agent as follows:

A travel agent, besides selling prepared package tours, also prepares individual itineraries. He arranges for hotels, motels, accommodation at resorts, meals, sightseeing, transfers of passengers and luggage between terminals and hotels; furthermore, he can provide the traveler with a host of other information (for example, on rates, quality and so on) which would normally be hard to get. The travel agent is paid for his services through commissions. For example, if a travel agent writes up an air ticket or makes a reservation in a hotel for a client, he gets paid by the carrier or the hotel in the form of a commission. In short, the travel agent saves the customer both time and money.

This definition is still true today except that some suppliers have reduced the commissions paid and a number of agents are charging fees to make up this lost revenue. In the future it is expected that the percentage of travel agent revenue from commissions will slowly decline and the percentage from fees will rise.

The latest *Travel Weekly* survey covers the two-year period from the end of 1995 through the end of 1997 and provides data on the agency marketplace, agency affiliations, agency automation, supplier relations, leisure market, agent training, and business market. A few of the highlights of the 220-page report are covered in the next section.

The Dimension of the Travel Agency Business

The *Travel Weekly* survey reported that at the end of 1997 there were 33,500 agency locations in the United States. For the first time, the number of travel agency locations decreased from one survey to the next, because the 1995 total was 33,593. However, this is still about 4.8 times the 5700 agencies reported in 1970 (see Figure 7.2).[1] Since airline deregulation took effect in 1978, the number of agency locations in the United States has more than doubled, from 14,804 to 33,500. Figure 7.2 illustrates the expansion of agency locations that began to slow down in the late 1980s has now stopped. The average agency has 6.5 full-time employees.

The *Travel Weekly* study found that the average salary for travel agents ranged from $16,604 for employees with less than a year's experience up to $29,543 for those with

---

[1] Louis Harris and Associates, *Travel Weekly*, 1998 U.S. Travel Agency Market Survey, Cahners Travel Group August 1998.

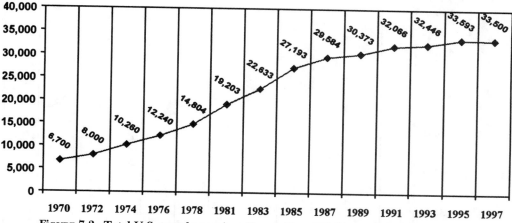

FIGURE 7.2. Total U.S. travel agencies. *(Source: Travel Weekly, copyright © 1998, Cahners Travel Group, a Division of Reed Elsevier, Inc.)*

a decade of experience. On average a manager on straight salary earned $49,740 a year. The highest-paid employees were managers of $5 million volume agencies who earned $74,292.

Even though the number of travel agencies has not grown, the dollar volume has increased dramatically. The annual estimated dollar volume for agencies reached $126.0 billion in 1997, an increase of 25 percent over the $101.1 billion reported in 1995 (see Figure 7.3). Today 17 percent of the agencies reach $5 million or more; 34 percent, $2 to 4.9 million; 30 percent, $1 to 1.9 million; and 19 percent, less than $1 million. The average revenue per agency is $3.8 million. The largest agencies account for the majority of the business. The 5618 agencies doing $5 million or more (17 percent of the total) account for 54 percent of the revenue. Leisure travel now accounts for 51 percent of agency revenue, up from 49 percent in 1995. It is expected that this trend will continue.

Travel agents are heavy users of automation. The *Travel Weekly* survey reports that many agencies are taking advantage of automation. Agencies are harnessing Internet power, because 82 percent of agents with Internet access are using it to research travel products or destinations. It is estimated that a quarter of all agencies had home pages in 1997 and that 42 percent will have their own sites by 1999. E-mail has become more important because in 1995, 55 percent used it to receive travel requests and 56 percent said they used it to confirm bookings, while in late 1997 those numbers were 72 percent and 73 percent, respectively. Among the 96 percent of agencies with CRSs, the average automated location has eight CRTs, up from six in 1995 and possibly a reflection of consolidation taking place. Fifty-two percent of the agent locations said that they owned PCs equipped with CD-ROM capabilities, which is up from 27 percent in 1995. Because of the need for increased buying power and benefits of consortiums the trend is toward affiliation with these organizations. According to the *Travel Weekly* survey, 54 percent of all agency locations were affiliated with a leisure-oriented consortium or marketing group. Twelve years ago in 1987, only 36 percent of agency locations had such affiliations.

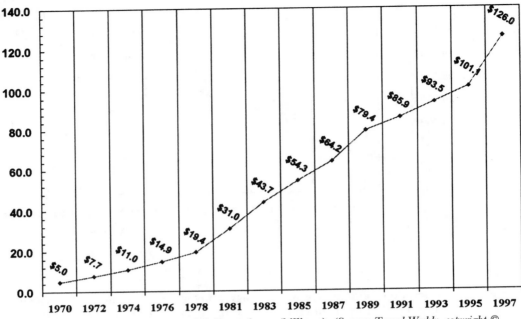

FIGURE 7.3. Agency annual dollar volume (billions). *(Source: Travel Weekly, copyright ©* *1998, Cahners Travel Group, a Division of Reed Elsevier, Inc.)*

Types of Travel Arrangements Made

As would be expected, the most common type of travel arrangement made is for air transportation. In 1997, 56 percent of total dollar volume was for air travel. Cruise sales accounted for 18 percent up from 14 percent in 1995. Much smaller proportions of the total dollar volume are attributable to lodging, car rentals, and miscellaneous arrangements; these activities accounted for 27 percent of total agency dollar volume (see Figure 7.4).

The Future of Travel Agents

One of the problems of being an intermediary (wholesaler or retailer) is that someone is always trying to eliminate you. So-called experts have been predicting for years that **intermediaries** would disappear and that with the current level of education, technology, and communication, consumers could conduct business directly with suppliers, and middlemen would gradually disappear because they were no longer needed. The experts have been wrong; intermediaries are doing more business than ever before, while at the same time there has been an increase in direct selling.

Popular questions being raised today are: Will there be a travel agent in the future? Will the web result in the demise of the travel agent? The questions are being raised because of the Internet, commission caps, commission cuts, and the changing world

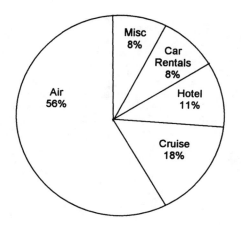

FIGURE 7.4. Sources of agency revenues by travel sector. *(Source: Travel Weekly, copyright © 1998, Cahners Travel Group, a Division of Reed Elsevier, Inc.)*

of travel. Ever since the Internet gave consumers the ability to plan and book their own travel, there has been speculation surrounding the viability of the traditional travel agent. Numerous articles have been written suggesting the downfall of the travel agent channel of distribution.

Despite the many predictions that the travel agent would disappear, the species is alive and well and will adapt to the changing marketplace and survive. Travel agents offer a valuable service that is valued by the majority of clients. The travel industry cannot get along without travel agents, and they will continue to save clients time and money far into the future.

Travel agents are the leading distributors of travel products and services. Agents book 80 percent of all air travel, 30 percent of hotel reservations, 95 percent of all cruise reservations, 50 percent of rental cars, 37 percent of rail, and 90 percent of tour packages. Agents are the best professionals to sort through nearly 100,000 daily changes in airfares alone. The authors, the television show 20/20, *Travel Trade* trade publication, and the U.S. Public Interest Research Group have all conducted tests to find the lowest price for travel, and travel agents have uncovered the best prices.

There is no question but what sales on the Internet will increase. A Travel Industry Association of America (TIA) study released in October 1997 stated that online sales amounted to $827 million in 1996 and that with future growth it will reach $8.9 billion by 2002. While that is a tremendous increase in online sales, it is not much in the total travel expenditure picture. Total travel expenditures were over $500 billion in 1998 and are expected to increase to $710 billion in 2002. If that happens, the online sales of $8.9 billion in 2002 would be 1.2 percent of the total. There is obviously room for both increased travel agents sales and online sales. The role of the Internet is examined in more detail later in this chapter.

Another factor supporting travel agents is that the industry is one of America's relatively few businesses that has used computers for years and knows the value of computer technology. John Naisbitt, in his best selling book, *Megatrends*, said "High tech requires high touch." In this day and age of the information superhighway, virtual reality, cyberspace, ticketless travel, e-mail, paging devices, and the Internet, it is the professional knowledgeable travel agent that can provide both high tech and high touch.

A large resort hotel, such as the Jasper Park Lodge in Canada, typically has a significant portion of its rooms sold through retail travel agencies. Tour companies that include the resort on their tour itineraries also bring in customers and represent another important distribution organization. *(Photo courtesy of Canadian Pacific Hotels.)*

A knowledgeable travel agent can provide time-saving, cost-saving, pleasure-adding ingredients that cannot be achieved via computer technology.

Travel agents are adapting to new ways of doing business. In spite of the Internet, commission caps, and commission cuts, agencies are continuing to achieve record travel sales volume. Travel agents are shifting their revenue sources from the airlines toward other suppliers, they are increasing in size, they are charging fees, and they are maintaining profitability in spite of cuts in their principal source of revenue. Travel agents are joining consortiums. They are creating their own web sites. While the Internet looms as a threat, it also represents an opportunity to reach a much larger audience. Fees are gaining acceptance by both agents and their clients. In a recent study by the American Society of Travel Agents (ASTA), 64 percent of agents nationwide say they now charge a fee for booking airline tickets and performing other services.

The consumer will continue to rely on agents for trip information, planning, and booking because they offer valuable professional services that save time and money. The travel industry's principal sales intermediary will not only survive, it will prosper.

Travel Agency Organizations

The **American Society of Travel Agents** (ASTA) is the largest association of travel and tourism professionals in the world with 26,500 members located in over 165 countries. Established in 1931, ASTA continues to serve the best interests of the travel industry and the traveling public. ASTA's purpose is:

- To promote and encourage travel among people of all nations
- To promote the image and encourage the use of professional travel agents worldwide
- To promote and represent the views and interests of travel agents to all levels of government and industry
- To promote professional and ethical conduct in the travel agency industry worldwide
- To serve as an information resource for the industry worldwide
- To promote consumer protection and safety for the traveler
- To sponsor and conduct educational programs for travel agents on subjects related to the travel industry
- To engage in any lawful activity that the members of the association shall deem fit and appropriate for the promotion of their common welfare

To be an active ASTA member, a travel agency must be currently accredited with the Airlines Reporting Corporation (ARC) or endorsed by the International Airlines Travel Agent Network (IATAN). All ASTA members agree to comply with the Society's Principles of Professional Conduct and Ethics.

ASTA is managed by a board of directors elected by travel agency members. Although travel agencies, through an official firm representative, are the voting members, other categories of membership include active associate, active associate independent, international, allied (includes most of the world's major travel suppliers), allied associate cruise-only, travel school, student, and senior. The association has 36 U.S. chapters and 87 international chapters; each with its own elected officers and appointed committees. All officers of ASTA are working travel agents. They are elected every two years by the society's active members. Day-to-day activities are administered by a staff of more than 90 professionals located at ASTA's world headquarters in the Washington, D.C., metropolitan area.

ASTA provides a wide range of services to its members and the travel industry, including educational seminars, the annual World Travel Congress and Trade Show, a consumer affairs program, publication of a monthly magazine (*ASTA Agency Management*) and a bimonthly newsletter (*Dateline ASTA*), a marketing services program, research and statistics programs, and a scholarship foundation. Visit the ASTA web site (**http://www.astanet.com**).

A smaller organization of travel agents is the Association of Retail Travel Agents (ARTA). The purpose of this organization is similar to that of ASTA, but ARTA does not supply the range of services provided to the members of ASTA. While ARTA addresses many travel agency issues at different levels, its two primary activities are providing education and training to its members and to lobby on their behalf. Visit their web site at **http://www.artaonline.com**. For specialized travel agencies that sell only cruises, there is the National Association of Cruise Only Agencies (NACOA). This group provides promotional and management assistance to its members. On a global scale, travel agent organizations include the International Federation of Travel Agencies, the Universal Federation of Travel Agents Association, and the World Association of Travel Agents.

Particularly in the British Commonwealth and in the United States, there are travel agents' organizations whose purpose is to raise business and professional competency and to award certification. In the United States, the Institute of Certified Travel Agents (ICTA) provides an educational and certification program leading to the designation CTC (Certified Travel Counselor) and CTA (Certified Travel Associate). The CTC curriculum covers three core areas: business development, contemporary issues, and professional development. CTC candidates are required to complete two core courses and two electives from each area, for a total of 12 CTC courses. The CTA program covers four critical skill areas. The institute has developed destination specialist courses, which cover destinations such as North America, the Caribbean, Western Europe, and the South Pacific. In addition, they have developed the Travel Agent Proficiency Test (TAP).

Similar programs are operated in the British Commonwealth by the Institute of Travel Agents in cooperation with the Association of British Travel Agents. The institute awards the designation M.T.A.I., indicating that the recipient has fulfilled the academic requirements by passing examinations leading to the certification.

INTERNET

In today's marketplace it is necessary to talk about the **Internet** as a channel of distribution. It makes direct selling from the supplier to the consumer more possible than ever before. There have always been direct sales in travel from suppliers to consumers via supplier's offices or the telephone. Telephone sales received a huge boost with the advent of 800 numbers; and at the time, 800 numbers were considered to be state-of-the-art technolgy. We have witnessed the coming of computers, central reservation systems (CRS), faxes, smart cards, videos, CD-ROMS, and the impact they have had on the travel distribution process. However, the newest technology entrant is attracting more attention and has more potential than any of its predecessors. It's the Internet. As an evolving communications tool, the Internet has vast potential because travel is an information-based product. The Internet, that vast network of computer networks around the world, confronts us with a bewildering blizzard of data. The World Wide Web is estimated to have over 64 million users in the United States and more than 320 million different pages of information. The Web gives consumers the information and power to plan and book their own travel. The Web also gives travel agents and tour operators the opportunity to have their own sites and greatly expands their reach. The Web gives suppliers (airlines, hotels, rental car companies, cruise lines, attractions, etc.) a direct sales channel that can reduce distribution costs by having the consumer do the booking, thereby eliminating travel agency commissions and computer reservation system fees. The Internet is both an information source and transaction source. Consequently, the Internet is a new marketing medium. It has the advantage that it can be used by virtually everyone in the tourism industry from the largest operator to the smallest. The airline giants and lodging giants have excellent web sites as do smaller scale businesses such as bed and breakfasts, dude ranches, ski areas, tour operators, travel agents, tourism organizations, and even restaurants. These travel suppliers have a new promotional tool to work with and one that promises cost-savings.

Electronic Commerce

E-commerce is coming of age. In fact, it is doubling every three months, according to Price Waterhouse. Electronic commerce is estimated to reach over one trillion dollars by the year 2000. Tourism-related services are one of the fastest-growing areas of Internet electronic commerce as the sales from online travel increase exponentially each year. Jupiter Communications (**http://www.jup.com**) has conducted a study for the Travel Industry Association of America entitled *Travel and Interactive Technology: A Five Year Outlook* that looks at the proliferation of travel related sites on the Internet and World Wide Web. They estimated that online revenue for 1996 reached $827 million and that by the end of 2002 these revenues will reach $8.9 billion. Jupiter is constantly updating their work, and at the June 1998 Travel and Tourism Research Association conference a representative reported that these figures are too conservative and that growth is occurring faster than earlier projections.

Creating this growth are suppliers' web sites and Internet booking services such as Microsoft's Expedia, Sabre's Travelocity, Internet Travel Network, Preview Travel, American Express, and Travel Web, which are full-service mega sites. While most airlines have sophisticated web sites for their own schedules and fares, these sites rarely show comparison rates. The consumer may find it easier to use services such as Travelocity (**www.travelocity.com**) to find helpful travel information and a comparison of fares and schedules among different airlines.

Small to medium-sized firms are using the global reach of the Web. It is serving as a great equalizer for small firms because travelers around the globe can seek out a small hotel or B & B just as easily as a five-star property. A small hotel in Amsterdam, unlisted in guidebooks, reported that 80 percent of their U.S. reservations came from the Web.

Online trends show rapid growth of online households. Estimated at 22 million in 1997, Jupiter projects that 57 million households will be online in 2002. The easiest prediction of all to make is that Internet technology and growth will become more rapid during the next five years as will the number of people who buy and sell on the Internet. The future appears bright for this new distribution channel.

Limitations

Despite its great potential, the Internet has limitations. While it is high tech, it is not high touch. It produces an overwhelming amount of information. More than the consumer can digest in many cases. It is a challenge to get the users attention long enough to deliver your message. A key to Web success is keeping information current, which is a formidable task. Nothing is worse than seeing outdated information on the Web. Speed and ease of use still need to be improved. Consumers have two major concerns about the Web. One is their right to privacy, and the other is the security of the site. Consumers question if it is safe to use their credit cards on the Internet even though it is probably much more secure than other places they are used. Travel distribution uses technology, but travel is not about technology. Travel is a complex service industry where the customer requires value. In the final analysis, consumer value will prevail over technology.

Beyond the Internet

In the ever-changing technological environment, it is essential that all components of the tourism industry, whether large or small, public or private, have the best intelligence on which to base decisions. One of the ways to do that is to tap the Internet as an information source. The day will come when a large segment of the market will communicate and transact business on the Internet as routinely as we talk on the phone today.

Another way is to think beyond the Internet. How soon will the Internet be old technology? How soon will consumers be able to book travel from all sorts of devices such as their television set or an appliance we don't know about yet in a networked home? Voice recognition systems are improving, and the price of hardware and software required to support them is declining. How soon will they become a part of the automated system? The smart agent or digital robot is a computer application that can complete specific tasks without human intervention. Will this application become commonplace?

CONSOLIDATORS

Consolidators are travel agencies that sell airline tickets at sizeable discounts. They specialize in this area and have contracts with one or more airlines to distribute discount tickets. Airlines work with consolidators to help fill what would otherwise be empty seats.

Some consolidators act strictly as wholesalers, selling their tickets only through other travel agencies. Others also sell directly to the public, usually at higher than wholesale prices. Thus, they function as both a wholesaler and a retailer.

Discount agencies sell consolidator tickets or other discounted travel services to the public. Some act as their own consolidators, while others buy from wholesale consolidators. It is now relatively easy to find a discounter that sells consolidator tickets. Consumer travel publications list consolidators, and consumers can also buy consolidator tickets from most full-service travel agencies.

THE TOUR WHOLESALER

The **tour wholesaler** (also called tour operator) puts together a tour and all its components and sells the tour through his or her own company, through retail outlets, and/or through approved retail travel agencies. Wholesalers can offer vacation packages to the traveling public at prices lower than an individual traveler can arrange because wholesalers can buy services such as transportation, hotel rooms, sightseeing services, airport transfers, and meals in large quantities at discounted prices.

Tour wholesaling became an important segment of the U.S. travel industry after World War II. It has expanded substantially since the 1960s, largely because air carriers wanted to fill the increasing numbers of aircraft seats. The tour wholesale business consists primarily of planning, preparing, and marketing a vacation tour, including making reservations and consolidating transportation and ground services into a tour assembled for a departure date to a specific destination. Tours are then sold to the public through retail outlets such as travels agents and airline ticket offices.

The independent tour operator has grown dramatically over the past decade and now numbers over 2000. A large portion of the business is concentrated in the hands of a small number of large operators.

Independent tour wholesalers provide significant revenue to transportation and ground service suppliers. They also provide the retailer and the public with a wide selection of tours to a large number of destinations at varying costs, for varying durations, and in various seasons. Furthermore, they supply advance notice and increased assurance of future passenger volumes to suppliers.

The independent tour wholesaler's business is characterized by relative ease of entry, high velocity of cash flow, low return on sales, and the potential for high return on equity because the investment necessary to start such a business is small.

Tour wholesaling businesses are usually one of four kinds: (1) the independent tour wholesaler, (2) the airline working in close cooperation with a tour wholesaling business, (3) the retail travel agent who packages tours for its clients, and (4) the operator of motor coach tours. These four entities, along with incentive travel companies and travel clubs, comprise the industry.

Figure 7.5 illustrates the position of the tour wholesaler in the basic structure of the travel industry. The public or the consumer is the driving force and can purchase travel services from a retail travel agent or directly from the suppliers of travel services: the airlines, hotels, and other providers of destination services. The tour wholesaler's

Motorcoach tours, both one-day and multi-day, are a significant component of the tour operator's business. *(Photo courtesy of Globus & Cosmos.)*

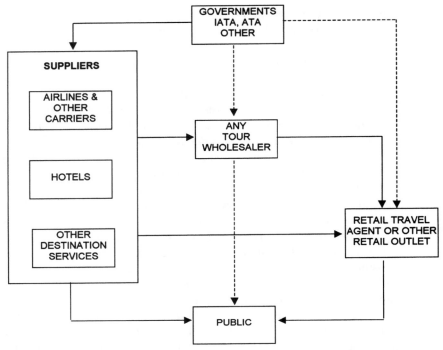

FIGURE 7.5. **Basic structure of the U.S. travel industry.** *(Source: Tour Wholesaler Industry Study, Touche, Ross & Co.)*

role is that of consolidating the services of airlines and other carriers with the ground services needed into one package, which can be sold through travel agents to the consuming public.

In 1996, the direct impact of the group tour industry in North America was estimated to be $11.6 billion in U.S. dollars. That $11.6 billion figure included an estimate of all expenditures by tour operators, both directly related to the tours they operate and for other transportation expenses, as well as the expenditures made by tour travelers white traveling.

Most of the impact was in the United States, with $9.6 billion in estimated direct impact in 1996. The impact of the tour industry in Canada was $2.0 billion in U.S. dollars.

The typical group tour of 40 passengers produces approximately $6270 in sales for each overnight stay in an average-sized North American city.

According to the United Motorcoach Association, more than 600,000 tours were operated by tour companies in the United States and Canada in 1996 (624,626), a 6.6 percent increase over 1995. The average number of passengers on one-day tours was 39.07, yielding a total of 13.3 million passenger days. Multi-day tour groups averaged 42.21 passengers, creating 12.0 million passengers on multi-day tours in 1996. In total there were 74.1 million tour passenger days in 1996. The group tour business creates a total of 194,149 full-time equivalent jobs.

Tour Wholesaler Organizations

The **National Tour Association** (NTA), founded in 1951, is the primary group tour industry association in North America. Its membership includes (a) group tour operators, who package and sell group tours in the United States, Canada, and Mexico, and (b) suppliers, whose businesses include hotels, attractions, restaurants, bus companies, airlines, passenger vessels, sightseeing companies, destination marketing organizations, and other travel and tourism entities.

The association provides marketing assistance, educational programs, governmental representation, and communications for its membership, and it annually produces the NTA Convention and Tour and Travel Exchange. This event is one of the largest travel industry gatherings held in North America, offering members the opportunity to conduct intensive business sessions and attend education seminars that increase professionalism in the industry. The association also produces the Spring Tour and Travel Exchange, which provides members with a second opportunity each year to conduct business and participate in educational programs.

NTA requires its members to adhere to a strict code of ethics that ensures proper business activity between individual members, for the ultimate good of the traveling public. The association acts as the primary advocate for consumers of the group tour product in North America and works to promote consumer awareness of that vacation alternative. NTA provides the traveling public protection through their Consumer Protection Plan. Visit their web site at **http://www.nta.online.com.**

The **U.S. Tour Operators Association** (USTOA) also represents tour operators. The goals of USTOA are to ensure consumer protection and education; to inform the travel industry, government agencies, and the public about tour operators' activities and objectives; to maintain a high level of professionalism within the industry; and to facilitate travel on a worldwide basis. USTOA's members must subscribe to the organization's strict code of ethics. Members are required to represent all information pertaining to tours, to maintain a high level of professionalism, and to state clearly all costs and facilities in advertising and promotional materials.

Most tour operators and wholesalers belong to the American Society of Travel Agents. Many also belong to the various promotional groups such as PATA (Pacific Asia Travel Association), ACTO (Association of Caribbean Tour Operators), and TIA (Travel Industry Association of America).

Local or short tours are conducted by sightseeing companies, and many of them are organized into American Sightseeing International and Grayline. These organizations aid sightseeing companies by providing local sightseeing services and competent personnel. Many sightseeing tour companies are also affiliated with the organizations already mentioned.

SPECIALTY CHANNELERS

Specialty intermediaries include such organizations as incentive travel firms, business meeting and convention planners, corporate travel offices, association executives, hotel representatives, travel consultants, and supplier sales offices. While specialty intermediaries are a small force in distribution compared to travel agencies, they have considerable

Tour operators plan and organize all elements of a trip, such as this photo safari in a Kenya national park. *(Photo by Richard Ryel; courtesy of International Expeditions, Inc.)*

power to influence when, where, and how people travel. Such groups, can represent either buyers or sellers, receiving either a commission or a salary from their employer. Specialty intermediaries are experts in their particular aspect of travel. As tourism becomes more specialized, these types of channelers will become increasingly important.

Incentive Travel Firms

Incentive travel has been enjoying significant growth because travel rewards are one of the most powerful motivators for increased employee performance. Companies can reward distributors, customers, and their employees. In the United States there are about 500 travel incentive planning firms selling their professional services of designing, promoting, and accomplishing incentive travel programs for buyers. They have a national trade association, the Society of Incentive Travel Executives (SITE). E. F. MacDonald and Maritz are leading companies.

Corporate Travel Departments

Just as many corporations have chosen to set up their own meeting planning departments, many also have travel sections. Growth in this area took place when the airline industry was deregulated in the late 1970s. Such in-house offices try to contain travel and entertainment costs by getting the best prices on travel. They typically provide the same services as those of travel agencies serving the corporate market.

Hotel Sales Representative Firms

Companies specialize in representing hotels, motels, resorts, and destination areas. This type of firm provides an alternative to a property hiring its own sales force and is an economical way to be represented in foreign markets. These firms are also active in the convention and meetings field.

Automated Distribution

Using telephone lines, the satellite ticket printer (STP) enables a travel agency to print tickets electronically in an office of a corporation that the agency serves thus eliminating the cost of delivering tickets. If this corporation wishes to use a particular agency's expertise, they can do so, regardless of the distance involved. Also, the corporation's travel expenses can be summarized into one periodic account—a beneficial arrangement. Automated ticketing machines (ATMs) are owned by airlines and located in major airports for passenger convenience. The customer inserts a credit card into the machine, which provides flight information, makes a reservation, and prints a ticket and boarding pass.

CHOOSING CHANNELS

Any marketing officer must decide on which combination of distribution channels would be most productive. One of his or her most important tasks is to research and identify distribution possibilities. Then the particular travel product can be integrated into the distributor's operation. Some channels are very evident, such as travel agencies. However, depending on the individual product, additional distributors, such as tour companies, specialty channelers, incentive travel firms, corporate travel departments, hotel sales reps, and associations, can be very sales-effective. Often, associations have huge numbers of members, which make them particualry good avenues for increasing sales.

SUMMARY

Tourism channels of distribution are organizational links in a travel product producer's system of describing, selling, and confirming travel arrangements to the buyer. Such channels are needed because it is impractical for any supplier to own sales outlets in every market city. It is much more feasible and productive to distribute the product, for example, through 30,000 retail travel agencies. A commission is paid for each sale made. There are specialty channelers of many kinds.

The Internet is a new force in the sale of travel today. It will grow in importance in the future and have an impact on the travel distribution system. Travel distribution channels are similar to those used in other industries. But tourism products are intangible. They cannot be stored and sold another time. An airplane seat, if not occupied for a trip, is revenue lost forever.

ABOUT THE READING

This reading was prepared by ASTA and answers the question: Why use an ASTA travel agent?

READING 7.1

WHY USE AN ASTA TRAVEL AGENT?

For savings and convenience. Planning a trip today can be confusing and time-consuming. A travel agent not only arranges the various modes of transportation, but also may be able to save you money with early booking discounts, special fares, accommodation details, and travel advisories. But don't just take our word for it. See what the President of Crystal Cruises has to say about using a travel agent.

Benefits of Using an ASTA Travel Agent

ASTA travel agents are knowledgeable professionals that uphold a strict code of ethics. The Society provides education, training, and resource materials to its members to equip them with the tools they need to offer you the highest quality of service. Knowledgeable ASTA travel agents keep up-to-date by attending industry events that offer educational seminars and networking opportunities.

The ASTA membership includes over 18,000 travel agencies across the United States and around the world. Most ASTA member agencies offer one-stop shopping for all travel arrangements. To find the ASTA member agency nearest you, search the ASTAnet Travel Directory.

ASTA's priority is fighting for your best interests. We have a long-standing record of fighting for consumer rights. Also, should you ever encounter a problem with an ASTA member, our Consumer Affairs Department is here to help you. We want you to have a safe and happy trip. Start by seeing your local ASTA member travel agency.

How Do You Find a Good Travel Agent?

Choose one like you would a doctor or lawyer. Get advice from friends and relatives who use an agent they trust. Because travel choices are personal decisions that reflect individual desires and lifestyles, you will want to visit or call several agencies to find the one that best suits your needs. Consider everything from the appearance of the office to the agent's willingness to answer questions. The best agents want to establish a long-term relationship with a client, not just make one sale.

What Should be the Determining Factor in Choosing a Travel Agency?

Your agency should belong to the American Society of Travel Agents, Inc. (ASTA). With over 26,500 members in 168 countries, ASTA is the largest and most influential travel trade association in the world. Membership includes travel agencies, airlines, hotels, railroads, cruise lines, tour operators, car rental companies, and travel schools. Through its continuing education and training programs, ASTA prepares its members to operate high-caliber, competitive businesses. Members also have the ASTA Travel Agent Manual, the only comprehensive guide to operating a travel agency. Due to the Society's on-going educational programs, resource materials and stringent Code of Ethics, ASTA travel agents are known as dedicated, hard-working professionals who provide superior service to their customers.

What Special Services Do Travel Agencies Offer?

As the industry grows more competitive, travel agencies increase the quality and type of services they offer. Agents can arrange all types of domestic and international travel, from hotel and resort accommodations to air and ground transportation, including car rental needs and tour packages. They can provide assistance with insurance protection, passport and visa applications, inoculation procedures, and other foreign travel requirements. Many have toll-free phone numbers and offer meeting planning and incentive travel services.

Some agents maintain automated individual profiles that include the client's frequent flyer number, airline seating preference, smoking or nonsmoking designation, and other specifications for a custom-designed trip. Boarding passes are often issued in advance as an added convenience. Arrangements can also be tailored to suit business and vacation objectives, personal interests, and budget concerns. Although most provide a wide range of services, some agencies may specialize in areas such as family travel, group travel, adventure travel, ecotourism, the mature market, incentive travel, or travel for the disabled.

How Do I Know If My Travel Agent Is Consumer-Conscious?

Membership in ASTA is a sign of consumer awareness. The Society works on behalf of its members to support pro-consumer issues. In addition to lobbying for consumer protection on issues like airline bankruptcy and travel safety, ASTA has an active Consumer Affairs Department that monitors travelers' problems and helps to find solutions. The Society works closely with other travel organizations to continually upgrade service and technology to better serve the traveling public.

How Do I Know If My Travel Agent Is Well-Trained?

Ask about your agent's professional background. Many have been trained in business management, travel and tourism, or geography. Others have supplemented their agency experience with extensive education and training courses, such as ASTA's Travel Management Academy, one of the most intensive programs in the industry. Some travel agents are Certified Travel Counselors (CTC), having completed an educational program with the Institute of Certified Travel Agents.

Benefits of Using an ASTA Travel Agent

Save Money: Strong working relationships with travel suppliers and the latest in computer reservations technology enable ASTA agents to access the most up-to-date information on how to get you the best value. *Traveler Advocates:* Your best interests are the priority. ASTA has a long-standing record of fighting for consumer rights, and ASTA travel agents are required to adhere to a stringent Code of Ethics. *Convenience:* The ASTA membership includes over 18,000 travel agencies across the country, most of which offer one-stop shopping for all travel arrangements. *Service:* ASTA travel agents are knowledgeable and active in the industry. The Society provides education, training, and resource materials to its members to equip them with the tools to offer the highest quality of service.

More About the Benefits of Using a Travel Agent

An Open Letter to Travel Editors from Joseph A. Watters, President, Crystal Cruises, June 11, 1998

Dear Travel Editor,

Why should I use a travel agent? As a veteran travel executive, that's a question I'm often asked. Today, with the overwhelming number of sources for travel information (the Internet, cable television, newspapers, magazines, guidebooks, etc.), it's no wonder the consumer is confused. Yet that's precisely why the services of a professional travel consultant are more valuable than ever.

In January, the television news magazine, 20/20, reported the results of a test in which travel agents beat consumers at uncovering the best airfares. However, it is much more than the "lowest fare" that provides the compelling argument for a good travel agent.

The best thing an agent can do is to match up a traveler with the vacation that's right for them. The professional travel consultant builds relationships with their clients to learn their interests and lifestyles, as well as their dispositions.

Below is a list of some of the important services, which are provided either free or for a nominal charge, by travel agents:

1. *Distilling the product information:* Through an ongoing and time-consuming process of familiarization, continuing education and customer feedback, the agent becomes a travel expert.

2. *Investigating and supplying competitive information:* No single supplier is going to advise a consumer that a better route or a better fare is available on a competing carrier.

3. *Staying abreast of the most current and timely promotions:* Via daily faxes, agent-only e-mail transmissions, and their relationships with their district sales managers, agents are obtaining the most current promotional information.

4. *Analyzing the current promotions:* The cheapest is not always the best.

5. *Clarifying the fine print, such as cancellation penalties and restrictions:* Again, the benefits of a professional's experience can save a traveler money . . . and headaches.

6. *Making recommendations for travel-related options:* Travel agents share the experience and knowledge they accumulate about a variety of travel topics—from where to eat, where to shop, and what to pack.

7. *Simplifying the research and subsequent transaction*: Like a personal shopper, agents can provide one-stop shopping for travelers who require air arrangements, rental cars, cruise accommodations, and hotel stays—with suggestions that are in the best interest of the client, not the supplier.

8. *Enhancing the trip with value-added benefits and amenities*: Agents can add to the clients' experience by sending a bottle of wine or providing a special land package, a specific escort, or other customer amenities.

9. *Using their clout to obtain the best possible in seemingly impossible situations*: Whether it's airline seats, hotel rooms or cruise space, the travel agent has more buying power than the consumer.

10. *Getting problems resolved*: The agent serves as the consumers' advocate in the event something inadvertently goes wrong. The use of outside service providers for many transactions, such as tax preparation, isn't questioned. Similarly, if one is going to spend hundreds or thousands of dollars, as well as a good chunk of valuable leisure time; it makes great sense to use a professional.

I hope you'll consider sharing this information in future consumer interest columns.

Sincerely,

JOSEPH A. WATTERS
President

KEY CONCEPTS

American Society of Travel Agents
automated distribution
choosing channels
corporate travel departments
distribution channels

domination of travel agencies
hotel sales representatives
incentive travel firms
intermediaries
Internet

National Tour Association
retail travel agencies
specialty channelers
tour wholesalers
U.S. Tour Operators Association

 ## INTERNET SITES

The Internet sites mentioned in this chapter are repeated here for convenience plus some selected additional sites. For more information, visit these sites. Be aware that Internet addresses change frequently, so if a site cannot be accessed, use a search engine. Also use a search engine to locate many additional sites that are available.

American Society of Travel Agents
http://www.astanet.com

Association of Retail Travel Agents
http://www.artaonline.com

Gray Line Worldwide
http://www.grayline.com

Internet Travel Network
http://www.itn.com

Jupiter Communications
http://www.jup.com

Microsoft Expedia
http://www.expedia.com

National Tour Association
http://www.ntaonline.com

Rocky Mountain International
http://www.RM1-RealAmerica.com

Society of Travel Agents in Government
http://www.government-travel.org

Travel Industry Association of America
http://www.ita.org

Travelocity
http://www.travelocity.com

Travel Technology Association
http://trav.org/tta

Travel Web
http://www.travelweb.com

Travel Weekly
http://www.twcrossroads.com

U.S. Tour Operators Association
http://www.ustoa.com

INTERNET EXERCISES

Activity 1

Site Name: Expedia Travel

URL: http://expedia.msn.com/daily/home/default.hts

Background Information: This site features comprehensive destination information, timely and relevant travel news, expert advice, the lowdown on deals, and much more.

Site Name: Travelocity

URL: http://www.travelocity.com/

Background Information: Travelocity, powered by the SABRE system, provides reservations capabilities for over 420 airlines, 40,000 hotels, and more than 50 car rental companies.

Exercise

1. Describe the features of these two sites and identify their role in the tourism distribution system.

Activity 2

Site Name: The National Tour Association

URL: http://www.ntaonline.com/

Background Information: The National Tour Association is a nonprofit organization of tour companies. Their mission is to foster professionalism in the tourism industry by supporting education, research, and industry relations for the benefit of the traveling public.

Exercise

1. As a reward for employees in your organization who met and exceeded a corporate goal, you have been asked to prepare a complete incentive travel package to a desirable location. Choose a travel destination, mode of travel to the destination, local transportation, accommodations, and restaurants in the area for this travel incentive package.

QUESTIONS FOR REVIEW AND DISCUSSION

1. As a producer of travel products, why not just sell your services directly to the consumer?

2. For what reasons do retail travel agencies dominate tourism distribution channels? What accounts for their remarkable growth in numbers?

3. Give some examples of marketing aids that a supplier might provide to your travel agency.

4. Some counselors are not really good salespersons. As manager of your agency, what skill-building program would you inaugurate if needed?

5. You are marketing director for a cruise line operating truly luxurious ships. These have superb service and cuisine. How would you proceed to identify the most promising distributors?

6. Air travel sales constitute the bulk of a travel agency's business. But auto travel makes up 80 percent of the intercity U.S. market. How could agencies increase their auto travel-related business?

7. As the president of a newly formed tour company, you must now decide if your tours are to be marketed through retail travel agencies or whether you should try to sell them directly to the consumer. Identify the advantages and disadvantages of each alternative. Would it be wise to do both? Discuss.

8. Why should an independently owned and operated travel agency become affiliated with one of the consortia, cooperatives, or franchise groups?

9. Could there be a difference in the functioning of a tour wholesaler and a tour operator? Explain.

10. List the advantages of a tour company becoming a member of USTOA.

11. Similarly, what advantages does a travel agency derive from its membership in ASTA?

12. A fairly large manufacturer of specialty electric products is located in your city. What steps would you take to sell this company on an incentive travel plan?

13. List the names of several prominent hotel rep firms. Explain how they function in behalf of an independently owned resort hotel. Would a Holiday Inn use such a firm? Why or why not?

CASE PROBLEMS

1. Joan S. and her husband are planning a vacation to a destination about which they know very little. They have seen an exciting ad for this area in a travel magazine. They respond to the ad, and subsequently they receive a group of fascinating brochures describing all the attractions, accommodations, shops, climate, and other allures. In the same magazine they saw an ad for an airline that serves this destination, including an 800 telephone number for reservations. Why should they seek the help of an travel agency?

2. A professor recently walked into a travel agency—his first visit there—and asked for a specific cruise brochure. The travel agent rose from her desk, found the promotional piece requested, and handed it to him. The professor thanked her and then asked, "How is the travel business these days?" She replied, "Business and corporate are OK but vacation travel is way off. Very few people are traveling now." She then sat down, looked into her CRS screen and said, "Have a nice day." Can you believe such a scenario? What *should* the conversation have been?

3. A prominent national columnist recently advised his readers that they should bypass their local travel agencies and obtain their air tickets and arrange their cruise vacations directly from these suppliers. This recommendation was intended to save the public money because, he explained, air and ship lines pay commissions to travel agencies whenever a sale is made. What's wrong with such advice?

4. An international tour company partnership is owned by Bill and Jane W. Bill is a rather deliberate, cautious type; Jane tends to be more aggressive and promotional in her day-to-day business relationships. The company's volume of business has declined somewhat during the past two years. Considering this problem, they recently had an extended discussion as to possible steps that might increase tour sales. Jane finally proposed that they should contact some of the largest travel agency cooperatives. These are also known as coops, consortia, franchisors, joint marketing organizations, stockholder licensee groups, and individual and corporate-owned chains. Jane thought that perhaps if their company could become a so-called "preferred supplier" to one or several of these groups, they would then increase their business considerably. Almost all of their tours are sold through retail travel agencies. Bill listened to this suggestion and then said. "I doubt that this idea would do us any good. The coop movement is not well established, and a lot of agencies are not members at all." Who's right? Why? Explain your position.

SELECTED REFERENCES

Buhalis, D., A.M. Tjoa, and J. Jafari, eds. *Information and Communication Technologies in Tourism: Enter 98.* Vienna: Springer-Verlag, 1998.

Duke, Charles R, and Margaret A. Persia. "Consumer-Defines Dimensions for the Escorted Tour Industry Segment: Expectations, Satisfactions, and Importance." *Journal of Travel and Tourism Marketing,* Vol. 5, Nos. 1 and 2, pp. 77–99, 1996.

Duvall, Patricia W., Ray M. Haynes, and Lawrence J. Truitt. "Evaluating Small Travel Agency Productivity." *Journal of Travel Research,* Vol. 31, No. 3, pp. 10–13, Winter 1993.

Evans, Nigel G., and Mike J. Stabler. "A Future for the Package Tour Operator in the 25th Century?" *Tourism Economics,* Vol. 1, No. 3, pp. 245–264, September 1995.

Friedheim, Eric. *Travel Agencies: From Caravans and Clippers to the Concorde* New York: Travel Agent Magazine Books, 1992.

Gilbert, D.C., and P. Houghton. "An Exploratory Investigation of Format, Design, and Use of UK Tour Operators' Brochures." *Journal of Travel Research,* Vol. 30, No. 2, pp. 20–25, Fall 1991.

Goldsmith, Ronald E., Leisa Reinecke Flynn, and

Mark Bonn. "An Empirical Study of Heavy Users of Travel Agencies." *Journal of Travel Research*, Vol. 33, No. 1, pp. 38–43, Summer 1994.

Hope, Christine, Robert Hope, and Lara Tavridou. "The Impact of Information Technology on Distribution Channels." *The Tourist Review*, No. 4, pp. 9–14, 1997.

Hoyle, Leonard, David C. Dorf, and Thomas J. Jones. *Managing Conventions and Group Business*. East Lansing, MI: Educational Institute of the American Hotel and Motel Association, 1989.

ICTA. "6th Annual Salary and Compensation Survey." Institute of Certified Travel Agents, *Travel Counselor*, pp. 20–52, August 26, 1996.

Illum, Steve, and Allen Schaefer. "Destination Attributes: Perspectives of Motorcoach Tour Operators and Destination Marketers." *Journal of Travel and Tourism Marketing*, Vol. 4, No. 4, pp. 1–14, 1995.

Jones, Peter, Simon Hudson, and Philip Costis. "New Product Development in the U.K. Tour-Operating Industry." *Progress in Tourism and Hospitality Research*, Vol. 3, No. 4, pp. 283–294, December 1997.

Jupiter Communications. *Online Travel Market: Five-Year Outlook*. New York: Jupiter Communications, 1997.

King, Brian. "Tour Operators and the Air Inclusive Tour Industry in Australia." *Travel and Tourism Analysis*, No. 3, pp. 66–87, 1991.

Laws, Eric. *Managing Packaged Tourism*. Boston: International Thomson Business Press, 1997.

Loban, Scott R. "A Framework for Computer-Assisted Travel Counselling." *Annals of Tourism Research*, Vol. 24, No. 4, pp. 813–834, October 1997.

Marcussen, Carl H. "Marketing European Tourism Products via the Internet/WWW." *Journal of Travel and Tourism Marketing*, Vol. 6, No. 3 and 4, pp. 23-34, 1997.

Morrell, Peter S. "Airline Sales and Distribution Channels: The Impact of New Technology." *Tourism Economics*, Vol. 4, No. 1, pp. 5–20, March 1998.

National Tour Foundation. *Group Travel Report*. Lexington, KY: NTF, 1990.

Oppermann, Martin. "Service Attributes of Travel Agencies: A Comparative Perspective of Users and Provides." *Journal of Vacation Marketing*, Vol. 4, No. 3, pp. 265–281, 1998.

Poon, A. *Tourism, Technology and Competitive Strategies*. Wallingford, Oxon, England: CAB International, 1993.

Quiroga, Isabel. "Characteristics of Package Tours in Europe." *Annals of Tourism Research*, Vol. 17; No. 2, pp. 185–207, 1990.

Reed Travel Group. *1998 Travel Weekly U.S. Travel Agency Market Survey*. Secaucus, NJ: Reed, 1998.

Renshaw, M. B. *The Travel Agent*. Sunderland, England: Business Education, 1997.

Runzheimer and Company. *1990–91 Survey and Analysis of Business Travel Policies and Costs*. Northbrook, IL: Runzheimer, 1991.

Rutledge, Joy L., and John F. Hunter. "Relation, by States, between Population and Number of Travel Agencies." *Journal of Travel Research*, Vol. 34, No. 4, pp. 73–76, Spring 1996.

Ryan, Chris, and Andrew Cliff. "Do Travel Agencies Measure Up to Customer Expectations? An Empirical Investigation of Travel Agencies' Service Quality as Measured by SERVQUAL." *Journal of Travel and Tourism Marketing*, Vol. 6, No. 2, pp. 1–32, 1997.

Sheldon, P. J. "Incentive Travel: Insights into Its Consumers." *Journal of Travel and Tourism Marketing*, Vol. 3, No. 2, pp. 19–34, 1994.

Sheldon, P. J. *Tourism Information Technology*. Wallingford, Oxon, England: CAB International, 1997.

Tjoa, A. M., ed. *Information and Communication Technologies in Tourism: Enter 97*. Vienna: Springer-Verlag, 1997.

TIA. *Travel and Interactive Technology: A Five-Year Outlook*. Washington D.C.: Travel Industry Association of America, 1997.

TIA. *Travelers' Use of the Internet*. Washington, D.C.: Travel Industry of Association of America, 1997.

TIA. *Technology and Travel*. Washington D.C.: Travel Industry Association of America, December 1998.

CHAPTER 8

ATTRACTIONS, ENTERTAINMENT, RECREATION, AND OTHER

- Examine the attractions sphere.

- Look at the role of theme parks.

- Understand the gaming industry.

- Describe public and commercial recreation facilities.

- Recognize shopping as a travel attraction.

◄ **LEARNING OBJECTIVES**

◄ *Preserved castles, mansions, and gardens are a popular tourist attraction throughout the continent of Europe. Shown here is Leeds Castle, in Kent, England. (Photo courtesy of the British Tourist Authority.)*

INTRODUCTION

One can make the argument that attractions are the reason people travel. If so, attractions are the most important component in the tourism system; and a case could be made that due to their importance in the tourism system, they should be covered in Chapter 1 rather than Chapter 8. There is no doubt that attractions are the main motivators for travel. Without attractions drawing tourists to destinations, there would be little need for all other tourism services such as transportation, lodging, food, distribution, and so on. However, as important as attractions are in motivating the tourist to travel, the attraction frequently receives the smallest portion of the tourist's expenditure. An example is the ski resort that sells only the lift ticket providing uphill transportation. This expenditure is the smallest of the travel experience, with the most expenditures going for air transportation, lodging, and food.

The list of attractions is extensive, and in many cases it is a combination of attractions that brings the tourist to a destination area. The opportunities for sightseeing, shopping, entertainment, gaming, culture, and recreation play an important role in determining the competitiveness of a destination.

ATTRACTIONS

Attractions can be classified in a number of ways (see Figure 8.1). One of the categories that first comes to mind is theme or amusement parks. The roots of these attractions go back to medieval Europe, when pleasure gardens were created. These gardens were the forerunner of today's parks, featuring rides, fireworks, dancing, and games. Today, theme parks are high-profile attractions made famous by Disney, Universal Studios, Busch Gardens, and others. They represent multimillion-dollar investments.

Natural attractions are the "mainspring" that drive many people to travel. The great national parks of the United States and other countries, such as those in Canada, India, Australia, and Japan, are examples. National forests in the United States attract millions of recreationists. State parks exist in many areas that have tourist appeal. The same is so for botanical, zoological, mountain, and seaside parks. Thus, these natural wonders lure travelers to enjoy the natural beauty, recreation, and inspiration that they provide.

Heritage attractions (such as historic sites) and prehistoric and archeological sites (such as the ancient monuments of Egypt, Greece, Israel, Turkey, Indonesia, India, Mexico, and Peru) also have appeal for those inspired to learn more about contemporary and long-vanished civilizations.

Recreation attractions maintain and provide access to indoor and outdoor facilities where people can participate in sports and other recreational activities. Examples include swimming pools, bowling alleys, ice skating rinks, golf courses, ski resorts, hiking trails, bicycle paths, and marinas.

Commercial attractions are retail operations dealing in gifts, handcrafted goods, art, and souvenirs that attract tourists. Recent surveys show that shopping is the number one activity participated in by both domestic and international visitors.

Industrial attractions cannot be overlooked. Wineries and breweries have long

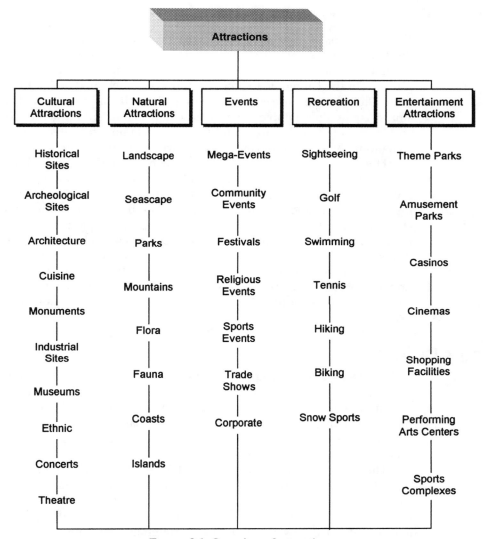

FIGURE 8.1 Overview of attractions.

been tourist attractions. Factory tours are growing in number, and manufacturers have developed elaborate facilities to handle tourists. An example is the Waterford Crystal Factory in Ireland, which houses a world-class crystal museum.

Great modern cities with their cultural treasures of many sorts provide powerful attractions to millions of visitors each year. Sightseeing tours are provided in most cities, giving easy access to the city's attractions. Theaters, museums, special buildings, zoos, aquariums, cultural events, festivals, shopping, and dining are some of the appeals.

Entertainment has become a powerful magnet. Musical entertainment has put Nashville, Tennessee and Branson, Missouri on the map.

The Attractions Industry

The attractions industry consists of fixed-location amusement parks and attractions in the United States and 40 other countries. They are primarily private businesses, although there are a number of publicly operated facilities. Amusement parks and attractions in the United States generate approximately $5.5 billion in annual revenues. Over 275,000 people are employed seasonally by the industry in the United States, and almost 265 million people visited amusement parks and attractions (including water parks, miniature golf courses, and family entertainment centers) according to the International Association of Amusement Parks and Attractions.

The attractions industry is dominated by Disneyland and Disney World, which have been two of the most successful attractions ever developed. However, while theme parks are a major tourist attraction, there are more than 10,000 natural scenic, historic, cultural, and entertainment attractions that appeal to travelers. Attractions include not only theme parks but also the entertainment park, amusement park, animal park, museum, scenic railway, historic village, preserved mansion, scenic cruise, natural wonder, restaurant, music festival, industry exhibit, cave, theater, historic farm, scenic overlook, resort complex, historic site, botanical garden, arboretum, plantation, hall of fame, water show, zoo, sports complex, cultural center, state park, national park, county park, outdoor theater, Native American reservation, and transportation exhibit.

Theme Parks

The **theme park business** has enjoyed spectacular expansion since the opening of Disneyland in 1955 in Anaheim, California. The opening of Disneyland changed the local amusement park business considerably because it expanded the concept of amusement parks from simply rides and carnival barkers to include shows, shops, and restaurants in theme settings with immaculate cleanliness, promising adventure, history, science fiction, and fantasy.

The success of Disneyland brought Disney World, the largest and grandest theme park in the world, with its Magic Kingdom as the focal point of the resort complex. The Magic Kingdom attracts over 17.0 million visitors annually (see Table 8.1). The Orlando site also has a 7500-acre conservation project for the preservation of fauna and wildlife of the everglades; an experimental prototype community of tomorrow (EPCOT); the Disney World Showcase, where several nations feature exhibits of their country's attractions and culture; Disney-MGM Studios; and Pleasure Island. Their newest attraction is Animal Kingdom.

As in the past, the Walt Disney Company's four theme parks hold down the top four positions in Table 8.1, accounting for a total of 53.6 million visits. Table 8.2 shows that Disney Paris also leads in European attendance.

As would be expected, the success of the Disney theme parks brought imitators and large corporations to the business. In addition to those listed in Table 8.1, other prominent theme parks are Sea World in San Antonio, Texas; Great America, Santa Clara, California; Canada's Wonderland, Toronto, Ontario; Busch Gardens, Williamsburg, Virginia; and Legoland, Carlsbad, California.

The nation's major theme parks appear to be concentrated in Florida and California. Disney has projects in both states, and the Orlando, Florida area has the largest

America's first theme park, Knott's Berry Farm, has 150 acres of rides, live shows, and family adventures, celebrating the lure and lore of the West. Snoopy is part of the magic at Knott's. Camp Snoopy is the official six-acre home of the Peanuts gang. *(Photo courtesy of Knott's Berry Farm.)*

TABLE 8.1
Top U.S. Theme Parks

Rank, 1997	Theme Park and Location	Attendance (in millions)
1	The Magic Kingdom, Orlando	17.0
2	Disneyland, Anaheim, California	14.3
3	Epcot, Orlando	11.8
4	Disney-MGM Studios, Orlando	10.5
5	Universal Studios, Orlando	8.9
6	Universal Studios, Los Angeles	5.4
7	Sea World of Florida, Orlando	4.9
8	Busch Gardens Tampa Bay, Tampa	4.2
9	Sea World of California, San Diego	4.0
10[a]	Six Flags Great Adventure, Jackson, New Jersey	3.7
10[a]	Knott's Berry Farm, Buena Park, California	3.7

[a] Tie.

Source: Amusement Business.

TABLE 8.2

Top European Theme Park Admissions

Rank, 1997	Park and Location	Attendance, 1997 (in millions)
1	Disneyland Paris, Marne la Vallee, France	12.6
2	Blackpool (U.K.) Pleasure Beach	7.8
3	Tivoli Gardens, Copenhagen	3.2
4[a]	De Efteling, Kaatsheuvel, the Netherlands	3.0
5[a]	Port Aventura, Salou, Spain	3.0
6	Gardaland, Castelnuovo del Garda, Italy	2.8
7[b]	Alton Towers, North Staffordshire, U.K.	2.7
7[b]	Europa Park, Rust, Germany	2.7
9	Liseberg, Goteborg, Sweden	2.5
10	Warner Bros. Movie World, Bottrop, Germany	2.1

[a] Tie.

[b] Tie.

Source: Amusement Business.

number of theme parks and attractions in any single location. This concentration is likely to continue, because new attractions or expansions are still taking place in the area.

Industry representatives predict that an area to watch for the future is the development of theme parks in conjunction with shopping malls. The activity at the West Edmonton, Canada mall complex and the Mall of America in Minnesota has encouraged this prediction.

Substantial attendance growth and expansion is taking place at amusement parks. Disney and Universal are leading the expansion, with multimillion-dollar investments in new theme parks.

One of the most expensive theme parks ever built, Disney's Animal Kingdom, opened to the public on April 22, 1998, to rave reviews and huge crowds. The 500-acre, $800 million park, located on the 47-mile Central Florida complex known as Walt Disney World, is expected to draw 10 million visitors annually. It's the fourth theme park on the Florida Disney property.

Visionland, near Birmingham, Alabama, is the other new park that opened in 1998. The $65 million park is unique in that it was developed by a consortium of 11 local governments who banded together to do something to help bring tourism to the Birmingham area. Visionland has a ride park, with a highly regarded wooden roller coaster, a water park, and an indoor family entertainment center.

There is also a great deal of excitement about the capital improvement programs and ride additions at existing parks. In all, there are nearly 40 roller coasters debuting in North America in 1998 and nearly 70 throughout the world.

Among the new coasters, Six Flags Theme Parks continue to cash in on the Batman theme, with four of its parks adding new coasters with the popular theme. They range from the Riddler-themed stand-up roller coaster at Six Flags Magic Mountain, near Los Angeles, to the twin racing steel coasters, Batman & Robin, at Six Flags Great Adventure in Jackson, New Jersey.

One of the tallest and fastest steel coasters in the United States has opened as

Miami Seaquarium, another type of theme park, features performances that constantly amaze visitors. Children and families are especially enthralled by the agility of the animals. *(Photo courtesy of Miami Seaquarium.)*

Mamba at Worlds of Fun in Kansas City, Missouri. The first hill has a drop of 205 feet, and riders go over 5600 feet of track at 75 miles per hour.

A new breed of roller coaster made its debut at Paramount's Great America in Santa Clara, California. Half of it is a boomerang-style, and the other half is an inverted looping coaster. Put them together and you have Invertigo. Liseberg Park in Gothenburg, Sweden has the only other Invertigo, which they named Hang Over.

Two big wooden coasters are making their premiers this summer. Roar has opened at Adventure World in Largo, Maryland as the most elaborate wooden coaster of the year with 12 banked curves, 20 crossovers, and six switches in direction, all within 3500 feet of track. Twin dueling wooden coasters will be opening at Kentucky Kingdom in Louisville, Kentucky. To be known as Twisted Sisters, two different coasters share the same loading station. They head out in different directions, Stella one way, Lola the other. They charge at each other four times, making it appear that a head-on collision is imminent.

The world's only half-coaster is the Journey to Atlantis at Sea World in Orlando, Florida. The ride starts out as a heavily themed water flume ride through the lost city of Atlantis. After the expected big splash, where you will get soaked, the boats head back inside, where they become roller coaster trains. After a drop and several steep turns, it becomes a flume again for the last of the ride. This is the first thrill ride at Sea World Orlando.

The largest nonride is the Twister attraction at Universal Studios Florida in Orlando. Based on the hit movie of the same name, guests experience—from only a few yards away—the world's largest indoor tornado. There's rain, there's thunder, there's lightning. It's truly an amazing attraction!

These are selected examples of the type of improvements that take place each year. The industry is constantly making annual improvements that range from fresh paint to multimillion-dollar rides to entire new parks.

International Association of Amusement Parks and Attractions

The world's largest amusement park and attractions association is the **International Association of Amusement Parks and Attractions** (IAAPA). The association, founded in 1918, has over 5000 members in 72 countries. It represents and serves operators of amusement parks, tourist attractions, water parks, miniature golf courses, family entertainment centers, and manufacturers and suppliers of amusement equipment and services. The association conducts research, compiles statistics, and publishes *Fun World, Family Entertainment Center* and an annual *International Directory and Buyers Guide.* They hold an annual convention and trade show. Located in Alexandria, Virginia, they can be reached at (703) 836-4800 or **www.iaapa.org.**

GAMING

The U.S. gaming–entertainment industry has seen tremendous change over the last 10 years. As recently as 1988, only two states permitted casino gaming—Nevada and New Jersey—and now, as we approach 2000, with Indian gaming included, 26 states have casino gaming. Today, there are only two states—Hawaii and Utah—that have no legalized gaming whatsoever.

Gambling, or the **gaming industry,** has become a major force in the tourism industry. The gaming industry has grown from a narrow Nevada base with limited acceptance in the financial and public sector to a recognized growth industry. While gaming has always been a popular form of recreation, it has also been controversial.

There is no question that gaming generates travel. Nevada has been the leader in gambling, which has made tourism the leading industry in the state. Las Vegas is considered the casino capital of the world. It is interesting to note the differences in the types of tourists and their modes of transportation when comparing Las Vegas and Atlantic City. Las Vegas attracts destination visitors from long distances who fly or drive, while Atlantic City is located in a densely populated area and attracts nearby (within 150 miles) residents. Atlantic City has successfully promoted short-duration motorcoach tours to increase its numbers. It is also now successfully promoting itself as a destination area.

Today, according to the American Gambling Association, the gaming industry is a $47.6 billion business that employs, directly and indirectly, more than one million men and women. This includes all forms of gaming, including casinos, Indian gaming, charitable organizations, the parimutuel industry, and lotteries. United States gaming revenue has grown an average of 11 percent annually between 1982 and 1996, and the casino industry's revenues alone have more than doubled since 1990. In 1996, casinos alone generated upwards of $25 billion in revenue. Over the past 20 years, the average economic growth rate in Nevada alone has been 4.6 percent com-

Gaming as a recreational pursuit is becoming more popular, especially in the United States. It is often combined with other types of entertainment such as night club shows and sports activities. *(Photo courtesy of Division of Tourism, Mississippi Department of Economic Development.)*

pared to the overall U.S. rate of 2.8 percent. Needless to say, the gaming industry is continuing to thrive.

The fact is that people enjoy gaming as an entertainment option in their lives. According to a 1996 survey, 92 percent of the American people view casino entertainment as acceptable for themselves or others. In 1996, there were 176 million visits made to casinos, up from 154 million in 1995—a 14 percent increase. As acceptance has grown, millions of Americans also understand the capital investment, tourism, public revenues, and employment impacts of casino gaming. According to the same survey, 70 percent of Americans seek casino gaming as an important part of the community's entertainment and tourism offering.

In 1993, the casino industry reached a milestone when more Americans went to casinos than visited major league baseball parks. Today, more Americans visit casinos than movie theaters, Broadway shows, and musical concerts. This entertainment trend is continuing as we find ourselves nearing the millennium.

The employment opportunities provided by the gaming–entertainment industry deserve special attention. In all, $8.5 billion in direct wages were paid by casino gaming, and another $12.5 billion were paid as a result of indirect jobs created by the industry.

As the growth in casino gaming has been widespread over the last several years, many individuals question how long such a phenomenon can last and what the limit should be. But according to a recent study, even if no new casinos open in the next ten years, direct employment in the casino industry will rise an average of 7.5 percent per year to reach nearly 700,000 by 2005. Based on a ten-year projection that conservatively assumes no new gaming facilities will open, the study projects that federal tax receipts will reach $17.7 billion in 2005 (compared to $5.9 billion in 1995), and state and local taxes will reach $3 billion in 2005 (compared to $2 billion in 1995). The study contains strong evidence that economic performance from gaming will continue to improve dramatically in the future.

In deciding whether or not to add casino gaming to a community or to the mix of gaming already in existence, it is important that voters and their elected representatives have the correct information, data, and statistics so that their decision, either pro or con, is an informed one. The National Gaming Impact Study Commission, signed into law in August 1996 to conduct a comprehensive study of the social and economic impacts of gaming in the United States, has the goal to provide objective information to assist in decision-making. Appointments were made to the Commission, and it started its work on April 29, 1997. The Commission has two years to complete its study.

Indian Reservation gaming in the United States became a growth industry in the past decade when the U.S. Supreme Court in 1987 recognized Indian people's right to run gaming: It ruled that states had no authority to regulate gaming on Indian land if such gaming is permitted outside the reservation for any other purpose. Congress established the legal basis for this right when it passed The Indian Gaming Regulatory Act (IGRA) in 1988. In 1997, the National Indian Gaming Commission reported that there were 115 tribes with gaming class III operations and 164 tribe/state compacts in 24 states. Less than one-third of the tribes in the United States have gaming operations. Indian Gaming is only 5 percent of the entire Gaming Industry. The IGRA mandates that tribal governments, not individuals, can have gaming operations. Thus, the entire proceeds of the industry go back to fund tribal government programs. Indian tribes are using gaming revenues to build houses, schools, roads, and sewer and water systems; to fund the health care and education of their people; and to develop a strong, diverse economic base for the future.

The Mashantucket Pequot Tribal Nation operates the Foxwoods Resort Casino, which is the largest casino in the United States. Foxwoods averages over 55,000 patrons each day and more than 20 million visitors each year. They employ over 10,000 people.

Gaming is available in many parts of the world, as well as on cruise ships. Well-known areas for casino gambling include Monaco, the Caribbean, London, Nice, Macau, and Rio de Janeiro.

As new casinos go up in Las Vegas, Atlantic City, New Orleans, Colorado, the Mississippi River, South Dakota, Indian reservations, and the Bahamas, one sees the impact of gaming on tourism and the local economy. Given the current growth in gaming, it is safe to predict that it will continue to play a role in tourism and economic development.

Gaming Organizations

The American Gaming Association (AGA) was formed in June of 1995 after President Clinton proposed a 4 percent gross receipts tax on the gaming industry. Realizing that this would have monumental repercussions, casino industry leaders decided that it was time to form an association to represent them on Capitol Hill. Although the bill didn't materialize, the AGA thrived and today has more than 100 member companies. Since the AGA's opening, when the first 14 members consisted exclusively of casino companies and gaming equipment manufacturers, the diversity of the association's members has expanded to include financial and professional services, suppliers and vendors, state associations, and publications.

The AGA's primary goal is to create a better understanding of gaming–entertainment by bringing the facts about the industry to the general public, elected officials, other decision-makers, and the media through education and advocacy. An integral part of AGA's mission is the commitment to address "problem" and underage gaming. The AGA is located in Washington, D.C. Phone (202) 637-6507, web site: **http://www.americangaming.org.**

The National Indian Gaming Association (NIGA) is also located in Washington, D.C. NIGA operates as a clearinghouse and educational, legislative and public policy resource for tribes, policymakers, and the public on Indian gaming issues and tribal community development. They have statistics and economic studies on Indian gaming. Phone (202) 546-7711, FAX: (202) 546-1755; e-mail: niga@dgsys.com; web site: **http://www.indiangaming.org.**

RECREATION

Recreation is a diverse industry, representing over $300 billion in expenditures each year. The industry generates millions of jobs in the manufacturing, sales, and service sectors. Nearly 50 percent of Americans describe themselves as "outdoor people." They enjoy a wide variety of activities to keep fit, to add excitement to their lives, to have fun with family and friends, to pursue solitary activities, and to experience nature firsthand.

The draw of recreation opportunities throughout the United States is one factor in the rise of domestic travel, as well as in the increase in international visits to the United States. Outdoor adventure travel is gaining in popularity, and travel professionals have better access to information on recreational travel options. People are seeking higher-quality services and amenities.

Illustrative of the range of businesses within the recreation industry are recreation vehicle (RV) manufacturers and dealers, boat manufacturers and dealers, full-line recreation product manufacturers, park concessioners, campground owners, resorts, enthusiast groups, snowmobile manufacturers, recreation publications, motorcoach operators, bicycling interests, and others.

Companies manufacturing recreation products tend to be large. For example, the manufacturing of new RVs is an $11.9 billion-per-year industry. According to the Recreation Vehicle Dealers Association, another $6.5 billion is generated through the used and rental RV markets and the sales of after-market parts, accessories, and services.

The **Recreation Vehicle Industry Association** (RVIA), located in Reston, Virginia, is a primary source of shipment statistics, market research, and technical data. The association also supplies campground directories, and publications covering RV maintenance, trip preparation, and safety issues (web site: **http://www.rvamerica.com/rvia**).

A family camping in Woodford State Park, near Bennington, Vermont. *(Photo courtesy of Vermont Department of Tourism and Marketing.)*

In contrast to the large companies involved in manufacturing RVs, boats, pools, mountain bikes, skis, and so on, the private service sector is made up primarily of small businesses, ranging from campgrounds to marinas to wilderness guides. There is also the public sector, providing services through the National Park Service, Forest Service, and state and local agencies.

Parks

Both private and government enterprises operate various kinds of **parks,** including amusement parks. National parks are often very important parts of a nation's or state's tourism. In some countries (e.g., Africa), national parks are their primary attractions. Typical are Kenya, Rwanda, Uganda, Tanzania, Botswana, and South Africa.

National and State Parks

The U.S. National Park system is one of the country's greatest tourist attractions appealing to both domestic and international visitors. U.S. National Parks recorded 275.2 million recreation visits in 1997. A recreation visit is the entry of one person, for any part of a day on lands or waters administered by the NPS for recreation purposes. The **National Park Service** (NPS) administers 376 parks, recreation areas, preserves, battlefields, historic sites, lakeshores, monuments, memorials, seashores, and parkways (see Figure 8.2) which encompass 80.7 million acres.

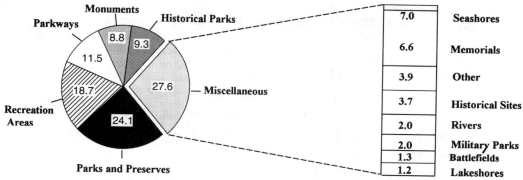

FIGURE 8.2 Types of areas administered by the National Park Service.

Ten parks accounted for over 30% of total visits to units of the national park system in 1997. The Blue Ridge Parkway (at 18.3 million visits) continued as the most visited unit of the system, and Great Smoky Mountains National Park continued as the most visited national park (at 9.9 million). Figure 8.3 shows the percentage of visits recorded by the NPS to 10 units of the park system. Commercial tour buses topped 302,000 entries into national park system units: Colonial National Historical Park (Jamestown, Williamsburg, Yorktown) received over 33,000 buses, and Grand Canyon received over 30,000.

Overnight stays in the concession lodges of the park topped 3.7 million, while campgrounds saw over 7 million overnight guests. Another 2 million visitors spent the night in a park backcountry site that they hiked into. Most park visitors are staying in facilities in "gateway communities" outside park boundaries or are simply day users.

While the most popular parks continue to experience a crowded peak summer season, the spring and fall are excellent times to visit the well-known areas, and there

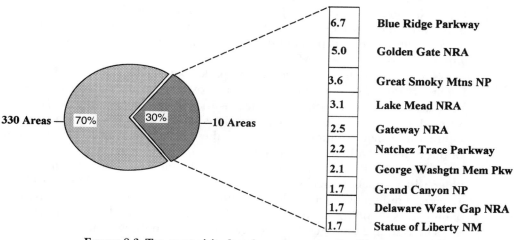

FIGURE 8.3 Ten most visited park areas account for 30 percent of all visits.

are a great many units of the national park system that are still underutilized. See the section entitled "Matching Supply with Demand" in Chapter 12.

Among the units of the national park system that have staff and facilities to serve more visitors than they currently receive are:

- Kenai Fjords National Park, Alaska
- Organ Pipe Cactus National Monument, Arizona
- Canyon de Chelly National Monument, Arizona
- Lassen Volcanic National Park, California
- Redwood National Park, California
- Voyageurs National Park, Minnesota
- Great Basin National Park, Nevada
- Guadalupe Mountains National Park, Texas
- Black Canyon of the Gunnison National Monument, Colorado
- Congaree Swamp National Monument, South Carolina
- George Washington's Birthplace National Monument, Virginia
- Fire Island National Seashore, New York
- Morristown National Historical Park, New Jersey
- Lowell National Historical Park, Massachusetts
- Canyonlands National Park, Utah

Early in 1997, the NPS opened the new Franklin Delano Roosevelt Memorial in Washington, D.C., a beautiful outdoor series of sculptured rooms that commemorate the Presidency of the only three-term President in American History. Visits topped 1.9 million in its first year. Most recently, in April 1998 the NPS opened the new Prisoners of War Museum in Andersonville, Georgia. At the site of the most infamous prison of the Civil War, the Museum honors all of the 800,000 Americans who have been captured in war from the American Revolution to the present.

Also in 1997, the NPS opened new visitor centers for both Everglades and Biscayne National Parks in south Florida. Each contains modern audio-visual presentations and interpretive exhibits on the ecosystems of the two national parks, as well as more traditional maps and bookstores. Hurricane Andrew destroyed both parks' old visitor centers in August 1992.

Not wishing to limit visitation to the parks, but needing to cope with the increasing number of cars attempting to enter the most popular parks in the peak season, the NPS has signed an important technical assistance agreement with the Federal Highways Administration. One of the first actions will be to implement mass transit plans within three major national parks over the next three years, including Yosemite, Grand Canyon, and Zion National Parks.

Visitors to NPS areas have a large economic impact on the surrounding communities, with estimated direct sales in 1996 of $7.8 billion. An additional $6.4 billion was generated indirectly from tourism expenditures, for a total economic impact of $14.2 billion. This spending by NPS visitors helped generate over 300,000 jobs.

The National Park Service publishes information on visits to national park areas in its annual report, *National Park Statistical Abstract*. They also publish biannually *The*

National Parks Index, which contains brief descriptions, with acreages, of each area administered by NPS.

In the United States many individual states operate park systems, some of the most outstanding being New York, California, Tennessee, Oregon, Indiana, Kentucky, Florida, and Michigan. The National Association of State Park Directors compile statistics for state parks. They issue an annual report called *Information Exchange*. They report that over 745.6 million people visited state parks in 1995. State parks generated $536 million in revenue from user fees, facilities, restaurants, concessions, beaches, pools, golf, and other sales. There are 5541 state parks totaling over 11.8 million acres in the nation.

Parks are also operated by other units of government, such as county or park districts like the Huron–Clinton Metropolitan Authority of the greater Detroit area in southeastern Michigan. This system has six parks within easy access of residents of the Detroit metropolitan area. Counties, townships, and cities also operate parks and often campgrounds as parts of parks.

National Forests

Visitors spent 345.1 million recreation visitor-days (12 visit-hours by one or more persons) in 1995, according to the U.S. Forest Service. Part of the Department of Agriculture, the U.S. Forest Service maintains 191 million acres in the National Forest System, with 156 national forests and 20 grasslands in 42 states and Puerto Rico. Especially popular activities are hiking, camping, hunting, fishing, canoeing, and skiing.

The state of Arkansas contains over 200 scenic hiking trails covering 750 miles. Here, two hikers take in the view from a trail in the Ouachita National Forest. *(Photo courtesy of Arkansas Department of Parks and Tourism.)*

The U.S. Forest Service reports that its developed recreation sites include 4389 campgrounds; over 328 swimming areas; 1496 picnic grounds; 1222 boating sites; and 277 interpretive, fishing, observation, and winter recreation sites.

Other Recreational Lands

The Bureau of Land Management (BLM) oversees more than 270 million acres of land. The BLM has nearly 2400 day-use and 16,698 family camp units on 50,000 acres. It also has 3179 miles of designated backcountry byways, 62,768 miles of roads suitable for highway vehicles, 90.8 acres open to off-highway vehicles, 54.4 million more acres open to limited off-highway vehicular use, and 19,000 miles of trails for motorized vehicles. The most popular recreational activities on BLM lands are camping and motorized travel.

The Corps of Engineers (COE) manages over 11 million acres of land and water in 42 states with approximately 456 water resource development projects. The COE is the nation's leading provider of water-based recreation and typically hosts over 375 million visitors each year. Some of the recreation facilities provided on the 11 million acres include 93,000 campsites, 55,000 picnic areas, 3500 boat launching ramps, 990 swimming areas, and 1900 miles of hiking trails.

The U.S. Fish & Wildlife Service (FWS) manages over 91 million acres of fish and wildlife habitats and provides recreation opportunities. According to the FWS, participants in hunting, fishing, bird watching, and other wildlife-related recreation spent $96.9 billion enjoying these activities.

Recreation.gov

A new multi-federal land recreation Internet web site address has been established. National Park Service, Bureau of Land Management, Fish & Wildlife Service, Forest Service, Corps of Engineers, and Bureau of Reclamation now have a fully integrated site on the Internet for the public to search for any recreation opportunities on the federal public lands. Launched in April 1998 as part of Vice President Gore's Reinventing Government, **recreation.gov** offers "one-stop-shopping" to the public for information about recreation on the federal public lands.

Adventure Travel

Many outdoor recreation activities are sports-related and have been classified in the adventure travel area. The National Sporting Goods Association conducts an annual study of sports participation by Americans seven years of age and older. They report that the top outdoor recreation adventure **activities** were overnight vacation camping (46.6 million participants), bicycle riding (45.1 million), fishing (44.7 million), hiking (28.4 million), hunting with firearms (17.0 million), on-road mountain biking (16.0 million), backpacking/wilderness camping (12.0 million), alpine skiing (8.9 million), off-road mountain biking (8.1 million), canoeing (7.1 million), water skiing (6.5 million), snorkeling (6.3 million), hunting with a bow and arrow (5.3 million), sailing (3.4 million), snowmobiling (3.4 million), kayaking/rafting (2.7 million), cross-country skiing (2.5 million), snowboarding (2.5 million), scuba diving (2.3 million), snowshoeing (0.7 million), and wind surfing (0.5 million).

The National Sporting Goods Association (NSGA) is the world's largest sporting goods trade association, representing more than 22,000 retail outlets and 3000 product manufacturers, suppliers, and sales agents. They are located at 1699 Wall Street, Suite 700, Mt. Prospect, IL 60056-5780, phone (847) 439-4000, FAX (847) 439-0111, e-mail: nsga 1699@aol.com, web site (**http://www.nsga.org**).

Another source of outdoor recreation information is the American Recreation Coalition (ARC). They conduct research on a regular basis, organize national conferences, and disseminate information on recreational needs, satisfaction, and initiatives. ARC monitors legislative proposals that influence recreation and works with government agencies. ARC is located at 1225 New York Avenue, N.W., Suite 450, Washington, D.C. 20005, phone (202) 682-9530, FAX (202) 682-9529, web site **http://www.funout doors.com.**

Winter Sports

Snow and winter sports tourism is an important component of the world tourism industry and is a key element for a better quality of life in many countries. Of the modern winter sports activities, skiing is by far the most popular. In the United States there were 507 ski resorts operating in the 1997–1998 season. Skier/snowboarder visits are one of the key performance indicators in the U.S. ski industry. On a nationwide basis, the number of visits have been relatively flat for the last two decades, hovering around 50 million. The peak year was 54.6 million visits in the 1993–1994 season. The total visits for the 1997–1998 season were 53.8 million according to the National Ski Areas Association (NSAA). A skier/snowboarder visit represents one person visiting a ski area for all or any part of a day or night and includes full-day, half-day, night, and complimentary, adult, child, season, and any other ticket types that gives one the use of an area's facility.

Snowboarding has been the growth portion of the ski industry representing over 21 percent of the total visits in 1997–1998. The compound annual rate of growth in snowboarding since the 1994–1995 season has been 20.7 percent.

Another trend is the emphasis on the multidimensional aspects of the snow resort experience. Today, ski areas are appealing to all on-snow participants whether they are down-hill skiers, snowboarders, telemarkers, cross-country skiers, snowshoers, or tubers. Vail Resorts has created "Adventure Ridge," which is an example of this trend. This facility, located at the top of Vail Mountain, offers snowshoeing, tubing, ice skating, laser tag, snowmobile tours, and four dining experiences until 10:00 p.m. every night.

Over the years the U.S. ski industry has grown and evolved just like other industries. Consolidations continue to take place, and ski resorts have developed into major destination resorts. Today, four companies have emerged at the forefront to consolidate ski areas under corporate banners. Large operations have become even larger. The resorts now in the hands of the big four—American Skiing Co., Vail Resorts, Inc., Booth Creek Ski Holdings, Inc., and Intrawest Corp—represent approximately 23 percent of the North American ski market based on 74 million skier days for North America in the 1996–1997 season.

Ownership consolidation will lead to more innovative development and marketing. We will see more emphasis on real estate with core village developments that feature shopping, attractions, conference facilities, and other amenities which create a year-round destination resort. On the marketing scene we will see interchangeable lift tickets, frequent skier programs, ski discount cards good at multiple resorts, and increased promotion. Increased size increases the opportunity to use media more effectively, especially television.

Snowsports Industries America (SIA) reports that $9.9 billion was spent on snow activities. Expenditures included travel and entertainment ($2.6 billion), skiing/snowboarding (1.9 billion), on-snow products ($1.8 billion), real estate ($1.7 billion), transportation ($1.6 billion), and ski area equipment ($0.3 billion).

The International Snowmobiling Manufacturers Association reports that 168,509 snowmobiles were sold in the United States in 1996. Snowmobilers use their snowmobiles for trail riding, touring on marked and groomed trails, and ice fishing.

Historic Sites

Historic sites have always been popular attractions for both domestic and international travelers. In 1997, TIA released a new report on historic travel. Over one-quarter of all adults (about 54 million) reported visits to historic places or museums in the past year. While travelers tend to engage in multiple activities when they travel, 19 percent of the historic travelers said these activities were the primary motive for the trip.

The National Park Service maintains an estimated 66,757 historic sites, as noted in the National Register of Historic Sites. Approximately 15 percent of these properties are historic districts, and about 1,015,434 are historic properties located within the sites.

Mount Vernon, the beloved plantation home of President George Washington and his wife Martha, is one of the most famous historic homes in America. *(Photo courtesy of the Virginia Tourism Corporation.)*

The National Trust for Historic Preservation provides leadership, education, and advocacy to save America's diverse historic places and revitalize communities. They own and manage 20 historic sites that are open to the public, and they offer study tours—namely, the Historic Hotels of America Program and the Heritage Tourism Program—to destinations all over the world. The National Trust is a nonprofit organization chartered by Congress in 1949 and has 275 members. Located in Washington, D.C., it can be reached by phone (202-588-6000) and by web site (**http://www.nthp.org**).

Zoos, "Jungles," and Aquariums

The menageries and aviaries of China, Egypt, and Rome were famous in ancient times. Today, **zoological parks** and **aquariums** continue to be popular attractions. A recent development in the United States has been the creation of indoor **rainforests.** Notable are the Lied Jungle in the Henry Doorly Zoo in Omaha, Nebraska and the Rainforest within the Cleveland, Ohio Metropolitan Zoo. The Lied Jungle is the world's largest indoor rainforest, with its $15 million cost financed by the Lied Foundation. It recreates rainforests as found in Asia, Africa, and South America. The "jungle" occupies 1.5 acres under one roof. It contains 2000 species of tropical plants and 517 animal species, and it attracts over 1.3 million visitors annually. This has become the biggest tourist attraction in Nebraska.

ENTERTAINMENT

Another powerful tourism magnet is **entertainment.** Live entertainment is often the main attraction for a vacation trip. The deadheads following the Grateful Dead concert tour are a prime example. Another is people traveling to Nashville, Tennessee to hear country and western music at the Grand Ole Opry. Branson, Missouri has put itself on the map as a music entertainment center and is now challenging Nashville. One of the centerpieces of the famous "I Love New York" advertising campaign was going to a Broadway play or musical. A theater tour to London is a powerful vacation lure. Large numbers of performing arts tours are offered.

Entertainment has risen to a new level in the vacation decision-making process. There is a growing influence of entertainment on vacation travel choices. Today the traveling public wants to have fun, to be entertained, to enjoy fantasy, and escape from the realities of everyday life. Think about these facts: The top two North American vacation destinations—Disney World and Las Vegas—are built around the appeal of entertainment. The growing cruise market features entertainment. Disney is featuring "edutainment" (combining education and entertainment). The growing influence of entertainment and the marriage of gaming, live entertainment, themed resorts, and theme parks are creating new careers in entertainment management.

The development of super entertainment complexes is a trend in the tourism industry. It's happening not only in Las Vegas and Atlantic City but also in other markets. Las Vegas mega resorts are designed to attract the family vacation market as well as gamblers. Table 8.3 shows the top 15 largest hotels in the world. It is interesting to note that 13 of them are in Las Vegas and the majority are not only hotels but attrac-

Hotel theaters and nightclubs along The Strip in Las Vegas, Nevada feature spectacular production shows. *(Photo courtesy of the Las Vegas News Bureau.)*

tions and entertainment centers as well. The Luxor, New York New York, Excalibur, and Treasure Island are all examples of themed resort hotels.

FESTIVALS AND EVENTS

Among the fastest-growing segments of tourism in the world are these types of celebrations. Countries and cities compete vigorously for mega-events such as the Olympics, World Cup, and World Fairs. **Festivals and events** are pervasive around the globe. Societies are always holding some kind of an event, whether it is a fair, festival, market, parade, celebration, anniversary, sports event, or a charitable endeavor.

Festivals and events are an important part of the tourism industry. They can serve

TABLE 8.3
World's Largest Hotels

Rank	Hotel	Number of Rooms
1	Ambassador City Jomtlen, Thailand	5,100
2	MGM Grand, Las Vegas	5,005
3	Luxor, Las Vegas	4,427
4	Excalibur, Las Vegas	4,032
5	Circus Circus, Las Vegas	3,741
6	Flamingo Hilton, Las Vegas	3,642
7	Las Vegas Hilton, Las Vegas	3,174
8	The Mirage, Las Vegas	3,049
9	Monte Carlo, Las Vegas	3,002
10	Treasure Island, Las Vegas	2,900
11	Bally's, Las Vegas	2,814
12	Harrah's, Las Vegas	2,699
13	Imperial Palace, Las Vegas	2,636
14	Hilton Hawaiian Village, Honolulu	2,523
15	Stardust, Las Vegas	2,431

Source: Las Vegas Convention & Visitors Authority.

as a powerful tool to attract tourists during the off-season and to create an image and awareness for an area.

Sponsorships have become an essential ingredient in festivals and events. Most events, whether local, national, or international, would have a difficult time existing without them. Sponsorship is when sponsors provide funds or "in-kind" contributions to promoters of events. Sponsorships have become big business today and involve the right to use logos and identify with the event.

Volunteers are one of the key factors in the success of events. The International Festivals and Events Association (IFEA) reports that the average weekend attendance at an event is approximately 222,000. It takes the hard work and support from community volunteers to ensure that a festival or event runs smoothly. With the average weekend event requiring up to 2000 volunteers, most events would not be able to take place without them.

There is a movement toward professional management of events and year-round operation of event offices. Event management is emerging as a field, becoming more professional, and providing a new source of job opportunities. As the number of events has grown by expanding in size and complexity, the number of staff and volunteers has mushroomed. This has given rise to professional associations, books, formal education, and training programs. Classes are being offered in event management in a number of tourism programs around the globe. George Washington University in Washington, D.C., offers a certificate program and a sequence in their Master's Degree program in event management. Dr. Joe Jeff Goldblatt heads this program and is also the author of a book entitled *Special Events,* which is in its second edition.

Donald Getz, University of Calgary, has written a book entitled *Festivals, Special Events and Tourism.* He states that festivals and events appeal to a very broad audience. However, elements of these or specific themes can be effectively targeted to desired

An annual event that attracts thousands of tourists and is broadcast on television is the New Year's Day Tournament of Roses Parade in Pasadena, California. *(Photo by Robert Holmes, courtesy of the California Division of Tourism.)*

tourist market segments. Festivals and events also have the ability to spread tourism geographically and seasonally. Special events allow a region or community to celebrate its uniqueness, promote itself, develop local pride, and enhance its economic well-being.

Events produce sizeable economic and tourism benefits. For example, SunFest, an annual festival in Florida, has a year-round staff of nine and a budget of $3 million. The 1996 SunFest generated an economic impact of approximately $21.5 million in the local community. The National Western Stock Show held in Denver each January for 12 days has a permanent staff of about 50 year-round employees who plan, organize, and market the event. During the stock show, this grows to 950 employees. They serve some 20,000 animals and 600,000 people attending the event. Considering both direct and indirect effects, it is estimated that the event provides a hefty $123 million boost to the Denver economy.

Even small communities can stage such events. Many local festivals originally designed to entertain local residents have grown to attract visitors from many miles away. Smaller communities that do not have convention bureaus and meeting space can turn to event tourism to seek tourism dollars by producing arts and craft shows, historical reenactments, music festivals, film festivals, food festivals, and the like. Consequently, events have shown tremendous growth as small and medium-sized towns seek tourism dollars through short-term events. The International Festivals Association estimates that every year there are between 50,000 and 60,000 half-day to one-day events and 5000 or more festivals of two days or longer.

The International Festival and Events Association (IFEA) has provided cutting-edge professional development and fund-raising ideas for the special events industry for 42 years. Through publications, seminars, annual conventions, trade shows, and ongoing networking, IFEA is advancing festivals and events throughout the world. More than 2400 events are currently members. IFEA is located in Port Angeles, WA 98362, phone (360) 457-3141, Fax (360) 452-4695, web site **http://ifea.com.**

SHOPPING

Shopping is an important part of any tourist's activities. Shopping leads as the number one activity while traveling for both domestic and international travelers. The Travel Industry Association of America (TIA) reports that shopping is an activity engaged in by 33 percent of domestic travelers, followed by outdoor recreation at 18 percent. Tourism Industries in the U.S. Department of Commerce reports that 90 percent of international visitors shopped in the United States in 1997 as part of their vacation activities.

An example of shopping's importance is the Bayside Marketplace. Launched in April 1987, the Rouse Company has created Miami–Dade County's number one visitor attraction, Bayside Marketplace. It has attracted more than 120 million visitors from South Florida and around the world. The Greater Miami Convention & Visitors Bureau has repeatedly identified Bayside as Miami–Dade County's number one visitor attraction, and *Florida Trend* magazine recently published a report naming Bayside as the fifth-most-visited attraction in the state of Florida.

Bayside has nearly 140 shops offering a variety of merchandise in both the North and South Pavilions and Pier 5 Marketplace. In addition, Hard Rock Café and nine additional full-service restaurants offer everything from Italian, Caribbean, Spanish,

Shopping leads as the number one activity while traveling. The Bayside Marketplace is Miami–Dade County's top visitor attraction. (*Photo courtesy of Bayside Marketplace.*)

Nicaraguan, Cuban, and American Cuisine. For visitors on the run, the International Food court offers 20 fast food eateries. Bayside is also the only entertainment venue in the city offering free concerts 365 days a year. The Rouse Company manages properties in 25 states, the District of Columbia, and Canada.

The Mall of America in Bloomington, Minnesota is the largest mall in the United States. It has proven to be a real tourist attraction. Excursion motorcoach tours in Minnesota and nearby states now feature packages with Mall of America as their destination. This mall is particularly attractive to children because it features Lego's gigantic space station, dinosaurs, a medieval castle, and other intricate creations. They can also enjoy Knott's Camp Snoopy and plenty of rides. There are 14 theaters in the Upper East Side entertainment district, plus a comedy club, sports bars, and a variety of nightclubs. While shopping at the **West Edmonton Mall** in Alberta, Canada, one can view sharks from a submarine, live a Roman fantasy, or soak in a bubble-filled spa near a volcano. This mall is the largest in the world. It even contains a full-scale replica of Columbus's ship *Santa Maria*, roulette wheels, the Ice Palace, and, of course, hundreds of stores, plus some theme parks.

Factory **outlet shopping malls** have become major attractions for U.S. and international travelers. TIA reports that 37 percent of all leisure and business travelers visited a discount outlet mall in 1997. This translates to 55 million discount outlet travelers out of a total of 149 million adult travelers annually. The 55 million includes 25 million men (46 percent) and 29 million women (54 percent). The TIA survey includes trips of 100 miles or more, one way, away from home.

One in ten discount outlet mall travelers (10 percent) cited the outlet shopping experience as the primary reason for their trip. Most (79 percent) said it was a secondary reason, while the rest (11 percent) said it was not a reason. Men and women were the same on this assessment.

Manufacturer's outlets are the fastest growing segment of retail trade. There are approximately 325 outlet centers scattered over the United States, occupying over 50 million square feet of space. Over 13,000 stores are open in factory outlets. An example of an outlet shopping mall is Sawgrass Mills, the 1.9-million-square-foot complex in Sunrise, Florida. It is the largest outlet mall combining retail and entertainment and is second only to Walt Disney World as the most popular tourist attraction in the state, according to the Mills Corporation, which developed it. In 1997, 25 million people tramped through a mile-long stretch of stores, from Bed, Bath and Beyond to the Ann Taylor Loft; about seven million shoppers came from abroad.

To make shopping as convenient as possible, many resorts and hotels provide shops featuring gift items, particularly local handicrafts and artwork. In the shopping areas of each community that caters successfully to tourists, there are high-quality gift and souvenir shops featuring items of particular interest to visitors. The chain hotel and motel companies have also organized gift shops as part of their operations. Airports have virtually become shopping centers.

EDUCATION

Suppliers of the tourism product look to educational organizations as sources of talent for their industries. These include secondary schools, vocational schools, junior or community colleges, four-year colleges and universities, and trade association schools and institutes. Most high schools, which are known by various terms in different countries, offer curricula and subjects of value to travel firms. Examples are native and foreign languages, geography, history, writing, use of computers, secretarial skills, bookkeeping, and food preparation. Many vocational schools produce entry-level employees for travel agencies, tour companies, airlines, accommodations, food service, and others, and junior and community colleges offer education and training in various skills applicable to the travel industry.

Trade associations and professional societies are also active in education. Examples of these are the educational programs and home study courses of the American Society of Travel Agents, the Institute of Certified Travel Agents, the Educational Institute of the American Hotel and Motel Association, the National Institute for the Foodservice Industry, and, in Britain, the Institute of Travel and Tourism. Most public carriers, especially the airlines, provide rigorous training and educational programs for their employees, as well as for those working for travel agencies and tour companies. The International Labour Organization (a U.N. affiliate in Geneva, Switzerland) has conducted numerous types of training programs in tourism-related vocations. Similarly, the World Tourism Organization conducts courses for those in official tourism departments.

Four-year colleges and universities provide instruction in similar skills and management education. In keeping with the diversity of the industry, courses are offered in schools of business and hotel and restaurant administration, colleges of natural resources, commercial recreation departments, sociology departments, geography departments, and anthropology departments. A number of schools are offering graduate programs in travel and tourism. In addition to courses and educational programs, universities and colleges conduct a great deal of research, which is available to the industry.

The Council on Hotel, Restaurant, and Institutional Education (CHRIE) lists 550 schools that offer two-year, four-year, and graduate study programs in the United States and abroad. The publication *A Guide to Programs in Hospitality and Tourism* provides a description of tourism programs and is available from CHRIE or John Wiley & Sons.

Finally, land-grant schools provide services through the Cooperative Extension Service, which operates in all 50 states. Educational services are available to managers of hotels, motels, restaurants, resorts, clubs, marinas, small service businesses, and similar enterprises from some state organizations. Short courses and conferences are sometimes held for managers of these businesses to make them more efficient and productive. These educational services are provided by the land-grant colleges and universities and the Cooperative Extension Service, which is supported in part by the U.S. Department of Agriculture.

Educational Organizations

The Travel and Tourism Research Association has over 150 educational members. In addition, educators' sessions are held at the annual conference. The National Park and Recreation Association has a section called the Society of Park and Recreation Educators (SPRE). This group works on appropriate curriculum and features programs on education and research. Hotel and restaurant educators formed the Council on

Hotel, Restaurant, and Institutional Education (CHRIE), which fosters improved teaching methods and aids in curriculum development for all educational levels, from high schools through four-year colleges and universities. The International Society of Travel and Tourism Educators holds an annual conference and publishes a newsletter. The Society strives to improve tourism teaching. Finally, there is the International Academy for the Study of Tourism, which seeks to improve tourism education and research.

PUBLISHING

Producers of printed news, feature articles, advertising, publicity, and electronic news constitute a very important type of business within tourism. Because the field is so fast-changing, such news and feature articles must be read in order to keep up to date, but also for current information needed for intelligent counseling and management.

Another vital group of publishers includes those who produce reference manuals, tariffs, guides, atlases, timetables, and operational handbooks both online and in hard copies. Without these, no travel organization could function. Counselors and others who contact travelers must be informed as to the nomenclature of their particular part of the business. They must also know rules and regulations, methods of operation, schedules, transit times, accommodations, equipment and service, tariffs, rates, commissions, and other, such as details of any travel destination. The list of these is long and varies for each country. No single publication could possibly cover the needed information for any particular branch of the industry. References can be grouped as follows:

1. Independently published references for the travel industry, such as the *Official Airline Guide, Hotel and Travel Index, AH & MA Red Book,* and the *Official Steamship Guide*
2. Publications of the national tourism organizations
3. Hotel chain or hotel representatives references
4. Guides published mainly for the public but used in the travel industry, such as Michelin, Fodor, Rand McNally, and Frommer
5. Specialized guides such as *Castle Hotels of Europe*

MARKETING AND PUBLICITY ORGANIZATIONS

Travel marketing consultants provide valuable assistance to any organization needing specialized sales services. A travel marketing consultant organization will provide assistance in planning a publicity and sales campaign, selecting markets, selecting media, providing market research, discovering new markets, and overall conducting of a sales and marketing program.

Most state-level tourism promotion programs are conducted through established advertising agencies. To conduct this program successfully, these agencies must do market analysis of the travel industry, and many of these agencies have developed an expertise in this field. The names of the advertising agencies serving the various state tourism organizations can be obtained by writing to the state organization. A list of the state tourism organizations appears in Appendix A or can be obtained from the Travel Industry Association of America, 1100 New York Avenue, N.W., Washington, D.C. 20005.

MISCELLANEOUS SERVICES

Many other organizations provide essential services to tourism. Examples are: hospitals and medical services; police services; sanitary trash pickup and disposal services; laundry services; construction services; retail stores such as department stores, drugstores, and clothing stores; newspapers (including tourist newspapers and special travel editions); travel writers; and magazines.

SUMMARY

The businesses and organizations that provide attractions, recreation, entertainment, shopping, and others comprise major parts of tourism. For example, trips just for entertainment constitute about one-fourth of all travel in the United States. There are many activities engaged in by tourists—a wealth of opportunities.

Theme parks such as Disneyland and Universal Studios also attract millions each year. Most of these are showing a steady rise in patronage. Gaming or gambling is also a growing industry. It has now been legalized in states other than Nevada and New Jersey, and attendance continues to rise. Parks come in all sizes and types. They serve both local and visitor recreational needs. National parks are of particular interest to both domestic and international visitors. National forests are very popular. Zoos, "jungles," and aquariums, usually located in parks, attract locals as well as millions of tourists. A new development is the recreation of tropical rainforests within zoological parks. An outstanding example is the Lied Jungle in Omaha, Nebraska.

Shopping continues to be a major attraction. Spectacular malls such as the Mall of America in Minnesota and the West Edmonton Mall in Alberta, Canada have become tourist destinations. They contain an amazing variety of recreational facilities as well as hundreds of shops. Festivals and events are attractions of great and growing importance. Mega-events such as the Olympics are sought-after awards to a city. Local festivals typically attract a wider audience once they become better publicized.

ABOUT THE READING

This is a fun reading that gives a brief history of the amusement park industry and lists some great (and not so great) moments in amusement park history.

READING 8.1

HISTORY OF AMUSEMENT PARKS

by Jim Futrell, Historian
National Amusement Park Historical Association

The roots of the amusement park industry go back to medieval Europe, when pleasure gardens began to spring up on the outskirts of major European cities. These gardens were a forerunner of today's amusement parks, featuring live entertainment, fireworks, dancing, games, and even primitive amusement rides. Pleasure gardens remained extremely popular until the 1700s, when political unrest caused many of these parks to close. However, one of these parks remains: Bakken, north of Copenhagen, opened in 1583 and now enjoys the status of the world's oldest operating amusement park.

In the late 1800s, the growth of the industry shifted to America. Following the American Civil War, increased urbanization gave rise to electric traction (trolley) companies. At that time, utility companies charged the trolley companies a flat fee for the use of their electricity. As a result, the transportation companies looked for a way to stimulate weekend ridership. This resulted in the amusement park. Typically built at the end of a trolley line, amusement parks initially were simple operations consisting of picnic facilities, dance halls, restaurants, games, and a few amusement rides. These parks were immediately successful and soon opened across America.

The amusement park entered its golden era with the 1893 World's Colombian Exposition in Chicago. This World's Fair introduced the Ferris Wheel and the amusement midway to the world. The midway, with its wide array of rides and concessions, was a huge success and dictated amusement park design for the next sixty years. The following year, Capt. Paul Boynton borrowed the midway concept and opened the world's first modern amusement park: Paul Boynton's Water Chutes on Chicago's South side. The success of his Chicago park inspired him to open a similar facility at the fledgling Coney Island resort in New York in 1895. The amusement park industry grew tremendously over the next three decades. The center of the industry was Coney Island in New York. Hundreds of new amusement parks opened around the world, while new innovations provided greater and more intense thrills to the growing crowds. By 1919, in the United States, over 1500 amusement parks were in operation. Unfortunately, this glory did not last.

In 1929, America entered the Depression; and by 1935, only 400 amusement parks still remained, struggling to survive. The industry was further hurt by World War II, when many parks closed and others refrained from adding new attractions due to the rationing.

With the end of World War II, America and the amusement park industry enjoyed postwar prosperity. Attendance and revenues grew to new records as new parks opened across America. A new concept, the Kiddieland, took advantage of the postwar baby boom, introducing a new generation to the joys of the amusement park. Unfortunately, this resurgence was short-lived.

As the 1950s dawned, television, urban decay, desegregation, and suburban growth began to take a heavy toll on the aging, urban amusement park. The industry was again in distress when the public turned elsewhere for entertainment. What was needed was a new concept, and that new concept was Disneyland.

When Disneyland first opened in 1955, many people were skeptical that an amusement park without any of the traditional attractions would succeed. But Disneyland was different. Instead of a midway, Disneyland offered five distinct themed areas, providing guests with the fantasy of travel to different lands and times. Disneyland was an immediate success; as a result, the theme park era was born. Over the next several years, there were many unsuccessful attempts to copy Disneyland's success. It wasn't until 1961, when Six Flags Over Texas opened, that another theme park was successful. Throughout the 1960s and 1970s, theme parks were built in many major cities across America. Unfortunately, while theme parks were opening across the country, many of the grand old traditional amusement parks continued to close in the face of increased competition and urban decay. However, some of the traditional parks were able to thrive during the theme park era because the renewed interest in amusement parks brought people back to their local park. In addition, many older traditional parks were able to borrow ideas from theme parks and introduce new rides and attractions to their long-time patrons.

As the 1980s dawned, the theme park boom began spreading around the world. Meanwhile, theme park growth slowed considerably in the United States due to the escalating costs and a lack of markets enough to support a theme park.

During the 1990s, the amusement park remains an international favorite. Many developing nations are experiencing the joys of the amusement park for the first time, while the older, more established amusement parks continue to search for new and different ways to keep their customers happy.

Founded in 1978, the National Amusement Park Historical Association is an international organization dedicated to promoting the preservation and enjoyment of the amusement and theme park industry—past, present, and future.

Great (and Not So Great) Moments in Amusement Park History

1550–1700: Pleasure Gardens begin to appear in Europe. These were the first permanent areas set aside specifically for outdoor entertainment. The attractions included fountains, flower gardens, bowling, games, music, dancing, staged spectacles, and a few primitive amusement rides.

1650: Large ice slides, supported by heavy timbers, become popular as a wintertime diversion in Russia. Small wooden sleds used iron runners to glide down hills in St. Petersburg and were quite elaborate. These simple amusements were the forerunner of today's roller coasters.

1846: The first looping gravity railway is exhibited at Frascati Gardens in Paris, France. The French called the device Chemin du Centrifuge.

1875: With the completion of the first railroad to Coney Island, Brooklyn, NY, it is fast becoming popular as a seaside resort. Coney's most popular attractions were located in pavilions built near the water. The attractions included cabaret entertainment, vaudeville acts, melodramas, fortunetellers, games, and rides such as small carousels.

1884: LaMarcus A. Thompson introduces his Switchback Gravity Pleasure Railway at Coney Island. This device is recognized as the first true roller coaster in America.

1889: Lina Beecher of New York constructs America's first vertical looping roller coaster in Toledo. It is later relocated to New York's Coney Island.

1893: Chicago's Columbian Exposition introduces the famous George Ferris Giant Wheel. A true wonder of the then modern world, the Ferris Wheel weighed in at over 4 million pounds and was 264 feet high. Also introduced at the Columbian Exposition was the Midway Plaisance (or White City Midway). The ornate building facades

and brilliant electric lights dictated amusement park design for the next 60 years.

1894: Chutes Park in Chicago opens. Built by Captain Paul Boynton, Chutes Park was the first amusement park to be enclosed and charge an admission. After relocating in 1896, Chutes Park closed in 1908. The park served as a model for Sea Lion Park at New York's Coney Island.

1895: Captain Paul Boynton's Sea Lion Park opens at Coney Island. Sea Lion Park inspired numerous amusement parks throughout the United States, including the three great Coney Island parks: Luna Park (1903–1947), Dreamland (1904–1911), and Steeplechase (1897–1964).

The Turn of the Twentieth Century: The late 1800s saw the beginning of a brand new industry, public transportation. Electric traction (trolley) companies began to appear in the urban United States. Electric light and power companies charged the traction companies a flat monthly fee for electricity on which they ran their trolleys. It didn't matter how much or how little the trolleys were used. Naturally, the trolley magnates became frustrated because little need existed to operate trolleys during the weekends, although they still had to pay for the electricity to operate their systems. A solution was to get the general public to ride the trolleys on Saturdays and Sundays, thus creating more revenue for the traction companies. How did they do this? By building an amusement park at the end of the trolley line, hence the term "Trolley Park," and a new era began. Soon hundreds of trolley parks were in operation throughout the United States. However, only twelve remain.

1903: Thompson and Dundy's Luna Park, Coney Island, opens on May 16th. The electrical "Arabian Nights" style of architecture attracted over 40,000 patrons that first evening. Luna Park burned down in 1947.

1910: By this date, more than 2000 amusement parks are operating throughout the United States.

1912: John Miller patents his design for the under-friction roller coaster. This new method of holding the coaster to the tracks, while reducing drag, would revolutionize the roller coaster, safely allowing for higher, steeper drops and faster speeds.

1915–1920: Many parks close, due to (a) the public's increased mobility caused by the invention of the automobile and (b) interest in new attractions such as motion pictures.

1920s: This is the golden age of amusement parks. Many larger cities had as many as six. Competition spawns the Great Wild Ride building boom that lasted until the end of the decade. Many of the best roller coasters of all time were built during this period.

1929–1933: The Stock Market Crash and Great Depression cause the closing of many more parks. The number of amusement parks in the United States decreases to less than 500 from over 2000 in 1910.

1940s: Amusement parks offer a diversion from the Second World War. Rationing and scarcity of supplies hamper the wartime growth of amusement parks.

1950s: Baby boomers come of age and a new innovation, Kiddielands, begin to spring up, near another postwar phenomenon, the shopping center. Due to rapidly rising property values, the boom in Kiddieland building is short-lived.

1955: Disneyland opens. Generally considered the nation's first theme park. Built at a cost of $17 million, Disneyland represented the largest investment for building an amusement park that had been made up to that time. In spite of skepticism over such a new concept, the park was an instant success, drawing 3.8 million visitors to its five themed areas during its first season.

1959: The Matterhorn premiers at Disneyland. The first major tubular steel roller coaster, it forever changes the face of roller coaster development.

1961: The first Six Flags park opens in Texas. This was the first successful regional theme park. In its first full season of operation, 1.3 million visitors pass through the turnstiles.

1963: Arrow Development introduces the Log Flume ride at Six Flags over Texas. The ride quickly became the most popular ride at the park, and soon the Log Flume was being built at theme and traditional parks around the world.

Late 1960s to Early 1970s: Large inner-city parks begin closing, reflecting changing times. As turmoil increases throughout large cities, parks feel similar pressures.

1970s: Large corporate-backed Theme Parks begin growing in numbers with such major corporations as Marriott Corp., Penn Central, Anheuser-Busch, Taft Broadcasting, Mattel, and Harcourt, Brace,

Jovanovich investing in theme parks. Many small family-owned traditional parks succumb to competitive pressures and go the way of the mom-and-pop grocery store. Still other traditional parks renovate and expand to compete with the new wave of theme parks. Examples include Kennywood, Pittsburgh, PA; Cedar Point, Sandusky, OH: Dorney Park, Allentown, PA: Geauga Lake, Aurora, OH: Lagoon, Farmington, UT; and Hersheypark, Hershey, PA.

1971: The opening of Walt Disney World on 27,500 acres of central Florida. Disney makes the biggest investment ever for an amusement resort, a whopping $250 million.

1972: Kings Island theme park near Cincinnati, Ohio opens and is credited with the revival of the classic wooden roller coaster by building the Racer. Wooden coasters, once numbering near 2000, had now dwindled to less than 100.

1981: Opening of Canada's Wonderland, Toronto, Canada. It was widely considered to be the last theme park to be constructed in North America for several years. With costs up and all major markets apparently taken, experts considered the American theme park markets saturated.

1982: EPCOT Center opens at Walt Disney World in Florida. Considered a permanent World's Fair, EPCOT is the first theme park to surpass $1 billion in cost.

1983: The opening of Disneyland in Tokyo. Other corporations in the amusement business are now looking to the Far East and Europe to expand their operations.

1988: Sea World of Texas opens in San Antonio. The first major theme park to open in North America since 1981, it reinvigorates a slumbering industry. Soon several other new parks are under development, although not at the frenzied pace of the 1970s. Other new parks include:

- Fiesta Texas, San Antonio (1992)
- Knott's Camp Snoopy, Bloomington, MN (1992)
- MGM Grand Adventures, Las Vegas, NV (1993)
- Hecker Pass, Gilroy, CA (1998)
- Disney's Wild Kingdom, Walt Disney World, FL (1998)
- Lego World, Carlsbad, CA (1999)
- Heartland America, Indianapolis, IN (1999)
- Universal's Islands of Adventure, Orlando, FL (1999)
- Jazzland, New Orleans, LA (2000).

1987: Kennywood and Playland in Rye, NY are listed on the National Register of Historic Places, the first operating amusement parks to be honored. This is symbolic of the renewed appreciation of the heritage of the amusement park industry.

1990: Boardwalk and Baseball in Florida closes. Opened in 1974 as Circus World, Boardwalk and Baseball was the first corporate theme park to close. Facing stiff competition from Walt Disney World, Busch Gardens, Cypress Gardens, and Sea World of Florida, the park never made a profit during its existence.

1992: Batman, the Ride opens at Six Flags Great America in Gurnee, IL. The first inverted roller coaster, in which the cars travel underneath the structure, is an immediate hit, and soon parks around the world are building them.

1997: Superman-The Ride opens at Six Flags Magic Mountain, Valencia, CA. This roller coaster breaks previously unthought of records for height (415 feet tall) and speed (100 miles per hour).

1998: Disney's Animal Kingdom opened April 22, 1998.

Source: National Amusement Park Historical Association. See their web site at **http://www.napha.org**

KEY CONCEPTS

activities
aquariums
attractions
entertainment
events
festivals
gaming or gambling

International Association of
    Amusement Parks and Attractions
"jungles" (rainforests)
national forests
National Park Service
outlet malls
parks

recreation
Recreational Vehicle
    Industry Association
shopping
theme parks
West Edmonton Mall
zoological parks

INTERNET SITES

The Internet sites mentioned in this chapter are repeated here for convenience, plus some selected additional sites. For more information, visit these sites. Be aware that Internet addresses change frequently; so if a site cannot be accessed, use a search engine. Also, use a search engine to locate many additional sites that are available.

American Gaming Association
http://www.americangaming.org

American Recreation Coalition
http://www.funoutdoors.com

Bureau of Land Management
http://www.blm.gov

Caesars Palace
http://www.caesars.com

**Council for Hotel, Restaurant, and
    Institutional Education**
http://www.chrie.org

EventSeeker!
http://www.eventseeker.com

Event Net
http://www.eventnet.aust.com

Foxwoods Resort Casino
http://www.foxwoods.com

Great Outdoor Recreation Pages
http://www.gorp.com/default.htm

**International Association of
    Amusement Parks and
    Attractions**
http://www.iaapa.org

**International Festival and Events
    Association**
http://ifea.com

International Society of Travel and Tourism Educators
http://www.istte.org

Multi-Federal Land Recreation Site
http://www.Recreation.gov

National Amusement Park Historical Association
http://www.napha.org

National Indian Gaming Association
http://www.indiangaming.org

National Park Service
http://www.nps.gov

National Sporting Goods Association
http://www.nsga.org

National Trust for Historical Preservation
http://www.nthp.org

Recreation Vehicle Industry Association
http://www.rvamerica.com/rvia

Tourist Railway Association
http://www.train.org

Travel and Tourism Research Association
http://www.ttra.com

U.S. Bureau of Reclamation
http://www.usbr.gov

U.S. Fish & Wildlife Service
http://www.fws.gov

USDA Forest Service Recreation
http://www.fs.fed.us/recreational

INTERNET EXERCISES

Activity 1

Site Name: Walt Disney World

URL:
http://disney.go.com/DisneyWorld/index2.html

Background Information: Everything you need to plan your Walt Disney World Resort vacation is at this site. Use this site to make all your Disney arrangements.

Site Name: Guide to Theme Parks

URL: http://themeparks.miningco.com/

Background Information: Provides links to theme parks and amusement parks worldwide.

Site Name: Recreation.GOV

URL: http://www.recreation.gov/

Background Information: Recreation.gov is a one-stop resource for information about recreation on federal lands. The site offers information from all of the federal land management agencies and allows tourists to search for recreation sites by state, by agency, or by recreational activity.

Site Name: National Park Service Net

URL: http://www.nps.gov/

Background Information: On August 25, 1916; President Woodrow Wilson signed the act creating the National Park Service, a new federal bureau in the Department of the Interior. The fundamental purpose of the National Park Service is to conserve the scenery, natural and historic objects, and wildlife in the parks, as well as to provide for the enjoyment of the National parks in such manner as will remain unimpaired for the enjoyment of future generations.

Exercises

1. What role do the above sites play in the tourism industry? How do these sites encourage people to travel?

2. Choose a commercial destination and a government sponsored destination from the above sites and describe how they differ? To whom would these sites appeal?

Activity 2

Site Name: Event Seeker

URL: http://w3.eventseeker.com/

Background Information: This site allows you to search business and leisure events (trade shows, conferences, festivals, carnivals . . .) all in one place. Once you find the event of your choice, simply click on the event icon, and automatically the event information is imported in popular calendaring software such as Netscape Calendar.

QUESTIONS FOR REVIEW AND DISCUSSION

1. Give some of the main reasons that attractions and entertainment places are enjoying growing popularity.

2. How important are these factors as pleasure travel motivators?

3. If you were planning a destination-type resort, how much attention would you give to its recreation and entertainment features?

4. Why have theme parks changed the amusement park business so drastically?

5. Identify the principal appeals of theme parks. Explain their growth trends.

6. What are the directions being taken in the U.S. gambling industry?

7. Is the ownership of recreational vehicles a passing fad?

8. Where are the most famous national parks located? (Select various countries).

9. Should the spectacular new shopping malls include a director of tourism?

10. Suppose that your firm was considering building a new theater or attraction in Branson, Missouri. Where would you seek information and data? What kind of data would be needed?

11. List the advantages to local people who sponsor a festival that subsequently becomes attractive to a wider market.

12. Evaluate the national forests as recreational resources.

CASE PROBLEM

Most of the states in the United States are experiencing budget crunches. A number of legislatures are considering legalizing gaming (gambling). Some states have already done so. As a state representative, you have decided to introduce legislation legalizing gaming, to bolster your state's budget. What would be your arguments supporting this bill? What opposition would you expect?

SELECTED REFERENCES

Au, Norman, and J. S. Perry Hobson. "Gambling on the Internet: A Threat to Tourism?" *Journal of Travel Research,* Vol. 35, No. 4, pp. 77–81, Spring 1997.

Braunlich, Carl G. "Lessons from the Atlantic City Casino Experience." *Journal of Travel Research,* Vol. 34, No. 3, pp. 46–56, Winter 1996.

Cammerman, James M., and Ronald Bordessa. *Wonderland Through the Looking Glass.* Ontario: Belsten, 1981.

Center for Survey and Marketing Research. *Attractions: The Heart of the Travel Product.* Kenosha, WI: CSMR, 1992.

Childress, Rebecca D., and John L. Crompton. "A Comparison of Alternative Direction and Discrepancy Approaches to Measuring Quality of Performance at a Festival." *Journal of Travel Research,* Vol. 36, No. 2, pp. 43–57, Fall 1997.

Choi, Hak. "Gambling in Hong Kong." *Journal of Travel Research,* Vol. 36, No. 2, pp. 23–28, Fall 1997.

Christiansen, Eugene Martin, and Julie Brinkerhoff-Jacobs. "Gaming and Entertainment: An Imperfect Union?" *Cornell Hotel and Restaurant Administration Quarterly,* Vol. 36, No. 2, pp. 79–94, April 1995.

Crompton, John L., and Lisa L. Love. "The Predictive Validity of Alternative Approaches to Evaluating Quality of a Festival." *Journal of Travel Research,* Vol. 34, No. 1, pp. 11–24, Summer 1995.

Deebow, Suzanne M. "Gone Gamblin." *Meeting News,* pp. 37–45, September 1993.

Deply, Lisa. "An Overview of Sport Tourism: Building Toward a Dimensional Framework." *Journal of Vacation Marketing,* Vol. 4, No. 1, pp. 23–28, January 1998.

d'Hauteserre, Anne-Marie. "Disneyland Paris: A Permanent Economic Growth Pole in the Francilian

Landscape." *Progress in Hospitality Research*, Vol. 3, pp. 17–33, 1997.

Eade, Vincent, and Raymond Eade. *Introduction to the Casino Entertainment Industry*. Upper Saddle River, NJ: Prentice-Hall, 1997.

Eadington, William R. "The Legalization of Casinos: Policy Objectives, Regulatory Alternatives, and Cost/Benefit Considerations." *Journal of Travel Research*, Vol. 34, No. 3, pp. 3–8, Winter 1996.

Eadington, William R., and Judy A. Cornelius. *Gambling Behaviour and Problem Gambling*. Reno, NV: University of Nevada Press, 1992.

Eadington, William R., and Judy A. Cornelius. *Gambling and Public Policy: International Perspectives*. Reno, NV: University of Nevada Press, 1991.

Finn, Adam, and Tulin Erdem. "The Economic Impact of a Mega-Multi-Mall." *Tourism Management*, Vol. 16, No. 5, pp. 367–373, August 1995.

Getz, Donald. *Event Management and Event Tourism*. Elmsford, NY: Cognizant Communication Corporation, 1997.

Gibson, Heather J., Simon P. Attle, and Andrew Yiannakis. "Segmenting the Active Sport Tourist Market: A Life-Span Perspective." *Journal of Vacation Marketing*, Vol. 4, No. 1, pp. 52–64, January 1998.

Goldblatt, Joe. *Special Events*. New York: Wiley, 1996.

Goldblatt, Joe. *The Dictionary of Event Management*. New York: Wiley, 1996.

Grado, Stephen C., Charles H. Strauss, and Bruce E. Lord. "Antiquing as a Tourism Recreational Activity in Southwestern Pennsylvania." *Journal of Travel Research*, Vol. 35, No. 3, pp. 52–56, Winter 1997.

Hall, C. Michael, and Christopher Hamon. "Casinos and Urban Redevelopment in Australia." *Journal of Travel Research*, Vol. 34, No. 3, pp. 30–36, Winter 1996.

Heung, Vincent C. S., and Hailin Qu. "Tourism Shopping and Its Contributions to Hong Kong." *Tourism Management*, Vol. 19, No. 4, pp. 383–386, 1998.

Janson-Verbeke, Myriam. "Leisure Shopping: A Magic Concept for the Tourism Industry?" *Tourism Management*, Vol. 12, No. 1, pp. 9–14, March 1991.

Jensen, Clayne R. *Outdoor Recreation in America*. Champaign, IL: Human Kinetics, 1995.

Kang, Yong-Soon, Patrick T. Long, and Richard R. Perdue. "Resident Attitudes Toward Legal Gambling." *Annals of Tourism Research*, Vol. 23, No. 1, pp. 71–85, 1996.

Kilby, Jim, and Jim Fox. *Casino Operations Management*. New York: Wiley, 1997.

King, Frank W. *It's How You Play the Game: The Inside Story of the Calgary Olympics*. Calgary: Script, 1991.

Lawson, Rob, Juergen Gnoth, and Kerry Paulin. "Tourists' Awareness of Prices for Attractions and Activities." *Journal of Travel Research*, Vol. 34, No. 1, pp. 52–58, Summer 1997.

Leiper, Neil. "Tourist Attraction Systems." *Annals of Tourism Research*, Vol. 17, No. 3, pp. 367–384, 1990.

Long, Patrick, Jo Clark, and Derek Liston. *Win, Lose, or Draw? Gambling with America's Small Towns*. Washington, D.C.: The Aspen Institute, 1994.

Marfels, Christian. "The Case for Casino Gambling." *Gaming Research and Review Journal*, Vol. 3, No. 1, pp. 5–26, 1996.

Marshall, Lincoln, and Denis P. Rudd. *Introduction to the Casino and Gaming Industry*. Des Moines, IA: NeoData Order Processing Center, 1995.

Mayer, Karl J., et al. "Gaming Customer Satisfaction: An Exploratory Study." *Journal of Travel Research*, Vol. 37, No. 2, pp. 178–183, November 1998.

Mayfield, Teri L., and John L. Crompton. "Development of an Instrument for Identifying Community Reasons for Staging a Festival." *Journal of Travel Research*, Vol. 33, No. 3, pp. 37–44, Winter 1995.

Mayfield, Teri L., and John L. Crompton. "The Status of the Marketing Concept among Festival Organizers." *Journal of Travel Research*, Vol. 33, No. 4, pp. 14–22, Spring 1995.

Milman, Ady. "The Role of Theme Parks as a Leisure Activity for Local Communities." *Journal of Travel Research*, Vol. 29, No. 3, pp. 11–16, Winter 1990.

Morrison, Alastair M., et al. "A Profile of the Casino Resort Vacationer." *Journal of Travel Research*, Vol. 35, No. 2, pp. 55–61, Fall 1996.

National Park Service. *National Park Service Statistical Abstract 1997*. Denver: National Park Statistical Office, 1998.

Nolan, Mary Lee, and Sidney Nolan. "Religious Sites as Tourism Attractions in Europe." *Annals of Tourism Research*, Vol. 19, No. 1, pp. 68–78, 1992.

Oppermann, Martin. "Visitation of Tourism Attractions and Tourist Expenditure Patterns—Repeat vs. First-Time Visitors." *Asia Pacific Journal of Tourism Research*, Vol. 1, No. 1, pp. 61–68, 1996.

Pearce, Philip L. "Analyzing Tourist Attractions." *The Journal of Tourism Studies*, Vol. 2, No. 1, pp. 46–55, May 1991.

Pigram, John J., and Ronald C. Sundell (eds.). *National Parks and Protected Areas: Selection, Delimitation, and Management*. Armidale, NSW, Australia: Center for Water Policy Research, University of New England, 1997.

Samuels, Jack B. "Trends in Growth and Segmentation of the Theme/Amusement Park Industry." *Visions in Leisure and Business*, Vol. 5, No. 1, pp. 6–12, Fall 1996.

Smeral, Egon. "Economic Aspects of Casino Gaming in Austria." *Journal of Travel Research*, Vol. 36, No. 4, pp. 33–39, Spring 1998.

Stokowski, Patricia A. *Riches and Regrets: Betting on Gambling in Two Mountain Towns*. Niwot, CO: University Press of Colorado, 1996.

Superintendent of Documents. *Outdoor Recreation: A Reader for Congress*. Washington, D.C.: U.S. Government Printing Office, 1998.

Swarbrooke, John. *The Development and Management of Visitor Attractions*. Woburn, MA: Butterworth-Heinemann, 1995.

TIA, *Adventure Travel: Profile of a Growing Market*. Washington, D.C.: Travel Industry Association of America, 1994.

TIA, *Profile of Travelers Who Participate in Gambling*. Washington, D.C.: Travel Industry Association of America, April 1996.

TIA, *The Adventure Travel Report, 1997*. Washington, D.C.: Travel Industry Association of America, 1997.

Toepper, Lorin K. "Assessing Historic Sites as Tourism Attractions: Implications for Public Policy." *Visions in Leisure and Business*, Vol. 10, No. 1, pp. 26–43, Spring 1991.

U.S. Bureau of the Census. *Statistical Abstract of the United States: 1997*. Washington, D.C.: U.S. Government Printing Office, 1997.

Van Sickle, Kerry, and Paul F. J. Eagles. "Budgets, Pricing, Policies, and User Fees in Canadian Parks' Tourism." *Tourism Management*, Vol. 19, No. 3, pp. 225–235, 1998.

Watt, D. *Event Management in Leisure and Tourism*. Essex, England: Longman, 1998.

PART 3

UNDERSTANDING TRAVEL BEHAVIOR

◄ *Travelers passing through a concourse in O'Hare airport near Chicago. (Photo courtesy of United Airlines.)*

CHAPTER 9

PLEASURE TRAVEL MOTIVATION[1]

- Define a manageable research question on why tourists travel.

- Appreciate the range of ideas on travel motivation, particularly historical accounts.

- Recognize the contribution of psychological theories/other models.

- Assess the value of survey approaches to travel motivation.

- Appreciate the need for and content of the travel experience ladder as a blueprint for travel motivation study.

◄ *While many people travel to France to experience the wonders of Paris or relax on the French Riviera, other recreational pursuits, such as this horseback ride in the Alps, can also be part of a vacation itinerary. (Photo courtesy of French Government Tourist Office.)*

---

[1] This chapter was prepared by Phillip L. Pearce. Department of Tourism, James Cook University, Queensland, Australia.

INTRODUCTION

To be successful, tourism practitioners must understand consumer motivation. **History** offers a glimpse of behaviors to study. Even the supposedly spiritually motivated medieval pilgrims were sometimes wont to succumb to temptations during the long journey! So, though crusaders' motivations might have been spiritual, they often succumbed to the need to increase immediate gratification. Thus, from ancient times until now, astute operators understand the importance of understanding the psychology of tourism. Such travel **motivation** studies include: consumer motivation, decision-making, product satisfaction, overall acceptability of holiday experiences, pleasure in the vacation environment, and interaction with the local inhabitants. In short, tourists travel for reasons including spirituality, social status, escape, and cultural enrichment. **Maslow's** hierarchy of needs provides insight into ways in which a trip may satisfy disparate needs. If these concepts are studied within a context, they can provide information into how visitors select activities and experiences to suit their personal psychological and motivational profiles.

A FOCUS ON CONSUMERS

An understanding of the **consumer** is at the core of successful business practice in the tourist industry. If the various facets of the tourism, travel, and hospitality world can meet the needs of the consumer, some chance of business success is possible provided that other financial and managerial inputs are appropriate. Thus, if a theme park can meet the needs of its customers, if a wilderness lodge can provide the kind of accommodation its users expect, and if an adventure tour operator can organize an exciting white-water rafting trip, there is the basis for a successful tourism business. When consumer expectations are met or exceeded by tourism operations, one can expect repeat business and positive word-of-mouth advertising, as well as the ability to maintain or even increase the current level of charging for the existing tourism service. Clearly, consumers matter to tourism businesses.

The general issue of understanding consumer needs falls within the area of the **psychology** of tourists' behavior. This study area is concerned with what motivates tourists, how they make decisions, what tourists think of the products they buy, how much they enjoy and learn during their holiday experiences, how they interact with the local people and environment, and how satisfied they are with their holidays.

Asking the Question

A major focus of consumer studies in the psychology of tourist behavior is the study of travel motivation. The question is often expressed simply as "Why do tourists travel?" One of the lessons of social science research is to learn to ask good questions—that is, questions that are stimulating and challenging to our understanding of the world but which can be answered with enough specificity and information to enhance our knowledge. The question "Why do tourists travel?" is not a good question. Instead, we need to think of why certain groups of people choose certain holiday experiences, because this more specific question focuses attention on the similarities among groups of people and the kinds of experiences they seek. It should be noted that we are not

Seeing a moose in its native natural environment is a thrill for visitors to national parks and wildlife preserves. *(Photo courtesy of the Wyoming Division of Tourism.)*

asking the question of why groups of people travel to a specific destination, such as Las Vegas or central Africa. It can be argued that destinations offer many kinds of holiday experiences, and it oversimplifies the world to assume that areas as diverse as resorts, cities, or countries are going to attract just one group of visitors with a certain narrow range of motivations. Additionally, the focus of this chapter is on pleasure travel rather than travel for sporting, military, political, or predominantly business reasons.

Background

There are three main sources of ideas that assist in answering questions concerning travel motivation. Historical and literary accounts of travel and travelers provides one such source. Additionally, the discipline of psychology and its long history of trying to understand and explain human behavior is a rich vein of writing for travel motivation. Finally, the current practices of tourism industry researchers, particularly those involved in surveying visitors, offer some additional insights concerning how we might approach travel motivation.

History and Literature

Historians provide a range of accounts concerning why travelers have set about their journeys over the centuries. Casson[2] and Wolfe[3] point out that the wealthier members of Athenian and Roman society owned summer resorts and used to holiday there to

---

[2] L. Casson, *Travel in the Ancient World* (London: Allen & Unwin, 1974).
[3] R. I. Wolfe, "Recreational Travel: The New Migration," *Geographical Bulletin*, Vol. 2 (1967), pp. 159–167.

avoid the heat of the cities and to indulge in a social life characterized by much eating and drinking. The stability of the Roman world permitted its citizens to interest themselves in some long-distant travel, and Anthony[4] reports that visiting the Egyptian monuments and collecting souvenirs from these sites was a well-accepted and socially prestigious practice. If motives such as escape, social interaction, and social comparison were popular in Roman times, the emergence of the pilgrimage in the Middle Ages can be seen as adding a serious travel motive to our historical perspective. The original pilgrimages were essentially journeys to sacred places undertaken because of religious motives. Travelers sought the assistance or bounty of their God and journeyed long distances to revere the deity. Rowling[5] has noted that later in the Middle Ages, revelry and feasting became important accompaniments to the journey, and "licentious living" among the pilgrims was not unknown. The legacy of the pilgrimage for understanding modern traveler motivation is not insignificant. The pilgrimage elevated the importance of travel as an activity in one's life and created the idea that certain key sites or attractions were of long-lasting spiritual benefit to the sojourner. Good times and spiritual times were, however, not always separate.

The seriousness of travel was further enhanced by the **Grand Tour,** an activity intended principally as a training ground for the young and wealthy members of the English courts of the Tudor times. By the end of the eighteenth century the Grand Tour had gained favor as an ideal finishing school for a youth's education, a theme not inconsistent with the analysis of much contemporary youth travel.

The effects of industrialization, urbanization, and improved transportation possibilities brought travel to the middle classes in the mid-nineteenth century, and strong elements of social status and class consciousness characterize the fashions of the railway and spa resorts of nineteenth-century Europe.[6] One of the first tourism scholars, Pimlott,[7] writing in 1947, noted: "In the present century holidays have become a cult. . . . For many they are the principal objects for life—saved and planned for during the rest of the year and enjoyed in retrospect when they are over."

Now, of course, tourism is a worldwide phenomenon with enormous differentiation in its available environments, host cultures, and types of visitors. Nevertheless, some of the chief motivations noted in this brief historical review—such as travel for escape, cultural curiosity, spirituality, education, and social status—must be accounted for in any summary of contemporary travel.

Much of the contemporary travel scene is eloquently described by literary figures and professional travel writers. Their accounts of travel motivation, both of themselves and others, is subjective rather than professional but can also be considered as a background for our understanding. The noted American John Steinbeck conceived of travel as an "itch," a disease or pseudomedical condition—"the travel bug"—which periodically drove him to "be someplace else." Additionally, the theme of traveling to discover oneself has a long literary tradition and is present in the works of Ovid, Chaucer, Spenser, and Tennyson, as well as in twentieth-century fiction such as that by Jack Kerouac, E. M. Forster, D. H. Lawrence, and Joseph Conrad. The professional travel

---

[4] I. Anthony, *Verulamium* (Hanley, Staffordshire, England: Wood Mitchell, 1973).

[5] M. Rowling, *Everyday Life of Mediaeval Travellers* (London: B. T. Batsford, 1971).

[6] E. Swinglehurst, *The Romantic Journey* (London: Pica Editions, 1974).

[7] J. A. R. Pimlott, *The Englishman's Holiday* (London: Faber & Faber, 1947).

writers of the last two decades, such as Paul Theroux, Jan Morris, and Eric Newby, have emphasized discovery and curiosity in their analysis of the motives of travelers.

The rich tapestry of ideas about travel motivation from historical accounts and literary sources can be supplemented by theories of motivation from the discipline of psychology.

The Contribution of Psychological Theory

Psychology, as a separate area of inquiry, is often considered as originating in 1879 with the creation of the first laboratory for the scientific study of behavior by Wilhelm Wundt in Germany. During their own travels as study tours of human behavior, psychology writers and researchers have frequently addressed the topic of human motivation. The scope of this research is impressive because it includes detailed studies of human physiology and the nervous system, through to approaches with a more cultural and anthropological orientation.

Many well-known theories in psychology have a strong motivational component. In many instances the discussion or study of motivation is a part of a broader theory directed at understanding human personality or, more simply, what makes individuals

The beauty of an unspoiled natural landscape is a strong travel motivator. These boys are on a rock overlooking Victoria Falls in Zimbabwe, one of southern Africa's most famous natural attractions.

different. A summary of some **major theories in psychology** that have been concerned in part with the topic of motivation is presented in Table 9.1. It must be noted that these psychology researchers and thinkers were not considering **travel** motivation directly when formulating these approaches. Nevertheless, the third column of Table 9.1 lists a number of human **needs** and **motives** that might usefully be applied to the question of why certain groups of travelers seek particular kinds of holiday experiences.

A direct application of these psychological theories for tourist motivation adds some new motives to the list obtained from the historical and literary review. In particular, such motives as personal control, love, sex, competence, tension reduction, arousal, achievement, acceptance, self-development, respect, curiosity, security, understanding, and self-actualization can be identified.

Current Market Research Practices

An understanding of travel motivation can also be approached by examining the kinds of motivation questions asked in surveys of travelers. Basic passport questions that are standardized around the world include only broad categories of motivation and are limited to distinctions such as whether the travel is for business reasons, as a holiday,

TABLE 9.1
Human Motives and Needs in Psychology Theory and Research[a]

Theorist/Researcher	Theoretical Approach	Motives or Needs Emphasized
Sigmund Freud	Psychoanalytic theory	Need for sex; need for aggression; emphasis on unconscious needs
Carl Jung	Psychoanalytic approach	Need for arousal; need to create and to self-actualize
Alfred Adler	Modified psychoanalytic	Need for competence; need for mastery to overcome incompetence
Harry Stack Sullivan	Modified psychoanalytic	Need for acceptance and love
Karen Horney	Modified psychoanalytic	Need to control anxiety; need for love and security
Clark Hull	Learning theory	Need to reduce tension
Gordon Allport	Trait theory	Need to repeat intrinsically satisfying behaviors
Albert Bambera	Social learning theory	Need for self-efficacy or personal mastery
David McClelland, John Atkinson	Social approaches	Need for achievement
Carl Rogers	Humanistic	Need for self-development
Abraham Maslow	Humanistic	Hierarchy of needs, from physiological needs to safety needs to love and relationship needs to self-esteem to self-actualization.
David Bertyne	Cognitive approaches	Need to satisfy curiosity; need to seek mental stimulation
Ron Harre	Ethogenic (social and philosophical)	Need to earn respect and avoid contempt of others
Stephen Cohen, Laurie Taylor	Sociological theory	Need to escape; need for excitement and meaning
George Kelly	Personal construct theory	Need to predict and explain the world
Mikhail Csikszentmihali	Humanistic approach	Need for peak experiences

[a] For clarity the terms motives and needs are used together in this summary table. Some writers prefer to see needs as more being physiologically based and motives as more socially oriented.

Most parents are motivated to provide their children with wholesome and memorable vacation experiences, such as a visit to see Fred Flintstone and Yogi Bear.
(Photo courtesy of Great America, Santa Clara, California.)

to visit friends and relatives, for a convention, or for other reasons. More specific market research questions are typified in studies of "travel benefits" or the rewards of travel. It can be argued that these travel benefits or rewards can be seen as the outcomes or satisfactions linked to tourists' motives for traveling. In a typical study of travel benefits, Loker and Perdue[8] studied visitors to North Carolina and factor-analyzed 12 benefit statements as part of a survey of summer travelers to that state. Using the two statistical sorting procedures of factor analysis and cluster analysis, the researchers argued that there were six segments of the market receiving different kinds of benefits from their holidays. The six categories included those who emphasized excitement and escape, pure adrenalin/excitement seekers, family- and friends-oriented group, naturalists (those who enjoyed natural surroundings), a group that emphasized the value of escape by itself, and a group that enjoyed all benefits. This kind of research, which has been repeated by several other scholars with slightly different benefit groups emerging for different settings, represents a summary of travel satisfaction for a particular destination. It is thus not a pure or clean analysis of travel motivation but helps us to understand the importance of travel motivation in tourism studies by emphasizing that for travel motivation analysis to be useful and

---

[8] L. E. Loker and R. Perdue, "A Benefit-Based Segmentation of a Nonresident Summer Travel Market," *Journal of Travel Research*, Vol. 31, No. 1 (Summer 1992), pp. 30–35.

TABLE 9.2
Motives and Destination Features from Market Survey Research

Canadian Government Travel Bureau (1970s)	Queensland (Australia) Domestic Market Segmentation Study (1990s)
Warm, friendly people	Good service
To visit friends or relatives	—
Relaxing atmosphere	—
Scenery	Lots of interesting countryside and wildlife
For oceans and beaches	Good beaches and lots of water activities
Sports facilities	Opportunity for sporting activities: golf, tennis, etc.
Good weather there	—
Not too many tourists	Seclusion
To get better buys	Good shopping
Low cost of vacations	Low-cost accommodation or good camping facilities
Good campsites	—
Good roads	—
Outstanding food	Good restaurants
Nightlife	Lots of nightlife
Easier to have fun there	—
Attractive customs, life	Wide variety of things to do
Foreigners	—
Cultural activities	Cultural things to do (theater, museums, etc.)
Attractive advertising	—
—	High-quality accommodation
—	Lots of things for the kids to do
—	Opportunity for adventure activities: rafting, rock climbing, etc.

meaningful, it must be put in a context. Thus, while the list of motives from psychology theories and the history/literature of travel provides a rich source of potential motives, an understanding of travel motivation makes sense only in a particular context—that is, when people are describing why they might seek certain holiday experiences.

Frequently, market survey organizations provide potential travelers with lists of items that the researchers believe are relevant to the question of why people travel to particular destinations. Echtner and Ritchie[9] provide a summary list of 34 attributes used in 14 leading studies of destination image. Of these 34 attributes, 24 were used in at least three studies. These lists are often a mixture of **attributes of the destination** and select motives of the traveler. Two examples of such lists are provided in Table 9.2. While such lists of motives and destination features mixed together are common in studies trying to explain the appeal of places, they have some limitations. In particular, the lists may not be comprehensive, but instead may reflect the biases of the researchers and may not explore the relative importance of the various features or reasons for visiting and assume incorrectly that all reasons are equally important. Additionally, the way in which the attributes are interrelated is not often considered. For example, the characteristics of "seclusion" and "exciting nightlife" may be mutually exclusive.

---

[9] C. M. Echtner and J. R. B. Ritchie, "The Meaning and Measurement of Destination Image," *Journal of Tourism Studies*, Vol. 2 No. 2 (1991), pp. 2–12.

The Need for a Theory

This review of travel motivation has stressed that there are three sources of information that can provide a list of motives concerning why people travel. The list of potential travel motivations is a long one and includes a range of needs, from excitement and arousal to self-development and personal growth. Additionally, the brief review of contemporary market research practice concerning destination image indicated that there were further lists of destination features that might be thought of as a mix of travel motives and destination characteristics.

Theories or models in social science research typically summarize or integrate knowledge in an area, as well as organize existing knowledge into a new perspective. Occasionally, the theory will enable prediction or specifications of future directions for human action and research. The area of tourist motivation requires a theoretical approach. There are lists of motives that need to be summarized; there are connections with other areas of inquiry, such as destination image studies, which need to be made; and there needs to be a new stimulus to challenge and enhance our current understanding. Pearce[10] has outlined seven features that are necessary for a good theory of tourist motivation. These are listed in Table 9.3.

The work of Plog[11] resulted in the psychocentric–allocentric model of travel mo-

TABLE 9.3
Requirements of a Sound Theory of Tourist Motivation

Element	Explanation
1. The role of the theory	Must be able to integrate existing tourist needs, reorganize the needs, and provide a new orientation for future research
2. The ownership and appeal of the theory	Must be appealing to specialist researchers, useful in tourism industry settings, and credible to marketers and consumers
3. Ease of communication	Must be relatively easy to explain to potential users and be universal (not country specific) in its application
4. Ability to measure travel motivation	Must be amenable to empirical study; the ideas can be translated into questions and responses for assessment purposes
5. A multimotive versus single-trait approach	Must consider the view that travelers may seek to satisfy several needs at once; must be able to model the pattern of traveler needs, not just consider one need
6. A dynamic versus snapshot approach	Must recognize that both individuals and societies change over time; must be able to consider or model the changes that are taking place continuously in tourism
7. The roles of extrinsic and intrinsic motivation	Must be able to consider that travelers are variously motivated by intrinsic, self-satisfying goals and at other times are motivated by extrinsic, socially controlled rewards (e.g., others' opinions)

---

[10] P. L. Pearce, "Fundamentals of Tourist Motivation," in D. G. Pearce and R. W. Butler, eds. *Fundamentals of Tourism Motivation* (London: Routledge, 1991), pp. 113–134.
[11] S. C. Plog, "Why Destination Areas Rise and Fall in Popularity," *The Cornell Quarterly*, Vol. 14, No. 4 (1974), pp. 55–58; and "Understanding Psychographics in Tourism Research," in J. R. B. Ritchie and C. Goeldner, eds., *Travel Tourism and Hospitality Research* (New York: Wiley, 1987), pp. 203–214.

Sailing on the Nile River in a felucca combines recreational activity, cultural appreciation, and natural beauty. *(Photo courtesy of the Egyptian Tourist Authority.)*

tivation. This work was historically important in providing one organizing theory of travel motivation. It does not, however, fulfill some of the criteria listed in Table 9.3 and is notably deficient in terms of offering only a single trait: a static and extrinsic account of tourist motivation. Additionally, it is not of universal application and is limited by its formulation in the tourism context of the early 1970s.

There are some new emerging theories of tourist and leisure motivation that fulfill more of the criteria described in Table 9.3. In particular, the intrinsic motivation–optimal arousal perspective of Iso-Ahola[12] and the travel needs model of Pearce[13] both add new perspectives to the tourist motivation field.

Iso-Ahola argues that tourist and leisure behavior takes place within a framework of optimal arousal and incongruity. That is, while individuals seek different levels of stimulation, they share the need to avoid either overstimulation (mental and physical exhaustion) or boredom (too little stimulation). Leisure needs change during the lifespan and across places and social company. He advises researchers to keep the motivation questions for leisure close to the actual participation in time and emphasizes the importance of participants' feelings of self-determination and competence to ensure satisfaction.

The **travel needs model** articulated by Pearce and co-workers is concerned more explicitly with tourists and their motives rather than with leisure, which is the focus of

[12] S. Iso-Ahola, "Toward a Social Psychological Theory of Tourism Motivation: A Rejoinder," *Annals of Tourism Research*, Vol. 9, No. 2 (1982), pp. 256–262.

[13] P. L. Pearce, *The Ulysses Factor: Evaluating Visitors in Tourist Settings* (New York: Springer-Verlag, 1988); and "Fundamentals of Tourist Motivation," in D. G. Pearce and R. W. Butler, *Fundamentals of Tourist Motivation* (London: Routledge, 1991), pp. 113–134.

Iso-Ahola's work. The travel needs model argues that people have a life cycle in their travel behavior which reflects a hierarchy of their travel motives. Like a career at work, people may start at different levels, they are likely to change their levels during their life cycle, and they can be inhibited in their travel needs by money, health, and other people.

The steps or levels on the travel needs model may be likened to a ladder, and this concept is built on Maslow's hierarchy of needs. By expanding and extending the range of specific needs at each ladder level which fit with Maslow's original formulation, a very comprehensive and rich catalog of the many different psychological needs and motives noted earlier in this chapter can be realized (see Figure 9.1). The travel needs ladder retains Maslow's ideas that lower levels on the ladder have to be satisfied

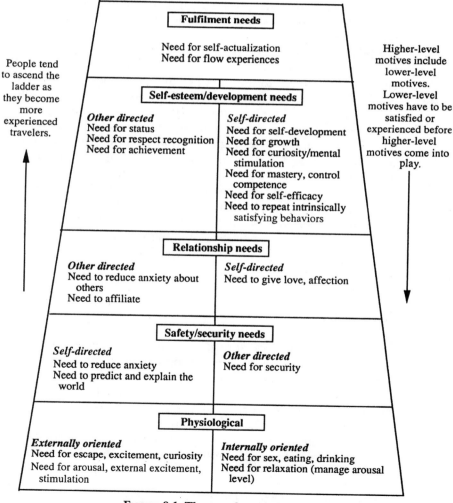

People tend to ascend the ladder as they become more experienced travelers.

Higher-level motives include lower-level motives. Lower-level motives have to be satisfied or experienced before higher-level motives come into play.

Fulfilment needs

Need for self-actualization
Need for flow experiences

Self-esteem/development needs

Other directed
Need for status
Need for respect recognition
Need for achievement

Self-directed
Need for self-development
Need for growth
Need for curiosity/mental
  stimulation
Need for mastery, control
  competence
Need for self-efficacy
Need to repeat intrinsically
  satisfying behaviors

Relationship needs

Other directed
Need to reduce anxiety about
  others
Need to affiliate

Self-directed
Need to give love, affection

Safety/security needs

Self-directed
Need to reduce anxiety
Need to predict and explain the
  world

Other directed
Need for security

Physiological

Externally oriented
Need for escape, excitement, curiosity
Need for arousal, external excitement,
  stimulation

Internally oriented
Need for sex, eating, drinking
Need for relaxation (manage arousal
  level)

FIGURE 9.1 The travel needs ladder.

before the person moves to higher levels of the ladder. Thus, travelers concerned with developing and extending their **relationships** while traveling will also have needs in terms of **safety** and **physiological** level factors but may not yet be particularly concerned with **self-esteem** and **self-development** needs. Importantly, the travel needs ladder emphasizes that people have a range of motives for seeking out holiday experiences. For example, a visitor to Canada who attends the Calgary Stampede might be motivated to do so by the pleasant, safe setting, to entertain a child and develop family experiences of togetherness, and to add to knowledge about Canadian culture. That is, several levels of the travel needs ladder are working together for a rich multi-motive picture of travel motivation. This flexibility and variability recognizes that motivation may change over time and across situations so that in visiting Britain, the same person might emphasize cultural understanding and curiosity motives more than relationship and family development motives.

In the travel needs model, destinations are seen as settings where vastly different holiday experiences are possible. Thus travelers' motives influence what they seek from a destination, and destinations will vary in their capacity to provide a range of holiday experiences.

In short, travelers do not visit a place with standard objective destination features but, instead, journey to a location where they select activities and holiday experiences among those offered to suit their personal psychological and motivational profile.

The travel needs model was formulated so that a dynamic, multimotive account of travel behavior could serve our understanding of tourism. It acts as a blueprint for the assessment of tourist motives and requires individual tailoring to specific situations. That is, the context or setting helps frame the way in which the travel needs ladder questions are asked. Pearce and McDermott[14], working in a theme park setting, were able to use the travel needs ladder to explain the motives of different consumers for that setting. This individual tailoring is done by taking sections of the travel needs ladder (e.g., the physiological level and the need for stimulation) and asking questions about the importance of rides and adventure activities in the theme park. Similarly, questions about the importance of going with friends were asked. In this way a full range of theme park motives is determined by linking travel motivation to other tourism studies.

SUMMARY

In this chapter we have argued that a theory of tourist motivation such as the travel needs ladder helps summarize existing statements and ideas about the motives of travelers. It can also be useful in answering several questions: "Why do certain groups of travelers seek particular holiday experiences?" and the related question "Why do certain groups of travelers travel to destination X?"

In this chapter we have stressed that there will not be one simple answer to these questions; instead, different groups of individuals will place different weightings on a structured set of answers consistent with their travel needs level. For example,

---

[14] P. Pearce and B. McDermott, *Dreamworld Report* (Townsville, Queensland, Australia: James Cook University of North Queensland, 1991).

young teenagers emphasize the motives of stimulation and relationships in visiting theme parks, while young couples emphasize developing relationships and the need for relaxation. For travelers exploring exotic locations and participating in more diverse forms of tourism, a wider range of motives, including self-development, mastery, curiosity, escape, and self-fulfillment, will be involved.

Travel motivation studies can be the basis of many consumer analyses in tourism. A good motivational profile of visitors should be of assistance in understanding how well the destination characteristics fit the needs of the travelers. The key to linking travel motivation studies to other tourism studies, such as destination choice, lies in analyzing the activities offered by the destination and the activities that fulfill the travelers' motives. Thus, if visitors strongly motivated by the need to enhance their understanding of art and history visit well-managed high-quality cultural attractions, satisfaction is likely. A mismatch can also occur, such as the unfortunate visitor to a tropical island who is seeking rest and relaxation only to be assaulted by a tourism product that is set up for those seeking stimulation, excitement, and new relationships. As tourism grows into an increasingly sophisticated consumer industry, the need to understand the needs of travelers will increase and the motivation of tourists will become a core part of all tourism studies.

ABOUT THE READING

The Reading, *Climbing Ayers Rock: Relating Visitor Motivation, Time Perception and Enjoyment,* examines how individual differences in motivation influence the experience of climbing Ayers Rock, a massive geological formation which is a tourist attraction located in north central Australia.

READING 9.1

CLIMBING AYERS ROCK: RELATING VISITOR MOTIVATION, TIME PERCEPTION AND ENJOYMENT

by Kerri-Anne Fielding, Philip L. Pearce, and Karen Hughes
James Cook University

Reprinted from *The Journal of Tourism Studies,* Vol. 3, No. 2 (1992).

Many famous tourist sites have become associated with particular activities (Pearce, 1991). Ayers Rock, for example, provides visitors with the opportunity to view magnificent sunsets, examine distinctive geological formations and, of course, climb to the summit. Every year an estimated 200,000 people of all ages and many nationalities attempt the arduous and sometime dangerous 1.5 kilometre trek to the top of the rock. Many of these people come to Central Australia solely for this purpose. The question to be asked is: why do

people climb Ayers Rock? and, even more importantly, do individual differences in motivation influence the climbing experience? Currently, consideration is being given to closing the climb, for environmental and cultural reasons. If such a closure takes place it will be important for the local tourism industry to have an understanding of why the climb matters and how individuals perceive it. Armed with such knowledge it might be possible to develop other activities in the vicinity of the rock which meet the tourists' needs and motives.

Additionally, an understanding of the links between visitor motivation and the visitor experience for challenging tourist activities has the potential to be very useful for market segmentation and management purposes. Hsieh, O'Leary and Morrison (1992) claim that the psychological benefits which individuals obtain from their tourist experiences represent one of the most subtle and innovative ways of seg-

Ayers Rock in Uluru National Park is a massive conglomerate rock formation rising over 1000 feet above the surrounding plain. It is located in central Australia in the Northern Territory. The rock is a popular tourist attraction, and climbing to its top is a challenging visitor activity. *(Photo courtesy of the Northern Territory Tourist Commission.)*

menting the visitor market, thus enhancing promotional efforts and facilitating product design and management for target groups.

The importance of motivation to the quality of general leisure experience is not new. In 1974 Neulinger proposed that individual differences in motivation play a major role in determining the intensity of leisure involvement. Ruskin and Shamir (1984) also pointed to the possibility that the activities engaged in and level of involvement may vary according to the individual's prime motivation. There have, however, been few empirical attempts to examine how individual differences in motivation influence the nature and quality of the leisure experience particularly in tourism settings (Hull & Harvey, 1989).

The purpose of the present study, therefore, is to examine whether individual differences in motivation influence the experience of climbing Ayers Rock. In particular, this study examines the differences in task enjoyment and time perception between tourists who are intrinsically motivated (that is, those climbing the rock for the sake of it) and tourists who are achievement motivated (that is, those climbing for the sole purpose of reaching the summit).

Intrinsically motivated activities are those for which there is no apparent reward other than the activity itself. That is, the activities are engaged in for their own sake, and not because they lead to an external reward (Deci, 1975). The rewards for behaviour motivated by intrinsic needs are inherent in the activity itself (e.g., the enjoyment derived from simply participating in the activity). Most leisure researchers argue that leisure is intrinsically motivated, that one does it for the sake of it, and does not expect a reward (Neulinger, 1974).

Several attempts have been made to examine the relationship between intrinsic motivation and leisure. Dichotomising motivation into intrinsic and extrinsic dimensions, these studies have consistently supported the notion that intrinsically motivated activities are more positively experienced than extrinsically motivated activities (Graef, Csikszentmihalyi, & Giannino, 1983; Samdahl, 1988).

The relationship between intrinsic motivation and loss of awareness of the passage of time has also been examined within the context of leisure. Mannell and Bradley (1986) found that people who were intrinsically motivated were more likely to experience time as passing quickly whereas extrinsically motivated individuals were more likely to perceive time to pass slowly. It appears that the major factor affecting perception of time is the degree to which one's attention is directed toward the passage of time itself. According to Gupta and Cummings (1986), when one is engaged in an absorbing activity, temporal awareness is minimised and time is perceived to pass relatively quickly. Thus, the more absorbing and enjoyable the activity, the less attention paid to temporal cues and the shorter the perceived duration of time (Gupta & Cummings, 1986).

Tourism activities and settings offer few possibilities for the study of extrinsic (that is, reward-related) motivation. Instead, a contrast may be drawn between intrinsic motivation and achievement motivation for tourism settings. While similar to intrinsic motivation in the sense that it is self-determined behavior (that is, the source of the motivation lies in the individual), achievement motivated behaviour differs from intrinsically motivated behaviour in a number of important ways. Firstly, unlike intrinsic motivation, the reward is the feelings of competence resulting from success in the activity (Deci, 1975; Atkinson, 1982). Secondly, achievement motivated individuals are especially sensitive to performance evaluation (Harackiewicz, Abrahams, & Wageman, 1987). This makes them more likely to be tense and apprehensive, particularly in situations where tasks competency is evaluated. Indeed, a number of studies have shown that achievement motivation tends to have a detrimental effect on task enjoyment. For example, Harackiewicz et al. (1987) reported a nonsignificant relationship between achievement motivation and enjoyment for a task (puzzle). Wankel and Kreisel (1985) measured ten factors said to be associated with sports enjoyment and found that while intrinsic motivation contributed mostly to enjoyment, winning the game and getting rewards, items which could be classified as outcome oriented (or achievement motivated) were of lesser importance to enjoyment. Shaw (1985) also found that for activities where the participant felt the outcome was being judged, tested or evaluated (as in the case of achievement situations) they were less likely to perceive that activity as leisure.

In relation to time perception, McClelland (1981) found subjects high in the need for achievement tended to overestimate time (that is, perceive time to pass more slowly than it actually does) whereas subjects low in need for achievement tend to underestimate time (perceive time to pass more quickly). According to Brown (1985), situations which involved heightened awareness of time, such as boredom, anticipation and impatience result in an apparent lengthening of time. This occurs because the individual wishes the unpleasant experience to finish, therefore the time passes slowly (Gupta & Cummings, 1986). It could be argued that the achievement situa-

tion is one which involves anticipation of achieving that goal and result in overestimation of time duration (Quigley, Combs, & O'Leary, 1984).

The above research suggests that intrinsically motivated tourists will tend to experience higher levels of enjoyment while climbing Ayers Rock than those who are achievement motivated. Furthermore, intrinsically motivated people were expected to perceive time as passing more quickly than actual time, whereas achievement motivated individuals were expected to perceive time as passing more slowly than real time.

This study also examines the relationship between enjoyment and time perception. Studies have repeatedly shown that pleasant psychological states result in underestimation of time while unpleasant experience produce an overestimation (Krus & Fletcher, 1988). The evidence suggests that regardless of activity, if it is evaluated as enjoyable, time seems to pass quickly, but if it is perceived to be dull or uninteresting, time seems to drag. From these findings it was postulated that tourists who enjoyed the climb would be likely to perceive time as passing quickly, whereas those who did not enjoy the climb would tend to perceive time as passing slowly.

Method

Study Site

Ayers Rock was chosen as the place of study because it provided access to large numbers of visitors within a confined area. Other studies in recreation have reported difficulties with sampling visitors at such highly mobile sites, as they tend to disperse over a wide area (Mills, Hodgson, McNeely, & Masse, 1981). At Ayers Rock, however, there is only one path to the summit. This enabled the researchers to position themselves at a point which all climbers must pass at the beginning and at the end of the climb. Secondly, climbing Ayers Rock was considered an appropriate activity to study as tourists were expected to be motivated by both intrinsic and achievement motives.

Participants: 187 tourists (97 males and 90 females) participated in this study. Participants ranged in age from 16 to 69 with a mean age of 26. They were mostly Australian (29%), European (30%), or British (28%).

Apparatus: Each participant was given a coloured, prenumbered ribbon which was attached to their clothing with a safety pin. Watches were used by the researchers to record the time each climber commenced and completed their climb. All other

Hikers descend from their climb to the top of Ayers Rock. The satisfactions and enjoyment of their climbing experience were determined by interviews at both the bottom and top of the rock climbing path. *(Photo courtesy of the Northern Territory Tourist Commission.)*

data were collected using a 2-page self report questionnaire, administered upon completion of the climb. This was designed to assess visitors' motivation for climbing, their level of enjoyment, and their estimates of the duration of the activity. Demographic details were also obtained.

Procedure: Data was collected on-site over a five day period from the 26th April to the 1st May, 1990. The procedure employed in the present study involved three stages: sampling and tagging of climbers, contact with tagged climbers at the summit, and contact again at the base upon completion of the climb. This procedure is similar to that employed by Mills and his associates in sampling participants at ski resorts (Mills, Hodgson, McNeely, & Masse, 1981) and has been found to result in good cooperation and high response rates.

Stage 1: Two researchers were situated at the base of the climb. As climbers approached to begin their climb, the researchers introduced themselves as students from James Cook University conducting research on the tourist experience at Ayers Rock. After briefly explaining the study, climbers were asked if they were willing to participate in the study. Those who agreed were given a highly visible coloured ribbon to pin to their clothing. Each ribbon was prenumbered, and this number, along with the time that the participant began the climb, was recorded.

To obtain the most representative sample possible and maximise the use of the survey team, the researchers were required to sample using the "next to pass" procedure (Gale & Jacobs, 1987). This meant that as soon as the last consenting climber had been tagged, the next individual to pass was sampled. This procedure began at 6.00 a.m. and continued until approximately 10.30 a.m., by which time most of the climbers for that day had already begun their climb.

Stage 2: Two researchers were situated at the top of Ayers Rock to identify tagged climbers as soon as they reached the summit. Participant's ribbon numbers and the time the climber arrived at the top were recorded.

Stage 3: The final stage involved distributing self-administered questionnaires to tagged participants upon completion of the climb. This was done at the base of Ayers Rock.

Operationalisation of Variables

Time Perception: The time it took for each person to climb the rock was calculated by subtracting the time they started from the time when they reached the summit. This was labelled 'actual time.' 'Perceived time' was determined by asking the subjects to indicate on the post-climb questionnaire how long they felt it took them to reach the top of the rock. Time judgements were then transformed into a ratio measure by dividing perceived time by actual time (see Brown, 1985). A value less than 1 represented a judgement shorter than the actual duration, while a value greater than 1 represented a judgement longer than the actual duration. This ensured that all scores existed on the same relative scale (Brown, 1985) and were not influenced by the actual time it took to reach the top.

Enjoyment: Enjoyment was measured using a 9 point graphic scale, ranging from very enjoyable to not at all enjoyable. Participants were asked to describe the climb by placing a tick next to the statement which best described their feelings about the climb.

Motivation: The method used to determine climbers' underlying motivation was similar to the one employed by Pearce and Caltabiano (1983) in that climbers' motives were measured indirectly on the basis of their response to an open-ended question. As the most significant distinction to be made in the present study was between intrinsic and achievement motivation, their coding scheme, based on Maslow's hierarchy, was not considered appropriate. For this study the following assessment procedure was implemented.

The present approach is closely related to the work of Pearce (1988, 1991) who has been developing a travel career ladder model of motivation. This particular study is seen as working within one rung or at one level of the ladder—the self-esteem, self-development level and contrasting an intrinsic versus an external (achievement) oriented approach at that level.

To determine climbers' underlying motivation, participants were asked to describe the best thing about the climb. The coding of responses into achievement motivation or intrinsic motivation involved a number of stages in an attempt to enhance both the reliability and validity of coding. Firstly, the researchers developed a list of potential reasons for wanting to climb Ayers Rock. This was done by asking

one hundred first-year university students enrolled in psychology to provide five reasons why they would want to climb Ayers Rock. A list of 50 different reasons were obtained, most of which were consistent with motives for outdoor recreation found in the literature (Driver & Brown, 1978; Crandall, 1980).

Twenty-three third-year psychology students were then asked to rate each reason on a seven point Likert-type scale (with a score of 1 indicating "not at all," and a score of 7 indicating "very much so") the extent to which they felt each reason represented an example of intrinsic motivation and an example of achievement motivation. The modal scores for both types of motivation were calculated for each of the fifty reasons. Each reason was then classified as either intrinsic or achievement motivation depending on the highest modal score.

Finally, participants' responses were then matched with the reasons given in Step 1, and the participant was identified as either intrinsically motivated or achievement motivated, based upon the coding in Step 2. If participants' responses were more elaborate and clearly did not fit into any one or combinations of the 50 listed reasons, two independent judges (fourth year psychology students) were asked to code the responses. The level of agreement reached between the judges was 86%. If responses belonged to both motivational categories, they were identified as multi-motivated and were excluded from the analysis.

On the basis of the above coding system, 52 participants were identified as being intrinsically motivated and 66 participants were identified as being achievement motivated.

Results

A regression analysis was used to assess the relationship between motivation and enjoyment. A moderate but significant correlation of $-.296$ ($p = .0012$) was found between motivation and enjoyment with motivation accounting for 9% of the variance in enjoyment. These results indicate that intrinsically motivated people were more likely to experience higher levels of enjoyment whereas achievement motivated people were more likely to experience lower levels of enjoyment. The relationship between motivational type and enjoyment was further examined using a contingency table, presented in Table 1.

From Table 1 it can be seen that 82.7% of intrinsically motivated climbers reported high levels of enjoyment, whereas only 61.5% of achievement moti-

TABLE 1
Relationship Between Motivation and Enjoyment

		Motivation		Total
		Intrinsic	**Achievement**	
Low enjoyment		**9**	**25**	**34**
	(row)	26.5%	73.5%	
	(col)	17.3%	38.5%	
High enjoyment		**43**	**40**	**83**
	(row)	51.8%	48.2%	
	(col)	82.7%	61.5%	
		52	**65**	**117**

Chi square = 6.271; p = 0.0123.

vated individuals reported this level of enjoyment. 73.5% of those who reported low levels of enjoyment were achievement motivated, whereas only 26.5% were intrinsically motivated. In the group experiencing high levels of enjoyment, 51.8% were intrinsically motivated and 48.2% were achievement motivated. While the differentiation between the motivational types was minimal, these findings do support the hypothesis that intrinsically motivated climbers would be more likely to experience higher levels of enjoyment than would achievement motivated individuals.

The relationship between motivation and time perception was examined in a similar manner. A regression analysis revealed a significant correlation of .312 (p = .0011) between motivation and time perception, indicating that people who were intrinsically motivated were more likely to perceive time as passing

quickly, whereas people who were achievement motivated were more likely to perceive time as passing slowly. Motivation accounted for 9.7% of the variance in time perception. This relationship is further clarified in Table 2.

It can be seen that 56% of those who perceived time as passing quicker than it actually did were intrinsically motivated, while 44% were achievement motivated. Conversely, of those who perceived time to pass slowly, 70% were achievement motivated whereas only 30% were intrinsically motivated. These results suggest that intrinsically motivated people tended to perceive time as passing more quickly than it actually did, whereas those who were achievement motivated were more likely to perceive time as passing more slowly.

Finally, the relationship between time perception and enjoyment was examined. A weak but significant

TABLE 2
Relationship Between Motivation and Time Perception

		Motivation		Total
		Intrinsic	**Achievement**	
Perceived time		**28**	**22**	**50**
less than	(row)	56.0%	44.0%	
actual time	(col)	54.9%	34.9%	
Perceived time		**8**	**6**	**14**
equal to	(row)	57.1%	42.9%	
actual time	(col)	15.7%	9.5%	
Perceived time		**15**	**35**	**50**
greater than	(row)	30.0%	70.0%	
actual time	(col)	29.4%	55.6%	
		52	**65**	**117**

Chi square = 7.829; p = 0.0199.

correlation of $-.148$ ($p = .0462$) was found between enjoyment and time perception, a relationship which is further clarified in Table 3.

Table 3 indicates that 78.2% of climbers who perceived time to pass quickly reported the highest levels of enjoyment. However, the prediction that people who perceived time to pass more slowly would report low levels of enjoyment was not supported, with 56.2% of these people also reporting high levels of enjoyment. Nevertheless, it can be seen that the majority (55.1%) of those who reported low levels of enjoyment felt that time has passed slower than it actually did.

Discussion

The results of the present investigation indicated a relationship between motivation and enjoyment, with intrinsically motivated people reporting higher levels of enjoyment than achievement motivated individuals (see Table 1). The close association between intrinsic motivation and enjoyment has been previously demonstrated (Roadburg, 1983; Shaw, 1985), however, few studies have examined the relationship between achievement motivation and task enjoyment. The present study indicates no significant relationship between achievement motivation and task enjoyment, supporting the findings of Harackiewicz et al. (1987). Furthermore, this research supports the argument that achievement motivation may have a detrimental effect on enjoyment of the leisure experience.

The relationship between motivation and perception of time was as hypothesised, with intrinsically motivated tourists perceiving time as passing quickly, and achievement motivated tourists experiencing time as passing slowly. These findings support the notion forwarded by Harackiewicz et al. (1987) that achievement motivated people tend to be apprehensive, tense, and aware of time passing, and are thus less able to become absorbed by the leisure experience. This occurs because participation in the activity is regarded as a means to an end, rather than an enjoyable experience in itself. Consequently, the time taken and actual involvement in the activity is seen as something of a barrier rather than an enjoyable aspect of the leisure experience. Several researchers (e.g. Harackiewicz et al., 1987; Shaw, 1985) have argued that achievement motivated individuals are particularly aware of their actions in situations where performance is evaluated.

Climbing Ayers Rock could be interpreted as such a situation involving performance evaluation. An obvious gauge of success is one's ability to reach the summit. Furthermore, almost all tourists climb between 7 a.m. and 11 a.m. and thus the activity is performed in the company of others. Additionally, the Ayers Rock climb takes place along a defined track and on busy days there is virtually a chain of human activity with climbers closely monitoring the efforts of others around them in the corridor of ascent. It is likely that achievement motivated people might interpret this setting as a competitive situation in which their performance was being evaluated by other climbers. Such an evaluation would heighten their awareness of performance which, in turn, would focus their attention on the time taken to complete the task. In this context

TABLE 3
Relationship Between Perception and Enjoyment

		Enjoyment		
		Low	**High**	**Total**
Perceived time		19	68	87
less than	(row)	21.8%	78.2%	
actual time	(col)	32.8%	54.8%	
Perceived time		7	15	22
equal to	(row)	31.8%	68.2%	
actual time	(col)	12.1%	12.1%	
Perceived time		32	41	73
greater than	(row)	43.8%	56.2%	
actual time	(col)	55.1%	33.1%	
		58	124	182

Chi square = 8.846; $p = 0.012$.

achievement motivated climbers would be keenly anticipating attaining the summit, therefore time taken would be regarded as a barrier to achievement of this goal (Quigley et al., 1984). This argument is also supported by the notion that events which induce anticipation engender overestimation of time involvement (Brown, 1985).

Intrinsically motivated individuals on the other hand, may have been involved in the activity itself. It has been argued that this group undertakes leisure activities because participation is enjoyable (e.g. Graef et al., 1983; Neulinger, 1974). Consequently, it seems logical to suggest that during participation, intrinsically motivated people will focus on other cues and perceive time to pass quickly. This supports the notion proposed by Gupta and Cummings (1986) that the more enjoyable the activity, the more quickly time passes.

The importance of the above findings in terms of tourism and leisure research lies in demonstrating that individual differences in motivation appear to have an influence on the quality of the visitor experience. In particular, people who are intrinsically motivated tend to become absorbed in the activity, experience higher levels of enjoyment, and perceive time as passing quickly. Conversely, achievement motivated individuals tend to report lower levels of enjoyment and perceive time to pass more slowly. From this, it would seem that the quality of the leisure experience is much greater for intrinsically motivated individuals than it is for achievement motivated individuals. These findings have important ramifications for the tourism industry, as they suggest that unless people are encouraged to involve themselves in the activity itself (that is, participate for the experience rather than merely achieving a goal), their enjoyment will be less than optimal. The management implications of these kinds of findings might extend to encouraging visitors to pay attention to sub goals of the total activity as well as heightening the need for interpretive information to add to all visitors' understanding of the settings being encountered. In particular tourism organisers, whether they be promoting long distance walks, white water rafting or managing the climb at Ayers Rock should pay attention to the work of Langer (1989). In her work on mindfulness, Langer notes that one can escape habitual behavioural routines and an achievement goal oriented approach to life by paying attention to the novel and unfamiliar and by adopting a questioning, analytic style to all our experiences. In brief, there may well be a case that some individuals have to learn to enjoy their leisure. Tourism managers

can play a role in this process by creating mindfulness inducing opportunities. Such an emphasis on interpretation and mindfulness might be necessary if the climb is closed and an alternate Ayers Rock walk is developed as a substitute experience for the climb.

It is also vital that tour operators, particularly those designing coach tour itineraries, provide visitors with enough time to pursue visitor activities in a relaxed, unhurried and mindful manner. Tight bus schedules and tour guide edicts that the activity must be completed in a short time (and this applies to the Ayers Rock climb) may artificially turn the setting into one where achievement motives emerge. As has been demonstrated in this study, visitors working to achievement oriented goals are less satisfied, overestimate the time they are taking and are likely to be more tense and anxious about their tourist activity. Reversing these trends would be a positive management step and allowing visitors ample time to experience the setting is a key tactic in this better management.

Finally, the methodological implications of this research should be addressed. As previously mentioned, one of the major difficulties in tourism and leisure research has been the practical difficulty of measuring the on-site leisure experience. This study revealed that the relationship between time perception and enjoyment was similar to that between time perception and motivation. This suggests that the time perception measure is a good indicator of enjoyment and intensity of involvement during leisure participation. Time measures have, of course, been used in behavioural observation studies in museums and visitor centres (Hockings & Moscardo, 1991) but the further development of time estimation, time perception and time ratio measures for on site tourist field settings offers much promise. In particular, the application of these motivational, satisfaction and time based studies with the emerging new tourism products in the ecotourism and adventure travel areas could develop a new body of tourist and leisure studies in the near future.

References

Atkinson, J. W. (1982). Attribution theory. In N. T. Feather (Ed.), *Expectations and actions*. Hillsdale, New Jersey: Lawrence Erlbaum.

Brown, S. W. (1985). Time perception and attention: The effects of prospective versus retrospective paradigms and task demands on perceived duration. *Perception and Psychophysics, 38*(2), 115–124.

Crandall, R. (1980). Motivations for leisure. *Journal of Leisure Research*, 12(1), 45–54.

Deci, E. L. (1975). *Intrinsic motivation*. New York: Plenum Press.

Driver, B. L., & Brown, P. J. (1978). The opportunity spectrum concept and behavioral information in outdoor recreation resource supply inventories: A rationale. In *Integrated inventories and renewable natural resources: Proceedings of workshop*. Fort Collins, Colo.: Rocky Mountain Forest & Range Experiment Station.

Gale, F., & Jacobs, J. (1987). *Tourists and the national estate*. Canberra: Australian Government Publishing Service.

Graef, R., Csikszentmihalyi, M., & Giannino, S. M. (1983). Measuring intrinsic motivation in everyday life. *Leisure Studies*, 2, 155–168.

Gupta, S., & Cummings, L. L. (1986). Perceived speed of time and task affect. *Perceptual and Motor Skills*, 63, 971–980.

Harackiewicz, J. M., Abrahams, S., & Wageman, R. (1987). Performance evaluation and intrinsic motivation: The effects of evaluative focus, rewards, and achievement orientation. *Journal of Personality and Social Psychology*, 53(6), 1015–1023.

Hockings, M., & Moscardo, G. (1991). The Cardwell Visitor Centre: Combining evaluation and design. In G. Moscardo & K. Hughes (Eds.), *Visitor centres: Exploring new territory* (pp. 121–237). Townsville: JCU Department of Tourism.

Hull, B. R., & Harvey, A. (1989). Explaining the emotion people experience in suburban parks. *Environment and Behavior*, 21(3), 323–345.

Hsieh, S., O'Leary, J. T., & Morrison, A. M. (1992). Segmenting the international travel market by activity. *Tourism Management*, 13, 209–223.

Krus, D. J., & Fletcher, S. H. (1986). Time: A speeding train or wind-driven sand? The estimation of fixed temporal intervals as related to images of time. *Perceptual and Motor Skills*, 62, 936–938.

Langer, E. J. (1989). *Mindfulness*. Reading, Mass: Addison-Wesley Publishing.

McClelland, D. C. (1961). *The achieving society*. Princeton: Van Nostrand.

Mannell, R. C., & Bradley, W. (1986) Does greater freedom always lead to greater leisure? Testing a person × environment model of freedom and leisure. *Journal of Leisure Research*, 18(4), 215–230.

Mills, A., Hodgson, R. W., McNeely, J. G., & Masse, R. F. (1981). An improved visitor sampling method for ski resorts and similar settings. *Journal of Leisure Research*, 13(3), 219–231.

Neulinger, J. (1974). *The psychology of leisure: Research approaches to the study of leisure*. Springfield: Charles C. Thomas.

Pearce, P. L. (1988). *The Ulysses Factor*. New York: Springer Verlag.

Pearce, P. L. (1991). Analysing tourist attractions. *Journal of Tourism Studies*, 2(1), 46–55.

Pearce, P. L., & Caltabiano, M. L. (1983). Inferring travel motivation from travellers' experiences. *Journal of Travel Research*, XXII, 16–20.

Quigley, J. J., Combs, A., & O'Leary, N. (1984). Sensed duration of time: Influence of time as a barrier. *Perceptual and Motor Skills*, 58, 72–74.

Roadburg, A. (1983). Freedom and enjoyment: Disentangling perceived leisure. *Journal of Leisure Research*, 15(1), 15–26.

Ruskin, H., & Shamir, B. (1984). Motivation as a factor affecting males' participation in physical activity during leisure time. *Society and Leisure*, 7, 141–161.

Samdahl, D. M. (1988). A symbolic interactionist model of leisure theory and empirical support. *Leisure Sciences*, 10, 27–39.

Shaw, S. M. (1985). The meaning of leisure in everyday life. *Leisure Sciences*, 7(1), 1–25.

Wankel, L., & Kreisel, P. S. (1985). Factors underlying enjoyment of youth sports: Sport and age group comparisons. *Journal of Sport Psychology*, 7, 51–64.

KEY CONCEPTS

consumers	Maslow	safety/security needs
destination attributes	motivation	self-esteem needs
discipline of psychology	needs	travel motivation analysis
fulfillment needs	physiological needs	travel needs model
Grand Tour	psychological theory	
history	relationship needs	

INTERNET EXERCISE

Site Name: Seniors Search

URL: **http://www.seniorssearch.com/**

Background Information: A search directory exclusively for the over 50 age group.

Site Name: Accessible Journeys

URL: **http://www.disabilitytravel.com/**

Background Information: Since 1985, Disability Travel has been designing accessible holidays and escorting groups on vacations exclusively for slow walkers, wheelchair travelers, and their families and friends.

Site Name: GrandTravel

URL: **http://www.grandtrvl.com/**

Background Information: Grandparents and grandchildren make outstanding travel companions! On a Grand Travel tour, grandparents are participating in the cultural enrichment of their grandchildren's lives and everyone has a wonderful time.

Site Name: Kids Go Too

URL: **http://www.kidsgotootravel.com/**

Background Information: Kids Go Too provides you with specific and meaningful information on lodging, activities, and restaurants that are perfectly suited to a unique and exciting vacation that is fun and satisfying to every member of the family.

Site Name: Eurocamp

URL: **http://www.eurocamp.com/**

Background Information: Visit this web site to find out more about self-drive camping holidays in Europe. You can search their campsite and regional databases.

Exercise

1. Choose at least two of the web sites indicated above. Describe how they are using travel psychology to motivate people to travel who may have barriers to travel.

QUESTIONS FOR REVIEW AND DISCUSSION

1. Why is it so important for tourism people to have a good understanding of travel motivation?

2. Explain the relationship of customer (tourist) satisfaction and travel motivation.

3. The author states that the question "Why do tourists travel?" is not a good starting point for research on this subject. Comment.

4. "Why do certain groups of people choose certain holiday experiences?" is a much better question. Why?

5. Identify five motivations for travel of Europeans during Roman times, the Middle Ages, and Tudor times. Do such motivations exist today?

6. How important are the motives of discovery and curiosity?

7. Are your travel benefits or rewards linked closely to your travel motives? Elucidate.

8. Provide a few examples of how a person's travel needs change over a lifespan.

9. Give an example of travel experience overstimulation (mental or physical exhaustion or both).

Similarly, give an example of boredom (too little stimulation).

10. Thinking about Pearce's five-level travel needs ladder provides some examples of externally and internally oriented physiological needs. Why are these needs at the bottom of the ladder?

11. Referring to the preceding question, provide similar representations of safety/security needs, relationship needs, self-esteem/development needs, and fulfillment needs.

12. Assume that you were employed by a nature (eco-tour) company and were planning a new tour to a newly established national park. Describe several ingredients of such a tour that meet most of these needs as shown in question 11.

13. How could a resort hotel's activities or social director help guests with their fulfillment needs? Give several cases in point.

14. Below is a short list of travel motivations. Suggest a travel experience or product that would match each motivation.

15. Rest/relaxation
16. Unspoiled natural environment enjoyment
17. Interesting countryside and wildlife study opportunities
18. Lots of nightlife and entertainment
19. Adventure activities
20. Good shopping and browsing
21. How important are a variety of available experiences at a destination?
22. Why would you want to climb Ayers Rock?
23. What were the climbers' motivational differences?

CASE PROBLEMS

1. You have been promoted to director of training of the Cruise Lines International Association. Reviewing the listed travel motivations, which would you select for a group of travel marketing sales seminars that will be sponsored by CLIA? (Attending would be travel agents and tour company reps.)

2. Referring to the preceding problem, after selecting the motivations, what kinds of instructional materials and teaching methods would you employ? Why?

3. Your first assignment after joining a tour company staff was to design a tour that would appeal to young singles. Obviously, you must create a tour that would probably motivate a market sufficiently large for your company to make a profit on it.

Identify the motivation(s) selected, then describe briefly your tour concept and the specific marketing elements you would feature in its promotion to reach this very promising market.

4. Pleasure travel motivation is often added to a business trip such as attending a convention. Give an example of such a combination. Identify the principal motivations involved. How would you sell this idea to the convention planning committee?

5. The holiday season is approaching. Jeff R. is trying to compose a direct-mail promotion letter to be sent to each person on his travel agency's mailing list. He's convinced that giving a gift of travel would be very appealing to many of his clients. What key phrases should he embody in this letter to motivate such giving?

SELECTED REFERENCES

Anthony, I. *Verulamium.* Staffordshire, England: Wood Mitchell, 1973.

Casson, L. *Travel in the Ancient World.* London: Allen & Unwin, 1974.

Crotts, John C., and W. Fred van Raaii (eds.). *Economic Psychology of Travel and Tourism.* Binghamton, NY: The Haworth Press, March 1995.

Echtner, C. M., and J. R. B. Ritchie. "The Meaning and Measurement of Destination Image." *Journal of Tourism Studies,* Vol. 2, No. 2, pp. 2–12, 1991.

Gnoth, Juergen. "Tourism Motivation and Expectation Formation." *Annals of Tourism Research,* Vol. 24, No. 2, pp. 283–304, April 1997.

Hill, Brian J., Cary McDonald, and Muzaffer Uysal. "Resort Motivations for Different Family Life Cycle Stages." *Visions in Leisure and Business,* Vol. 8, No. 4, pp. 18–27, Winter 1990.

CULTURAL AND INTERNATIONAL TOURISM FOR LIFE'S ENRICHMENT

- Recognize that travel experiences are the best way to learn about other cultures.

- Identify the cultural factors in tourism.

- Appreciate the rewards of participation in life-seeing tourism.

- Become aware of the most effective promotional measures involving an area's cultural resources.

- Realize the importance of cultural attractions to any area promoting itself as a tourist destination.

- Evaluate the contributions that international tourism can make toward world peace.

◄ **LEARNING OBJECTIVES**

◄ *The Palace of the Arts in Mexico City. (Photo courtesy of the Mexican Government Tourism Office.)*

INTRODUCTION

The highest purpose of tourism is to become better acquainted with people in other places and countries, because this furthers the understanding and appreciation that builds a better world for all. International travel also involves the exchange of knowledge and ideas—another worthy objective. Travel raises levels of human experience, recognition, and achievements in many areas of learning, research, and artistic activity.

Tourism goes beyond dependable transportation and comfortable hotels; it necessitates enhancing all the avenues through which a country presents itself. They include educational, cultural, media, science, and meeting/congress activities. To increase accessibility, cultural institutions need to adapt to meet visitors' needs, sometimes providing multilingual guides and signage. Tourists can then more easily choose the purposeful activities that will match their interests.

Travel experiences vary according to the varieties of humankind and their geographical distribution. To classify destinations so that a systematic discussion of tourism motivation can be undertaken, Valene L. Smith has identified six categories of tourism: (1) ethnic tourism, (2) cultural tourism, (3) historical tourism, (4) environmental tourism, (5) recreational tourism, and (6) business tourism. Obviously, destinations can, and usually do, provide more than one type of tourism experience.

IMPORTANCE

While **culture** is only one factor that determines the overall attractiveness of a tourism region (see Figure 10.1, Stage 1), it is a very rich and diverse one. The elements of a society's culture are a complex reflection of the way its people live, work, and play (Figure 10.1, Stage 2).

Cultural tourism covers all aspects of travel whereby people learn about each other's ways of life and thought. Tourism is thus an important means of promoting cultural relations and international cooperation. Conversely, development of cultural factors within a nation is a means of enhancing resources to attract visitors. In many countries, tourism can be linked with a "cultural relations" policy. It is used to promote not only knowledge and understanding but also a favorable image of the nation among foreigners in the travel market.

The channels through which a country presents itself to tourists can be considered its cultural factors. These are the entertainment, food, drink, hospitality, architecture, manufactured and handcrafted products of a country, and all other characteristics of a nation's way of life.

Successful tourism is not simply a matter of having better transportation and hotels but of adding a particular national flavor in keeping with traditional ways of life and projecting a favorable image of the benefits to tourists of such goods and services.

A nation's cultural attractions must be presented intelligently and creatively. In this age of uniformity, the products of one nation are almost indistinguishable from those of another. There is a great need for encouraging cultural diversity. Improved techniques of architectural design and artistic presentation can be used to create an expression of originality in every part of the world.

Taken in their narrower sense, cultural factors in tourism play a dominant role

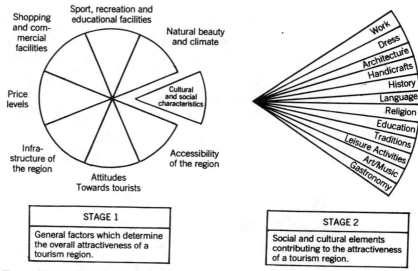

FIGURE 10.1 **Variables influencing the attractiveness of a tourism region.**
[*Source:* **J. R. Brent Ritchie and Michel Zins, "Culture as Determinant of the Attractiveness of a Tourism Region,"** *Annals of Tourism Research* **(April–June 1978), p. 256.**]

chiefly in activities that are specifically intended to promote the transmission or sharing of knowledge and ideas. Consider the following factors:

1. Libraries, museums, exhibitions
2. Musical, dramatic, or film performances
3. Radio and television programs, recordings
4. Study tours or short courses
5. Schools and universities for longer-term study and research
6. Scientific and archaeological expeditions, schools at sea
7. Joint production of films
8. Conferences, congresses, meetings, seminars

In addition, many activities that are not educational or cultural in a narrow sense provide opportunities for peoples of different nations to get to know each other.

LIFE-SEEING TOURISM

Traditionally, a person "sees the high points" of a given location and thus feels that he or she has "seen" this area. However, there is a growing belief among tourism specialists that such an approach, although traditionally valid, is by no means the best approach. Purposeful activities that match the travelers' interests are becoming more commonly accepted and recognized. (In popular tourist areas, such arrangements may have to be limited to the off-season periods of the year.) For example, a physician

Experiencing new cultures, along with their architecture, food, and dress, is a strong travel motivation. This mosque in the Arab community of Singapore presents striking architecture. *(Photo by the author.)*

on a vacation might be interested in talking with local physicians and viewing interesting or progressive medical installations or facilities. He or she may wish to participate in a symposium or some type of educational endeavor there or have lunch with a group of physicians interested in the same particular specialty or in public health or medical practices in general. The visitor may also wish to visit the home of a well-known physician to exchange ideas.

Suggestions made by the travel agent and machinery provided to make such experiences come about are of growing importance to successful tourism. Any place that wishes to become a successful tourist destination must have more activities for visitors than the traditional recreational activities such as lying on the beach or patronizing a night club or visiting popular tourist attractions.

Axel Dessau, former director of the Danish National Tourist Office, is credited with this concept of **"life-seeing tourism."** In Denmark, for example, the visitor is met by a graduate student or other person who is technically familiar with the field of interest that a visitor may have. This guide then arranges for purposeful visits in a schedule suited to the visitor.

For example, the visitor might be interested in reviewing social problems and city government. An expert in these matters would plan to visit city planning offices, schools, social welfare establishments, and rehabilitation centers; to attend meetings or seminars at which problems of this nature are discussed; and to provide other opportunities for the visitor to learn firsthand what is happening in his or her field in Denmark.

The plan is usually set up on a half-day basis, with the visitor spending afternoons visiting tourist highlights, shopping, and pursuing other traditional recreational activities. The mornings would be devoted to making visits to organizations and establishments with programs planned by a special expert guide. A travel agent can make these arrangements.

Another aspect of life-seeing tourism is the opportunity to have social intercourse with families. These families host the visitor or the visitor's family in the evening after dinner for conversation and sociability. Or the visitor can stay in a private home—an excellent way in which to become acquainted with the culture and lifestyle of persons in a different locality.

In the Bahamas, visitors can discover the island group's people and culture in a very personal way through their People-to-People Program. This stimulating and exciting program is organized by the Ministry of Tourism. It matches visitors with Bahamian volunteers who host visitors having similar professions or interests. The Bahamian host or host family may choose to take guests to a local theater performance or a Sunday church service or may invite them to a home-cooked Bahamian dinner. A wide variety of other activities may be included, depending on the interests of the visitor(s). Such opportunities substantially increase visitor appreciation and understanding of the culture they are visiting, and often bring about lasting friendships.

THE ROMANCE OF PLEASURE TRAVEL

Perhaps the strongest of all individual travel motivations is simply that of satisfying a need for pleasure. Travel has the unique quality of being able to satisfy this desire to an extremely high degree. Not all trips are pleasurable, but some are more pleasurable than anticipated. The planning and anticipation period prior to the trip can be as enjoyable as the trip itself. Discussing prospects of the trip with friends and pursuing research, educational, and shopping activities relating to the trip and the area to be visited is a most important part of the total pleasure travel experience. In the formulation of marketing programs and advertising, in particular, the pleasurable aspects of the trip need to be emphasized. The prospective traveler should be told how much fun it is to go to the popular, as well as some of the most uncommon, destinations.

The romance of the trip is also a strong motivation, particularly in relation to honeymoon travel and for those who are thrilled with the romantic aspects of seeing, experiencing, and enjoying the culture of strange and attractive places. Thus, the romance and pleasure of the trip are primary attributes of the travel experience and need to be emphasized far more than they have been in the past. Sharing experiences with members of the family or friends is another integral part of the enjoyment of the trip. A trip can become a fine medium through which additional pleasure, appreciation, and romance is experienced.

DEVELOPMENTAL AND PROMOTIONAL MEASURES

Measures taken to develop and promote the cultural elements in tourism through special activities can be considered from several different points of view.

Development of Methods and Techniques

The examples just listed involve specialized methods, techniques, and skills, all of which can be developed in their own right, without any direct reference to the promotion of tourism. Theaters, libraries, museums, and other such national institutions are not usually created with tourism in mind, but they are a great asset in attracting the interest of visitors. Museums and monuments, especially, are among the expected features of a tourist itinerary. These and other activities that can assist in the development of tourism may also be desirable elements in the cultural development of the nation. The methods and techniques associated with each of the examples listed constitute a whole field of specialized knowledge. As in the most other fields of expert knowledge, information and ideas can be acquired from abroad and adapted to national situations.

Even when the necessary facilities exist, it may be desirable to adapt them to the needs of tourism. Special courses will often have to be created for foreigners. Multilingual guides must be trained. Captions and instructions in museums and cinemas should be provided in at least two languages. Special arrangements may be made for tourists to be given free or inexpensive access to institutions of interest to them. Lifeseeing arrangements can also be made.

Improvement in Educational and Cultural Content of Tourism

There is always room for improvement in what a tourist may learn abroad. This applies chiefly to books, pamphlets, films, and all types of illustrated information material. There is a great need for the services of experts in such matters, not only in assembling material on the history or geography of a country, but also in the attractive and accurate presentation of the material in several languages.

Consideration might be given to the development, on a regional basis, of **"cultural identity card"** systems, such as that operated successfully by the Council of Europe, which would introduce the tourist to experts in the fields of education, science, and the arts.

Heritage interpretation as an academic discipline can be very useful in tourism. Courses can be developed to enable local citizens to become authentic interpreters of their area's cultural, historical, and natural heritage. Achievement of such knowledge builds a person's ability to become a fully qualified interpreter. One example might be a 40-hour course entitled "Tourism—Keeper of the Culture." Those who successfully complete the course would be fully aware of their area's resources and thus would be capable of providing guide services or other services in which their knowledge can be useful. All forms of tourism, from group to individual, can, in various ways, benefit from the assistance of such informed, enthusiastic individuals.

Such an educational effort, when publicized, also creates a new self-awareness and pride in the community and a resulting improvement in the quality of life. Local art events, for example, can be organized to be attractive to the community and tourists alike. "Heritage Trails" or "Cultural Highways" can be designated. "Art in the Park" and festivals with various cultural themes help show off the area's resources and help to lengthen the season or fill in low spots in visitor demand. From the tourist's standpoint, engaging in such culturally oriented activities builds a heightened appreciation and respect for the qualities and abilities of their hosts.

Concentration of Activities Around Important Themes

In recent years, much has been done to link up tourist-related activities with themes or events of widespread interest, as in the case of festivals that bring together a variety of dramatic, musical, or cinema performances. An example is the successful Quebec, Canada, Winter Festival. Another way is to focus attention on large exhibitions or fairs. Events such as these give an opportunity for the combined sponsorship of many different types of activity. International congresses or meetings can be held at the same time as the exhibitions or festivals. Youth festivals or "jamborees" can take place to coincide with important sporting events or large conventions.

Another way of stimulating interest is through **"twinning,"** whereby towns, communities, or regions in different countries establish relations with each other and send delegations to events arranged by their partners. Special attractions such as EPCOT near Disney World in Florida bring together in one location large-scale cultural exhibits and entertainment of several countries. Another example is the Polynesian Cultural Center in Hawaii. A map of the center is shown in Figure 10.2.

Uses of Mass Media

Mass media are always important in the development of tourism. Whether for use outside a country as a means of attracting tourists or to inform and entertain them after

Beijing Workers' Stadium played host to the preliminary and final soccer matches of the 11th Asian Games. The stadium, which seats 70,000, has witnessed several important large-scale events in modern China's history.

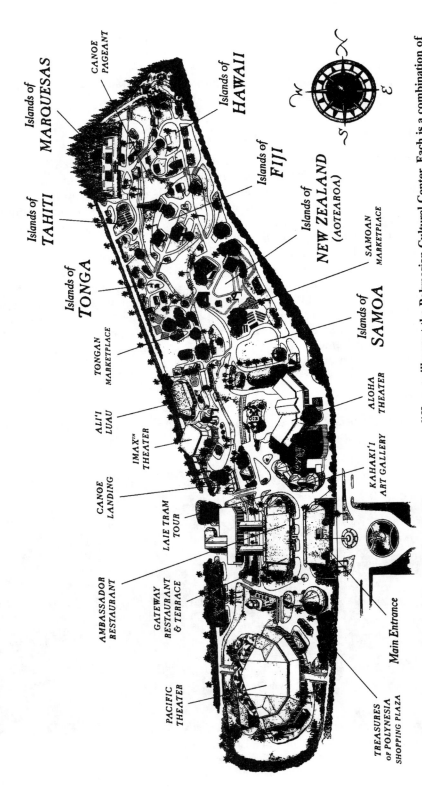

FIGURE 10.2 Polynesian Cultural Center, Hawaii. There are many different villages at the Polynesian Cultural Center. Each is a combination of buildings, gardens, activities, and people as you would find them if you were to travel to the various island groups represented.

their arrival, there is a great need for high-quality products by journalists, film producers, and artists. In many countries there are some who already specialize in the field of tourism whose services can be used to advantage. The Society of American Travel Writers is one professional group dedicated to good travel journalism.

Development of Out-of-Season Tourism

Educational and cultural activities are particularly well adapted to the "out-of-season" tourism development. International meetings and study courses do not depend on good weather and entertainment. Often, their sponsors are glad to take advantage of off-season rates in hotels. Efforts should therefore be made to develop facilities and publicity to attract suitable activities and events. Theater tours are a good example.

ANTHROPOGRAPHY (GEOGRAPHY OF HUMANKIND)

Anthropography is defined as the branch of anthropology that describes the varieties of humankind and its geographical distribution. One of the most important motivations for travel is interest in the culture of other peoples. The Mexicans are not like the Swiss, and the Balinese are not like the Eskimos. Our natural curiosity about our world and its peoples constitutes one of the most powerful travel-motivating influences. A travel agent or other travel counselor must be familiar with the basic differences in culture among the peoples of the world, where accessible examples of such cultures are located, and which of these cultures (or groups of culture) would be most interesting to a particular would-be traveler.

Most of the earth's 5 billion people are concentrated in a limited number of geographical areas. These population concentrations provide attractions in themselves. On the other hand, areas of the earth that are largely empty—such as Canada, parts of western United States, Siberia, western China, Australia, most of Africa, and much of South America—have appeal because of the absence of humans. The landscape, with its towns and villages and rural (and perhaps nomadic) cultures, provides interesting contrasts to urban centers. Visits to primitive cultures are enriching and exciting travel experiences. In the United States, such cultural groups as the Amish in Pennsylvania or the American Indian have tourist appeal.

TYPES OF DESTINATIONS—TRAVEL EXPERIENCES

The spatial and characteristic diversity among destinations has become so great that it is important to classify destinations so that a systematic discussion of tourism psychology and motivation can be undertaken. One way to do this is to build on Valene L. Smith's identification of several types of tourism.[1] That is, a classification of destina-

---

[1] Valene Smith, *Hosts and Guests* (Philadelphia: University of Pennsylvania Press, 1977), pp. 2–3.

A pyramid on the "Ruta Maya" at Chichen Itza in Mexico is a constant source of amazement to visitors and offers a unique challenge to those who wish to climb to the top. *(Photo by Mark Ritchie.)*

tions can be developed on the basis of the types of travel experience provided at the various destinations.

Smith identified six categories of tourism:

1. *Ethnic tourism* is traveling for the purpose of observing the cultural expressions and lifestyles of truly exotic peoples. Such tourism is exemplified by travel to Panama to study the San Blas Indians or to India to observe the isolated hill tribes of Assam. Typical destination activities would include visits to native homes, attending dances and ceremonies, and possibly participating in religious rituals.

2. *Cultural tourism* is travel to experience and, in some cases, participate in a vanishing lifestyle that lies within human memory (Figure 10.3). The picturesque setting or "local color" in the destination area are the main attractions. Destination activities, typically, include meals in rus-

FIGURE 10.3 The Maya Route is a proposed system of paved roads, dirt roads, and trails connecting archeological sites of the magnificent culture shaped by people called the Maya. Between C.E. 250 and 900 "the Maya created one of the most distinguished civilizations of all antiquity" according to *National Geographic* author George Stuart. How the Maya raised their enormous pyramids and stone temples is one of the many mysteries confronting investigators. The Maya Route plan would also introduce visitors to Spanish Colonial architecture, marvelous tropical forests teeming with wildlife, miles of pristine beaches, excellent snorkeling, and villages of great charm. Preliminary work is now underway for creating and promoting this four-nation ecocultural tourism circuit. *(Map courtesy of National Geographic magazine.)*

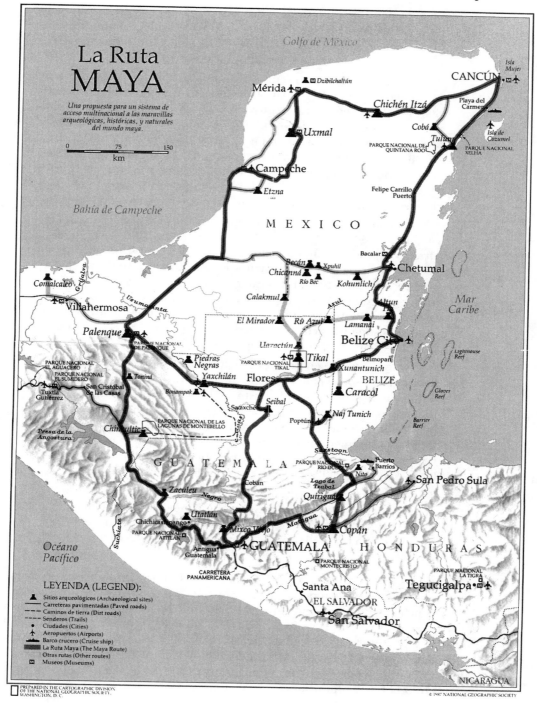

La Ruta MAYA

Una propuesta para un sistema de acceso multinacional a las maravillas arqueológicas, históricas, y naturales del mundo maya.

0   75   150
km

Golfo de México

Isla Muje

CANCÚN

Dzibilchaltún

Mérida

Chichén Itzá

Playa del Carmen

Uxmal

Cobá

Isla de Cozumel

PARQUE NACIONAL DE QUINTANA ROO

Tulum

PARQUE NACIONAL XELHA

Campeche

Etzna

Felipe Carrillo Puerto

Bahía de Campeche

M E X I C O

Bacalar

Becán

Xpuhil

Chetumal

Chicanná

Río Bec

Kohunlich

Comalcalco

Calakmul

Altun

Mar Caribe

Villahermosa

El Mirador

Río Azul

Lamanai

Palenque

PARQUE NACIONAL DE PALENQUE

Uaxactún

Belize City

PARQUE NACIONAL EL AGUACERO

Piedras Negras

Tikal

PARQUE NACIONAL TIKAL

Belmopán

Lighthouse Reef

PARQUE NACIONAL EL SUMIDERO

Toniná

Yaxchilán

Flores

Xunantunich

BELIZE

San Cristóbal de las Casas

Bonampak

Caracol

Glover Reef

Tuxtla Gutiérrez

Sayaxché

Seibal

Naj Tunich

Barrier Reef

Presa de la Angostura

PARQUE NACIONAL DE LAS LAGUNAS DE MONTEBELLO

Poptún

Chinkultic

G U A T E M A L A

Sarstoon

PARQUE NACIONAL RÍO DULCE

Puerto Barrios

Nito

San Pedro Sula

Cobán

Lago de Izabal

Zaculeu

Negro

Quiriguá

Chichicastenango

Utatlán

Mixco Viejo

Motagua

Copán

H O N D U R A S

PARQUE NACIONAL ATITLÁN

Suchiate

GUATEMALA

Antigua Guatemala

PARQUE NACIONAL MONTECRISTO

PARQUE NACIONAL LA TIGRA

Océano Pacífico

CARRETERA PANAMERICANA

Tegucigalpa

Santa Ana

EL SALVADOR

San Salvador

LEYENDA (LEGEND):

▲ Sitios arqueológicos (Archaeological sites)
━━ Carreteras pavimentadas (Paved roads)
--- Caminos de tierra (Dirt roads)
····· Senderos (Trails)
• Ciudades (Cities)
✈ Aeropuertos (Airports)
⚓ Barco crucero (Cruise ship)
▬ La Ruta Maya (The Maya Route)
▬ Otras rutas (Other routes)
Ⓜ Museos (Museums)

NICARAGUA

PREPARED IN THE CARTOGRAPHIC DIVISION OF THE NATIONAL GEOGRAPHIC SOCIETY, WASHINGTON, D.C.

© 1987 NATIONAL GEOGRAPHIC SOCIETY

tic inns, costume festivals, folk dance performances, and arts and crafts demonstrations in "old-style" fashion. Visits to Williamsburg, Virginia and Greenfield Village in Dearborn, Michigan or to Mystic Seaport, Connecticut are examples of cultural tourism.

3. *Historical tourism* is the museum–cathedral tour that stresses the glories of the past—Rome, Egypt, and Greece. Civil War sites in the United States such as Gettysburg, Pennsylvania, and Chancellorsville, Virginia are other examples. Guided tours of monuments, visits to churches and cathedrals, and sound and light performances that encapsulate the lifestyle of important events of a bygone era are favored destination activities. Such tourism is facilitated because the attractions are either in or are readily accessible from large cities. Typically, such attractions seem particularly adaptable to organized mass tourism.

4. *Environmental tourism* is similar to ethnic tourism, drawing tourists to remote areas. But the emphasis here is on natural and environmental attractions, rather than ethnic ones. Travel for the purposes of "getting back to nature" and to appreciate (or become sensitive to) people–land relationships falls in this category. Environmental tourism is primarily geographic and includes such destinations as Niagara Falls, the Grand Canyon, Yellowstone National Park, and other natural wonders. Typical destination activities include photography, hiking, mountain climbing, canoeing, and camping.

5. *Recreational tourism* centers on participation in sports, curative spas, sun bathing, and social contacts in a relaxed environment. Such areas often promote sand, sea, and sex through beautiful color photographs that make you want to be there on the ski slopes, on palm-fringed beaches, on championship golf courses, or on tennis courts. Such promotion is designed to attract tourists whose essential purpose is to relax. Las Vegas epitomizes another type of recreational travel—gambling, spectacular floor shows, and away-from-home freedom.

6. *Business tourism* as characterized by conventions/meetings/seminars is another important form of travel. (The United Nations includes the business traveler in its definition of a tourist.) Business travel is frequently combined with one or more of the types of tourism already identified.

This classification system is by no means unassailable. Destination areas can, and in most cases do, provide more than one type of tourism experience. For example, Las Vegas, which essentially provides recreational tourism, is also a popular convention destination. Resorts in Hawaii provide recreational, environmental, and cultural tourism, depending on what types of activities the tourist desires. A tourist vacationing in India, in addition to recreational tourism on one of the spectacular beaches in that country, has the opportunity for ethnic tourist experiences. Visits can be made to the villages to observe the lifestyles of remote populations.

Conversely, a tourist can select from myriad destinations that provide the same basic type of tourism. For instance, a tourist with an interest in historical tourism may travel to any country that has historical appeal.

OTHER TOURIST APPEALS

Other representative expressions of a people provide powerful attractions for travel. Art, music, architecture, engineering achievements, and many other areas of activity have tourist appeal.

Fine Arts

Such **cultural** media as painting, sculpture, graphic arts, architecture, and landscape architecture constitute an important motivation for travel. As a specific example, recall the beauty of art forms such as cloisonné or scroll paintings.

A recent trend in resort hotel operations has been the display of local art and craft objects within the hotel or in the immediate vicinity so that the guests may become acquainted with the art of the local people. These objects may be for sale and thus become valued souvenirs. Art festivals often include various types of fine arts together with other cultural expressions to make them more broadly appealing. There are many examples of these, such as the Edinburgh Festival in Scotland. This festival features not only displays of art, but also other forms of craft work, music, pageants, ceremonial military formations, and other cultural attractions.

Music and Dance

The **musical** expression and resources of a country are among its most appealing and enjoyable aspects. In fact, in some countries or states the music is a major source of enjoyment and satisfaction to visitors. Hawaii, Mexico, Haiti, Spain, various sections of the continental United States, and the Balkan states are examples.

Resort hotels, particularly, can bring to the guests opportunities for enjoyment of local music at its best. Evening entertainment programs, concerts, recordings, and sound reproduction systems all aid in presenting this aspect of the art of the country. Community concerts, parades, and welcoming ceremonies are appreciated by visitors. Phonograph or tape recordings that the visitor can purchase provide another effective means of keeping in touch with the culture of a particular area.

Ethnic dancing is another exciting and appealing aspect of a country's culture. The color, costumes, music, setting, and skill of forms and execution add to the appeal. Almost all countries have native or ethnic dancing. Local shows, nightclubs, and community programs present additional opportunities. Illustrations show a popular community festival scene and an example of ethnic dancers.

Notable examples of dance as a cultural expression are those of Polynesian dancers, the Ballet Folklorico of Mexico, the Russian ballet, folk dances of the Eastern European countries, dances of many African nations, Thai dancing, the Kabuki dancers of Japan, and Philippine country dancing.

Handicraft

To satisfy tourists, gifts and souvenirs offered for sale should be **handcrafted** or manufactured in the country or region where the purchase is made. There is much dissatisfaction in purchasing a craft article that you later discover was made in another

Dancing is a form of cultural entertainment found throughout the world. Here, a Manohra dancer from Southern Thailand performs. *(Photo courtesy of the Tourism Authority of Thailand.)*

country thousands of miles away. There is no substitute for genuineness. If the locally produced article is useful and appealing, it should be made available in conveniently located shops. A visit to shops where handicraft products for sale are actually being made is another effective form of guest entertainment.

Industry and Business

The **industrial** aspects of an area provide important motivation for travel. A large proportion of travelers, particularly international travelers, are intellectually curious about the economy of any state or country. They are interested in the country's industry, commerce, manufactured products, and economic base.

Industry tours are a good way to develop an interest in the culture of the area and provide a potential market for the product being made. Tourist organizations should encourage tours to factories or processing plants when such visits are appropriate and pleasant experiences. Lists of such industrial installations can be maintained by tourist promotional organizations, chambers of commerce, resort hotels, motels, restaurants, or other establishment or service organizations where tourist contacts are made.

These handicrafts made in Thailand are an example of souvenirs that represent the culture of the country. *(Photo courtesy of the Tourism Authority of Thailand.)*

Industrialists from one country are often interested in the industry of another. Group tours can be organized for manufacturers of a particular product who visit another country to see how the manufacture of that or a similar product is accomplished. Such visits are mutually beneficial because each country's representatives learn from the other.

Chambers of commerce or other business or industrial groups often conduct tours to become acquainted with markets and processors in other countries in an effort to develop more interest in their products and to increase sales in various market areas. Business establishments, particularly retail stores, are of considerable interest to visitors. Excellent examples are shopping centers near resort areas, where a wide variety of stores are concentrated so that the visitor can readily find the products or services desired.

Shopping is one of the most important elements in tourism. Attractiveness, cleanliness, courtesy, and variety of products are among the most significant elements of the success of any shopping area. In fact, much goodwill can be created by courteous and devoted store clerks who assist the visitor in finding just what is being sought. Probably the world's most notable example of businesses that cater to the tourist is Hong Kong, where shopping and business activity are probably the most important aspect of any visitor's experience.

Agriculture

The **agriculture** of an area may be of interest to visitors. The type of farming conducted—livestock, poultry, dairy, crops, vineyards and wine production, fresh fruits

Souvenirs that bring back memories of a travel experience can be a lifelong treasure. Those based on authentic craftsmanship from a local artisan can be especially valuable. *(Photo courtesy of the Malaysia Tourism Promotion Board.)*

and vegetables—is an interesting aspect of the culture. Farmer's markets such as the well-known Los Angeles Farmer's Market or roadside stands that offer local agriculture products are also an important part of tourist services in many areas. This is particularly true of stands selling fresh fruits, vegetables, honey, wine, cider and other drinks, and products from nearby farms readily enjoyed by the traveler.

Exemplary agricultural systems provide a point of interest for farm groups who may wish to visit a particular industry from another part of the country. Denmark, with its outstanding pork industry, is of great interest to hog farmers in many parts of the world.

Local tours should include agricultural developments and services so that visitors can see the agricultural products and operations within the country and perhaps try some of the products. On the one-day tour of Oahu in Hawaii, visitors have a chance to sample field-ripened pineapple at a stand adjacent to a great pineapple plantation. State and country fairs and livestock shows also have interesting tourist attractions.

Education

Citizens of one country are concerned with **education systems** of another. The college and university campuses of any country provide important attractions to tourists.

Many of these are beautifully landscaped and attractively situated for a pleasant and enlightening visit. Well-known universities in England such as Oxford or Cambridge are in themselves important tourist attractions.

The operation of high schools and grade schools as well as private schools and other types of vocational training institutions are features of the culture of the area that can be utilized to a considerable degree as attractions for visitors. International education centers provide still another dimension of the relationship between tourism and education. Many universities conduct adult education programs within the university's continuing education service. Such educational opportunities attract learners from other states within their own country or from many countries around the world. This provides an incentive for travel. International conferences of business and industrial groups as well as scientific and educational organizations are often held on the campuses of colleges, universities, or other educational institutions.

Outstanding examples of this type of operation are the adult education centers similar to Kellogg Center at Michigan State University and the East–West Center at the University of Hawaii. These centers attract thousands of adults each year for continuing education courses, conferences, and meetings of an educational nature. "Elderhostel" educational programs for senior citizens are held at many colleges and universities around the world. These are short programs embracing a wide range of subject matter.

Literature and Language

The **literary** achievements of a state or country, though having more limited appeal than some cultural aspects, still constitute a significant element of travel motivation. Books, magazines, newspapers, booklets, pamphlets, and other printed literary works are among the most important expressions of the culture of the country. Interestingly, the availability or absence of certain literature is indicative of the political system of the area. Consider the restriction on distribution of literature from various areas of the world practiced by some countries.

Libraries are favorite cultural institutions for the visitor. Many have well-appointed reading lounges and comfortable, attractive surroundings. Particularly on rainy days, the visitor can enjoy reading about the history, culture, arts, and folkways of the host area. Often guest entertainment programs will feature the reading of poetry or the discussion of various books or other literary works as a cultural enrichment opportunity for visitors.

A well-educated person is likely to speak or at least have studied more than one language. Interest in the language of another nation or state is a motivating force for travel. This is particularly true of students traveling to a particular area to practice the language and to become better acquainted with its colloquial usage.

Travel–study programs are particularly valuable learning experiences. Receiving instruction in a foreign language abroad might well be integrated into any comprehensive travel–study curriculum. Language study institutes flourish all over the world. They can be private or associated with universities. Some examples of the latter are the University of Geneva, Switzerland; University of Grenoble, France; and the University of California at Berkeley in the United States. Sophomore or Junior Year Abroad programs for college students provide excellent opportunities to learn a different language. Such programs are numerous in Europe and in other parts of the world. Elderhostel learning opportunities for senior citizens provide another example of travel–study in which a foreign language can be pursued.

Most travelers like to learn at least some of the language to use while they are in a foreign country. Usually, this is in the form of expressions related to ordering food in a restaurant or in talking with hotel or other tourism employees. Classes in language could be included in an entertainment or activities program within a tourist area.

Science

The **scientific** activities of a country constitute an interest to visitors, particularly those in technical industries, education, or scientific research. Organizations responsible for tourist promotion can serve the scientific community by offering facilities for the exchange of scientific information, organization of scientific seminars, visits to scientific installations, and other activities that provide access to scientific information by visitors.

The most popular scientific appeals include museums of science and industry, planetariums, and visits to unusual scientific installations such as atomic power plants and space exploration centers. Zoos and aquariums are also popular.

An outstanding example is the John F. Kennedy Space Center in northeastern Florida. This installation attracts substantial numbers of visitors each year and provides educational and scientific knowledge for even the most unsophisticated visitor. Another is the Air and Space Museum in Washington, D.C.

Government

Systems of **government** vary throughout the world. Persons interested in political science and government find visits to centers of government, such as capitals, particularly valuable and highly motivating. Whenever a person visits another area, he or she is made aware of the type of government system in effect and notes the differences between this and the home country. Persons from Western countries are particularly aware of the differences between their form of government and that of Eastern Europe or the former Soviet Union, for example. Probably the world's best example of this was the city of Berlin, which was divided between a Western democratic government and an Eastern totalitarian government before the wall came down.

Persons interested in politics and the ways in which other countries and areas solve their political problems represent another part of the market. Lawmakers often visit another state or country to observe the procedures developed to solve social or economic problems.

A visit to Washington, D.C., can show visitors the lawmaking process in the House of Representatives and in the Senate. Hearings on various proposed regulations or statutes are often open to visitors. As the center of the government of the United States, this city provides educational opportunities in many areas to both American and foreign travelers.

Religion

Another motivation for travel through all of recorded history is the **religious** pilgrimage. Probably the best known are those to Mecca. Large numbers of people go to the

The renowned pilgrim center at Sainte-Anne-de-Beaupré in Quebec, Canada has attracted millions of people for over three centuries. A sign on the chapel commemo-
rates the first church to be built at Sainte-Anne in 1662.

headquarters of their church organizations and to areas well known in their religious
literature. Often these are group trips, for example, a group of Protestants visiting
magnificent churches and headquarters of various church denominations in different
parts of the world. Similarly, missionaries travel with a religious mission. The large
amount of travel to Israel is in part based on religious motivation, as are travels to the
Catholic centers at Vatican City in Rome, Oberammergau, Lourdes, and Mexico City.
Visits to prominent houses of worship of all forms of religious doctrine are an impor-

tant motivation for travel. Notre Dame cathedral in Paris, Saint Peter's basilica in Rome, and the sacred mosque at Mecca are examples.

Food and Drink

Food and **drink** of a country are among its most important cultural expressions. The tourist enjoys native foods, particularly items of a local or ethnic nature. When traveling, trying out local dishes is part of the fun.

Restaurants and hotels can make a favorable impression on the tourist if they feature local dishes and also perhaps an explanation on the menu about what the dish consists of and how it is prepared. Of particular appeal is the type of restaurant in which the atmosphere complements the type of food being served, such as seafood restaurants on the wharf.

The purchase of local food and drink is another source of tourist revenue. Advertising messages that include reference to local food are highly effective. The tourist considers eating and drinking important aspects of a vacation. How these foods and drinks are prepared and presented are of great importance. Among the happiest memories may be the experience of dining in a particularly attractive or unusual eating place where local foods were prepared and served.

Encouragement from tourist organizations for restaurants and hotels to feature local foods is highly recommended.

History and Prehistory

The cultural heritage of an area is expressed in its **historical** resources. See Figure 10.3. Some tourist destination areas are devoted to history such as the Mackinaw City area of northern Michigan, St. Augustine, Florida, the Alamo and San Juan Mission in San Antonio, Texas, old gold-mining tours in many western states, Machu Picchu in Peru, and the spectacular archeological find at Xian in east central China.

The preservation of history and the quality and management of museums is of utmost importance for successful tourism. Becoming familiar with the history and prehistory (archaeology) of an area can be one of the most compelling of all travel motivations. One of the principal weaknesses observed in historical museums is that the explanations of the exhibits are provided in only one language. This is a serious limitation to many tourists' enjoyment of such historical exhibits.

The hours of operation of historical points of interest and museums are significant and should be arranged to provide access for visitors at convenient times. Admittance fees to museums and points of historical interest should be kept as low as possible to encourage maximum attendance. Promotion is necessary, and tourist contact organizations such as chambers of commerce, tourist information offices, hotels, resorts, restaurants, and other businesses should have available literature that describes the point of interest, hours, admittance fees, special events, and any other information needed by the tourist to visit this historical attraction.

Some notable examples of museums include the National Museum of Anthropology at Mexico City, the American Museum of Natural History of New York City, the various branches of the British Museum in London, the Hermitage in Leningrad, and the various museums of the Smithsonian in Washington, D.C.

Other types of historical preservation are national historic parks and monuments

History and culture can come alive in venues such as the Utah Shakespearean Festival. Held every summer, the festival offers performances of Shakespearean plays; afternoon shows featuring Elizabethan dancers, musicians, and puppeteers; and morning seminars. *(Photo courtesy of the Utah Travel Council.)*

and national parks with a history or prehistory theme, such as Mesa Verde National Park, Colorado. Another type is the "living history" farms in Iowa and Illinois.

Among the most outstanding innovations in the presentation of history are the "sound and light" programs found mainly in Europe, the Mediterranean countries, and Mexico. A series of loudspeakers, broadcasting recorded voices in several languages with sound effects, tell the history of an unusually significant structure or place. Varying lights intensify the effect and focus the attention of the audience on various parts of the location.

At the Forum in Rome, the history of Rome is presented at night in half a dozen languages. Visitors can hear the voices of the emperors and hear the crackling flames as Rome burns. At the pyramids of Teotihuacan, about 20 miles northeast of Mexico City, famous actors relate the history of the area in another sound and light presentation given in Spanish and English language versions. Egypt offers similar programs at its ancient monuments.

TOURISM AND PEACE

Tourism is believed to have a positive effect on world **peace.** When people travel from place to place with a sincere desire to learn more about their global neighbors, knowledge and understanding grow. Then at least a start has been made in improving world communication, which seems so important in building bridges of mutual appreciation, respect, and friendship.

Tourism: A Vital Force for Peace

In October 1988, the first global conference on the theme "Tourism: A Vital Force for Peace" was held in Vancouver, B.C., Canada. Some 500 delegates from 65 countries attended. The purpose of the conference was to explore ways in which the world's hundreds of millions of international travelers could, by increasing interests, improving attitudes, and engaging in various social and other activities, contribute to better mutual **understanding and appreciation**—an important contribution toward world peace.

The conference provided a forum to examine tourism and its many dimensions as a force for peace. It brought recognition that tourism has the potential to be the largest peacetime movement in the history of humankind because tourism involves people: their culture, economy, traditions, heritage, and religion. Tourism provides the contacts that make understanding possible among peoples and cultures. The conference clearly demonstrated that tourism has the potential to make the world a better place in which to live.

One of the outcomes of the conference was distribution of the following:

Credo of the Peaceful Traveler

Grateful for the opportunity to travel and to experience the world, and because peace begins with the individual, I affirm my personal responsibility and commitment to:

- Journey with an open mind and gentle heart
- Accept with grace and gratitude the diversity I encounter
- Revere and protect the natural environment which sustains all life
- Appreciate all cultures I discover
- Respect and thank my hosts for their welcome

- Offer my hand in friendship to everyone I meet
- Support travel services that share these views and act upon them and, by my spirit, words and actions
- Encourage others to travel the world in peace

A Philosophy of Tourism and Peace

Great leaders in many fields have extolled the social benefits to humanity that result from travel. Travel is one of the noblest human occupations. In 550 B.C. the famous Greek statesman, Solon, recommended that we travel "in order to see." To see is to increase understanding and appreciation of other peoples, other cultures, and other lands. Jason, leader of the Argonauts—those incessant sailors in Greek mythology who were searching for the Golden Fleece—said, "The essential thing is not to live, the essential thing is to navigate."

Marco Polo became a prince of merchants, papal envoy, governor of a Chinese city, favorite of Kublai Khan, master of exotic languages, war correspondent, and the

Meeting people from other parts of the world and partaking in their culture and customs can be one of the most rewarding aspects of travel. Enjoying a coffee in Morocco is one example. *(Photo by the author.)*

first travel writer. His book describing his adventures, written in A.D. 1296, established the first bond between East and West. Polo was wonderstruck at splendors that he saw and of which he heard. During the Renaissance, his book was the chief and almost the sole Western source of information on the East.

This brief dip into history and mythology has but one purpose—to emphasize that travel—and written accounts of it in later years have often done more to create bonds and mutual understanding between various peoples of the world than any other single force throughout civilization's long existence.

There's no better way in which to gain a panoramic view of civilization than making a trip around the world. Being a guest for dinner is probably the best way to sense the unity that exists among peoples throughout the world. Here, people joined by blood or friendly spirit gather to break bread under the same roof. A few examples might include a dinner with a Japanese family, marveling at the swift movement of chopsticks gracefully picking rice from small snow-white porcelain bowls. Or a meal with Thais in the floating markets of Bangkok, where sampans loaded with pyramids of tropical fruits, vegetables, and fish ply the klongs in search of buyers. With Arabs in Tunisia, it may be having a delicious lunch in the shade of a tent out on the Sahara desert—in a landscape of stark, wild beauty, enriched by the lively warm hospitality of these friendly people.

Whatever happens in any home—be it a modest wooden house furnished with straw mats and rice paper windows in Kyoto, a solemn British mansion on Victoria Hill, a mud hut on the banks of the Nile, a Cape Cod bungalow, or a Rio de Janeiro apartment—being born, living, eating, drinking, resting, and dying are the same the world over. These similarities reflect the basic unity of people. This unity is really well understood by people but, alas, is too often forgotten by nations and their rulers and leaders.

There are many ways in which a traveling family can meet and become acquainted with families in other lands. One of the best known of these plans is the "people-to-people" program. Arrangements can be made by a travel agent through a local contractor, say, in Copenhagen, to provide a program of social contacts and other activities to enrich the visitor's acquaintanceship and understanding of the Danish people. Arrangements can be made to stay in a private home or to attend a seminar or similar program. Such opportunities can be and are operating in hundreds of places, in many parts of the world. A greater awareness of such possibilities and more widespread use of this type of program would increase understanding, friendship, and appreciation of other people.

A tourist standing on the balcony of a $100 to $200 per-day hotel room looking at the passersby below obtains little real knowledge of the people in the country being visited. However, if opportunities are readily available for social contacts with locals of that country, increased understanding and appreciation for the people of that area will take place.

Can tourism contribute to peace? If understanding and increased appreciation for other people's way of life, mores, culture, and language make us more a part of a world community, then the answer must be "yes." This is especially so if at least casual acquaintance can be made with residents of the host country. Tourism provides a vehicle whereby people from one area become acquainted with people of another. Ef-

In Malaysia, visitors can observe local carvers creating works of art. Such opportunities for interaction increase cultural understanding and awareness. *(Photo courtesy of the Malaysia Tourism Promotion Board.)*

forts to build that acquaintance will contribute to understanding, and understanding is at least the first step in creating and maintaining friendly national relationships.

Countries whose leaders understand and encourage tourism are making an effort to improve the personal relationship between their citizens and those of other countries. Although economic considerations may be uppermost, the importance of social contacts is also recognized.

Tourism flourishes in a climate of peace and prosperity. Political unrest, wars, depressions, recessions, and civil strife discourage tourism.

Tourism, if properly planned, organized, and managed, can bring understanding, appreciation, prosperity, and a better life to all who are involved. Let it grow and its positive effects increase. Tourism, if not a passport to peace, is at least a worthy effort toward building peace. Wherever and whenever visitor and host meet and greet each other with mutual appreciation, respect, and friendship, a movement toward peace has been made.

The Holiday Inn Passport, which lists and describes worldwide properties associated with this company, contains this statement:

> In today's shrinking world, neighbors are across the ocean, down the continent, and in every corner of the world. Time is different. So is dress, language, even food. But for all to live as neighbors, mankind must understand each other.

Understanding is impossible without communication. That which is unknown often seems forbidding, even wrong. People must learn other ways of life besides their own.

Only travel and communication closes this gap of knowledge. By world tourism it is possible to discover distant neighbors, how they live and think as human beings.

World tourism and understanding go hand in hand. For travel is the way to knowledge. So let everyone do his part, traveling about the earth, keeping his mind and heart open. And the world will become a better place for all.

SUMMARY

The cultural expressions of a people are of great interest to most travelers. These include fine arts, music and dance, handicrafts, food and drink, industry and business, agriculture, education, literature and language, science, government, religion, history, and prehistory. Tourists' experiences are enriched when they make a sincere effort to become better acquainted with local people.

Any country or area that seeks to attract tourists must plan and develop facilities and promote programs that invite access to such cultural expressions. A useful concept is "life-seeing tourism," a structured local program that arranges evening visits to local homes by tourists or, alternatively, a plan whereby interested tourists are accommodated for a few days in local homes.

Cultural interpretation in any area that hosts foreign tourists requires bilingual provisions. These include foreign language ability by guides, bilingual signs, labels, and literature.

Examination of the interrelationships of the cultural backgrounds of visitors and cultural expressions of the host society as provided by this chapter should provide useful guidance to hosts.

Because tourism can lead to better understanding among people, it has the potential to contribute to a more peaceful and better world.

ABOUT THE READINGS

There are four readings in this chapter. The first deals with the concept of community interpretation and appropriate tourism through heritage interpretation. Based on the application of heritage interpretation skills, these concepts are proposed as an approach to aid in the perpetuation of an area's unique heritage. The writer gives examples of the empowerment of local hosts in facilitating heritage experiences for guests. Also discussed is the potential applicability of the appropriate tourism concept at all levels of tourism development.

The second reading is by John Poimiroo, Deputy Secretary for Tourism in California, and stresses the importance of cultural tourism in today's marketplace.

The third reading features the Mashantucket Pequot Museum and Research Centre. The tribe's museum, which opened in 1998, is expected to be a major attraction.

The fourth reading discusses the claim of tourism creating understanding, trust, and goodwill among peoples of the world and contributing to peace and asks whether there exists a causal relationship between tourism and peace or simply a co-relationship with tourism as a beneficiary.

READING 10.1

COMMUNITY INTERPRETATION:

THE KEY TO APPROPRIATE TOURISM ("STORIES NEW AND STORIES OLD, STORIES KEPT AND STORIES TOLD")

by Gabriel J. Cherem
Department of Geography and Geology,
Eastern Michigan University

Perpetuating Community Stories

I would like to outline two closely related concepts today: community interpretation and appropriate tourism. A decade ago, Barbara Cherem and I, having given the broad applicability of heritage interpretation a great deal of thought, asked the questions: Why should we confine interpretation only to sites (Cherem, 1977) such as parks, museums, historic sites, and zoos? Why couldn't we interpret the heritage of an entire community to its residents and to its visitors? In response to these questions the concept of "community interpretation" was created in 1980 (B. Cherem, 1981; G. Cherem, 1982; McLennan, 1984; Cherem, 1988b; Gee et. al., 1989).

We defined community interpretation as "telling the natural and cultural stories of a community to its residents and visitors." The term *story* is key here, because we believe that the story is the basic unit or building block of community interpretation programs. Indeed, psychologist Rene Fuller has suggested "that the story may be the basic building block, the engram . . . of human learning" (Zemke, 1990). We use the term *story* to mean a narrative of factual content embedded into "vivid events and images that carry strong emotional coloring" (Egan, 1989).

In 1982 we were able to apply the community interpretation concept to Rochester, New York, and spent 18 months preparing a community interpretation plan for that city of 250,000 people. We then were able to produce a community interpretation plan for Chelsea, Michigan, which is a small town of 5,000.

In 1984, I was invited by Ray Tabata and Jane Yamashiro of the University of Hawaii to come to Hawaii to deliver two seminars on the community interpretation concept. One seminar was delivered in Honolulu, and one on the Big Island (Klemm, 1984). Interest in the concept was very strong in Hawaii. As one result a program called "Interpret Hawaii" was initiated by Glen Grant at Kapiolani Community College. The program was designed to empower local hosts to interpret their own heritage. Tour guides, docents, hotel activity coordinators, and others were provided a background in Hawaiian natural and cultural heritage. Many of these local hosts, albeit growing up in the islands, did not have this heritage background. Training was also provided for these hosts in presentational and interpretive skills. The local hosts were thus empowered to become their own best ambassadors for Hawaii when working with visiting guests.

As development of the community interpretation concept progressed, I wanted to more directly link community interpretation to tourism. In 1987, I developed the concept of "appropriate tourism" (Cherem, 1988a; Cherem, 1990). Appropriate tourism was envisioned as the analog of the appropriate technology concept that was popular in the 1960s. It was envisioned as tourism that was appropriate to the scale, values, and unique heritage of a community or locality. It was defined as "tourism that springs from and helps perpetuate the heritage identity of an area." The area's heritage identity (Cherem, 1988a) includes both its cultural heritage and its natural heritage—in other words, its "sense of place."

In 1989, I was asked by Glen Grant of the Interpret Hawaii program to lead an Interpretation Institute in Honolulu on the appropriate tourism concept as applied to Pacific tourism. Attendees were working professionals at museums, hotels, parks, visitor attractions, historic sites, and academic institutions in Hawaii. A preliminary listing of 11 principles of appropriate tourism was produced.

Appropriate Tourism Principles

1. Actively aids in the perpetuation of an area's heritage—cultural, historical, and natural

2. Emphasizes and showcases the heritage identity of an area as unique in the world

3. Is based on the application of heritage interpretation skills

4. Empowers local hosts to interpret their own heritage to guests

5. Builds the pride of local hosts in their heritage and improves their guest relations and service skills

6. Helps perpetuate local life-styles and values

7. Empowers local hosts to plan and facilitate authentic and meaningful multidimensional heritage experiences for their guests

8. Is "transcultural," in that both host and guest receive a mutually rewarding enrichment experience

9. Represents programming that can be implemented at any level of tourism development and in virtually any tourism setting

10. Represents a "value-added" approach to tourism, in that it increases the level and depth of genuine service provided to guests

11. Represents an approach to sustainable tourism development, because it respects and emphasizes an area's heritage and empowers its people as the true basis for tourism development

Taken together, the concepts of community interpretation and appropriate tourism were at the very core of the Honolulu Charter (see the box), which was drafted for delegate signature at the 1991 Third Global Congress of Heritage Interpretation International. The Charter outlined the relationship of heritage interpretation and the perpetuation of community place identities to the international travel industry. Two hundred and thirty delegates from thirty countries signed the document, and in January of 1992 the Charter was transmitted to the United Nations Educational, Scientific and Cultural Organization and to the United Nations Environment Program.

The Story Matrix

Every community, area, or locality of the world has a unique heritage identity—which includes both its cultural heritage and natural heritage, through time and into the future. To help document and organize the cultural and natural stories of an area, I have developed a tool called the heritage identity matrix, or more simply the "story matrix" (Figure 1). It is divided into cultural heritage (or cultural tourism resources) and natural heritage (or ecotourism resources). The matrix also has a timeline, so we are able to look at cultural heritage, for example, as either in the future, contemporary, historic, or pre-historic. We can do the same thing for the natural heritage of an area.

The cultural heritage portion of the story matrix is broken into four categories. The *first* of these is "non-material culture." By this is meant all of the values, attitudes, beliefs, norms, and other aspects of culture that are held within the heads and within the hearts of a particular group of people. Those non-material elements help define that culture and make it unique in the world.

The *second* category is "selected persons." By this is meant a selected individual, either well known or not, who in some way embodies an important element of that culture. The selected person could be a master artist or a master craftsperson. The selected person could be a well known figure, male or female, who embodies characteristics highly valued by that culture. The selected person could also be an everyday individual who through his work habits, living patterns, and/or religious habits embodies what is seen as being very valued in that culture. Selected persons are embodiments of the non-material culture.

The *third* category, "material culture," is the easiest to grasp. Material culture represents the tangible objects, artifacts, buildings and various other structures that a culture produces. All of the material culture elements are totally dependent on the non-material culture. Different non-material cultures, ways of believing, ways of thinking, will give us different material cultures.

The last category is that of "cultural landscapes," which is really an intersection category between cultural heritage and natural heritage. Put very simply the cultural landscape is the imprint of humankind on the land. It is another expression of the non-material culture. The cultural landscape is the configuration of buildings, structures, farmscapes, and other landscape features that the particular culture superimposed upon the natural environment. The cultural landscapes category bridges us into the natural heritage portion of the story matrix.

The natural heritage categories of the story matrix are fairly straightforward. Flora and fauna are ad-

	Nonmaterials Culture	Selected Person	Material Culture	Cultural Landscapes	Plants	Animals	Land	Water	Climate
Future	1	5	9	13	17	21	25	29	33
Contemporary	2	6	10	14	18	22	26	30	34
Historic	3	7	11	15	19	23	27	31	35
Prehistoric	4	8	12	16	20	24	28	32	36

Cultural Heritage
(Cultural Tourism Resources)

Natural Heritage
(Ecotourism Resources)

FIGURE 1 Story (heritage identity) matrix.

HONOLULU CHARTER

▼

The Honolulu Charter was drafted by the Congress organizers as a statement to the international travel industry of the relationship of heritage interpretation and preservation. A total of 230 Congress attendees from 35 countries supported the intent of the Charter and signed the document. In January 1992, the following Honolulu Charter was transmitted to the United Nations:

> The undersigned—having gathered in Honolulu, Hawaii, during November 3–8, 1991 for the "Joining Hands for Quality Tourism" Congress of Heritage Interpretation International— do hereby assert and endorse the indispensable roles of heritage interpretation and preservation in the provision of quality tourism experiences for visiting guests at every community and locality in the world.
>
> We assert and endorse that the unique heritage identity of each community and locality, including its natural and cultural resources, must be perpetuated to maintain the biological and cultural diversity, and thereby the diversity of place identities, of the entire planet. Further, such unique local heritages must be interpreted, not only to visiting guests, but to community residents themselves.
>
> We assert and endorse that heritage interpretation principles and practices, and heritage identity preservation, are at the very core of tourism development approaches such as cultural tourism and ecotourism.
>
> We hereby call upon and encourage both public and private groups to join hands in the perpetuation of global diversity and unique place identities—through the application of heritage interpretation principles and practices in all communities and localities of the world. We transmit this document to the United Nations Educational, Scientific and Cultural Organization (UNESCO) and to the United Nations Environment Program (UNEP) with a call for governments to take actions that permit and encourage the implementation of the principles of this Charter.

dressed by the categories of "plants" and "animals." The category of "land" takes in topographic elements, landform, and soils of the area. The category of "water" takes in not only open bodies of water, whether they be ocean coastlines or lakes or streams or rivers, but also the situation underneath the ground in terms of the availability of water resources in the groundwater table. The last category of "climate" involves the broad sun/cloud and temperature patterns, weather patterns, precipitation patterns, and other regular seasonal variations of the area.

(While expressed as separate categories for organizational purposes, all the natural heritage categories are obviously interrelated in the ecosystems of the area. Further, the evolution of any area's cultural heritage is inextricably tied to the natural heritage of the area.)

Storykeepers and Storytellers

The story matrix is an organizing tool to document and categorize in a balanced manner all of the heritage identity stories of an area through time. In categorizing an area's stories, it is further necessary to say that all areas have living stories, sleeping stories, and dying stories. It is the purpose of community interpretation and appropriate tourism programs to discover, to revive, to tell, and to perpetuate as many of these stories as possible—because collectively those stories define the area's unique sense of place. I call people who are responsible for discovering, rediscovering, and reviving an area's stories "storykeepers." These are people who are actively involved in the study, documentation, preservation, and conservation of both the natural and the cultural stories of an area.

Traditionally, most societies have had persons responsible for safeguarding its stories. As an example, Alex Haley in *Roots* refers to the "griot" as serving this role in certain African cultures. In contemporary times, anthropologists, biologists, historians, ecologists, preservationists, and conservationists are among those serving roles of "storykeepers."

"Storytellers," by extension then, are those persons who are involved as interpreters, as local hosts and guides, as writers and photographers in community interpretation and appropriate tourism programs.

They take the stories that have been revived and kept by the storykeepers, and they tell those stories to both area residents and visiting guests.

When the unique heritage identity stories of an area are realized, organized, kept and told—to residents and visitors alike—we have the sound basis of a community interpretation and appropriate tourism program.

Literature Cited

Cherem, Barbara, 1981. "Community Interpretation in Chelsea." *The Historical Society of Michigan Newsletter,* Vol. 7, No. 2 (July–August 1981).

Cherem, Gabriel J. 1977. "The Professional Interpretor: Agent for an Awakening Giant." *Journal of Interpretation,* Vol. 2, No. 1, 3–16.

Cherem, Gabriel J. 1982. "Life Space Analysis in Interpretation." *Proceedings of the Interpretation Canada National Workshop.* Banff, Alberta.

Cherem, Gabriel J. 1988a. "Interpretation as the Vortex: Tourism Based on Heritage Experiences." *Proceedings of the Interpretation Canada National Conference.* Ottawa, Ontario.

Cherem, Gabriel J. 1988b. "Community Interpretation and Tourism." Presented at the Second World Congress on Heritage Presentation and Interpretation. Warwick, England (August–September).

Cherem, Gabriel J. 1990. "Appropriate Tourism Through Heritage Interpretation." In McIntosh, Robert W. and Goeldner, Charles R., *Tourism Principles, Practices, Philosophies,* Sixth Edition. Wiley, New York.

Egan, Kieran. 1989. "Memory, Imagination, and Learning: Connected by the Story." *Phi Delta Kappan* (February).

Gee, Chuck Y., Makens, James C., and Choy, Dexter J. L. 1989. *The Travel Industry.* Library of Congress. Van Nostrand Reinhold.

Haley, Alex. 1976. *Roots.* Doubleday.

Klemm, R. 1984. "Community Interpretation—Not Just Another Tourist Trap." *Makai* 6(11) (November). University of Hawaii.

McLennan, Marshall. 1984. "New Opportunities in Historical Geography." *The Geographical Bulletin,* Vol. 26 (November).

Zemke, Ron. 1990. "Storytelling: Back to a Basic." *Training* (March).

READING 10.2

CULTURAL TOURISM: NO JOKE

by John Poimiroo,
Deputy Secretary for Tourism
California Trade and Commerce Agency,
Division of Tourism

In jest, followed by a host of cat calls from the audience, I suggested at the recent Far West Cultural Tourism Leadership Forum in Los Angeles, that California's definition of cultural tourism was "to visit a frozen yogurt store."

My humor was understood by this body for the absurdity I intended. California is kidded for its bigger-than-life popular culture, yet a vast population of Californians enjoy a cultural scene that is second to no other state or nation. Cultural tourism in California is no joke. It is as rich, multifaceted and powerful as is our state.

Market research has long established that more California travelers visit historic sites, festivals, the arts and museums than see professional sports or visit theme parks. Cultural tourism is among California's strongest draws. Given the diversity of our product, it is easy to see why.

California is rich with ethnic tourism. Diverse festivals and communities flourish across our state. They showcase foods, music, arts and dance that reflect the innumerable ethnic groups that call California their home. Latino, African-American, Chinese, Japanese, Polynesian, Thai, Indo-Pakistani, Hmong, Vietnamese, Jewish, Native-American, Italian, German, French, Irish, Portuguese, English, Scottish, and on and on.

California, as the entertainment capital of the world, is blessed with exceptional entertainers. This is exhibited in a wealth of performing arts. Opera, rock concerts, symphonies, theater companies, summer stock, blue-grass festivals, ballet, comedy, jazz clubs, melodramas, modern dance, ad infinitum. It is said there are more theater companies in Los Angeles than in New York City.

California's modern history spans 400 years. Its ancient history goes back nearly 10,000 years.

English exploration, the California Missions, Russian fur-trading outposts, the Mexican era, the Mexican-American War, the Gold Rush, western outlaws and lawmen, the buffalo soldiers, agricultural bounty, Hollywood, car culture, the development of popular culture and the technological age are all part of California heritage. Yet, while visiting historic places is a prime reason people travel, many California visitors are unaware of this multidimensional heritage.

California is home to many of the world's finest museums and art galleries, exhibiting the visual arts in everything from posh, treasure-filled castles overlooking land and sea, to tiny shops hidden in alleys exhibiting the work of great artists. The Getty, the Palace of the Legion of Honor, the Huntington, the Autry, the Museum of Tolerance, the M. H. de Young, the Crocker, the Norton Simon, the Peterson and countless artist studios open to visits are among a pantheon of celebrated California treasuries.

Given this wealth of cultural venues, it is surprising that cultural tourism is only beginning to be recognized for the force it is. About 200 tourism and cultural leaders from across the western U.S. addressed the issue. It was not always an easy discussion. Some involved in cultural development are critical of tourism marketers for having ignored them. Some involved in tourism development are critical of cultural managers for expecting a free promotional ride.

Despite the division, the two groups found common ground when crafting a vision for California cultural tourism development.

Their first recommendation was to create a coalition for cultural tourism in California that meets regularly. Representatives of the California Division of Tourism, California Council for the Humanities, California Arts Council and California Office of Historic Preservation will begin this process shortly, developing lists of local and regional representatives who will seed this "grass roots" effort.

Their seeding tasks will be to:

- Inventory existing research materials and methods, assess needs and disseminate a consolidated report that will aid cultural tourism managers and tourism marketers.

- Identify core values (i.e., cultural integrity, community involvement).

- Create a communications vehicle so that cultural tourism managers and tourism marketers can exchange information (i.e., web site, newsletter, intranet, billboards).

- Investigate funding.

Once formed, the coalition will also pursue putting cultural tourism on the agenda of already existing association conferences, such as the California Conference on Tourism in 1998. Both the arts and tourism industry associations will be asked to include cross-training about how to attract tourism or how to utilize cultural venues as an attraction for tourism.

Finally, the coalition will ask for the addition of cultural tourism representatives to the California Tourism Commission's Marketing Advisory Committee. In response, we have begun adding representatives from those who attended the Leadership Forum.

Through these steps, cultural tourism will gain in stature and assume its proper place within California tourism. Then, the only laughter will be at one of our comedy clubs.

READING 10.3

MASHANTUCKET PEQUOT MUSEUM AND RESEARCH CENTER

Source: Mashantucket Pequot Tribal Nation, Connecticut

In 1998 the Mashantucket Pequot Tribe will open the country's largest, most innovative and technically interactive museum devoted to Native American history and culture.

The exhibits will be divided into three segments portraying survival, hardship and rebirth. First, the glacial era 20,000 years ago to European contact. Second, the era of increasing aggression by the Europeans leading to the Pequot Massacre in 1637 and finally, a look at Mashantucket life over the past 360 years.

Beginning with an escalator trip through a simulated glacier, complete with sounds of cracking ice and the feel of icy air, visitors will enter a 9,000-year-old prehistoric era, including a diorama of a caribou hunt.

Visitors may then travel in the footsteps of Pequot ancestors living about 3,000 years ago, when the climate began to warm up. At this time native people began cultivating and harvesting plants for food and medicine. Displays will illustrate the use of herbs and plants indigenous to the region and explain the importance of the marine environment to native culture.

A recreated Pequot village from the early 1600s is one of the museum's highlights. Visitors can experience the sights and sounds of a sunny August afternoon, and even smell food cooking.

The Cedar Swamp, a key part of the Tribe's history, is another highlight. The swamp was a place of refuge for Pequots who survived the 1637 Massacre. A large, framed glass, circular "Gathering Space" offers expansive views of the swamp. Two circular theaters will show a 20-minute film portraying the Massacre, in which a small force of English soldiers and native warriors killed up to 700 Pequots in less than an hour at Mystic Fort.

The 308,000-square-foot facility will be the largest of its kind in the United States. The cultural research center will offer a 30,000-square-foot library capable of holding 150,000 volumes on native history and culture. It will have climate controlled research laboratories and storage rooms, an herbarium and photo/technical rooms, a restaurant, a 300-seat auditorium, two 100-seat theaters and gift shops. The facility will also include a 175-foot tower, where people can view the surrounding land.

READING 10.4

TOURISM: THE WORLD'S PEACE INDUSTRY?

by Stephen W. Litvin
Wanyang Technological University, Singapore

Reprinted from the *Journal of Travel Research*, Vol. 31, No. 1, August 1998, pp 63–66, copyright © 1998 by Sage Publications. Reprinted by permission of Sage Publications, Inc.

I have watched the cultures of all lands blow around my house and other winds have blown the seeds of peace, for travel is the language of peace.

—*Mahatma Gandhi, cited in Theobald (1994)*

Travel has become one of the great forces for peace and understanding in our time. As people move throughout the world and learn to know each other, to understand each other's customs and to appreciate the qualities of individuals of each nation, we are building a level of international understanding which can sharply improve the atmosphere for world peace.

—*John F. Kennedy (1963)*

The promotion of travel for pleasure between countries contributes not only to economic growth but to interchange between citizens which helps to achieve understanding and cooperation.

—*Ronald Reagan (1985)*

There is no shortage of handy quotes from well-known political figures extolling the virtues of tourism as a conduit to peace, tolerance, and understanding in our "global village." While reviewing the literature for this article, the above three quotations, among others, were enjoyed.

Much academic literature touts the virtues of the tourism industry as an integral component in the world's quest for peace. During a review of the tourism-for-peace literature, it was interesting to note the temerity of each author's regarding the relationship of tourism and peace, with much of the writing leaning toward the polemic. Most articles did not seem to suggest that tourism leads to peace. Instead, the arguments were presented as absolutes—the author's view of the "true word."

The arguments used in the literature are, however, predominantly conjectural. For example, D'Amore's (perhaps the leading tourism-peace guru) well-written and well-argued articles include "Tourism—The World's Peace Industry," which was published in this journal (D'Amore, 1988).

This article is presented as a counterpoint to the notion that tourism is a generator of peace. It is my belief that the "tourism creates peace" camp has a serious problem with the basic research axiom that distinguishes between co-relational and causal relationships. Does tourism create peace or is tourism, along with many other industries, a fortunate beneficiary of peace? This article argues that the latter is true.

There is no contention to the belief that tourism flourishes in an environment of peace; clearly there exists a co-relation between successful tourism and the absence of war, terrorism, and internal strife. But does tourism create peace, or does peace generate tourism? If a causal relationship exists, as much of the literature indicates, then does the literature properly distinguish action from reaction?

I recognize that this article will not resolve the argument. Believing such would be folly: Debating tourism virtues is much like any other moralistic debate, where no argument can change the fact that individuals will decide what they consider correct based on their hearts and not their heads. However, it is hoped that by adding to the debate and inviting contemplation, the views of some readers may be swayed.

Arguments from the Peace-Tourism Camp

Louis D'Amore chaired the First Global Conference: Tourism-A Vital Force for Peace in 1988, attracting more than 1,000 delegates to Canada to discuss the role of the tourism industry in promoting global understanding, trust, and world peace. In discussing the role of tourism in his conference overview, D'Amore (1988) states that tourism plays an integral part in world diplomacy by "spreading information about the personalities, beliefs, aspirations, perspectives, cultures and politics of the citizens of one country to the citizens of another," providing "the opportunity for individuals to gain first-hand knowledge of the larger world" (p. 38).

D'Amore (1988) adds that the collective outcomes of the world's "travel and tourism experiences help all humankind to appreciate the meaning of the 'Global Village' and the bonds that people everywhere have with one another" (p. 39). He concludes that tourism represents "a powerful force for the improved relations among people and nations of the world; relations which emphasize a sharing and appreciation of cultures rather than a lack of trust bred by isolation" (p. 39).

Similar thoughts are held by Khamouna and Zeiger (1995), who open their article "Peace Through Tourism" with the statement that "worldwide tourism has been recognized as a social force that can promote international understanding, cooperation and global fraternity . . . as one of the great forces for peace and understanding in our time" (p. 81). They conclude that "tourism is becoming that social force that will help peoples and nations to shape the outcome of their future," playing " a major role in the coming together of people from all walks of life and backgrounds in a spirit of goodwill and brotherhood" (p. 86).

Knopf (1991) supports tourism's virtue as a "vehicle for effecting change in our imperfect world" and states that tourism has the ability to "strengthen national pride, to dissipate barriers among people, to build communication, and to spread understanding. In fact such concepts have been appreciated to the point where tourism is frequently posited as the fundamental key to world peace" (p. 62).

Holland (1991) escalates the argument to a somewhat higher plane, stating that "tourism could be the equivalent of atomic energy by being a positive force for world peace . . . effect[ing] social change on a global scale by building bridges of understanding and acceptance through the peace ambassadors [i.e., tourists]" (p. 80). Holland does, however, temper his argument via the self-disclosure that his view is that of an idealist.

Caneday (1991), while not specifically using the term *peace*, states that "tourism has within its attributes the ability to bring people and nations together to mutual understanding and respect" (p. 91).

As quoted in an article titled "PATA: Travel Paves Way for Peace," Pacific Asia Travel Association (PATA) president Inder Sharma called for tourism industry leaders to become more active in presenting the tourism-for-peace platform to political, economic, and tourism policy makers (MacDonald 1993).

McIntosh, Goeldner, and Ritchie (1995), in their widely used tourism text, ask "Can tourism contribute to peace?" They reply that "if understanding and increased appreciation of other people's way of life, mores, culture and language make us more a part of a world community, then the answer must be yes," and they conclude that "tourism, if not a passport to peace, is at least a worthy effort toward building peace" (pp. 489–90).

Clearly, there is a breadth and depth of arguments in support of the peace power of the tourism industry. But do these arguments hold up to objective scrutiny?

Definitions

When discussing peace and war, it is probably worthwhile to discuss definitions that would have applicability in tourism research. D'Amore (1994) indicates that our current definition of *peace* is simply "the absence of war" and calls for a new "*positive* concept of peace accepting the perspective of an organic and interconnected world" (p. 113). Although I have no problem with this simplistic definition and am awaiting the development of a positive alternative, for the purposes of this article the term peace, in addition to the absence of war, also includes the absence of acts of terrorism and random violence.

It is of interest to note that in the three quotations at the beginning of this article, neither the word tourist nor tourism is used. Instead, each author uses the term *travel* or *traveler*. This is a semantic difference, perhaps, but in tourism literature this can create a major chasm.

A vast body of tourism literature argues the negative social, cultural, environmental, and economic impacts of tourism (versus travel). These discussions go beyond the scope of reference for this article. However, if we are looking for tourism to be the guiding light of peace at the same time the industry focuses on numbers (if not in spirit then certainly in actuality), then often creating a product in which the "chance for real human contact between holiday makers and locals could hardly be less hopeful" (Krippendorf 1990, p. 58). If tourism has in many cases been reduced to "museumization" (MacCannell 1976), and if tourists often visit destinations within the comforts of mass tourism's "environmental bubble" (Cohen 1995), then how can we expect tourism to create understanding, let alone peace?

Interactions and sharing may happen between travelers and hosts. But real understanding between tourists and locals is not likely. The problem with relying on travelers to be change agents in this tumultuous world is that they visit in very small numbers and abandon a destination before the mainstream tourists arrive (e.g., Plog's [1991] Allocentrics or Cohen's [1995] Explorers and Drifters).

Points for Consideration

First, tourism is clearly a beneficiary of peace, but as tourism is never successful in the absence of peace, it cannot, therefore, be a generator of peace.

While reviewing academic and trade literature for this article, never was a reference found that indicated that the emergence (or reemergence) of an indigenous tourism industry in any way led to conflict reconciliation. There is no shortage of examples in which pacification has led to increases in tourism (e.g., Northern Ireland, the Middle East, even Ethiopia and Nicaragua), but no examples were uncovered in which tourism, or tourists, brought differing sides to a peace table.

Numerous articles indicate that peace and tourism are related, but the health of tourism is always the result of peace, never the cause of peace. By way of example, the following headlines, related to the Northern Ireland conflict, serve as a point of reference:

- "Peace Brings Hilton to Northern Ireland" (Selwitz 1994),
- "Peace Brings Tourism to Northern Ireland" (Selwitz 1996),
- "The Economic Consequences of Peace in Ireland" (Gray 1995), and
- "The Spoils of Peace" (Shallcross 1994).

This is not to say that the economic benefits of tourism, following pacification, may not be one of many motivations for ending conflict. But this is far different than implying that tourism creates peace.

Clearly, the incumbent powers during times of strife may look longingly beyond the conflict to when sanity again rules and tourists again visit, but do the rebel or foreign forces creating the strife feel the same? Does the existence of tourists, in the present or in the past, create for these rebel or foreign forces an understanding of the folly of conflict? Does the existence of tourists, in the present or past, cause them to reconsider their actions? Has having had tourists in their midst somehow changed or altered their cause?

It is not believable that the dysfunctional youth in Miami who robs and kills a tourist cares much about tourism. It is not reasonable to assume that an IRA or Palestinian soldier fighting for a homeland would respond to the argument that tourism will lead to peace. Clearly, Rabuka did not let the argument that his coup in Fiji would wipe out the tourism industry overnight stand in the way of his political agenda. René did not hesitate to do the same in the Seychelles, despite his nation's almost total reliance on the tourist trade. A robust tourism trade did not stop the conflict in Balkans. Cambodia is in a classic start-and-stop-again tourism development mode, with each new conflict putting the nascent industry back to square one.

It simply seems illogical to think that neither the enlightenment from past tourism nor the prospects of future tourism had much or any impact in these aforementioned situations.

Second, tourism, rather than as a protector of stability, is likely to be held hostage in times of relative peace, causing a degeneration of the peace process.

We often see tourism used as a tool of aggression, as tourism guerrilla tactics create headlines and threaten an economy. A definitive example of this is the recent terrorist acts in Egypt. Egypt was, of course, the first Middle Eastern nation to recognize Israel. As a result, Egyptian tourism flourished.

However, as tourism became a major strength of the Egyptian economy, it also became an attractive target of extremists, whose terrorist acts threatened the safety of tourists and cost the nation at least U.S. $1 billion in tourism ("Egypt: Staying Away" 1994).

Likewise, threats to tourists (and foreigners in general) that are made or carried out in Kashmir, the Philippines, and Algeria have diminished, if not wiped out, these markets for tourism.

Does tourism help the peace process in these cases? It seems the converse is true. Instead, tourism provides relatively easy targets for terrorists or subversive factions. These attacks give them hope that their cause can be won through crippling the industry by holding hostage the flow of export dollars that tourism can generate.

Third, tourism can regenerate when "peace breaks out," but this does not imply that tourism creates peace. Rather, this is a testimony to the resiliency of the tourism industry.

Examples abound of destinations where, once the bullets stopped flying, tourists came visiting again. The memories of the television sound bites often take a long time to fade, but tourism, like a spring flower, generally regenerates. But in these cases, was tourism the cause of peace breaking out? Again, it would seem that tourism is not the cause but rather the beneficiary, a peace dividend, of the resolution of conflict. For example, see the following tourism trade article headlines:

- "The Peace Dividend for Israel and Jordan" (Rossant et al. 1994),
- "Peace Brings Hope for Travel Boom" (Middle East) (Pames 1994),
- "Peace Dividend II" (Angola's hopes for tourism) (1994), and
- "Ireland-Peace Dividend" (Carey 1996).

None of these headlines is meant to make light of the contention that the prospect of tourism dollars is an inducement to seek peace, an argument made by D'Amore (1988); McIntosh, Goeldner, and Ritchie (1995); and others. If, in fact, the rewards of peace can somehow become a reward sufficient to halt conflict, wonderful. It seems more logical, however, that tourism is but one of numerous benefits accruing to an environment absent of war or civil unrest. To elevate the benefits of tourism above the benefits to the farmer who can return to the fields without worrying about land mines, the factory worker who can stop worrying about mortars, or the mother who can again feel safe about sending her children to school seems myopic.

Need for Further Research

The beginning of this article stated that the prior body of writing on the topic of peace and tourism has been conjectural in nature. This article has attempted to "raise the bar" with a rebuttal that has been largely anecdotal. The next step in the process should be a research-supported article, which may hopefully elevate any further debate to a higher plane.

One such study that would aid in understanding the relationship between peace and tourism would be an empirical analysis comparing, in a time-series, a destination's tourism receipts and visitor counts with the destination's levels of peace and conflict. The goal of this research would be to learn if a statistical and predictable correlation exists between these variables.

An additional research avenue would be an empirical study of the opinions of the scholarly and professional tourism communities on the topic. Survey data could reveal whether most agree or disagree with various aspects of the debate.

It is not a given that either of these studies or other researchable ideas could be conclusive or able to sway those individuals on the fence. However, the topic is of sufficient importance that it deserves further review and warrants findings that go beyond opinion, conjecture, and anecdotal evidence. I hope that this article is an impetus for such work.

Conclusion

Before concluding, it is important to say that this is not the first article questioning the tourism-as-peacemaker theorem. Brown (1989), in a persuasive editorial titled "Is Tourism Really a Peacemaker?" asks researchers to "eschew their rhetoric" (p. 271), and instead of praising virtues not real, he urges the industry to invest its effort in finding ways to create a tourism product that creates a better world in which to live. Despite Brown's solid arguments, tourism literature and, perhaps more important, tourism texts remain a decade later largely unchanged in their tone and rhetoric, as demonstrated in this article.

The intent of this article is clearly not to denigrate the importance of tourism, both to the global economy and to the human psyche. Furthermore, I do not wish to be viewed as "anti-tourist" (Taylor 1993,

p. 254). However, it is important that a realistic and non-glorified vision of the impacts—social, economic, environmental, and political—of this mega-industry be maintained.

Tourism, as a social science, is often subject to healthy and lively debate. But within the context of debate, we, as tourism academics, must not forget to remain true to our standards and must demand of ourselves the same rigor we expect of other disciplines.

It is my opinion that tourism proponents who overlook the important distinction between co-relation and causality when discussing peace and tourism are guilty of overglamorizing the industry and of championing arguments that simply do not ring true when viewed objectively in the light of history.

History is littered with conflicts, the causes of which defy intuition, logic, and sanity. In reality, it is governments, not people, that chose war over peace and conflict over conciliation, and it is at such times of insanity that tourism, far from being a savior, becomes a victim.

A wonderful quote by former U.S. President Dwight D. Eisenhower that was included in an article by D'Amore (1994) articulates the power of peace:

> I'd like to believe that people in the long run are going to do more to promote peace than are governments. Indeed, I think that people want peace so much that one of these days, governments had better get out of their way and let them have it. (p. 113).

As travel and tourism professionals and academics, we are some of the people Eisenhower was referring to. As such, whether our industry causes peace, in some way adds to cultural tolerance and understanding, or simply makes the human journey more enriching, we can be proud of our contributions.

References

Brown, F. (1989). "Is Tourism Really a Peacemaker?" *Tourism Management,* December: 270–71.

Caneday, L. (1991). "Tourism: Recreation of the Elite." In *Tourism and Leisure: Dynamics and Diversity,* edited by J. Zeiger and L. Caneday. Alexandria, VA: National Recreation and Parks Association, pp. 83–91.

Carey, R. (1996). "Ireland-Peace Dividend." *Successful Meetings,* 45 (2): 131.

Cohen, E. (1995). "Toward a Sociology of International Tourism." In *Tourism; Principles, Practices and Philosophies,* 7th ed., edited by R. McIntosh, C.

Goeldner, and J. Ritchie. New York: John Wiley, pp. 24 1–50.

D'Amore, L. (1988). "Tourism—The World's Peace Industry." *Journal of Travel Research,* 27 (Summer): 35–40.

———(1994). "Tourism: The World's Peace Industry." In *Tourism: An Exploration,* 3rd ed., edited by Van Harssel. Englewood Cliffs, NJ: Prentice Hall, pp. 112–17. Note: this article, reproduced in entirety by Van Harssel, was referenced as having been first published in *Recreation Canada,* without additional detail. Note also that although the title of this article is identical (except punctuation) from the 1988 article referenced above, they are, in fact different articles.

"Egypt: Staying Away." (1994). *Economist,* 330 (February 19): 4546.

Gray, A. (1995). "The Economic Consequences of Peace in Ireland." *Accountancy Ireland,* 27 (5): 23–24.

Holland, S. (1991). "Recreation and Tourism: Evolution of the Social Mission." In *Tourism and Leisure: Dynamics and Diversity,* edited by J. Zeiger and L. Caneday. Alexandria, VA: National Recreation and Parks Association, pp. 66–81.

Kennedy, J. F. (1963). *The Saturday Review,* January 5.

Khamouna, M., and Zeiger, J. (1995). "Peace through Tourism." *Parks and Recreation,* 30 (9): 80–86.

Knopf, R. (1991). "Harmony and Convergence between Recreation and Tourism." In *Tourism and Leisure: Dynamics and Diversity,* edited by J. Zeiger and L. Caneday. Alexandria, VA: National Recreation and Parks Association, pp. 53–66.

Krippendorf, J. (1990). *The Holiday Makers.* Oxford, UK: Heinernann.

MacCannell, D. (1976). *The Tourist: A New Theory of the Leisure Class.* London: Macmillan.

MacDonald, J. (1993). "PATA: Travel Paves Way for Peace." *Hotel and Motel Management,* 208 (10): 1, 26.

McIntosh, R., C. Goeldner, and J. Ritchie (1995). *Tourism: Principles, Practices and Philosophies,* 7th ed. New York: John Wiley.

Parnes, S. (1994). "Peace Talks Bringing Hope for Travel Boom." *Advertising Age,* 65 (3): 1–2.

"Peace Dividends II." (1994). *Business Africa,* 4 (1): 1–15.

Plog, S. (1991). *Leisure Travel, Making it a Growth Market . . . Again!* New York: John Wiley.

Reagan, R. (1985, April 18). Correspondence to 25th Session of the Executive Council of the World Tourism Organisation. Washington, DC: The White House.

Rossant, J., N. Sandier, A. Borris, and S. Reed (1994). "The Peace Dividend for Israel and Jordan." *Business Week*, issue 1984, August 8, pp. 36–37.

Selwitz, R. (1994). "Peace Brings Hilton to Northern Ireland." *Hotel and Motel Management*, 209 (19): 90.

———(1996). "Peace Brings Tourists to Northern Ireland." *Hotel and Motel Management*, 211 (7): 8, 40.

Shallcross, M. (1994). "The Spoils of Peace." *Corporate Location*, November/December: 16–21.

Taylor, J. (1993). "Travelers, Tourists, and Transients All-Learning to See." *The Sewanee Review*, 101 (2): 248–256.

Theobald, W., ed. (1994). *Global Tourism, The Next Generation*. Oxford, UK: Butterworth-Heinemann.

KEY CONCEPTS

agriculture
anthropography
appreciation
appropriate tourism
community interpretation
cultural attractions
cultural identity card
cultural tourism
education

fine arts
food and drink
government
handicraft
heritage interpretation
history and prehistory
Honolulu Charter
industry and business
life-seeing tourism

literature and language
music and dance
peace
religion
science
story matrix
twinning principle
understanding

INTERNET SITES

Ethnoloque Database
http://www-ala.doc.ic.ac.uk/~rap/Ethnologne

National Park Service
http://www.nps.gov.

Smithsonian Institute Museums
http://www.si.edu

National Geographic
http://www.nationalgeographic.com

National Trust for Historic Preservation
http://www.nthp.org

World Heritage
http://www.unesco.org/whc

INTERNET EXERCISE

Site Name: National Geographic Society

URL: http://www.nationalgeographic.com/

Background Information: The National Geographic Society is propelled by new concerns: the alarming lack of geographic knowledge among our nation's young people and the pressing need to protect the planet's natural resources. The Society continues to develop new and exciting vehicles for broadening their reach and enhancing their ability to get people in touch with the world around them.

Exercise

1. Visit the National Geographic Society and search its database for two destinations where you think there would be a cultural tourism attraction. Collect data on these destinations and design an advertisement that would appeal to individuals who have cultural tourism in mind.

QUESTIONS FOR REVIEW AND DISCUSSION

1. Evaluate culture as a travel motivator.

2. Give an example of a cultural experience that would be most satisfying to a visitor in a country much different from his or her own.

3. Create a life-seeing tourism program in a familiar community.

4. What type of life-seeing experience would you particularly enjoy?

5. How much cultural difference can most tourists tolerate? Give examples.

6. Identify some of the rewards that international travel can bring to a perceptive, sensitive traveler.

7. For what reasons did the Minister of Tourism for the Bahamas promote their People-to-People Program?

8. Referring to question 7, identify some other countries where a similar program would be equally successful.

9. A philosopher states that culture is what we know. Research changes our viewpoint. Thus new discoveries make us change. Do you agree?

10. Does your community possess some distinctive cultural attraction?

11. Can you apply the concept of "appropriate tourism" to any tourist destination area? Give examples.

12. Explain the benefits tourists would enjoy if they participated in a heritage experience led by a graduate of a heritage interpretation training program of excellent quality.

13. How significant will be the Honolulu Charter?

14. In what way can world peace be enhanced by tourism?

CASE PROBLEMS

1. An attractive lakeside community of 5000 persons is presently a popular tourist center, primarily due to its appeal to sports enthusiasts and its proximity to a magnificent state park. However, tourist expenditures are low due principally to the lack of entertainment in the community. The movie theater closed three years ago, and there is virtually no entertainment except that to be found in a couple of beer taverns. The town and surrounding countryside are rich in history, but the only museum is a small one in the front part of a bar. How could a museum and other entertainment be provided?

2. As the director of an area tourism organization, you have been approached by a fine arts group to consider the feasibility of promoting a Shakespearean Festival in your community similar to the long-established festival at Stratford, Ontario, Canada. What factors would you consider in evaluating this request, and how would you work with your state and national tourism organizations to determine how this cultural event could be publicized?

SELECTED REFERENCES

Alley, Kelly D. "Heritage Tourism and Urban Development in India." *Practicing Anthropology,* Vol. 14, No. 2, Spring 1992.

Black, Neil, and Joy Rutledge, eds. *Outback Tourism: The Authentic Australian Adventure.* Townsville, Queensland, Australia: James Cook University, Department of Tourism, 1995.

Bohnet, Gerald V. "The Polynesian Cultural Center: A Multi-cultural Theme Park Experience." *Visions in Leisure and Business,* Vol. 9, No. 1, pp. 51–60, Spring 1990.

Boniface, P. *Managing Quality Cultural Tourism.* London: Routledge, 1995.

Brokensha, Peter, and Hans Guldberg. *Study of Cultural Tourism in Australia.* Canberra, Australia: Government Printing Office, 1992.

Brown, Vanessa. "Heritage, Tourism and Rural Regeneration: The Heritage Regions Programme in

Canada." *Journal of Sustainable Tourism,* Vol. 4, No. 3, pp. 174–182, 1996.

Butler, R. and T. Hinch, eds. *Tourism and Indigenous People.* London: ITBP, 1996.

Centre for Travel and Tourism. *Tourism and Culture: Towards the 21st Century.* Sunderland, England: Business Education Publishers, Ltd., 1996.

Chambers, Erve. *Tourism and Culture: An Applied Perspective.* Albany, NY: State University of New York Press, 1997.

Chen, Joseph S. "Travel Motivation of Heritage Tourists." *Tourism Analysis,* Vol. 2, Nos. 3 and 4, pp. 213–215, 1997.

Cohen, Erik. "Pilgrimage Centers: Concentric and Eccentric." *Annals of Tourism Research,* Vol. 19, No. 1, pp. 33–50, 1992.

Craik, Jennifer. "Are There Cultural Limits to Tourism?" *Journal of Sustainable Tourism,* Vol. 3, No. 2, pp. 87–98, 1995.

Davis, Derrin, and Betty Weiler. "Kakadu National Park: Conflicts in a World Heritage Area." *Tourism Management,* Vol. 13, No. 3, pp. 313–320, September 1992.

Edwards, J. Arwel. "Mines and Quarries: Industrial Heritage Tourism." *Annals of Tourism Research,* Vol. 23, No. 2, pp. 341–363, 1996.

Evans-Pritchard, Deirdre. "Ancient Art in Modern Context." *Annals of Tourism Research,* Vol. 20, No. 1, pp. 9–31, 1993.

Farrell, Bryan H. *Hawaii, the Legend That Sells.* Honolulu: University Press of Hawaii, 1982.

Fitzgibbon, M., and A. Kelly. *From Maestro to Manager: Critical Issues in Arts and Culture Management.* London: Oaktree Press, 1997.

Foley, M., J. Lennon, and G. Maxwell, eds. *Hospitality, Tourism and Leisure Management: Issues in Strategy and Culture.* London: Cassell, 1997.

Gee, Chuck Y., and Eduardo Fayos-Sola, eds. *International Tourism: A Global Perspective.* Madrid, Spain: World Tourism Organization, 1997.

Graburn, Nelson H. H. "The Anthropology of Tourism." *Annals of Tourism Research,* Vol. 10, No. 1, pp. 9–33. Special Issue on the Anthropology of Tourism, 1983.

Graburn, Nelson H. H. *Ethnic and Tourist Arts.* Berkeley, CA: University of California Press, 1976.

Hall, C. M., and S. Macarthus. *Integrated Heritage Management.* London: Stationery Office, 1998.

Harkin, Michael. "Modernist Anthropology and Tourism of the Authentic." *Annals of Tourism Research,* Vol. 22, No. 3, pp. 650–670, 1995.

Harrison, Julia. "Museums and Touristic Expectations. *Annals of Tourism Research,* Vol. 24, No. 1, pp. 23–40, 1997.

Herbert, D.T. "Artistic and Literary Places in France as Tourist Attractions." *Tourism Management,* Vol. 17, No. 2, pp. 77–86, March 1996.

Herbert, David T. ed. *Heritage, Tourism and Society.* New York: Cassell, 1995.

Hobson, J.S. Perry and Barry Mak. "Home Visit and Community-Based Tourism: Hong Kong's Family Insight Tour." *Journal of Sustainable Tourism,* Vol. 3, No. 4, pp. 179–190, 1995.

Johnson, Barbara R. "Anthropology's Role in Stimulating Responsible Tourism." *Practicing Anthropology,* Vol. 14, No. 2, Spring 1992.

Johnson, Peter and Barry Thomas. "Research Report–Capital Investment in the United Kingdom Arts, Sport, and Heritage Sectors: An Evaluation of Statistics." *Tourism Economics,* Vol. 4, No. 1, pp. 51–70, March 1998.

Kerstetter, Deborah, John Confer, and Kelly Bricker. "Industrial Heritage Attractions: Types and Tourists." *Journal of Travel and Tourism Marketing,* Vol. 7, No. 2, pp. 91–104, 1998.

Kimmel, James R. "Art and Tourism in Santa Fe, New Mexico." *Journal of Travel Research,* Vol. 33, No. 3, pp. 28–30, Winter 1995.

Leslie, David. "Northern Ireland, Tourism and Peace." *Tourism Management,* Vol. 17, No. 1, pp. 51–55, February 1996.

Litvin, Stephen W. "Tourism: The World's Peace Industry?" *Journal of Travel Research,* Vol. 37, No. 1, pp. 63–66, August 1998.

Masberg, Barbara A. and Lois H. Silverman. "Visitor Experiences at Heritage Sites: A Phenomenological Approach." *Journal of Travel Research,* Vol. 34, No. 4, pp. 20–25, Spring 1996.

McBoyle, Geoff. "Culture and Heritage: Keys to the Success of Scottish Malt Whisky Distilleries as Tourist Attractions," in *Culture as the Tourist Product,* Mike Robinson, Nigel Evans, and Paul Callaghan, eds. Sunderland, UK: Business Education Publishers, 1996.

McGehee, Nancy Gard, and Alison C. Meares. "A Case Study of Three Tourism-Related Craft Marketing Cooperatives in Appalachia: Contributions to Community." *Journal of Sustainable Tourism,* Vol. 6, No. 1, pp. 4–25, 1998.

Moscardo, Gianna. "Mindful Visitors: Heritage and Tourism." *Annals of Tourism Research,* Vol. 23, No. 2, pp. 322–340, 1996.

Moskin, Bill and Sandy Guettler. *Setting the Stage.* Sacramento, CA: California Arts Council, September 1998.

Nash, Dennison, and Valene L. Smith. "Anthropology and Tourism." *Annals of Tourism Research,* Vol. 18, No. 1, pp. 12–25, 1991.

Nash, Dennison. *Anthropology of Tourism.* London, UK: Pergamon Press, 1996.

Nuryanti, Wiendu. "Heritage and Postmodern Tourism." *Annals of Tourism Research,* Vol. 23, No. 2, pp. 249–260, 1996.

Richards, Greg. *Cultural Tourism in Europe.* New York: CAB International, 1996.

Rudd, Michelle Andreadakis and James A. Davis. "Industrial Heritage Tourism at the Bingham Canyon Copper Mine." *Journal of Travel Research,* Vol. 36, No. 3, pp. 85–89, Winter 1998.

Ryan, Chris. "Maori and Tourism: A Relationship of History, Constitutions, and Rites." *Journal of Sustainable Tourism,* Vol. 5, No. 4, pp. 257–278, 1997.

Silverberg, Ted. "Cultural Tourism and Business Opportunities for Museums and Heritage Sites." *Tourism Management,* Vol. 16, No. 5, pp. 362–365, 1995.

Smith, Randell A., and John D. Lesure. "Don't Shoot the Messenger: Forecasting Lodging Performance." *Cornell Quarterly,* Vol. 37, No. 1, pp. 80–88, February 1996.

Smith, Valene L. *Hosts and Guests: The Anthropology of Tourism.* Philadelphia: University of Pennsylvania Press, 1989.

Smith, Valene L. "Managing Tourism in the 1990s and Beyond." *Practicing Anthropology,* Vol. 14, No. 2, Spring 1992.

Smith, Valene L. "War and Tourism: An American Ethnography." *Annals of Tourism Research,* Vol. 25, No. 1, pp. 202–227, January 1998.

Steffen, Barbara D. "Tourism as an Instrument of Peace—Is Cross-Cultural Preparation the Answer? Rationale and Methodology." *Visions in Leisure and Business,* Vol. 16, No. 1, pp. 26–35, 1997.

TIA. *Profile of Travelers Who Participate in Historic and Cultural Activities: Results from the TravelScope Survey.* Washington D.C.: Travel Industry Association of America, August 1997.

Tian, Shu, John L. Crompton, and Peter A. Witt. "Integrating Constraints and Benefits to Identify Responsive Target Markets for Museum Attractions." *Journal of Travel Research,* Vol. 35, No. 2, pp. 34–45, Fall 1996.

Tunbridge, J. E. and G. J. Ashworth. *Dissonant Heritage: The Management of the Past as a Resource in Conflict.* London, UK: Wiley, 1995.

UNESCO. *World Decade for Cultural Development 1988-1997.* Paris: United Nations Educational, Scientific, and Cultural Organization, 1996.

van der Borg, Jan, Paola Costa, and Giuseppe Gotti. "Tourism in European Heritage Cities." *Annals of Tourism Research,* Vol. 23, No. 2, pp. 306–321, 1996.

Vukonic, Boris. *Tourism and Religion.* London, UK: Pergamon Press, 1996.

Walle, Alf H. "Habits of Thought and Cultural Tourism." *Annals of Tourism Research,* Vol. 23, No. 4, pp. 874–890, October 1996.

Walle, Alf H. *Cultural Tourism: A Strategic Focus.* Boulder, CO: Westview Press, 1998.

Weiler, Betty, and Michael Hall. *Special Interest Tourism.* New York: Wiley, 1992.

Yale, P. *From Tourist Attractions to Heritage Tourism.* London, UK: Elm, 1998.

Yamashita, Shinji, Kadir H. Din, and J. S. Eades (eds.). *Tourism and Cultural Development in Asia and Oceania.* Selangor D. E., Malaysia: Penerbit Universiti Kebangsaan Malaysia, 1997.

Zeppel, Heather, and C. Michael Hall. "Selling Art and History: Cultural Heritage and Tourism." *Journal of Tourism Studies,* Vol. 2, No. 1, pp. 29–45, May 1991.

CHAPTER 11

SOCIOLOGY OF TOURISM

- Appreciate the inordinate social impact that travel experiences make on the individual, the family or group, and society as a whole—especially the host society.

- Recognize that a country's indigenous population may resent the presence of visitors, especially in large numbers. Also recognize that the influence of these visitors may be considered detrimental—both socially and economically.

- Discover that travel patterns change with changing life characteristics and social class.

- Become familiar with the concept of social tourism and its importance in various countries.

- Perceive that there are four extremes relating to the travel preferences of international tourists. Also, recognize that a sociologist has identified a typology of four tourist roles in international tourism.

◀ LEARNING
OBJECTIVES

◀ *Travel experiences have an impact on people, whether it is a visit to a bustling city or a climb to the top of a remote mountain. (Photo courtesy of Arkansas Department of Parks & Tourism.)*

INTRODUCTION

Sociology is the science of society, social institutions, and social relationships. Visitors to a community or area create social relationships that typically differ greatly from the affiliations among the indigenous population. In this chapter we identify and evaluate tourist–host relationships and prescribe methods of managing these to create significant advantages for both groups. The ultimate effects of travel experiences on the population in areas of origin as well as in places of destination should determine to what extent societies encourage or discourage tourism.

EFFECTS ON THE INDIVIDUAL

Someone who travels, particularly to a strange location, finds an unfamiliar environment not only geographically but personally, socially, and culturally. Thus, the traveler faces problems for which a solution must be found if the trip is to be fully enjoyable and rewarding. Travelers must manage their resources of money and time in situations much different from those at home. They also must manage their social interactions and social relations to obtain sustenance, shelter, and other needs and possibly to find companionship. Determining the extent of the **"cultural distance"** they may wish to maintain results in decisions as to just how unfamiliar the traveler wants his or her environment away from home base to be. People who travel do so with different degrees of contact with the new cultures in which they may find themselves. Life-seeing tourism, for example, is a structured method for those who wish deeper immersion in local ways of life to acquire such enrichment. Some travelers prefer a more selective contact experience as might be arranged by a tour company. Tours designed around cultural subjects and experiences such as an anthropological study tour or participation in an arts and crafts festival are examples. Regardless of the degree of local participation, the individual traveler must at least superficially study the country to be visited and reach some level of decision on how these problems in environmental differences are to be resolved. Advance preparation is an intelligent approach. Travel experiences have a profound effect on the traveler as well as on society, because travel experiences often are among the most outstanding memories in the traveler's life.

EFFECTS ON THE FAMILY

As a **family** is growing and the children are maturing, the trips taken as a family are highlights of any year. The excitement of preparation and anticipation and the actual travel experience are memorable occasions of family life. Travels with a measure of adventure are likely to be the most memorable. Family travel may also be educational. The more purposeful and educational a trip becomes, the more beneficial it is. Study before taking the trip and expert travel counseling greatly add to a maximization of the trip's benefits.

Family vacation fun is provided by a ride on the Alpine Slide at Stowe, Vermont.
(Photo courtesy of Vermont Department of Tourism and Marketing.)

EFFECTS ON SOCIETY

Travel has a significant influence on national understanding and appreciation of other people. Government policies in progressive and enlightened nations encourage travel, particularly domestic travel, as a means of acquainting citizens with other parts of their country and building appreciation for the homeland.

The presence of visitors in a country affects the living patterns of indigenous peoples. The way visitors conduct themselves and their personal relationships with citizens of the host country often have a profound effect on the mode of life and attitudes of local people. Probably the most pronounced effects of this phenomenon are noted when visitors from North America or Western Europe travel in an emerging country that has a primitive culture or a culture characterized by a low (economic) standard of living and an unsophisticated population.

Conversely, the visitor is influenced by the contrast in culture. Generally, however, this brings about an increased appreciation for qualities of life in the society visited that may not be present at home.

A favorable situation exists when visitors and those of the host country mingle socially and become better acquainted. This greatly increases the awareness of each other's character and qualities, building appreciation and respect in both groups.

Tourism: Security and Crime

Unfortunately, tourists can be easy prey for criminals. Tourists do not know about dangerous areas or local situations in which they might be very vulnerable to violent crimes. They become easy marks for robbers and other offenders because they are readily identified and are usually not very well equipped to ward off an attack.

Sometimes popular tourist attractions such as parks or beaches are within walking distance from hotel areas. However, a walking tour from the hotel may bring the tourist into a high-crime area lying directly in the path taken to reach this attraction. If such high-crime areas exist, active efforts must be made to inform visitors and guests. Hotels and others that publish maps of walking tours should route such tours into safe areas only. Also, they should warn guests of the danger that could arise if the visitor undertakes certain activities.

Crimes against tourists result in bad publicity and create a negative image in the minds of prospective visitors. Thus, tour companies tend to avoid destinations that have the reputation for crimes against tourists. Eventually, no matter how much effort is applied to publicize the area's benefits and visitor rewards, decreasing popularity will result in failure.

Pizam, Reichel, and Shieh found that tourism expenditures had a negligible effect on crime.[1] However, they suggested that tourism could be considered a potential determinant of crime, negatively affecting the quality of the environment. The tourist industry cannot be held responsible for the occurrence of crime. But one must be aware that tourists are a potential target of crime. Protecting them from offenders is essential to the survival and growth of the industry. See Reading 11.2 for further discussion of safety and security.

Resentments

Resentment by local people toward the tourist can be generated by the apparent gap in economic circumstances, behavioral patterns, appearance, and economic effects. Resentment of visitors is not uncommon in areas where there is conflict of interests because of tourists. For example, in North America, local people may resent visiting sports enthusiasts because they are "shooting our deer" or "catching our fish." The demand for goods by tourists may tend to increase prices and cause bad feelings.

---

[1] Abraham Pizam, Arie Reichel, and Chia Fian Shieh, "Tourism and Crime: Is There a Relationship?" *Journal of Travel Research*, Vol. 20, No. 3 (Winter 1982), pp. 7–10.

Another form of resentment may result in a feeling of inferiority among indigenous groups because of unfavorable contrasts with foreign visitors. Local persons employed in the service industries catering to visitors may be better paid and, thus, exhibit feelings of superiority toward their less fortunate fellow citizens. This creates a poor attitude toward the entire visitor industry.

Financial dislocations can also occur. While a tourist may give a young bellhop a dollar tip for delivering bags, the bellhop's father may be working out in the fields as a farm laborer for a total daily wage of only a dollar or a dollar and a half.

As a rule, both hosts and guests in any society can learn from each other. Beneficial social contact and planned visits to observe local life and culture do much to build appreciation for the indigenous culture. At the same time, the visitors' interest in their ways of life increases the local people's respect for these visitors and gives them a feeling of pride in their own accomplishments.

Tourism often facilitates a transition from rigid authoritarian social structure to one that is more sensitive to the individual's needs. When societies are "closed" from outside influences, they tend to become rigid. By encouraging visitors, this policy is changed to a more moderate one, for the benefit of hosts and guests. The preservation of wildlife sanctuaries and parks as well as national monuments and other cultural resources is often encouraged when tourism begins to be a force in the society.

One-to-one interaction between hosts and guests can break down stereotypes, or the act of categorizing groups of people based upon a single dimension. By "labeling" people, often erroneously, individualism is lost. When a visitor gets to know people personally and is aware of their problems, hopes, and ways in which they are making life more pleasant, this visitor becomes much more sensitive to the universality of humankind. It is much easier to distrust and dislike indistinguishable groups of people than to distrust and dislike individuals one has come to know personally.

Some problems are often rooted in economic problems, such as unemployment or underemployment. The economic contributions of tourism can help to moderate such social difficulties. **Negative social effects on a host society** have been identified as follows:

1. Introduction of undesirable activities such as gambling, prostitution, drunkenness, and other excesses

2. The so-called "demonstration effect" of local people wanting the same luxuries and imported goods as those indulged in by tourists

3. Racial tension, particularly where there are very obvious racial differences between tourists and their hosts

4. Development of a servile attitude on the part of tourist business employees

5. "Trinketization" of crafts and art to produce volumes of souvenirs for the tourist trade

6. Standardization of employee roles such as the international waiter—same type of person in every country

7. Loss of cultural pride, if the culture is viewed by the visitor as a quaint custom or as entertainment

8. Too rapid change in local ways of life due to being overwhelmed by too many tourists

9. Disproportionate numbers of workers in low-paid, menial jobs characteristic of much hotel and restaurant employment

Many, if not all, of these negative effects can be moderated or eliminated by intelligent planning and progressive management methods. Tourism can be developed in ways that will not impose such a heavy social cost. Strict control of land use by zoning and building codes, enlightened policies on the part of the minister of tourism or similar official organization, and proper phasing of supply components such as infrastructure and superstructure to match supply with demand for orderly development are some of the measures needed. Education and good public relations programs can accomplish much. Enforcing proper standards of quality in the marketing of local arts and crafts can actually enhance and "rescue" such skills from oblivion. As cited in the book *Hosts and Guests*,[2] the creative skills of America's Indians of the Southwest were kept alive, enhanced, encouraged, and ultimately expanded to provide tourists with authentic Indian rugs and turquoise jewelry particularly, but other crafts as well. The Fred Harvey Company, which still bears his name, is credited with encouraging Indians to continue these attractive crafts so that he could market them in his hotels, restaurants, and gift shops.

Changing Population and Travel Interests

People change, group attitudes change, and populations change. All these factors affect travel interests. Travel interests also change. Some countries grow in travel popularity; others wane. World events tend to focus public attention on particular countries or regions of the world. The emergence of Japan and Korea as travel destinations following World War II and the Korean War and interest in visiting the Caribbean area, as well as Israel, Spain, Morocco, and East Africa, are examples. Currently, travel to China and Australia is of great interest. There is an old saying among travel promotors that "mass follows class." This has been proven beyond a doubt. Travel page publicity concerning prominent persons visiting a particular area inevitably produces a growth of interest in the area and subsequent increases in demand for travel to such well-publicized areas.

The growth of communication systems, particularly network and cable television, has broadened the scope of peoples' interests in other lands and other peoples. To be able to see, as well as hear, has a powerful impact on the viewer's mind and provides acquaintanceship with conditions in another country that may develop a desire for a visit. As communications resources grow, awareness and interest also grow.

LIFE CHARACTERISTICS AND TRAVEL

Rising standards of living, changes in the population age composition, the increasing levels of educational attainment, better communication, increased social conscious-

---

[2] Valene L. Smith (ed.), *Hosts and Guests* (Philadelphia: University of Pennsylvania Press, 1977), p. 176.

To reflect the travel patterns of different age groups, some cruise lines offer special theme cruises and trips for those with specific interests. *(Photo courtesy of Carnival Cruise Lines.)*

ness of people relating to the welfare and activities of other people throughout the world, and the psychological shrinking of the world by the jet plane have combined to produce an interest among nations in all other nations.

Travel Patterns Related to Age

With age (late sixties and upward) the traveler may become more passive. Family recreation patterns are associated with life stages of the family. The presence of young children tends to reduce the number of trips taken, whereas married couples with no children are among the best travel prospects. As the children mature, however, families increase their travel activities, and families with children between the ages of 15 and 17 have a much higher family travel pattern than do those with younger children. As the children grow up and leave home, the married couple (again without children) renews interest in travel. Also, couples in this life stage are more likely to have more discretionary income and are financially able to afford more travel. Persons living in urban centers are more travel inclined than are those in rural areas.

Senior Citizen Market

A major trend is the growth of the over-65 senior citizen market and the semi-senior citizen market—that is, those over 55 years old. Many have dubbed this the mature market, senior market, retirement market, or elderly market. Others look at it as the 50-plus market because 50 is the age for American Association of Retired Persons (AARP) membership.

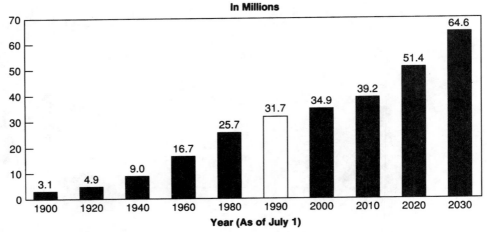

In Millions

FIGURE 11.1 **Number of persons 65 and over, 1900–2030** *(Source: U.S. Bureau of the Census and AARP.)*

Whatever it is called, it is an important and growing market. The over-65 group totaled 25.7 million in 1980, 31.7 million in 1990, and 33.9 million in 1995. Then, because of the small birth cohorts of the Great Depression, the group will grow more slowly to 36.2 million in 2005. After that, it is expected to grow rapidly to 64.6 million in 2030 as the baby boomers reach this age (see Figure 11.1).

Income

Buying power is another factor for the tourism manager to consider. People must have buying power to create a market. There is no question that a large and increasing percentage of the population today has sufficient discretionary **income** to finance business and pleasure travel, although some families may be limited to inexpensive trips. The frequency of travel and the magnitude of travel expenditures increase rapidly as income increases. All travel surveys, whether conducted by the Census Bureau, U.S. Travel Data Center, market research firms, or the media, show a direct relationship between family income and the incidence of travel. The greater the income, the more likely a household will travel. The affluent spend more on just about everything, but spending on travel is particularly strong. The value placed on time increases with household income, which is one of the reasons air travel attracts the higher-income consumer.

How the travel dollar is spent obviously depends on income. When the income of the population is divided into fifths, less than 33 percent of the lowest fifth report an expenditure for travel, whereas 85 percent of those in the top fifth report a travel expenditure. Almost half of all consumer spending for vacation and pleasure trips comes from households in the top fifth of the income scale. The affluent spend more on lodging, all-expense-paid tours, food, and shopping, but transportation expenditures are a smaller share of their total travel outlays than with those at the bottom of the income scale—32 percent versus 43 percent. This results from the fact that it is more difficult to economize on transportation than on food, lodging, and miscellaneous expenses.[3]

If current trends continue, the U.S. population will be wealthier by the year 2000. The Bureau of the Census reports that median family income rose to $40,611 in 1995. Since 1982, real median family income (after adjusting for inflation) increased by 11.8 percent. In addition to a rise in real wage rates, an exceedingly important factor was the growth in dual wage earners. The increase in the number of women who work outside the home has been dramatic and has boosted household income. Both husband and wife are employed in about half of all marriages (51 percent), an increase over the less than 29 percent in 1960. This trend is expected to continue, with 57 percent of families having both partners working by the year 2000. As incomes increase, it bodes well for travel; but with husbands and wives both working, it may be more difficult to find time for travel and vacation. It is believed that this is one of the reasons for the trend toward shorter and more frequent vacations.

Travel expenditures historically have had an income elasticity exceeding unity; as per capita real incomes continue to rise, consumers should spend an increasing proportion of their incomes on travel. Besides making more trips in the future, increasing numbers of consumers can be expected to choose air travel over other modes of travel. Income and education are closely correlated. We discuss this relationship below.

Education

Another factor deserving attention from tourism managers is education because it tends to broaden peoples' interests and thus stimulate travel. People with college educations take more pleasure trips than do those with high-school educations, and those with high-school educations take more trips than do those with grade-school educations. Educators are forecasting continued increases in the average educational level, which would result in a continued positive impact on pleasure travel.

Studies uniformly show that well-educated individuals account for the most travel and the most dollars spent for vacation and pleasure trips. Only about 50 percent of the homes where the household head did not earn a high-school diploma report an expenditure for vacation trips. Where the head holds a high-school diploma, about 65 percent report vacation expenditures; where the head has some college, 75 percent spend on vacations; and where the head has a degree, 85 percent report vacation expenditures. Income accompanies education as an important factor. In the approximately 35 percent of the homes where the head of the household has had some college, approximately 55 percent of the expenditures for vacation travel are made. Where the head has more than four years of college, vacation expenditures run two to three times the U.S. average. There appears to be no question that increased education levels heighten the propensity to travel; and with expanding higher education levels within the population, air travel should also expand.

The nation's educational level continues to rise. Fifty years ago, a high-school diploma was nearly as rare a credential as a four-year college degree is today. As of

---

[3] Fabian Linden, "The Business of Vacation Traveling." *Across the Board*, Vol. 27, No. 4 (April 1980), pp. 72–75.

Education often motivates travel, and it is an important factor in the number and types of pleasure trips taken. *(Photo courtesy of Maine Office of Tourism.)*

1996, 81.7 percent of all adults 25 years of age and older had completed four years of high school. The proportion of the population completing college has also increased considerably. In 1950, only 7.3 percent of men and 5.2 percent of women had completed college. In 1996 the proportion of persons 25 and over completing four years of college or more grew, so that 26.0 percent of men and 21.4 percent of women were college graduates. Today, the majority of college students (55.5 percent) are women.[4] Education is closely correlated with income and occupation, so the rising level of education should help to increase the demand for travel.

---

[4] U.S. Bureau of the Census, *Statistical Abstract of the United States*, 1997, 117th edition (Washington, D.C.:U.S. Government Printing Office, 1997), pp. 159–181.

TABLE 11.1
Physical or Mental Conditions Limiting Travel

Condition	Number of Conditions	Percentage of Respondents
Heart condition	20	33
Crutches	6	10
Old age	5	8
Wheelchair	3	5
Stroke victim	3	5
Recent major surgery	3	5
Diabetes	3	5
Leg braces	2	3
Blindness	2	3
Other[a]	15	23
	62	100
		(n = 60)

[a]For example, phobia of mountains, mental retardation, pregnancy, bad leg, dizziness, sprained back, flu, and stomach virus.

Travel and the Handicapped

In the United States alone, there are about 47 million physically **handicapped** people—almost twice the total population of Canada.[5] This group constitutes an excellent potential market for travel if the facilities and arrangements are suitable for their use and enjoyment. Woodside and Etzel made a study of the degree to which physical and mental conditions restricted travel activities by households and how households with one or more handicapped persons were likely to adjust their vacation travel behavior.[6]

Findings in Table 11.1 indicate that many of the physical or mental conditions that limited travel were unobservable (such as heart condition or diabetes) by other travelers or by employees of tourist facilities. But this high percentage of disabled persons creates a substantial potential for emergency situations, and the planning and management of travel equipment and facilities must aim for a major reduction or elimination of such possibilities.

The effect of the presence of handicapped persons in a family on lengths of stays is summarized in Table 11.2. The number of nights away from home differed considerably between those traveling with handicapped persons and those traveling without handicapped persons.

Many households reported little difficulty in using accommodations due to careful planning before making the trip. The majority of difficulties encountered seemed to be at recreational facilities.

[5] Michael Quigley, "Cruise Lines Under Jurisdiction of Americans with Disabilities Act," *Handicapped Travel Newsletter* (June/July/August 1993), p. 1.

[6] Arch G. Woodside and Michael J. Etzel, "Impact of Physical and Mental Handicaps on Vacation Travel Behavior," *Journal of Travel Research*, Vol. 18, No. 3 (Winter 1980), pp. 9–11.

TABLE 11.2

Number of Nights away from Home (as a Percentage of Total)

	Travel Parties	
Nights	**With Handicapped Persons**	**Without Handicapped Persons**
1–3	37	42
4–6	24	31
7–9	15	15
10–12	5	5
13–15	7	3
16 or more	12	4
Number of respondents	60	530

Americans with Disabilities Act

Substantial improvements have been made by the tourist industry to serve this segment of the market over the years. Activity accelerated with the enactment of the Americans with Disabilities Act (ADA) on July 26, 1990. ADA contains five titles, or sections: Employment, Public Services, Public Accommodations and Services Operated by Private Entities, Telecommunications, and Miscellaneous Provisions. Included in these titles are mandates for accessible public transit and complementary paratransit; accessible intercity (Amtrak) and commuter rail; accessible stations; accessible public accommodation (private entities), including inns, hotels, motels, restaurants, bars, theaters, concert halls, auditoriums, convention centers, all kinds of stores, service establishments, offices, terminals and depots, museums, libraries, galleries, schools, and so on, and telecommunications relay services for hearing- and speech-impaired persons.

Although the act is not specifically a travel law, travel agencies, lodging establishments, motorcoach operators, museums, and restaurants fall into the broad category of public accommodation that are required to make their facilities accessible to disabled persons. As the Justice Department and the Transportation Department issue final regulations and firms comply, easier travel for the disabled will result.

EMERGENCE OF GROUP TRAVEL PATTERNS

Travel Clubs

These are groups, sometimes with a common interest (if only in travel), that have formed travel organizations for their mutual benefit. For example, some purchase an aircraft and then arrange trips for their members. Others join international membership clubs such as Club Méditerranée, which owns resort properties in many countries and provides package-type holidays at usually modest cost.

Special hobbies and interests, such as fishing, provide another strong motivation for travel, either individually or in groups. *(Photo courtesy of Arkansas Department of Parks & Tourism.)*

Low-Priced Group Travel

Many tour companies cater to common interest groups such as the members of a religious group or professional or work group. A tour is arranged, often at reasonable cost, and is promoted to members of the group.

Public Carrier Group Rates and Arrangements

Airlines and other public carriers make special rates available for groups—a common number is 15 at discounted rates. A free ticket is issued to the group's escort or leader. Chartering all or part of a public transportation vehicle, aircraft, or ship is also a special effort on the part of the carrier to accommodate travel groups.

Incentive Tours

One of the fastest-growing group arrangements is that of incentive tours provided by a company to members and their spouses who are successful in achieving some objective, usually a sales goal. At the destination, the group is sometimes asked to review new products and receive some company indoctrination.

Special-Interest Tours

Special-interest group travel is another segment growing in importance. Tours are arranged for those interested in agriculture, archaeology, architecture, art, bird watching, business, industry, castles and palaces, ethnic studies, fall foliage, festivals, fishing, hunting, flower arranging, gardening, gems and minerals, music, golf, history, literature, nature, opera, photography, professional interests, psychic research, safaris, skiing, skin diving, social studies, sports, study, theater, and wine, to name a few examples.

Social and fraternal organizations also are traveling more in groups. Some private clubs are taking group trips. Some are extensive trips around the world or trips lasting up to 60 days. Women's groups, social groups, youth groups, alumni, and professional societies commonly take extended trips together as a group. Preconvention and postconvention trips are also popular.

SOCIAL (SUBSIDIZED) TOURISM

Although there is as yet no agreed definition of **social tourism,** there has been considerable study of the question. W. Hunziker at the Second Congress of Social Tourism held at Vienna and Salzburg in 1959 proposed the following definition: "Social tourism is a type of tourism practiced by low income groups, and which is rendered possible and facilitated by entirely separate and therefore easily recognizable services." Another definition, that of M. Andre Poplimont, is as follows: "Social tourism is a type of tourism practiced by those who would not be able to meet the cost without social intervention, that is, without the assistance of an association to which the individual belongs."

From these definitions and from the reports of the three International Congresses on Social Tourism, it is clear that certain elements may be described. First is the idea of "limited means." Second, social tourism is subsidized by the states, local authorities, employers, trade unions, clubs, or other associations to which the worker belongs. Third, it involves travel outside the normal place of residence, preferably to a different environment that is usually within their own country or sometimes to a country nearby.

Holidays with Pay

Paid holidays are now established all over the world, and in most countries a minimum duration (one, two, or three weeks) is specified either by law or by collective agreement. Some, however, consider this institution only a first stage, and they believe that attention should now be turned to the way in which these holidays are used. One of the great subjects of discussion by twentieth-century sociologists is (a) the use of the increased leisure time now available to workers and (b) the cultural and educational development that such leisure time makes possible.

Large numbers of workers are obliged to spend their holidays at home, partly because of their lack of means or tourist experience and partly because of lack of information, transport difficulties, or shortage of suitable accommodation. Organized social tourism, if efficiently managed, can overcome most of these problems: finance through subsides and savings schemes, experience and information through contacts elsewhere in the country concerned or abroad, transport problems through package deals with carriers, and accommodation through contracts with resorts. Thus, organizations can bring tourism within the reach of many who would otherwise be unable to travel. There will be some, however, who for reasons of age, health, family responsibility, or disinclination are unwilling to join in such holidays even when all arrangements are made for them.

Determination of Needs

Some countries carry out research in this field. In Belgium it was discovered that almost 60 percent of the respondents to an inquiry preferred a continuous stay to moving from place to place, but this preference was more marked among older people than among younger ones. In the Netherlands, another inquiry revealed that about a million holiday makers preferred not to rely on the hospitality of relatives if other facilities within their means were provided. It was evident that existing facilities of this kind were inadequate.

It was also found that the tendency to take holidays away from home was increasing and that more attention should be given to the educational and cultural aspects of tourism. Studies in France and Italy have found orders of preference between the countryside, the seaside, the mountains, health resorts, and other places; and in Sweden and Italy, inquiries have been carried out into the types of accommodations favored.

Examples of Social Tourism

Leysin, in Switzerland, is one of the best-known examples of holiday centers for social tourism. Originally a famous health resort, advances in medicine meant that its clientele would gradually diminish; but with the cooperation of certain organizations, including the Caisse Suisse de Voyage, the resort was adapted to attract a new type of tourist. A small golf course, a swimming pool, tennis courts, and arrangements for skiing were established, and sanatoria and hotels were converted to meet the new demands. A publicity campaign was begun, and in its first year over 2000 tourists arrived and spent more than 50,000 bed-nights in the resort.

Camping and staying at hostels are popular with younger tourists and are also used by families. In recent years there has been a considerable development of caravan camps, particularly in Great Britain. Camping has the advantage of being one of the least expensive forms of holiday and makes possible more mobility. Financial aid is given to camps by the state in France and other countries. In Greece, camps are operated by some large industrial firms for the benefit of their employees; and in most countries, they are run by camping clubs and youth associations.

Provision of Information

In the development of social tourism, other problems arise, but these are largely common to tourism in general. The provision of information, however, deserves brief mention here, because many of the beneficiaries of social tourism will have little knowledge of the special attractions of different resorts. In some countries, government authorities, trade unions, national tourist organizations, and other bodies have given attention to this question. In the United States, for example, there are tourist information offices in the large cities, and publications are issued advising workers how they can spend their holidays. In Canada, bulletins are sent to the trade union offices and other organizations.

To date, most progress has been made in domestic tourism only; and although many workers are already traveling abroad, there is great opportunity for joint action between the official travel organizations of different states. Proposals have been made in some regions as how best to promote foreign travel by the lower-income groups, and the Argentine national tourist organization has invited the correspondent bodies in other South American states to arrange programs on a reciprocal basis.

SUMMARY OF THE PRINCIPAL SOCIAL EFFECTS OF TOURISM

1. The vacation and special business trips a person takes are often among life's most vivid memories.

2. For families, vacation trips taken together are among the highlights of the year's activities.

3. The presence of visitors in a particular area can affect the living patterns of local people. The extent to which a local population is affected depends on the diversity of the mixing groups, including factors such as obvious differences in wealth, habits, appearance, and behavior.

4. On a national basis, people of a particular country can have their lives changed by tourism, particularly if there are large numbers of tourists in proportion to the indigenous population. Visitors may influence ways of dressing, consumption patterns, desire for products used by tourists, sexual freedoms, and a broadening outlook on the world.

5. For both hosts and guests, the most satisfying relationships are formed when they can meet and interact socially at a gathering such as a reception; a tea, or a cultural event; in "people-to-people" programs (home visitation); or in life-seeing tourism (a structured learning–leisure program).

6. Tourism's effects on crime are negligible, but tourists can become easy victims of crime. Hosts must help them avoid dangerous places and areas.

7. Resentment of visitors by local (indigenous) people can occur. There may be conflicts over the use (or abuse) of local facilities and resources. Consumer prices may rise during the "tourist season."

8. Extensive tourism development can bring about undesirable social effects such as increased prostitution, gambling, drunkedness, rowdyism, unwanted noise, congestion, and other excesses.

9. Domestic and international tourism increases for people in a country that has a rising standard of living, a population age distribution favoring young adults or young marrieds with no children, and an increasing population of older, affluent adults.

10. People living in cities are more interested in travel than those living in small towns or rural areas.

11. Wealthy people and those in higher social classes are greatly inclined to travel.

12. Increase in the educational level in a population brings about an increase in travel.

13. Catering to handicapped persons substantially increases markets.

14. Group travel and tours are popular ways to travel.

15. Social tourism is a form of travel wherein the cost is subsidized by the traveler's trade union, government, public carrier, hotel, or association. Travelers thus assisted are in low-income groups or older age groups, or they are workers in organizations authorized to receive such subsidies or vacation bonuses.

THE INTERNATIONAL TOURIST

International travel largely emanates from countries with a comparatively high standard of living, with high rates of economic growth, and with social systems characterized by declining inequality of incomes and a sizable urban population. In addition, these international travelers come from countries where large-scale industry and commerce comprise the foundations of the economy and where the communications and information environment is dominated by the mass media. The international market is largely made up of middle-income people, including the more prosperous minority of the working class, who normally live in large cities and earn their living in managerial, professional, white-collar, supervisory, and skilled occupations.

There are four extremes relating to the preferences of the international tourist: (1) complete relaxation to constant activity, (2) traveling close to one's home environment to a totally strange environment, (3) complete dependence on group travel to traveling alone, and (4) order to disorder. These extremes are not completely separate, and for most travelers there may be any number of combinations on any given trip. For example, a traveler may take a peaceful river cruise and then enjoy a strenuous swim in a quiet pool.

Relaxation Versus Activity

Historically, the first wave of mass international travel (the interwar and postwar years) occurred at a time when there was a sharp differentiation between work and leisure and when the working week for most people, including the middle class, was long and exhausting. Under these circumstances, it was not surprising that the demand concentrated on holidays that offered relaxation, recuperation, and rest. Essentially they provided an opportunity for winding down and getting fit for the next 49 weeks of arduous activity. Since then, the balance between work and leisure has shifted sharply in favor of the latter. Usually the weekend is free, and the annual holiday leave for some workers has been lengthened. In other words, over the past decades people have become used to greater slices of leisure time. Relaxation is possible throughout the year, and there is less need to use a holiday exclusively for this purpose.

With the arrival of year-round leisure, there seems to be a surfeit of opportunities for relaxation, so that increasingly the people have started to use their nonholiday leisure time to acquire and exercise new activity skills: sailing, climbing, sports, horseback riding. It is reasonable to forecast that the balance between leisure and work will continue to move in the direction of leisure and that the relative demand for activity-oriented travel will increase.

Familiarity Versus Novelty

Most people, when they make their first venture abroad, tend to seek familiarity rather than novelty: people speaking the visitors' language, providing the meals and beverages they are accustomed to, using the same traffic conventions, and so on. Having found a destination where the traveler feels at home, this sort of tourist, at least for the first few ventures abroad, will be a "repeater," going back time and again to the same

A great deal of international travel is conducted to experience the novel. A striking example is the well-known floating market in Bangkok. (*Photo courtesy of the Tourism Authority of Thailand.*)

place. Not until more experience is gained will the traveler want to get away from a normal environment—to mix with people who speak differently, eat differently, dress differently.

In the Western world the general change in social conditions seems to be in the direction of speeding up the readiness for novelty. Where previously the social climate and rigid structure of society had reinforced a negative attitude to change, we now find increasingly a positive attitude to change. People accept and seek innovation in industry, education, family life, the arts, social relationships, and the like.

In particular, in countries with high living standards, manufacturers faced with quickly saturated markets concentrate on developing new products and encouraging the consumer to show greater psychological flexibility. More and more markets are dependent on the systematic organization of rapid change in fashion to sustain and expand. With the blurring of class differences and rising standards of living, travel demand will likely reflect this climate and express fragmentation of the total market as people move away from the traditional resorts to a succession of new places.

Dependence Versus Autonomy

A widely accepted analysis of modern industrial society is based on the concept of alienation in work. Briefly, this view states that most people are inevitably employed in work that, though perhaps well paid, is not intrinsically rewarding and satisfying and that from this frustration results, among other things, a general sense of powerlessness, a withdrawal from political and social activities, and the pursuit of status symbols. In the field of leisure, this work alienation should lead to a demand for passive, time-killing holidays or for holidays where the main gratification is the achievement of easily recognized status. Fundamental absence of significance in work, in other words, would lead to holidays during which the same sense of powerlessness and dependence would prevail—organized holiday camps, organized package trips, mass entertainment, and so forth.

In fact, there has been very little empirical research to substantiate this description of an industrialized society. Indeed, the data available suggest the contrary—that many industrial workers, backed by strong trade unions and state-created full employment, feel that as workers they wield considerable power. Certainly, industry and social organization is moving in the direction of providing work that is intrinsically rewarding and satisfying, which should enhance life for today's workers, leading to a sense of personal autonomy in all aspects of their lives, including their leisure time: They are likely to seek holidays during which they feel independent and in control of what they do and how they do it. One would expect that for some time ahead, economic and social circumstances should generate a greater proportion of autonomous participants in the total demand for travel.

Order Versus Disorder

Until recently in most Western societies, the training of children has been based on control and conformity, defined and enforced by an all-embracing circle of adult authority figures: parents, teachers, police officers, clergy, employers, civil authorities. With such a background, it is not surprising that most tourists sought holidays that reinforced this indoctrination: set meals at fixed times, guidebooks that told them the "right" places to visit, and resorts where their fellow tourists were tidy, well-behaved, "properly" dressed, and so on. They avoided situations where their sense of orderliness might be embarrassed or offended.

More recently, child-rearing practices have changed in the direction of greater permissiveness, and the traditional incarnations of authority have lost much of their Victorian impressiveness. The newer generation of tourists no longer feels inhibited about what to wear and how to behave when on holiday; differences of others, opportunities for unplanned action, and freedom from institutionalized regulations are distinctive characteristics of the contemporary traveler.

Summing up, then, one would predict that because of deep and persisting social and economic changes in modern Western society, the demand for travel will be based less on the goals of relaxation, familiarity, dependence, and order and increasingly on activity, novelty, autonomy, and informality. One should not, of course, ignore the fact that, since international travel is a rapidly growing market, each year's total consumers will always include a minority who value familiarity, dependency, and order.

BARRIERS TO TRAVEL

While travel has become a popular social phenomenon, there are a number of reasons why people do not travel extensively, or do not travel at all. The reasons, products of psychological analysis, are not meant to be ultimate answers as to why people travel where they do. We can, however, look at the more concrete reasons why those studied did not go on a trip during a certain period of time. For most of these studies, barriers to travel fall into six broad categories:

1. *Cost.* Consumers operate within monetary constraints, and travel must compete with other allocations of funds. Saying that travel is too expensive is an indirect way of saying that travel is not important, but, even allowing this interpretation, costs are a principal reason for staying home.

2. *Lack of time.* Many people cannot leave their businesses, jobs, or professions for vacation purposes.

3. *Health limitations.* Poor health and physical limitations keep many persons at home.

4. *Family stage.* Parents of young children often do not travel because of family obligations and inconveniences in traveling with children. Widows and singles sometimes do not travel because of the lack of a traveling companion.

5. *Lack of interest.* Unawareness of travel destinations that would bring pleasurable satisfaction is a major barrier.

6. *Fear and safety.* Things unknown are often feared; and in travel, much is often not familiar to the would-be traveler. Wars, unrest, and negative publicity about an area will create doubt and fear in the mind of the prospective traveler. Terrorism has reared its ugly head in the last decade and is a deterrent to travel.

When motivation to travel is sufficiently powerful, the barriers may be overcome, but these forces may still influence means of travel and destinations selected.

Although travelers may be able to overcome the first four variables listed, tourism marketers need to modify the fifth barrier—lack of interest. This is a challenge for tourism marketing managers. To illustrate just how widespread this barrier is, the following approach was taken where the cost barrier was eliminated. The respondents were asked this incomplete sentence: "Mr. and Mrs. Brown were offered an expense-free tour of the United States, but they didn't want to go because . . ." Forty-two percent of the respondents said that the Browns wanted to go on the trip but couldn't due to job reasons, poor health, age, or responsibilities for children. However, 26 percent indicated that the Browns did not want to go on the trip at all; they would rather stay home, or they did not like to travel, or they were afraid to travel. It is evident that in spite of widespread desires to travel, some people would rather stay home. For others, a weak desire to travel is compounded by nervousness or fear of what the experience may bring. Such a reluctance to travel runs counter to the tide, but this segment is too large a group to be overlooked. With the proper motivational tools, a significant percentage of this untapped group of potential travelers might be convinced that there are places or things of interest outside the world in which they are now existing.

When analyzing some of the psychological reasons contributing to the lack of interest in travel, at least some are related to conflicts between exploration and safety needs. A person's home is safe and is a place thoroughly known, and he or she is not required to maintain a facade there. On the other hand, the familiarity of home can also produce boredom and the need to explore. A person is thus possessed of two very strong drives—*safety and exploration*—and he or she needs to reduce this conflict.

One way to do this is by traveling in areas that the person knows well. He or she may to go the same cottage at the same lake with the same people that he or she has known for years. Thus, a new experience that may threaten the need for safety is avoided, but this approach reduces the exploration need by the persons leaving home and traveling to a different place even though it is familiar.

SUMMARY

Sociologists are interested in tourism because travel profoundly affects individuals and families who travel, inducing behavioral changes. The new insights, understandings, and appreciations that travel brings are enlightening and educational.

A person who travels to a strange environment encounters problems that must be resolved. How well the traveler solves these problems will largely determine the degree of the trip's success. In planning a trip the traveler must decide how much cultural distance (from the home environment) he or she desires. Tourists differ greatly in this regard.

In this chapter we have described various social phenomena related to mass tourism. Included are social tourism, international travel behavior extremes, barriers to travel, and a typology of four tourist roles. Your understanding of these can help to provide a basis for determining tourist volume policy. Consideration must be given to the likely influence that masses of tourists will have on their hosts. Furthermore, applying the procedures explained in this chapter should minimize the negative sociological influences and enhance the positive effects of large numbers of tourists on their host society. Although tourism expenditures have a negligible effect on crime, tourists are potential targets for crime. It is essential that they be protected as much as possible.

ABOUT THE READINGS

As you become educated in tourism, you will develop a growing awareness that international tourists differ greatly in their travel objectives, their manner of traveling, their spending habits, and their relationship to the tourist business establishment and to the citizens of the host country.

Each tourist must decide to what extent he or she wishes to become immersed into a different society when on a vacation trip. The degrees of involvement are divided or classified into a typology of four tourist roles by a sociologist, and these are described in detail in Reading 11.1, which has become a classic. Once understood, the classifications become very useful criteria for making decisions about who we wish to attract as tourists and what kinds of supply components are appropriate for each type of tourist.

Reading 11.2 addresses the question of safety and security of tourists. It examines law enforcement agencies treatment of tourists.

READING 11.1

TOWARD A SOCIOLOGY OF INTERNATIONAL TOURISM

by Erik Cohen
Department of Sociology and Social Anthropology
The Hebrew University of Jerusalem
Reprinted from *Social Research*, Vol. 39, No. 1 (Spring 1972).
In recent years, there has been an enormous rise in both the number of people traveling for pleasure and the number of countries and places visited regularly by tourists.[1] Sociologists, however, seem to have neglected the study of tourism as a social phenomenon of international tourism, one which includes a typology of tourists on the basis of their relationship to both the tourist business establishment and the host country.[2]

Varieties of Tourist Experience
"After seeing the jewels of Topkapi, the fabled Blue Mosque and bazaars, it's awfully nice to come home to the Istanbul Hilton" (Advertisement in *Time* magazine)

Tourism is so widespread and accepted today, particularly in the Western world,[3] that we tend to take it for granted. Traveling for pleasure in a foreign country by large numbers of people is a relatively modern occurrence, however, dating only from the early nineteenth century.[4]

It seems that mass tourism as a cultural phenomenon evolves as a result of a very basic change in man's attitude to the world beyond the boundaries of his native habitat. So long as man remains largely ignorant of the existence of other societies, other cultures, he regards his own small world as the cosmos. What lies outside is mysterious and unknown and therefore dangerous and threatening. It can only inspire fear or, at best, indifference, lacking as it does any reality for him.

A tremendous distance lies between such an orientation and that characteristic of modern man. Whereas primitive and traditional man will leave his native habitat only when forced to by extreme circumstances, modern man is more loosely attached to his environment, much more willing to change it, especially temporarily, and is remarkably able to adapt to new environments. He is interested in things, sights, customs, and cultures different from his own, precisely because they are different. Gradually, a new value has evolved: the appreciation of the experience of strangeness and novelty. This experience now excites, titillates, and gratifies, whereas before it only frightened. I believe that tourism as a cultural phenomenon becomes possible only when man develops a generalized interest in things beyond his particular habitat, when contact with and appreciation and enjoyment of strangeness and novelty are valued for their own sake. In this sense, tourism is a thoroughly modern phenomenon.

An increased awareness of the outer world seems to lead to an increased readiness to leave one's habitat and to wander around temporarily, or even to emigrate to another habitat. Although we have little real knowledge of the way in which this awareness grows, it would seem that the technological achievements of the past two centuries have been prime determinants. While the invention of increasingly effective means of communication and the increasingly widespread availability and use of these means helped make man more aware of the outside world, at the same time a parallel phenomenon occurred in transportation, making travel less arduous, less dangerous, and less time-consuming. Also, the creation and growth of a monied middle class in many societies made traveling for pleasure a possibility for large numbers of people, whereas even as recently as the early nineteenth century only the aristocracy could afford the necessary expenditure in money and time.

Though novelty and strangeness are essential elements in the tourist experience, not even modern man is completely ready to immerse himself wholly in an alien environment. When the experience becomes too strange he may shrink back. For man is still basically molded by his native culture and bound through habit to its patterns of behavior. Hence, complete abandonment of these customs and complete immersion in a new and alien environment may be experienced as unpleasant and even threatening, especially if prolonged. Most tourists seem to need something familiar around them, something to remind them of home, whether it be food, newspapers, living quarters, or another person from their native country. Many of today's tourists are able to enjoy the experience of change and novelty only from a strong base of familiarity, which enables them to feel secure enough to enjoy the strangeness of what they experience. They would like to experience the novelty of the macroenvironment of a strange place from the security of a familiar microenvironment. And many will not venture abroad but on those well-trodden paths equipped with familiar means of transportation, hotels, and food. Often the modern tourist is not so much abandoning his accustomed environment for a new one as he is being transposed to foreign soil in an "environmental bubble" of his native culture. To a certain extent he views the people, places, and culture of that society through the protective walls of his familiar "environmental bubble," within which he functions and interacts in much the same way as he does in his own habitat.[5]

The experience of tourism combines, then, a degree of novelty with a degree of familiarity, the security of old habits with the excitement of change.[6] However, the exact extent to which familiarity and novelty are experienced on any particular tour depends upon the individual tastes and preferences of the tourist as well as upon the institutional setting of his trip. There is a continuum of possible combinations of novelty and familiarity. This continuum is, to my mind, the basic underlying variable for the sociological analysis of the phenomenon of modern tourism. The division of the continuum into a number of typical combinations of novelty and familiarity leads to a typology of tourist experiences and roles. I will propose here a typology of four tourist roles.[7]

The Organized Mass Tourist: The organized mass tourist is the least adventurous and remains largely confined to his "environmental bubble" throughout his trip. The guided tour, conducted in an air-conditioned bus, traveling at high speed through a steaming countryside, represents the prototype of the organized mass tourist. This tourist type buys a package tour as if it were just another commodity in the modern mass market. The itinerary of his trip is fixed in advance, and all his stops are well-prepared and guided; he makes almost no decisions for himself and stays almost exclusively in the microenvironment of his home country. Familiarity is at a maximum, novelty at a minimum.

The Individual Mass Tourist: This type of tourist role is similar to the previous one, except that the tour is not entirely preplanned, the tourist has a certain amount of control over his time and itinerary and is not bound to a group. However, all of his major arrangements are still made through a tourist agency. His excursions do not bring him much further afield than do those of the organized mass tourist. He, too, does his experiencing from within the "environmental bubble" of his home country and ventures out of it only occasionally—and even then only into well-charted territory. Familiarity is still dominant, but somewhat less so than in the preceding type; the experience of novelty is somewhat greater, though it is often of the routine kind.

The Explorer: This type of tourist arranges his trip alone; he tries to get off the beaten track as much as possible, but he nevertheless looks for comfortable accommodations and reliable means of transportation. He tries to associate with the people he visits and to speak their language. The explorer dares to leave his "environmental bubble" much more than the previous two types, but he is still careful to be able to step back into it when the going becomes too rough. Though novelty dominates, the tourist does not immerse himself completely in his host society, but retains some of the basic routines and comforts of his native way of life.

The Drifter: This type of tourist ventures furthest away from the beaten track and from the accustomed ways of life of his home country. He shuns any kind of connection with the tourist establishment, and considers the ordinary tourist experience phony. He tends to make it wholly on his own, living with the people and often taking odd-jobs to keep himself going. He tries to live the way the people he visits live, and to share their shelter, foods, and habits, keeping only the most basic and essential of his old customs. The drifter has no fixed itinerary or timetable and no well-defined goals of travel. He is almost wholly immersed in his host culture. Novelty is here at its highest, familiarity disappears almost completely.

The first two tourist types I will call *institutionalized* tourist roles; they are dealt with in a routine way by the tourist establishment—the complex of travel agencies, travel companies, hotel chains, etc., which cater to the tourist trade. The last two types I will call *noninstitutionalized* tourist roles, in that they are open roles, at best only very loosely attached to the tourist establishment.

The Institutionalized Forms of Tourism:

The Organized and the Individual Mass Tourist[8]
"Where were you last summer?"

"In Majorca."
"Where is that?"
"I don't know, I flew there."
(Conversation between two girls, reprinted in a German journal)

Contemporary institutionalized tourism is a mass industry. The tour is sold as a package, standardized and mass-produced.[9] All transportation, places to be visited, sleeping and eating accommodations are fixed in advance. The tourist establishment takes complete care of the tourist from beginning to end. Still, the package tour sold by the tourist establishment purportedly offers the buyer the experience of novelty and strangeness. The problem of the system, then, is to enable the mass tourist to "take in" the novelty of the host country without experiencing any physical discomfort or, more accurately, to observe without actually experiencing.

Since the tourist industry serves large numbers of people, these have to be processed as efficiently, smoothly, and quickly as possible through all the phases of the tour. Hence, it is imperative that the experience of the tourist, however novel it might seem to him, be as ordered, predictable, and controllable as possible. In short, he has to be given the illusion of adventure, while all the risks and uncertainties of adventure are taken out of his tour. In this respect, the quality of the mass tourist's experiences approaches that of vicarious participation in other people's lives, similar to the reading of fiction or the viewing of motion pictures. The tourist establishment achieves this effect through two interrelated mechanisms that I will call the *transformation of attractions and the standardization of facilities.*

Every country, region, or locality has something which sets it apart from all others, something for which it is known and worth visiting: scenic beauty, architecture, feasts or festivals, works of art, etc. In German there is a very appropriate term for these features, *Sehenswurdigkeiten,* or "things worth seeing," and I will call them "attractions." Some attractions are world renown, and become the trademark of a place; these attract tourists naturally. In other cases, they are created artificially—they are contrived "tourist attractions."[10]

The main purpose of mass tourism is the visiting of attractions, whether genuine or contrived. However, even if they are genuine, the tendency is to transform or manipulate them, to make them "suitable" for mass tourist consumption. They are supplied with facilities, reconstructed, landscaped, cleansed of unsuitable elements, staged, managed, and otherwise organized. As a result, they largely lose their original flavor and appearance and become isolated from the ordinary flow of life and natural texture of the host society.[11] Hawaiian dancing girls have to be dressed for public decency—but not much, so that they remain attractive; natural sights have to be groomed and guarded until they look like well-kept parks; traditional festivals have to be made more colorful and more respectable so tourists will be attracted but not offended. Festivals and ceremonies, in particular, cease being spontaneous expressions of popular feelings and become well-staged spectacles.[12] Even still-inhabited old quarters of otherwise modern cities are often turned into "living museums" to attract tourists, like the old town of Acre in Israel, Old San Juan, and Old Town in Chicago.

While the transformation of attractions provides controlled novelty for mass tourism, the standardization of facilities serves to provide him with the necessary familiarity in his immediate surroundings. The majority of tourists originate today from the affluent Western countries, the U.S. and Western Europe, and increasingly from Japan. Hence, whatever country aspires to attract mass tourism is forced to provide facilities on a level commensurate with the expectations of the tourists from those countries. A tourist infrastructure of facilities based on Western standards has to be created even in the poorest host countries. This tourist infrastructure provides the mass tourist with the protective "ecological bubble" of his accustomed environment. However, since the tourist also expects some local flavor or signs of foreignness in his environment, there are local decorations in his hotel room, local foods in the restaurants, local products in the tourist shops. Still, even these are often standardized: the decorations are made to resemble the standard image of that culture's art, the local foods are made more palatable to unaccustomed tongues, the selection of native crafts is determined by the demands of the tourist.[13]

The transformation of attractions and the standardization of facilities, made necessary by the difficulties of managing and satisfying large numbers of tourists, have introduced a basic uniformity or similarity into the tourist experience. Whole countries lose their individuality to the mass tourist as the richness of their culture and geography is reduced by the tourist industry to a few standard elements, according to which they are classified and presented to the mass tourist. Before he even begins his tour, he is conditioned to pay attention primarily to the few basic attractions and facilities advertised in the travel literature or suggested by the travel agent, which are catalogued and sometimes even assigned a level of "importance."[14] This induces a peculiar kind of selective awareness; the tourist tends to become aware of his environment only when he reaches spots of "interest," while he is largely oblivious to it the rest of the time.[15] As a result, countries become interchangeable in the tourist's mind. Whether he is looking for good beaches, restful forests, or old cities, it becomes relatively unimportant to him where these happen to be found. Transportation by air, which brings him almost directly to his destination without his having to pass through other parts of the host country, contributes to the isolation of the attractions and facilities from the rest of the country—as well as the isolation of the tourist. And so mass tourism has created the following paradox: though the desire for variety, novelty, and strangeness are the primary motives of tourism, these qualities have decreased as tourism has become institutionalized.

In popular tourist countries the tourist system or infrastructure has become separated from the rest of the culture and the natural flow of life. Attractions and facilities which were previously frequented by the local population are gradually abandoned. As Greenwich Village became a tourist attraction, many of the original bohemians moved to the East Village. Even sites of high symbolic value for the host society may suffer a similar fate: houses of government, churches, and national monuments become more and more the preserve of the mass tourist and are less and less frequented by the native citizen.

The ecological differentiation of the tourist sphere from the rest of the country makes for social separation; the mass tourist travels in a world of his own, surrounded by but not integrated in, the host society. He meets the representatives of the tourist establishment—hotel managers, tourist agents, guides—but only seldom the natives.[16] The natives, in turn, see the mass tourist as unreal. Neither has much of an opportunity to become an individual to the other.

A development complementary to the ecological differentiation of the tourist sphere is the gradual emergence of an international tourist system, reaching across political and cultural boundaries. The system enjoys a certain independence and even isolation from its immediate surroundings, and an internal homogeneity in spite of the wide variations between the countries with which it intersects. The autonomy and isolation can be most clearly seen in those cases where tourists enjoy some special facilities that are out of bounds to the members of the host society, such as spas and nightclubs in Eastern European countries serving exclusively foreigners or the Berionka (dollar shop) in the Soviet Union, which caters only to tourists.

The isolation of the mass tourist from the host society is further intensified by a general communication gap. Tourist publications and travel literature are ordinarily written in the spirit of the tourist establishment—and often not by a native of the country—whose prime motive is selling, not merely informing. Such literature colors the tourist's attitudes and expectations beforehand. But probably more responsible than any other single factor mentioned thus far in creating and maintaining the isolation of the tourist is the fact that he seldom knows the language of the country he is traveling in. Not knowing the language makes forming acquaintances with the natives and traveling about on one's own so difficult that few tourists attempt it to any extent. Even worse, it leaves the tourist without any real feel for the culture of people in the country.

The sad irony of modern institutionalized tourism is that, instead of destroying myths between countries, it perpetuates them. The tourist comes home with the illusion that he has "been" there and can speak with some authority about the country he has visited. I would hypothesize that the larger the flow of mass tourists becomes, the more institutionalized and standardized tourism becomes and consequently the stronger the barriers between the tourist and the life of the host country become. What were previously formal barriers *between* different countries become informal barriers *within* countries.

The Noninstitutionalized Forms of Tourism: The Explorer and the Drifter

Boorstin's vivid description of the evolution of the aristocratic traveler of yesterday into the tourist of modern times oversimplifies the issue to make a point. For Boorstin, there exists either the mass tourist or the adventurer, who contrives crazy feats and fabricates risks in order to experience excitement.[17] Even Knebel's less tendentious analysis postulates little variety in the role structure of the contemporary tourist. Both writers seem to have overlooked the noninstitutionalized tourist roles of explorer and drifter.

While the roles of both the explorer and the drifter are noninstitutionalized, they differ from each other chiefly in the extent to which they venture out of their microenvironment and away from the tourist system, and in their attitudes toward the people and countries they visit.

The explorer tries to avoid the mass tourist route and the traditional tourist attraction spots, but he nevertheless looks for comfortable accommodations and reliable means of transportation. He ventures into areas relatively unknown to the mass tourist and explores them for his own pleasure. The explorer's experience of the host country, its people, places and culture, is unquestionably much broader and deeper than that of the mass tourist. He tries to associate with the people he visits and to speak their language, but he still does not wholly immerse himself in the host society. He remains somewhat detached, either viewing his surroundings from an aesthetic perspective or seeking to understand the people on an intellectual level. Unlike the drifter, he does not identify with the natives emotionally or try to become one of them during his stay.

Through his mode of travel, the explorer escapes the isolation and artificiality the tourist system imposes on the mass tourist. Paradoxically, though, in his very attempts at escape he serves as a spearhead of mass tourism; as he discovers new places of interest, he opens the way for more commercialized forms of tourism, the managers of which are always on the lookout for new and unusual attractions. His experiences and opinions serve as indicators to other, less adventurous tourists to move into the area. As more and more of these move in, the tourist establishment gradually takes over. Thus, partly through the unwitting help of the explorer, the scope of the system expands.

As the tourist system expands, fewer and fewer areas are left that have mass tourist potential in terms of the traditional kinds of attractions. Recently, however, the ability of an area to offer a degree of privacy and solitude has, in itself, become a commodity of high value. Indeed, much of the mass tourist business today seems to be oriented to the provision of privacy per se. Obviously, mass tourism here reaches a point at which success is self-defeating.

While the explorer is the contemporary counterpart of the traveler of former years, the drifter is more like the wanderer of previous times. The correspondence is not complete, though. In his attitude toward and mode of traveling, the drifter is a genuine modern phenomenon. He is often a child of affluence, who reacts against it. He is young, often a student or a graduate, who has not yet started to work. He prolongs his moratorium by moving around the world in search of new experiences, radically different from those he has been accustomed to in his sheltered middle-class existence. After he has savored these experiences for a time, he usually settles down to an orderly middle-class career.

The drifter seeks the excitement of complete strangeness and direct contact with new and different people. He looks for experiences, happenings, and kicks. His mode of travel is adapted to this purpose. In order to preserve the freshness and spontaneity of his experience, the drifter purposely travels without either itinerary or timetable, without a destination or even well-defined purpose. He often possesses only limited means for traveling, but even when this is not true, he usually is concerned with making his money last as long as possible so as to prolong his travels. Since he is also typically unconcerned with bodily comfort and desires to live as simply as possible while traveling, he will travel, eat, and sleep in the most inexpensive way possible. He moves about on bicycle or motorcycle or hitchhikes rides in autos, private planes, freighters, and fishing boats. He shares rooms with fellow travelers he has met along the way or stays with a native of the area who has befriended him. When necessary, and often when not, he will sleep outdoors. And he will cook his own meals outdoors or buy food on the street more often than eat in a restaurant. If, in spite of such frugality, his money runs out before his desire to travel does, he will work at almost any odd-job he can get until he has enough to move on.

The particular way of life and travel of the drifter brings him into contact with a wide variety of people; these usually belong to the lower social groups in the host society. Often the drifter associates with kindred souls in the host society. In my study of a mixed Jewish–Arab town in Israel, I encountered a great deal of association between drifters and local Arab boys who also wanted to travel.[18]

An international subculture of drifters seems to be developing. In some places drifters congregate and create an ecological niche of their own. On the shore of the Red Sea in Eilat, Israel's southernmost port, there is a "permanently temporary" colony of squatters locally called "beatniks," who drifted there from many parts of the world. Similarly, the National Monument on the Dam, in the very center of Amsterdam, serves as a mass meeting place for young people who flock there from all over Europe and the U.S.

The drifter discards almost completely the familiar environment of his home country and immerses himself in the life of the host society. Moreover, as explained above, the drifter differs significantly from the explorer in the manner in which he relates to the host society. The drifter is, then, the true rebel of the tourist establishment and the complete opposite of the mass tourist.

Discussion

So far I have formulated a general approach to the sociology of tourism based on a typology of tourist roles. Here I will develop some implications of this approach and propose several problems for further research.

The fundamental variable that forms the basis for the fourfold typology of tourist roles proposed here is strangeness versus familiarity. Each of the four tourist roles discussed represents a characteristic form of tourist behavior and a typical position on the strangeness/familiarity continuum. The degree to which strangeness or familiarity prevail in the tourist role determines the nature of the tourist's experiences as well as the effect he has on the host society.

Initially, all tourists are strangers in the host society. The degree to which and the way they affect each other depends largely on the *extent* and *variety* of social contacts the tourist has during his trip. The social contacts of the mass tourist, particularly of the organized mass tourist, are extremely limited. The individual mass tourist, being somewhat more independent, makes occasional social contacts, but his conventional mode of travel tends to restrict them to the close periphery of the tourist establishment, thus limiting their number and their nature. The social contacts of the explorer are broader and more varied, while those of the drifter are the most intensive in quality and the most extensive in quantity.

The extent to which the tourist role is predefined and the social expectations of it spelled out determines to a large degree the *manner* in which tourists interact with members of the host society, as well as the images they develop of one another. The mass tourist generally does not interact at all, but merely observes, and even that from within his own microen-vironment. The explorer mixes but does not become involved in the lives of members of the host society. Here the length of *time* spent in one place is as important a determinant of social involvement as attitude. The drifter, unlike the mass tourist, does not set a limit beforehand on the length of time he will spend in any one place; if he finds an area that particularly pleases him, he may stop there long enough for social involvement to occur.

Tourism has some important aggregate effects on the host society, in terms of its impact on the division on labor and on the ecology or the land-use patterns of that society. As the tourist role becomes institutionalized, a whole set of other roles and institutions develop in the host country to cater to his needs—what we have called the tourist establishment. This development gradually introduces a new dimension into the ecology of the host society, as attractions and facilities are created, improved, and set aside for tourist use. This primary impact of tourism has important secondary and tertiary consequences.[19] Predominantly agricultural regions may become primarily tourist areas, as agriculture is driven out by tourist facilities, and the local people turn to tourist services for their living. The "tourist villages" in the Austrian Alps are an example. Conversely, stagnant agricultural areas may receive a boost from increased demands for agricultural products in nearby tourist regions, such as the agricultural boom that has occurred in the hinterland of the Spanish Costa Brava. Without doubt, the impact of large-scale tourism on the culture, style of life, and world-view of inhabitants of tourist regions must be enormous. To my knowledge, however, the problem has not yet been systematically studied.[20]

The explorer and the drifter do not affect the general division of labor in the host society to the same degree as the mass tourist does, and consequently do not have the same aggregate impact on that society. Their effect on the host society is more subtle, but sometimes considerable, as I found in my own study of the impact of drifting tourist girls on Arab boys in a mixed Jewish–Arab city.

It is understood that foreign travel can have a considerable impact upon the traveler himself, and, through him, on his home country. In premodern times, travelers were one of the chief means through which knowledge and innovations were diffused and information about other countries obtained. How does the impact vary with the different kinds of expe-

riences yielded by each type of tourist role, on the tourist himself, and, through him, on his own society? Is his image of his own society and his own style of life changed? In what ways? These are some of the questions that future studies of tourism might be organized around.

We also know very little about the way preferences for countries and localities are formulated in the mind of the tourist and later translated into the ways the tourist system expands or contracts geographically.[21] I have dealt with the role of the explorer in the dynamics of growth of the tourist system, but other mechanisms are undoubtedly at work, such as the planned creation of new attractions to foster mass tourism, like the building of Disneyland. It might be worthwhile to differentiate between the organic and the induced growth of the tourist system and look into the differential effect of the modes of expansion on the workings of the tourist system and the host society.

The problems raised in this paper have been dealt with in a most general form; any attempt to explore them in depth will have to make use of a comparative approach. Though tourism could be studied comparatively from several angles, the most important variables of comparison are probably the differences between the cultural characteristics of the tourist and the host[22] and the manner in which tourism is embedded in the institutional structure of the host country.[23]

Conclusion

Growing interaction and interpenetration between hitherto relatively independent social systems is one of the most salient characteristics of the contemporary world. In K. Deutsch's phrase, the world is rapidly becoming a "global village." No far-off island or obscure primitive tribe manages to preserve its isolation. Tourism is both a consequence of this process of interpenetration and one of several mechanisms through which this process is being realized. Its relative contribution to the process—in comparison to that of the major transforming forces of our time—is probably minor, though it seems to be increasing rapidly. Tourism already serves as the chief source of foreign currency in several countries, and its scope is growing at an accelerating rate.

It is interesting to speculate, then, about some of

the broader sociological consequences of the increase in the scope of tourism for the society of the future. The picture which emerges is complex. On the one hand, as the numbers of mass tourists grow, the tourist industry will become more and more mechanized and standardized. This, in turn, will tend to make the interaction between tourist and host even more routinized. The effect of the host country on the mass tourist will therefore remain limited, whereas his effect on the ecology, division of labor, and wealth of the country will grow as his numbers do. On the other hand, as host societies become permeated by a wide variety of individually traveling tourists belonging to different classes and ways of life, increased and more varied social contacts will take place, with mixed results for international understanding.[24] Like-minded persons of different countries will find it easier to communicate with each other and some kind of new international social groupings might appear. Among the very rich such groups always existed; the fashionable contemporary prototype is the international "jet-set." And only recently drifter communities have emerged in many parts of the world, comprised of an entirely different kind of social category. The effect of such developments may well be to diminish the significance of national boundaries, though they also create new and sometimes serious divisions within the countries in which such international groups congregate. Some indication of the emergence of new foci of conflict can already be seen in the recent riots between drifters and seamen in Amsterdam, the hub of the European "drifter community."

Finally, the differential impact of tourism on various types of societies should be noted. As Forster pointed out,[25] the impact of tourism on a society with an unbalanced, developing economy might be much more serious than its impact on a mature, well-developed society. As tourism is eagerly sought for by the developing nations as an important source of revenue, it may provoke serious disruptions and cause ultimate long-range damage in these societies. The consequences cannot yet be fully foreseen, but from what we already know of the impact of mass tourism it can safely be predicted that mass tourism in developing countries, if not controlled and regulated, might help to destroy whatever there is still left of unspoiled nature and of traditional ways of life. In this respect, the easy-going tourist of our era might well complete the work of his predecessors, also travelers from the West—the conqueror and the colonialist.

Reading Endnotes

1. This paper was first written while I was a visiting scholar at the Institute of Urban Environment, Columbia University, New York. Thanks are due to the Institute as well as to Dr. R. Bar-Yoseph, Prof. Elihu Katz, and Dr. M. Skokeid, for their useful comments.

2. There exist very few full-length studies of tourism. One of the most comprehensive studies is that by H. J. Knebel, *Soziologische Strukturwandlungen* in *Modernem Touriusmus* (Stuttgard: F. Enke Verl, 1960). By far the most incisive analysis of American tourism has been performed by D. Boorstin, *The Image* (New York: Atheneum, 1961), pp. 71–117. There is a chapter on tourism in J. Dumazedier, *Towards a Society of Leisure* (New York: Free Press, 1967), pp. 123–128, and in M. Kaplan, *Leisure in America: A Social Inquiry* (New York: Wiley, 1960), Ch. 16.

3. For the contemporary tourist boom see S. K. Waters, "The American Tourist," *The Annals of the American Academy of Social Science*, 368 (November 1966), pp. 109–118.

4. Dumazedier, op. cit., p. 125n. For the scarcity of tourists even as late as 1860, see Boorstin, op. cit., p. 84.

5. Knebel speaks, following von Uexkull, of a *"touristische Eigenwelt,"* from which the modern tourist can no longer escape; op. cit., p. 147.

6. For a similar approach to modern tourism, see Boorstin, op. cit., pp. 79–80.

7. For a different typology of tourist roles ("travelers"), see Kaplan, op. cit., p. 216.

8. For a general description of the trends characteristic of modern mass tourism, see Knebel, op. cit., pp. 99ff.

9. See Boorstin, op. cit., p. 85.

10. Ibid., p. 103.

11. In Boorstin's language, they become "pseudo-events."

12. "Not only in Mexico City and Montreal, but also in the remote Guatemalan Tourist Mecca of Chichecastenango, out in far-off villages of Japan, earnest honest natives embellish their ancient rites, change, enlarge and spectacularize their festivals, so that tourists will not be disappointed." Ibid., p. 103.

13. Boorstin, talking of the Hilton chain of hotels, states: "Even the measured admixture of carefully filtered local atmosphere [in these hotels] proves that you are still in the U.S." Ibid., pp. 98–99.

14. For an analysis of travel literature, see Knebel, op. cit., pp. 90–97. On the development of the guidebook, particularly the Baedeker, see Boorstin, op. cit., pp. 109ff, and Knebel, op. cit., pp. 24–26.

15. The tendency of the mass tourist to abide by the guidebook was noticed a hundred years ago by "A Cynic" who wrote in 1869: "The ordinary tourist has no judgment; he admires what the infallible Murray orders him to admire. . . . The tourist never diverges one hair's breadth from the beaten track of his predecessors, and within a few miles of the best known routes in Europe leaves nooks and corners as unsophisticated as they were fifty years ago; which proves that he has not sufficient interest in his route to exert his own freedom of will." "A Cynic: Vacations," *Cornhill Magazine*, August 1869, reported in *Mass Leisure*, E. Larrabee and K. Meyersohn (eds.), (Glencoe, IL.: Free Press, 1952), p. 285

16. Boorstin, op. cit., pp. 91ff.: Knebel, op. cit., pp. 102–104; see also Knebel's discussion of the primary tourist group, op. cit. pp. 104–106.

17. Boorstin, op. cit., pp. 116–117.

18. E. Cohen, "Arab Boys and Tourist Girls in a Mixed Jewish–Arab Community," *International Journal of Comparative Sociology*, Vol. 12, No. 4 (1971), pp. 217–233.

19. For some of these see J. Forster, "The Sociological Consequences of Tourism," *International Journal of Comparative Sociology*, Vol. 5, No. 2 (1964), pp. 217–227.

20. A study of this problem is in progress now in the region of Faro in southern Portugal; this is a backward region in which the sudden influx of mass tourism seems to have some serious disruptive effects.

21. This problem is discussed with reference to the rather special conditions of Hawaii and other Pacific Islands, by Forster, op. cit.

22. W. A. Sutton, "Travel and Understanding: Notes on the Social Structure of Touring," *International Journal of Comparative Sociology*, Vol. 8, No. 2 (1967), pp. 218–223, touches upon this point in a discussion of factors which make for harmony and tension in the tourist–host encounter.

23. Forster's argument about the differential impact of tourism on a society with an underdeveloped as against an advanced economy is one example of such an approach. Another would be to compare the effects of tourism on closed (totalitarian) as against open (democratic) societies.

24. See Sutton, op. cit.

25. See Forster, op. cit.

READING 11.2

MAKING TOURISTS FEEL SAFE: WHOSE RESPONSIBILITY IS IT?

by Abraham Pizam, University of Central Florida; Peter Tarlow, Tourism & More Consulting Services; and Jonathan Bloom, University of Stellenbosh

Reprinted from *Journal of Travel Research*, Vol. 36, No. 1 Summer 1997, pp. 23–28, Copyright (c) 1997 by Sage Publications. Reprinted by permission of Sage Publications.

The evidence from many parts of the world suggests that safety and security are a necessary condition for a prosperous tourism industry. Researchers such as Ryan and Kinder (1996), Schiebler, Crotts, and Hollinger (1996), Lankford (1996), Prideaux (1996), Cohen (1996), Bloom (1996), Tarlow and Muehsam (1996), Pizam and Mansfeld (1996), and others have written about how incidences of violence and crimes against tourists negatively affect the tourism industry. Most tourists select their destinations not only on the basis of price and destination image, but, most importantly, on personal safety and security. Destinations that gain notoriety as crime hot spots are likely to experience difficulty in retaining their tourism industry (Prideaux 1996, p. 59).

In recent years tourist destinations such as Rio de Janeiro, Brazil; Florida; Papua New Guinea; Johannesburg; Republic of South Africa; and others have suffered significant declines in overseas visitation in response to widely reported incidents of crime. In Florida, an outbreak of crimes against tourists in 1993, caused a decline of 11% in the number of overseas tourists and a 16% decline in the number of Canadian tourists, in the first seven months of 1994. The number of European visitors declined nearly 20%—from 1.3 million to 1.05 million. Tourism from Great Britain and Germany, the top European markets for Florida and the two countries that had a number of their citizens who visited Florida attacked or murdered, declined by 22%. Altogether, Florida's total share of foreign visitors to the USA declined from 23% to 20% in the first seven months of 1994 (Pizam and Mansfeld 1996, p. 1).

The media traditionally have highly publicized crimes against international tourists in a given destination, even when the number of such crimes are constantly decreasing. Such media coverage often results in panic among potential visitors. For example, the tragic murders of a pregnant German mother in Miami, Florida and a male English tourist near Tallahassee, Florida, followed by a string of other incidents of random violence throughout the remainder of the state, generated considerable national and international media attention suggesting that crime against Florida's tourists was rampant and on the increase. During this same time period, however, official state tourist crime statistics told another story. The number of reported crimes against nonresidents had declined from a high in 1990 of 37,949 to 31,299 in 1993. Unfortunately, "perception becomes reality" in the travel business and these official statistics have done little to calm the apprehensions of those at risk as indicated by the decline in Florida tourism during 1994 (Schiebler, Crotts, and Hollinger 1996, pp. 37–38).

It has been suggested that tourists have been disproportional victims of crimes because they are

- Tempting targets (carry large sums of money and other forms of portable wealth),

- Involved in risky behavior (i.e., frequent nightclubs and bars at late hours, travel to remote and unfamiliar places, venture into "unsafe" areas; consume alcohol and drugs), ignorant of local language(s)/dialect, signage, and/or customs,

- Lack local support groups and/or local resources,

- Perceived to be aggressive and insensitive to local norms and customs, and

- Bring notions about safety and the role of law enforcement agencies based on their experience at home (Tarlow and Muehsarn 1996; Chesney-Lind and Lind 1986; Sparks 1982; Fujii and Mak 1979; McPheters and Stronge 1974).

Violent crimes of both a social nature (murder, rape, armed robbery) and a political nature (acts of terrorism) have made many individuals afraid of travel in general and afraid of travel to particular destinations that are perceived to be unsafe. Violence directly affects a nation's image internally and internationally, it destroys the fabric of a society, and it interferes with the free flow of people and ideas. Few people travel to places where they feel threatened. When people are afraid to travel, isolation begins, xenophobia reigns, and cross-cultural fertilization ceases. Furthermore, the effects of crime on host communities could lead to additional socioeconomic negative impacts, such as

- Increased expenditures on law enforcement during the tourist season;

- Monetary losses from burglary and larceny, property damage from vandalism, commercial embezzlement, tax dodging and the growth of black markets;

- Heightened tension; and

- The visible presence of the law may lead to a false sense of security (Mathieson and Wall 1982, p. 151.)

It is evident that if the world's travel industries cannot promote a safe and worry-free travel experience, then nations suffering from the social cancer of crime will be hurt not only economically but will also be damaged sociologically, morally, and spiritually.

Tourism leaders have only recently begun to address the issue of crimes against visitors. All of them admit that crimes against tourists can have a devastating effect on their industry. However, many assert that it is beyond their capability to correct the situation and suggest that only law enforcement agencies and public policy makers can take the necessary action. Some scholars have even suggested that because tourists are strangers in these destination communities and may lack political clout, law enforcement agencies are not as diligent in prosecuting offenders who are involved in tourist crimes as they would be in prosecuting offenders against local residents. Criminal justice data from Hawaii indicated that "when the victim was a visitor, a large proportion of the arrestees were released without being charged (57.9%) than when the victim was a resident (17.4%)" (Chesney-Lind and Lind 1986, p. 178).

Contrary to this opinion, law enforcement officials in many parts of the world suggest that, if anything, the tourism industry is receiving preferential treatment in crime protection. These officials criticize the tourism industry for being too lax in applying well-established strategies for crime prevention or crime reduction. They imply that many industry executives do little to aid in the fight against crime and instead expect law enforcement agencies to do the "whole job" for the tourism industry.

In trying to resolve this question, Cohen (1987) maintains that, on the one hand, it is possible that "representatives of the law enforcing agencies may . . . feel less obligation to deal fairly with the tourists, especially if the latter have a reputation of . . . being naive or innocuous, so that they can be safely extorted or otherwise victimized." However, "there are also grounds to assume that the tourist will be given preferential treatment and enjoy the protection of the . . . representatives of the law" (Cohen 1987, p. 185). Based on his observations in Thailand, he concludes that conventional tourists, being a principal source of income to the hosts, enjoy special protection and considerations from the Thai law enforcement agencies, as evidenced by the establishment of a special tourist police force whose sole responsibility is the protection of tourists.

Recently, there is a growing recognition that the prevention of violent acts against tourists is the joint responsibility of the tourism industry *and* the public sector. The World Tourism Organisation (WTO), in its *Best Practice Manual on Traveler Safety and Security* (WTO 1995), and the White House Conference on Travel and Tourism (WHCTT) have reinforced this opinion. Objective 5 of the WHCTT calls for "mobilizing the industry to respond to concerns about traveler safety and security, through community partnerships and disaster preparedness programs. The Traveler Safety Task Force of the WHCTT recommended that "by January 1997 [the industry] adopt guidelines such as those published by WTO that provide for the safe handling of visitors... and by January 1997, IACVB, in cooperation with the National Conference of Mayors and national law enforcement organizations, should develop guidelines for the development of Community Safety Plans" (White House Conference on Travel and Tourism 1995, pp. 18–20).

Objective

This study's overall objective was to determine how law enforcement agencies in three large tourist communities perceive their role in preventing crimes against tourists. More specifically, the aim was to understand how local police departments view their responsibility vis-à-vis the tourism industry and whether they deal with crimes against tourists differently than crimes committed against residents. An additional purpose of this study was to learn how local law enforcement agencies structure their organizations for the purpose of reducing and preventing crimes against tourists.

Methodology

Destinations

Law enforcement officials were interviewed in three major tourism destinations: metropolitan Orlando, Florida; New Orleans, Louisiana; and Cape Town, Republic of South Africa (RSA). These tourism destinations were selected as case studies because of their position of prominence in the tourism industry and because all three sites suffered from the effects of crimes aimed specifically against tourists.

Metropolitan Orlando is the leading tourism destination in the United States. In 1994, Orlando received a total of 15 million out-of-state tourists, of which 2.3 million were international visitors. The majority of the domestic tourists (8.1%) came for leisure purposes and stayed an average of 5.7 nights, while international tourists stayed an average of 7.2 nights. The top four origin markets for Orlando's international tourism, which together generated more than 50% of the total, are the United Kingdom, Brazil, Germany, and Venezuela. The Orlando/Orange County Convention and Visitors Bureau estimates the direct economic impact to be U.S. $10.67 billion for domestic tourism and U.S. $0.73 billion for international tourism (Orlando/Orange County Convention and Visitors Bureau 1995). Moreover, Orlando, because it is in Florida, has suffered from the overall negative effect caused by violent crimes against tourists in that state.

New Orleans was chosen because it is one of the major tourist destinations in the United States and its police department received a great deal of negative publicity during the latter part of 1995 and early 1996. In 1994 a total of 9.6 million domestic trips were made to New Orleans, and the average length of stay was 4.0 nights. That same year 570,000 international tourists visited the city and stayed an average of 6.6 nights (Chacko 1996).

Cape Town was included in the study because it is

major South African destination that had minimal crime under the former apartheid regime. Since the end of apartheid, Cape Town has experienced a significant increase in crime rates, especially in crimes aimed at tourists. It is estimated that in 1995 a total of 504,000 international tourists visited the Cape Town metropolitan area (out of a total of 4.2 million international tourists who visited South Africa) and stayed an average of 8.8 nights. Of those tourists, 87% came for leisure purposes and the remaining 13% visited for business purposes (South African Tourism Board 1995a). The size of the 1995 domestic market was estimated to be 1.56 million trips or 3.12 million tourists. The South African Tourist Board estimates total domestic expenditures to be R1.69 billion, which is equivalent to U.S. $365 million (South African Tourism Board 1995b).

Research Instrument

An open interview guide was developed to interview law enforcement officials in all three cities. The guide was developed to permit officials in each location the freedom to speak about their own locale, while facilitating cross-locale comparisons. Each of the three investigators first developed a number of suppositions about their own city, then exchanged these suppositions with the other two investigators. The final narrowing of suppositions permitted research to be conducted simultaneously by three different people who focused on common issues. The methodology was designed to give each investigator the liberty to delve into his location without restricting answers due to cultural or political differences. All interviews were conducted orally, and each interviewer requested the right to conduct follow-up interviews to clarify and to corroborate answers. Multiple interviews with several officials were conducted in each of the cities. The multiple interviews enabled the researchers to be exposed to diverse opinions and to conduct interjudge reliability checks. Answers were then shared and commonalities were sought. After listing commonalities among the three police departments, an applied program action model was developed in the form of common solutions to problems.

Limitations of Study

It is important to emphasize that this research is exploratory in nature. Because of its design and the limited sample size, it is not possible to claim that the findings obtained in this study are representative of the entire tourism community or that they are applicable elsewhere. It is hoped that this study will generate further hypotheses so that higher levels of nomothetic applied theory may be developed.

Crimes Against Tourists in Orlando, New Orleans, and Cape Town

Both metropolitan Orlando and New Orleans are major U.S. tourism cities that have suffered either directly or indirectly from crime. Whereas Orlando suffers the effects of negative publicity caused by violence against tourists in other Florida locations, New Orleans has been negatively affected because tourists have been victims of violent crimes, and the national media have portrayed the city's police force in a very unflattering way. Recent articles that have appeared in magazines such as *Playboy* and newspapers such as the *Houston Chronicle* paint the picture of a corrupt police force that is as capable of murder as it is of law enforcement. Cape Town is one of its nation's major tourism centers. During what South Africans call their "festive season" (December to the middle of January) at least 10 of the 85 reported muggings involved tourists, and one out of every 10 robberies or pick-pocketing crimes was committed against a tourist in 1995-96. The South African situation may be even more serious in that tourist-related crime statistics focus more on the international tourist, while the authorities classify domestic occurrences of crimes against tourists in the national crime statistics rather than as a separate item. Because of the media's focus on South Africa, and because South African government officials view tourism as a way to reenter the world's stage in the post-apartheid era, tourism plays a major role in the nation's socioeconomic struggle for reconstruction and development. All three cities then have the following in common:

- Tourism is a major contributor to each city's economy.

- Each community has suffered from negative media publicity due to crimes against tourists.

- Each community has a crime problem that negatively affects its tourism industry and the economic and social well-being of its citizens.

- Each community's police force has been specifically charged with protecting not only its citizens and tourists, but also its community's economic welfare.

Interviews with Law Enforcement Representatives from Each Community

Cape Town

Cape Town, the mother city of South Africa and the seat of its parliament, is a major tourist attraction in the southern part of the African continent. Cape Town has recently formed a special police unit to protect tourists. Government officials project that this special unit will be subsumed into the Cape Town Metropolitan Police Force. City officials realize that their city currently lacks credible statistics on crimes against tourists. Crimes against tourists are underreported or not reported, and law enforcement agencies lack an orientation toward tourists' needs, guidelines for addressing tourism-related crimes, resources, and personnel.

In Cape Town, crimes against tourists are often seen as a national problem rather than a local one. It is important, however, to place this situation in the context of the centralized nature of decision making within the South African Police Services (SAPS). The SAPS operates tourism units in five major tourism centers, one of which is Cape Town. Additionally, the local tourism industry is beginning to note that crime threatens its well-being. Tourism assistance units are being formed with foreign language-trained personnel who patrol highly frequented tourism areas on foot. There is a belief among SAPS officials that improved liaisons between the tourism assistance unit, the community police, and tourism-related and other commercial interests have contributed to a significant reduction in tourist-related crime. However, the success of the new "policing umbrella," which entails the foot patrols and various other crime prevention measures, can only succeed if all crime prevention efforts are integrated and coordinated through police structures that are sensitive to the needs of tourists and the manner in which businesses, both directly and indirectly associated with tourism, cooperate to address crime and violence.

The SAPS has embarked on an initiative, facilitated by the Tourism Security Task Group, to decrease the potential for tourist-related crime that may occur during transfers from various points of entry into South Africa, including Cape Town International Airport. The aim of the project is to ensure that when travelers arrive at particular destinations

they are approached by youths who assist them with requests that can range from accommodation and transportation to package tours and other unique experiences. The safety of tourists would be assured as far as possible and the uncertainty related to their arrival and transfers significantly reduced. It must be stressed that a major difference between Cape Town and the two U.S. cities studied is that in Cape Town the issue of crime and violence is locally or regionally driven, but the planning in terms of personnel, policy, and national tourism police strategy is coordinated at the national level.

Metropolitan Orlando

"If it [crime] happens in Florida, it's news in the world." The Orange County Sheriff's office is very sensitive to the fact that even if a tourist is murdered almost 30 miles from Orlando, world newspaper headlines will indicate that Orlando's attractions may not be safe. Such deep recognition of the importance of keeping tourists safe has forced the Orange County Sheriff's Department to institute a number of programs and to take a highly proactive stance. Orange County was one of the first communities in the United States to form what it calls a tourist-oriented policing unit (TOPS). TOPS comprises some 60 officers (of which 12 were hired with the aid of a federal grant) who patrol and aid in the city's principal tourist zones (i.e., the Disney World Center and Sea World). Additionally, the sheriff's office has established a full-time "victim advocate" whose only job is to help victims of crime, especially visitors and their families.

The sheriff's office recognizes that the way one "would go about policing [a tourist area] is different than what you [the police] do in a neighborhood." "Although a law enforcement representative noted staff shortage problems based on low budgets, he emphasized the need for police presence. Citing the example of high-profile patrols during the hosting of the World Cup soccer games, Ray Wood of the Orange County TOPS division stated that "high profile [police] visibility does, indeed, reduce crime." Wood also believes that this high-profile police visibility has a bonus or residual effect that lasts for approximately an additional 10 weeks. TOPS is unique in that its officers put major emphasis on working with, and not just alongside, the tourism industry. TOPS, which is represented on the board of the local hotel/motel association, has developed hotel/motel security standards. Officers in the unit teach local attraction and hotel/motel property owners how to incorporate security devices into capital improvement budgets that will make their properties crime-unfriendly and help owners learn how to verify the honesty of their employees.

Another unique aspect of Orange County's crime prevention program is the shift away from measuring law enforcement's success by counting the number of crimes against tourists (body counts) to evaluating how well the office prevents crimes from happening. Regarding crimes against tourists, the sheriff's office counts a "nonevent" as a success. Under this scenario the questions that are asked are not how many crimes were committed this year versus last year, but rather "did we reduce crime, have we kept it reduced, and are we working to reduce it further?"

New Orleans

Perhaps no police force in the United States has received as much negative publicity as the New Orleans Police Department (NOPD). Not only does the department have to cope with negative national publicity, but it is also often cited by other police departments as the "police department with troubles par excellence." Despite its officers' low morale, low training budget, and even lower pay, the NOPD has developed a number of innovative programs for crime reduction and prevention, and it takes its obligation to protect citizens and tourists very seriously. In 1985 a special police district (8th district) was formed specifically to protect the city's major tourist areas (the French Quarter and the downtown development district).

Adopting the attitude that good policing requires "communication, dialogue, discretion, and networking," NOPD handpicks some 60 officers and specially trains them to deal with tourist crimes. When one considers the extraordinary low amount of money budgeted to training, this fact demonstrates how seriously the NOPD views the need to protect tourists. Many of these officers are younger, and some are multilingual, speaking a variety of languages from Spanish to Vietnamese. A tourist information bureau is even located in the 8th district's headquarters. The bureau, which is staffed by volunteers, is open seven days a week during regular business hours. Lt. Marlon A. Defillo of the NOPD stated that his department sees tourism as a major industry to be protected.

To cooperate with the tourism industry, the NOPD holds monthly meetings with the New Orleans Hotel Motel Association and attends metropolitan New Orleans Convention and Visitors Bureau meetings. The department has also established an interhotel/motel fax alert. Defillo notes that the NOPD has a special obligation to the city's tourist zones, not only because some 10 million out-of-town visitors significantly affect New Orleans' economy, but also because its tourist areas are heavily frequented by the local citizenry. Just as in the case of metropolitan Orlando, New Orleans' law enforcement agency does not get all of the media support that it would like. While the people in the media will turn an incident of a crime against a tourist into a major event, they rarely publish items such as "how to protect yourself against crime." Defillo sees police presence as the number one tool in fighting crime. The use of foot patrols, mounted patrols, and bicycle patrols have had a major effect in cutting down on the incidence of teenage harassment and have helped make tourists feel welcome and safe. Because New Orleans is a "party city," the NOPD often is placed in the position of being as much a "parent" as a law enforcement agency.

New Orleans makes sure that its police officers use discretion in how they handle such cases as a drunken tourist. Police officers are expected to decide if a drunken tourist should be booked or simply taken back to a hotel room and put to bed. Defillo notes that, despite its best efforts, the police department cannot be everywhere at all times and therefore must depend on the community for help. For this reason, the NOPD encourages local restaurants and bars to put inebriated tourists in cabs and asks that the city's hotel employees take a proactive stance in keeping rooms safe. Finally, just as the police departments in Cape Town and metropolitan Orlando do, the NOPD encourages visitors to stay in "safe" areas rather than tell them where not to go.

Common Problems

Interviews with spokespersons for law enforcement agencies in all three study cities indicated certain common problems.

- *Lack of finances.* Representatives of the three law enforcement agencies who were interviewed stated that, despite the importance of tourism to their local economy, city, state, provincial, or national governments did not provide the agencies with the proper level of funding. There was a common perception that governments want tourists to receive extraordinary services within the confines of ordinary budgets. Often law enforcement agents suffer from low morale due in part to low pay and lack of resources.

- *Staff shortages.* *All* three police departments indicated that adding staff is a major means of preventing crime. However, due to budget constraints and, in the case of the United States, federal regulations regarding compensation time, efforts by police department employees are limited.

- *Lack of cooperation from the media.* Law enforcement agencies state that the media find stories about crime a good way to sell newspapers or increase ratings. Often the media are insensitive to the damage done to a community and to an agency's morale when only negative news items are reported. Inaccurate reporting destroys media credibility with law enforcement agencies.

- *Need for greater community cooperation.* Law enforcement agencies cannot completely eradicate crime. They must depend on the local population, and the tourism industry in particular, to help them prevent crime. Law enforcement agencies see prevention as their best tool.

- *Poor statistics* and a *lack of standardization.* Currently there is no international standard definition of a crime against a visitor, who a visitor is, or how records are to be kept. Law enforcement agencies are well aware that the industry does not always report crimes and that the statistics often lack credibility.

Common Solutions and Methodologies

Interviews with law enforcement representatives revealed that all three communities share some common methodologies, including:

- *High police visibility.* All three law enforcement agencies require their officers to be highly visible. They maintain that the traveling public is better protected by police officers on foot, on horseback, or on a bicycle rather than in a car.

- *Gregarious police officers.* Tourist police units need extroverted officers who understand that part of their job is to "shmooz" with their community's guests. These informal conversations not only permit the police to have a better idea about what is on a person's mind, but they also create the perception that the community is safe enough for the police officer to have the time to talk with an out-of-towner.

- *Proactive participation on tourism boards.* By working with local hotel/motel associations, convention and visitor bureaus, and chambers of commerce, law enforcement agencies have developed joint programs to stop crime before it begins.

Some of the most effective programs were found to be

- *Visible policing.* All three cities' officials take the position that there is a direct negative correlation between the number of police officers on the street and the number of crimes that take place in a particular neighborhood.

- *Coordination on a national level and help from national law enforcement agencies.* South Africa is ahead of the United States in realizing that often crime must be dealt with on a national or state/provincial basis rather than merely at the local level. Pockets of criminals just outside of a community's limits will not hesitate to attack tourists. Furthermore, a crime committed within a community's tourism radius may be presented in the media as if it had taken place within that community.

- *Inspections of properties with minimal safety standards.* The interviews revealed that hoteliers and owners of attractions can learn a great deal from local law enforcement agencies. Police are very concerned about such issues as old-fashioned numbered guestroom keys and easy access doorways. From the perspective of law enforcement officers, it may be easier to prevent a crime than to deal with it ex post facto.

- *Personnel checks.* Law enforcement officers suggested that some people who work in the tourism industry may have "less than sterling" backgrounds. Therefore, they recommended that each new employee's background be checked. Furthermore, they insisted that those who are found to be guilty of crimes be heavily punished. Ray Wood of Orange County's Sheriff's Office may have said it best when speaking of his county's policy concerning crimes committed by hotel workers: "If they get caught stealing from a guest, they are going to go to jail."

- *Employee security training.* All three police forces encourage security training for anyone who works in places or areas frequented by tourists.

- *Police tourism training.* Police officers who work in tourism areas need to be sensitive to the special needs of the transient person. Sociologically it is known that tourists suffer from higher than normal levels of anomie and are often "sitting ducks" for criminals. Police need to know how to comfort tourists when they are victims of a crime and how to help tourists so that they have a lower probability of becoming crime victims.

- *Integrated efforts.* Law enforcement representatives from all three cities noted that they alone cannot keep all citizens safe. Law enforcement agents recognize that they need the support of their community. Innovative programs such as national nights-out against crime, restaurant and bar taxi services, and interhotel and attraction crime alerts all make the job of law enforcement easier.

Conclusions

The results of this study suggest that in all three destinations, law enforcement agencies are seriously committed to preventing and reducing crimes against tourists. To accomplish this goal, police authorities have set up special units whose sole responsibility is the protection of tourists and have selected and trained their officers to deal specifically with tourist matters. From this point of view it is possible to conclude that, rather than discriminating against tourists and the tourism industry, these law enforcement agencies give the industry preferential treatment and make immense efforts to prevent crimes against tourists. Despite this, it is evident that to succeed in preventing crime, the tourism industry must join with law enforcement agencies in a partnership for safety. Partnership implies two-way cooperation. Tourism operators should take all the necessary steps to prevent crimes from occurring on their properties and make every possible political effort to ensure that law enforcement agencies have the personnel and resources they need to do their jobs. Additionally, law enforcement agencies should work with the industry to train and assist its operators in the never-ending task of crime prevention and reduction.

Future Research

As previously indicated, this research was exploratory in nature and conducted with a limited sample size. To confirm its findings and expand its boundaries it is recommended that national surveys be conducted of tourism operators and law enforcement agencies in tourist destinations. The purpose of these studies would be to discover what, if any, crime prevention strategies have been put in place by both law enforcement agencies and tourism operators and to estimate their costs and benefits.

References

Bloom, J. (1996). "A South African Perspective of the Effects of Crime and Violence on the Tourism Industry." In *Tourism, Crime and International Security* Issues, edited by A. Pizam and Y. Mansfeld. London: John Wiley and Sons, pp. 91–102.

Chacko, Harsha (1996). Personal communication with authors, June 10.

Chesney-Lind, A., and L. Y. Lind (1986). "Visitors as Victims: Crimes Against Tourists in Hawaii." *Annals of Tourism Research,* 13(2): 167–91.

Cohen, E. (1987). "The Tourist as Victim and Profit of Law Enforcement Agencies." *Leisure Studies,* 6 (2): 181–98.

———(1996). "Touting Tourists in Thailand: Tourist Oriented Crime and Social Structure." In *Tourism, Crime and International Security Issues,* edited by A. Pizam and Y. Mansfeld. London: John Wiley and Sons, pp. 77–90.

Fujii, E. T., and J. Mak (1979). "The Impact of Alternative Regional Development Strategies on Crime Rates: Tourism vs. Agriculture in Hawaii." *Annals of Regional Science,* 13(3): 42–56.

Lankford, S. V. (1996). "Crime and Tourism: A Study of Perceptions in the Pacific Northwest." In *Tourism, Crime and International Security Issues,* edited by A. Pizam and Y. Mansfeld. London: John Wiley and Sons, pp. 51–58.

Mathieson, A., and G. Wall (1982). *Tourism, Economic, Physical and Social Impacts.* London: Longman.

McPheters, L. R., and W. B. Stronge (1974). "Crime as an Environmental Externality of Tourism: Florida." *Land Economics,* 50:192–288.

Orlando/Orange County Convention and Visitors Bureau (1995). *1994 Research Report.* Orlando, FL: Orlando/Orange County Convention and Visitors Bureau.

Pizam, A., and Y. Mansfeld (1996). *Tourism, Crime and International Security Issues.* London: John Wiley and Sons.

Prideaux, B. (1996). "The Tourism Crime Cycle: A

Beach Destination Case Study." In *Tourism, Crime and International Security Issues,* edited by A. Pizam and Y. Mansfeld. London: John Wiley and Sons. pp. 77–90.

Ryan, C., and R. Kinder (1996). "The Deviant Tourist and the Crimogenic Place—The Case of the Tourist and the New Zealand Prostitute." In *Tourism, Crime and International Security Issues,* edited by A. Pizam and Y. Mansfield. London: John Wiley and Sons, pp. 23–36.

Schiebler, S. A., J. C. Crotts, and R. C. Hollinger (1996). "Florida Tourists' Vulnerability to Crime." In *Tourism, Crime and International Security. Issues,* edited by A. Pizam and Y. Mansfield. London: John Wiley and Sons, pp. 37–50.

South African Tourism Board (1995a). *A Survey of South Africa's International Tourism Market Compiled by Surveys International, Pretoria.* Pretoria: SATOUR.

———(1995b). *The South African Domestic Tourism Market Compiled by Markinor.* Pretoria: SATOUR.

Sparks, R. F. (1982). *Research on Victims of Crimes: Accomplishments, Issues and New Directions.* Department of Health and Human Services Publication No. (ADM) 82-109. Washington, DC: Government Printing Office.

Tarlow, P., and M. Muehsam (1996). "Theoretical Aspects of Crime as They Impact the Tourism Industry." In *Tourism, Crime and International Security Issues,* edited by A. Pizam and Y. Mansfield. London: John Wiley and Sons, pp. 11–22.

White House Conference on Travel and Tourism (1995). *Proposed National Tourism Strategy.* Washington, DC: U.S. Travel and Tourism Administration.

World Tourism Organisation (1995). *Best Practice Manual on Traveler Safety and Security.* Madrid: World Tourism Organisation.

KEY CONCEPTS

contrasting cultures and cultural distance
democratization of travel
drifter
effects of travel experiences
group travel arrangements
handicapped travelers
income
individual mass tourist
isolation of the mass tourist
negative social effects on host society
organized mass tourist

population changes and travel interests
resentment toward visitors
social tourism
sociology
standardization of facilities
strangeness versus familiarity
tourism and crime
travel patterns change with age, family
travel preferences of international tourists
world as a global village

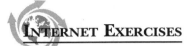 ## INTERNET EXERCISES

Site Name: World Heritage

URL: http://www.unesco.org/whc/nwhc/pages/home/pages/homepage.htm

Background Information: UNESCO's World Heritage mission is to (1) encourage countries to sign the Convention Concerning the Protection of the World Cultural and Natural Heritage and thereby ensure the protection of their own natural and cultural heritage and (2) encourage parties to the Convention to nominate sites within their national territory for inclusion on the World Heritage List.

Exercises

1. What is the World Heritage Convention, and what impact does it have on cultural tourism?

2. What does the Convention contain?

QUESTIONS FOR REVIEW AND DISCUSSION

1. As a manager of a resort hotel popular with families, what social and/or educational activities would you offer your guests?

2. You have decided to take a trip to a country whose culture is very much different from your own. Would you participate in a group tour or go alone? Why?

3. Would a child's learning experience during a trip to another part of his or her country be comparable to school learning for that period of time? In what ways might parents maximize the educational benefits of such a trip?

4. Describe how a hotel's food and beverage manager might avoid the "universal waiter uniform" image.

5. Discuss the effects of television news coverage of global and national events on tourism.

6. Give some examples of how tourism suppliers accommodate handicapped travelers. How important is this segment of the market?

7. Is there a potential for increased social tourism in your country?

8. How might the four extremes relating to the preferences of present-day international tourists affect a resort hotel's social and recreational program? Give some specific examples.

9. How do your travel interests differ from your parents'? from your grandparents'?

10. You are president of a tourist promotion association. Which of Cohen's four tourist types would you try to attract? Why?

11. Do you feel governments have a responsibility for encouraging and supporting social tourism?

CASE PROBLEMS

1. Alfred K. is a widower 67 years old. He has not had an opportunity to travel much, but now as a retiree he has the time and money to take extensive trips. As a travel counselor, what kinds of travel products would you recommend?

2. Sadie W. is president of her church missionary society. She has observed that many visitors to her fairly small city in England are interested in the local history. Her church is a magnificent cathedral, the construction of which began in the year 1083. Mrs. W. and her colleagues believe that missionary work begins at home. By what methods could her group reach and become acquainted with the cathedral visitors?

3. A U.S. group tour conductor wishes to maximize the mutual social benefits of a trip to an underdeveloped country. Describe possible kinds of social contacts that would be beneficial to the hosts and to the members of the tour group.

4. A popular beach resort hotel is located in a tropical country which, unfortunately, has a high crime rate. One section of the city nearby has some "South Seas" atmosphere gambling casinos. Many guests would like to visit them. How might the hotel's staff control this situation?

5. Nadia P. is Minister of Tourism for a small West African country. This country has become a very popular winter destination for Scandinavians. The tourists seem to be mainly interested in the beaches, which are among the finest in the world. However, it is customary for these visitors to wear very scanty clothing, especially when bathing. In fact, nude bathing is occasionally practiced. About 90 percent of the indigenous population of the host country are Moslems. The appearance and sometimes behavior of the visitors, especially when shopping and otherwise contacting local citizens, often seems improper to their hosts. Tourism is increasing each year. The economic benefits are considerable and are very much needed. However, the social problem is becoming more acute. What should Ms. P. do about this?

SELECTED REFERENCES

Borocz, J. *Leisure Migration: A Sociological Study on Tourism.* London, UK: Pergamon Press, 1996.

Clift, S. and P. Grabowski. *Tourism and Health: Risks, Research and Responses.* London: Pinter, 1997.

Cohen, Erik. "Traditions in Qualitative Sociology of Tourism." *Journal of Travel Research,* Vol. 15, No. 1, pp. 29–46, 1988.

Cohen, Erik. "Tourism-Related Crime: Towards a Sociology of Crime and Tourism." *Visions in Leisure and Business,* Vol. 16, No. 1, pp. 4–14, Winter 1997.

Dann, Graham, and Erik Cohen. "Sociology and Tourism." *Annals of Tourism Research,* Vol. 18, No. 1, pp. 155–169, 1991.

Dann, Graham M.S. *The Language of Tourism: A Sociolinguistic Perspective.* New York: CAB International, 1996.

deKadt, Emanuel. "Social Planning for Tourism in the Developing Countries." *Annals of Tourism Research,* Vol. 6, No. 1, pp. 36–48. Special Issue on Sociology of Tourism, January/March 1979.

Farrell, Bryan H. *The Social and Economic Impact of Tourism on Pacific Communities.* Santa Cruz, CA: Center for South Pacific Studies, University of California at Santa Cruz, June 1977.

Goeldner, Charles R., Gin Hayden, and Carol Krismann. *Mature Traveler Bibliography: An Information Source Guide.* Lexington, KY: National Tour Foundation, 1997.

Goodrich, Jonathan N. "Socialist Cuba: A Study of Health Tourism." *Journal of Travel Research,* Vol. 32, No. 1, pp. 36–41, Summer 1993.

Jafari, Jafar. "Tourism and Social Science: A Bibliography." *Annals of Tourism Research,* Vol. 6, No. 2, pp. 149–195. Special Issue on Sociology of Tourism, April/June 1979.

Jurowski, Claudia. "Tourism Means More Than Money to the Host Community." *Parks and Recreation,* Vol. 31, No. 9, pp. 110–118, September 1996.

Jurowski, Claudia, Muzaffer Uysal, and Daniel R. Williams. "A Theoretical Analysis of Host Community Resident Reactions to Tourism." *Journal of Travel Research,* Vol. 36, No. 2, pp. 3–11, Fall 1997.

Kerstetter, Deborah, Kelly Bricker, and Richard Gitelson. "The Influence of a Spouse or Partner in Travel Decision-Making." *Visions in Leisure and Business,* Vol. 15, No. 2, pp. 40–44, Summer 1996.

Lindberg, Kreg, and Rebecca L. Johnson. "The Economic Values of Tourism's Social Impacts." *Annals of Tourism Research,* Vol. 24, No. 1, pp. 90–116, 1997.

MacCannel, Dean. *The Tourist: A New Theory of the Leisure Class.* New York: Schocken Books, 1976.

Milman, Ady. "The Impact of Tourism and Travel Experience on Senior Travelers' Psychological Well-Being." *Journal of Travel Research,* Vol. 37, No. 2, pp. 166–170, November 1998.

Milman, Ady, and Abraham Pizam. "Social Impacts of Tourism in Central Florida." *Annals of Tourism Research,* Vol. 15, No. 2, pp. 191–205, 1998.

Murray, M., and J. Sproats. *The Disabled Traveler: Tourism and Disability in Australia.* Townsville, Australia: James Cook University, 1990.

Pizam, Abraham, and Y. Mansfield, eds. *Tourism, Crime and International Security-Issues,* New York: Wiley, 1995.

Pizam, Abraham, Peter E. Tarlow, and Jonathon Bloom. "Making Tourists Feel Safe: Whose Responsibility Is It?" *Journal of Travel Research,* Vol. 36, No. 1, pp. 23–28, Summer 1997.

Ryan, C. "Crime, Violence, Terrorism, and Tourism: An Accidental or Intrinsic Relationship." *Tourism Management,* Vol. 14, No. 3, pp. 173–183, 1993.

Ryan, Chris, and Rachel Kinder. "Sex, Tourism and Sex Tourism: Fulfilling Similar Needs?" *Tourism Management,* Vol. 17, No. 7, pp. 507–518, November 1996.

Salmon, J. P. S. *Accommodating All Guests: The Americans with Disabilities Act and the Lodging Industry.* Washington, D.C.: American Hotel and Motel Association, 1992.

Sönmez, Sevil F. "Tourism, Terrorism, and Political Instability." *Annals of Tourism Research,* Vol. 25, No. 2, pp. 416–456, 1998.

Transport Canada. *Access for All.* Ottawa: Transport Canada, 1991.

Turner, Louis, and John Ash. *The Golden Hordes.* London: Constable, 1975.

USTDC. *The 55+ Traveler.* New York: U.S. Travel Data Center, April 1995.

Verhoven, Peter J., and Lynn A. Masterson. "The Impact of Select Socio-Demographic and Life-cycle Variables on the Importance Ratings of Vacation Enjoyment Attributes." *Visions in Leisure and Business,* Vol. 15, No. 2, pp. 15–26, Summer 1996.

WTO. *Tourist Safety and Security: Practical Measures for Destinations.* Madrid: World Tourism Organization, 1996.

———"Social Tourism for All: The Swiss Travel Saving Fund." *Tourism Management,* Vol. 4, No. 3, pp. 216–219, September 1983.

PART 4

TOURISM SUPPLY, DEMAND, POLICY, PLANNING, AND DEVELOPMENT

◀ *Hotel facilities built to accommodate visitors to Ayers Rock (seen in the distance), one of Australia's most famous landmarks.*

361

CHAPTER 12

TOURISM COMPONENTS AND SUPPLY

- Know the four major supply components that any tourist area must possess.

- Become familiar with the newer forms of accommodations: condominium apartments and timesharing arrangements.

- Be able to use the mathematical formula to calculate the number of guest rooms needed

for the estimated future demand.

- Develop the ability to perform a task analysis in order to match supply components with anticipated demand.

- Discover methods of adjusting supply components in accordance with fluctuating demand levels.

◄ **LEARNING OBJECTIVES**

◄ *Delicious food, enjoyable entertainment, and unique transportation all make for a winning vacation experience. (Photo courtesy of the Delta Queen Steamboat Company.)*

INTRODUCTION

Considering that tourism is a composite of activities, services, and industries that deliver a travel experience, it is important to identify and categorize its supply commonents. The quality and quantity of these determine tourism's success in any area.

In Chapter 1 (Figure 1.3) you observed that tourism was a complex phenomenon—the composite of activities, policies, services, and industries involving many players that deliver the travel experience. The purpose of this chapter is to take a look at just one segment of the tourism phenomenon by examining the physical supply side of tourism. It is important for a tourist area to identify and categorize its supply components and compare them with the competition because the quality and

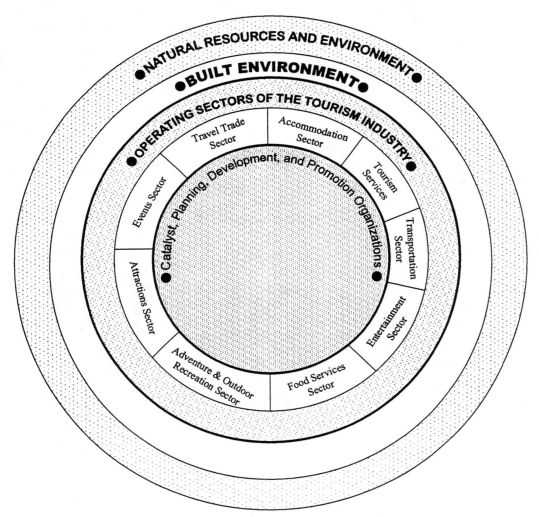

FIGURE 12.1 Components of tourism supply.

quantity of supply components are a critical factor in determining tourism's success. Figure 12.1 extracts the supply components from Figure 1.3 and provides the basis for discussion in this chapter. However, it is important to recognize that no segment operates in a vacuum and that supply is interrelated to all other aspects of tourism. It must be matched with demand (see Chapter 13). It is an important part of policy considerations. Chapter 15 on tourism policy discusses tourism supply policy focusing on physical resources, human resources, organizational resources, and program/activity resources policy. While this chapter focuses on physical and human resources that the tourist comes in contact with, it must be remembered that earlier policies in the finance, organization, and program areas made it possible for the physical resources to be there for the tourists to enjoy. See Chapter 15, pp. 443–511.

SUPPLY COMPONENTS

Tourism **supply components** are classified into four broad categories for discussion in this chapter.

1. *Natural resources and environment.* This category constitutes the fundamental measure of supply—the **natural resources** that any area has available for the use and enjoyment of visitors. Basic elements in this category include air and climate, physiography of the region, land forms, terrain, flora, fauna, bodies of water, beaches, natural beauty, and water supply for drinking, sanitation, and similar uses.

2. *The built environment.* This includes the infrastructure and superstructure discussed in Chapter 1. This component has been developed within or upon the natural environment. One of the most base elements of the built environment is the **infrastructure** of the region that consists of all underground and surface developmental construction such as water supply systems, sewage disposal systems, gas lines, electrical lines, drainage systems, roads, communications networks, and many commercial facilities. The tourism **superstructure** includes facilities constructed primarily to support visitation and visitor activities. Primary examples are airports, railroads, roads, drives, parking lots, parks, marinas and dock facilities, bus and train station facilities, resorts, hotels, motels, restaurants, shopping centers, places of entertainment, museums, stores, and similar structures. For the most part, the operating sectors of the industry are part of the built environment and provide much of the superstructure or facilitate access to the physical supply.

3. *Transportation.* Included are items such as ships, airplanes, trains, buses, limousines, taxis, automobiles, cog railroads, aerial tramways, and similar passenger transportation facilities. Because nothing happens until someone leaves home, **transportation** is a critical component. Without transportation, the tourist would be unable to reach and enjoy the natural and built environment so this component is given attention.

4. *Hospitality and cultural resources.* Pervading all of the foregoing physical elements of the built infrastructure and superstructures is the social foundation of the destination—its culture, which consists of the language, customs, and religions of the residents of the region, as well as their work- and leisure-related behaviors. It is the people and the cultural wealth of an area that makes possible the successful hosting of tourists. Examples are the tourist business employees' welcoming spirit "aloha" in Hawaii, attitude of the residents toward visitors, courtesy, friendliness, sincere interest, willingness to serve and to get better acquainted with visitors, and other manifestations of warmth and friendliness. In addition, the cultural resources of any area are included here: fine arts, literature, history, music, dramatic art, dancing, shopping, sports, and other activities.

There is a wide range of tourist resources created by combining cultural resources. Such examples would be sports events and facilities, traditional or national festivals, games, and pageants.

NATURAL RESOURCES

A great variety of combinations of natural resource factors can create environments attractive to tourism development. Thus, no general statements can be formulated. Probably the most noticeable are the pronounced seasonal variations of temperature zones and the changes in demand for recreational use of such areas. To even out demand, the more multiple-use possibilities, the better. For example, it is more desirable that an area be used for golf, riding, fishing, hunting, snow skiing, snowmobiling, mushroom hunting, sailing and other water sports, nature study, and artistic appreciation such as painting and photography than for hunting alone. The wider the appeal throughout the year, the greater the likelihood of success.

Another highly important consideration is that of location. As a rule, the closer an area is to its likely markets, the more desirable it is and the more likely to have a high demand. User-oriented areas (e.g., golf courses) should be close to their users. By contrast, an area of superb natural beauty such as a U.S. national park could be several thousand miles from major market areas and yet have very satisfactory levels of demand.

Productivity of the natural resources of the area for tourism is a function of the application of labor and management. The amounts and proportions of these inputs will determine the quality and quantity of the output. The terrain, vegetation, and beaches of the natural resources will be affected by the intensity of use. Proper planning, taking such concentrations of use under consideration, and planning accordingly for permanent aesthetic appreciation will help to maintain the quality of the natural resources for the enjoyment of present and future users.

The quality of the natural resources must be maintained to sustain tourism demand. Proper levels of quality must be considered when planning is undertaken, and the maintenance of quality standards after construction is undertaken is absolutely necessary for continued satisfaction of the visitor. In fact, tourism is very sensitive to the quality of recreational use of natural resources, and unless high standards are

Golfing at the Jasper Park Lodge in Canada offers recreation, relaxation, and scenic beauty. *(Photo courtesy of Canadian Pacific Hotels.)*

maintained, a depreciation of the demand will inevitably result. Thus, ecological and environmental considerations are vital.

INFRASTRUCTURE AND SUPERSTRUCTURE

The ground and service installations described as infrastructure are of paramount importance to successful tourism. These installations must be adequate. For example, the diameters of the pipes in various utility systems should be ample for any future increase in use. Electrical installations, water supply systems, communications installations, waste disposal, and similar service facilities should be planned with a long-term viewpoint so that they can accommodate future expansion. Airport runways should be built to adequate standards for use by the newest group of jets so that future costly modifications will not be necessary.

Hotel or lodging structures are among the most important parts of the super-structure. The goal should be to produce an architectural design and quality of construction that will result in a distinctive permanent environment. A box-like hotel typical of any modern city is not considered appropriate for a seaside resort dominated by palms and other tropical vegetation, nor is it likely to attract tourists.

A tourist is often more attracted by a facility designed in conformance with local architecture as a part of the local landscape than by the modernistic hotel that might be found at home. Attention must be given to this subject because people often travel to immerse themselves in an environment totally different from their own. Modern amenities such as air conditioning, central heating, and plumbing, however, should be used in buildings otherwise characteristic of a particular region.

Interior design should also be stimulating and attractive. Lodging structures need local decor and atmosphere as well as comfort. To minimize the expense of obsolescence, high-quality materials and furnishings and first-rate maintenance are necessary. Infrastructure is expensive and requires considerable time to construct.

Rental car companies provide essential ground transportation services. Rental cars are often found at or near airports all over the world, to facilitate ease of travel throughout a trip. *(Photo courtesy of Budget Rent-A-Car Corporation.)*

Auto Traveler Services

In developed countries, automobile transportation is most common. As the economy of a country develops, the usual pattern is from walking, to using horses or other working animals, to bicycles, to motorcycles, and finally to small and then larger automobiles, augmented by public transport. In the case of roads, they should be hard, all-weather surfaced, be properly graded and drained, and be built to international standards for safe use. Small, inadequate roads will only have to be torn up and replaced with better and more adequate systems.

Auxiliary services, such as gasoline stations, roadside eating facilities, motels, roadside parks, roadside picnic facilities, rest parks that have toilet facilities, scenic turnouts, marked points of interest within easy access of the road, and auto repair and service facilities are all needed for successful auto tourism. The number and spacing of essential services depend on the nature of the area, but a spacing of about one hour's driving distance is recommended.

Road Planning and Road Signs

In the planning of new roads, long-term consideration must be given to "tourist" or "scenic routes" that present the most impressive scenery. A good example is the scenic Mississippi River route in the United States. Such routes should have specially colored markers and be indicated on road maps as "scenic tourist routes" or some similar designation. The marking or sign program for the roads should show points of interest—including directions—and have sufficient information concerning availability of food, lodging, and gasoline.

Some type of classification for such signs indicating the nature of the accommodations and services available is desired. One method is to provide signs with the logos of the various hotel, motel, restaurant, and gasoline service stations. This type of sign identifies for the traveler the type of facilities he or she can expect. Adequate sign facilities including the international auto-road symbols are essential as are adequate supplies of maps that translate road signs into the most needed language of visitors.

Another aspect of signs concerns their control along the highways. It is the authors' belief that the most satisfactory way to provide information (and advertising) for the tourist and at the same time protect the beauty of the countryside is to control the placement of signs as follows:

Within one mile (1609 meters) from the outskirts of the city or community, signs along the highways will be permitted. These signs will be located in any convenient place, with one stipulation—that signs be maintained in excellent physical condition. No obvious deterioration of the signs will be allowed, and if such deterioration takes place, the highway authorities would have the mandate to remove the sign at the expense of the owner. The countryside between cities beyond the one-mile radius of each city would have no advertising signs. Only highway marker signs to indicate road conditions, curves, warning signs, and similar highway directional information would be found in this area.

An exception to these rules might be made in the case of major intersections where highway directional signs exist and a cluster of informational signs of tourist accommodations and other tourist services could be permitted.

Roadside Parks

Auto tourists use and enjoy roadside parks, picnic tables, rest areas, scenic turnouts, and similar roadside facilities. These facilities are sometimes abused by inconsiderate motorists who litter the area with their trash. Thus, the rule "If you can't maintain it, don't build it" is a cardinal principle of tourism development, and regular maintenance to keep the park in an orderly condition is essential. If the parks are not properly maintained, the tourist is disappointed and the investment in the park is largely wasted.

Some states provide deluxe roadside parks with a fine information building, free refreshments, tourist hosts and hostesses, and rest rooms. These parks are equipped with supplies of folders, maps, pictures, and other amenities for a refreshing informative stop.

Gasoline Stations

Service stations should be provided in sufficient quantity to avoid delays for service. An automobile patron should not wait more than five minutes for service. Station attendants need to be schooled in courteous service and in the importance of friendliness, hospitality, and knowledge of the tourist attractions in the immediate vicinity

Auto travelers find observing wildlife in parks or on safaris to be a major attraction. In all cases, respect for animals is a must. *(Photo courtesy of South Dakota Tourism.)*

(such as within a radius of 50 miles). They should be knowledgeable concerning accommodations, shopping, and entertainment in their community.

Accommodations

For successful tourism, **accommodations,** must be available in sufficient quantity to match the demand of the travelers who arrive at the destination. Given access accommodations should precede any other type of development; their importance cannot be overemphasized.

Hotels vary tremendously in their physical facilities, level of maintenance and cleanliness, and services provided. Unless all of these factors are at satisfactory levels, tourism cannot succeed. The hotels must provide the physical facilities, price ranges, locations, and services that meet the expectations, wants, and needs of the travelers. Should the quality of facilities and services drop, demand will fall off—a serious blow to the tourism industry in the area.

Types of Accommodations

Hotels

Hotels are of several types: commercial, resort, motor, airport, and residential. In relation to tourism, residential hotels are probably not important, although there are

The personal greeting of guests conveys a feeling of warmth and professionalism at the Sheraton New York Hotel and Towers. (*Photo courtesy of Sheraton Hotels of New York.*)

usually some rooms available to tourists in most residential hotels. The primary type is the resort hotel situated in attractive surroundings and usually accompanied by a large mix of services, including entertainment and recreational activities for the traveler and vacationer. The commercial hotel is usually a downtown structure located conveniently for the business traveler, convention attender, and vacationer.

The demand for accommodations varies according to the price guests are willing to pay, services required, and similar considerations. Many successful tourism areas have no multistoried, expensive, contemporary-looking hotels. For example, a bungalow-type accommodation constructed with native materials, built to modern standards of comfort and safety, and kept immaculately clean will be acceptable to a large segment of the market.

The motor hotel is of primary importance for tourists traveling by car and is of major importance in the United States, Canada, and Mexico. Suitable accommodations should be available for all segments of the market. American companies such as Marriott, Ramada, Hilton, and Choice now offer accommodations under different names that are aimed at specific price levels of the market. Thus, they compete for various segments of the travel market. Expensive hotel accommodations may be demanded by those who "want the best" and are willing and able to pay accordingly. On the other hand, youth tourism and adults unable or unwilling to pay for top-level accommodations should have facilities available, such as hostels, pensions, and bed and breakfast. Camping or caravanning facilities are often needed. Other types of accommodations include marina hotels, airport hotels, gambling resort hotels, and rustic cabins in wilderness areas. All accommodations should be harmonious with one another.

Certain places are known as expensive destination areas, and travelers expect to find higher-quality accommodations there. Conversely, other areas are expected to be inexpensive, and the high-priced hotel would be out of place in such a locality.

Condominium Apartments

Individual buyers of condominium units typically use the apartment for their own enjoyment, or they rent it to tourists for all or part of the year. This form of accommodation has become increasingly important and, in some resort areas, constitutes considerable competition to the resort hotels. Real estate management firms often manage such apartments or groups of "condos" within a building or complex and thus serve as agents for the owners. They rent the condos as managers of the group, charging a fee for this service to the absent owner. Such arrangements can be made through a local travel agent in the prospective traveler's home city. The agent will book the reservation through the real estate management firm.

Timesharing

Timesharing is a technique for the multiple ownership and/or use of resort and recreational properties. Timesharing has been applied to hotels, motels, condominiums, townhouses, single-family detached homes, campgrounds, and even boats and yachts. It involves both new construction and conversion of existing structures, along with properties devoted solely to timesharing and projects that integrate timesharing and nontimesharing properties. While most programs may be classified as either ownership or nonownership (right to use), there are wide variations in program and legal format.

The attraction of timesharing is simple: It permits purchasers to own or have occupancy rights at a resort accommodation for a period of time each year for a fraction of the purchasing price of the entire unit. Timeshare owners pay for exactly what they plan on using, and when they leave they don't have to think about where they'll be vacationing next year. Another option or advantage of timesharing is the exchange program. The exchange system affords vacation flexibility by allowing owners to trade or swap their timeshares for other locations and times. Finally, a well-designed timeshare program can be a hedge against inflation in resort accommodations.

The benefits of timesharing are substantially borne out by the high degree of consumer satisfaction it has achieved. In a survey of approximately 10,000 timeshare buyers, conducted by the National Timesharing Council, 86.3 percent of the respondents said they were "very satisfied" or "satisfied" with their purchase. About 40 percent indicated that they were interested in purchasing additional timeshares. Additional information on timesharing is available from the National Timesharing Council, 1220 L Street N.W., Suite 510, Washington, D.C. 20005. Also see the discussion in Chapter 6.

Hotel Management

As mentioned in the preceding section, the management of a hotel should ideally be the same group that was involved in the planning and construction of the hotel. To

The concierge provides personalized services to guests at the Great Wall Sheraton Hotel in Beijing, China. Their knowledge of the local scene is especially valuable to visitors who do not have time to familiarize themselves with a city's special treasures. *(Photo courtesy of Starwood Hotels and Resorts Worldwide, Inc.)*

do otherwise is unadvisable because the hotel business is not overly profitable, and any efficiency that can be built into the design or layout of the hotel as recommended by an experienced management group helps to ensure a better chance of success. For best results, the manager should be a graduate of a hotel school so there is a proper depth of understanding and appreciation of the industry as well as training for the job.

All decisions pertaining to the management of the hotel should begin with the customers and guests. What is the likely reaction to each management decision? Implementation of such a policy favors success for the hotel as the policy most likely to produce a high measure of guest satisfaction.

Success in hotel management also depends on organization and the functioning of each department. Each department head should be considered a manager of his or her own department. The goals of each should affect and support the overall goals of the hotel. The personal goals of each employee should contribute to and buttress the goals of the department. Each employee should be taught high standards of service, sanitation, and personal conduct, essential for the success of the hotel.

Thorough training sessions must be conducted for new employees, and recurring training should be provided for all employees. A wide selection of home study courses (also suitable for group use) is available, in English, from the Educational Institute of the American Hotel and Motel Association, 2113 North High Street, Lansing, Michigan 48906.

Assistance in training staff and managers can also be obtained from colleges and universities, state departments of education and public instruction, trade associations, and private management institutes or associations as well as from resources from within the organization or from larger affiliates or chain staff personnel.

Local Charm

A principal appeal of travel is the enjoyment of people of other cultures, and guests will inevitably become acquainted with the staff of the hotel. In fact, at a resort hotel, the guest probably gets to know his or her waiter or waitress better than anyone else in the hotel or local area.

Tourists expect all hotel personnel to serve them with courtesy and efficiency. Thus, all hotel employees should be indoctrinated into the importance of this relationship and its success-building potential. The use of local costumes, the retention of unsophisticated charm, and the practice of friendliness and cleanliness are integral to achieving good hotel management.

Inspection

The most common types of hotel inspection relate to water supplies, sewage and waste disposal, general cleanliness, kitchen and food storage, and safety. Such inspection can be accomplished by local-, area-, or state-level authorities. Inspections of these conditions should be made no less than annually, and semiannually would be preferred.

Inspection to prevent fires is also important. Rigid inspections of electrical sys-

Accommodations vary tremendously from luxury properties to charming hostels, such as this one in Galway, Ireland. *(Photo by the author.)*

tems, heating systems, ventilating systems, air-conditioning systems, fuel storage, elevators, and storage areas are all important. Cleanliness and orderliness are essential ingredients in the prevention of fires. Fire prevention systems such as automatic sprinklers or similar warning devices should be inspected, and installation of fire prevention devices should be encouraged, if not required.

Regulations

Regulations of hotels take many forms depending on local conditions and requirements. Regulations often relate to fairness and minimum standards of wages, hours, and ages of employees. Others relate to the licensing for selling alcoholic beverages; various tax structures for hotels; the disposal of wastes; hours of operation for public eating and drinking facilities; registration of guests; the importation of various food and drink items; equipment, unemployment, and disability insurance and other staff benefits; passport identification; zoning and building regulations; and fair employment and civil rights regulations. Many states regulate the sale of alcoholic beverages and the licensing of serving establishments, usually via a special agency.

Hotel Classification

Hotels are classified using a number of different systems. Then, too, many tourist countries have no classification system whatsoever. Many in the industry prefer the five-star rating system, which grades hotels according to specific criteria (usually by the national tourist organization) from the highest (five stars) to the most modest accommodations (one star) suitable for travelers. Countries such as Spain also classify nonhotel accommodations, such as pensions. Criteria used for star ratings are public rooms, bathrooms, climatization, telephone, bar, dining rooms, and other characteristics. The inspections and classifications in Spain are conducted by the director general of Touristic Enterprise and Activities.

Other classifications are deluxe, superior, and good, or super deluxe, and first-class reasonable. Still another classification is A, B, C, D, or E. A uniform worldwide classification truly indicative of the grades of hotels in any country would be a real plus to tourism. Of course, differences in general standards of development in various countries would be understood. A five-star hotel in a highly developed country would likely be more deluxe than would a five-star hotel in a less developed area.

Promotion Through Referral and Franchise Groups

A substantial number of U.S. hotels and motels belong to some kind of an endorsing or referral association. Examples are Best Western, American Automobile Association (AAA), or Preferred Hotels. The main purpose of group membership is to obtain substantial numbers of reservations from other properties in the group and from the association's computerized reservation system.

Accommodations firms can also hold a franchise such as Holiday Inns, Hilton Inns, or Marriott Inns. All members of the franchise encourage their guests to make free reservations at another property in the group. Franchise companies operate sales offices in major cities (called hotel rep firms) and also provide national and international reservations services. All of this effort is aimed at increasing members' annual volume of reservations.

TRANSPORTATION

All factors concerning transportation should be considered in developing tourism, beginning with taxis, limousines, and bus service from the place of lodging to the departure terminals. Such services must be adequate and economical.

Air

As described in Chapter 5, the airline industry dominates public intercity transportation systems, capturing over 92 percent of the common-carrier passenger mile market. Thus, planners looking to improve tourism must evaluate the adequacy of air transportation. Flight frequencies as well as size and type of aircraft are important. Air service from important origins for tourists is, of course, essential.

Airport facilities must be adequate. Major problems frequently encountered are the accessibility to the airport and the loading–unloading parking space sequence. Newly built airports seem to have solved these to a considerable degree and also reduced walking distances due to design improvements. There is also frequent shuttle bus service for interline passengers.

Motorcoach

Motorcoaches intended for tour use should have large windows, air conditioning, comfortable seats, and rest room facilities. Springs or other suspension systems in the coaches should be designed so that the joggling of passengers is kept to a minimum or eliminated. Multilingual guide service or multilingual tape recording facilities with earphones for each passenger are desirable in communities or on tours where an interpretation of the points of interest is desirable.

Personnel assigned to buses should be selected for suitable temperament, courtesy, and spirit of hospitality. For example, if a bus is staffed by a driver and an interpreter, the interpreter can assist passengers on and off the bus as well as inform them of local environment, particularly attractions of interest. Interpreters or guides should be trained and educated for this duty. Too often, the interpretation of points of interest is superficial (and inaccurate). A program of certification for guides should be conducted by a special school or provided in the curriculum of an institution of higher learning. In such a program, competent instructors should educate potential guides in the history, archeology, ethnology, culture, and economic system of the area in which the tour is being conducted. Competency in the various languages commonly encountered with tourists is also an essential qualification.

Ship and Boat

Water travel is a major part of tourism and contributes considerably to the development of travel on land and by air. Forms of water travel include cruise ship, passenger travel on freighters, ferryboats, river stern wheelers, chartered boats and yachts, houseboats, and smaller family boats and canoes.

Cruise ships and other large vessels need convenient piers and good land–air transportation connections for their passengers. Smaller boats need docks and loading–unloading ramps for easy accessibility to water. Charter boat operators must have reliable weather forecasting and ready availability of needed supplies and repair services. Where rental canoes are popular, delivery and pickup services are often necessary as are campgrounds in wilderness areas where canoeists can stay overnight. Persons owning their own boats appreciate good public access points for launching.

Rail

Travelers worldwide often prefer rail travel, particularly because of its unparalleled safety record and the convenience and comfort of viewing the scenery from

Cruise sailing is a special component of the cruise market. The Wind Spirit is shown here under full sail. *(Photo by Harvey Lloyd; courtesy of Windstar Cruises.)*

an air-conditioned car. Also, the frequent schedules of trains in many countries appeal to travelers. The recent advent of high-speed trains further enhances their appeal. Some trains have stewardesses or hostesses, which travelers seem to appreciate.

Adequate taxi, limousine, or bus service from the railroad station to hotels and downtown points is essential. Such transportation service must be frequent enough to get the traveler to the destination promptly. Conversely, the traveler should be able to get to the railroad station in ample time to make connections with the train as well.

Taxis

Adequate taxi and limousine services are essential in a tourist area. Ideally, taxis should have removable and washable seat covers so the car always presents a clean appearance to the passenger. Also, the taxi driver, to make the best impression, should

The growing popularity of "heritage tourism" has created a desire to preserve and enjoy early railway equipment, such as the 1880 train in Hill City, South Dakota. *(Photo courtesy of South Dakota Tourism.)*

dismount from the driver's seat and open the door for the passenger. He or she also should assist in stowing the luggage in the trunk or elsewhere in the cab and be courteous at all times.

Taxi drivers that are multilingual are highly desirable and, in fact, essential if tourism is to be an important element of the economy of the state. Training taxi drivers in foreign languages should be no more difficult than training of tourist guides or front desk clerks. Where taxi drivers have no foreign language ability, hotels may provide written directions for the tourist to give to the driver concerning the destination and the return to the hotel at the end of the excursion.

HOSPITALITY AND CULTURAL RESOURCES

The development of **hospitality resources** is perhaps the most important factor in tourism. The finest physical facilities will be worthless if the tourist feels unwelcome. For example, we suggest having a welcoming sign and a special reception area for visitors at airports and other entry points. A favorable attitude toward the visitor can be created through programs of public information and propaganda. Public relations and publicity designed to convince local citizens of the importance of tourism are helpful. Courses at tourist hospitality schools for all persons who have direct contact with visitors are useful. In these schools, store clerks, gasoline station attendants, hotel clerks, and other persons who are directly in contact with the visitor are given indoctrination on the importance of tourism to their community and are taught the location of important points of interest. Other parts of the program include the importance of appearance and good grooming, greeting of visitors, providing information, and being helpful, gracious, friendly, and cooperative.

Cultural programs such as "Meet the Danes" (home visitation arrangements) help greatly in this respect. Adequate training of personnel by tourist hospitality businesses can also create the desired hospitable attitude.

Activities Tourists Enjoy Most

One of the most important functions of a tourism promotion organization is to ascertain what activities visitors would enjoy. When substantial data are accumulated, the findings should be reported to those who accommodate and entertain. Thus, they are guided into more successful methods and programs. Table 12.1 shows some of tourists' favorite things.

The best method of obtaining this information is by interviewing both the visitors and their hosts. Questionnaires can also be placed in guests' rooms. Public contact

TABLE 12.1
Tourists' Favorite Things: What European-Bound Travelers Plan on Doing

Activity	Percent Citing It
Dining at restaurants	86.2
Shopping	76.9
Visiting a historical site	67.5
Visiting a small town	53.6
Sightseeing in a city	51.8
Touring the countryside	47.0
Visiting an art gallery/museum	40.1
Visiting a cultural heritage site	38.3
Visiting a nightclub/dancing	21.4
Taking a guided tour	21.0
Attending a concert/play	20.2
Visiting an ethnic heritage site	13.3
Participating in water sports/sunbathing	10.7
Visiting an amusement park	8.1
Visiting a national park	6.7
Taking a cruise	6.4
Camping/hiking	4.9
Playing golf/tennis	4.9
Visiting a casino	4.8
Attending a sports event	3.8
Skiing	2.9
Participating in an ecological excursion	2.5
Hunting/fishing	1.4

Source: Travel Weekly, European Travel Commission, and Tourism Industries, U.S. Department of Commerce.

employees can be instructed to inquire politely as to guests' interests and entertainment preferences. Careful recording and thorough analysis of these data will result in findings of real value. When those responsible for attracting and hosting visitors provide the requested entertainment activities, the community will likely be a preferred destination area. There is no better advertising than a satisfied visitor (see Chapter 18).

Shopping

Shopping is an important tourist activity and thus an essential element in the tourism supply because it affects the success of the tourist destination area. The most important single element in shopping is the authenticity of the products offered for sale as they relate to the local area. A product that is supposedly a "native handicraft" should be that. If it is an import, the purchaser may be disappointed if he or she expected an authentic, locally made item.

Tourists who are shopping are particularly interested in handicraft items that are typical or indigenous to the particular locale or region. Of course, they are also interested in essential items such as toothpaste, but our discussion here is confined to purchases that tourists make as souvenirs or special gifts.

Tourists can be encouraged to spend more money on shopping if displays are high quality, imaginative, and attractive. Hotels are excellent places for shops; and if these shops are exquisitely furnished and stocked, the tourist is attracted to the shop and is more likely to make purchases.

Native Marketplaces

Another shopping experience concerns the local market or so-called "native marketplace." Such areas are rich in ethnicity and have much local color. They are popular with visitors, even though the visitor may not understand the language and may have trouble making a purchase. Although many persons in native shopping places do not understand any foreign languages, the sign language of bargaining is fairly universal.

Shops and Clerks

Shopkeepers and clerks themselves should be amiable and courteous. Furthermore, the shopkeeper should not be so anxious to close a sale that the tourist is pressured. A tourist who is courteously served in a store and who makes a good purchase will tell friends back home. Thus, future business can be developed in this way. Salespeople should also take the time to explain the value of the item and relate something of its history that would be otherwise unknown to the purchaser. Of course, this information should be accurate and truthful.

Salespersons must have sufficient language ability to conduct conversations with the visitors. The most common language is English, but a knowledge of other languages that are commonly spoken by tourists who visit a particular area is a necessary qualification of clerks who serve these visitors. Salespersons must be patient and understanding and try to help the prospective purchaser cheerfully at all times.

The many colors and varieties of products in foreign markets makes shopping a unique and enjoyable experience for visitors. *(Photo courtesy of Malaysia Tourism Promotion Board.)*

Prices and Unethical Practices

One of the most important considerations in shopping is the pricing of the goods. Probably resented more than any other single factor of tourism is higher prices for tourists than for local residents. Because many shoppers compare prices from one store to another, prices should be as consistent as possible and in line with costs.

If the shopkeeper resorts to unethical methods of selling such as deception, selling imitation goods or products of inferior quality, refusing to exchange damaged goods, or short-changing or short-weighting, the seller is hurting the tourist trade and should be prosecuted by local authorities.

Entertainment, Recreation, and Other Activities

The recreation and other activities engaged in by tourists at their destination comprise a major component of tourism. Thus, considerable thought and effort should be devoted to the type of activities that visitors are likely to enjoy.

Entertainment

The most satisfying entertainment for visitors is native to the area. In any country, there are expressions of the culture in the music, dance, drama, poetry, literature, motion pictures, television, ceremonies, festivals, exhibits, shows, meetings, food and beverage services, and tours (or local excursions) that portray the best the area has to offer.

Not all forms of entertainment can be successfully described or illustrated in tourist promotional literature. One of the best ways to bring these entertainment opportunities to the attention of the visitor is with a social director whose desk is in the lobby of hotels, resorts, and other forms of accommodation so that the visitor can readily find out what is going on and make arrangements to attend. In European hotels, this desk is traditionally staffed by the concierge, who provides an amazing amount of information concerning all types of entertainment and activities available. An appropriate substitute is a knowledgeable person at the front desk to provide information concerning recreation and entertainment.

Bulletin board displays or posters and verbal announcements of outstanding events made in the dining room or other areas where guests gather can also provide entertainment information. A local newspaper that features articles concerning everyday as well as special entertainment events and opportunities is a valuable method of distributing information. These newspapers or bulletins are presently provided in popular vacation destination areas such as Miami Beach and Honolulu, but the idea is not widespread. In metropolitan centers, a weekly magazine is normally provided to hotel guests to give current information on entertainment, recreational, and cultural opportunities in the city.

Special Events

Entertainment can be provided very effectively as a special promotional event to attract visitors during an off-season. One of the best examples of this is "Aloha Week," which was inaugurated in Hawaii in the early 1960s to bolster tourist traffic in the fall. This festival is enthusiastically supported by local tourism interests and is very successful in attracting tourists. Musicians, dancers, exhibits, floral displays, and special programs are assembled and give the visitor an unusual opportunity to enjoy the beauty and excitement of cultural expression that this state offers. Once created, such events become annual and typically grow in visitors and importance. Expositions and festivals are very attractive to visitors and deserve adequate promotion.

Museums and Art Galleries

Museums and art galleries are another major attraction for tourists. They provide some of the highlights in many of the world's most important tourist destinations such as New York, Washington, D.C., Chicago, Paris, London, Madrid, Rome, Singapore, Tokyo, Buenos Aires, Mexico City, and many others. The quality and magnitude of these institutions are an important consideration for attracting and satisfying tourists.

Sports

Golf and sports such as tennis, surfing, swimming, mountain climbing, skiing, hunting, fishing, hiking, prospecting, or any other outdoor sports activity require properly

Western culture in Canada and the United States finds rodeos a popular entertainment venue. Bareback bronco riding is a featured event in many localities. *(Photo courtesy of Wyoming Division of Tourism.)*

publicized facilities and services. Guides, equipment, charter boats, and other services needed to enjoy these sports must be readily available at fair prices. Convenience and accessibility are key factors in this type of entertainment.

Matching Supply with Demand

Providing an ample tourism supply to meet anticipated demand is a challenge for the planner. Supply functions are always constrained by demand. The following formula can be used to calculate the number of hotel rooms (or other types of lodging) required:

$$\text{room demand per night (100\% occupancy)} = \frac{\text{no. tourist} \times \text{\% staying in hotels} \times \text{average length of stay}}{365 \times \text{average no. persons per room}}$$

$$R = \frac{T \times P \times L}{S \times N}$$

where

T = number of tourists

P = percentage staying in hotels

N = average number of persons per room (obtained from hoteliers); this is the total number of guest nights divided by the number of guests, during any period of time

R = room demand per night, at 100 percent occupancy

O = hotel occupancy used for estimating (for 70 percent occupancy); divide number of rooms needed at 100 percent occupancy by 70 percent

S = number of days per year in business

L = average length of stay

Illustration of application of the formula:

T = 1,560,000 visitors

P = 98%

L = 9 days

N = 1.69

O = 70%

S = 365 days per year open for business

$$R = \frac{1,560,000 \times 0.98 \times 9}{365 \times 1.69} = \frac{13,759,200}{616.85} = 22,306 \text{ (rooms needed at 100\% occupancy)}$$

$$= \frac{22,306}{0.70} \text{ (as more rooms will be needed at 70\% occupancy than at 100\%)}$$

$$= 31,866 \text{ rooms needed}$$

Infrastructure factors in supply will be determined largely by the number of guest rooms as well as restaurants, stores, and similar installations. Infrastructure appropriate to the size of the development is an engineering problem and is readily ascertained as the plans are developed. Transportation equipment is generally supplied by commercial firms as well as publicly owned or quasi-public transportation facilities and services.

Regarding hospitality resources, the recruiting and training of staff for the various elements of supply is a critical one. The traveler generally enjoys being served by unsophisticated local persons who have had proper training and possess a hospitable attitude. Such persons may be recruited through government and private employment agencies as well as through direct advertisement to the public. Newly hired employees must be indoctrinated in the importance of tourism, how it affects their own personal welfare as well as that of their community, the importance of proper service to the visitors, and how their economic welfare is closely related to their performance.

Museums, art exhibits, festivals, craft shows, and similar cultural resources are usually created by community cooperation and the willing assistance of talented people. A chamber of commerce or tourism body is the best mechanism for organizing the creation of these hospitality resources.

Task Analysis

The procedure used in matching supply with demand is called a task analysis. Suggested steps are as follows:

1. Identification of the present demand
   a. By mode of transportation and by seasons of the year
   b. For various forms of tourism such as activities, attendance at attractions, and similar categories
   c. For special events such as conventions, celebrations, fairs
   d. Group and tour visitors
   e. Family and individual visitors
   f. Business visitors
2. A quantitative and qualitative inventory of the existing supply
3. The adequacy of present supply with present demand
   a. Natural resources
   b. Infrastructure
   c. Transportation and equipment
   d. Hospitality and cultural resources
4. Examination of present markets and the socioeconomic trends
   a. Geographic market segmentation and orientation
   b. Demographic market segmentation and orientation
      i. Population age, sex, occupation, family life stages, income, and similar data
      ii. Leisure time and work patterns
   c. Psychographic market segmentation
      i. Motivations, interests, hobbies, employment orientation, skills, professional interests
      ii. Propensity to travel, responsiveness to advertising
5. Forecast of tourism demand
   a. Computer systems simulation method
   b. Trend analysis
   c. Simple regression—linear least squares
   d. Multiple regression—linear least squares
   e. Executive judgment or Delphi method
6. Matching supply with anticipated demand
   a. If adequate, no further action necessary
   b. If inadequate, inauguration of planning and development procedures

To perform the task analysis, certain skills are required, with statistical research techniques employed to identify and quantify the present demand. Suggestions for doing this are provided in Chapter 13.

When making a quantitative and qualitative inventory of the existing supply, the aid of specialists and experts is usually needed. For example, the adequacy of the present supply in relation to present demand requires the work of tourism specialists such as travel agents, tour company and hotel executives, tourism promotion people, ground operators (companies that provide baggage transfers, taxi services, local tours, and similar services), shopkeepers, and perhaps a sample of the tourists themselves.

Examining the present markets and the socioeconomic trends that will affect future markets requires specialized market research activities. These should include determination of market characteristics, development of market potentials, market share analysis, sales analysis, competitive destination studies, potentials of the existing and possibly new markets, short-range forecasting, and studies of travel business trends. A number of sophisticated techniques are now available. The engagement of a reputable market research firm is one way to obtain this information.

Forecasting tourism demand is a perilous business. However, a well-structured statistical analysis coupled with executive judgment is most likely the best approach to this difficult problem. See Chapter 13 for several methods for accomplishing this.

Finally, matching supply with the anticipated demand must be done by knowledgeable planners. A tourism development plan within the master plan is recommended. Supply items are essentially rigid. They are elaborate and expensive and, thus, cannot be expanded rapidly. An exception would be transportation equipment. Additional sections of planes, buses, trains, or cars could be assembled quite rapidly to meet an unusually high-demand situation.

Peaks and Valleys

The foregoing discussion dealt with matching supply and demand in a long-run context. Another important consideration is that of fluctuations in demand in the short run (**seasonality**) and the resulting **peaks and valleys** in demand. This is a vexing problem.

The reason for this is simply that tourism is a service, and services cannot be placed in inventory. If a 400-room hotel rents (sells) 350 rooms on a particular night, it cannot place the other 50 rooms in inventory, for sale the following night. Regardless of how many rooms went unoccupied in the past, a 400-room property can only rent up to 400 rooms on any given night. By way of contrast, consider the case of some tangible good, say, television sets. If some television sets are not sold in one month, the storekeeper can keep them in inventory and sell them the next month. Of course, the storage charges, interest payments, and other expenses incurred in inventorying a particular item reduces the item's economic value. But in tourism, the economic value of unsold items such as the 50 hotel rooms mentioned is exactly zero.

Thus, it should be clear that while in most cases, firms selling tangible goods can deal with demand fluctuation through the inventory process, this option is not available to firms providing travel services. In the travel industry, an effort must be made to reduce seasonal fluctuations as much as possible. Because of the high economic cost involved, no effort should be spared in attempting to limit the amount of seasonal variations in demand. Nor can the problem be dealt with by simply selecting an appropriate supply level. The following charts illustrate various supply situations associated with fluctuating demand levels.

Suppose that the demand for a particular destination exhibits the seasonal pattern depicted in Figure 12.2*a*. If no action is taken to "level off" the demand, then three possible levels of supply can be considered. In Figure 12.2*b*, the level of supply is provided so that demand in the peak season is fully satisfied. This

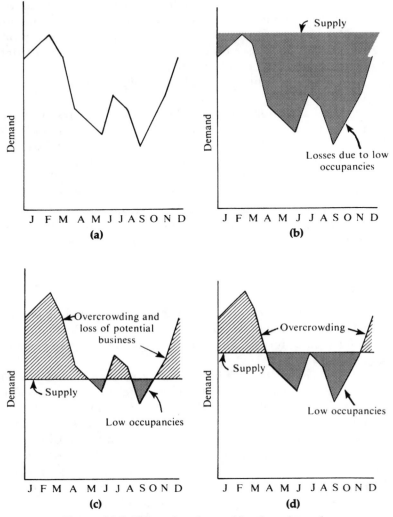

FIGURE 12.2 Fluctuating demand levels and supply.

implies that tourists coming to the destination in the peak season will be accommodated comfortably and without overcrowding. However, during the slack season, the destination will suffer from extremely low occupancy levels, with obvious implications for profitability. If, on the other hand, the supply is set at a low level (Figure 12.2c), the facilities during the peak season will be overcrowded enough to detract from the tourist experience. Visitor satisfaction will be at a low level, and the future of such a resort area will be doubtful. Last, if supply is set in between the level of demand during the peak season and the off-season (Figure 12.2d), the problems are somewhat mitigated. Nevertheless, low occupancy will result during low demand periods, and overcrowding will result in peak periods—neither is desirable. To maximize customer satisfaction and to utilize the facilities year-round, some action must be taken. Two strategies for dealing with this situation are as follows:

1. **Multiple use.** This involves supplementing peak-season attractions of a destination with other attractions that would create demand for travel to that destination during off-season periods. In effect, the peak season for the destination is extended. Examples of such efforts abound. In Michigan, for example, the current demand for off-season travel (during the fall, winter, and spring) has been successfully increased and sustained at much higher levels than 10 years ago. While Michigan was once viewed primarily as a summer destination, the development and promotion of winter sports in resort areas, foliage tours, and superb salmon fishing in the fall and spring have created new markets for these off-season periods. Festivals, special celebrations, conventions, and sports activities sponsored and promoted during off-seasons are other examples of multiple-use strategies.

2. **Price differential.** This technique, as contrasted with the multiple-use strategy, creates new markets for the off-season periods by employing price differentials as a strong tool to shift demand away from the peak season in favor of the off-season. Florida and destinations in the Caribbean have used this strategy rather effectively. The prices in these destinations during the off-seasons are considerably less than during the peak seasons. In addition, the development of promotional fares by airlines and other carriers, along with the expansion of the number, timing, and variety of price-discounted tours, has helped to stimulate demand in the off-season. Increased efficiency and effectiveness of promotional campaigns and better marketing also tend to offset the traditional seasonal patterns of demand. Yield management techniques used in the airline and lodging industries are very effective in using price differentials to match supply and demand.

In addition to these strategies implemented by destination areas, some trends in the employment and leisure patterns of Western societies contribute further to the leveling of demand between off-seasons and peak seasons. The staggering of holidays, the increasing popularity of three-day weekends with a holiday on Friday or Monday, and the splitting of vacations between various seasons of the year all lend themselves to leveling the demand for travel. Once the demand is evened out, the destination is then able to maximize customer satisfaction during the peak season and during the off-season. Also, facilities are utilized at a considerably higher level than previously. The importance of boosting off-season demand and, therefore, utilization level is further underscored by the fact that in most tourist service businesses, fixed costs are quite high in relation to op-

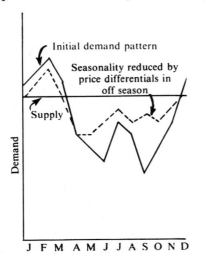

FIGURE 12.3 **Reducing seasonality through price differentials.**

erating costs. This implies that increasing total yearly revenue, even modestly, produces proportionally larger profits. There may be some softening of demand during the peak season due to those who might switch to the off-season because of the lower prices (see Figure 12.3). However, this is believed to be minimal. When off-season demand is boosted by the multiple-use strategy, peak-season demand is unaffected. Therefore, overall demand for the entire year will be substantially higher (see Figure 12.4).

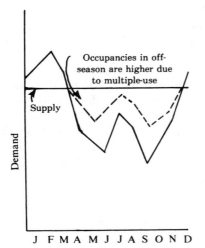

FIGURE 12.4 **Reducing seasonality through multiple use.**

SUMMARY

Certain broad classifications of supply components must be provided by any area that is attractive to tourists. The components consist of natural resources, infrastructure, transportation–transport equipment, and hospitality and cultural resources. These factors may be combined in many ways to create the environment, facilities, and services that the planners hope will attract and please the customers.

Creation of supply components necessarily involves financing—a critical element. Ideally, all the supply components perfectly match the demand at any given time. However, this is unrealistic. Too much supply means unused facilities, which is uneconomic. Too little supply results in overcrowding with resultant depreciation of the vacation experience. A moderate supply level is recommended.

Supply can be matched with demand using a mathematical formula. When confronted with a supply problem, the proper level of supply to meet the anticipated demand can be estimated by using the formula provided in this chapter. The process is refined and completed by a six-step task analysis.

KEY CONCEPTS

accommodations
cultural resources
entertainment, recreation, and other activities
hospitality resources
hotel management
infrastructure
multiple use
natural resources
peaks and valleys of demand

price differentials
seasonality
shopping
superstructure
supply components
task analysis
timesharing
transportation

INTERNET SITES

American Automobile Association
http://www.aaa.com

American Hotel and Motel Association
http://www.ahma.com

American Public Transit Association
http://www.apta.com

American Resort and Development Association
http://www.arda.org

Cruise Lines International
http://www.cruising.org

Fodor's Guidebooks
http://www.fodors.com

International Air Transport Association
http://www.iata.org

**International Association of
     Amusement Parks and Attractions**
http://www.iaapa.org

**International Civil Aviation
     Organization**
www.ca.org/ICAO

Lonely Planet Online
http://www.lonelyplanet.com

Microsoft: Expedia
http://www.expedia.com

National Restaurant Association
http://www.restaurant.org

Tourist Railway Association
http:www.train.org

Travel Web
http://www.travelweb.com

Virtual Tourist
http://www.vtourists.com/webmap

Virtual Tourist II
http://www.vtourist.com/vt

Welcome to the Avis Group
http://www.avis.com

INTERNET EXERCISES

Activity 1

Site Name: Fodor's Travel Publications

URL: http://www.fodors.com/

Background Information: Fodor's Travel Publications is a subsidiary of Random House, Inc. and is the largest publisher of English-language travel information in the world. Fodor's now publishes 14 guidebook series and more than 290 books on destinations around the world.

Exercise

1. Using the four major supply components your textbook indicates that any tourist area must possess, discuss how the Fodor's web site addresses each of these areas for the potential tourist.

Activity 2

Site Name: The Lonely Planet Online

URL: http://www.lonelyplanet.com/

Background Information: Lonely Planet publishes some of the world's best guidebooks for independent travelers. Their books are known worldwide for reliable, insightful travel information, maps, photos, and background historical and cultural information.

Exercise

1. Choose a destination or analyze one provided by the instructor. How does this site address the four components of travel for the potential tourist?

QUESTIONS FOR REVIEW AND DISCUSSION

1. In planning supply components for a development in an entirely new area, which one of the four components should be considered first? Last? Why?

2. When a gorgeous new hotel is opened for business, are the attractive physical facilities more important than the quality and training of the staff?

3. As a resort hotel manager, do you believe there is any need to educate your guests about environmental protection? Is there a need to educate your staff?

4. In a poor, developing country, a world-class hotel uses about half of the community's water supply. This requires rationing of water by the local people, which creates resentment. Suggest a partial solution to this problem.

5. For new developments, should the access roads be supplied by a government agency, the developer, or both? If both, who should supply what?

6. What might be appropriate costumes and uniforms for waiters and waitresses in various localities?

7. A motor hotel manager states, "I can't seem to sell any souvenirs that cost over $5." How could this situation be improved?

8. The sports director of a large resort hotel has been instructed to upgrade the hotel's physical fitness program. Provide some suggestions as to how this might be done.

9. Is changing the prices of hotel rooms, meals, and entertainment the best way to mitigate fluctuating levels of demand? Are there nonprice methods? Could combinations of methods be used?

CASE PROBLEMS

1. To maintain and hopefully enhance the appeal and quality of its area's natural resources, the city council had decided that it needs to enact protective laws to help ensure its future tourism success. What specific laws and regulations might these be?

2. Resort City is anxious to attract more tourists. The chamber of commerce has been successful in attracting several new tourist firms to the community. These firms plan to develop new hotels, motels, shops, and restaurants. However, an influential member of the chamber of commerce expresses the viewpoint that the community should enact some strict zoning and building code laws before these construction projects get under way.

The prospective developers and many other members of the chamber disagree. What do you think should be done to resolve this situation, and why?

3. A national tourism organization is seeking ways in which to improve the proficiency of accommodations management. It is exploring the possibility of installing a computer-based accommodations information system. This system provides data comparisons between similar operations considering size, location, and countrywide averages. What do you see as advantages for implementing such a system? How might the system be implemented in your country? What other management improvement incentives or programs could be provided?

SELECTED REFERENCES

Arbel, Avner, and Abraham Pizam. "Some Determinants of Urban Hotel Location: The Tourist Inclinations." *Journal of Travel Research,* Vol. 15, No. 3, pp. 18–22, Winter 1977.

Bonn, Mark A., H. Leslie Furr, and Muzaffer Uysal. "Seasonal Variation of Coastal Resort Visitors: Hilton Head Island." *Journal of Travel Research,* Vol. 31, No. 1, pp. 50–56, Summer 1992.

Clawson, Marion, and Jack L. Knetsch. *Economics of Outdoor Recreation.* Baltimore: Johns Hopkins University Press, 1966.

Maguire, Patricia A. "Tourism Supply: A U.S. Perspective." *Tourist Review,* No. 3, pp. 2–6, July/September 1990.

Manning-Shaw, Janet. "The Channel Tunnel." *Tourism Management,* Vol. 12, No. 1, pp. 5–7, March 1991.

McCool, Stephen F. "Recreation Use Limits: Issues for the Tourism Industry." *Journal of Travel Research,* Vol. 17, No. 2, pp. 2–7, Fall 1978.

Moulin, Claude, "Appreciating the Built Environment through Cultural Tourism." *The Tourist Review,* No. 2, pp. 7–13, 1996.

Smith, Darren L., and Nancy V. Kniskern. *The Traveller's Sourcebook.* Detroit: Omnigraphics, September 1996.

Smith, Stephen L. "Room for Rooms: A Procedure for the Estimation of Potential Expansion of Tourist Accommodations." *Journal of Travel Research,* Vol. 15, No. 4, pp. 26–29, Spring 1977.

OTD. *Travel Signing in Oregon.* Salem, OR: Oregon Tourism Division, 1989.

Trowbridge, Keith W. *Resort Timesharing.* New York: Simon and Schuster, 1981.

Var, Turgut, R. A. D. Beck, and Patrick Loftus. "Determination of Tourist Attractiveness of the Tourist Areas in British Columbia." *Journal of Travel Research,* Vol. 15, No. 3, pp. 23–29, Winter 1977.

Waddell, Joseph M. "Hotel Capacity: How Many Rooms to Build?" *Cornell Hotel and Restaurant Administration Quarterly,* Vol. 18, No. 2, pp. 35–47, August 1977.

World Bank. *Tourism Supply in the Caribbean Region.* Washington, D.C.: The Bank, November 1974.

CHAPTER 13

MEASURING AND FORECASTING DEMAND

- Know the definition of demand and its application and importance in tourism development planning.

- Understand the factors determining the magnitude and fluctuations of demand.

- Become able to apply various methods to measure and forecast demand.

◄ *Travelers enjoying Connoisseur Class service on United Airlines. (Photo courtesy of United Airlines.)*

INTRODUCTION

Economists define **demand** as a schedule of the amount of any product or service that people are willing and able to buy at each specific price in a set of possible prices during some specified period of time. Thus there exists at any one time a definite relationship between the market price and the quantity demanded.

WHY DEMAND IS IMPORTANT

The amount of demand for travel to a particular destination is of great concern to anyone involved in tourism. Vital demand data include (1) how many visitors arrived, (2) by what means of transportation, (3) how long they stayed and in what type of accommodations, and (4) how much money was spent. There are various measures of demand; some are much easier to obtain and are usually of more general interest than are others. Techniques also exist for making forecasts of future demand. Such estimates are of great interest to anyone planning future tourism developments. The availability of financing will depend largely on reliable forecasts of the future gross sales or revenues from the project to determine if the proposal will be financially feasible.

Marketing and sales promotion programs are, of course, aimed at increasing demand. Sometimes this effort focuses on increasing demand at certain times of the year or to a particular market. But the basic purpose is the same—to increase demand.

DEMAND TO A DESTINATION

In somewhat more specific terms, the demand for travel to a particular destination will be a function of the person's **propensity** to travel and the reciprocal of the **resistance** of the link between origin and destination areas. Thus,

$$D = f(\text{propensity, resistance})$$

where D is demand.

Propensity can be thought of as a person's predisposition to travel—in other words, how willing the person is to travel, what types of travel experiences he or she prefers, and what types of destinations are considered. A person's propensity to travel will, quite obviously, be determined largely by his or her psychographic profile and travel motivation, as discussed in previous chapters. In addition, a person's socioeconomic status will have an important bearing on propensity. It follows that to estimate a person's propensity to travel, we must understand both psychographic and demographic variables concerning the person. Propensity is *directly* related to demand.

Resistance, on the other hand, relates to the relative attractiveness of various destinations. This factor is, in turn, a function of several other variables, such as economic distance, cultural distance, the cost of tourist services at destination, the quality of service at destination, effectiveness of advertising and promotion, and seasonality. Resistance is *inversely* related to demand.

Economic Distance

Economic distance relates to the time and cost involved in traveling from the origin to the destination area and back. The higher the economic distance, the higher the resistance for that destination and, consequently, the lower the demand. It follows, conversely, that between any origin and destination point, if the travel time or travel cost can be reduced, demand will increase. Many excellent examples of this are available, such as the introduction of the jet plane in 1959 and the introduction of the wide-bodied jets in the late 1960s. They first cut travel time between California and Hawaii, for example, from 12 hours to 5 hours, and demand grew dramatically. A similar surge in demand was experienced with the introduction of the wide-bodied planes for transatlantic flights. The introduction of these planes cut the travel cost by almost 50 percent between the United States and most countries of the European continent.

Cultural Distance

Cultural distance refers to the extent to which the culture of the area from which the tourist originates differs from the culture of the host region. In general, the greater the cultural distance, the greater will be the resistance. In some cases, however, the relationship might be the opposite. For example, the higher the cultural distance be-

Many tourists seek familiarity while others seek new cultural experiences where they can mingle with the population and enjoy local food from a vendor such as this one in Morocco. *(Photo by the author.)*

tween particular origin and destination areas, the more an allocentric person may wish to travel to that destination, to experience this extreme difference.

Cost of Services

The higher the **cost of services** at a destination, the higher the resistance to travel to that destination will be and, therefore, the lower the demand. This variable captures the familiar inverse relationship between the price of a good or service and demand for it.

Quality of Service

Clearly, the higher the **quality of service** at a destination, the lower the resistance will be for travel to that destination. Although the relationship between quality of service and demand is straightforward enough, a difficulty arises in the interpretation and evaluation of "quality." Evaluation of quality is a highly personal matter, and what is quality to one tourist is not necessarily quality to another. Second, if a tourist does not have previous travel experience at a destination, can the tourist accurately judge the quality of services there? In such a case, the tourist must select a destination based on what the quality of service is *perceived* to be. Often, due to misleading advertisements or inaccurate input from others, the tourist's perception of the quality of service may not be realized at the destination. Such a situation has serious implications for establishing a repeat clientele, which is an important ingredient for success in the tourist business. Consequently, a destination area must be meticulous in projecting an accurate image.

Seasonality

The effect of **seasonality** on demand is quite apparent. The relative attractiveness of a given destination will depend on the time of year for which a vacation is planned. For a ski resort, for example, the demand will be at the highest level during the winter months. Resistance is at a minimum in this season.

The following illustrates the relationship between propensity, resistance, and demand, in terms of these variables as just described:

$$\text{demand} = f\,(\text{propensity, resistance})$$

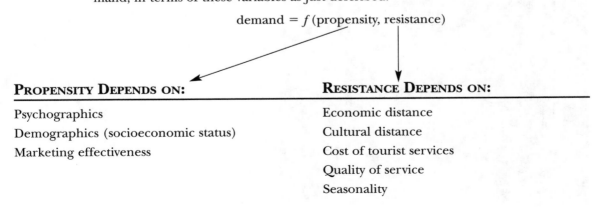

PROPENSITY DEPENDS ON:	RESISTANCE DEPENDS ON:
Psychographics	Economic distance
Demographics (socioeconomic status)	Cultural distance
Marketing effectiveness	Cost of tourist services
	Quality of service
	Seasonality

MEASURING DEMAND

Demand is strongly affected and limited by the supply. If the supply aspects are not taken into consideration when using demand figures, planners might be led into the false assumption that in a particular area, the supply should be increased to meet the demand when, in actuality, the increased supply may be needed much more elsewhere.

There are several measures of actual demand:

1. Visitor arrivals
2. Visitor-days or visitor-nights
3. Amounts spent

Visitor Arrivals

Simply counting the number of people who arrive at a destination is a measure of demand, although not a particularly adequate one. However, when visitors arrive by ship or aircraft, for example, to an island, quite accurate data are obtainable. Those who

Visitor-days or visitor-nights are a convenient way of measuring travel demand.
(Photo courtesy of United Airlines.)

are en route to someplace else should not be included in the arrival data. **Visitor arrivals** are the easiest type of data to obtain, especially if public transportation is the principal mode used. Regular reporting of visitor arrivals is of value in measuring broad changes in demand. Variation in the number of arrivals month by month is quite significant because it indicates the rise and fall of demand during the course of a year.

Arrival data become more of a problem if a large proportion of visitors arrive by private automobile on many major highways. In this case, a sampling method is employed, sometimes involving a tourist information center. Those stopping at the center are asked to fill out a card with data about their trip. The total number of visitors is then estimated, based on the sample obtained.

Visitors coming through seaports should be classified according to the United Nations' definition of tourists and excursionists. Excursionists remain in an area for less than 24 hours, whereas tourists stay 24 hours or longer. Arrival statistics should not include those who illegally enter the country, air travelers who do not leave the airport transit area, or analogous cases.

Visitor-Days or Visitor-Nights

Data on **visitor-days and visitor-nights** are much more valuable to tourism planners than are data on the number of arrivals. To calculate the former, the number of visitors is multiplied by their average length of stay. Public park planners and beach managers are interested in visitor-day figures. Hotel and other accommodations people want data on visitor-nights. When such data are obtained, it is not difficult to make an estimate of the likely expenditures made per visitor per day or night. But these expenditure figures are at best only estimates and need to be used carefully. Data on visitor-days and visitor-nights are of great benefit to planners who are working on public facilities for tourists such as utility systems, parking, and recreation areas. Similarly, private developers planning new hotels or other accommodations or services want and need visitor-night information. Thus visitor-days and/or visitor-nights are the most practical data to obtain and are useful to tourism people.

$$D = \text{no. of visitors} \times \text{avg. no. of days or nights at destination}$$

Amounts Spent

Amount spent is the most meaningful measure of demand if determined accurately. However, it is *the most difficult measure* to obtain. Statistics of this type tend to be hidden or partially forgotten by the visitor. Thus, they are not as accurate as desired. However, to members of legislatures and the public, total tourist expenditures are the most easily understood and the most impressive.

The most common method of estimating tourist expenditures is to multiply visitor-days or visitor-nights by the average per day or per night expenditure. Thus,

$$D(\$) = \text{no. of visitor-days or visitor-nights} \times \text{avg. expenditures per day/night}$$

Total expenditures in an area consists of the visitor-day and visitor-night total expenditures over a specified period of time.

Measuring Tourism Expenditures Through Tax Collections

Many states have a **sales and use tax** on consumer items. These tax collections provide a statistical base for calculating tourist expenditures. Suppose that a state has a 4 percent use tax on hotel and motel rooms. If we know what percentage of the average tourist dollar is spent for lodging, we could make an estimate of how much is spent on lodging and total expenditures, as illustrated in the following hypothetical example:

Rooms tax collections   = $5 million

Rooms use tax rate   = 4 percent

Total lodging spending = $5 million ÷ 0.04 = $125 million

Lodging expenditures   = 25 percent of total spending

Total expenditures   = $125 million ÷ 0.25 = $500 million (visitor-nights)

Estimated spending of those not using commercial lodging
+ visitor-day spending   = $600 million

Total $D(\$)$ = $500 million + $600 million = $1.1 billion

Research in Measuring Demand

Considerable interest exists in improving methods of measuring current demand. Tourism is a labor-intensive service industry. As such, it is looked upon by state governments as a promising business to relieve unemployment. But one of the main problems is to determine its present financial dimensions.

Official tourism organizations are typically charged with the responsibility of undertaking research to measure economic impact and current demand. In this task they are assisted greatly by the U.S. Travel Data Center. Details on research are provided in Chapter 18. The next research task is to make an estimate of what the future demand might be should certain steps be taken by the destination area.

PROJECTION METHODOLOGY

Several statistical methods or econometric analyses can be used to project demand. All require a degree of statistical or mathematical sophistication, familiarity with computers, and a clear understanding of the purpose (and limitations) of such projections. Listed are several such methods with brief explanations. (For a more complete review, see the references at the end of this chapter.)

Trend Analysis Method

This method involves the interpretation of historical demand data. For instance, if a record of the number of tourist arrivals in an area on an annual basis is available, then demand for future years can be projected using this information. The first step is to plot the available data on a graph: time (in years) against the tourist arrivals. Once this has been done, a linear trend can be established, which best captures the changes in demand levels in the past. Demand projections for future years can now be made by extending the trend line up to the relevant year and reading the demand estimate off the graph. Figure 13.1 illustrates this procedure. The points represent the levels of demand for the six-year period for which data are available.

A linear trend in demand levels can then be determined (say, line *AB*). If a demand projection for year 10 were needed, the trend line *AB* can be extended to a point such as *C*. Finally, the projected demand level in year 10 can be determined to be approximately 180,000 arrivals as shown in Figure 13.1.

The advantage of using trend analysis is that the data needed are rather basic and easy to obtain. Only one data series is required: visitor arrivals, or some other measure of demand on a quarterly or on an annual basis for the past few years. In addition, the method is simple and does not require a great deal of mathematical sophistication. Characteristically, however, the simplicity of the model is to a large extent a trade-off for the usefulness of the results. For instance, the future demand estimates obtained in this manner should be interpreted with a great deal of caution. There are several reasons for this. First, trend analysis does not "explain" demand in any way. In other words, if demand changes from year to year, we would expect this to be due to changes in the components of demand (propensity and resistance, as discussed earlier in this chapter). Trend analysis does not acknowledge the influence that these variables have on demand levels and, therefore, cannot explain why it changed. Second, to *extrapolate* from a linear trend (extending the trend line *AB* to point *C*) is to assume that past growth trends will continue without change. Such an assumption is tentative at best. Estimates based on a constant growth rate tend to become very unrealistic in rather short periods of time, due to the nature of compounding.

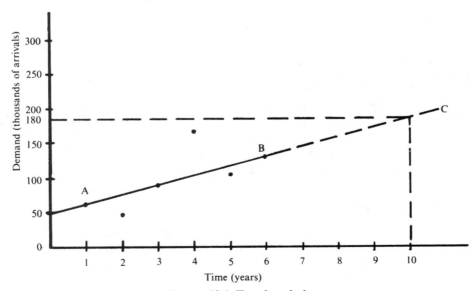

FIGURE 13.1 **Trend analysis.**

Simple Regression: Linear Least Squares Method

In this method, information on demand levels for past years is plotted against one important determinant of demand, say, income or prices. Then, through the application of a statistical technique called **least squares** regression, a straight line is used to "explain" the relationship between demand and the particular variable being considered (such as income levels of tourists). Consider, for example, the hypothetical data in Table 13.1 for demand levels for 10 years and the income levels of tourists for these same years.

By plotting the pairs of arrivals—income data on a graph—we obtain a relationship between income and travel demand, illustrated in Figure 13.2. The points represent the annual observations, and the line *AB* represents the line of "best fit." It is obtained by the least squares method. We can now obtain demand projections from this method based on what we expect income levels to be in the future. Suppose we wish to estimate demand for year 15. In this year, income is projected to be $8300 per capita. As shown in the figure, the estimate of demand for this income level is 128,000.

Because income is a major determinant of demand, simple regression "explains" demand to some extent. It is superior to trend analysis for this reason. Besides, the methodology is still relatively simple and can be presented visually. Data needed for this method are relatively easy to collect, when compared to the data needs of the two following projections methods.

Multiple Regression—Linear Least Squares Method

The major drawback of simple regression is that only one variable can be considered at a time. In reality, demand is affected by all the factors that influence propensity and resistance, as discussed earlier. It may not be feasible to include all these variables at one time, but it is certainly practical to isolate a few that are particularly relevant to determining demand and deal with these in one model. Multiple regression is one way to do this. It is essentially the same as simple regression, except that now more than one variable can be used to explain demand. Through a mathematical formula, a re-

TABLE 13.1
Demand and Income Data

Year	Number of Tourist Arrivals (thousands)	Per Capita Income of Tourists (dollars)
1	75	6300
2	90	7200
3	100	7000
4	105	7400
5	95	6800
6	110	7500
7	105	7500
8	100	7200
9	110	7600
10	120	7900

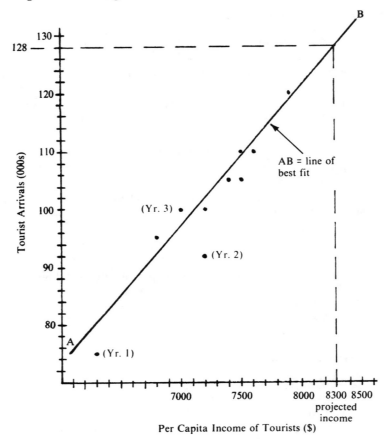

FIGURE 13.2 Relationship between income and travel demand.

lationship is established between demand and the variables that we have chosen to consider in the model. For example, suppose that we had data on the prices of tourist services at a destination in addition to the incomes of the tourists. We could then regress demand on these two variables (income and prices) and obtain a mathematical relationship between them. To estimate future demand, projected income and price levels for the relevant year can simply be substituted into the mathematical formula. The resulting estimate of demand will be more reliable than will one obtained by the simple regression method, because the former incorporates the *combined* effect of income and price on demand.

Indeed, the analysis is not restricted to these two variables alone. Conceptually, any number of variables can be used to explain and predict demand levels. But there are some practical limitations. As the number of "explanatory" variables increases, the calculations become increasingly complex. In addition, the costs involved in collecting the additional data and solving the mathematics of the technique are consider-

Cruise travel is forecasted to continue to be the fastest growing sector of the travel industry. This forecast is based on survey research, past trends, demographics, customer satisfaction, marketing efforts, and new ships joining the fleet. *(Photo by Andy Newman; courtesy of Carnival Cruise Lines.)*

able. In some instances, the incremental reliability of the estimates may not justify these expenses, because estimates are after all only estimates, and not certain to materialize—no matter how comprehensibly they may be calculated.

In addition to the expense involved, another drawback of multiple regression is that the relationships cannot be depicted graphically, as the results of the two earlier methods can be. The reason is, of course, that we get into multidimension planes. Up to three dimensions can be depicted visually; but beyond that, it becomes impossible.

Computer Simulations and Models

The essence of this approach is building a computer model that will simulate tourist demand. Typically, the demand for tourism to a particular area is a function of factors such as levels of income of tourists, the cost of travel from the tourists' homes to the destination, price levels, competition, currency exchange rates, and distance or journey time. These relationships are usually identified using multiple regression, as discussed above.

Simulation models include a complex set of equations that will usually combine both the trend-line extrapolation methods and the regression techniques models into a more comprehensive systems simulation. Relationships between many variables are specified through interrelated equations. Simulation models rely on historical data for input and model calibration. Once a model gives reasonably accurate distributions for past years, it can be used to predict probable future distributions.

Simulation models require specially trained personnel with a high degree of technical expertise to set up original model and data processing programs. Knowledge of time-series, cross-sectional, and causal relationships and change processes is required. Also, powerful computing resources and high data precision are necessary. These are serious problems that have to be faced by any tourism organization that might consider using this approach. Simulation forecasting is best suited for a problem that is complex with known and quantifiable relationships and some feedback effects. It is also suitable for long forecast horizons.

Executive Judgment (Delphi) Method

Mathematical and statistical models are most useful and often produce accurate results. However, the combined experience of tourism executives is also valuable. The **Delphi method,** in essence, consists of a systematic survey of such experts. A series of questions is asked, and then the results, as a consensus, are reached.

Mathematical–statistical tools cannot incorporate the influences of variables not explicitly included in the model. For example, under multiple regression, income and travel prices were the only two variables used to predict demand. However, other factors such as the political situation, fuel situation, changes in taste, amounts of leisure, and the effectiveness of promotion campaigns obviously have an impact on demand levels. By the Delphi method, the combined effects of all such factors are carefully considered from the base of the executive's experience. For estimating tourism demand, then, *a combination of various mathematical statistical methods and the Delphi method* is believed to produce the most reliable demand estimates in any given situation.

SUMMARY

Demand, without doubt, is the fundamental measure of any area's success in attracting visitors. All planning activities are ultimately intended to increase or control demand. Marketing programs are aimed at increasing demand, sometimes at certain periods during the year, and/or to attract particularly identified market segments.

Understanding demand requires a knowledge of its definition, what comprises demand, what affects the levels of demand, and how future demand can be identified and estimated. Thus, use of demand data is essential in any tourist business situation.

Development of a destination area, whether by public authority, private developers, or both, requires demand data that are as accurate as possible. Providing such data is one of the most important responsibilities of an official tourism organization. Similar data are provided by research organizations and consulting firms, usually when commissioned to make feasibility studies. Any development proposal must have ample estimates of expected demand before any financing can be committed.

Becoming familiar with methods of measuring or estimating present and future demand, as described in this chapter, should enable you to produce such data. With the current high cost of land and construction, reasonably accurate demand statistics are of paramount importance.

KEY CONCEPTS

amounts spent	executive judgment (Delphi method)	seasonality
arrivals	linear least squares method	simple regression
computer simulation	multiple regression	tax collections
cost of services	projection methodology	trend analysis
cultural distance	propensity	visitors
demand	quality of service	visitor-days
economic distance	resistance	visitor-nights

INTERNET SITES

**Organization for Economic
    Cooperation and Development**
http://www.oecd.org

Tourism Industries
http://tinet.ita.doc.gov

Travel Industry Association of America
http://www.tia.org

World Tourism Organization
http://www.world-tourism.org

World Travel and Tourism Council
http://www.wttc.org

INTERNET EXERCISES

Activity 1

Site Name: Tourism Policy Council

URL: http://tpcnet.doc.gov/main/index.html

Background Information: The Tourism Policy Council was established to "ensure that the United States' national interest in tourism is fully considered in Federal decision making." It coordinates programs, policies, and issues related to tourism, recreation, or national heritage resources involving federal departments, agencies, or other entities. It is charged with developing areas of cooperative program activity and assisting in resolving interagency programs and policy conflicts.

Exercise

1. What statistical data are available at this web site that would help a tourism professional determine the demand for travel and tourism?

Activity 2

Site Name: STAT-USA/Internet

URL: http://www.stat-usa.gov/

Background Information: STAT-USA/Internet, a service of the U.S. Department of Commerce, is a site for the U.S. business, economic, and trade community, providing authoritative information from the Federal government.

Exercises

1. What information does the National Trade Data Bank (NTDB) provide?

2. What publications are available to the public from this organization?

QUESTIONS FOR REVIEW AND DISCUSSION

1. Why are demand data so important? Give examples. By whom are demand data used?

2. Explain why resistance to make a trip is inversely related to demand. Are there situations with which you are familiar? Explain.

3. Describe in detail the three factors that determine propensity to travel. Create an example using all three of these major elements.

4. What determines the degree of resistance to travel experiences? Considering the five factors described in this chapter, give an example involving (1) an irresistible travel offer and (2) a seasonal travel product.

5. Using the three measures of demand presented, describe a situation in which each one of these would be the most meaningful.

6. A state tourism director wants to convince the legislature to increase the promotion budget for the next fiscal year. What measure of demand should be used? How might these data be obtained?

7. How much faith should be placed in mathematical models of demand projection? What characteristics of input data affect the degree of reliability?

8. A national lodging chain is planning expansion. What are the best methods for estimating future demand?

9. How valuable is trend analysis?

10. What is the Delphi method?

CASE PROBLEMS

1. Assume that the federal government has imposed an increase in the gasoline tax of 50 cents per gallon, effective in three months. How might a motel franchise headquarters organization estimate the effect on demand that this new tax would have for their member motels, which are located in all parts of the country? How could a restaurant chain organization operating turnpike food services make such an estimate? How could a regional airline?

2. Byron C. is director of development for a major hotel systems firm. His company has formulated a new concept in resort-type overnight and longer-stay accommodations. The new suites will possess an exciting array of electronic entertainment features, including a large screen, stereo sound, movies, compact discs, and cassette players. Understandably, these suites are quite expensive to build. Thus, reasonably accurate demand forecasts are essential. Byron C. has tentatively selected your city as a location for the first of these new suite concepts. As executive vice-president of your city's convention and visitors bureau, what method would you use to assist Mr. C. in making these crucial demand estimates?

SELECTED REFERENCES

Crouch, Geoffrey I. "The Study of International Tourism Demand." *Journal of Travel Research,* Vol. 32, No. 4, pp. 41–53, Spring 1994.

Crouch, Geoffrey I. "The Study of International Tourism Demand: A Review of Findings." *Journal of Travel Research,* Vol. 33, No. 1, pp. 12–23, Summer 1994.

Crouch, Geoffrey I. "A Meta-Analysis of Tourism Demand." *Annals of Tourism Research,* Vol. 22, No. 1, pp. 103–118, 1995.

Cruz, Tony Dela. "Forecast' 98." *Hotels: The Magazine of the Worldwide Hotel Industry,* Vol. 32, No. 1, pp. 48–56, 1998.

Edwards, Anthony. *Asia-Pacific Travel Forecasts to 2005.* London: The Economist Intelligence Unit, 1995.

Faulkner, Bill, and Peter Valerio. "An Integrative Approach to Tourism Demand Forecasting." *Tourism Management,* Vol. 16, No. 1, pp. 29–37, February 1995.

Frechtling, Douglas C. *Practical Tourism Forecasting.* Oxford, UK: Butterworth-Heinemann, 1996.

Johnson, Peter, and Barry Thomas. *Choice and Demand.* London: Mansell Publishing, 1992.

Lim, Christine. "An Economic Classification and Review of International Tourism Demand Models." *Tourism Economics,* Vol. 3, No. 1, pp. 69–82, March 1997.

Lim, Christine. "Review of International Tourism Demand Models." *Annals of Tourism Research,* Vol. 24, No. 4, pp. 835–849, October 1997.

Morley, Clive L. "A Microeconomic Theory of International Tourism Demand." *Annals of Tourism Research,* Vol. 19, No. 2, pp. 250–267, 1992.

Morley, Clive L. "A Comparison of Three Models for Estimating Tourism Demand Models." *Tourism Economics,* Vol. No. 3, pp. 223–235, September 1996.

Morley, Clive L. "An Evaluation of the Use of Ordinary Least Squares for Estimating Tourism Demand Models." *Journal of Travel Research,* Vol. 35, No. 4, pp. 69–74, Spring 1997.

Morley, Clive L. "A Dynamic International Demand Model." *Annals of Tourism Research,* Vol. 25, No. 1, pp. 70–84, January 1998.

Moutinho, Luiz, and Stephen F. Witt. "Forecasting the Tourism Environment Using a Consensus Approach." *Journal of Travel Research,* Vol. 33, No. 4, pp. 46–50, Spring 1995.

Pearce, Douglas G. "Analyzing the Demand for Urban Tourism: Issues and Examples from Paris." *Tourism Analysis,* Vol. 1, pp. 5–18, 1996.

Schwartz, Zvi, and Stephen Hiemstra. "Improving the Accuracy of Hotel Reservations Forecasting: Curves Similarity Approach." *Journal of Travel Research,* Vol. 36, No. 1, pp. 3–14, Summer 1997.

Sheldon, Pauline J. "The Demand for Incentive Travel: An Empirical Study." *Journal of Travel Research,* Vol. 33, No. 4, pp. 23–28, Spring 1995.

Smeral, Egon, and Stephen F. Witt. "The Impacts of Eastern Europe and 1992 on International Tourism Demand." *Tourism Management,* Vol. 13, No. 4, pp. 368–376, December 1992.

Smeral, Egon, and Stephen F. Witt. "Econometric Forecasts of Tourism Demand to 2005." *Annals of Tourism Research,* Vol. 23, No. 4, pp. 891–907, October 1996.

Spotts, Daniel M., and Edward M. Mahoney. "Understanding the Fall Tourism Market." *Journal of Travel Research,* Vol. 32, No. 2, pp. 3–15, Fall 1993.

Travel Industry Association of America. *1998 Outlook for Travel and Tourism.* Washington: D.C.: TIA, 1997.

Turner, L. N. Kulendran, and H. Fernando. "The Use of Composite National Indicators for Tourism Forecasting." *Tourism Economics,* Vol. 3, No. 4, pp. 309–318, 1997.

U.S. Travel Data Center. *National Travel Survey: Full-Year Report.* Washington, D.C.: USTDC, annual.

Uysal, Muzaffer, and John L. Crompton. "An Overview of Approaches Used to Forecast Tourism Demand." *Journal of Travel Research,* Vol. 23, No. 3, pp. 7–15, Spring 1985.

Waters, Somerset R. *Travel Industry World Yearbook: The Big Picture.* New York: Child and Waters, annual.

Witt, Stephen F. "Tourism Forecasting: How Well Do Private and Public Sector Organizations Perform?" *Tourism Management,* Vol. 13, No. 1, pp. 79–84, March 1992.

Witt, Stephen F., and Christine A. Martin. "Econometric Model for Forecasting International Tourism Demand." *Journal of Travel Research,* Vol. 25, No. 3, pp. 23–30, Winter 1987.

Witt, Stephen F., and Christine A. Witt. *Modeling and Forecasting Demand in Tourism.* London: Academic Press, 1992.

Zalatan, Antoine. *Forecasting Methods in Sports and Recreation.* Toronto: Thompson Educational Publishing, Inc., 1994.

CHAPTER 14

TOURISM'S ECONOMIC IMPACT

- Know the economic generators and impact of tourism.
- Perceive the economic importance of tourism in various regions of the world.
- Know about tourism satellite accounts.

- Understand multipliers.
- Know about balance of payments.
- Comprehend elasticity and inelasticity.

◀ **LEARNING OBJECTIVES**

◀ *The bustling Nakamise shopping lane of Sensoji Temple.*
(Photo courtesy of the Japan Information Center.)

INTRODUCTION

Tourism is a powerful economic force providing employment, foreign exchange, income, and tax revenue. The generators of **economic impact** for a city, a state, a province, a country, or a destination area are visitors, their expenditures, and the multiplier effect. The economic impact of tourism spending is a function of the numbers of domestic and international visitors and their expenditures. Because of the economic importance of tourism, the World Tourism Organization (WTO) maintains statistics by region and country on tourism arrivals (visitors) and both tourism expenditures (what a country spends) and receipts (what a country receives from visitor expenditures). Tourism destinations are becoming increasingly competitive as more and more destinations look at tourism to become the new economic generator replacing declining activity in agriculture, mining, and manufacturing.

NUMBER OF VISITORS AND RECEIPTS

WTO reports that there were 612,835,000 tourist arrivals in 1997. Table 14.1 shows world tourism arrivals and receipts by region. These are key indicators of economic performance and important benchmarks to trace growth or decline from. While the growth of tourists arrivals slowed from a dramatic 5.5 percent in 1996 to a solid 3.0 percent in 1997 largely due to the Asian economic problems, this was an increase of over 18 million arrivals. World tourism receipts grew from $434 billion to $444 billion, for a 2.3 percent increase.

An analysis of regional performance shown in Table 14.1 reveals the following.

Africa

Arrivals rose by 9.2 percent to more than 23 million in 1997, while receipts increased by 4.5 percent to $8.7 billion. The best-performing regions were Southern Africa, led by strong growth in South Africa, Eastern Africa, and the Indian Ocean islands as well as more traditional destinations such as Zimbabwe and Tanzania.

Americas

Growth fell below the world average, with arrivals increasing by 2 percent to 119 million and receipts climbing by over 6 percent to $120 billion in 1997. In North America, the United States showed the strongest growth, up 5.5 percent in terms of arrivals and 7.4 percent in terms of receipts. Arrivals to the Caribbean region grew by 6.8 percent to 15.4 million in 1997, largely due to increasing cruise passenger arrivals. South America also fared well, with arrivals climbing by 6.5 percent to 15.4 million.

East Asia and the Pacific

Tourism arrivals rose by only 1.1 percent in 1997 and receipts grew only 2 percent, with the poorest results coming from Northeastern Asia.

TABLE 14.1

International Tourist Arrivals and Receipts by Region

	Tourist Arrivals (thousands)		Percent Change		Tourist Receipts (US$ million)		Percent Change	
	1996	1997	97/96	96/95	1996	1997	97/96	96/95
World	594,827	612,835	3.0	5.5	433,863	443,770	2.3	8.1
Africa	21,553	23,537	9.2	7.1	8,334	8,712	4.5	14.8
Americas	116,673	119,056	2.0	5.5	112,854	120,251	6.6	9.7
East Asia/Pacific	89,186	90,163	1.1	9.6	81,3352	83,153	2.2	10.1
Europe	348,999	360,774	3.4	4.5	219,670	218,918	-0.3	6.2
Middle East	14,084	14,759	4.8	4.6	7,739	8,585	10.9	8.8
South Asia	4,332	4,546	4.9	3.1	3,914	4,151	6.1	11.1

Source: World Tourism Organization (WTO).

413

Europe

A good tourism year was experienced by European countries in 1997, with arrivals growing by 3.4 percent to almost 361 million and receipts down slightly (0.3 percent) to $219 billion. Traditional destinations in Western and Northern Europe were preferred, especially France (+7 percent), Switzerland (+4.5 percent), Ireland (+4.9 percent), and the United Kingdom, which showed an increase of 2.6 percent in arrivals despite its very strong currency. The emerging destinations of Eastern and Central Europe fared less well in 1997, but Southern European and Mediterranean countries had another season of solid growth, especially Spain (+7 percent), Greece (+11 percent), Cyprus (+6.9 percent), and Turkey (+13.5 percent).

Middle East

Spurred by a good winter season in 1996–1997, tourist arrivals to the Middle East grew by 4.8 percent to nearly 15 million and receipts climbed by 10.9 percent to $8.6 billion in 1997. Egypt, which accounts for half the region's arrivals, reports an increase of 3.7 percent in arrivals and 20 percent in receipts, despite cancellations at the end of the year due to violence in Luxor. Arrivals to Jordan were up by 7.4 percent, and the Gulf countries continued to show strong gains in tourism. The only exception was Israel, which suffered a drop of nearly 2 percent in tourist arrivals.

South Asia

An increase in arrivals of 4.9 percent, to 4.6 million, and an increase of 6.1 percent in receipts to $4.1 billion marked a very positive year for tourism in South Asia. India, which accounts for half of all arrivals, showed an increase of 3.9 percent. Sri Lanka showed a spectacular turnaround, posting gains of 23.5 percent in arrivals and 35.7 percent in earnings. Tourism to the Maldives and Nepal grew steadily in 1997, while Pakistan declined for a third consecutive year.

EMPLOYMENT

The world tourism industry is not only important as a generator of income, but also as a generator of **employment.** The World Travel and Tourism Council (WTTC) argues that tourism is overlooked as an employer by those unfamiliar with tourism, its workforce, and its potential for growth. WTTC anticipates 100 million jobs being created in the tourism sector within the next decade. They estimate that tourism's economic activity generated about 231 million jobs in 1998, or about one in nine workers worldwide. WTTC projects that 328 million jobs to be generated by tourism jobs will increase faster than traditional industries by as much as 59 percent.

Tourism provides both direct and indirect employment. Firms such as hotels, restaurants, airlines, cruise lines, and resorts provide direct employment because their employees are in contact with tourists providing the tourist experience. Employees of firms providing goods and services to the direct employment firms such as aircraft manufacturers, construction firms, and restaurant suppliers create indirect employment.

The impact of this can be illustrated using a United States example. In 1996 the TIA Foundation sponsored a study entitled "A Portrait of Travel Industry Employment in the U.S. Economy." Table 14.2 shows that in 1995, travel and tourism directly generated 6.6 million jobs in the U.S. economy and illustrates employment by sector.

Travelers in the United States produce "secondary" impacts over and above that of their original expenditures. These secondary outputs (sales) and earnings (wage and salary income), supported by this **"indirect"** and **"induced"** spending, add an additional 8.9 million jobs to the U.S. economy. With the almost 5.7 million jobs in 1995 generated directly by domestic travel spending, and the 970,000 employment opportunities generated directly by the international travel to the United States, total U.S. employment created by the travel and tourism industry was 15.5 million in 1995.

TOURISM SATELLITE ACCOUNTS

The World Tourism Organization (WTO), the World Travel and Tourism Council (WTTC), the Canadian Tourism Commission (CTC), the Travel Industry Association of America (TIA), and others have attempted to measure the economic impact of tourism for some time only to be met with complaints such as: "All the hype about tourism's contribution to economic growth and job creation is a gross exaggeration."

TABLE 14.2
Direct Travel-Generated Employment by Industry Category, 1994 and 1995p[a]
(Employees in Thousands)

	1994	1995p	Percent of Total	Percent Change
Public transportation	890.9	931.0	16.5	4.5
Auto transportation	225.9	229.3	4.1	1.5
Lodging	1059.1	1076.0	19.0	1.6
Foodservice	1926.8	2000.0	35.4	3.8
Entertainment/recreation	831.6	894.8	15.8	7.6
General retail	301.4	312.3	5.5	3.6
Travel planning	204.3	210.6	3.7	3.1
Total	**5440.0**	**5654.0**	**100.0**	**3.9**
International visitor-generated[b]	947.9	970.4	2.4	2.4
Grand total	**6387.9**	**6624.4**	**100.0**	**3.7**

[a] p = preliminary.

[b] Data on employment generated by International visitor spending not available by category.

Source: Travel Industry Association of America; Tourism Industries/International Trade Administration.

Consequently, ways have been sought to provide data on national tourism industries that are creditable, consistent, and comparable to statistics provided for other industries.

The answer appears to be **Tourism Satellite Account** (TSA). The purpose of the travel and tourism satellite accounts is to provide a framework for analyzing tourism expenditures in a systematic and consistent way that links tourism demand expenditures to the industries that produce tourism goods and services. The tourism satellite account is a relatively new practice adapted by some countries and now embraced by WTO and WTTC, who have cooperated to develop an international standard for travel and tourism satellite accounting. WTTC believes the development of travel and tourism satellite accounting is perhaps the most important event in the study of tourism economics in recent times. See Reading 14.1 for a brief discussion and a model of the WTTC/WEFA tourism satellite account.

Some of the earliest TSA work has been done in Canada. The British Columbia Ministry of Development, Trade and Tourism, British Columbia, Canada, has developed a tourism satellite account and a separate input–output model designed to display tourism's contributions based on the overall input–output model for the province. A TSA has also been developed by Statistics Canada to assess the economic contribution of tourism to Canada. Similar accounts have been developed in Sweden and the United States.

There are a number of descriptions of TSA available; however, the articles and monographs are written for technical audiences and do not provide an easy introduction to the subject. One article that is highly recommended is "The Tourism Satellite Account: Perspectives of Canadian Tourism Associations and Organizations" by Stephen L. J. Smith in *Tourism Economics.*

The TSA holds great promise for the future. It should lead to more reliable, credible tourism impact estimates and forecasts. The advantages of the tourism satellite accounts are as follows:

- TSA provides the individual components of tourism with their first system of National Accounts (SNA) based portrait of the industry as a totality. This will contribute to greater credibility as internationally agreed SNAs are used.

- TSA provides a comprehensive picture of the size and scale of tourism in a province or country that will assist both business and government to determine the value of tourism to the economy.

- TSA can support certain types of simulation analyses. It can be used to improve the accuracy of local economic impact models by providing national ratios of expenditure for accommodation, food and beverages, transportation, and so on.

OPTIMIZATION

Economics is concerned with the attainment of an **optimum** return from the use of scarce resources. Whether it is a person seeking psychological benefit from travel, or a business interested in providing tourists goods and services at a profit, or a host community government viewing tourism in terms of the economic benefits resulting from tourist expenditures, the principle is the same. Economic agents seek to fulfill psychological and physical wants (which, as a rule, are limited). The problem that economics attempts to solve is how these scarce resources should be allocated in the pursuit of a variety of unfulfilled needs and wants.

Hawaii is a beehive of economic activity, with visitors filling hotels, renting cars, enjoying the beach, eating at restaurants, and purchasing souvenirs. (*Photo courtesy of American Airlines.*)

Goals

As indicated, at least three major goals can be identified in tourism:

1. Maximize the amount of psychological experience for tourists.
2. Maximize profits for firms providing goods and services to tourists.
3. Maximize the **direct** (primary) and **indirect** (secondary) impacts of tourist expenditures on a community or region.

These goals are often compatible; maximizing psychological experience creates happy clientele, which causes them to return, to spend money, and to make everyone in the industry and the region satisfied. In certain situations, they can also be incompatible. A short-run profit-maximizing goal may cause the development of facilities beyond capacity of the site, thus leading to overuse and a decline in psychic enjoyment. Extreme emphasis on tourism as an element in economic development might have the same result. There can also be clashes between use of resources for tourism and for other kinds of development.

Constraints

The second half of the optimizing situation is occupied by those factors that place obstacles in the way of goal attainment. We assume that it is desirable to have unlimited amounts of psychic enjoyment, profits, and local impacts. But that is not possible because something is always getting in the way. Tourism, being extremely broad and diverse, must deal with a large number of constraints. To make an analysis of relationships, it will be necessary to classify them.

Demand

Every firm providing goods and services to tourists is constrained by the **demand** functions of its customers. These relate quantity purchased to price, wealth, and income.

Supply of Attractive Resources

Possibly one of the most important constraints faced by the industry as a whole is the limited amount of resources available for tourist enjoyment. This is particularly true when geographic distribution of these sites is considered. Some areas are simply better attractions for tourists than others.

Technical and Environmental Constraints

These are usually related to a particular site or situation. They involve such things as the relationship between sewage effluent disposal and the environment, numbers of fish and numbers of fishermen, number of people who can walk in a given area without causing unacceptable damage, number of elephants supportable on a wildlife range, impact on lions' behavior of observing them from a car, number of campsites possible in a given area without harming the environment, and so on.

Time Constraints

The amount of vacation time available limits what the vacationer can do. The length of the tourist season influences profitability of tourist-oriented businesses and the impact of tourist expenditures on the local economy.

Indivisibilities

Many times it is necessary to deal with all of something or nothing. It is not possible to fly half an airplane, even though the seats are only half filled. It may not be profitable to build a hotel under a given size. A road has to be built all the way from one point to another.

Legal Constraints

There are several types of legal constraints affecting tourism. Activities of the government tourist bureau might be one. Laws concerning environmental problems could be another. Zoning and building codes may influence the construction of facilities. Laws concerning contractual relations may limit activities.

Self-Imposed Constraints

This type of constraint arises from a need to reconcile conflicting goals. The conflicts may arise within a firm or among firms, government agencies, and so on, that are seeking to develop a particular area or concept.

Lack of Knowledge

Many activities are limited because little is known about particular situations. Businesspeople are used to living with a certain amount of uncertainty, but there are inevitable limits to the amount they are willing to countenance. Ignorance influences governmental operations as well.

Limits on Supportive Resources

There are always limits to the amount of money, managerial talent, workers, construction materials, social capital, and so on. And these, in turn, limit chances to provide psychic experiences, take advantage of profit-making opportunities, or develop local attractions.

Many times these individual constraints interact, creating compound constraints on given activities.

Optimizing the Experience

Maximization of the tourist experience is subject to a number of constraints and is manifested in the demand function. Demand for tourist experience is peculiar in the sense that the product being purchased is not easy to identify directly and is frequently purchased sight unseen.

The tourist is particularly constrained by time and budget. To optimize the experience, it is necessary to determine the combination of destinations preferred and then the possibilities within the money and time constraints. This explains some of the popularity of package tours, where both time and cost can be known in advance. There are some exceptions. Retired persons and young people often have time but limited resources. A few people have neither constraint.

Optimizing Returns to Businesses

Because goods and services provided to tourists are really inputs to the process of producing the experience, demand for them is derived from demand for tourism as a whole. Some goods and services are complementary, and their demand is interrelated in a positive fashion. Others are substitutes and are characterized by limited area competition.

Packaged tours have the characteristic of putting all parts and services together, so they become complementary. Competition occurs among tours. Tour operators can maximize profits by selling tours of different value and costs, in order to cater to as many people as possible along the demand curve. The number of people to be accommodated can be determined from the marginal cost of the tour and the marginal revenue to be derived from a given price level.

Goods and services sold to tourists are subject to severe peaking in demand. That is, the heaviest tourist season is usually limited. During that period, demand is intense and must be met with facilities that are excess in the off-season. This means that investment necessary to provide the excess capacity must be paid for from revenues received during the peak period. During off-peak periods, only variable cost is of interest, but, because demand is low, some capacity will not be utilized.

As owner of the facilities, firms are concerned with providing adequate long-run capacity and with choosing those investments that will give optimum returns. In the tourist industry, a number of interrelationships must be considered. Sometimes, low benefit–cost investments are made so that higher yielding investments can succeed. Consequently, it is not always true that investors choose the highest-yielding opportunities.

Generally, it is considered the long-run business of the firm to remove constraints on operations. But in tourism there are a number of constraints to expansion. These include demand for the tourist experience and environmental constraints.

Optimizing for the Local Economy

Tourism affects a region during periods of intense investment activity and afterward when the investments are producing. The effects depend on linkages among economic units. Money spent for investment will go to construction and a few other industrial sectors. These will have links to economic units varying from households to manufacturing plants. Money spent by tourists will also be introduced through a few sectors that will also be linked to the economy.

The **multiplier** effects in both cases are dependent upon the strength of the linkages. The multiplier reflects the amount of new economic activity generated as basic income circulates through the economy. Some sectors have strong links to other sectors in an economy and a large multiplier effect. Others have weak links and small multipliers. It is possible to have a thriving tourist industry and abject poverty in the local populace, if there are not links. For example, linkages will be strong and the income multiplier high if the year-round resorts in a particular destination area hire all local labor; buy their flowers, fruit, and vegetables and poultry products from local farmers; hire local entertainers; and buy furnishings for guest rooms from local manufacturers. Linkages would be weak if most of these goods and services were imported from another state or country.

North Americans traveling in Morocco spend money in the country and bring travel experiences home with them. By doing so, these tourists create export income for Morocco. *(Photo by the author.)*

Tourism Exports and Imports

The host region is defined loosely as a country, a state, or a nation, depending on the level at which the problem is being considered. For a county-level government, the income of the county is of primary interest. A state government would perceive the maximization of the combined income of the entire state to be its objective, and so on. Regardless of which definition of host region is being considered, expenditures in this area by tourists coming from another region represent injections into the area's economy.

Japanese traveling to the United States presumably earned their income in Japan. When spending money in the United States as tourists, they are "injecting" money into our economy that wasn't here before. As such, expenditures by foreigners in this country (for travel purposes) represent tourism **exports** for the United States. This may be somewhat confusing because we are accustomed to thinking of something leaving the country as an export. When we export computers or cars, for example, these commodities are sent out of the United States. In the example of the Japanese tourists, the tourists are coming into this country. So how is it an export? There seems to be a contradiction in terminology. As the astute student would note, however, when tourists come into this country, they are purchasing travel experiences. When they leave, they take these experiences back with them. We have exported travel experiences, which are, after all, what tourism is all about.

Figure 14.1 clarifies this concept. When U.S. tourists travel to Japan and spend money there, this becomes a tourism **import** to the U.S. economy. For the Japanese, their money spent in the United States is a tourism import for the Japanese economy.

In tourism exports, the flows of tourists and payments are in the same direction, whereas in commodity exports, the two flows are in opposite directions. Therein lies the confusion. However, if one were to look at the *direction of payment flow* to determine what is an export, there is no contradiction between the two cases. When payment flows into the United States, something has been exported—

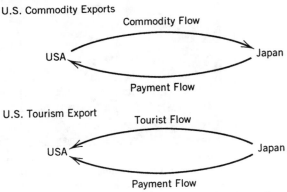

FIGURE 14.1 Economic comparison—commodity flows and tourist flows.

travel experiences, for instance, or commodities. Both payment flows are in the same direction.

Balance-of-Payments Effects

Tourism is one of the world's largest international industries. As such, it has a noticeable impact on the **balance of payments** of many nations. We have heard much about the balance-of-payments problems of the United States, and, indeed, tourism imports do affect the balance of payments and economic conditions generally. We define tourism imports as those expenditures made by American tourists in foreign countries. An easy way to remember this is "Who got the money?" If, for example, Britain received American funds, it makes no difference whether we bought some English china or an American tourist visited England.

Our balance-of-payments situation directly affects the gross national product of the United States (Y). The formula is

$$Y = C + I + G + (X - M)$$

where

Y = GNP

C = consumer expenditures

I = investments

G = government expenditures

X = exports

M = imports

By looking at the formula, we can see that if imports (M) exceed exports (X), it will be a negative number and Y will thus be smaller. Thus, it is advantageous to us in our American economy to attract more visitor spending in the United States. These "tourism exports" are like credits and help our economy. It is economically better to have foreign visitors come to the United States than it is to have U.S. citizens travel abroad. However, this should be tempered with the realization that the situation is not entirely positive or negative.

Expenditures by U.S. tourists abroad make possible purchasing power in foreign countries for those countries to buy American-made products. For example, most airlines of the world use American-made equipment. Purchase of these aircraft, parts, supplies, repair services, and so forth, makes an important contribution to the export trade of the United States; thus, we cannot charge the U.S. international traveler with a total negative balance of payments. The purpose of the foregoing discussion is simply to point out the relationships.

Tourism exports become very desirable as far as the gross national product and the prosperity of the country are concerned. Efforts on the part of National Tourism Offices to attract foreign visitors have a great impact on the balance-of-payments situation. Business firms, which serve the foreign visitor, provide desired services, and stimulate sales, materially help our national economy. However, during periods when the U.S. dollar is high against foreign currencies, a dampening effect occurs on our tourism exports because this situation is seen as unfavorable by prospective foreign visitors. Conversely, if the dollar is low, more foreign tourists will visit the United States. This increases our tourism exports, improves our balance of payments, and raises the gross national product. These same relationships of comparable currency values exist between any country that exports tourism and the countries of its tourists' origin.

In 1998 the value of the Canadian dollar was low in comparison to the U.S. dollar and illustrated this principle. Americans visiting Canada to take advantage of the exchange rate increased dramatically (see box). This contributed positively to Canada's balance of payments.

Investment Stimulation

The tourist industry has a unique structure. It is characterized by, and, in fact, is, an agglomeration of a large number of very small units, covering a variety of different service trades—the small restaurants, motels, guest houses, laundries, arts and crafts shops, and others. Thus, investment in infrastructure and sometimes expensive superstructure by the government stimulates investment in numerous smaller businesses. Because of the small size of these businesses, capital requirements are relatively low and investment generally proceeds at a rapid pace. In this respect, too, governments view tourism rather favorably. The initial investment in tourism brings forth a large investment in supporting and tertiary industries. This also includes large investments in major hotels, restaurants, shopping centers, marinas, airports, and so on.

Tourism Increases Tax Revenue

Tourists must pay **taxes** like most other people. Because they come from other regions or countries, their expenditures represent an increased tax base for the host govern-

---

AMERICAN TOURISTS FLOCKING TO CANADA
▼

"Canada has never seen anything like it. More tourists are pouring across our borders and spending more money than ever before. "It is extremely clear to us we are heading for a record year," said Canadian Tourism Commission spokesman John Olsthoorn. "Our deficit is already lower than its been in 10 years, and we are only talking January to June. We haven't even got to the summer months of July and August." The depressed value of the Canadian dollar is one clear reason for the massive swing in the American market. But Mr. Olsthoorn suggests there are other factors. "Americans are being lured here because they are becoming more and more aware of what we have to offer," he said. "They are travelling because their economy is good and because we have what they want to see and do." "There is a raised awareness that we are a preferred destination for Americans. And once they get here, they discover what their dollar can buy them. Honestly, most of them don't realize this before they arrive." "Consequently, they are spending more and staying longer.'"

Source: The Ottawa Citizen, September 11, 1998.

ment. In addition to the usual sales tax, tourists sometimes pay taxes in less direct ways. Airport taxes, exit fees, customs duty, and charges assessed for granting visas are just a few examples of commonly used methods of taxing tourists. The wisdom of imposing such special taxes on tourists is questionable, because it merely serves to reduce demand. In some countries, for instance, the room rate at a hotel can be different for tourists (generally higher) than for residents. This is a questionable practice, because it leaves the tourist with a feeling that he has been "taken." Apart from these special cases, the usual taxes collected from both tourists and residents increase due to tourism expenditures.

Is tourism, then, a panacea for all the economic woes of a region or country? It has been claimed that tourism increases incomes, employment, investment, tax revenues, and so forth, so it might indeed appear to be one. However, there are constraints that limit the extent to which governments can maximize the benefit from these aspects of tourism. These constraints are of two types: social and economic. The social constraints have already been discussed. The economic constraints are in the form of potential economic costs that the tourism industry may impose. These merit further scrutiny to gain a better understanding of the government's optimization problem.

Inflationary Pressure

Tourists inject money (earned elsewhere) into the destination economy. While this increases the income of the region (as discussed earlier), it also might cause **inflationary pressures.** Tourists typically have a higher expenditure capability than the residents do—either because tourists have higher incomes or because they have saved for the trip and are inclined to "splurge" while on vacation. Hence, they are able to somewhat bid up the prices of such commodities as food, transportation, and arts and crafts. This causes inflationary pressures, which can be detrimental to the economic welfare of residents of the host community. This is particularly true when inflation affects the prices of essentials such as food, clothing, transportation, and housing. Land prices have been known to escalate rapidly in tourist destination areas. The prices that foreigners are willing to pay for "vacation homes" in the area can decrease the demand for "first homes" by residents.

Lundberg[1] notes that as the tourist industry developed in an area, land prices rose sharply. In a particular underdeveloped area, the amount of investment in land constituted just 1 percent of the total investment for a hotel project. By contrast, this ratio increased to 20 percent in an area where tourism was already overdeveloped. With such increases in land prices, it can be expected that local residents (with their lower incomes) are effectively "chased out" of the housing market in a tourism-developing section.

---

[1] Donald E. Lundberg, "Caribbean Tourism," *The Cornell Hotel and Restaurant Administration Quarterly*, Vol. 14, No. 4 (February 1974), pp. 30–45.

ECONOMIC MULTIPLIERS

Direct Effect

In addition to the direct impact of tourism expenditures on an area, there are also indirect impacts. The indirect or **multiplier** impact comes into play as visitor spending circulates and recirculates. The direct effects are the easiest to understand because they result from the visitor spending money in tourist enterprises and providing a living for the owners and managers and creating jobs for employees.

Indirect Effect

This visitor expenditure gives rise to an income that, in turn, leads to a chain of expenditure–income–expenditure, and so on, until leakages bring the chain to a halt.

The money spent by tourists circulates and recirculates, creating an economic multiplier. *(Photo courtesy of Vermont Department of Tourism and Marketing.)*

Consequently, the impact of the initial income derived from the tourist's expenditure is usually greater than the initial income, because subsequent rounds of spending are related to it. For example, a skier purchases a lift ticket for $40. This money received by the ski area will be used to pay the wages of the lift operators. The lift operator spends the money on groceries; the grocer uses the money to pay part of his rent to the local landlady; the landlady uses it to pay for her dry cleaning; the dry cleaner spends it in a restaurant for a dinner; the restaurant owner spends it for steaks shipped in from Kansas City; and the cycle stops as the money is lost to the local economy. This last transaction is known as "leakage" from the economy.

The combination of the direct and indirect effects of an expenditure pattern determines the impact. In a typical situation, not all of the income generated in each round of expenditure is respent. Some portion tends to be saved, and some portion tends to be spent outside the local economy. The greater the proportion of income spent locally, the greater will be the multiplier.

The degree to which a local area is able to retain tourist income depends on how self-sufficient the local economy is. If the local economy is able to produce the goods and services tourists buy, the greater will be the multiplier effect. The more goods that have to be imported from outside the region, the smaller the multiplier will be.

From the discussion, it is clear that when a tourist's spending injects funds into the economy of a host area, an economic effect occurs that is a specified number of times what was originally spent. Initially, this effect is thought of as an *income multiplier*, as tourist expenditures become income directly and indirectly to local people. However, there are additional economic phenomena. Increased spending necessitates more jobs, which results in an *employment multiplier*. Because money changes hands a number of times during a year, there is a transactions multiplier. This is of particular interest to governmental tax officials where sales taxes are imposed. As business grows in a tourist destination area, more infrastructure and superstructure are constructed. This results in a *capital multiplier*. Examples are provided here of how an employment multiplier and an income multiplier were determined.

Employment Multiplier

This multiplier varies from region to region depending on its economic base. In a study entitled *Recreation as an Industry*, by Robert R. Nathan Associates, county employment multipliers calculated for the Appalachian region provide a good illustration of what typical multipliers are and how they work.[2]

The multipliers estimated in this study were based on county employment data. They represent the approximate measure of the direct and indirect employment associated with each addition of direct employment to the export sector of a county. There are 375 counties and 3 independent cities for which multipliers were estimated. The smallest multiplier was 1.13 and the highest was 2.63. Thus, the county with the smallest multiplier value would provide other employment opportunities for

---

[2] *Recreation as an Industry* (Washington, D.C.: Robert R. Nathan Associates and Resource Planning Associates, 1966), p. 57.

approximately 0.13 person for each person directly employed in servicing export demand, and the county with the highest multiplier value would provide other employment opportunities for approximately 1.63 persons for each person directly employed in servicing export demand. In general, county employment multipliers vary directly with the population or total employment size of the counties: As county population size grows, so does the multiplier value. This relationship is as might be expected, insofar as import leakages would tend to be less where diversity of occupations is greater, and diversity is positively associated with county population or total employment.

Income Multiplier

Jobs mean income, which stimulates the economy of the area in which the development occurs. How much stimulation depends on several factors. Using a hotel as an example, the management takes one of two actions concerning the revenue earned:

TABLE 14.3
Formula for the Multiplier

$$\text{Multiplier} = \frac{1}{1 - MPC}$$

where
M = marginal (extra)
P = propensity (inclination)
C = consume (spending) MPC
S = savings (money out of circulation) MPS
Suppose \$1000 of tourist expenditure and an MPC of 1/2. Then

\$1000.00	
+	
500.00	$1/2 \times 1000$
+	
250.00	$(1/2)^2 \times 1000$
+	
125.00	$(1/2)^3 \times 1000$
+	
62.50	$(1/2)^4 \times 1000$
+	
31.25	$(1/2)^5 \times 1000$
+	
15.63	$(1/2)^6 \times 1000$
+	
7.81	$(1/2)^7 \times 1000$
...	

$\overline{\text{\$2000.00 (approx.)}}$

Multiply: $\dfrac{1}{1 - 1/2} \times \$1000$, or $2 \times \$1000 = \$2000$

Thus, the original \$1000 of tourist expenditure becomes \$2000 of income to the community.

It either spends the money on goods and services, or it saves part of such funds. Economists refer to such action as *MPC* (marginal propensity to consume) or *MPS* (marginal propensity to save—removing funds from the local economy). Such removal of these marginal (extra) funds can be made in two ways: (1) They can be saved and thus not loaned to another spender, or (2) they can be used to purchase imports. In either case, so doing removes the funds and thus does not stimulate the local economy.

Economic research is needed in a tourist destination area to determine what these income relationships are. If the results of such economic research were made available, many beneficial results might be possible. For example, governmental bodies might be more inclined to appropriate additional funds for tourism promotion to their areas if they knew more about the income that was generated by tourist expenditures. Also, improved and added developments of facilities to serve tourists might be more forthcoming if prospective investors could have more factual data upon which to base decisions.

To understand the multiplier, we must first make some approximation as to what portion of the tourist dollars that are received in a community are spent (consumed) and saved (leakage). To illustrate this, suppose that we had a total of $1000 of tourist spending in a community and that there was an *MPC* of 1/2. The expenditure pattern might go through seven transactions in a year. These are illustrated in Table 14.3. The other formula for the multiplier is 1/*MPS*. This is a simpler formula, because it is the reciprocal of the marginal propensity to save. If the marginal propensity to save were 1/3, the multiplier would be 3. This is shown in Table 14.4.

Leakage, as defined, is a combination of savings and imports. If we spend the money outside our country for imports, obviously it does not stimulate the economy locally. Also, if it is put into some form of savings that are not loaned to another spender within a year, it also has the same effect as imports—not stimulating the economy. Thus, to get the maximum benefits economically from tourist expenditures, we should introduce as much of the tourist funds as possible into the local

TABLE 14.4
"Leakage"

$$\text{Leakage} = \begin{cases} \text{Savings} \\ \text{Imports} \end{cases}$$

where

Savings = not loaned to another spender

Imports = spending on tourism needs in sources outside country (state)

$$\text{Multiplier} = \frac{1}{MPS}$$

$$MPS = 1/3$$

$$\text{Multiplier} = \frac{1}{1/3}$$

$$\text{Multiplier} = 3$$

economy for goods and services rather than save the proceeds or buy a large amount of imports.

Here, also, more economic research is needed. Some studies have indicated that the multiplier might be as high as 3 in some areas, but economic research in other localities indicate that it may be more typically lower than this.

Economic Benefits Widely Distributed

Using a conceptual approach, you should realize that tourism is characterized by the existence of a large number of very small businesses that support and are ancillary to the industry. The receipts from tourism quickly filter down to an extremely broad cross section of the population, so that the entire community shares the economic benefits. Table 14.5, based on a partial hypothetical example, illustrates how quickly tourism receipts seep through the economy and the diversity of the businesses that benefit from tourism. As the figure indicates, the tourism dollar is shared by over 70 distinguishable types of enterprises in just two rounds of spending.

Structural Changes

In countries that primarily rely on a single industry, such as agriculture, the introduction of tourism has often led to a decrease in the agricultural base of the country. Agriculture is an extremely low-productivity industry in the developing countries. The promise of much higher wages in the tourism industry draws people away from farming. Agricultural output declines as a result, just when the demand for food is increasing due to the influx of tourists. The inflationary pressure on food prices is further aggravated and can lead to considerable social upheaval. In the mid-1970s, some Caribbean countries experienced a wave of protests and even direct attacks on tourists, as the resident population expressed its dissatisfaction over rising prices.

Another major implication of the structural change is that instead of diversifying its economic base, the country's tourism sector merely "cannibalizes" its other major economic sector. Diversity is the foundation of economic stability. When one sector (or industry) is experiencing a slump, another sector is booming, thus reducing the probability of a severe depression and, indeed, reducing its impact if a depression does occur. Thus, tourism, instead of diversifying an economy, sometimes replaces agriculture as a "subsistence" sector.

Dependence on Tourism

Permitting tourism to become the subsistence industry is not desirable for a number of reasons. First, tourism is by its very nature subject to considerable seasonality. While seasonal fluctuations in demand can sometimes be reduced, they cannot be eliminated. Thus, when tourism is the primary industry in an area, the off-season periods inevitably result in serious unemployment problems. Such areas find that the seasonal character of tourism leaves severe economic and social effects on the host region.

Another very important reason relates to the source of demand for tourism. The

TABLE 14.5
Distribution of Tourism Expenditures

Visitors Spend for	Travel Industry Spends for	Ultimate Beneficiaries
Lodging	Wages and salaries	Accountants
Food	Tips—gratuities	Advertising and public relations
Beverages	Payroll taxes	Appliance stores
Entertainment	Commissions	Architects
Clothing, etc.	Music and entertainment	Arts and crafts producers
Gifts and souvenirs	Administrative and	Attorneys
Photography	general expenses	Automobile agencies
Personal care	Legal and professional	Bakers
Drugs and cosmetics	services	Banks
Internal	Purchases of food,	Beach accessories
transportation	beverages, etc.	Butchers
Tours and	Purchases of goods sold	Carpenters
sightseeing	Purchases of materials and	Cashiers
Miscellaneous	supplies	Charities
	Repairs and maintenance	Chemists
	Advertising, promotion,	Clerks
	and publicity	Clothing stores
	Utilities—electric gas,	Clubs
	water, etc.	Confectioners
	Transportation	Contractors
	Licenses	Cooks
	Insurance premiums	Cultural organization
	Rental of premises and	Dairies
	equipment	Dentists
	Interest and principal	Department stores
	payments of borrowed	Doctors
	funds	Dry cleaning establishments
	Income and other taxes	Electricians
	Replacement of capital	Engineers
	assets	Farmers
	Return to investors	Fishermen
		Freight forwarders
		Garages and auto repairs
		Gardeners
		Gift shops
		Government
		Education
		Health
		Roads and railroads
		Utilities
		Development and others
		Greengrocers
		Grocery stores
		Financiers
		Furniture stores
		Importers
		Insurance agencies
		Landlords
		Laundries

TABLE **14.5** *(Continued)*

Visitors Spend for	Travel Industry Spends for	Ultimate Beneficiaries
		Manufacturing agents
		Managers
		Motion picture theaters
		Newspapers, radio, etc.
		Nightclubs
		Office equipment suppliers
		Painters
		Pastoralists
		Petrol stations
		Plumbers
		Porters
		Printers—sign painters
		Publishers
		Real estate brokers and developers
		Resorts
		Restaurants
		Room maids
		Shareholders
		Sporting events
		Transportation
		Travel brokers
		Taxi—hire car services
		Unions
		Wholesale establishments

Source: Pannell Kerr Forster and Belt Collins and Associates.

demand for tourism depends largely on the income and the tastes of tourists, both of which are beyond the control of the host region. If the American economy is going through a slump, demand for travel to a foreign destination by Americans will fall off. There is precious little a destination area can do, in this case, to increase the level of demand. If the tastes of the people in the tourist-generating area change—that is, they decide to travel to a new destination—tourism in the old area will decline, causing economic and social problems. Again, there will be little or nothing the destination can do to avoid this. In fact, as Plog[3] points out, there is reason to believe that such a decline in an area's popularity may be largely inevitable. Quite clearly, then, tourism should not be allowed to grow to an extent that the destination area becomes totally dependent on it.

In other words, total dependence on a single industrial sector is undesirable. If it cannot be avoided, then dependence on domestic agriculture is in many ways preferable to dependence on tourism. The country has presumably adapted itself economically and socially to dependence on agriculture over several centuries. The demand for agriculture output is also unlikely to suffer from a secular decline because people

---

[3] Stanley C. Plog, "Why Destination Areas Rise and Fall in Popularity," *The Cornell Hotel and Restaurant Administration Quarterly*, Vol. 14, No. 4 (February 1974), pp. 55–58.

Seasonal fluctuations in tourism result in an uneven source of revenue. During the winter months, skiers enjoy the powder snow of Aspen, Colorado and make a significant contribution to the Colorado economy. *(Photo courtesy of the Aspen Skiing Company.)*

must eat. Also, it is the residents, not foreigners as in tourism, who directly benefit from agricultural production.

Investment Priorities

Sometimes, governments of developing countries take an overly optimistic view of tourism. They undertake aggressive investment programs to develop tourism, assigning it top priority in their development plans. In extreme cases, such an approach can lead to the neglect of more fundamental investment needs of the country. For example, funds can be channeled into tourism development at the cost of education, health, and other social services. The education, health, and other aspects of the social well-being of the population should be of primary concern for a developing country. Not only is undue glamorization of tourism unwise because it usurps this position, but such a strategy only speeds up the process of dependence on tourism, which, as discussed earlier, is itself undesirable. Moreover, investment in tourism at the cost of health and education programs also slows down the rate at which the local population is assimilated into the modern market economy of the country. Under certain circumstances, it may actually retard development rather than enhance it.

The conclusion is that although tourism has tremendous potential as a tool in economic development, it is no panacea. Governments should attempt to optimize (not maximize) the benefits that tourism provides, being ever mindful of the costs that it can impose. It should be noted also that the probability and the intensity of the economic costs of tourism are greater for developing nations (or regions) than for wealthy ones. Wealthy nations, by definition, possess robust economies that can more easily absorb the cost of tourism. Typically, such economies are well-diversified, and government investment programs are not so central to development efforts.

The social benefits and costs of tourism should be viewed similarly. While the host community seeks to maximize the benefits, it must weigh these against the social costs. The social costs are likewise higher in both probability and magnitude when tourism is being considered for development in an area that still possesses a traditional social structure.

Quantity Demanded and Price Elasticity

For some products, even a large change in price over a certain range of the demand curve results in only a small change in quantity demanded. In this case, demand is not very responsive to price (Table 14.6). For other products, or for the same product over a different range of prices, a relatively small change in price elicits a much larger relative change in quantity demanded. Demand can be classified as inelastic or elastic on the basis of the relative responsiveness of quantity demanded to changes in price. Specifically, price elasticity of demand may be defined as the percentage change in demand resulting from a given percentage change in price. Most tourism products are price elastic. During 1992, when U.S. airlines began offering one-half fares, the number of air travelers increased to record-high levels.

TABLE 14.6
Relationships Between Price Elasticity and Total Revenue (TR)

	Elastic Demand ($|\epsilon p| > 1$)	Unitary Elasticity ($|\epsilon p| = 1$)	Inelastic Demand ($|\epsilon p| < 1$)
Price rises	TR falls	No change	TR rises
Price falls	TR rises	No change	TR falls

Income Elasticity of Demand

As income rises, more travel is demanded at any given price. Thus, the relationship between income and demand is positive. The responsiveness of demand to changes in income is called **income elasticity** of demand. It is defined as the percentage change in quantity demanded in response to a given percentage change in income, price remaining unchanged.

SUMMARY

Domestic and international tourism are major economic strengths to many of the world's countries, states, cities, and rural areas. Thus, those who live there are affected by the economic results of tourist spending. In this chapter we explain why these resulting effects vary greatly and what brings about a large measure of benefits or possible detriments to a community. The main economic phenomena described are various multipliers, balance of payments, investments, tax consideration, employment, economic impact generators, travel expenditures, dependence on tourism, price and income elasticity as related to buying travel experiences, and optimization. A new method of measuring tourism economic impact, the satellite account, is discussed.

Many people do not understand or appreciate the economics of tourism. The following list summarizes the principal economic effects:

1. Expenditures by foreign visitors in one's country become exports (mainly of services). The economic effects are the same as those derived from exporting tangible goods. If there is a favorable exchange rate (foreign currency buying appreciably more of one's own country's currency), the country that has the devalued currency will experience a higher demand for visitor services than before devaluation.

2. If citizens of one's country spend money in foreign countries, these expenditures become imports for the tourists' originating country.

3. Sums of the values of national exports and imports are used when calculating a nation's balance of payments. A plus balance results when exports exceed imports; thus increasing a nation's gross national product (GNP).

4. Tourism developments typically require large investments of capital. Thus, local economies where the developments take place are stimulated by such investments.

5. Tourists pay various kinds of taxes directly and indirectly while visiting an area. Thus, tax revenues are increased for all levels of government.

6. Because tourists usually spend more per day at a destination than they do while at home, these extra expenditures may cause inflationary pressures and rising prices for consumer goods in the destination area.

7. Tourism expenditures injected into the economy produce an income multiplier for local people. This is due to the diversity of expenditures made by those receiving tourist payments. Tourist receipts are used to buy a wide variety of goods and services over a year's time. The money turnover creates additional local income.

8. The amount of income multiplication, however, will depend on how much leakage takes place. Leakages are a combination of (1) imported goods and services purchased by tourism suppliers and (2) savings made of tourist receipts not loaned to another spender within one year of receipt. Thus, the more tourist goods that are supplied locally, the higher will be the multiplier.

9. Income multiplication caused by tourist expenditures necessitates hiring more people. Thus, they also effect an employment multiplier.

10. As increased spending produces more financial transactions, they cre-

ate a transactions multiplier. These are of particular interest to governments that have a sales or value-added tax on such transactions.

11. As a tourist area grows, more capital is invested in new facilities. This results in a capital multiplier.

12. It is an unwise policy for a society to place too much dependency on tourism as a subsistence industry.

13. Although tourism often has an excellent potential in economic development, it is not a panacea for economic ills. Its economic benefits should be optimized rather than maximized.

14. We believe that tourism products are mainly price elastic, meaning that as prices rise, the quantity demanded tends to drop.

15. In general, we believe that tourism is income elastic. This means that as family income rises, or a particular market's income rises, and tourism prices do not rise proportionally, the demand for travel to that particular area will increase.

ABOUT THE READING

This reading describes the WTTC/WEFA development of a National Travel and Tourism satellite account.

READING 14.1

MEASURING TRAVEL & TOURISM'S IMPACT ON THE ECONOMY

Prepared by the World Travel and Tourism Council.

What is a Satellite Account?

Countries measure economies—GDP, employment, capital formation, tax revenue etc.—using an internationally agreed System of National Accounts (SNA) which identifies all elements of supply and demand with specific industries. Because Travel & Tourism is one of the new service industries which have developed in the latter half of the 20th century, it was never properly organised in the SNA framework. Satellite Accounting has therefore been established to compile those elements relevant to Travel & Tourism without disturbing the established SNA structure.

Since 1991, WTTC and WEFA have developed and implemented Satellite Accounting research to mea-sure the economic impact of Travel & Tourism. This work has broken new ground and helped to change the mindset about the real economic value of Travel & Tourism. We have conducted some 20 detailed national, regional and global economic impact analyses during this period, with presentations to public, private and media audiences.

During the same period we have cooperated, under the auspices of the World Tourism Organization, to develop an international standard for Travel & Tourism Satellite Accounting which will be considered at an International Conference in 1999.

In supporting this framework and in order to operationalise it around the world, we have strengthened our partnership with WEFA to help countries with this new research effort in order that they are able to create national Travel & Tourism Satellite Accounts.

From 1998, all WTTC/WEFA economic research has been restructured and restated in line with the proposed international standard. This provides greater insight into the economic make-up of the "Travel & Tourism Industry" and the linkages into the broader "Travel & Tourism Economy."

The "Travel & Tourism Industry" shows the narrow production-side equivalent: the "Travel & Tourism Economy" captures the "economy-wide" impact (including capital formation, collective government expenditures and trade exports).

Satellite Accounting—Economic Concepts

Tracking Demand

The Travel & Tourism Satellite Account is based on a "demand-side" concept—the economic activities of travellers. Travel & Tourism is a collection of products and services ranging from cruise-ship fares, to restaurant meals, entertainment, purchases and gifts. Since many of these services are also bought by residents—for example restaurant meals—the Satellite Account captures the economic activities of travellers only.

The Travel & Tourism Satellite Account starts with consumption.

- *Personal Consumption.* The expenditures of residents of a country related to their domestic and international leisure trips. This includes expenditures on Travel & Tourism services such as lodging, transportation, entertainment, meals, financial services and the like. It also includes goods used for Travel & Tourism. Some of these are non-durable goods like photographic film, gasoline or food, which are consumed immediately, While others are durable goods like luggage, cameras and vehicles, which are used over time.

- *Business and Government Individual Consumption.* Expenditures undertaken by travellers in the course of their work.

- *Government Collective Consumption.* Expenditures by government agencies on behalf of travellers. These expenditures include sums given to cultural institutions like museums or national parks to cover actual visitor costs over and above entry fees. It also includes services like customs and immigration provided to travellers.

- *International Visitor Consumption.* Exports on goods and services. In economic terms, visitor exports (i.e. travellers arriving from other countries) are as important as traditional manufacturing, agricultural or commodity-based exports.

In aggregate, these four elements comprise the demand-side concept of Travel & Tourism consumption.

From Demand to Supply

By employing input/output analysis to this aggregate, the Satellite Account identifies:

- *Direct.* Value Added (GDP) and Employment created by the Travel & Tourism "industry."

- *Indirect.* Value Added (GDP) and Employment created by "industry" suppliers.

- *Imported.* Goods and services from abroad.

All three components are important:

- *Direct Value Added and Employment.* For comparative purposes with other industries, Value Added can be further disaggregated into its components which include: wages and compensation, operating surplus, depreciation, indirect taxes and subsidies to provide even greater detail and information about "industry" economics.

- *Indirect Value Added.* To identify the economic impact of suppliers such as fuel companies, food service suppliers, accounting/legal services, etc.

- *Industry Imports.* To show imports consumed by travellers and reflect GDP created at home and abroad.

The Economic Impact

The full economic impact of Travel & Tourism is calculated by incorporating 3 elements of indirect consumption flowing from traveller demand.

- *Non-Market Products.* Essentially, general government expenditures made on behalf of travellers and the industry—covering such items as promotion, aviation administration, security services, sanitation services and the like.

- *Non-Visitor Exports.* Essentially, consumer goods sent abroad for sale ultimately to travellers, or capital goods sent abroad for use by travel companies. This incorporates aircraft, cruise-ships, automobiles and fuel where these are used for Travel & Tourism purposes.

- *Capital Formation.* By both public and private sectors to provide facilities, equipment and infrastructure to travellers. The capital investments in this category range from computer

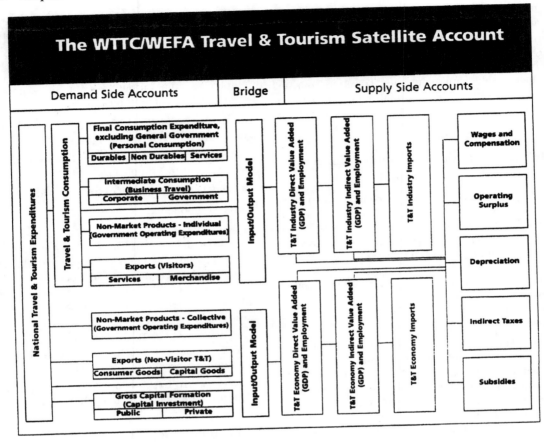

equipment, to commercial aircraft and resort infrastructure.

These three elements, together with consumer demand, provide the full demand-side picture collectively known as *National Travel & Tourism Expenditure.*

Satellite Accounting in this form allows two important policy analysis to be undertaken:

• Comparison of Travel & Tourism industry GDP with other sectors of the economy

• Examination of the flow-through effect of Travel & Tourism across the economy and the dynamic interlinks with related sectors

KEY CONCEPTS

balance of payments	income elasticity	optimization
demand	indirect impact	price elasticity
direct impact	inflationary pressure	price inelasticity
economic impact	leakage	tax revenue
employment	multipliers	tourism satellite account
exports and imports		

INTERNET SITES

**Asia-Pacific Economic
Cooperation**
http://www.apecsec.org.sg

Canadian Tourism Commission
http://www.canadatourism.com

Economist Intelligence Unit
http://www.i-trade.com

**Organization for Economic Cooperation
and Development**
http://www.oecd.org

World Tourism Organization
http://www.world-tourism.org

World Travel & Tourism Council
http://www.wttc.org

INTERNET EXERCISES

Site Name: World Travel and Tourism Council

URL: http://www.wttc.org/

Background Information: The World Travel & Tourism Council (WTTC) is the Global Business Leaders' Forum for travel and tourism. Its central goal is to work with governments to realize the full economic impact of the world's largest generator of wealth and jobs—travel and tourism.

Exercises

1. Review the economic research for a particular region selected by either you or your instructor. What are the economic forecasts for that region?

2. What are the overall tourism forecasts worldwide?

3. What do the statistical data reveal about the United States?

4. What are the regional statistics for the region where you live?

5. What are the employment projections?

6. What are the projections for the number of U.S. citizens traveling abroad versus foreign tourists visiting the United States? How does the difference affect the balance of trade?

QUESTIONS FOR REVIEW AND DISCUSSION

1. What is meant by *optimization*?

2. Discuss how an airline executive might use tourism economics relating to passenger load factors, ticket prices, discounts, frequent flyer programs, joint fares, and flight frequencies.

3. Selecting one form of public transportation, enumerate the economic constraints that affect this business.

4. A full-service restaurant is considering having an elaborate buffet dinner three nights a week. What constraints are likely to bear on this consideration?

5. Define tourism exports and imports in terms of national economies.

6. Explain how international tourism could assist in reducing the current sizable U.S. trade deficit. How could it increase the deficit?

7. Give several reasons why a hotel's purchasing director should be familiar with the income multiplier phenomenon.

8. Trace how tourist expenditures in a community provide financial support to the public library.

9. Enumerate various methods by which a tourist-dependent community can at least partially overcome seasonality of tourism demand.

10. Why is tourism satellite account considered to be the best way to measure tourism's impact on the economy?

CASE PROBLEMS

1. Mr. and Mrs. Henry B are considering taking their first trip abroad. Deciding to buy a group tour, they find that some countries in which they are interested seem to offer a much better value than do others. Assuming that the ingredients of the tours being considered are very similar, what factors are likely to account for this price difference?

2. A western U.S. state is quite popular with tourists, hosting about 6 million visitors per year. The state's director of sales and use taxes has recently advised the governor that a special 5 percent hotel and motel rooms tax should be added to the present 4 percent use tax, making a 9 percent total rooms tax. Currently, the state's budget is in the red. Thus, an increase in revenue is badly needed. What economic advice should the governor seek?

SELECTED REFERENCES

Boskin, Michael J. "National Satellite Accounting for Travel and Tourism: A Cold Review of the WTTC/WEFA Group Research." *Tourism Economics*, Vol. 2, No. 1, pp. 3–12, March 1996.

Braun, Bradley M. "The Economic Contribution of Conventions: The Case of Orlando, Florida." *Journal of Travel Research*, Vol. 30, No. 3, pp. 32–37, Winter 1992.

Briassoulis, Helen. "Methodological Issues in Tourism Input–Output Analysis." *Annals of Tourism Research*, Vol. 18, No. 3, pp. 485–495, 1991.

Bull, Adrian. *The Economics of Travel and Tourism*. Essex, England: Longman, 1995.

Deply Lisa, and Ming Li. "The Art and Science of Conducting Economic Impact Studies." *Journal of Vacation Marketing*, Vol. 4, No. 3, pp. 230–254, 1998.

Dwyer, Larry, and Peter Forsyth. "Economic Impacts of Cruise Tourism in Australia." *Journal of Tourism Studies*, Vol. 7, No. 2, pp. 36–45, December 1996.

Eadington, William R., and Milton Redman. "Economics and Tourism." *Annals of Tourism Research*, Vol. 18, No. 1, pp. 41–56, 1991.

Fenich, George G. "The Uses and Abuses of Multipliers: A Current Case." *Hospitality Research Journal*, Vol. 20, No. 1, pp. 101–108, 1996.

Freeman, Daniel, and Esther Sultan. "The Economic Impact of Tourism in Israel: A Multi-Regional Input–Output Analysis." *Tourism Economics*, Vol. 3, No. 4, pp. 341–360, 1997.

Grado, Stephen C., Charles H. Strauss, and Bruce E. Lord. "Economic Impacts of Conferences and Conventions." *Journal of Convention and Exhibition Management*, Vol. 1, No. 1, pp. 19–34, 1998.

Henry, E. W. and B. Deane. "The Contribution of Tourism to the Economy of Ireland in 1990 and 1995." *Tourism Management*, Vol. 18, No. 8, pp. 535–554, December 1997.

Ioannides, D., and K. G. Debbage (eds). *The Economic Geography of the Tourist Industry: A Supply-Side Analysis*. London: Routledge, 1998.

Johnson, Daniel G., and Jay Sullivan. "Economic Impacts of Civil War Battlefield Preservation: An Ex-ante Evaluation." *Journal of Travel Research*, Vol. 32, No. 1, pp. 21–29, Summer 1993.

Johnson, Peter, and Barry Thomas. *Tourism, Museums and the Local Economy: The Economic Impact of the North of England Open Air Museum at Beamish.* Brookfield, VT: Ashgate Publishing Co., 1992.

Lundberg, Donald E., M. Krishnamoorthy, and Mink H. Stavenga. *Tourism Economics*. New York: Wiley, 1995.

Mak, James. "Taxing Hotel Room Rentals in the U.S." *Journal of Travel Research,* Vol. 27, No. 1, pp. 10–15, Summer 1988.

Mak, James, and Edward Hishimura. "The Economics of a Hotel Room Tax." *Journal of Travel Research*, Vol. 17, No. 4, pp. 2–6, Spring 1979.

Mules, Trevor. "Decomposition of Australian Tourist Expenditure." *Tourism Management*, Vol. 19, No. 3, pp. 267–271, 1998.

Nördstrom, Jonas. "Tourism Satellite Account for Sweden 1992–93." *Tourism Economics*, Vol. 2, No. 1, pp. 13–42, March 1996.

Okubo, Sumiye, and Mark Planting. "U.S. Travel and Tourism Satellite Accounts for 1992." *Survey of Current Business*, July 1998.

Schulmeister, Stephan. *Tourism and the Business Cycle.*

Vienna: Austrian Institute for Economic Research, 1979.

Smith, Stephen. "The Tourism Satellite Account: Perspectives of Canadian Tourism Associations and Organizations." *Tourism Economics,* Vol. 1, No. 3, pp. 225–244, September 1995.

Smith, Stephen J., and David Wilton. "TSAs and the WTTC/WEFA Methodology: Different Satellites or Different Planets?" *Tourism Economics,* Vol. 3, No. 3, pp. 249–264, 1997

Taylor, David T., Robert R. Fletcher, and Trish Clabaugh. "A Comparison of Characteristics, Regional Expenditures, and Economic Impact of Visitors to Historical Sites with other Recreational Visitors." *Journal of Travel Research,* Vol. 32, No. 1, pp. 30–35, Summer 1993.

TIA. *A Portrait of Travel Industry Employment in the U.S. Economy.* Washington D.C.: Travel Industry Association of America, 1996.

TIA. *The Economic Review of Travel in America:* 1996 Edition. Washington D.C.: Travel Industry Association of America, 1997.

TIA. *1995 Impact of Travel on State Economies.* Washington D.C.: Travel Industry Association of America, 1997.

TIA. *Travel and Tourism Congressional District Economic Impact Study.* Washington D.C.: Travel Industry Association of America, 1998.

TIA. *Tourism Works for America, 1998 Annual Report.* Washington, D.C.: Tourism Works for America Council, TIA, annual.

Tribe, John. "Tourism Economics: Life after Death?" *Tourism Economics,* Vol. 1, No. 4, pp. 329–339, December, 1995.

Vellas, Francois, and Lionel Becherel. *International Tourism: An Economic Perspective.* Hamptonshire, UK: Macmillan Press, 1995.

Wager, John E. "Estimating the Economic Impacts of Tourism." *Annals of Tourism Research,* Vol. 24, No. 3, pp. 592–608, July 1997.

Wanhill, Stephen. "The Measurement of Tourism Income Multipliers." *Tourism Management,* Vol. 15, No. 4, pp. 281–283. August 1994.

WTO. *Barometer of Travel and Tourism.* Madrid: World Tourism Organization, 1998.

WTO. *Compendium of Tourism Statistics.* Madrid: World Tourism Organization, 1998.

WTO. *Tourism Economic Report.* Madrid: World Tourism Organization, 1998.

WTO. *Tourism Highlights 1997.* Madrid: World Tourism Organization, 1998.

Zhou, Deying, et al. "Estimating Economic Impacts from Tourism." *Annals of Tourism Research,* Vol. 24, No. 1, pp. 76–89, 1997.

CHAPTER 15

TOURISM POLICY: STRUCTURE, CONTENT AND PROCESS

- Demonstrate the critical importance of tourism policy to the competitiveness and sustainability of a tourism destination.

- Outline the structure and content of a typical policy framework for a tourism destination.

- Describe a process for the formulation of a destination tourism policy.

- Identify some of the methods, techniques, and approaches used to assist in tourism policy formulation.

◀ **LEARNING OBJECTIVES**

◀ *Developing new tourism destinations and successfully maintaining existing ones requires a policy that combines competitiveness and sustainability. Shown here is an aerial view of Flims, a popular winter resort in the Grisons, Switzerland. (Photo courtesy of Switzerland Tourism.)*

INTRODUCTION

This chapter addresses a relatively new dimension of tourism—one that is being increasingly acknowledged for the impact it can have on the long-term success of a tourism destination. Although the concept of "master planning" has been around for some time, the need for high-level strategic planning involving the explicit definition of major policies reflecting an ongoing consensus among all the stakeholders in a tourism destination is the outgrowth of social changes in which all citizens are demanding a greater level of participation in the formulation of policies and programs and development which affects their daily lives.

Tourism has not escaped the pressure of this social change. As a consequence, this chapter plays several important roles in enhancing our understanding of tourism in future years. It also discusses two other global forces that all tourism destinations must now face: (1) the growing competition from both established and emerging destinations and (2) the pressure to maintain the ecological integrity of regions affected by tourism. These two pressures together have led to the overall need to strive to build **"competitive** and **sustainable"** destinations (see Figure 15.1).

The chapter starts by defining **tourism policy** and its overall purpose. It then demonstrates the broad scope of stakeholders who are affected by tourism policy—be it good or bad. Subsequent discussion focuses on the specific functions of tourism policy and describes the many areas that must be addressed by a comprehensive tourism policy.

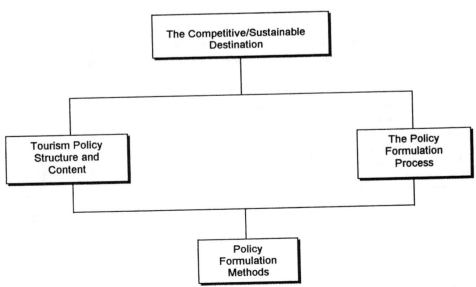

FIGURE 15.1 The competitive/sustainable tourist destination: A managerial framework.

Tourism Policy: A Definition

Tourism policy can be defined as follows:

A set of regulations, rules, guidelines, directives, and development/promotion objectives and strategies that provide a framework within which the collective and individual decisions directly affecting tourism development and the daily activities within a destination are taken.

The Purpose of Tourism Policy: Providing Maximum Benefits to the Stakeholders of the Region While Minimizing Negative Impacts

The hosting of visitors by a tourism destination is undertaken to provide its stakeholders (see Figure 15.2) with a broad range of economic and social benefits—most typically employment and income. This employment and income allows stakeholders to reside in and to enjoy the quality of the region. Tourism policy seeks to ensure that the hosting of visitors is done in a way that maximizes the benefits to stakeholders while minimizing the effects, costs, and impacts associated with ensuring the success of the destination. In effect, tourism policy seeks to provide high-quality visitor experiences that are profitable to destination stakeholders while ensuring that the destination is not compromised in terms of its environmental, social, and cultural integrity.

Why Is Tourism Policy Important?

The area of tourism policy is often overlooked in terms of its importance in ensuring the success of a tourism destination. Perhaps its most important role is to ensure that

---

- Residents of the "host" destination
- Local/municipal/regional/provincial/national governments
- Local/regional/national environmental groups
- Local visitors/excursionists
- Remote visitors/tourists
- Tourism industry sectors:
  - Transportation
  - Accommodation
  - Food service
  - Attractions
  - Entertainment
  - Events
  - Commercial outdoor recreation
  - Commercial visitor service
- Destination management organization (DMO)
- Culture/heritage groups
- Social/health/education groups

Figure 15.2 Examples of the many "stakeholders" in tourism within a given destination/region.

a given destination has a clear idea as to where it is going or what it is seeking to become in the long term. In parallel, it must strive to create a climate in which collaboration among the many stakeholders in tourism is both supported and facilitated. In more specific terms, tourism policy fulfills the following functions:

1. It defines the rules of the game—the terms under which tourism operators must function.

2. It sets out activities and behaviors that are acceptable.

3. It provides a common direction and guidance for all tourism stakeholders within a destination.

4. It facilitates consensus around specific strategies and objectives for a given destination.

5. It provides a framework for public/private discussions on the role and contributions of the tourism sector to the economy and to society in general.

6. It allows tourism to more effectively interface with other sectors of the economy.

In light of the foregoing, it is important to keep in mind that tourism policy affects the extent to which all our day-to-day operational activities—such as marketing, event development, attraction operations, and visitor reception programs—are successful. As such, it is not just a theoretical concept—it has very real implications in day-to-day practice.

Areas Addressed by Tourism Policy

In general terms, a formal tourism policy for a given destination will address such areas as (at the national level):

1. The roles of tourism within the overall socioeconomic development of the destination region

2. The type of destination that will most effectively fulfill the desired roles

3. Taxation—types and levels

4. Financing for the tourism sector—sources and terms

5. The nature and direction of product development and maintenance

6. Transportation access and infrastructure

7. Regulatory practices (e.g., airlines, travel agencies)

8. Environmental practices and restrictions

9. Industry image, credibility

10. Community relationships

11. Human resources and labor supply

12. Union and labour legislation

13. Technology

14. Marketing practices
15. Foreign travel rules

THE FOCUS OF TOURISM POLICY: THE COMPETITIVE/SUSTAINABLE DESTINATION

In a complex world of many jurisdictions, it is important to explicitly identify the geographic area to which a tourism policy applies. We refer to the "generic" entity in question as the "Tourism Destination." A tourism destination, in its simplest terms, is a particular geographic region within which the visitor enjoys various types of travel experiences.

Types and Levels of "Tourism Destinations"

Tourism destinations are most commonly defined in formal terms by recognized political jurisdictions such as:

1. A nation or country.
2. A macro region, consisting of several countries (e.g., Europe) or other groupings that either transcend national borders (such as the European "Riviera") or reflect economic trade zones (e.g., NAFTA and the Americas).
3. A province or state within a country.
4. A localized region within a country such as "Western Canada" or the U.S. "Northwest."
5. A city or town.
6. A very unique locale, such as a National Park, a historic site, or memorial which is in itself sufficiently significant to attract visitors. Examples include substantive and readily identifiable institutions such as Disney World in Orlando, the Hermitage in St. Petersburg, and St. Paul's Cathedral in Rome. These may, in themselves, exert sufficient drawing power to be classified as a destination.

The Major Parameters of Tourism Destination Management— Competitiveness and Sustainability

While the task of tourism destination management (TDM) is a complex, multidimensional challenge, there are, when all the rhetoric is stripped away, two primary parameters that must be satisfied if the destination is to be successful. These are competitiveness and sustainability. Either alone is not sufficient. They are both essential and mutually supportive.

The **competitiveness** of a destination refers to its ability to compete effectively and profitability in the tourism marketplace. **Sustainability** pertains to the ability of a destination to maintain the quality of its physical, social, cultural and environmental resources while it competes in the marketplace. A major concern in this regard is to avoid the false appearance of economic profitability, a profitability that is derived from the subtle, often invisible (in the short run), depletion of the destination's "natural capital." Conversely, sustainability may be viewed as encouraging "natural capital investment"—that is, refraining from current consumption in order to restore capital stocks (those that are renewable), thus ensuring the availability of resources for future consumption (Prugh, 1995).

Viewed in the above light, we can see that successful TDM involves traditional economic/business management skills balanced with environmental management capabilities (Figure 15.3). The economic business skills required are those related to effective Resource Development and Deployment. They include strategic planning for destination development, the marketing of the destination, the management of the human resources necessary to deliver quality visitor experiences, the management of the financial resources/investment required to support development, and the ability to develop the organizational capacity to coordinate and ensure the delivery of essential services.

The environmental management capabilities are those that are critical to effective destination stewardship. Traditionally, these have included the knowledge and skills essential for ensuring the protection of air and water, forest and plants, and wildlife management.

More recently, the concept of stewardship has been expanded to encompass management practices designed to both maintain and enhance the commemorative, social, and cultural integrity of the destination. It also involves the ability to effectively manage the human presence within the boundaries of the destination. This human presence has two main components: visitor management and resident/community management.

Finally, the tasks of resource deployment and resource stewardship are linked by the shared need for a **tourism destination management information system** (TDMIS) to support policy formulation, strategic planning, day-to-day decision-making, and

COMPETITIVENESS	**SUSTAINABILITY**
[*Resource Deployment*]	[*Resource Stewardship*]
Business/Economic Management Skills	Environmental Management Capabilities
• Marketing	• Water quality management
• Financial management	• Air quality management
• Operations management	• Wildlife management
• Human resources management	• Forest/plant management
• Information management	• Visitor management
• Organization management	• Resident/community management
• Strategic planning	• Commemorative integrity
Information Management	
Destination Monitoring	**Destination Research**

FIGURE 15.3 Some elements of successful "total tourism destination management" (TTDM).

overall performance evaluations. Information management has, in turn, two major components. The monitoring component provides stakeholders, and particularly the DMO, with an ongoing assessment of destination performance across a broad range of indicator variables. These indicator variables should be carefully chosen so as to be representative of the "overall" health of the destination in terms of both competitiveness and sustainability. Monitoring also includes an environmental scan component that seeks to identify unusual or "emerging" trends and forces that have the potential to significantly affect the competitiveness or sustainability of a destination.

The research component of the TDMIS is normally structured to play several distinct roles. One of these is to provide **research for policy formulation**. Policy research is characterized by analysis of the overall destination situation. It is undertaken with a view to providing information that assists in developing well-defined but broad guidelines that serve to establish priorities to direct the activities of the destination.[1] More specifically, policy research seeks to gather and interpret macro-level data related to present values and the evolution of trends of major economic, social, technological, and political factors, which bear on the success of the destination.

A Model of the Competitive Destination

Regardless of the size or scope of a destination, it is useful to view it from a holistic perspective in which the structure management processes are explicit defined and examined. One framework that attempts to do this has been developed by Ritchie and Crouch.[2,3] From the standpoint of this model, the purpose of tourism policy is to ensure a common, agreed-upon purpose for tourism and to establish the broad parameters for planning and coordinating the efforts of all tourism stakeholders, those whose well-being relates in some way to the success of tourism in the destination.

A Warning: The Tourism Destination and Tourism Policy Do Not Exist in a Vacuum

In all of the foregoing discussions, it needs to be kept in mind that tourism policies are but part of the social, economic, and political policies that govern and direct the functioning of the overall society within which tourism exists and functions.

In brief, there are a number of more general policies (regulations, rules, directives, objectives, strategies) that are controlled by governments, as well as other industry sectors and organizations, and they may have a significant effect on the success of tourism and tourism destinations. These include:

- Taxation—affects costs and thus profitability
- Interest rate policy—affects costs and thus profitability
- Bilateral air agreements—determines foreign visitor access

---

[1] Ritchie, J. R. B., and C. R. Goeldner, *Travel Tourism & Hospitality Research: A Handbook for Managers and Researchers,* New York: Wiley & Sons, 1994.

[2] Ritchie, J. R. B., and Geoffrey I. Crouch, "Competitiveness in International Tourism—A Framework for Understanding and Analysis." *AIEST Conference Proceedings,* Argentina, pp. 23–71, 1993.

[3] Crouch, Geoffrey I., and J. R. B. Ritchie, "Tourism, Competitiveness and Societal Prosperity." *Journal of Business Research,* Vol. 4, No. 3, March 1999.

The White House tourism conference in the United States was a major tourism event where policy recommendations were made and are still being implemented. *(Photo courtesy of the Washington, D.C. Convention and Visitors Association.)*

- Environmental policy—limits growth and access to attractive but sensitive areas
- Customs and immigration policy—can facilitate or hinder international visitation
- Communications policy—can restrict use of certain advertising media
- Minimum wage policy—can affect labor markets
- Welfare policy—can influence nature and behavior of workforce
- Education policy—can affect quality of workforce
- Cultural policy—can affect preservation and promotion of national heritage
- Foreign investment policy/regulations—can affect availability of investment capital
- Local zoning policy/by-laws—can restrict or encourage tourism facility development
- National/provincial/local policy re: funding support for major public facilities (e.g., stadiums, convention centers, museums, parks)—can drastically affect destination attractiveness
- Infrastructure policy—can make destination safer for visitors, or restrict resident travel to foreign destinations
- Currency/exchange rate policies—directly affects destination cost competitiveness

• Legal system—determines consumer/visitor protection legislation (e.g., liability for failing to deliver advertised facilities/tours/experiences)

To summarize, there are a whole range of social, economic, legal, and technological policies that greatly affect the appeal, attractiveness, competitiveness, and sustainability of a tourism destination. Some are under the control of the tourism sector (such as visitor satisfaction, guarantee policy, truth in advertising policy), but the great majority are not. Thus, the challenge facing tourism managers is to try to influence global policies where they can—and adapt to them as effectively as possible where they cannot.

The Many "Influences" on Tourism Policy

As stressed above, tourism does not exist in a vacuum. It can only function smoothly if it shares, cooperates, and dialogues effectively with many other sectors of society and of the economy (Figure 15.4). Many of these sectors have little understanding of, or explicit interest in, tourism in the region—unless, of course, visitor activity somehow appears to detract from the functioning or well-being of another sector. Tourism/other sector conflicts most commonly arise when there is competition for a shared resource base (e.g., the extractive industries), where there is a common need for specific individuals or type of individuals (e.g., entertainment, technology, education), or where there may exist a divergence of philosophical views (e.g., the environment, transportation sectors).

Each of these interfaces can pose either a threat or an opportunity for tourism. The Environmental sector and the extractive industries have traditionally viewed

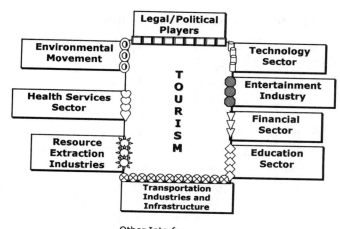

Other Interfaces:

• Manufacturing Sector
• International Relations
• Agricultural Sector

FIGURE 15.4 Tourism: Some of its multiple interfaces with other sectors of the economy and society.

tourism as a competing force; the technology, entertainment, and transportation sectors most often perceive tourism as an ally or business opportunity.

In order to dialogue and to present its case effectively at each interface, the tourism sector must be as capable, as well trained, and as well prepared as the professionals of any specific sector at any given point in time. Otherwise, tourism risks being undermined and weakened. Consequently, it may miss a critical market opportunity or may fail to establish an innovative alliance or partnership. All too often, tourism's lack of sophistication and preparedness has resulted in government decisions and policies that significantly weaken its ability to compete—or to do so more profitability. In certain cases, the tourism sector has never been aware of the extent to which it has been disadvantaged by its naivete or by a failure to proactively and adequately prepare its case. This can be particularly disastrous in public forums where both the issue at hand and the industry's long-term credibility can be lost.

The Multidisciplinary Nature of Tourism and Tourism Policy

As explained in Chapter 1, tourism is, by its very nature, a multidisciplinary phenomenon (see Figure 1.3). The tourism experience is impacted by a range of economic, psychological, societal, technological, legal, and political forces.[4,5] It follows that, in order to formulate policies that accommodate or address these multiple forces, those involved must appreciate the complexities of each discipline and their interactions in any given situation. The disciplines of psychology, economics, sociology, and law are but some of the disciplines that can enhance our understanding of international marketing. The environmental sciences, political science, and the behavioral sciences are essential to the formulation of National Park policy that defines the levels and types of tourism that are appropriate and desirable.

Some Other Characteristics of Tourism Policy

In addition to the multidisciplinary nature of tourism policy, it also possesses several other essential characteristics:

1. It must focus on macro-level policies—that is, be concerned with societal views of the direction that tourism development should take at the subnational, national, and even transnational level.

2. It must be designed to formulate policies having a long time perspective.

3. It must concentrate on how critical and limited resources can best respond to perceived needs and opportunities in a changing environment.

4. It must recognize the intellectual nature of the process of policy formulation. As such, it must incorporate tacit knowledge and personal experience as important sources of information, in addition to more conventional methods of research and study.

---

[4] Jafari, J. and J. R. B. Ritchie (1981). "Toward a Framework for Tourism Education: Problems and Prospect," *Annals of Tourism Research*, 8(1): 13–34.

[5] Echtner, C. and T. B. Jamal (1997). "The Disciplinary Dilemma of Tourism Studies," *Annals of Tourism Research*, 24(4): 868–883.

5. It must encourage and stimulate organized creativity so as to avoid policies based on stereotyped or outmoded perceptions.

6. It must be constructed to permit and facilitate a continuing dynamic social process requiring inputs from multiple sources.

7. It must break down the traditional boundaries between industry sectors in tourism.

8. It must relate policies of the tourism subsystem to those of the total socioeconomic system of a nation or region of which it is a part.

9. It must acknowledge the destination roles of both competition and cooperation, and seek to identify situations where each is appropriate. The judicious application of either or both in tourism policy has given rise to use of the term "coopetition."[6]

TOURISM POLICY: STRUCTURE, CONTENT, AND PROCESS

In discussing tourism policy, it is helpful to clearly distinguish among the overall structure of a policy and the specific policy content found within that structure. In the same vein, readers must distinguish between (a) the static concepts of policy structure and content and (b) the dynamic concept of **policy formulation.** Structure and context define the "what" of tourism policy; the process of policy formulation describes the "how" of defining the structure of a destination's policy and determining the content of policy found within that structure. In tourism the process, or the "how," provides the following:

- An overview of the different stages or steps involved in the policy formulation process
- A review of the various possible methodologies that might be used within, or across, the stages of policy formulation

The Structure of Tourism Policy

While there is no "single" model defining the content of tourism destination policy, Figure 15.5 provides one framework for tourism policy (i.e., a set of guidelines for successful destination development and operations).

Total System and Tourism "Mega Policy"

Macropolicy, or what some have referred to as megapolicy, involves determination of the postures, assumptions, and main guidelines to be followed by specific policies. They are a kind of master policy, clearly distinct from detailed discrete policies.[7] In

---

[6] Edgell, D. L. S., *World Tourism at the Millennium; An Agenda for Industry, Government and Education.* Washington, D.C.: USTTA, U.S. Department of Commerce, 1993.

[7] Dror, Y. *Design for Policy Sciences,* New York: American Elsevier, 1971.

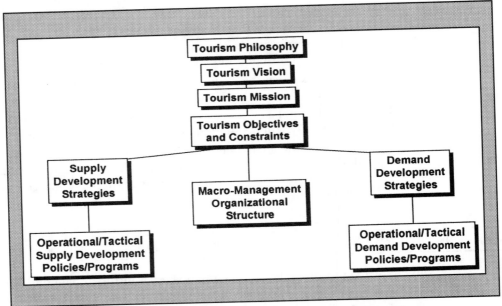

FIGURE 15.5 The structure and composition of tourism policy.

this regard, tourism policy is viewed as being directly based upon and derived from the policies that direct the total socioeconomic system of the nation or region in which the tourism subsystem is located. In fact, it is the general content of these total system policies that provides much of the basis upon which to derive the tourism philosophy of the destination region in question.

Tourism Philosophy

An explicit tourism philosophy is an essential foundation on which to develop a coherent policy. In general, a "philosophy" may be defined as "a system for guiding life, as a body of principles of conduct, beliefs or traditions; or the broad general principles of a particular subject or field of activity." Adapting this general definition for present purposes, a tourism philosophy may be defined as: "a general principle or set of principles which indicates the beliefs and values of members of a society concerning how tourism shall serve the population of a country or region, and which act as a guide for evaluating the utility of tourism related activities."

It is important to stress the critical role that the values of destination residents exert in determining the context of tourism policy. In effect, the values of residents provide the foundation on which the policy and its various components rest. In the end, tourism policies that do not reflect the values of the destination stakeholders, or "hosts," will inevitably fail to gain ongoing popular, or political support. Policies that do not maintain long-term political support are doomed to failure.

The philosophical distinction sometimes made between "value-driven" and "market-driven" destinations, while conceptually appealing, is, in practice, somewhat ambiguous. No destination can be competitive unless it succeeds in appealing to profitable segments of the market over the long term. By the same token, no destination can be sustainable unless, while it generates economic rewards, it also succeeds in maintaining the value-driven legitimacy required by a democratic society.

The Destination Vision

Although a "tourism philosophy" sets out the overall nature of tourism in a destination, it is the **destination vision** that provides the more functional and more "inspirational portrait of the ideal future" that the destination hopes to bring about in some defined future (usually 5, 10, 20, or 50 years).

Visions can take many different forms. Some are very concise (the equivalent of a corporate "mission statement"); others are much more extensive and idealistic. Typically, however, a destination vision is structured as shown in Figure 15.6.

The preamble sector of a vision sets the tone and provides the context and rationale for the vision being developed. The core vision, as the name implies, attempts to capture the overall essence of the "ideal future" for the destination in question. The values component of the vision statement seeks to provide an understanding of the "deeply held enduring beliefs" of the stakeholders formulating the vision. It is these values that effectively drive—or provide a foundation—for the vision statements that are enunciated by individuals. One cannot understand or appreciate a vision without understanding and appreciating the values on which it is based.

The elements of the vision are the means by which the essence or idealism of the vision (the core vision) is linked to reality of the destination. In effect, they provide the means by which operational components of the vision can be defined. The nature of these components is dependent upon the specific destination in question. In the example in Figure 15.6, the core vision for a Canadian National Park gave rise to six vision elements.

Finally, once the **core vision** and its elements have been agreed upon, it is fre-

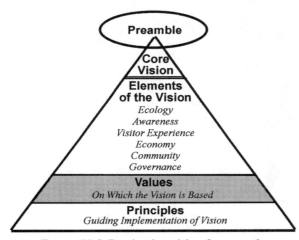

FIGURE 15.6 Destination vision framework.

quently useful to provide a statement of principles designed to provide guidance as to how the vision and its elements should be interpreted and implemented.

Tourism Objectives and Constraints

Component three of a tourism policy consists of a statement of the objectives of the tourism system. Objectives are defined as: "operational statement(s) of the specific results sought by the tourism system within a given time frame."

The objectives of the tourism system should possess a number of important characteristics. First, because the objectives are formulated in light of the tourism vision, their achievement should clearly contribute to the fulfillment of this vision. Second, in order that the objectives can be qualified as "operational," it is essential that managers are able to measure the extent to which desired results have or have not been attained. This implies that we must have some explicit means of quantifying appropriate performance standards. Third, we must ensure that the measures selected with respect to each objective are indeed valid indicators of the desired results—that is, they measure what we truly want to achieve. Fourth, in the common situation where the tourism system has multiple objectives, it is advisable to indicate an order or priority among objectives. This indication of relative importance provides a basis for decision-making should different strategies or programs for achieving the objective be in conflict. Fifth, the objectives must be related to a given time period as is directly stated

Tourism promotion policy often features trying different ethnic foods as one of the pleasures of travel. *(Photo courtesy of the Malaysia Tourism Promotion Board.)*

in the above definition. Finally, the objectives that are stated must be reasonable. While they should serve to offer a real challenge, goals that are virtually impossible to attain quickly become a negative rather than a positive source of motivation.

One further remark concerning the formal statement of objectives is in order. Objectives identify those events or results that we wish to bring about. While not necessarily so, the word "objective" implies that the results are positive entities, such as a certain number of travelers. In fact, the managers of a tourism system may be seeking goals with respect to what they do not want to happen as a consequence of their activities. Examples include the avoidance of environmental and cultural pollution. These types of results could be stated as specific objectives of the tourism system. While very important, the essentially negative nature provides little incentive for management action. An alternative and more satisfactory manner of dealing with effects that one wishes to avoid is to express them in the form of constraints. A common approach to formally stating constraints on system activities is to specify, where possible, the maximum level of each undesirable outcome (e.g., pollution) that can be tolerated as a result of tourism activity. Even where it is difficult to quantify the tolerable levels of undesirable outcomes, constraints can be formulated so as to at least provide explicit indications as to the type of outcomes to be minimized or avoided.

"Crafting" versus "Formulating" a Vision

The preparation, formulation, or "crafting" of a destination vision is a stimulating, intellectual process that often attracts and involves the relevant stakeholders of a destination. However, the implementation, or "realization," of the vision is always a demanding process that requires the acceptance of responsibility, the search for funding, and the allocation of a considerable amount of energy and resources. It goes without saying that most of the effort in crafting a vision is wasted if a commitment to realizing the vision is not made. The first step in translating the vision into reality is to identify the specific destination development strategies that clearly define what must be done in terms of both supply (destination facilities and services) and demand (destination marketing development).

TOURISM DESTINATION DEVELOPMENT STRATEGIES

Tourism development strategies may be viewed as specific major actions or patterns of action over time designed to attain the objectives of the tourism system of a country or region. For both analytical and managerial purposes, these strategies can be divided into three broad categories: supply development strategies, demand development strategies, and organizational structure strategies.

Supply Development Strategies

Strategies in this category are concerned with major actions related to five main categories of resources (Figure 15.7), each of which is required to provide an attractive, viable tourism destination. These are: physical resources, human resources, financial resources, information resources, and program/activity resources.

When formulating tourism resource development strategies, it is essential that attention be paid to identifying the relative strengths and weaknesses of each of these categories and their component elements in determining the principle actions necessary to upgrade the quality of each component/element of attractiveness. In so doing, it should be remembered that different destinations can (and normally do) arrive at satisfactory levels of attractiveness for each of the nine elements in different ways. Strategy formulation involves careful selection and development of those elements in each category that offer the greatest potential for the destination in question.

The physical resources of a tourism destination represent perhaps the most fundamental determinant of its attractiveness. For strategic planning purposes, these determinants of attractiveness can be viewed as falling into three major categories. These categories and the elements they contain are given in Figure 15.7a. The first category of elements in value includes those that reflect the very nature of the destination and its people. These fundamental elements offer little or no possibility of modification for tourism purposes. A second type includes those defined by the economic base of the destination or region. These include the overall level of economic activity and associated price levels as well as the general infrastructure and the basic services infrastructure. Finally, the third type includes those components of destination attractiveness that are directly related to, and largely controlled by, the tourism system. These components are visitor access and transport facilities, residential tourism plant, receptive tourism plant, and, to a lesser degree, attitudes toward visitors. Clearly, the ability of the tourism manager to directly influence the desirability of a destination increases as one moves from Type 1 to Type 3 components of attractiveness.

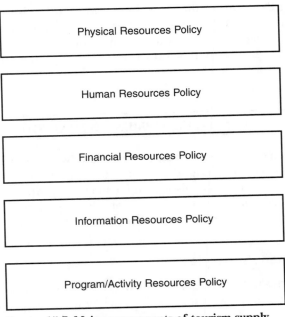

FIGURE 15.7 **Major components of tourism supply policy.**

Very few attractions are as striking as the North American pronghorn antelope. Developing policies to promote tourism while ensuring the protection of wildlife demands commitment on the part of planners and sensitivity on the part of tourists.
(Photo courtesy of Wyoming Division of Tourism.)

Human resources represent a second major category of supply resources that must be considered when formulating supply development strategies in tourism (Figure 15.7*b*). Concern here must focus on the quantity, the quality, and the mix of personnel available to meet the tourism needs of the country or region in question. Quantity measures the number of persons wishing to work in tourism-related activities and is, to a large extent, determined by the attractiveness of working conditions in the

---

Fundamental Nature of the Destination
- Natural/physical beauty
- Climate
- Social characteristics

Economic Base of Destinations
- General infrastructure
- Basic services infrastructure
- Economic activity and overall price levels

Tourism System Resources
- Visitor access & transportation facilities
- Residential tourism plan
- Attitude toward visitors

FIGURE 15.7*a* Physical resources policy: Dimensions of policy.

Quantity Dimension

Level/number of personnel required by the tourism system of the destination

Quality Dimension

Technical, professional, and managerial competence of personnel required by the destination

Human Resource Mix Dimension

Achieving the proper balance in terms of personnel types
Achieving a proper balance in terms of seasonality of demand
Flexibility, adaptability of personnel

Institutional Capability

Ensuring the availability of institutions capable of providing education/training to our human re-

---

Figure 15.7b Human resources policy: Dimensions of policy.

tourism field relative to those provided by other opportunities. Strategic actions in this regard must therefore be directed at improving the desirability of tourism careers in terms of both their monetary and nonmonetary dimensions. Quality, as it refers to human resources in tourism, is a more complex issue. It refers first to the technical, professional, and managerial competence of personnel as reflected in their ability to perform the tasks essential to the provision of a broad range of necessary skills. These skills are difficult to define and even more difficult to measure. In essence, these human resources skills are those that give the tourist the feeling that their presence is both welcome and appreciated, and that service is being provided willingly and with enthusiasm. From a strategic management standpoint, the question of the quality of tourism personnel must be addressed through education and training programs designed to improve both professional and human relations skills. Finally, the mix of human resources is a term that describes the distribution of available tourism personnel throughout the tourism system in terms of both quantity and quality. An imbalance in the mix exists when the number of personnel having particular skills is either insufficient or exceeds the requirements of particular sectors of the tourism system. Strategic management of human resources must therefore be focused in two main directions. First, it must concentrate on forecasting human resource needs in order that educational and training activities can be appropriately adjusted. Second, in a field as diverse and seasonal as tourism, strategic human resource planning must be also concerned with developing flexibility among personnel in order to offer individuals greater opportunity while at the same time improving the performance of the total system.

Once the quantity, quality, and mix dimensions of human resource policy have been formulated, it then becomes essential to determine how these needs will be met—either through the education and training of destination residents or by means of foreign labor. Given a policy of self-determination, it then becomes necessary to define and develop the institutional capabilities that will be needed to deliver the education and training that is required to support human resource policy needs of the destination.

Financial resource policy (Figure 15.7c) is another component of tourism supply

Financial Needs Policy

- Capital investment needs
- Operational capital needs
- Source of capital policy
  - Public versus private capital
  - Domestic versus foreign capital
  - Debt versus equity capital
- Special incentives policy

Figure 15.7c Financial, resources policy: Dimensions of policy.

development strategies. Once the strategic development requirements have been identified with respect to physical and human resources, it becomes necessary to find the capital to implement the chosen strategy. In making this statement, it is recognized that the formulation of physical and human resource development strategies could not originally have been carried out without some reference to the possibilities of funding. As such, the process tends to be an iterative one that necessarily recognizes the interdependence of physical, human, and financial resources. Given this situation, financial resource planning involves decisions concerning amounts of capital, sources of capital, and the conditions under which it is obtained. The amounts of capital required depend on the size and scope of the actions planned for physical and human resource development. These capital needs will also depend on the amount required for *investment* (or destination facility development) and the amount required for *operating* purposes.

Identifying and selecting *sources of capital* is a complex issue and one that takes heavily into account the tourism philosophy and objectives of the country or region, as well as its available economic resources. As such, strategic decisions concerning sources of capital must consider the extent to which private or public funding is desired, whether foreign capital is to be sought or permitted, and whether funding is available from special sources such as international development agencies. Finally, decisions must also be made concerning the conditions under which funding will be provided to projects in both the public and private sectors. Examples of strategic decisions in this area are those regarding the desired mix of debt and equity capital, the optimal length of borrowing periods and the desirability or necessity of incentives, or public subsidization, for specific forms of development.

Information Resources Policy

Another critical support area of supply policy is that of information resources. While information may have been regarded as somewhat of a luxury in the past, DMOs are now fully aware of the vital role of relevant and timely information. The ability to respond to shifting market demands and growing social pressure on tourism is totally dependent on an awareness and understanding of these factors.

The "awareness" factor of information policy is typically fulfilled by an ongoing monitoring of market conditions and public opinion. This monitoring is commonly referred to as "environmental scanning," a process by which exceptions to managerial expectations serve as a "trigger" for DMO actions. In contrast to monitoring, the "understanding" factor of information policy is met by more focused and more in-depth research on critical topics identified by the environmental scanning process or by issues that emerge on a "crisis" basis.

Program/Activity Policy

The final component of supply policy represents somewhat of a consolidation of all the dimensions. Program or activity policy defines the various focused activities of a DMO that ensures that policies, ideas, and concepts get translated into reality on a very practical basis. Examples include membership development programs that seek to expand and strengthen the membership of a DMO, as well as membership support programs (training, access to financing). Other programs that might be envisaged are collaborative promotions and consolidated purchasing programs.

To conclude, it must be emphasized that once overall supply and demand development strategies have been enunciated, and appropriate organizational structures put in place, these strategies must be translated into specific policies and programs of an operational nature. At this level, the management process becomes one of detailed planning and implementation of the many tasks necessary to provide the individual tourist with the satisfying yet challenging experience that he/she is seeking. While detailed discussion of tourism planning is beyond the scope of this chapter, the need to effectively translate strategic ideas into real world actions cannot be too strongly stressed. Without effective execution, even the most brilliant policies will prove of little value.

Demand Development Strategies

Demand development strategies in tourism involve decisions with respect to three primary components and three secondary components. These are (see Figure 15.8) as follows:

Primary Components
- The overall level of marketing support that should be provided
- The identification of a strategic **destination positioning** in the marketplace
- The selection of strategic target markets

Overall Level of Marketing Support

The total *level* of expenditures for demand development should ideally be derived from an analysis of the effort needed to meet the demand objectives in each target market. Commonly, however, this "ideal" amount will exceed the maximum total of funds that are available to support such efforts. In these instances, the actual level of funds available may be defined by some arbitrary figure, possibly some percentage of total tourism receipts. In any event, the amount that is finally available is especially critical in that it limits the extent to which the destination can compete against its many rivals.

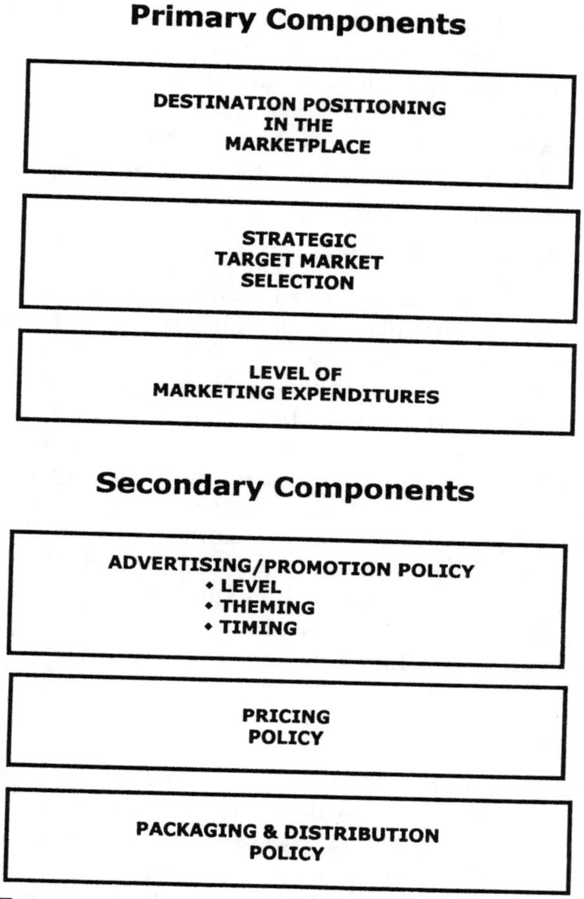

Primary Components

DESTINATION POSITIONING
IN THE
MARKETPLACE

STRATEGIC
TARGET MARKET
SELECTION

LEVEL OF
MARKETING EXPENDITURES

Secondary Components

ADVERTISING/PROMOTION POLICY
◆ LEVEL
◆ THEMING
◆ TIMING

PRICING
POLICY

PACKAGING & DISTRIBUTION
POLICY

FIGURE 15.8 Major components of tourism demand policy.

Selection of Strategic Target Markets

The selection decision concerning appropriate *targets* of demand development activities is also critical because it determines which markets are excluded from future consideration. Given the importance of this decision, it is essential that it be based on the best possible information concerning the potential of alternative markets and the feasibility of tapping each market. Once the most desirable target markets have been identified, one then proceeds to define demand objectives that should be met for each market segment. These objectives form the basis for the ultimate evaluation of demand management efforts.

The determination of the appropriate *mix* of demand management efforts within each target market requires an in-depth understanding of the information needs and decision-making processes of the members of each market segment. For certain types of markets, such as the corporate travel market, a highly selective personal selling approach may prove most effective. In the case of special interest groups, careful selection of print media may offer the greatest returns. In yet other markets, where awareness of a destination is low, traditional mass media advertising, accompanied by public relations press articles, may prove to be an essential first step in demand development. Most target markets can be most effectively attacked through a judiciously chosen combination of all available techniques.

Destination Positioning in the Marketplace

The positioning of a destination in the minds of potential visitors or strategic market segments is a particularly challenging task that demands considerable creativity. As such, it requires accurate and current information concerning market perceptions of each destination and its competitors. Because the perceptions of any destinations are not infrequently determined by factors largely outside the control of destination managers (such as schooling, press reports, television programming, and previous experiences), we should not overestimate the ability of a destination to define its image in the marketplace. Nevertheless, DMOs can have some meaningful influence on how potential visitors view their destination. Creative advertising, carefully orchestrated press stories, the hosting of major events, and the judicious choice of symbols and icons can raise the profile and modestly modify the image of a city, state, or country. And finally, a bit of good luck in world events can prove to be highly fortuitous and, unfortunately, also highly negative.

Secondary Components

While decisions regarding (1) promotion policy, (2) pricing policy, and (3) packaging and distribution policy may be termed "secondary" from a strategic perspective, they are nevertheless not to be dismissed lightly. Although the decisions tend to be somewhat more "operational" in nature, they very directly impact the nature and structure of demand development. If not executed properly, they can negate the value of a "brilliant" overall policy.

Advertising/Promotion Policy

Decisions concerning the allocation of available funds for destination advertising and promotion across target markets is directly related to the mix of efforts selected. Certain types of promotional activity may be more expensive relative to others. In addition, they may require some minimum or threshold level of expenditure to achieve any impact at all. Despite these complexities, decisions must be made concerning how to divide total available funds across markets which offer different potential returns and which may be at different stages of development in terms of their current propensity to visit a given country or region. These different stages may require advertising and promotion designed to simply increase *awareness* of the destination as a potential vacation site. Somewhat better known destinations will place a greater stress on enhancing knowledge and understanding of the destination. In cases where the destination is very well known in a specific target market, advertising and promotion expenditures will more likely focus on influencing more immediate decisions regarding destination choice for specific travel experiences.

Prior to the national transportation policy creating the Interstate highway system, many family summer vacations were enjoyed traveling on the legendary Route 66, which has been immortalized by song and television. *(Photo by Robert Holmes; courtesy of the California Division of Tourism.)*

Finally, decisions must be made concerning the most appropriate *timing* for the implementation of demand development efforts and the most appropriate *theming* within each target market. Given the variations in demand across different time periods that are commonly found in tourism, along with the highly variable mentalities of target markets, it is essential that strategies be developed to ensure that demand development efforts are being instituted when they are likely to have the greatest impact. Similarly, the message conveyed must be relevant and meaningful for each potential visitor.

Pricing Policy

One look at the advertisements in the Travel Section of any newspaper will highlight the importance that the travel industry places on "visible prices" in the marketplace. One should not, however, be misled. The travel market is becoming increasingly sophisticated. With every passing year, the well-traveled elements of the market are increasingly able to discern true value in travel, and they cannot be duped in most circumstances. Accordingly, destinations that are seeking to be competitive on a sustainable basis must offer "value for money." It follows that the pricing of travel experiences, to the extent that they are controllable by a destination, must be kept realistic in relation to alternative offerings. This requires high-quality information concerning visitor needs and competitive pricing, as well as an ability to deliver travel experiences in an efficient manner.

Packaging and Distribution

As discussed very early in this text, the nature of distribution of the travel product is evolving at an alarming speed. The traditional distribution channels (through travel wholesalers and retailers) are being constantly challenged by technologically driven alternatives. While all this is happening, however, destination managers and travel industry operators need to keep clearly in mind that they are selling unique travel experiences to many different individuals, who realize these experiences one at a time. Because of this, the need for simplification and for human concern in the delivering of tourism services are underlying forces that will never be totally replaced by high tech solutions.

Organizational Policy

Organizational policy (see Figure 15.9) is yet another area that, until recently, has received little formal attention. In effect, the organizational capability for developing and implementing tourism policy has often been, essentially, left to "chance." Today, however, the importance of the critical roles played by the Destination Management Organization (DMO) (see box) are well-established.[8] Without the effective leadership and coordination of a committed CVB, a destination is ill-equipped to be either competitive or sustainable. The entity to which this responsibility falls is referred to as the Destination Management Organization (or DMO). The exact name of this DMO depends on the level and type of destination in question:

- At the country level, the organization is normally referred to as the National Tourism Organization (NTO). An example is the British Tourism Authority (BTA).
- At the state or provincial level, the organization is most commonly referred to as the State Tourism Office or the Provincial Department of Tourism.
- At the city or municipal level, the organizational structure that dominates is most frequently identified as a Convention & Visitor Bureau (CVB).

DMOs can be either a public sector agency, or a private sector driven organization. Whatever the nature of the organization, it must be constituted in a manner that provides it with certain key characteristics. Among these are:

1. It must be clearly identifiable as the organization responsible for coordinating and directing the efforts of the many pacts of the diverse and complex tourism system.

---

[8] Getz, Donald, Don Anderson, and Lorn Sheehan, *The Roles and Activities of Visitor and Convention Bureaus in Destination Planning and Product Development*. Working Paper Submitted to Calgary Convention and Visitors Bureau, 1997.

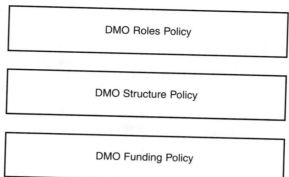

FIGURE 15.9 Major components of organizational policy.

ROLES, TASKS, AND RESPONSIBILITIES OF THE DESTINATION MANAGEMENT ORGANIZATION (DMO)
▼

- Serve as the body responsible for coordinating the marketing and promotional efforts of the destination

- Provide leadership concerning the overall nature and direction of tourism planning and development for the destination

- Act as a catalyst to initiate and facilitate the realization of destination development priorities

- Serve as an effective voice of the tourism sector in efforts to enhance the awareness and understanding of both governments and the general public concerning the economic and social importance of tourism

- Act as a representative of the tourism sector in all public and private forums where the views and position of the tourism sector need to be presented and explained

- Provide an easily recognizable and easily accessible interface between tourism and other sectors of the economy

- Coordinate the identification and delivery of commercial visitor services (such as information/service centres)

- Coordinate the identification and meeting of the information/research needs of the tourism sector with the destination

- Attempt to ensure that the education and training needs of the tourism sector are adequately met

- In certain cases, act as an investor, owner, or operator of tourism facilities considered essential to the development and well-being of the destination

- Identify and coordinate the establishment of partnerships and alliance that strengthen the competitiveness of the destination

- Where possible and appropriate, assist in the search for sources of financial assistance for members of the tourism sector of the destination

2. It must command the support of all important sectors and all major actors in the tourism system.

3. It must be capable of influencing the decisions and actions of the many public sector agencies/departments and private firms that directly determine the nature and quality of the tourism experience provided to visitors.

4. It must possess the tools necessary to stimulate or discourage the type and amount of supply development that is required by the overall tourism megapolicy.

5. It must be sufficiently independent and flexible to develop innovative strategies that can be implemented in a timely manner in response to rapidly evolving market and environmental conditions.

Following a review of the above requirements, it becomes more evident why it is generally felt that the most effective organizational form is an independent organization, be it a ministry of tourism or CVB. In cases where such a ministry or bureau does not exist, the explanation usually derives from two main sources. It may be that tourism is a relatively unimportant economic factor in the country/region/city in question and as such does not merit the expenditure of funds necessary to support an independent ministry/bureau. In these cases, tourism policy and development responsibilities are commonly subsumed within some larger ministry or city department, such as economic development, parks and recreation, or even cultural affairs. A second major reason why a ministry/bureau does not exist may reflect the political philosophy of the country, region, or city. In certain countries, notably the United States, the diversity of the country and the existence of relatively strong private sector associations in tourism has led to a low level of public sector leadership with respect to tourism development. In addition, this situation appears to be strongly enhanced by a lower level of government regulation of both supply and demand development activities than is found in many other countries.

In addition to defining DMO roles, organizational policy should also provide guidance concerning the appropriate structure for the destination management organization. Several alternatives are possible. Some DMOs are primarily based on individual membership; others tend to be structured as a federation of supporting organizations (such as chambers of commerce, hotel associations, restaurant associations, and other city "booster groups"). The structure of others reflects the fact that they are, in reality, a department of the municipal government.

It is interesting to note that few, if any, countries/regions have experimented with more novel forms of organization lying somewhat between the public and the private model. For example, the public corporation has been used in a number of countries/regions to direct and coordinate national/provincial efforts in such diverse fields as air service, petroleum development, postal services, rural services, venture development, and hydroelectric power. The important common characteristics of all these fields is that most are primarily involved in the provision of services rather than the manufacture of products. Also, most depend heavily on the use of public or natural resources, and all must satisfy some minimum standards of economic performance. Currently, the Korean Tourism Corporation is one of the most prominent examples of this approach.

Conversely, increasing pressures for the privatization of the tourism system in some destinations has led to the creation of some "hybrid" organizational forms. In Canada, the Canadian Tourism Commission (CTC), while "private sector-driven," depends very heavily on public sector funding. In addition, it has incorporated into itself many of the resources and personnel of the former federal government department, known as "Tourism Canada."

The organizational structure that is adopted has a major impact on DMO funding policy. Membership-based DMOs rely heavily on membership fees, and federation-based structures are usually financed by constituents of the federation. Municipal department DMOs, as might be anticipated, are highly dependent on local taxation for funding. These tax funds may come directly from city coffers, or indirectly by means of a local hotel tax—which may be either voluntary or compulsory (the norm).

THE PROCESS OF TOURISM POLICY FORMULATION

Discussion to this point in the chapter has focused on the structure and content of tourism policy. In this section, attention is directed toward understanding the process by which the structure and content of policy, as presented in Figure 15.5, may be developed. This process is conceptualized as containing 11 distinct stages grouped into four main phases (Figure 15.10). These phases are identified as the definitional phase, the analytical phase, the operational phase, and the implementation phase.

Definitional Phase

The definitional phase of tourism policy formulation is concerned with the development of explicit statements that define the content and direction of the overall tourism system in question. As shown in Figure 15.10, these statements deal with four different topics.

Defining the Tourism System

The definition of the destination tourism system represents the critical first step in the process of policy formulation. Despite its importance, this phase is frequently overlooked or implicitly assumed. As a result, it is common to find widely varying perceptions among policymakers and tourism officials concerning the nature and structure of the entity that they propose to manage. The consequence of this lack of perceptional congruence is that the subsequent thought process of policymakers is frequently focused on divergent components of the tourism system. The most serious aspect of this phenomenon is that the individuals involved may not recognize these perceptual differences and assume that other policymakers view the tourism system in a manner consistent with their own perception.

The above statements are not meant to imply that a tourism system cannot be conceptualized and defined in different ways, because such is clearly not the case. Indeed, the fact that this is possible reinforces the need for a particular region to adapt a spe-

Definitional Phase	**Analytical Phase**	**Operational Phase**	**Implementation Phase**
Definition of tourism destination system Explication of a tourism philosophy Crafting of a destination vision Specification of destination Objectives and constraints	*Internal Analysis* • Review of existing policies and programs • Resource audit • Strategic impact analysis *External Analysis* • Macro-level analysis of current and future demand • Micro-level analysis of current and future demand and behaviors • Review of competitive and supportive tourism development and promotion policies	Identification of strategic conclusions Implications of conclusions for supply and demand development Policy/program recommendations	Implementation of strategy for destination development, promotion, and stewardship Allocation of responsibilities for recommendation implementation Identification of sources of funding to support competitive initiatives and stewardship programs Specification of timing for recommendation implementation

Figure 15.10 The process of tourism policy, strategy formulation and implementation.

cific definition of its tourism system so that a common frame of reference is acknowledged by those involved in the policymaking process.

Figure 1.3 in Chapter 1 provides one model that might be useful as the basic framework for defining a tourism system. It views the tourism system as being constructed of two major components, namely, the operating sectors and the planning/catalyst organizations. These in turn contain various subcomponents which form the basis for identifying and classifying the individual organizations and actors (the stakeholders) that make up a given tourism system. It is essential that each region develop such a model that is generally accepted by the policymakers concerned. Once agreed to, this model should become a constant frame of reference for discussion and decisionmaking.

The need to explicitly define the stakeholders in the tourism system has led certain countries to set up a separate framework and an associated system of accounts that clearly identifies the supply-side components of the tourism industry and their individual contributions to the gross domestic product (GDP). This special system of accounts is commonly referred to as a "satellite account."[9] See Chapter 14.

The remaining three components of the definitional phase (Figure 15.10) involve the explication of a tourism philosophy, the formulation of a destination vision, and

---

[9] Smith, S. L. J., "The Tourism Satellite Account: Perspectives of Canadian Tourism Associations and Organizations." *Tourism Economics*, Vol. 1, No. 3, pp. 225–244, 1995.

State capitols are an important seat of tourism policy formation. Shown here is the state capitol building in Pierre, South Dakota. *(Photo courtesy of South Dakota Tourism.)*

the determination of tourism objectives and constraints for the destination. Previous discussion has described the content of these policy components; attention here focuses on issues concerning the process involved in specifying this content. In this regard, three comments are particularly relevant. First because the specification of these components has implications that go beyond the tourism system itself, the process employed must ensure that inputs are obtained from the total environment. This environment may include many entities, but particular importance must be attached to the overall views of the government of the day and those of the general public. Second, while a broad range of inputs must be sought and listened to, the goal of the process is not necessarily consensus, because a high level of agreement from such a wide range of inputs is rarely achieved. Rather, what is required is a series of clear statements that reflect the desires of destination stakeholders, while at the same time being realistic and capable of implementation. Finally, once agreed to by the majority of policymakers, there must be a clear commitment to these statements as the basis for policymaking by all concerned for an extended period of time. While these statements should be reviewed periodically to assess their continued relevance, such a review should not occur too frequently. Constant questioning of the fundamental directions of a tourism system only serves to divert energies from the important implementation tasks that must follow.

Explicating a Destination Philosophy

The explication of a tourism philosophy for the destination is a phase in which all destination stakeholders are forced to carefully assess their personal values with a view to reaching consensus on the fundamental role that tourism should play in the life of the region. Traditionally, tourism has been viewed primarily as a generator of economic well-being (income, employment). While an economic philosophy still tends to underlie the rationale for most tourism-related development, some destinations now incorporate social, cultural, environmental, and even concerns for world peace thinking into their destination philosophy. It may well be that pragmatic factors have stimulated the explication of these multidimensional philosophies. Whatever the reasons, we have seen a broadening of the philosophy justification for tourism development in recent years.

Crafting a Destination Vision

Perhaps the single most important and most challenging component of this phase of policy formulation is the "crafting" of a tourism destination vision. The use of the term "crafting" is very deliberate.[10] Whereas strategic planning has in the past been viewed as a highly deliberate and structured process, current thinking emphasizes the intuitive and interactive nature of effective strategy planning and policy formulation. Nowhere in the policy process is this truer than in the preparation of a destination vision statement.

Specifying Destination Objectives

As noted earlier, a destination vision paints an inspirational portrait of an ideal future at some relatively distant point in the future. The visioning process is therefore a creative and value-laden one. In contrast, the process of specifying destination objectives requires a less idealistic process that is closer in touch with immediate realities. While still consensus-oriented, the objective setting process seeks to define measurable goals, most frequently tied to visitation and revenue levels as well as organizational performance (effectiveness and efficiency). As well, the time frames involved are much shorter and more tightly defined.

Specifying Destination Constraints

The process of specifying policy constraints must also be considerably more "hard-nosed" than visioning. It is here where common agreement on the negative possibilities that simply cannot be tolerated is necessary. While environmental groups often play a dominant role in this area, the realities of the marketplace and human nature

---

[10] Mintzberg. H, "Crafting Strategy." *Harvard Business Review,* July–August issue, 1987.

are also major determinants of the constraints that are placed on tourism development within a destination.

Analytical Phase

The analytical phase of tourism policy development, while perhaps less stressful than the previous one from a managerial standpoint, involves considerably greater amounts of effort. The definitional phase requires fundamental, value-based decisions concerning the nature and direction of tourism development in a region. The analytical phase accepts these decisions as a given and proceeds to carry out the extensive collection and assessment of information needed to identify and assess the desirability of alternative means of attaining the destination vision and to achieve the goals defined by the vision.

The overall process of analysis is best viewed as being composed of two major subprocesses: (1) an internal or supply-oriented analysis and (2) an external or demand-oriented analysis.

The internal/supply analysis consists of a thorough review and analysis (frequently termed an "audit") of two major elements. The first element relates to existing policies and programs for the development of the various components of tourism supply. These policies/programs must be critically reviewed to determine the extent to which they are both consistent with, and effective in, developing the type of tourism facilities and services that are likely to achieve the goals of the region, given the nature of demand facing that region. As can be quickly seen, this statement implies a di-

Tourism policy formation is a complex, creative process that requires the active participation of a broad spectrum of stakeholders to be successful. *(Photo courtesy of Denver Metro Convention and Visitors Bureau.)*

rect interaction between the supply analysis and the demand analysis. In effect, the analytical phase involves parallel, iterative forms of analysis that must constantly be related one to the other.

A second element of the supply analysis is termed a "resource audit." A resource audit should be conducted with two goals in mind. First, it should provide a comprehensive cataloguing of the quantity and distribution of tourism facilities and services within the tourism system. Such information is basic to an understanding of the current state of affairs of supply development. Second, the resource audit should provide some assessment of the quality of existing facilities and services. Again, the execution of the audit to assess the adequacy of the quantity, distribution, and quality of supply can only be meaningful if it is eventually related to the analysis of demand. There are no absolute measures of desirability in terms of supply; *only those that relate to a given demand at a given point in time for a given market segment are relevant.*

The third form of internal analysis is a strategic impact analysis. This analysis seeks to provide policymakers with well-defined benchmarks as to the extent to which tourism is currently impacting the destination in economic, ecological, social, and cultural terms. Economic benchmarks have traditionally been the most requested forms of impact analysis because both managers and politicians seek to measure and understand both the level of tourism receipts and the incomes and employment they create. Virtually any proposal for investing in tourism development is required to provide at least a global estimate of the economic benefits and taxes to be generated. More comprehensive economic impact analyses will also estimate the possible negative impacts such as increases in land prices resulting from increased tourism as well as additional taxes that may be required to build a facility such as a municipal convention centre.

In addition to economic reviews, ecological (or environmental) impact analysis is increasingly becoming another standard requirement for meaningful policy formulation. Typically, a "State of the Ecology" report is a starting point for tourism policy formulation in any region that is in any way environmentally sensitive. In such cases, these "state of" reports are normally complemented by an environmental impact assessment (EIA) for all proposed tourism developments.

In certain instances, social and cultural impact benchmarks and analyses may also be requested. These are typically, but not always, restricted to situations where a culture is threatened or where a community feels increased tourism will negatively impact its way of life (see Chapter 11).

The external/demand analysis is composed of three distinct types of analytical activity. The first involves macro-level analysis of data that describes and defines the overall nature and structure of current tourism demand as well as those markets having a potential for future demand. This form of analysis relies heavily on aggregate statistics measuring the flows of tourists and travel-related expenditures within a region; it must not, however, limit itself to such historical data. In addition, macro-level analysis must be future-oriented and attempt to constantly monitor the environment in order to identify shifts or trends in social, political, or technological factors that might significantly affect the region's success in its field of tourism.

The second type of external/demand analysis is termed "micro-level analysis." Here, rather than focusing on aggregate trends in tourism demand, attention is directed toward gaining an understanding of the motivations and behavior of the different segments of the total tourism market. The purpose of gaining this understanding is to provide those responsible for supply development with the information needed to design facilities and services that will appeal most to each of the various demand segments. In addition, such data facilitates the task of those responsible for the promotion of existing facilities and services.

The final component of external/demand analysis involves a review and evaluation of competitive and supportive tourism development and promotion policies and programs. Competitive analysis is a common form of managerial investigation. In this case, it is designed to produce a clear picture concerning the identity, strength, and strategies of those tourism destinations most likely to be appealing to the same segments of demand as those of interest to the tourism region in question. Such information is essential if a region is to effectively counter the efforts of such competitors from the standpoint of both supply development and demand modification.

The analysis of supportive policies and programs is an activity that is frequently neglected in the highly competitive world of tourism. As a result, policymakers may overlook potential sources of synergy that may be developed by cooperating with either other tourism regions or other public/private sector organizations within the region, but in nontourism fields. While care must be exercised in deciding what forms of cooperation are most likely to be attractive, failure to explore such avenues may deprive a region of the possibility of appealing to new or distant markets.

Operational Phase

Once the various types of analysis have been carried out, policymakers must move to develop specific strategies and action plans that can be implemented. As shown in Figure 15.10, this operational phase is envisaged to contain three conceptually different types of activity; in reality, these different activities are executed almost simultaneously.

The identification of strategic conclusions flows directly out of the analytical phase, and its goal is to synthesize the large amounts of information obtained into a limited number of major conclusions. In addition to specifying the major findings from each type of internal and external analysis, this process also must attempt to provide conclusions that assess the impact of the trade-offs that inevitably are made when attempting to match supply and demand.

The strategic conclusions themselves may be viewed as reasonably factual information; that is, they are the result of a logical process of analysis that would give rise to generally similar findings irrespective of the investigator. In contrast, the drawing of "implications of the conclusions for supply-and-demand development strategies" involves a high degree of judgment on the part of the individuals involved. The goal of this process is to attempt to assess the significance of each conclusion for tourism in the region. While the actual conclusions may be clear, the implications of these facts for the kind of policies and programs needed to deal with them involves a considerable level of interpretive skills derived from both experience and a creative mind.

The subsequent stage of the policy formulation process is the identification of specific "policy/program recommendations for supply/demand development." For present purposes, this rather complex activity has been oversimplified in reality; a range of policy options would normally be developed which attempt to respond to alternative implications or alternative scenarios. Some judgment would then be exercised as to which implications or scenarios are most likely to occur. Policy/program recommendations most appropriate to the most likely events would probably, although not necessarily, be adopted.

Finally, for a destination tourism policy to truly succeed, it is essential to include an implementation phase. At a minimum, such a strategy must (1) identify the individual groups or organizations that will assume responsibility for each major dimension of the policy realization, (2) establish initial estimates of the financial requirements, and (3) provide preliminary timelines for the launching of all major facilities, events, and programs that support the destination vision.

Policy Formulation Methods

While a detailed examination of policy, planning, and research methods is beyond the scope of this text, it is important to be aware of some of the most popular and most effective approaches currently in use:

- Delphi technique
- Brainstorming
- Focus groups
- Nominal group technique
- Household surveys
- Industry expert interviews
- Evaluation research
- Impact analysis (economic, environmental, social, cultural)
- Panel research
- Interest-based negotiation
- Destination visioning

References for readings providing an understanding of each of these approaches are included at the end of the chapter.

SUMMARY

This chapter points out that (a) tourism policy is needed for destinations at all levels and for all types of political jurisdictions, (b) in all cases, competitiveness and sustainability must be the primary goal of policy, and (c) the effective pursuit of each of these goals requires a different set of skills and capabilities. With this background firmly in place, the chapter then fulfills two major roles.

The first of these roles is to provide a framework describing the structure and composition of a formal tourism policy. The primary components discussed are the philosophy for tourism and the formulation of a long-term vision for the destination. This vision provides important guidance for the definition of specific objectives for a tourism destination, as well as for identifying any constraints that must be observed as tourism is developed. These objectives, in turn, provide a basis for formulating long term development strategies for the region. The detailed components of supply-and-demand development strategies are then discussed.

Finally, the chapter focuses on the process of policy formulation, the process by which all of the foregoing components of policy are defined. The chapter identifies the major components of tourism policy and strategy formulation and implementation and discusses the activities involved in each.

ABOUT THE READINGS

The first reading represents a rare document in tourism: a policy framework that is not only well thought out, but which appears to be used in practice as an important guiding force for California's ongoing efforts to market the state and its many attractions around the world.

The increasing commitment of national governments to the funding of their tourism administrations' marketing activities abroad has been accompanied by demands for more rigorous evaluations of the effectiveness of these activities. More rigorous and comprehensive approaches to evaluation are also required to furnish a more solid foundation for strategic decisionmaking. The second reading proposes a framework for systematically integrating a range of techniques to accomplish evaluation.

READING 15.1

"CALIFORNIA TOURISM POLICY ACT," CALIFORNIA DIVISION OF TOURISM, 1997 ANNUAL REPORT, MARCH 1, 1998.

The People of the State of California Do Enact as Follows: California Government Code—California Tourism Policy Act

15364.50. The Legislature finds and declares that:

a. Tourism is a major source of jobs, income, and tax revenues in California, and the expansion of this industry is vital to the overall growth of California's economy.

b. The tourism, travel, and recreational industries are important to the state, not only because of the numbers of people they serve and the vast human, financial, and physical resources they employ, but because of the benefits which tourism, recreation, and related activities confer on individuals and on society as a whole.

c. There is a need to invest state resources to provide a more effective means of promoting and marketing travel to, and within, the state, and to optimize the considerable investment of time, energy, capital, and resources being made by the tourism industry.

d. Existing state government involvement in tourism and related activities needs to be better coordinated at the state level, as well as with local government and the private sector, if the economic and employment benefits of the industry are to be maximized.

e. The entire state could benefit from promotion of lesser known and underutilized destinations within the state and additional state resources may be effectively utilized to assist such localities in order that they can participate in, and benefit from, a tourism promotion.

15364.51. It is the intention of the Legislature in enacting this part or amending this part to add Chapter 2.2 (commencing with Section 15372.60) to do all of the following:

a. Reaffirm a commitment to the fostering of the economic activity inherent in tourism promotion as delineated as a mandate to the agency and to the Office of Tourism, and, in furtherance of those goals and pursuant to the supervision and oversight of the secretary, further specific state governmental goals, as established by the Legislature, to result in a promotion program that produces non ideological and commercial communication that bears the characteristics of, and is entitled to all the privileges and protections of, government speech.

b. To provide the state with an effective means of promoting and marketing the State of California as a destination for tourists on a worldwide basis, to provide the private sector with a more effective means of promoting tourism efforts and a forum for removing obstacles to overall tourism growth in order for California to remain competitive in world and national tourism marketplaces.

c. Optimize the contribution of the tourism-related industries to the state's economic prosperity and to expand employment opportunities.

d. Make the opportunity for, and benefits of, tourism in the state accessible to its residents and visitors and ensure that present and future generations are afforded adequate tourism resources and attractions.

e. Encourage the preservation and use of California historic and scenic environments to enhance the state's appeal as a destination for domestic and international tourism.

f. Encourage California residents to take maximum advantage of travel and tourism opportunities within the State of California by enabling them to obtain accurate, timely, up-to-date travel and tourism information benefiting both urban and rural travelers in various regions of the state.

g. Contribute to personal growth, health, education, and intercultural appreciation of the geography, history, arts, and ethnicity of the State of California.

h. Encourage the free and welcome entry of individuals traveling to the state in order to enhance international understanding and goodwill, consistent with immigration laws, the laws protecting the public health, and laws governing the importation of goods into the United States and state law.

i. Encourage investment in new tourism facilities and renovation of older facilities.

j. Assist in the collection, analysis, and timely dissemination of data that accurately measure the economic and social impact of tourism to, and within, the state in order to facilitate planning in the public and private sectors.

k. Harmonize, to the maximum extent possible, all state activities in support of tourism and recreation with the needs of the general public, local governments, and the private sector, and to give leadership to all concerned with tourism in California.

15364.52.

a. There is hereby created in state government a California Tourism Commission, located within the Trade and Commerce Agency, which shall consist of the Secretary of Trade and Commerce who shall serve as the chairperson of the commission; the Director of the Office of Tourism, who shall serve as vice chairperson of the commission and nine other members appointed as follows:
1. Five members shall be appointed by the Governor who are able persons, professionally active in the tourism industry representing diverse segments of that industry.
2. One Member of the Senate shall be appointed by the Senate Committee on Rules and one Member of the Assembly shall be appointed by the Speaker of the Assembly. These members shall be ex officio, nonvoting members of the commission.
3. Two members, who are able persons professionally active in the tourism industry representing diverse segments of that industry, shall be appointed one each by the Senate Committee on Rules and the Speaker of the Assembly.

b. The Assistant Director of the Office of Tourism shall serve as secretary to the commission, a nonvoting position, and shall keep the minutes and records of all commission meetings and provide staff and whatever supportive services necessary to the activities of the commission.

c. The commission shall meet quarterly and at other times and places as the chairperson may designate for the purpose of transacting the commission's business. Each commission member shall serve without compensation but shall be reimbursed for traveling and other expenses necessarily incurred in the performance of duties.

d. The commission shall, in cooperation with the Office of Tourism and the agency, adopt, and annually update, a tourism marketing plan for the State of California that includes both domestic and international tourism promotion. The plan shall, to the extent practical and feasible, do all of the following:

1. Serve as a guide for effectuating the California Tourism Policy Act, within available resources.
2. Include an assessment of the activities and accomplishments of the Office of Tourism.
3. Outline the intended program of tourism promotion and visitor service activities for the oncoming year.
4. Delineate the ways, means, and programs by which tourism shall be promoted, including any cost-effective marketing methods and techniques to be employed.
5. Identify resources as are reasonably necessary, from all sources both public and private, to accomplish these promotion and marketing activities.
6. Identify and articulate cooperative or shared cost programs, or opportunities for these ventures, with private entities.
7. Identify licensing opportunities, including licensing agents.
8. Contain other information, data, or recommendations that may be germane to the marketing efforts of California pursuant to the intent of this chapter.

e. The commission, in cooperation with the Office of Tourism, may convene committees consisting of qualified professionals and experts in various segments of the tourism industry that may be required to aid in the preparation of, or revision of, the marketing plan, or parts thereof, and as may from time to time be appropriate to the commission shall work to the maximum extent practicable with governmental organizations and private for profit and nonprofit associations, corporations, organizations, or other entities, or all of these, whose purpose includes the promotion, representation, or development, or all of these, of travel and tourism.

f. The commission established by this chapter shall be inoperative while the California Travel and Tourism Commission established pursuant to Chapter 2.2 (commencing with Section 15372.60) is in existence. The commission established by this chapter shall resume operation on the date the California Travel and Tourism Commission established by Chapter 2.2 (commencing with Section 15372.60) terminates.

15364.53. In addition to the intent of the Legislature expressed in Section 15364.51, and those functions of the Office of Tourism and the California Tourism Commission specified in Section 15364.52, the Office of Tourism and the California Travel and Tourism Commission established pursuant to Chapter 2.2 (commencing with Section 15372.60):

a. Shall take advantage of particular promotional opportunities as may be presented.
b. Shall facilitate travel and visitorship to, and within, California to the maximum extent feasible.
c. May identify and assist in the development of a user-directed, computer-based, public-access information system serving the needs of the traveling and tourist public in urban and rural areas in California.
d. Shall develop and publish research to determine sources and characteristics of present and future visitors to California and measure the effectiveness of marketing and service programs.
e. Shall represent the state at domestic and international travel trade shows that provide an opportunity to promote a significant amount of travel to, and within, California.
f. Shall cooperate with the federal government in the development and the promotion of the United States as a destination for international tourism.
g. Shall implement the Tourism Marketing Plan.

15364.54. The director shall report on or before March 1 of each year to the Governor, the Legislature, and the California Tourism Commission. Each report shall do all of the following:

Detail the tourism marketing plan that been adopted for the upcoming fiscal year. If the California Tourism Commission established pursuant to Section 15364.52 is inoperative, the secretary shall detail the marketing plan described in Section 15372.75.

a. Assess the effectiveness of the previous calendar year's tourism marketing program.
b. Document the directly attributable benefits of the previous calendar year's tourism marketing program.
c. Identify methods of promoting travel to the state's lesser known and underutilized destinations.
d. Measure the annual size (for the most recent measurable year) in aggregate and by county of the following:

1. Travel and tourism spending in California.
2. Travel and tourism employment in California.
3. Travel and tourism generated state and local tax revenues.

e. Identify additional data to be collected to assess further and adequately the benefits of the tourism marketing program.

f. Establish standardized and accurate methods to measure annually California's share of the domestic and international tourism.

g. Report on the income and expenses of the commission and otherwise generally with respect to its financial affairs. The portion of the report pertaining to the topics described in this subdivision shall be audited.

15364.55. State agencies and departments may, in their discretion, detail to temporary duty with the office, such personnel as the director may request for carrying out the purposes of this act, each such detail to be without loss of seniority, pay or other employee status.

The People of the State of California Do Enact as Follows: California Government Code—Chapter 2.2. California Tourism Marketing Act

Article 1. Legislative Intent

15372.60. This chapter shall be known and may be cited as the California Tourism Marketing Act.

15372.61. The Legislature hereby finds and declares all of the following:

a. Tourism is among California's biggest industries, contributing over fifty-two billion dollars $52,000,000,000 to the state economy and employing nearly 700,000 Californians in 1995.

b. In order to retain and expand the tourism industry in California, it is necessary to market travel to and within California.

c. State funding, while an important component of marketing, has been unable to generate sufficient funds to meet the threshold levels of funding necessary to reverse recent losses of California's tourism market share.

d. In regard to the need for a cooperative partnership between business and industry:

1. It is in the state's public interest and vital to the welfare of the state's economy to expand the market for, and develop, California tourism through a cooperative partnership funded in part by the state that will allow generic promotion and communication programs.

2. The mechanism established by this chapter is intended to play a unique role in advancing the opportunity to expand tourism in California, and it is intended to increase the opportunity for tourism to the benefit of the tourism industry and the consumers of the State of California.

3. Programs implemented pursuant to this chapter are intended to complement the marketing activities of individual competitors within the tourism industry.

4. While it is recognized that smaller businesses participating in the tourism market often lack the resources or market power to conduct these activities on their own, the programs are intended to be of benefit to businesses of all sizes.

5. These programs are not intended to, and they do not, impede the right or ability of individual businesses to conduct activities designed to increase the tourism market generally or their own respective shares of the California tourism market, and nothing in the mechanism established by this chapter shall prevent an individual business or participant in the industry from seeking to expand its market through alternative or complementary means, or both.

6. (A) An individual business's own advertising initiatives are typically designed to increase its share of the California tourism market rather than to increase or expand the overall size of that market. (B) In contrast, generic promotion of California as a tourism destination is intended and designed to maintain or increase the overall demand for California tourism and to maintain or increase the size of that market, often by utilizing promotional methods and techniques that individual businesses typically are unable, or have no incentive, to employ.

7. This chapter creates a mechanism to fund generic promotions that, pursuant to the required supervision and oversight of the secretary as specified in this chapter, further specific

state governmental goals, as established by the Legislature, and result in a promotion program that produces nonideological and commercial communication that bears the characteristics of and is entitled to all the privileges and protections of, government speech.

8. The programs implemented pursuant to this chapter shall be carried out in an effective and coordinated manner that is designed to strengthen the tourism industry and the state's economy as a whole.

9. Independent evaluation of the effectiveness of the programs will assist the Legislature in ensuring that the objectives of the programs as set out in this section are met.

e. An industry-approved assessment provides a private-sector financing mechanism that, in partnership with state funding, will provide the amount of marketing necessary to increase tourism marketing expenditures by California.

f. The goal of the assessments is to assess the least amount per business, in the least intrusive manner, spread across the greatest practical number of tourism industry segments.

g. The commission shall target an amount determined to be sufficient to market effectively travel and tourism to and within the state.

h. In the course of developing its written marketing plan pursuant to Section 15372.75, the commission shall, to the maximum extent feasible, do both of the following:

1. Seek advice and recommendations from all segments of California's travel and tourism industry and from all geographic regions of the state.

2. Harmonize, as appropriate, its marketing plan with the travel and tourism marketing activities and objectives of the various industry segments and geographic regions.

i. The commission's marketing budget shall be spent principally to bring travelers and tourists into the state. No more than 15 percent of the commission's assessed funds in any year shall be spent to promote travel within California, unless approved by at least two-thirds of the commissioners.

Article 2. Definitions

15372.65. Unless the context otherwise requires, the definitions in this section govern the construction of this chapter.

a. "Appointed Commissioner" means a commissioner appointed by the Governor.

b. "Assessed business" means a person required to pay an assessment pursuant to this chapter, and until the first assessment is levied, any person authorized to vote for the initial referendum. An assessed business shall not include a public entity or a corporation when a majority of the corporation's board of directors is appointed by a public official or public entity, or serves on the corporation's board of directors by virtue of being elected to public office, or both.

c. "Commission" means the California Travel and Tourism Commission.

d. "Elected Commissioner" means a commissioner elected pursuant to subdivision (d) of Section 15372.70.

e. "Industry category" means the following classifications within the tourism industry:
1. Accommodations.
2. Restaurants and retail.
3. Attractions and recreation.
4. Transportation and travel services.

f. "Industry segment" means a portion of an industry category. For example, rental cars are an industry segment of the transportation and travel services industry category.

g. "Office" means the Office of Tourism, also popularly referred to as the Division of Tourism, within the Trade and Commerce Agency.

h. "Person" means an individual, public entity, firm, corporation, association, or any other business unit, whether operating on a for a profit or nonprofit basis.

i. "Referendum" means any vote by mailed ballot of measures recommended by the commission and approved by the secretary pursuant to Section 15372.100, except for the initial referendum, which shall consist of measures contained in the selection committee report, discussed in Section 15372.66.

j. "Secretary" means the Secretary of Trade and Commerce.

k. "Selection Committee" means the Tourism Selection Committee described in Article 3 (commencing with Section 15372.66).

Article 3. Tourism Selection Committee

15372.66.

a. The Governor shall appoint a Tourism Selection Committee based upon recommendations from established industry associations. The committee shall consist of 25 representatives, with no fewer than six from each industry category. In selecting the representatives, the Governor shall, to the extent possible, give recognition to the diversity within each industry category. The committee shall select a chairperson from among its members. The office shall provide staffing for the committee.

b. The selection committee shall convene on or before March 1, 1996. Not later than 150 days following the initial convening of the committee, the committee shall issue a report listing the following:
   1. Industry segments that will be included in the initial referendum.
   2. The target assessment level for the initial referendum.
   3. Percentage of funds to be levied against each industry category and segment. To the extent possible, the percentages shall be based upon quantifiable industry data, and amounts to be levied against industry segments shall bear an appropriate relationship to the benefit derived from travel and tourism by those industry segments.
   4. Assessment methodology and rate of assessment within each industry segment, that may include, but is not limited to, a percentage of gross revenue or a per transaction charge.
   5. Businesses, if any, within a segment to be assessed at a reduced rate, which may be set at zero, whether temporarily or permanently.
   6. Initial slate of proposed elected commissioners. The number of commissioners elected from each industry category shall be determined by the weighted percentage of assessments from that category.

c. Nothing in this section shall preclude the selection committee from setting the assessment rate for a business within a segment at a lower rate, which may be set at zero, than a rate applicable to other businesses within that segment if the selection committee makes specific findings that the lower rate should apply due to unique geographical, fi-

nancial, or other circumstances affecting the business. No business for which a zero assessment rate is set pursuant to this subdivision shall be sent a ballot or entitled to participate in the initial referendum, or in any subsequent referendum in which its rate of assessment is set at zero.

d. The committee members for each industry category, also referred to as a subcommittee, shall prepare a recommendation for the entire committee on how the items specified in subdivision (b) should be determined for the industry segments within their industry category. The recommendations shall not include a discussion of industry category levies, which shall be determined solely by committee. In the event that the subcommittee cannot agree on one or more of the items specified in subdivision (b), no recommendation shall be given in that category. The recommendations shall be presented to the full committee, which shall address each of the items contained in subdivision (b).

e. In order to be assessed, an industry segment must be defined with sufficient clarity to allow for the cost-effective identification of assessed businesses within that segment.

f. It shall be the responsibility of the office to advertise widely the selection committee process and to schedule public meetings for potential assessed businesses to provide input to the selection committee.

g. The recommendations developed by the committee pursuant to subdivision (b) shall be reviewed and approved by the secretary.

h. The selection committee process and report are exempt from the requirements of the Administrative Procedure Act (Chapter 3.5 (commencing with Section 11340) of Part 1).

Article 4. Commission

15372.70.

a. Upon approval of the initial referendum, the office shall establish a nonprofit mutual benefit corporation named the California Travel and Tourism Commission. The commission shall be under the direction of a board of commissioners, which shall function as the board of directors for purposes of the Nonprofit Corporation Law.

b. The board of commissioners shall consist of 37 commissioners comprising the following:

1. The secretary, who shall serve as chairperson.
2. Twelve members, who are professionally active in the tourism industry, representing each of the 12 officially designated tourism regions and diverse elements of the industry, shall be appointed by the Governor. Appointed commissioners are not limited to assessed businesses.
3. Twenty-four elected commissioners, including at least one representative of a travel agency or tour operator that is an assessed business.

c. The commission established pursuant to Section 15364.52 shall be inoperative so long as the commission established pursuant to this section is in existence.

d. Elected commissioners shall be elected by industry category in a referendum. Regardless of the number of ballots received for a referendum the nominee for each commissioner slot with the most weighted votes from assessed businesses within that industry category shall be elected commissioner. In the event that an elected commissioner resigns, dies, or is removed from office during his or her term, the commission shall appoint a replacement from the same industry category that the commissioner in question represented, and that commissioner shall fill the remaining term of the commissioner in question. The number of commissioners elected from each industry category shall be determined by the weighted percentage of assessments from that category.

e. The secretary may remove any elected commissioner following a hearing at which the commissioner is found guilty of abuse of office or moral turpitude.

f. With the exception of the secretary, no commissioner shall serve for more than two consecutive terms.

g. Except for the original commissioners, all commissioners shall serve four-year terms. One-half of the commissioners originally appointed or elected shall serve a two-year term, while the remainder shall serve a four-year term. Every two years thereafter, one-half of the commissioners shall be appointed or elected by referendum.

h. The selection committee shall determine the initial slate of candidates for elected commissioners. Thereafter the commissioners, by adopted resolu-

tion, shall nominate a slate of candidates, and shall include any additional candidates complying with the procedure described in Section 15372.102.

i. The commissioners shall elect a vice chairperson from the elected commissioners.

j. The commission may lease space from the office.

k. The commission and the office shall be the official state representatives of California tourism.

l. All commission meetings shall be held in California.

m. No person shall receive compensation for serving as a commissioner, but each commissioner shall receive reimbursement for reasonable expenses incurred while on authorized commission business. (2) The commission's annual budget shall be subject to the review and approval of the secretary. However, any decision of the secretary related to the budget may be overridden by a vote of three-fifths or more of the commissioners then in office.

n. The commission shall maintain a report on the percentage assessment allocation between industry categories and industry segments. The report shall also specify the reasons and methodology used for the allocations. This report shall be updated every time the assessment allocations are amended. The report shall be made available to any assessed business.

15372.75.

a. The commission shall annually prepare, or cause to be prepared, a written marketing plan. In developing the plan, the commission shall utilize, as appropriate, the advice and recommendations of the industry marketing advisory committee or committees established pursuant to subdivision (a) of 15372.77. The commission may amend the plan at any commission meeting. All expenditures by the commission shall be consistent with the marketing plan.

b. The plan shall promote travel to and within California, and shall include, but not be limited to, the following:
   1. An evaluation of the previous year's budget and activities.
   2. Review of California tourism trends, conditions, and opportunities.

3. Target audiences for tourism marketing expenditures.

4. Marketing strategies, objectives, and targets.

5. Budget for the current year.

c. Before final adoption of the plan, the commission shall provide each known destination marketing organization in California notice of the availability of the proposed marketing plan and suitable opportunity, which may include public meetings, to review the plan and to comment upon it. The commission shall take into consideration any recommendations submitted by the destination marketing organizations, except that the final determination as to the nature, extent, and substance of the plan shall in all respects rest solely within the ultimate discretion of the commission, except as provided in subdivision (d).

d. The final adoption of the plan shall be subject to the review and approval of the secretary. However, any decision of the secretary related to the plan may be overridden by a vote of three-fifths or more of the commissioners then in office.

15372.76. Commissioners and employees of the commission are not responsible individually in any way whatsoever to any person for liability for any good faith activity of the commission.

15372.77.

a. The commission shall establish one or more industry marketing advisory committees, which may include noncommissioners as members. The industry marketing advisory committees shall be structured so that, in the aggregate, they include, to the maximum extent feasible and reasonable, representation from every geographic region of the state and every segment of the state's travel and tourism industry. The commission shall establish procedures for the operation of the industry marketing advisory committees that will provide appropriate opportunity for every geographic region of the state and every segment of the travel and tourism industry to offer advice and recommendations to the commission relative to the development of its written marketing plan pursuant to Section 15372.75.

b. The commission may also establish from time to time any other committees it deems appropriate, and may appoint noncommissioners to the committees.

15372.78. If the commission believes that the administration of the marketing plan will be promoted thereby, the commission may borrow money, with or without interest, to carry out the provisions of the marketing plan, and may hypothecate anticipated assessment collections.

15372.79. The commission may by written contract accept a voluntary assessment from any person in a travel and tourism related business who is not an assessed business. The contract shall apply solely to the person in question and not to any other person in a travel and tourism related business who is not an assessed business. The contract shall provide that the voluntary assessment be equivalent to the assessment that would be levied if the person were an assessed business under this chapter, shall permit that business to vote on any referendum conducted under this chapter as if that person were an assessed business, and shall have a term concurrent with the effective period of any referendum on which the person votes. Individual voluntary assessments under this section shall be enforceable only under the terms of the respective contracts to which they pertain. This section shall not be construed to preclude donations to, or cooperative marketing activities of any kind with, the commission. Notwithstanding the foregoing, the commission shall not enter into any contract for a voluntary assessment with a person whose primary business is gaming, as defined in Chapter 10 (commencing with Section 330) of Title 9, Part 1 of the Penal Code.

Article 5. Secretary

15372.85.

a. The marketing of California tourism is hereby declared to be affected with the public interest. This chapter is enacted in the exercise of the police powers of this state for the purpose of protecting the health, peace, safety, and general welfare of the people of this state.

b. The police powers shall be used to collect assessments not paid by the deadlines established by the secretary.

15372.86.

a. The following powers shall be the responsibility of the secretary:

   1. Call referenda in accordance with the procedures set forth in Article 6 (commencing with Section 15372.100) and certify the results.

   2. Collect and deposit assessments.

3. Exercise police powers.

4. Pursue actions and penalties connected with assessments.

b. Except as otherwise specified in this chapter, the secretary shall have veto power over the actions of the commission, following consultation with the commission, only under the following circumstances:

1. Travel and expense costs.

2. Situations where the secretary determines a conflict of interest exists, as defined by the Fair Political Practices Commission.

3. The use of any state funds.

4. Any contracts entered into between the commission and a commissioner.

15372.87.

a. Except as otherwise specified in Section 15372.111, the commission may be terminated at any time after the initial four years of operation by referendum of the assessed businesses.

b. Notice of the termination shall be mailed to all assessed businesses.

c. Upon termination, the commission shall continue its existence as a nonprofit corporation for purposes of winding up its affairs and dissolution.

d. Upon termination of the commission established pursuant to this chapter, the California Tourism Commission authorized pursuant to Section 15364.52 shall advise the office, and conduct all other tasks authorized by the California Tourism Policy Act.

15372.88. The secretary may require any and all assessed businesses to maintain books and records that reflect their income or sales as reflected in the assessment, and to furnish the secretary with any information that may, from time-to-time, be requested by the secretary, and to permit the inspection by the secretary of portions of books and records that relate to the amount of assessment.

15372.89. Information pertaining to assessed businesses obtained by the secretary pursuant to this chapter is confidential and shall not be disclosed except to a person with the right to obtain the information, any attorney hired by the secretary who is employed to give legal advice upon it, or by court order. Information obtained by the secretary in order to determine the assessment level for an assessed business is exempt from the California Public Records Act (Chapter 3.5 (commencing with Section 6250) of Division 7 of Title 1).

15372.90. For the purpose of carrying out Section 15372.86, the secretary may hold hearings, take testimony, administer oaths, subponea witnesses, and issue subpoenas for the production of books, records, or documents of any kind.

15372.91. A person shall not be excused from attending and testifying, or from producing documentary evidence, before the secretary in obedience to the subpoena of the secretary pursuant to the authority granted in Section 15372.90 on the ground, or for the reason, that the testimony or evidence, documentary or otherwise, which is required of him or her may tend to incriminate the person or subject that person to a penalty. A natural person shall not, however, be prosecuted or subjected to any penalty on account of any transaction, matter, or thing concerning which he or she may be required to testify, or produce evidence, documentary or otherwise, before the secretary in obedience to a subpoena. A natural person testifying shall not, however, be exempt from prosecution and punishment for perjury committed in so testifying.

15372.92. Any funds appropriated to the office may be used to implement the tourism marketing plan specified in Section 15372.75 or, if the commission is not in existence, Section 15364.52. In addition to any other authority for the office to spend funds, state funds may be used for the following: research, conducting and advertising referenda, administration of state funds, policing, collection of assessments, and contracting for assistance in obtaining information on businesses to be assessed.

15372.93. The office may contract with the commission in order for the commission to undertake marketing activities utilizing state funds, and Section 10295, and Article 4 (commencing with Section 10335) and Article 5 (commencing with Section 10355) of Chapter 2 of Part 2 of Division 2 of the Public Contract Code shall not apply to those agreements.

Article 6. Referendum

15372.100.

a. The initial referendum shall cover, but not be limited to, the following subjects:

1. The proposed assessment level, based upon specified assessment formulae, together with necessary information to enable each assessed

business to determine what its individual assent would be.

2. Election of commissioners.
3. Whether to have an assessment.

b. A referendum shall be called every two years, commencing on the second anniversary of the initial referendum.

c. The first referendum following the initial referendum shall solely determine the new set of commissioners by adopted resolution. At that referendum, the assessment target shall remain at the same level as utilized in the initial referendum. The assessment formula shall remain the same and the commission shall continue its existence. As used in this article and Article 7 (commencing with Section 15372.105) "assessment level" means the estimated gross dollar amount received by assessment from all assessed businesses on an annual basis, and "assessment formula" means the allocation method used within each industry segment (for example, percentage of gross revenue).

d. Commencing with the third referendum, the commission shall, by adopted resolution, determine the slate of individuals who will run for commissioner. The resolution shall also cover, but not be limited to, the proposed assessment level, based upon specified assessment formulae, together with necessary information to enable each assessed business to determine what its individual assessment would be; and termination of the commission. The resolution may also include an amended industry segment allocation formula and the percentage allocation of assessments between industry categories and segments. The commission may specify in the resolution that a special, lower assessment rate that was set pursuant to subdivision (c) of Section 15372.66 for a particular business will no longer apply due to changes in the unique circumstance that originally justified the lower rate. The resolution may include up to three possible assessment levels, from which the assessed businesses will select one assessment level.

e. The commission shall deliver to the secretary the resolution described in subdivision (b) or (c). The secretary shall call a referendum containing the information required by subdivision (b) or (c) plus any additional matters complying with the procedures of subdivision (b) of Section 15372.102.

f. When the secretary calls a referendum, all assessed businesses shall be sent a ballot for the referendum. Every ballot that the secretary receives by the ballot deadline shall be counted, utilizing the weighted formula adopted initially by the selection committee, and subsequently amended by referendum.

g. If the referendum includes more than one possible assessment rate, the rate with the plurality of weighted votes shall be adopted.

h. The initial referendum shall, if possible, be held within 180 days of receipt by the Governor of the selection committee report, or, if not possible, as soon as practicable thereafter. The secretary shall call the referendum.

15372.101.

a. The costs of marketing and promoting the initial referendum shall be provided by private payments. The costs of the initial referendum shall be paid by the office. The office shall coordinate the referendum to ensure that it is unbiased and factually correct. In the event that the initial referendum fails in the first attempt at passage, subsequent attempts at passage, of the initial referendum shall be permitted, except that the costs of conducting the subsequent attempts at passage along with the costs of marketing and promoting those attempts at passage, shall be provided by private payments. Subsequent attempts at passage shall be conducted in the manner specified in this subdivision. In the event that the initial referendum passes, whether on the first attempt at passage or a subsequent attempt at passage, the private payers and the office shall be reimbursed for all of their respective initial referendum costs from assessments first received.

b. The ongoing referendum costs shall be paid by the commission.

15372.102.

a. Commencing with the third referendum, assessed businesses may place on a referendum additional candidates for commissioner, a different assessment level, or both.

b. Except for the referendum that occurs four years from the initial referendum, a minimum of 20 percent of the assessed businesses (calculated by weighted percentages) must signify their agreement to add different assessment levels to the items included in the referendum. For the referendum occurring four years from the initial referendum, a minimum of 10 percent of the assessed businesses (calculated by weighted percentages) must signify agreement.

c. A minimum of 10 percent of the assessed businesses (calculated by weighted percentages) must signify their agreement to add candidates for commissioner to the items included in the referendum.

15372.103.

a. Upon receipt of the resolution required by Section 15372.100, including any assessed business referendum request pursuant to Section 15372.102, the secretary shall establish a referendum period not to exceed 60 days. If the secretary determines that the referendum period so established does not provide sufficient time for the balloting, the secretary may extend the referendum period not more than 15 additional days. At the close of the referendum period, the secretary shall count and tabulate the ballots filed during the referendum period.

b. The secretary shall establish a deadline for adoption of the resolution described in subdivision (a). If the commission fails to meet this deadline, or if the adopted resolution fails to meet the requirements of this chapter, then assessed businesses may present a slate of candidates to the secretary not later than 60 days following the deadline established for the commission resolution. A minimum of 10 percent of weighted voters must sign the document presenting the slate.

c. In the event that the secretary does not receive a resolution required by Section 15372.100 from the commission by the deadline established pursuant to subdivision (b) or the resolution does not comply with the requirements of this chapter and the assessed businesses fail to present a slate pursuant to subdivision (b), then the secretary shall select a slate of commissioners and this slate, added to any assessed business referendum requests pursuant to Section 15372.102, shall constitute the items included in the referendum.

15372.104.

a. Each assessed business is entitled to a weighted vote in each referendum. In calculating weighted votes, each assessed business receives a vote equal to the relative assessment paid by that business. An assessed business paying nine hundred dollars ($900) in annual assessments has three times the weighted vote of a business paying three hundred dollars ($300). Weighted votes are used to determine all issues on the referendum. The initial referendum, and any referendum item to terminate the commission, must be approved by a majority of the weighted votes cast at the referendum. The amount of assessment and selection of commissioners is determined by the most weighted votes, whether or not there is a majority.

b. For purposes of voting in any referendum, each assessed business is part of one industry category and one industry segment, and for voting purposes only, a business with revenue in more than one industry category or industry segment shall only be included in the category and segment in which it earns the most gross revenue.

c. Each assessed business is eligible to vote for each item on the referendum, except that an assessed business can only vote for commissioners representing its industry category, and industry segment formulae for its industry segment.

d. A business is not eligible to vote unless it has paid all assessments and fines outstanding as of a date established by the secretary.

Article 7. Assessments

15372.105.

a. Each industry category shall establish a committee to determine the following within its industry category: industry segments, assessment formula for each industry segment, and any types of business exempt from assessment. The initial segment committees shall consist of the subcommittee for that category as described in subdivision (c) of Section 15372.66. Following approval of the assessment by referendum, the committees shall be selected by the commission, based upon recommendations from the tourism industry. Committee members need not be commission members.

b. The committee recommendations shall be presented to the commission or selection committee, as applicable. The selection committee may adopt a resolution specifying some or all of the items listed in subdivision (a), plus an allocation of the overall assessment among industry categories. The commission may adopt a resolution specifying one or more of the items listed in subdivision (a), plus an allocation of the proposed assessment. The selection committee and commission are not required to adopt the findings of any committee.

c. The initial industry category and industry segment allocations shall be included in the selection committee report required by subdivision (b) of Section 15372.66. Changes to the industry segment allocation formula may be recommended to the commission by a segment committee at the biennial commission meeting scheduled to approve the referendum resolution pursuant to Section 15372.100. At the same meeting, the commission may amend the percentage allocations among industry categories. Any item discussed in this section that is approved by resolution of the commission, except amendments to the percentage allocations among industry categories, shall be placed on the next referendum, and adopted if approved by the majority of weighted votes cast.

d. Upon approval by referendum, the office shall mail an assessment bill to each assessed business. The secretary shall determine how often assessments are collected, based upon available staffing resources. The secretary may stagger the assessment collection throughout the year, and charge businesses a prorated amount of assessment because of the staggered assessment period. The secretary and office shall not divulge the amount of assessment or weighted votes of any assessed businesses, except as part of an assessment action.

e. An assessed business may appeal an assessment to the secretary based upon the fact that the business does not meet the definition established for an assessed business within its industry segment or that the level of assessment is incorrect. An appeal brought under this subdivision shall be supported by substantial evidence submitted under penalty of perjury by affidavit or declaration as provided in Section 2015.5 of the Code of Civil Procedure. If the error is based upon failure of the business to provide the required information in a timely manner, the secretary may impose a fee for reasonable costs incurred by the secretary in correcting the assessment against the business as a condition of correcting the assessment.

f. Notwithstanding any other provision of law, an assessed business may pass on some or all of the assessment to customers. An assessed business that is passing on the assessment may, but shall not be required to, separately identify or itemize the assessment on any document provided to a customer. Assessments levied pursuant to this chapter and passed on to customers are not part of gross receipts or gross revenue for any purpose, including the calculation of sales or use tax and income pursuant to any lease. However, assessments that are passed on to customers shall be included in gross receipts for purposes of income and franchise taxes.

g. For purposes of calculating the assessment for a business with revenue in more than one industry category or industry segment, that business may elect to be assessed based on either of the following:

  1. The assessment methodology and rate of assessment applicable to each category or segment, respectively, as it relates to the revenue that it derives from that category or segment.

  2. With respect to its total revenue from all industry categories or segments, the assessment methodology and rate of assessment applicable to the revenue in the category and segment in which it earns the most gross revenue.

15372.106. The initial assessment level shall be the amount that the selection committee recommends in its report to the Governor pursuant to Section 15372.66, which may be less than twenty-five million dollars ($25,000,000). This assessment level is a target, and shall serve as the basis for setting application of the assessment formulae, but the actual amount of collected assessments may be more or less than the assessment level.

15372.107. Assessments may be used in furtherance of the purposes set forth in Section 15372.71, or to fund the costs pursuant to Section 15372.92. Assessments may be used to fund these costs regardless of whether the work was performed by the office or commission.

15372.109.

a. The secretary shall establish a list of businesses to be assessed and the amount of assessment owed by each. The secretary shall collect the assessment from all assessed businesses, and in collecting the assessment the secretary may exercise the police powers and bring enforcement actions.

b. Funds collected by the secretary shall be deposited into the account of the commission. This account shall not be an account of the state government.

c. Any costs relating to the collection of assessments incurred by the state shall be reimbursed by the commission.

15372.110.

a. The office shall develop a list of California businesses within each segment included within the report required by subdivision (b) of Section 15372.66, periodically updated. Other state agencies shall assist the office in obtaining the names and addresses of these businesses.

b. The office shall mail to each business identified pursuant to subdivision (a) a form requesting information necessary to determine the assessment for that business. Any business failing to provide this information in a timely manner shall be assessed an amount determined by the secretary to represent the upper assessment level for that segment.

c. The office, in consultation with the commission, shall establish by regulation the procedure for assessment collection.

15372.111.

a. Funding for the commission is a cooperative venture. Because of the benefits that accrue to the state and to its residents by virtue of having the travel and tourism industry participate cooperatively with the state for the purpose of effectively marketing travel and tourism to and within the state, it is the intent of the Legislature that the state shall be responsible for appropriating a minimum of seven million three hundred thousand dollars ($7,300,000) each fiscal year for travel and tourism, and the industry shall be responsible for targeting the level of assessments for each fiscal year at the amount determined to be appropriate by the commission and approved by referendum. However, that assessment level shall ultimately reach at least

twenty-five million dollars ($25,000,000). The industry may terminate the commission by referendum at any time, including during the initial four years, if the state fails to appropriate seven million three hundred thousand dollars ($7,300,000) in any fiscal year,

b. The assessed funds shall be audited annually.

c. The assessed funds shall be under the control of the commission, which shall spend the funds consistent with commission policies and the tourism marketing plan. The state shall have no interest in the fund except the general state interest that the state has in nonprofit corporations.

15372.112. Any assessment levied as provided in this chapter is a personal debt of every person so assessed and shall be due and payable to the secretary. If any assessed person fails to pay any assessment, the secretary may file a complaint against the person in a state court of competent jurisdiction for the collection of the assessment.

15372.113. If any assessed business that is duly assessed pursuant to this chapter fails to pay to the secretary the assessed amount by the due date, the secretary may add to the unpaid assessment an amount not to exceed 10 percent of the unpaid assessment to defray the cost of enforcing the collection of the unpaid assessment. In addition to payment for the cost of enforcing a collection, the assessed business shall pay to the secretary a penalty equivalent to the lesser of either the maximum amount authorized by Section 1 of Article XV of the California Constitution or 5 percent for each 30 days the assessment is unpaid, prorated over the days unpaid, commencing 30 days after the notice has been given to the assessed business of his or her failure to pay the assessment on the date required, unless the secretary determines, to his or her satisfaction, that the failure to pay is due to reasonable cause beyond the control of the assessed business.

15372.114. The secretary may require assessed businesses to deposit with him or her in advance the following amounts:

a. An amount for necessary expenses.

b. An amount that shall not exceed 25 percent of the assessment to cover costs that are incurred prior to the receipt of sufficient funds from the assessment.

c. The amount of any deposit that is required by the

secretary shall be based upon the estimated assessment for the assessed business.

15372.115. In lieu of requiring advance deposits pursuant to Section 15372.114, or in order generally to provide funds for defraying administrative expenses or the expenses of implementing the tourism marketing plan until the time that sufficient moneys are collected for this purpose from the payment of the assessments that are established pursuant to this chapter, the secretary may receive and disburse for the express purposes contributions that are made by assessed businesses. If, however, collections from the payment of established assessments are sufficient to so warrant, the secretary shall authorize the repayment of contributions, or authorize the application of the contributions to the assessment obligations of persons that made the contributions.

15372.116. Upon termination of the commission, any remaining funds that are not required by the secretary to defray commission expenses shall be returned by the secretary upon a pro rata basis, to all persons from whom the assessments were collected unless the secretary finds that the amounts to be returned are so small as to make impractical the computation and remitting of the pro rata refund to the appropriate persons. If the secretary makes a finding that returning the remaining funds would be impractical, he or she may use the moneys in the fund to defray the costs of the office.

15372.117. Any check or warrant that is drawn against the funds of the commission that remains unclaimed or uncashed for a period of six months from the date of issuance shall be canceled and the money retained for disbursement to the original payee or claimant upon satisfactory identification a period of one year from the time the check or warrant is canceled. The money so retained, if not claimed within the period of one year, shall be used for administration of the commission, and in furtherance of the tourism marketing plan.

15372.118. A business is exempt from the assessments provided for in this chapter if any of the following apply:

a. The business is a travel agency or tour operator that derives less than 20 percent of its gross revenue annually from travel and tourism occurring within the state. A travel agency or tour operator that qualifies for this exemption may participate as an assessed business by paying an assessment calculated on the same basis applicable to other travel agencies or tour operators, respectively, and by filing a written request with the secretary indicating its desire to be categorized as an assessed business.

b. The business is a small business. For purposes of this section, "small business" means a business location with less than $1,000,000 in total California gross annual revenue from all sources. A business exempted pursuant to this subdivision may enter into a contract for voluntary assessments pursuant to Section 15372.79.

c. The assessments provided for in this chapter shall not apply to the revenue of regular route intrastate and interstate bus service: provided, however, that this subdivision shall not be deemed to exclude any revenue derived from bus service that is of a type that requires authority, whether in the form of a certificate of public convenience and necessity, or a permit, to operate as a charter-party carrier of passengers pursuant to Chapter 8 (commencing with Section 5351) of Division 2 of the Public Utilities Code.

Article 8. Actions and Penalties

15372.120. Any action for any penalty or other remedy that is prescribed under any provision of this chapter shall be commenced within three years from the date of the alleged violation.

15372.122. Any person who files false information concerning an assessment is civilly liable in an amount of not more than ten thousand dollars ($10,000), in addition to any amount owed as the assessment.

15372.123.

a. When the secretary makes a determination that an assessment is deficient as to the payment due, the secretary may determine the amount of the deficiency, including any applicable penalty, as provided in this chapter. After giving notice that a deficiency determination is proposed and an opportunity to file a report or provide supplemental information is provided, the secretary may make one or more deficiency determinations of the amount due for any reporting period based on information in the secretary's possession. When an assessed business is discontinued, a deficiency determination may be made at anytime thereafter as to the liability arising out of the operation of that business.

b. The secretary shall give notice of the proposed deficiency determination and the notice of deficiency determination by mailing a copy of the deficiency to the assessed business at the current address for that business on file with the secretary. The giving of notice is complete at the time of deposit in the United States mail. In lieu of mailing, a notice may be served personally by delivering it to the person to be served.

c. Except in the case of fraud or failure to file required information, a notice of a deficiency determination shall be given within four years of the accrual of the deficiency.

d. The person against whom a deficiency determination is made may petition the secretary for redetermination within 30 days after the serving of the notice of deficiency determination. If a petition is not filed within 30 days, the deficiency determination shall become final.

e. A petition for redetermination shall be in writing, state the specific grounds upon which it is based, and be supported by applicable records and declarations under penalty of perjury that the information supporting the petition is accurate and complete. If a petition for redetermination is duly filed, the secretary shall reconsider the deficiency determination and may grant a hearing thereon. The secretary shall, as soon as practicable, make an order on redetermination, which shall become final 30 days after service of notice of the order of redetermination upon the petitioner. The notice of the order shall be served in the same manner as the notice of the original deficiency determination.

f. If any amount required to be paid pursuant to a deficiency determination or redetermination is not paid within the time specified in the notice thereof, the secretary may, within four years thereafter, file in the Superior Court in the County of Sacramento, or the superior court in any other county, a certificate specifying the amount required to be paid, the name and address of the person liable as it appears on the records of the secretary, and a request that judgment be entered against the person in that amount 30 days after the filing. Notice of the filing shall be given in the same manner as for the

notice of deficiency determination. The court shall enter a judgment in conformance with the secretary's certificate 30 days after its filing, unless a petition for judicial review has been filed within the 30-day period.

g. An abstract of the judgment, or a copy thereof, may be filed with the county recorder of any county. From the time of filing of the judgment, the amount of the judgment constitutes a lien upon all of the property in the county owned by the judgment debtor. The lien has the force, effect and priority of a judgment lien and shall continue for 10 years from the date of the judgment, unless sooner released or otherwise discharged. The lien imposed by this section is not valid insofar as personal property is concerned against a purchaser of value without actual knowledge of the lien.

h. Execution shall issue upon the judgment upon request of the secretary in the same manner as execution may issue upon other judgments, and sales shall be held under execution as prescribed in the Code of Civil Procedure.

i. The person named in a notice of deficiency determination or redetermination may, within 30 days of the notice of filing with the superior court, file an action for judicial review thereof, as provided herein, in the Superior Court in the County of Sacramento or, with the secretary's consent, the superior court in any other county. As a condition of staying entry of judgment or granting other relief, the court shall require the filing of a corporate surety bond with the secretary in the amount of the deficiency stated in the certificate. In any court proceeding, the certificate of the secretary determining the deficiency shall be prima facie evidence of the fee and the amount due and unpaid.

j. The provisions of this section are supplemental to any other procedures for collection and imposition of fees and penalties provided by this chapter.

k. In lieu of proceeding pursuant to this section, the secretary may file a complaint for collection of unpaid assessments as provided by law.

15372.124. It is a violation of this chapter for any person to willfully render or furnish a false or fraudulent report, statement, or record that is required by the secretary pursuant to any provision of this chapter.

15372.125. Any suit brought by the secretary to enforce any provision of this chapter, or any regulation, or rule and regulation, that is issued by the secretary shall provide that the defendant pay to the secretary the costs that were incurred by the secretary and by the commission in the prosecution of the action in the event the secretary prevails in the action. Any money that is recovered shall reimburse the account or accounts used to pay the costs.

Article 9. Miscellaneous

15372.130. In any civil or criminal action or proceeding for violation of any of the following, proof that the act that is complained of was done in compliance with the provisions of this chapter is a complete defense to the action or proceeding:

a. The Cartwright Act, Chapter 2 (commencing with Section 16700) of Part 2 of Division 7 of the Business and Professions Code.

b. The Unfair Practices Act, Chapter 4 (commencing with Section 17000) of Part 2 of Division 7 of the Business and Professions Code.

c. Any rule of statutory or common law against monopolies or combinations in restraint of trade.

15372.131. If any section, sentence, clause, or part of this chapter or the application thereof to any person or circumstance is for any reason held to be invalid, that invalidity shall not affect the remaining provisions or applications of this chapter that can be given effect without the invalid provision or application, and to this end the provisions of this act are severable. The Legislature hereby declares that it would have passed this chapter and each section, sentence, clause, and part of this chapter despite the fact that one or more sections, sentences, clauses, or parts of this chapter is declared invalid.

Section 19559 is added to the Revenue and Taxation Code:

19559.

a. Subject to the limitations of this section and federal law, the Franchise Tax Board may provide the Secretary of Trade and Commerce, when that person is acting in any capacity authorized by Chapter 2.2 (commencing with Section 15372.60) of Part 6.7 of Division 3 of Title 2 of the Government Code, with all of the following:

1. The names and addresses or other identification or location information from income or franchise tax returns or other records required under Part 10 (commencing with Section 17001), Part 11 (commencing with Section 23001), or this part, solely for the purposes of establishing and maintaining an accurate list of businesses to be assessed pursuant to Chapter 2.2 (commencing with Section 15372.60) of Part 6.7 of Division 3 of Title 2 of the Government Code.

2. Sufficient financial data from income and franchise tax returns solely for purposes of verifying the base upon which the assessment is determined.

b. Neither the Trade and Commerce Agency, nor its agents, nor any of its current or former officers or employees, nor any current or former members, employees, or agents of the California Tourism Marketing Commission, shall disclose or use any information obtained pursuant to this section except as provided in this section. Any disclosure not authorized by this section is a misdemeanor.

c. The Franchise Tax Board may from time to time review the use of information provided to the Secretary of Trade and Commerce pursuant to this section and the Secretary of Trade and Commerce shall provide the Franchise Tax Board with access for that purpose. The reviews shall be limited to ensuring that the Secretary of Trade and Commerce uses the information provided by the Franchise Tax Board only in the manner specified in subdivision (a). The Franchise Tax Board shall report all findings to the Secretary of Trade and Commerce.

SEC. 7. No reimbursement is required by this act pursuant to Section 6 of Article XIIIB of the California Constitution because the only costs that may be incurred by a local agency or school district will be incurred because this act creates a new crime or infraction, eliminates a crime or infraction, or changes the penalty for a crime or infraction, within the meaning of Section 17556 of the Government Code, or changes the definition of a crime within the meaning of Section 6 of Article XIIIB of the California Constitution. Notwithstanding Section 17580 of the Government Code, unless otherwise specified, the provisions of this act shall become operative on the same date that the act takes effect pursuant to the California Constitution.

SEC. 22. Notwithstanding Section 17610 of the Government Code, if the Commission on State Mandates determines that this act contains costs mandated by the state, reimbursement to local agencies and school districts for those costs shall be made pursuant to Part 7 (commencing with Section 17500) of Division 4 of Title 2 of the Government Code. If the statewide cost of the claim for reimbursement does not exceed one million dollars ($1,000,000), reimbursement shall be made from the State Mandates Claims Fund. No reimbursement is required by provisions of this act pursuant to Section 6 of Article XIIIB of the California Constitution because the only costs that may be incurred by a local agency or school district will be incurred because this act creates a new crime or infraction, eliminates a crime or infraction, or changes the penalty for a crime or infraction, within the meaning of Section 17556 of the Government Code, or changes the definition of a crime within the meaning of Section 6 of Article XIIIB of the California Constitution.

Notwithstanding Section 17580 of the Government Code, unless otherwise specified, the provisions of this act shall become operative on the same date that the act takes effect pursuant to the California Constitution.

SEC. 24. The Legislature finds and declares that the provisions of this act further the purposes of the Political Reform Act of 1974 within the meaning of subdivision (a) of Section 81012 of the Government Code.

READING 15.2

"A MODEL FOR THE EVALUATION OF NATIONAL TOURISM DESTINATION MARKETING PROGRAMS"

by Bill Faulkner
Griffith University (Gold Coast) Australia.

Reprinted from *Journal of Travel Research*, Vol. 36, No. 3, Winter 1997, p.p. 23–32, copyright 1997 by Sage Publications. Reprinted by permission of Sage Publications.

The increasing commitment of national governments to the funding of their tourism administrations' marketing activities abroad has been accompanied by demands for more rigorous evaluations of the effectiveness of these activities. More rigorous and comprehensive approaches to evaluation are also required to furnish a more solid foundation for strategic decision making. However, many evaluations to date have been ad hoc in the sense that they have relied on one or two techniques that address only part of the problem. A framework for systematically integrating a range of techniques is proposed as a way to overcome this deficiency, while an alternative approach to market share analysis is described in an effort to add to the battery of techniques in this field.

With the emergence of tourism as a major growth sector in the global economy, national governments have become increasingly aware of the role this industry can play in enhancing a country's trade performance. Many have thus sought to improve their competitive position with respect to the international tourism market by either increasing funding allocations to their existing national tourism administration (NTA) or establishing and funding such bodies. Given the number and diversity of private sector concerns usually involved in the delivery of tourism product, NTA activities in general have involved a considerable emphasis on developing a coordinated approach to promoting their destination abroad. The fundamental objective of the NTA in this process, and the main parameter by which its performance is ultimately judged, is to increase the country's market share beyond that which might otherwise have been achieved.

The increased commitment of many governments to tourism marketing, however, has coincided with a general trend toward greater fiscal restraint in the policy environment. As a consequence, NTAs are under increasing pressure to carry out more systematic and rigorous evaluations of their activities so that the investment of public funds can be fully justified in terms of outcomes and competing priorities (WTO 1994). The stakeholders in this process are not just the government and the general public to whom it is ultimately accountable, but also the industry constituency with whom the NTA is working. This is particularly so where the NTA is involved in cooperative marketing programs with industry partners.

In one sense, evaluation can be construed as a tool for ensuring accountability in the use of public resources at a national level and, in this regard, it is in the NTAs' interest to develop credible methodologies for demonstrating their contribution simply because continued funding depends on them doing so. However, well-structured evaluation procedures also have an important internal role to play by virtue of the contribution they can make to the organization's ongoing planning and management processes. The introduction of systematic evaluation procedures as a routine component of an organization's activities provides a framework for monitoring and assessing its performance with respect to the environment within which it operates and a rational basis for the identification of priorities and allocation of resources. Evaluation keeps an organization in touch with changes in its environment and its performance with respect to this environment and is thus an essential prerequisite for responsiveness and adaptability.

Therefore, evaluation is important both as a proactive means of providing information for rational decision making and as a retrospective means of assessing the outcomes of decisions and their associated programs (Stufflebeam and Shinkfield 1985). This dual purpose of evaluation (i.e., accountability and management information enhancement) has been emphasized in national government guidelines on program evaluation (e.g., Australian Government Department of Finance 1989) and noted specifically in the tourism context by Burke and Lindblom (1989) and Davidson and Wiethaupt (1989). Meanwhile, the external pressures mentioned previously, combined with the growing recognition of strategic management requirements, have been instrumental in the growing interest in evaluation research in the tourism field noted by Cook and Azucenas (1994).

One of the problems confronting NTAs wishing to incorporate more rigorous evaluation procedures in their planning and management is that, in the tourism context, evaluation is of necessity a multilayered process. It is multilayered first because NTAs are generally engaged in a range of activities that are each intended to play a role in a loosely connected chain of events leading to decisions by consumers to visit a destination. A multilayered approach is also necessary because, at this stage, there is no single approach that can unequivocally substantiate and quantify the impact of tourism marketing programs on visitor numbers and, indeed, the limitations of individual approaches suggests that a combination of methods needs to be applied so that a composite picture can be produced. Another related problem arises from the complexity of the research necessary to investigate linkages between program initiatives and the market's response and the difficulties this creates in the translation of research into meaningful management information.

These problems imply that action is required on three fronts. First, a framework for structuring the evaluation process needs to be developed to enable relationships between individual facets of the process to be understood and to facilitate the application of a range of techniques in a way that enables their individual strengths and weaknesses to be appreciated. Second, the battery of available techniques needs to be expanded so that a range of techniques that are complementary in terms of their respective strengths and limitations can be applied. Finally, it is important that methods for presenting and explaining the information produced by these techniques be improved to make them more useful to decision makers.

This article takes a step toward addressing each of these requirements. After clarifying the principles, underlying dimensions, and structure of the evaluation process, a broad framework for evaluating tourism destination marketing programs is proposed. An alternative approach to assessing market performance outcomes is then described to add to the range of techniques available. This approach uses graphical techniques that enable the performance of individual countries in specific markets to be more readily compared.

The Dimensions and Structure of the Evaluation Process

As emphasized in public sector documents on the subject, evaluation can be simply defined as a systematic process for objectively assessing an organization's (or program's) performance (New South Wales Office of Public Management 1991). Three key criteria are used to assess an organization's (or program's) performance in this process.

(1) Appropriateness (i.e., the extent to which stated program objectives and priorities match the needs of clients and stakeholders);

(2) Effectiveness (i.e., the extent to which the program achieves its objectives); and

(3) Efficiency (i.e., the extent to which the program outcomes are achieved at a reasonable cost and within a reasonable time frame).

The basic ingredients of the evaluation process involve the four overlapping procedures described in Figure 1, where the appropriateness question is addressed mainly in the program review stage and effectiveness is assessed on the basis of examining outputs and outcomes in Stages 2 and 3. In these stages, one of the most challenging methodological issues concerns the establishment of causal linkages between the immediate impacts of the NTA's initiatives and the market's response. This issue is considered further in the next section. The bottom line in any evaluation is to establish and, if possible, quantify the net benefits of the program in question. However, as Hunt (1991) emphasizes, the general nature of NTA activities complicates this process.

> Measuring return on investment for governmental or public tourism organisations is complicated because most are unable to be particularly product-specific or narrow in their marketing efforts. Most of these organisations are required to develop and promote a rather generic or general destination product comprised of a large package of diverse products, services and attractions over which they have little or no control. (p. 2)

The appropriateness issue, specifically, requires some consideration at this stage because this helps define the orientation of NTA program activities and thus the focus of the discussion that follows. Most NTAs would view their overriding mission as being to boost their country's foreign exchange earnings by in-

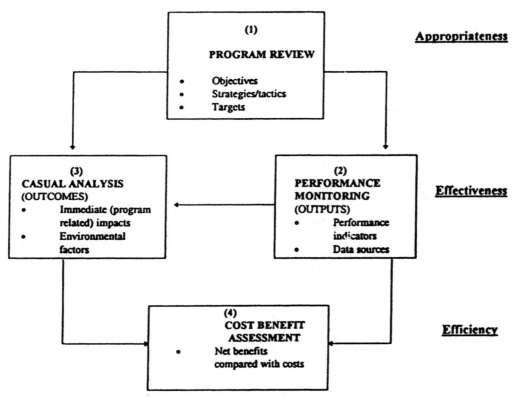

FIGURE 1 The structure of the evaluation process *(Source: Faulkner, 1992).*

creasing its share of the international tourism market. However, a mission such as this is subject to several qualifications.

First, the focus on increasing international tourism market share usually means that NTA activities tend to be preoccupied with promotional aspects of marketing to the exclusion of a broader marketing and management role (March 1994). However, there are inevitably situations where continuing growth of visitor numbers is inappropriate because the limits of the destination's social or environmental carrying capacity is being approached and, as a consequence, further increases are neither in the interest of the community nor consistent with long-term sustainability of the tourism industry (Cooke 1982; Getz 1994; Inskeep 1991; Woodley 1993; Zehnder 1976). This consideration has been recognized in the charter of some NTAs (e.g., the Australian Tourist Commission 1991), where responsibility for the minimization of adverse environmental and social impacts of international tourism is included.

Second, NTA international market share targets are generally expressed in terms of visitor numbers, even though a country's income from tourism can be increased by means other than simply increasing the number of visitors. Indeed, there is a strong case for using indicators other than this as a basis for evaluating results. Paraskevopoulos (1977), for instance, suggests that visitor nights is a more basic parameter for tourism demand, while O'Hagan and Harrison (1984) propose that the ultimate basis for measuring economic outcomes is clearly tourist expenditure. However, as comparable visitor expenditure data across many markets and destinations are not usually available, most discussion on international demand patterns is in terms of tourist numbers (Barry and O'Hagan 1972). Visitor numbers are thus emphasized in the following discussion, despite the limitations of this measure.

The application of the evaluation process described in Figure 1 to the NTA situation is outlined in the framework described in Figure 2. Here, a range of strategies that are commonly employed by NTAs are identified (Stage 1), along with corresponding performance or output indicators (Stage 2). Some of the issues associated with the analysis of outcomes are explored in the next section.

The Analysis of Outcomes

A meaningful evaluation of the NTA's overall marketing effectiveness eventually requires some conclusions to be drawn about the extent to which the market's response is actually attributable to the organization's actions. A positive relationship between marketing initiatives described in terms of the (Stage 2) outputs and favorable market trends (immediate impacts) is not, in itself, proof of a causal relationship. As emphasized by Hunt (1991), a range of factors that are quite independent of those under the control of the NTA and its various strategies have the potential to influence travel simultaneously. These need to be identified and factored into the assessment of the NTA's program. This phase of the evaluation might, therefore, involve two steps:

(1) Assessment of the impact of immediate program related factors (i.e., as identified by the output measures described in Figure 2); and

(2) Identification and analysis of broader environmental factors that have the potential to impact visitor numbers.

Most of the methods currently used and identified in Stage 3 of the framework (i.e., tracking studies, conversion studies, and market share analysis) are limited in terms of the second of the above requirements and, therefore, need to be used in conjunction with other methods (such as multivariate analysis and experimental or quasi-experimental approaches) if causal relationships are to be established. An examination of these aspects of evaluation research sharpens the appreciation of the limitations associated with these methods and, in the process, reinforces the argument for a multilayered approach such as that described in Figure 2.

Tracking and Conversion Studies

In the first instance, tourism marketing campaigns aim to influence the consumer's predisposition to visit a destination, while the ultimate objective is to ensure that this is translated into actual visitation. Output performance indicators, such as those referred to in Stage 2 of the framework, provide some evidence of the exposure and response levels achieved by various initiatives, but they provide little information about the influence these have on the consumer. Methods that take us a step closer to understanding these impacts include tracking studies, conversion studies, and market share analyses. Tracking and conversion studies are, in essence, concerned with identifying the immediate impacts of programs, while market share analysis is concerned more with isolating shifts in the

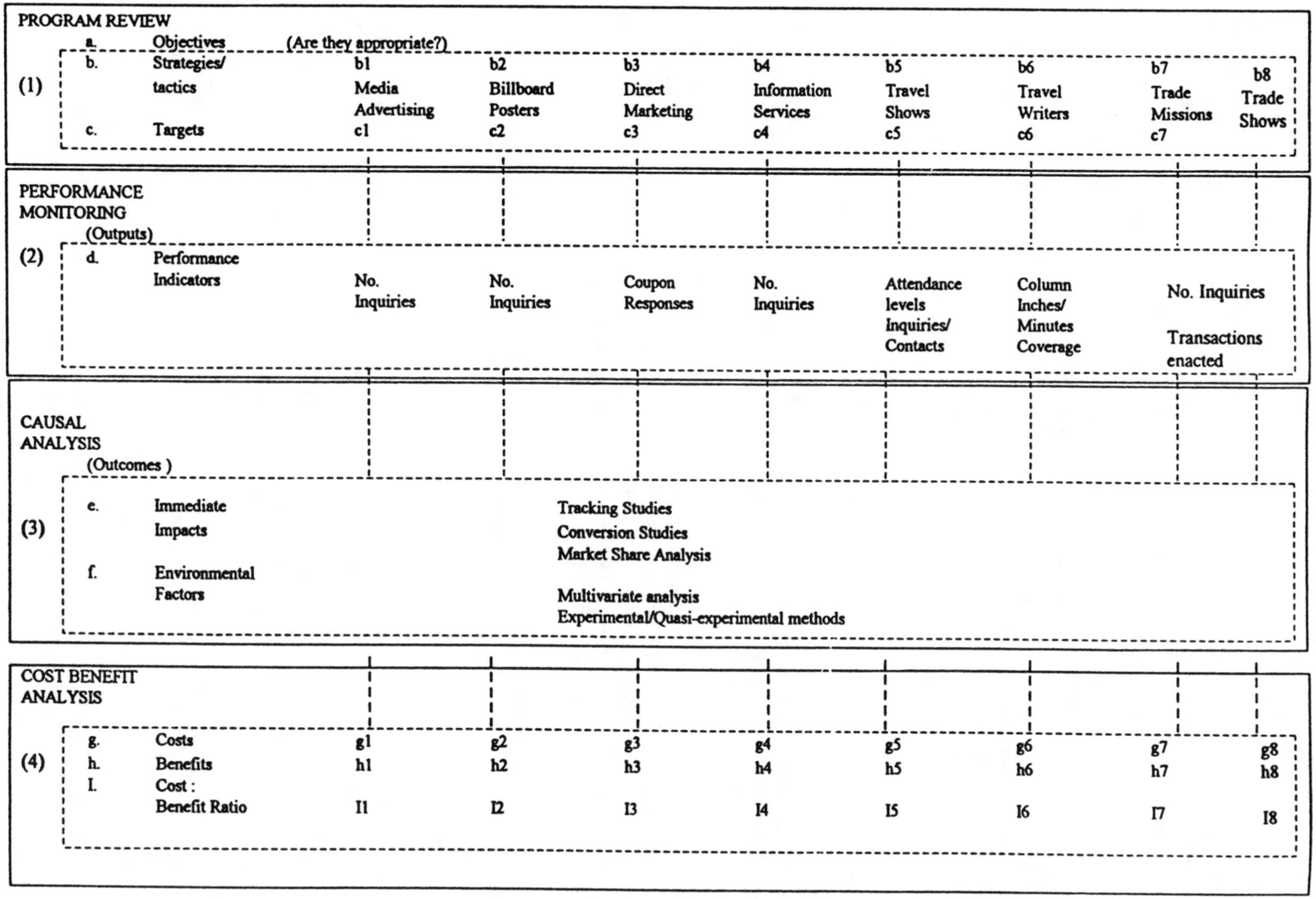

PROGRAM REVIEW

	a. Objectives/ Strategies/ tactics (Are they appropriate?)	b1 Media Advertising	b2 Billboard Posters	b3 Direct Marketing	b4 Information Services	b5 Travel Shows	b6 Travel Writers	b7 Trade Missions	b8 Trade Shows
(1) b.		b1	b2	b3	b4	b5	b6	b7	b8
c. Targets		c1	c2	c3	c4	c5	c6	c7	

PERFORMANCE MONITORING (2) (Outputs)

	b1	b2	b3	b4	b5	b6	b7	b8
d. Performance Indicators	No. Inquiries	No. Inquiries	Coupon Responses	No. Inquiries	Attendance levels Inquiries/ Contacts	Column Inches/ Minutes Coverage	No. Inquiries / Transactions enacted	

CAUSAL ANALYSIS (3) (Outcomes)

e. Immediate Impacts

f. Environmental Factors

Tracking Studies
Conversion Studies
Market Share Analysis

Multivariate analysis
Experimental/Quasi-experimental methods

COST BENEFIT ANALYSIS

(4)	g1/h1/I1	g2/h2/I2	g3/h3/I3	g4/h4/I4	g5/h5/I5	g6/h6/I6	g7/h7/I7	g8/h8/I8
g. Costs	g1	g2	g3	g4	g5	g6	g7	g8
h. Benefits	h1	h2	h3	h4	h5	h6	h7	h8
I. Cost : Benefit Ratio	I1	I2	I3	I4	I5	I6	I7	I8

FIGURE 2 A framework for the evaluation of NTA programs

marketplace that may or may not reflect these impacts.

Tracking studies attempt to monitor changes in the markets' awareness, interest, preference, and intentions as a consequence of exposure to advertising campaigns. The importance of such studies in the evaluation process is high-lighted by Davidson (1994).

> In essence, the science of predicting human behavior—of which advertising evaluation research is a branch—is at best imprecise. The relationship between message and a change in the mind set is more direct and easier to study; and if the effect of advertising begins in the potential customer's mind then advertising evaluation research should also begin in the potential customer's mind.
> (p. 538)

Davidson also draws attention to the tendency of evaluation research to often focus on the immediate impact tourism advertising has on awareness of, and interest in, a destination, rather than on the final sales achieved. He attributes this to two factors that emphasize both the strengths and limitations of tracking studies.

(1) The lead times involved in travel decisions mean that the impact of advertising often takes a long time to be expressed. More immediate feedback on the effectiveness of the program is often required and tracking studies serve this purpose; and

(2) The final decision to travel to a destination is influenced by many other factors apart from the advertisement.

On the role of tracking studies, Siegel and Ziff-Levine (1994) therefore conclude that

> It is only rarely that definitive conclusions can be drawn about the impact of advertising on travel behavior. Instead, tracking research is more valuable, from a diagnostic perspective, in pinpointing the strengths and weaknesses of a campaign for the fine-tuning of creative development and media buying. (p. 563)

In finally assessing the impact of a campaign on the bottom line (i.e., increased volume of visitors), tracking studies play a necessary, but not sufficient, role. They are necessary if the first link in the causal chain is to be verified, but a change in the predisposition of the market toward a particular destination does not necessarily translate into actual trips.

Conversion studies can be seen as taking the evaluation process a step further, to the extent that they provide an estimate of the proportion of those responding to advertisement who actually travel to the destination. Considerable emphasis has been placed on the use of conversion studies as a basis for evaluating tourism advertising campaigns (Mok 1990). A common approach is linked with advertising campaigns where there is a direct response component that involves providing additional information to the public through mail coupons or toll-free telephone calls. This enables the researcher to contact respondents to ascertain the extent to which advertising material was, in fact, instrumental in stimulating their travel to the destination. Alternatively, random samples of the relevant population are carried out.

Many authors have drawn attention to methodological deficiencies in the application of conversion studies to the tourism field (e.g., Ballman et al. 1984; Burke and Gitelson 1990; Burke and Lindblom 1989; Davidson 1994; Ellerbrock 1981; Hunt and Dalton 1983; Mok 1990; Siegel and Ziff-Levine 1994; Sunday 1975; Woodside 1981, 1990), and several others have highlighted the tendency of the methods used to exaggerate the impact of the advertising program (Ballman et al. 1984; Ellerbrock 1981; Hunt and Dalton 1982; Woodside 1981). Common deficiencies itemized by Ballman et al. (1984) and later by Mok (1990) include

(1) The failure to use proper sampling techniques and a tendency not to take the implications of sampling error into account in the interpretation of results;

(2) The failure to allow for the effect of nonresponse bias. As those who visit a destination are more inclined to respond to a survey than those who have not (Ellerbrock 1981), the lower the response rate the higher the potential for an inflated measure of conversion rates. The extent of inflation due to this factor has been estimated to be as high as 40 to 50% (Ballman et al. 1984; Hunt and Dalton 1982);

(3) In conversion studies associated with destination information services, there has been a tendency not to factor out those respondents who had decided to visit the destination prior to being exposed to the advertisements and for whom the advertisements simply facilitated the collection of

information for planning purposes. Again, this results in conversion rate being inflated and, according to Ballman et al. (1984), highlights the need to put advertising effects into the context of various extraneous sources of information that influence decisions (e.g., word of mouth, relatives and friends who live at potential destinations, media news and events); and

(4) Failure to include all costs associated with the development of advertising campaigns.

With these limitations in mind, Burke and Lindblom (1989) and Burke and Gitelson (1990) have concluded that conversion studies provide useful diagnostic information for the destination marketer, but they are potentially misleading if relied on to produce figures on the return on investment.

Multivariate Analysis

Multivariate analysis has the potential to provide the foundation to assess return on investment by providing the ability to identify and quantify the relative impact of a range of factors. Any change in the market's response coinciding with a promotional campaign or more general marketing initiatives needs to be considered in the context of broader environmental factors, which may also have a bearing on propensities and capacities to travel. The inclination to travel in a particular market at any point in time is dependent on a combination of social and economic conditions that vary in the degree to which they can be quantified.

Relevant social conditions range from prevailing social mores, attitudes, and tastes affecting holiday choices to more variable (in time) levels of consumer confidence, which in turn tend to reflect economic conditions, unemployment levels, and the political climate at home and abroad. In addition, events such as the Chernobyl disaster, the Gulf War, and various Olympic Games have demonstrated how ephemeral political, environmental, and hallmark events can have profound short-term effects on patterns of world travel (Faulkner 1990).

Among the range of factors that have a bearing on travel, economic factors have probably been the most systematically investigated and, as a consequence, their influence is arguably better understood. Economic conditions, in general, affect both the capacity to travel through their impact on disposable incomes and the affordability of travel. The latter is governed by such factors as relative inflation and exchange rates. Economic conditions that potentially have a more direct bearing on propensities to travel include those that affect such items as the availability of air services, fare levels; and accommodation rates.

In their review of more than 50 studies that have attempted to model international tourist movements over the past 30 years, Crouch and Shaw (1990) and Crouch (1994) have noted the general dependence on econometric and, to a lesser extent, gravity model approaches. According to Crouch (1994), the most frequently analyzed independent variables have been income levels (in 89% of studies), tourism product price levels (70%), costs of transportation (58%), and exchange rates (33%). Special events and terrorist incidents were incorporated as dummy variables in 58% of the studies examined. Although the possible influence of marketing variables (e.g., expenditure on marketing programs) has been frequently acknowledged, as Witt and Martin (1987) note, few studies have actually attempted to take this factor into account. Among those studies that have, however, the results have been inconclusive.

Uysal (1983) and Uysal and Crompton (1984) analyzed the impact of promotional expenditure by the Turkish Ministry of Tourism and Culture and concluded that, relative to other determinants of demand, promotional expenditure appeared to have minimal effect on tourist flows to that country. In their study of promotional effects on British tourism to Ireland, Barry and O'Hagan (1972) concluded that income and price were more important, while Uysal and O'Leary (1986) arrived at a similar conclusion in their analysis of tourism in Yugoslavia and Greece. On the other hand, Papadopoulos (1987) concluded that promotional expenditure by the Greek National Tourist Organization did have an impact on tourist arrivals, although the strength of this impact varied among the major markets. Similarly, Crouch, Schultz, and Valerio (1992) cite Clark (1978) as concluding that the impact of Barbados' promotional effort varied according to the class of hotel and origin of visitors.

Witt and Martin's (1987) critique of several of the above studies drew attention to such problems as the exclusion of potentially important explanatory variables (especially costs), multicollinearity of data, and inaccuracies associated with the derivation of marketing expenditures. It was also noted that as promotional programs have impacts over periods beyond the units of time used for analytical purposes, the isolation of these effects is compounded. A similar problem has been referred to in relation to the interpretation of shift share analysis in the previous section.

In a more recent study, which included marketing expenditure among the variables used to model international visitor flows to Australia, Crouch, Schultz, and Valerio (1992) concluded that the international marketing of the Australian Tourist Commission played a statistically significant role in influencing inbound tourism to that country. However, the authors also emphasized that statistically significant relationships, such as those revealed by regression analyses, do not necessarily imply causal linkages. Industry Canada (1994) has since adopted a similar approach to the analysis of Tourism Canada's advertising programs and concluded that advertising has had a small but significant effect on the U.S. and Japanese markets.

In a noneconometric approach involving a comparison of 15 NTAs actively engaged in promotions in the U.S. market, Hunt (1991) noted that in general those with above average marketing expenditure achieved better growth rates in their share of this market. A similar, earlier study in the same market by Sunday (1975) concluded that the effect of advertising seemed quite small when compared with the array of factors that influence tourism. The same author, however, also observed that as the absolute magnitude invested by the individual countries concerned was relatively small, the amount invested could be justified by a very small number of additional visitors.

Experimental and Quasi-Experimental Design

The myriad of external factors that impinge on the market's response, along with the interaction of specific promotions with other elements of the marketing mix (Park, Roth, and Jacques 1988), highlights the complexities associated with the effort to link specific NTA initiatives with changes in the destination's performance. Under these circumstances, the experimental or quasi-experimental methodologies are potentially the more convincing approach to establishing cause and effect relationships.

To prove that a tourism marketing program has actually been responsible for a positive response in the market, it is necessary to demonstrate that the program preceded the supposed changes in the market,

that the supposed cause and effect co-vary, and no alternative explanations of the effect exist apart from the assumed cause (Posavac and Carey 1992). The combination of methods described above satisfies the first two criteria, but is generally deficient with respect to the last one. Greater internal validity can only be achieved by adopting an experimental or quasi-experimental approach with the ability to

(1) Observe individuals in the marketplace both before and after the implementation of the program in question;

(2) Observe additional people (i.e., control groups) who have not been exposed to the program; and

(3) Take into account a wide variety of variables to ensure that other factors with the potential to influence responses can be detected.

Experimental and quasi-experimental approaches involve a level of control that enables all three of the above conditions to be observed, with the main distinction between the two approaches being that the latter does not involve the random assignment of individuals to treatment and nontreatment groups (Cook and Campbell 1979).

Woodside (1990) has advocated the application of experimental methods to evaluate tourism marketing campaigns and has, in particular, argued that experimental design principles should routinely be built into marketing plans so that their impacts can be properly assessed. This approach draws on the principles of Caples' (1974) tested advertising methods, which have been applied more generally. In his evaluation of the effectiveness of Hawaii's print media destination advertising in 13 U.S. midwestern states, Woodside attempted to factor out extraneous effects by adopting a "quasi-experimental" approach involving comparisons with 16 other (nontargeted) states. He concluded that the program affected demand for trips to Hawaii only slightly, and the retentive effect was only evident after the second advertising campaign.

One problem associated with quasi-experimental design in this context is that the targeting of areas for promotion is itself influenced by an assessment of the likely responsiveness of populations in these areas, which in turn compounds comparisons with control groups in nontargeted areas. As Cook and Campbell (1979) observe, the challenge "confronting the persons who try to interpret the results from quasi-experiments is basically one of separating the effects of a treatment from those due to the initial incomparability between the average units in each treatment group." (p. 6)

Cost-Benefit Analysis

As emphasized earlier, the bottom line in any evaluation is, ultimately, the cost-benefit ratio achieved by the program. A useful overview of the issues involved in this aspect of the process is provided by Dwyer and Forsyth (1995). For the purposes of this study, it is sufficient to note that cost-benefit ratios have been produced at the broader level (i.e., with respect to advertising expenditures in general) in the form of elasticities derived from some regression analyses. Here, advertising expenditures were included as an explanatory variable (e.g., Crouch, Schultz, and Valerio 1992; Industry Canada 1994; Papadopoulos and Witt 1985; Uysal and Crompton 1984). However, in view of the difficulties encountered in isolating and quantifying the final effects of individual strategies, it appears that the derivation of cost-benefit ratios to the degree depicted in the final phase of the figure is far from being achievable at this stage.

Market Share Analysis

As noted in previous sections, the role of market share analysis in the evaluation process is central as an indicator of the extent to which the NTA has achieved its fundamental objective, but it is limited as a basis for attributing outcomes specifically to the NTA's actions. Nevertheless, this form of analysis provides a useful basis for monitoring the performance of a destination vis-à-vis competitors and particular target markets, and, in this sense, it also provides valuable diagnostic information for strategic planning. This is especially so when used in conjunction with other methods referred to in the framework.

Indices based on rankings provide a broad indication of the relative effectiveness of an NTA's programs, but there are several reasons for caution in the way they should be interpreted. First, the relative position of a destination is often largely a reflection of geographical and historical factors that are outside the control of the NTA and its programs. Second, partly for the same reason, infrastructure and/or carrying capacity constraints may put a ceiling on how far up in the rankings a particular destination should rise. Finally, in any case, it is not so much the destination's ranking at a particular point in time that is im-

portant, but rather the progress it makes over a period of time.

Following on from the last point, it would seem that what is required is an index that reflects the dynamics of the marketplace and changes in the destination's performance with respect to this market, while at the same time allowing for the "givens" that place broad limits on the destination's overall competitiveness. Toward this end, an approach analogous to shift-share analysis of regional economics is promising.

Shift-share analysis was originally widely applied during the 1960s to compare the economic development of regions vis-à-vis a larger reference group comprising the national or global economies (Houston 1967). Historically, this form of analysis has concentrated on supply side factors, such as employment, manufacturing output, and income (e.g., Andrikopolous, Bronx, and Carvalho 1990; Beck and Herr 1990; Ledebur and Moomav 1983; Tervo and Okko 1983), as it has in the one application to tourism by Sirakaya, Uysal, and Toepper (1995). By contrast, since the focus of this article is on market share trends, this application will have a demand side emphasis.

The main strength of the shift-share approach with respect to the assessment of a destination's performance is that it depicts outcomes in terms of the change in market share achieved, and this is viewed in the context of overall change in the market. In addition, by focusing on change over a period of time, rather than by providing a snapshot as in the case of most other indices, the possibility of ephemeral or random events distorting the picture is reduced. Indeed, Vanhove and Klaassen (1987) emphasize the importance of applying techniques such as shift-share analysis over a period of time to ensure that enduring trends can be isolated. Finally, long-term trends in the level and profile of international visitors are used as a basis for factoring in limits imposed by the geographical and historical context. This is not intended to imply that these limits are insurmountable. They merely allow comparisons to be made within realistic "aspiration levels."

For the purposes of explaining and illustrating this application of the shift-share approach, the following discussion will refer to visitor numbers only as a basis for analysis, even though this approach can be just as readily based on the other parameters. In general, data considerations make the definition of markets in terms of visitor numbers and country of origin most convenient, although as noted previously, other criteria (e.g., nights, expenditure, age, sex, purpose of trip, psychographic orientation) might be equally or more relevant for marketing purposes.

As implied by the term "shift-share," the primary objective of the approach is twofold.

(1) To enable a destination's position with respect to its share of a particular market to be established; and

(2) To provide an indication of the extent to which the destination is improving its position with respect to a particular market relative to overall movements in that market.

There are, therefore, two dimensions of the analysis.

(1) *An index of market share with respect to each major market.* To neutralize the scale of the destination's overall involvement in international tourism, this dimension is expressed in terms of a "market bias index" (*B*), which reflects the degree to which the destination's market share with respect to a particular market deviates from its share of visitors overall. The derivation of this index is as follows:

$$B_{ik} = \frac{\left[X_{ijk} / \sum_{i=1}^{n} X_{ijk} \right] - 1.0}{\left[\sum_{j=1}^{n} X_{ij(k)n} / \sum_{i=1}^{n} \sum_{j=1}^{n} X_{ij(k)n} \right]}$$

where

B_{ik} = Market bias index for destination i in year k,

X_{ijk} = Visitor numbers to destination i from market j in year k, and

n = Number of markets (origin) and destinations.

(Alternatively, B_{ik} can be described in the following terms: B_{ik} = Destination i's market share with respect to market j in year k × 100/Destination i's total market share with respect to all markets, j . . . n, in year k.)

Thus, if destination i's share of a particular market (j) is on a par with its share of visitors overall, B_{ij} = 0. If its share of another market (*l*)

exceeds what would be received on a pro rata basis, then $B_{ij} > 0$.

The market bias index complements Hudman's country potential generation index (Hudman 1979, 1980; Hudman and Davis 1994) in the sense that where the latter is concerned with the relative propensity of a country to generate trips, the market bias index looks at the relative importance of a particular country of origin from the receiving country's point of view.

(2) *An index of change (C) in the visitors received from each market relative to the change in that market overall.*

$$C = [(X_{ijk} / X_{ijl}) \overset{k=1}{\underset{}{-}} 1] - [(X_{jk} / X_{jl}) \overset{k=1}{\underset{}{-}} 1]$$

where

X_{ijk} = Visitor numbers to destination i from market j in year k,

X_{jk} = Total outbound visitors from market j in year k, and

1 . . . k = Years 1988 (l) to 1992 (k).

(Alternatively, Bik can be described in the following terms: Bik = Destination i's market share with respect to market j in year k × 100/Destination i's total market share with respect to all markets, j . . . n, in year k.)

If the destination in question achieves a growth rate for market (j) that is consistent with the growth of that market overall, then Cij = 0. If the growth achieved by the destination with respect to another market (*l*) exceeds the growth of that market overall, then Ci*l* > 0.

To illustrate this approach to market share analysis, indices have been calculated for the top 40 countries in terms of tourism promotional expenditure as indicated by the WTO's survey of NTA budgets (WTO 1994). For the purposes of this exercise, it is assumed that these countries account for the whole international tourism market, whereas in fact they account for 87%. The change index is based on the average annual change over the period 1988 to 1992, while the reference year for the market bias index is 1992. There may be some merit in also using average annual figures for the latter index, as this would alleviate any problems associated with the sensitivity of the analysis to the base year used. However, there is also value in relying on the most recent picture of the market bias profile to assess the situation.

The potential value of these two indices in assisting in the assessment of an NTA's performance with respect to a range of markets lies in the way the results can be graphically represented. In Figure 3, Australia's status vis-à-vis the various markets is plotted on a graph that has the market bias index (B) on the horizontal axis and the change index (C) on the vertical axis. Within this framework, markets can be classified in the following way:

(1) Performing markets (Quadrant I: +B, +C), where the country's share of the market in ques-

tion exceeds its overall share of the total market and where it has achieved a higher than average growth rate for this market;

(2) Emerging markets (Quadrant II: −B, +C), where an above average growth in the market has been achieved, but the share of this market still falls behind that expected on a pro rata basis;

(3) Declining markets (Quadrant III: +B, −C), where market share exceeds the pro rata level, but this position is being eroded by lower than average growth; and

(4) Stagnant markets (Quadrant IV: −B, −C), where the market share is below the pro rata level, and this situation is exacerbated by lower than average growth.

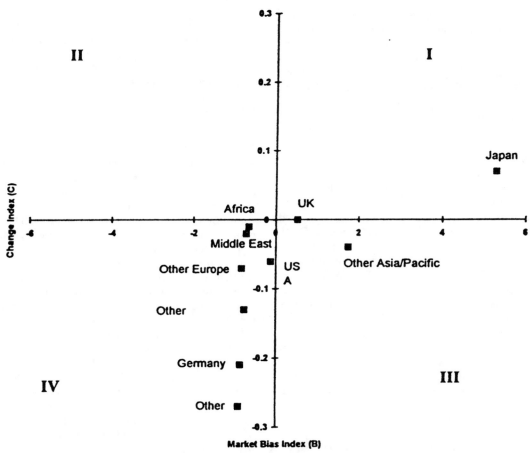

FIGURE 3 Australia's international tourism marketing performance, 1988–92

The presentation of the market share analysis in this format highlights the parallels between this approach and the applications of portfolio analysis to tourism by Calantone and Mazanec (1991) and McKercher (1995). Calantone and Mazanec plotted country of origin markets to a destination according to growth rate on the vertical axis and relative market share on the horizontal axis to produce a classification of markets comparable with that provided in Figure 3. The main differences between the two approaches are that the market bias and change indices referred to previously are modified to reflect relative position of the destination in the global market as a whole and the performance of different destinations can be more readily compared.

As far as Australia is concerned, Figure 3 reveals that Japan stands out as the market in which the best results have been achieved, while Australia's relatively strong historical position as a destination for the U.K. market has been maintained. On the other hand, Australia's position with respect to some of the other markets is more problematic. The WTO's survey of NTA budgets (WTO 1994) indicates that priority in the allocation of Australia's tourism promotional budget in 1991 was given to the United States, Europe, Asia, Japan, and the United Kingdom, respectively. The positions in the graph of the U.S. and European markets in particular, and to a less extent the Other Asia market, suggest a less than satisfactory outcome. However, some caution needs to be exercised in the interpretation of these results, because much of the reference period associated with the indices predates 1991 and allowance needs to be made for a gestation period for promotional effects. On the other hand, it is also relevant to note that Australia targeted the U.S. and European markets over much of the period from 1988 to 1992. The interpretation of analyses such as those presented in Figure 3 also need to take into account instances where resource allocation in the NTA concerned is motivated by strategic decisions aimed at arresting the stagnation of important markets. Whether this is an appropriate response is, of course, open to debate. Apart from these considerations, the discussion elsewhere in this article highlights the need to examine market share patterns in the context of a range of indicators before a proper understanding of their implications can be developed.

The graphical representation of indices also provides a useful basis for comparing a country's performance in relation to a specific market with that of competitors who have also targeted this market. This can be done by plotting the indices for the target market registered by the countries concerned on one graph. Thus, in Figure 4, the performance of countries that have assigned first or second priority to the U.S. market in the allocation of promotional funds (WTO 1994, Table 8) is compared with others.

Notwithstanding the above cautionary note regarding the gestation period for promotional effects and strategic considerations, the results are nevertheless somewhat disconcerting. Historically, those countries targeting the U.S. market have generally not been performing any better than the remainder. Indeed, if anything, the opposite is the case. However, it appears that Mexico has succeeded in consolidating its obvious geographical advantage with respect to the market, while China has gained ground. China, however, still has less than a pro rata share of the market. Although Canada, Bermuda, and Barbados each enjoy a relatively high market share by virtue of their geographical proximity, it appears that they are losing ground. It also appears that Greece, Switzerland, Italy, Portugal, and Australia have all registered mediocre results over the reference period, despite the priority they have each assigned to the U.S. market.

Conclusion

The range of activities in which NTAs engage constitutes just a few of the extensive array of factors that affect international tourism flows. Some of these factors are quantifiable and have thus been taken into account in conventional forms of analysis. However, many potentially important variables are excluded from analysis because adequate data are not available and/or they are simply not quantifiable. Those analyses that have been carried out have, therefore, been able to isolate the impacts of advertising and other contributing factors in a partial sense only, and attempts to identify the relative contribution of the NTA's programs have been frustrated by this problem.

The process of attributing market trends to the actions of NTAs is further complicated by the fact that many of the variables influencing tourists' decisions in general, and the attractiveness of the destination in particular, are simply beyond the NTA's control. Therefore, whatever criteria are adopted as indicators of success in the marketplace, extreme caution must be exercised in the extent to which outcomes are attributed specifically to the NTA's actions.

After recognizing these problems, and the fact that

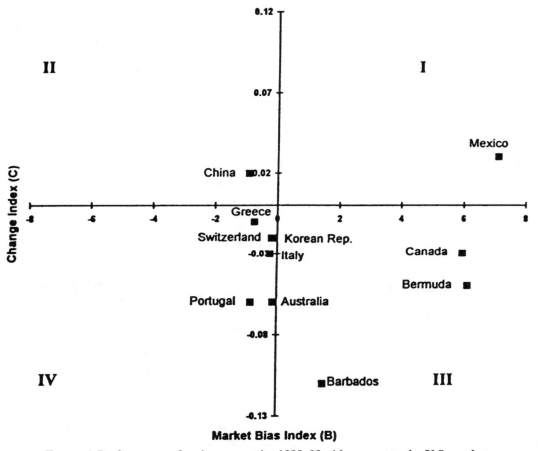

FIGURE 4 Performance of various countries 1988–92 with respect to the U.S. market

any single method that might be employed is deficient in some respect and therefore "subject to numerous caveats," the Australian Tourist Commission (1991, p. 3) resolved to adopt a "weight of evidence" approach to the evaluation of its programs in 1991. This approach involved the conduct of several parallel studies that would each have a different set of strengths and limitations. It was thus believed that, in combination, collaborative results providing evidence of the benefits derived from the Commission's activities would be obtained.

One of the main implications of the analysis contained in this article is that while the weight of evidence approach is a step in the right direction, it is an incomplete response to the problem. A more systematic approach is necessary with a range of studies being carried out so that each facet of the evaluation

process is addressed and the chain of events in the marketing process is examined comprehensively. The model presented in Figure 2 represents an attempt to provide a framework for the more coherent methodology that is required to achieve this.

The other issue examined previously concerns the development of more techniques to fill gaps in the framework and to support the strategic planning role of the evaluation process by providing a basis for generating more diverse insights into aspects of the destination's performance. An important consideration in the development of these techniques is to devise means for communicating research findings that enhance their usefulness to decision markers. It is hoped that shift-share approach to market share analysis will be seen as a contribution in both these respects.

References

Andrikopolous, A., J. Bronx, and E. Carvalho (1990). "Shift-Share Analysis and the Potential for Predicting Regional Growth Patterns: Some Evidence for the Region of Quebec, Canada." *Growth and Change,* 21 (1): 1–10.

Australian Government Department of Finance (1989). *Program Evaluation: A Guide for Program Managers.* Canberra: Australian Government Department of Finance.

Australian Tourist Commission (1991). *Evaluation of the Australian Tourist Commission's Marketing Impact.* Sydney: Australian Tourist Commission.

Ballman, G., J. Burke, U. Blank, and D. Korte (1984). "Toward Higher Quality Conversion Studies: Refining the Numbers Game." *Journal of Travel Research,* 22 (Spring): 28–33.

Barry, K., and J. O'Hagan (1972). "An Economic Study of Tourist Expenditure in Ireland." *Economic and Social Review,* 3 (2): 143–61.

Beck, R. J., and W. McD Herr (1990). "Employment Linkages from a Modified Shift-Share Analysis: An Illinois Example." *Review of Regional Studies,* 20 (3): 38–45.

Burke, J. L., and R. Gitelson (1990). "Conversion Studies: Assumptions, Applications, Accuracy and Abuse." *Journal of Travel Research,* 28 (Winter): 46–51.

Burke, J. L., and L. A. Lindblom (1989). "Strategies for Evaluating Direct Response Tourism Marketing." *Journal of Tourism Research,* 28 (Fall): 33–37.

Calantone, R. J., and J. A. Mazanec (1991). "Marketing Management and Tourism." *Annals of Tourism Research,* 18 (1): 101–19.

Caples, J. (1974). *Tested Advertising Methods.* 4th ed. Englewood Cliffs, NJ: Prentice Hall.

Clark, C. D. (1978). *An Analysis of the Determinants of Tourism Demand in Barbados.* Ph.D. diss. Fordham University (as referred to in Crouch, Schultz, and Valerio, 1992).

Cook, S. D., and V. Azucenas (1994). "Research in State and Provincial Travel Offices." In *Travel Tourism and Hospitality Research: A Handbook for Managers and Researchers,* 2d ed., edited by J. R. Brent Ritchie and C. R. Goeldner. New York: John Wiley and Sons, pp. 165–80.

Cook, T. D., and D. T. Campbell (1979). *Quasi-Experimentation.* Boston: Houghton Mifflin.

Cooke, K. (1982). "Guidelines for Socially Appropriate Tourism Development in British Columbia." *Journal of Travel Research,* 21 (Summer): 22–28.

Crouch, G. I. (1994). "The Study of International Tourism Demand: A Survey of Practice." *Journal of Travel Research,* 32 (Spring): 41–55.

Crouch, G. I., L. Schultz, and P. Valerio (1992). "Marketing International Tourism to Australia: A Regression Analysis." *Tourism Management,* 13 (2): 196–208.

Crouch, G. I., and R. N. Shaw (1990). "Determinants of International Tourism Flows: Findings from Thirty Years of Empirical Research." *Proceedings of the 21st Annual Conference of the Travel and Tourism Research Association.* Lexington, KY: Travel and Tourism Research Association, pp. 45–60.

Davidson, T. L. (1994). "Assessing the Effectiveness of Persuasive Communications." In *Travel Tourism and Hospitality Research: A Handbook for Managers and Researchers,* 2d ed., edited by J. R. Brent Ritchie and C. R. Goeldner. New York: John Wiley and Sons, pp. 537–43.

Davidson, T. L., and W. B. Wiethaupt (1989). "Accountability Marketing Research: An Increasingly Vital Tool for Travel Marketers." *Journal of Travel Research,* 27 (Spring): 42–45.

Dwyer, L., and P. Forsyth (1995). "Assessing the Net National Benefits from Promotion in Inbound Tourism." *Proceedings of the 26th Annual Travel and Tourism Research Association Conference.* Lexington, KY: Travel and Tourism Research Association, pp. 123–33.

Ellerbrock, M. (1981). "Improving Coupon Conversion Studies: A Comment." *Journal of Travel Research,* 19 (Spring): 37–38.

Faulkner, H. W. (1990). "Swings and Roundabouts in Australian Tourism." *Tourism Management.* 11 (1): 29–37.

——— (1992). "The Anatomy of the Evaluation Process." In *Evaluation of Tourism Marketing,* edited by H. W. Faulkner and R. Shaw. BTR Occasional Paper No. 13. Canberra: Bureau of Tourism Research, pp. 6–9.

Getz, D. (1994). "Residents Attitudes Toward Tourism: A Longitudinal Study in Spey Valley, Scotland." *Tourism Management,* 15 (4): 247–58.

Houston, D. B. (1967). The Shift-Share Analysis of Regional Growth: A Critique." *The Southern Economic Journal,* 34: 577–81.

Hudman, L. E. (1979). "Origin Regions in International Tourism." *Weiner Geographische Schrifium,* 53/54: 43–49.

——(1980). *Tourism: A Shrinking World.* Columbus: Grid.

Hudman, L. E., and J. A. Davis (1994). "World Tourism Markets: Changes and Patterns." *Proceedings of the 25th Annual Tourism and Travel Research Association Conference.* Lexington, KY: Travel and Tourism Research Association, pp. 127–45.

Hunt, J. D. (1991). "The Impact of National Tourism Organisation Advertising Expenditures on the United States Traveller Market." Appendix G in *Evaluation of the Australian Tourist Commission's Marketing Impact.* Sydney: Australian Tourist Commission.

Hunt, J. D., and M. J. Dalton (1983). "Comparing Mail and Telephone for Conducting Coupon Conversion Studies." *Journal of Travel Research,* 21 (Winter): 16.

Industry Canada (1994). *An Economic Evaluation of Tourism Canada's International Advertising.* Unpublished internal report. Ottawa: Financial and Economic Analysis, Corporate and Industrial Analysis Branch.

Inskeep, E. (1991). *Tourism Planning: An Integrated and Sustainable Development Approach.* New York: Van Nostrand.

Ledebur, L. C, and R. L. Moomav (1983). "A Shift-Share Analysis of Regional Labor Productivity in Manufacturing." *Growth and Change,* 14 (1): 2–9.

March, R. (1994). "Tourism Marketing Myopia." *Tourism Management,* 15 (6): 411–15.

McKercher, B. (1995). "The Destination-Market Mix: A Tourism Market Portfolio Analysis Model." *Journal of Travel and Tourism Marketing,* 4 (2): 23–40.

Mok, H. R. (1990). "A Quasi-Experimental Measure of the Effectiveness of Destination Advertising: Some Evidence from Hawaii." *Journal of Travel Research,* 28 (Summer): 51–55.

New South Wales Office of Public Management (1991). *New Requirements and Guidelines for Program Management.* Sydney: NSWOPM.

O'Hagan, J. W., and M. J. Harrison (1984). "Market Shares of U.S. Tourism Expenditure in Europe: An Economic Analysis." *Applied Economics,* 16 (6): 919–31.

Papadopoulos, S., and S. F. Witt (1985). "A Marketing Analysis of Foreign Tourism in Greece." In *Proceedings of the Second World Marketing Congress,* edited by S. Shaw, L. Sparks, and E. Kaynak. University of Stirling, pp. 682–93.

Papadopoulos, S. (1987). "Strategic Marketing Techniques in International Tourism." *International Marketing Review,* Summer: 71–84.

Paraskevopoulos, G. N. (1977). *An Economic Analysis of International Tourism.* Lecture Series 31. Athens: Centre for Planning and Economic Research.

Park, C. W., M. S. Roth, and P. F. Jacques (1988). "Evaluating the Effects of Advertising and Sales Promotion Campaigns." *Industrial Marketing Management,* 17: 129–40.

Posavac, E. J., and R. G. Carey (1992). *Program Evaluation: Methods and Case Studies.* 4th ed. Englewood Cliffs, NJ: Prentice Hall.

Siegel, W., and W. Ziff-Levine (1994). "Evaluating Tourism Advertising Campaigns: Conversion versus Advertising Tracking Studies." In *Travel Tourism and Hospitality Research: A Handbook for Managers and Researchers,* 2d ed., edited by J. R. Brent Ritchie and C. R. Goeldner. New York: John Wiley and Sons, pp. 559–64.

Sirakaya, E., M. Uysal, and L. Toepper (1995). "Measuring Tourism Performance Using A Shift-Share Analysis: The Case of South Carolina." *Journal of Travel Research,* 34 (Fall): 55–61.

Stufflebeam, D. L., and A. J. Shinkfield (1985). *Systematic Evaluation.* Boston: Kluver-Nijhoff.

Sunday, A. A. (1975). "Estimation of the Effectiveness of International Tourism Promotion by Selected Countries in American Media." Ph.D. diss., University of Illinois at Urbana-Champaign.

Tervo, H., and P. Okko (1983). "A Note of Shift-Share as a Method of Estimating the Employment Effects of Regional Economic Policy." *Journal of Regional Science,* 23 (1): 115–21.

Uysal, M. (1983). "Construction of a Model Which Investigates the Impacts of Selected Variables on International Tourist Flows to Turkey." Ph.D. diss., Texas A&M University (as reported in Crouch, Schultz and Valerio 1992).

Uysal, M., and J. L. Crompton (1984). "Determinants of Demand for International Tourist Flows to Turkey." *Tourism Management,* December: 288-97.

Uysal, M., and J. T. O'Leary (1986). "A Canonical Analysis of International Tourism Demand." *Annals of Tourism Research,* 13 (4): 651–55.

Vanhove, N., and P. Klaassen (1987). *Regional Policy: A European Approach.* Aldershot, England: Gower.

Witt, S. F., and C. A. Martin (1987). "International

Tourism Demand Models. Inclusion of Marketing Variables." *Tourism Management,* 8 (1): 33–40.

Woodley, A. (1993). "Tourism and Sustainable Development: The Community Perspective." In *Tourism and Sustainable Development: Monitoring, Planning, Management,* edited by J. G. Nelson, R. Butler, and G. Wall, Waterloo, Ontario: University of Waterloo Heritage Resource Centre, pp. 137–47.

Woodside, A. G. (1981). "Measuring the Conversion of Advertising Coupon Inquiries into Visitors." *Journal of Travel Research,* 19 (Spring): 38–41.

———(1990). "Measuring Advertising Effectiveness in Destination Marketing Strategies." *Journal of Travel Research,* 29 (Fall): 3–8.

WTO (World Tourism Organisation) (1994). *Budgets of National Tourism Administrations.* Madrid: WTO.

Zehnder, L. E. (1976). "Tourism and Social Problems: Implications for Research and Marketing." *Proceedings of the 7th Annual Travel and Tourism Research Association Conference.* Lexington, KY: Travel and Tourism Research Association, pp. 211–12.

KEY CONCEPTS

competitive destinations
content of tourism policy
core vision
demand development strategies
destination positioning
destination vision
implementation strategy
multidisciplinary tourism policy
policy formulation
policy formulation methods
process of policy formulation

research for policy formulation
structure of tourism policy
supply development strategies
sustainable destinations
total system policy
tourism constraints
tourism destination management
   information system (TDMIS)
tourism objective
tourism policy

INTERNET SITES

Asia Pacific Economic Corporation
http://www.apecsec.org.sg

Australia Tourist Commission
http://tourism.gov.au/welcome.html

British Tourist Authority
http://www.bta.org.uk

California Tourism Policy Act
http://gocalif.ca.gov/tma/ctpa.html

Canadian Tourism Commission
http://canadatourism.com

Caribbean Tourism Organization
http://www.caribtourism.com

Embassy Page
http://www.embpage.org

European Travel Commission
http://www.visiteurope.com

European Union
http://www.europa.eu.int

German National Tourist Office
http://www.germany-tourism.de

International Air Transport Association
http://www.iata.org

International Association of Convention and Visitor Bureaus
http://www.iacvb.org

International Civil Aviation Organization
http://www.ca.org/CAO

International Labour Organization
http://www.ilo.org

Organization for Economic Cooperation and Development
http://www.oecd.org

Organization of American States
http://www.oas.org

Pacific-Asia Travel Association
http://www.pata.org

Tourism Industries (U.S.)
http://tinet.ita.doe.gov

Tourism Offices Worldwide Directory
http://www.mbnet.mb.ca/lucas/travel

Tourism Policy Council
http://tpcnet.doc.gov./main/index.html

Tourism Policy Group, Ministry of Commerce, New Zealand
http://www.moc.govt.nzl

Travel Industry Association of America
http://www.tia.org

UNESCO
http://www.unesco.org

United Nations
http://www.un.org

World Tourism Organization
http://www.world-tourism.org

World Travel and Tourism Council
http://www.wttc.org

 **INTERNET EXERCISES**

Activity 1

Site Name: Tourism Policy in Turkey
URL: http://www.turizm.net/economy/touris~1.htm
Background Information: In 1983, the government of Turkey amended its tourism policy to encourage Turkish and foreign investment companies to participate more effectively in the development of Turkey's tourism sector.

Exercise

1. Compare the Turkish tourism policy with the elements of a good tourism policy as described in the textbook. What similarities and differences can you find?

Activity 2

Site Name: World Travel and Tourism Tax Policy Center (TPC)

URL: http://traveltax.msu.edu/
Background Information: The World Travel & Tourism Tax Policy Center (TPC) is dedicated to strengthening the travel and tourism industry and the world's economy by providing timely information and analysis of tax policy issues and considerations for government policymakers, industry leaders, and the general public.

Exercises

1. Using information from the site, explain why a tax policy would be important to the travel and tourism industry.

2. How does travel and tourism as a "product" differ from more conventional types of products that can be taxed by government agencies?

QUESTIONS FOR REVIEW AND DISCUSSION

1. What is a "tourism policy" and why is it important for a tourism destination to have a formal policy?

2. Why might a major stakeholder not wish to participate in the policy process?

3. How might tourism policy differ from countries, states/provinces, and cities? Why might it differ?

4. How would you identify and choose the stakeholders who should be involved in the formulation of a tourism policy for a region? Is there anyone that you feel should be excluded from the process?

5. What are the implications of no involvement in policy formulation by a major stakeholder?

6. What is the difference between a tourism policy and a tourism strategy?

7. Who should be "in charge" of policy formulation?

8. What are the most important "interfaces" of tourism policy; that is, which other sectors of the economy and society need to be aware of tourism policy or might have a significant impact on the success of tourism policy?

9. What do you see as the major barriers to successful policy formulation for tourism?

10. Must there be total consensus by all stakeholders on the content of a region's tourism policy? If not, how would you determine if there was adequate support for the different components of a policy?

11. How frequently should the policy formulation process take place for a destination? Why?

12. Why is a "vision" especially important for policy formulation? How long into the future should a vision attempt to define a "ideal future"?

13. Implementation of policy recommendations is often a problem. What do you see as the major barriers to the implementation of policy? Why do they exist? How might these barriers be overcome?

SELECTED REFERENCES

Ashworth, G. J., and Dietvorst, A. G. J., eds. *Tourism and Spatial Transformations: Implications for Policy and Planning.* London: CAB International, 1995.

Bramhan, P., et al. *Leisure Policies in Europe.* London: CAB International, 1993.

Bramwell, Bill, and Adrian Fearn. "Visitor Attitudes to a Policy Instrument for Visitor Funding of Conservation in a Tourism Area." *Journal of Travel Research,* Vol. 35, No. 2, pp. 29–33, Fall 1996.

Brewton, Charles, and Glenn Withiam. "United States Tourism Policy: Alive, but Not Well." *Cornell Quarterly: Hotel Restaurant and Administration,* Vol. 39, No. 1, pp. 50–59, February 1998.

Clare, Harry. "Australian Tourism Industry Policy: A New View." *Tourism Economics: The Business and Finance of Tourism and Recreation,* Vol. 3, No. 4, pp. 361–378, 1997.

Craigwell, Roland, and Kelvin Dalrymple. "The Effect of Domestic Policies on Tourism Demand: A Theoretical Analysis." *Tourism Analysis: An Interdisciplinary Journal,* Vol. 1, No. 1, pp. 55–60, 1998.

Datzira-Masip, Jordi. "Tourism Policy in Spain: An Overview." *The Tourist Review,* Vol. 53, No. 1, pp. 41–50, 1998.

Deegan, J., and D. A. Dineen. *Tourism Policy and Performance: The Irish Experience.* London: ITBP, 1997.

Denzin, N. K., and Y. A. Lincoln, eds. *Handbook of Qualitative Research.* Thousand Oaks, CA: Sage Publications, 1994.

Edgell, D. L. S. *Coopetitive World Tourism at the Millennium: An Agenda for Industry, Government and Education,* Washington, D.C.: USTTA, U.S. Department of Commerce, 1993.

Edgell, David L., and R. Todd Haenisch. *Coopetition: Global Tourism Beyond the Millennium.* Kansas City, MO: Midpoint National, 1995.

Elliot, J. *Tourism: Politics and Public Sector Management,* London: Routledge, 1997.

Faulkner, Bill. "A Model for the Evaluation of National Tourism Destination Marketing Programs." *Journal of Travel Research,* Vol. 35, No. 3, pp. 23–32, Winter 1997.

Fayos-Sola, Eduardo. "Tourism Policy: A Midsummer Night's Dream?" *Tourism Management,* Vol. 17, No. 6, pp. 405–412, 1996.

Greenbaum, T. L. *The Practical Handbook and Guide to Focus Group Research.* Lexington, MA: Lexington Books, 1988.

Groves, R. M., et al., eds. *Telephone Survey Methodology.* New York: Wiley, 1988.

Hall, C. M. *Tourism and Politics: Policy, Power and Place.* New York: Wiley, 1994.

Hall, C. M., and J. M. Jenkins. *Tourism and Public Policy.* London: ITBP, 1995.

Hobson, J. S. Perry, and Goldwyn Ko. "Tourism and Politics: The Implications of the Change in Sovereignty on the Future Development of Hong Kong's Tourism Industry." *Journal of Travel Research,* Vol. 32, No. 4, pp. 2–8, Spring 1994.

Laarman, Jan G., and Hans M. Gregersen. "Pricing Policy in Nature-Based Tourism." *Tourism Management,* Vol. 17, No. 4, pp. 247–255, June 1996.

Laws, Eric. *Tourism Destination Management: Issues, Analysis and Policies.* New York: Routledge, 1995.

Lewis, Robert C. *Cases in Hospitality Strategy and Policy.* New York: Wiley, 1998.

Linstone, H. A., and M. Turoff. *The Delphi Method:*

Techniques and Applications. London: Addison-Wesley Publishing Company, 1975.

Myers, James, Peter Forsberg, and Donald Holecek. "A Framework for Monitoring Global Travel and Tourism Taxes: The WTTC Tax Barometer." *Tourism Economics: The Business and Finance of Tourism and Recreation,* Vol. 3, No. 1, pp. 5–20, March 1997.

NPS. *National Parks for the 21st Century: The Vail Agenda.* Washington, D.C.: National Parks Service, 1995.

Oral, M., and O. Kettani, eds. *Globalisation and Competitiveness: Implications for Policy and Strategy Formulation.* Ankara, Turkey: Bilkent University, 1997.

Prugh, Thomas. *National Capital and Human Economic Survival.* Solomons, MD: ISSE Press, 1995.

Ritchie, J. R. B. "Crafting a Destination Vision: Putting the concept of resident-responsive tourism into practice." *Tourism Management,* Vol. 14, No. 5, pp. 379–389, 1993.

Ritchie, J. R. B. "Crafting a Value-driven Vision for a National Tourism Treasure." *Tourism Management,* Vol. 20, No. 3, pp. 273–282, 1999.

Rosenberg, M. *The Logic of Survey Analysis.* New York: Basic Books, 1968.

Sindiga, Isaac. "Wildlife-Based Tourism in Kenya: Land Use Conflicts and Government Policies over Protected Areas." *Journal of Tourism Studies,* Vol. 6, No. 2, pp. 47–55, December 1995.

Smeral, Egon. "The Impact of Globalization on Small and Medium Enterprises: New Challenges for Tourism Policies in European Countries." *Tourism Management,* Vol. 19, No. 4, pp. 371–380, 1998.

Smith, Ginger. "Implications of the North American Free Trade Agreement for the US Tourism Industry." *Tourism Management,* Vol. 15, No. 5, pp. 323–326, October 1994.

Soteriou, E. C., and C. Roberts, "The Strategic Planning Process in National Tourism Organizations." *Journal of Travel Research,* 37(August): 21–29, 1998.

Taylor, Gordon D. "The Implications of Free Trade Agreements for Tourism in Canada." *Tourism Management,* Vol. 15, No. 5, pp. 315–318, October 1994.

Templeton, J. F. *Focus Groups: A Guide for Marketing and Advertising Professionals.* Chicago: Probus Publishing Company, 1987.

Tyler, Duncan, Martin Robertson, and Yvonne Guerrier. *Managing Tourism in Cities.* New York: Wiley, 1998.

Veal, A. J. *Leisure Policy and Planning.* Essex, UK: Longman, 1994.

Wanhill, Stephen. "Peripheral Area Tourism: A European Perspective." *Progress in Hospitality Research,* Vol. 3, pp. 47–70, 1997.

Weed, M. E., and C. J. Bull. "Integrating Sport and Tourism: A Review of Regional Policies in England." *Progress in Tourism and Hospitality Research,* Vol. 3, No. 2, pp. 127–148, June 1997.

Wilkinson, Paul F. *Tourism Policy and Planning: Case Studies from the Commonwealth Caribbean.* Elmsford, NY: Cognizant Communication Corporation, 1998.

WTO. *How & Why Governments Need to Stay Involved in Tourism.* Madrid: World Tourism Organization, 1997.

Yueh-Hsiu, and Nigel Hemmington. "The Impact of Environmental Policy on the Tourism Industry in Taiwan." *Progress in Hospitality Research,* Vol. 3, pp. 35–45, 1997.

CHAPTER 16

TOURISM PLANNING, DEVELOPMENT, AND SOCIAL CONSIDERATIONS

◀ **LEARNING OBJECTIVES**

- Relate tourism planning to tourism policy.

- Discover what the goals of tourism development should be.

- Recognize that there are some serious barriers to tourism development that must be overcome if a desired growth is to occur.

- Learn the political and economic aspects of development, including those related to developing countries.

- Appreciate the importance of architectural design and concern for heritage preservation, local handicrafts, and use of indigenous materials in creating tourist facilities.

◀ *Good planning is necessary for a luxury resort to come together and work for management, guests, and the surrounding community. (Photo courtesy of The Phoenician.)*

INTRODUCTION

Good tourism planning goes far beyond schemes to maximize profit. While profitable development brings positive economic and social benefits to the community, it also carries inevitable drawbacks. Therefore, developers must incorporate ways to enhance human welfare and happiness. These include insistence on quality architectural, landscape, and environmental design; planning for transportation; and energy conservation and education.

If such diverse goals are to be achieved, planners must implement a model that will guide their thinking by incorporating each aspect (including various political aspects) into a master plan. These include: zoning, road maintenance, water and sewage treatment systems, and promotional expenses. An official body, financed through tourist earnings, is useful in keeping abreast of socioeconomic activities in the industry as well as dealing with other problems like stabilizing prices, forecasting demand, keeping an inventory of potential national tourists resources, and arranging publicity campaigns.

Resort development also necessitates working out financial arrangements that will not only enable the developer to take out loans for construction but also to be given reduced or forgiven taxes for a period of time in order to improve the venture's financial success.

RELATING TOURISM PLANNING TO TOURISM POLICY

The previous chapter provided an understanding of the role of tourism policy in providing a set of guidelines for the development and promotion of a tourism destination. It also describes the structure and content of a formal tourism policy, as well as the process of **policy formulation.**

Because tourism policy formulation and tourism planning are very directly related to one another, it is important to distinguish between the two, to identify their similarities and their differences in a tourism context.

Their similarities are as follows:

1. They both deal with the future development of a tourism destination or region.
2. They both emphasize the strategic dimensions of managerial action, although planning must also address a number of tactical concerns.

Their differences are listed below:

1. Policy formulation is definitely very "big picture," while much of planning is characterized by an attention to detail.
2. Policy formulation is a creative, intellectual process, while planning is generally a more constrained exercise.
3. Policy, and particularly its visioning component, has a very long-term strategic emphasis, while planning tends to be more restrictive in its time horizon. A one-year planning cycle is not uncommon, although

three- to five-year plans are a possibility. In contrast, destination visions may have a 5-, 10-, 50-, or even a 100-year time horizon.

4. Policy formulation must allow for as yet unseen circumstances and technologies to be considered. In contrast, planning tends to assume current conditions and technologies, with some allowances for predictable (i.e., evolutionary) change.

5. Policy formulation tends to emphasize a systematic determination of "what" should be done in long-term tourism development, while planning tends to emphasize the "how" for the achievement of specific destination goals.

The reader should keep these distinctions in mind when reviewing the rest of this chapter. While policy formulation and planning appear to have certain commonalties, they are, in effect, quite distinct processes. Failure to acknowledge this reality has been quite limiting in the past.

It should be noted that the definitions and distinctions related to policy, strategy, goals, objectives and planning are ongoing sources of debate in the management literature. Different scholars and managers frequently debate the exact meaning of these terminologies. While the debate is not inconsequential, it should not stand in the way of creative thinking or managerial action.

Integrating Policy and Planning

Although policy formulation and destination planning are different types of processes, they must nevertheless be seen as integrated components of an ongoing process of destination management. This need is reflected in Table 16.1 on page 521.

WHY TOURISM PLANNING IS NECESSARY

The decision to develop tourism or expand present tourism development in a community, a region, or a country must be studied carefully. The socioeconomic benefits from tourism are powerful. Tourism development looks attractive to both developed and underdeveloped countries with the right preconditions—some combination of natural, scenic, historical, archaeological, cultural, and climate attractions. Tourism is a growth industry; and while that growth may show some slowing in the short run, the long run prospects are good. The expected continued growth is based on continually rising per capita incomes, lower travel costs, increased leisure time, and changes in consumers' tastes and preferences toward travel, recreation, and leisure goods and services.

Many advocates look at tourism as a panacea for solving an area's development problems. This view is unrealistic because benefits may be accompanied by detrimental consequences. A review of some advantages and disadvantages from Chapter 1 arising from tourism development will indicate why careful planning is necessary. Major arguments for tourism are that it:

1. Provides employment opportunities, both skilled and unskilled, because it is a labor-intensive industry

2. Generates a supply of needed foreign exchange

3. Increases incomes

4. Creates increased gross national product

5. Requires the development of an infrastructure that will also help stimulate local commerce and industry

6. Justifies environmental protection and improvement

7. Increases governmental revenues

8. Helps to diversify the economy

9. Creates a favorable worldwide image for the destination

10. Facilitates the process of modernization by education of youth and society and changing values

11. Provides tourist and recreational facilities that may be used by a local population who could not otherwise afford to develop facilities

12. Gives foreigners an opportunity to be favorably impressed by a little-known country or region

Some disadvantages of tourism are that it:

1. Develops excess demand

2. Creates leakages so great that economic benefits do not accrue

3. Diverts funds from more promising forms of economic development

4. Creates social problems from income differences, social differences, introduction of prostitution, gambling, crime, and so on

5. Degrades the natural physical environment

6. Degrades the cultural environment

7. Poses the difficulties of seasonality

8. Increases vulnerability to economic and political changes

9. Adds to inflation of land values and the price of local goods and services

Consequently, tourism is not always a panacea. On the contrary, overdevelopment can generate soil and water pollution and even people pollution, if there are too many visitors at the same place at the same time. Consider automobile and bus traffic congestion, inadequate parking, hotels dwarfing the scale of historic districts, and the displacement of the local community serving businesses by tourist-serving firms leading to degradation of the quality of life rather than improving it.

Furthermore, too many visitors can have a harmful impact on life in the host country and on the visitors themselves. A beautiful landscape can suffer through thoughtless and unwise land development and construction methods. And customers and crafts can be vulgarized by overemphasis on quantity and cheapness.

These responsibilities cannot really be blamed on tourism, but rather on over-commercialization. Tourism is one of the world's greatest and most significant social and economic forces. But government officials and business people must weigh the economic benefits against the possible future degradation of human and natural resources.

Tourism development must be guided by carefully planned policy, a policy not built on balance sheets and profit and loss statements alone, but on the ideals and principles of human welfare and happiness. Social problems cannot be solved without a strong and growing economy that tourism can help to create. Sound development policy can have the happy result of a growing tourist business, along with the preservation of the natural and cultural resources that attracted the visitors in the first place.

Planning is critical to having sustainable development and protecting the environment. For that reason the next chapter has been devoted to "tourism and the environment" to expand the discussion on how to have development and, hopefully, both protect and enhance the environment.

Viewed comprehensively, the relationship between tourism and the community, state, regions, and countries requires consideration of many difficult issues: the quality of architecture, landscape, and environmental design; environmental reclamation and amenity; natural conservation; land-use management; financial strategies for long-term economic development; employment; transportation; energy conservation; education, information and interpretation systems; and more.

These are the reasons why sound tourism planning is essential. Planning can ensure that tourist development has the ability to realize the advantages of tourism and reduce the disadvantages.

THE PLANNING PROCESS

Proper planning of the physical, legal, promotion, finance, economic, market, management, social, and environmental aspects will help to deliver the benefits of tourism development.

Good planning defines the desired result and works in a systematic manner to achieve success. The following steps briefly describe a logical sequence:

Define the system. What is the scale, size, market, character, and purpose?

Formulate objectives. Without a set of objectives the development concept has no direction. The objectives must be comprehensive and specific and should include a timetable for completion.

Data gathering. Fact finding, or research, provides basic data that are essential to developing the plan. Examples of data gathering are preparing a fact book, making market surveys, undertaking site and infrastructure surveys, and analyzing existing facilities and competition.

Analysis and interpretation. Once collected, the many fragments of information must be interpreted so the facts gathered will have meaning. This step leads to a set of conclusions and recommendations that leads to making or conceptualizing a preliminary plan.

Preliminary planning. Based on the previous steps, alternatives are considered and alternative physical solutions are drawn up and tested. Frequently, scale models are developed to illustrate the land-use plans; sketches are prepared to show the image the development will project; financial plans are drafted from the market information, site surveys, and the layout plan to show the investment needed in each phase of the project and the cash flow expected; and legal requirements are met.

Denver International Airport exemplifies good planning for traveler convenience. The modern terminal building has separate drop-off levels for passengers arriving in private and commercial vehicles, close-in parking, and trains to shuttle passengers from the terminal to three concourses. *(Photo courtesy of Denver International Airport.)*

Approving the plan. The parties involved can now look at plans, drawings, scale models, estimates of costs, and estimates of profits and know what will be involved and what the chances for success or failure will be. While a great deal of money may have been spent up to this point, the sum is a relatively small amount compared to the expenditures that will be required once the plan is approved and master planning and implementation begin.

Final plan. This phase typically includes: a definition of land use; plans for infrastructure facilities such as roads, airports, bike paths, horse trails, pedestrian walkways, sewage, water, and utilities; architectural standards; landscape plans; zoning and other land-use regulations; and economic analysis, market analysis, and financial programming.

Implementation. Implementation carries out the plan and creates an operational tourism development. It also follows up and evaluates. Good planning provides mechanisms that give continuing feedback on the tourism project and the levels of consumer satisfaction achieved.

Good planning should eliminate problems and provide user satisfaction. The final user is the judge in determining how successful the planning process has been.

Figure 16.1 shows a model for the tourism planning and development process and

FIGURE 16.1 Model for the tourism planning and development process.

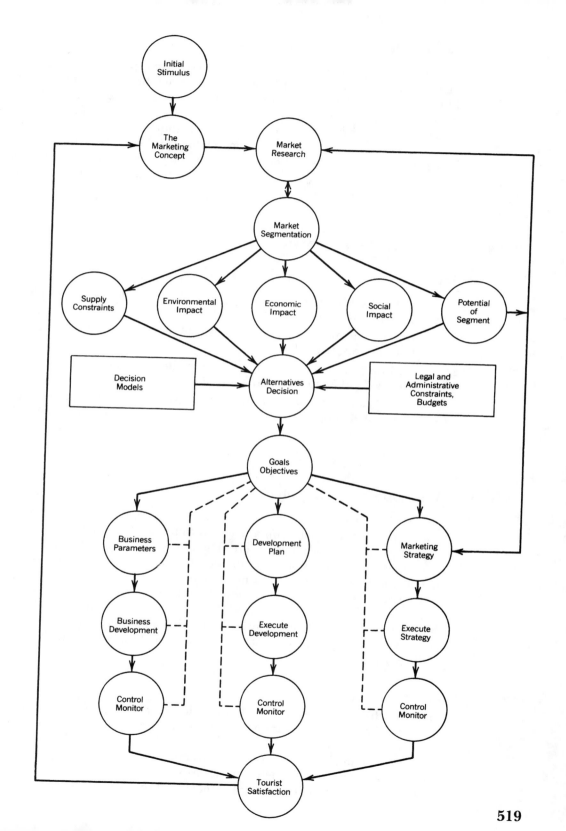

519

illustrates the large number of variables that come into play. The advantage of utilizing such a model is that it requires the planner to view the total picture and guides the thinking process. While no model can depict all interrelated facts of a planning process or eliminate all guesswork, such a model deserves inclusion in the initial phases of planning as a tool that helps to order, coordinate, and control the process.

Table 16.1 shows an integrated approach to planning. Again it serves as a guide to asking the right questions and making sure that the process is complete. It also illustrates that there are a number of approaches to tourism planning. There is no single magic approach.

GOALS OF TOURISM DEVELOPMENT

Tourism development should aim at:

1. Providing a framework for raising the living standard of the people through the economic benefits of tourism
2. Developing an infrastructure and providing recreation facilities for visitors and residents alike
3. Ensuring types of development within visitor centers and resorts that are appropriate to the purposes of those areas
4. Establishing a development program consistent with the cultural, social, and economic philosophy of the government and the people of the host country or area
5. Optimizing visitor satisfaction

Obstacles to Development of Supply

The first **obstacle** to overcome in turning potential supply into actual supply is the lack or inadequacy of transportation and access routes to the tourist nucleus or center. It is, of course, not enough to get there. The tourist should also be induced to stay. To this end, another basic obstacle to the development of actual supply should be overcome: the lack or shortage of accommodation.

Tourists inevitably require a series of goods and services. Some may be found on the spot and may be economically flexible enough to adapt to the fluctuations of demand. The infrastructure capacity must meet maximum demand. Financing can be a major obstacle. Finally, we cannot overlook the need for sufficiently trained and hospitable personnel.

Internal Obstacles

These are the obstacles found within the destination area that can be corrected or eliminated by direct, voluntary means. They may occur in incoming as well as outgoing or internal tourism.

As tourism in all its forms absorbs consumer goods, prices in this field tend to be extremely sensitive to movements in the prices of goods. The rising price of tourism has the same effect as a decrease in the income of the potential tourist. Consequently,

TABLE 16.1
TOURISM PLANNING: AN INTEGRATED APPROACH

Planning Activity	Organizational Development	Community Involvement	Tourism Product Development	Tourism Product Marketing
		Where Are We Today?		
1. Gather Information	Evaluate existing group composition. Identify potential representatives that could or should be involved.	Identify both tourism and nontourism interests that may be affected by the proposed tourism development. Determine key issues and concerns of the various stakeholders.	Conduct an inventory and assessment of the area's tourism resources, services, and infrastructure. Estimate existing levels of use and carrying capacity.	Profile the existing markets in terms of geographic origin, demographics, family life cycle, spending patterns, needs, and interests.
		Where Do We Want to Go?		
2. Identify community values	Tourism organization members express community values by answering questions related to quality of life now and in the future.	Community representatives express their values by answering questions related to quality of life now and in the future.	Values expressed by the tourism organization and community representatives begin to form the foundation upon which future tourism development and resource allocation decisions will be based.	Values expressed by the tourism organization and community representatives begin to form the foundation upon which future tourism marketing decisions will be based.
3. Create a vision	Tourism organization members create an image of how the community should look, feel, and be, now and in the future.	Community representatives create an image of how the community should look, feel, and be, now and in the future	The descriptive "story" about future development and quality of life in the community further strengthens the foundation and guides tourism development and resource allocation decisions.	The descriptive "story" about future development and quality of life in the community further strengthens the foundation and guides tourism marketing decisions.

TABLE 16.1 (*Continued*)

Planning Activity	Organizational Development	Community Involvement	Tourism Product Development	Tourism Product Marketing
4. Identify concerns and opportunities	Tourism organization members brainstorm a list of concerns and opportunities that the group or community may be facing. Similar ideas are combined and narrowed down to reflect (1) those related to tourism and (2) those the tourism organization *should* handle.	Community representatives brainstorm a list of concerns and opportunities the community may be facing. Similar ideas are combined and narrowed down to reflect (1) those related to tourism and (2) those that can be addressed by the tourism organization or through tourism initiatives.	The major concerns and opportunities will provide direction for tourism development initiatives. Ideas expressed should be revisited as more concrete plans for developing or enhancing tourism attractions, services, and infrastructure are being considered.	The major concerns and opportunities will provide direction for tourism development initiatives. Ideas expressed should be revisited as more concrete plans for marketing tourism resources and services are being considered.
5. Develop a mission	Tourism organization members articulate their purpose for existing and determine who they are serving. It is important to recognize not only the visitor, but also community needs during this activity.	The tourism organization's mission serves as a vehicle to inform the community about the group's purpose for existing.	The mission, along with the values, vision, concerns, and opportunities helps guide the tourism development effort.	The mission, along with the values, vision, concerns, and opportunities helps guide the tourism marketing effort.
		Where Do We Want to Go?		
6. Develop goals	Based on the tourism organization's values, vision, concerns, opportunities, and mission, *goals* relative to the structure and	Goals related to community education and involvement in the tourism development effort are developed. Most	Based on the expressed values, vision, concerns, opportunities, and mission, goals for the physical development	Based on the plans for tourism product development and/or enhancement, goals for tourism marketing are developed.

	Organizational	Community education	Tourism product development	Tourism marketing
	administration of the organization are developed.	likely, goals will center on ways to involve the public in the planning process.	and/or enhancement of tourism resources, traveler services, and infrastructure are developed.	

How Are We Going to Get There?

	Organizational	Community education	Tourism product development	Tourism marketing
7. Develop objectives	Tourism organization members develop action-oriented statements that propose how to achieve each *organizational* goal. The number of objectives for each goal will vary depending on the group's stage of development and available human, physical, and financial resources.	Tourism organization members develop action-oriented statements that propose how to achieve each *community education and involvement* goal. The number of objectives for each goal will vary depending on the community's level of interest and involvement in the tourism initiatives, and the available human, physical, and financial resources.	Tourism organization members develop action-oriented statements that propose how to achieve each *tourism product development* goal. The number of objectives for each goal will vary depending on the community's stage of development, the quantity and quality of existing tourism resources, services, and infrastructure, and available human, physical, and financial resources.	Tourism organization members develop action-oriented statements that propose how to achieve each *tourism product marketing* goal. The number of objectives for each goal will vary depending on the quantity and quality of existing tourism marketing activities and available human, physical, and financial resources.
8. Develop actions	Tourism organization members define strategies and tactics which outline specifically how each *organizational*	Tourism organization members define strategies and tactics which outline specifically how each *community education*	Tourism organization members define strategies and tactics which outline specifically how each *tourism product*	Tourism organization members define strategies and tactics which outline specifically how each *tourism marketing*

TABLE 16.1 (*Continued*)

Planning Activity	Organizational Development	Community Involvement	Tourism Product Development	Tourism Product Marketing
	development objective will be achieved. This includes exploring funding and technical assistance alternatives, identifying timelines, and assigning tasks.	*and involvement* objective will be achieved. This includes exploring funding and technical assistance alternatives, identifying timelines, and assigning tasks.	*development objective* will be achieved. This includes exploring funding and technical assistance alternatives, identifying timelines, and assigning tasks.	objective will be achieved. This includes exploring funding and technical assistance alternatives, identifying timelines, and assigning tasks.
How Did We Do?				
9. Evaluate progress	Organization members conduct a periodic review of the organization's activities and progress. A report is written and copies submitted to appropriate governing bodies, funding agencies, and the general public.	Organization members conduct a periodic review of key public involvement activities. A report is written and copies submitted to appropriate governing bodies, funding agencies, and the general public.	Organization members conduct a periodic review of tourism product development and implementation activities and progress. A report is written and copies submitted to appropriate governing bodies, funding agencies, and the general public.	Organization members conduct a periodic review of tourism product marketing activities and progress. A report is written and copies submitted to appropriate governing bodies, funding agencies, and the general public.
10. Update and modify plan	Based on new information or changing circumstances, revisions to the organizational development plan are made.	Based on new information or changing circumstances, revisions to the plan for community involvement are made.	Based on new information or changing circumstances, revisions to the plan for tourism product development are made.	Based on new information or changing circumstances, revisions to the plan for tourism marketing are made.

Source: Jonelle Nuckolls and Patrick Long, *Organizing Resources for Tourism in Rural Areas* (Boulder, CO: University of Colorado, 1993).

when considering costs and planning a holiday, the tourist will choose to go—if the value is the same—where money goes the furthest.

Another major obstacle is the attitude of government and business leaders in the destination area. If this leadership is resistant or even passive toward tourism, development will lag.

POLITICAL ASPECTS OF TOURISM DEVELOPMENT

Like any significant element of an area's economy, there are **political aspects** that can and often do have major influences on the creation, operation, and survival of tourism projects. Many examples can be cited. One is the land-use regulations (zoning) for commercial or public tourism developments, which can be emotionally and politically sensitive topics. Another is the degree of involvement of governmental agencies in creating and maintaining tourism infrastructure. A third is the type and extent of publicity, advertising, and other promotional efforts.

Land Use (Zoning)

Zoning ordinances specify the legal types of **land use.** But the final determination of the land use and the administration of the zoning ordinances are typically assigned to a publicly employed zoning administrator and a politically appointed or elected zoning board. Thus, the government decides on how land is to be used, and it also rules on any request for changes in the zoning districts or rezoning to accommodate a nonconforming proposed development.

Attitudes of these public bodies toward tourism development will be influenced by the general public's perception (if any) of the desirability of a specific development. Creating a favorable public image is the responsibility of the developer and the managers of all tourism supply components. The public tourism promotion organization bears responsibility as well. If the public feels that tourism is desirable, rational zoning regulations and administration should result. Furthermore, if principles of tourism planning and development, as presented in this chapter, are faithfully implemented, the result should be well-planned projects. These will be accepted in the community as welcome sources of employment and tax revenues.

Creation and Maintenance of Infrastructure

Any tourism development will need **infrastructure.** Whether this is provided by government agencies or the private developer, or both, is basically a political question. What troubles many local people is that their taxes are spent in part to provide roads, water systems, sewers, airports, marinas, parks, and other infrastructure that they perceive as benefiting mainly tourism. Is this fair or desirable from their point of view? Those having a common concern in tourism must realize that it is their responsibility to convince the public that such expenditures by governmet *are* desirable and *do* benefit the local economy. One way to achieve this understanding is through an intelligent lobbying effort. Another approach is to address service clubs, social organizations, and school groups. A third method shows how much money was spent by tourists or convention delegates.

Maintenance policies are also a vital factor in successful tourism development. Any element of infrastructure, once created, needs maintenance. The level of this maintenance can greatly affect successful tourism. An example is the promptness and adequacy of snow removal from public roads servicing ski resorts. Another is the quality and adequacy of public water and sewage systems. Many other examples could be given. Political influence to obtain good maintenance can be brought to bear by hotel and motel associations, chambers of commerce, convention and visitors' bureaus, and promotion groups. Such efforts can be very effective, because public service agencies tend to be receptive if the demands are frequent and forceful.

Government and private industry *must* interact cooperatively if tourism development is to be successful. Political friction can develop when government officials think that private industry should do more to help itself and businesspeople believe that the government should do more to assist them. A knowledgeable outside consulting firm can study the situation and make recommendations in the best interests of both factions.

Promotional Efforts

Publicly funded promotional programs are an essential part of the industry. However, the level or degree of participation in such publicity is largely a political process. To convince lawmakers and local political decision makers of the desirability of tourism, produce accurate data on the economic impact of tourism spending. An "investment" concept is the preferred way to view government programs. Pointing out industry diversification in the economy is another good approach. Other benefits cited could be employment, income multipliers, additional investments, and preservation and enhancement of local industries, crafts, and the arts, as well as building local pride and recognition.

Lobbying efforts need to be convincing and persistent. Organizations representing tourism must have both moral and monetary support in sufficient measure to bring about successful political influence. Nothing succeeds like success. If tourism booms, the politicians can well take pride in their important contribution. We repeat: As in all other aspects of the tourist business, cooperation pays!

DEVELOPMENT OF TOURIST POTENTIAL

Official Tourism Body

A **tourism body or organization** should be created to keep abreast of socioeconomic developments in the various market countries or areas to provide a reasonably early forecast of the size, type, and structure of probable tourism demand. It would be equally useful to have a report on developments in the tourist industry of supplying centers or areas and on activities and projects undertaken to promote development.

Because tourism is such a complex phenomenon, distinct ministerial departments are responsible for finding solutions to developmental problems.

The stabilization of general and tourist prices should be a constant objective, because rising prices automatically reduce the volume of demand. Land speculation should be discouraged.

The inventory of potential national tourist resources (parks, attractions, recreational facilities, and so on) should be kept up to date and extended so that these resources may be duly incorporated into actual tourist trade in accordance with quantity and quality forecasts of demand.

Tax pressures that directly affect operating costs also influence prices. Because of the export value of tourism, a fiscal policy similar to that applied to the conventional or classical export trade should be devised.

Publicity campaigns should be organized and implemented every year according to the forecasts. These should be to the point, detailed, and constructive and should zero in on socioeconomic developments and activities in the market. Financing to cover this activity should be obtained from annual tourist earnings and other identifiable funds at a rate of not less than 1 percent and perhaps not more than 4 percent of total earnings. Customs facilities should be as lenient as possible while ensuring control and maintenance of order and avoiding fraud or other crimes.

For their own benefit, host countries should make the tourists' sojourn as agreeable as possible. But proof that tourists have the financial means to cover the costs of their stay may be desired.

The seasonal nature of mass tourism causes congestion in the use of services required by tourists. Some services, such as accommodation, cannot adapt easily to seasonal fluctuation. On the other hand, some, such as transportation and communications, can adapt. Government provision of public services is important for development.

Transportation

Because of its role in tourist development, the following measures with regard to **transportation** are recommended:

1. Continual, detailed study of transport used for tourism with a view toward planning necessary improvements and extensions.

2. Establishing a national or international plan of roads relevant to tourism, building new roads if necessary, improving those in a deficient state, and improving road sign systems. Such activities should be included in the general road plans with priorities according to economic necessity and the significance of road transport in tourism.

3. Improving rail transport (where needed) for travelers on lines between the boundary and the main tourist centers and regions as well as short-distance services in these regions of maximum tourist influx.

4. Improving road frontier posts, extending their capacity to ensure smoother crossings, organizing easier movement of in- and outgoing tourist flows. Crossing the frontier is always either the prologue or the epilogue to any journey between countries and is therefore important for the favorable impression the tourist will retain.

5. Providing adequate airport services and installations to meet demand.

Transportation is an important component of tourism planning. This steam train carries visitors to the Grand Canyon National Park in Arizona. It not only provides a unique travel experience, but also helps to alleviate road congestion and reduce auto pollution in an environmentally sensitive area. *(Photo by James B. Winters.)*

The rapid progress of technology in air transport makes reasonable forecasts possible.

6. Planning for ports and marinas equipped for tourism.

7. Extending car-hire services (with and without drivers) for tourists who arrive by air or sea.

Accommodations

Accommodations must be properly placed in the regional plan. Hotels are permanent structures and grace the landscape for a long time. Planning considerations are vital. Figure 16.2 shows a specific site development plan.

One of the first considerations to be made by any planning body should be where hotels will be located. This can be accomplished by using zoning laws. Hotels are commonly allowed in "commercial" zones. Also to be decided is the number of hotel rooms needed in relation to the anticipated demand. Then to be considered is a provision for expansion of hotels as demand increases.

One consideration in hotel planning is intelligent spacing of hotels in a given area. Hotels spaced too close together tend to have a mutual value-reducing effect. Views are cut off or inhibited, and structures are lowered in value.

Also important is the ratio of the number of persons on the beach to the number of rooms in the hotel. Research in the Department of Natural Resources of the state of Michigan indicates that the optimum capacity of an average-sized ocean or Great Lakes beach is approximately 1000 persons for each 400 lineal feet of beach. Typically, about 50 percent of those vacationers in a resort or beach area will actually be on the beach; and of this group, 25 percent will be in the water and 75 percent will be on the beach.

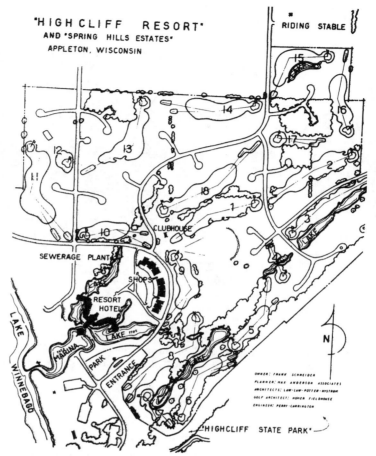

"HIGH CLIFF RESORT"
AND "SPRING HILLS ESTATES"
APPLETON, WISCONSIN

RIDING STABLE

CLUBHOUSE

SEWERAGE PLANT

SHOPS

RESORT HOTEL

LAKE WINNEBAGO

MARINA

PARK

ENTRANCE

N

OWNER: FRANK SCHNEIDER
PLANNER: MAX ANDERSON ASSOCIATES
ARCHITECTS: LAW-LAW-POTTER-NYSTROM
GOLF ARCHITECT: HOMER FIELDHOUSE
ENGINEER: PERRY-CARRINGTON

"HIGHCLIFF STATE PARK"

FIGURE 16.2 Example of "planning for private tourism development adjacent to a state park." Note integration of infrastructure and recreational facilities. *(Source: Recreational Land Development, Wisconsin Department of Natural Resources, Division of Resource Development, Bureau of Recreation)*

Another consideration is the topography. In rolling or hilly country, more accommodations can be placed close together without a feeling of interference with one another than in a flat area. Also, the type of vegetative cover affects the density of the accommodations. A heavy, thick cover tends to obscure the view, and more accommodations can be successfully placed in a limited area than if the vegetation is sparse or absent entirely (see Figure 16.3).

Clusters of accommodations in reasonably close proximity, surrounded by extensive natural areas, is recognized as superior planning, as opposed to spreading out accommodations over a wide area. The beauty of the natural environment can be more fully appreciated in such an arrangement.

Before any investment in hotels and similar lodging facilities is made, the traveling and vacation habits of the prospective guests should be studied to tailor the facili-

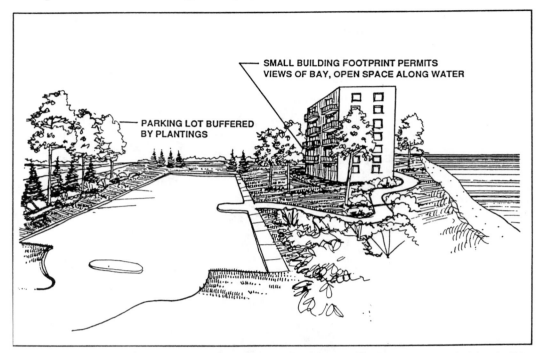

SMALL BUILDING FOOTPRINT PERMITS VIEWS OF BAY, OPEN SPACE ALONG WATER

PARKING LOT BUFFERED BY PLANTINGS

FIGURE 16.3 "Better approach" planning principles of "buffering and minimizing building site space to open scenic views." *(Source: Grand Traverse Bay Region Development Guidelines.)*

ties to the requirements and desires of guests. This is extremely important and conforms to the "market orientation" concept in which major decisions on investment begin with the desires of the potential customers. Another factor is the harmony required between the various elements of the travel plan, the local environment, and infrastructure.

Finally, when resort development is to be limited (and it usually is), it is best to select the most desirable location and create a hotel of real distinction at this site. Then, later, if proper planning and promotion have been accomplished, expansion to other nearby sites can be achieved. Distinctive design of other hotel sites will encourage the visitor to enjoy the variety, architectural appeals, and other satisfactions inherent in each resort hotel.

Financing

Possible procedures for financing construction include a mortgage guarantee plan and direct loans from a variety of sources.

Mortgage Guarantee Plan

Under this plan the government would guarantee mortgage loans up to 80 percent of the approved and appraised value of the land, building, furnishings, and equipment

Hotel accommodations should be planned to blend in with the surrounding environment to enhance the tourist experience. The cabins shown here provide accommodations for guests at the Jasper Park Lodge in the Canadian Rockies. *(Photo courtesy of Canadian Pacific Hotels.)*

when the resort is completed. The approved mortgage would carry interest at prevailing mortgage rates and would require a schedule of amortization for the full retirement of the loan in not more than perhaps 30 years.

A guarantee fund would be established that at all times would be maintained at 20 percent of the total outstanding principal amount of mortgages guaranteed under this plan. The guarantee fund would be managed by trustees who would make any payments of interest and principal certified to them by the agency in charge of the mortgage loan plan. This agency would supervise the status of all approved loans and would investigate the facts and situations whenever it might become necessary to rely upon the guarantee fund to make the required interest and amortization payments. In such cases, an assignment of assets and income would be taken from the resort in default, which would have to be made up from subsequent earnings before any other use could be made of it.

Under this plan, the investor in the resort project would secure a mortgage loan from a lending institution or issue bonds or mortgage certificates to one or more sources of the borrowed capital. With the guarantee of payments of interest and principal and the existence of the guarantee fund for that purpose, mortgage loans under this plan should be attractive to lending institutions and other sources of borrowed capital.

With an approved resort development project and a guaranteed mortgage loan equivalent to 80 percent of the total financing required for land, building, furniture and equipment, 20 percent of the cost could be invested as equity risk capital. The ability to finance on this basis would provide incentive to those directly interested in the business, as well as other investors, to participate in new resort development projects.

Financing Procedures

A group interested in building a resort must convince the local city, regional, or national authorities that the resort should be built. The next step is to obtain a suitable site designated for construction under a previously completed tourist development plan for the area. A third-party feasibility study should be undertaken.

To indicate that this group is seriously interested in building a resort, architects, engineers, consultants, and other specialists should be contacted during the planning phase. The organization that is to operate the resort should be the same group that builds the hotel. An important planning ingredient is the recommendation of experienced resort managers concerning design and layout of the project.

The next step is to obtain construction capital either from local sources or from government or foreign sources. Also, capital must be secured for equipment, supplies, and services, including opening expenses and pre–break-even expenses. Government aid in obtaining imported supplies and equipment is often necessary. Governmental consideration should be given for reduction or elimination of taxes for an adequate length of time to help ensure the financial success of the resort venture. Elimination of import duties on materials needed to build and run resorts is also desirable.

SUMMARY

The quality of tourism planning and development will determine the ultimate success and longevity of any destination area. Thus, time, effort, and resources devoted to planning are essential investments.

Thoughtful planners have formulated the goals for tourism development, and these should be guiding principles everywhere. Obstacles must be overcome by sound planning augmented by political means, if growth is desired. This is often accomplished by the official tourism body. Tourism development should be a part of the overall regional or urban land-use development plan.

Tourism developments almost always involve both government and private developers. Each sector can best contribute certain parts of a project. Government typically provides the infrastructure, such as roads, water supply, sewers, public transportation terminals, and parks. Private developers supply superstructure, such as hotels, restaurants, recreation facilities, and shopping areas.

Government can also help considerably in making financing available. The private sector must deem an investment in a tourist facility attractive from the standpoint of financial return and risk before funds will be committed.

ABOUT THE READING

Allison's article emphasizes the wisdom of incorporating local architectural designs, materials, decor, handicraft products, and other manifestations of local culture into tourist facilities. Doing so helps to make the developments an asset to the country instead of a detriment.

READING 16.1

SPECIAL PLACES IN SPECIAL PLACES

by Gerald L. Allison, FAIA, RIBA
President, Wimberly Allison Tong and Goo Architects, Ltd.
Special places in special places—redundant? Not really. In the context of resort travel, those words are a fair description of what we all seek when we become travelers for pleasure. Certainly when we head for a resort in anticipation of cherished days of respite, we look forward to finding a special place within a special place.

Furthermore, this expectation often influences travel decisions even when the primary purpose is not an unalloyed holiday. Otherwise, why would resort hotels offer extensive convention facilities or corporate conferences be held in exotic places?

Speaking for myself—with everything else being equal—I am far more likely to accept an invitation to speak in Portugal, for example, over the same opportunity in Chicago. I have never experienced Portugal. It holds great promise of pleasure. I have been to Chicago and experienced Chicago. I stayed in a Chicago hotel. And I also stayed in a Chicago hotel in Hong Kong. And in Tokyo. And in Singapore. A couple of them in Sydney, another in Auckland, and a whole list of other places around the world. Also Athens, the wellspring of architectural history. It is truly amazing how widespread Chicago hotels are. Even in Kuala Lumpur and Bali you can wake up in the morning and say, "What a nice hotel—for Chicago."

That's what I want to talk about—how it is not necessary or even desirable to design Chicago hotels around the world. They belong in Chicago.

Please understand, this is not meant to denigrate Chicago, the city. Or special places appropriate to Chicago, where they reflect the special character of that city.

The repetition of the architecture of any particular place—over and over in other places—and mindlessly superimposed out of context—inevitably adds up to sameness and usually inappropriateness. This homogenizing sameness means, at best, overlooking the vast potential that awaits sensitive, responsible development. Sameness in hotel design has the effect of watering down the individuality of place—the very thing that should be enhanced, spotlighted. This sameness is—by inference—disrespectful of the character and culture of the host community. Further, it tends to limit rather than contribute to guest opportunities to experience the place chosen for special qualities. These clone hotels are anything but special places.

I concede they routinely offer the basics for comfortable travel—plumbing that works, hot water for bathing, safe water for drinking, and clean sheets—but not deeply rewarding travel.

And I would gladly accept a little sag in the bed in exchange for a little lift of the spirit.

Do you think this is a bit overstated? I don't think so. There are highly successful premium priced resorts in which all rooms have views and none have telephones, radios, TVs, or mini-bars. Let's consider the implications of "travel for pleasure." What does it mean? It means that for reasons of pleasure we leave one place to go to another. Why? The expectation of change, relaxation, escape, newness, excitement, enrichment, fantasy. Rejuvenating experience.

A successful resort, then, is one that satisfies these expectations. Put another way: The realization of these expectations is what sells hotel rooms and dining seats. And that's really what spells success in the hospitality industry; because if you don't fill those rooms and those seats, you are destined for failure.

So what are we talking about in terms of satisfying this wish list of expectations?

First—and I know this is repetitive—one thing we are not talking about is cookie cutter sameness, because change, not sameness, is what the pleasure traveler seeks.

Note of caution, however. Never underestimate the power of the cookie cutter. As rich as the possibilities are for individuality and appropriateness in hotel design, the cookie cutter mold is an ever-present temptation. It's always there, available, quick, cost efficient (in the short haul), ready to stamp out more and more copies of itself. It is often sneaked in under the guise of expediency, among other things. Perhaps one of the most heavily weighted reasons for reliance on cookie cutter hotels has been guest acceptance. Fortunately, this is eroding. Discrimination in matters of taste is an acquired, or developed, attribute. Jet travel, growing affluence, the opening up of heretofore undeveloped areas, renovation of the grand old hotels of Europe and America, and a rapidly expanding inventory of truly fine new hotels worldwide all contribute to the growing pool of pleasure travelers who grow more and more discriminating as they amass travel experiences. Thus, the more success the travel industry enjoys, the more dedicated to excellence it must become—to keep pace with the enlightened, discriminating traveler it is in the process of producing.

If we disdain cookie cutter hotels, we endorse hotels that are an expression of their particular environment and its people, that have a vibrant sense of place, and provide guests a rich array of optional pleasures. These hotels work, in part, because they recognize the name of the game is "pleasure" and they do afford guests the means whereby their individual expectations of pleasure can be realized. And because people are as individual in their preferences as in their personalities, the potential for creating uniquely wonderful—special—places is limitless.

While the ideal site for your special place may be in the Swiss or New Zealand Alps or mountains of Colorado, my fantasies may focus on the shores of Bora Bora or Cannes.

Australian rain forests and desert sands of the American Southwest have strong appeal.

Country lanes and, surely, city streets have allure.

Both the exoticism of Bangkok and the familiarity of American apple pie in Memphis attract, as surely as the warmth of the California or Riviera sunshine, or Scandinavia's bracing winds and weather.

History and culture buffs are drawn, as if by a magnet, to Williamsburg and New Orleans, London and Paris, Rome and Lisbon. . . .

How about castles in Spain? Or—Italy? Surely they too capture the imagination.

Fly to the Pacific for safe viewing of primeval furies of Hawaii's volcanoes; or, to the Atlantic for leisure listening to mellifluous songs and vibrant rhythms of the Caribbean.

Sip a Singapore Sling at fabled Raffles Hotel and talk about the tiger that was killed in the bar and the writers who created legends there.

Small jewel-like resorts—simple to sophisticated, informal and formal, each catering to a single facet of recreation—are cutting a nice niche in the marketplace—for example, the European and African resorts of Serena Hotels.

Leave your *istana* (ancient palaces of Malaysian sultans) inspired quarters in Trengganu to watch the ageless ritual of a giant sea turtle lumbering ashore, laying and burying her eggs and then with silent dignity returning to the deep from whence she came.

Is the picture emerging? Growing in your mind's eye?

You ask, am I talking business or am I caught up in my own dreams and imaginations?

The answer is—both!

The business of pleasure travel is the business of creativity, creating special places in special places—to translate everyone's dreams into reality. Call it the Pleasure Principle, if you like. But never lose sight of this very real fact: In this business, pleasure is paramount. Believe it—there is a correlation between the degree of success we achieve in pleasing people and the color of the bottom line.

To deviate slightly, I would like to encourage you to feel good about all this "leisure." Americans as a group are probably burdened excessively with our Puritan work ethic. Hotel management attracts many Germans, who may have originated the super disciplined approach to work. Unless, of course, it was of Chinese derivation. Whatever the roots of our dedication to work, I think we sometimes need reminding that it's OK—even desirable for good health—for humans to indulge, on a regular basis, in periods of pure pleasure. Recreation, in the sense of recreation.

This business we're engaged in has a very valid raison d'être. It is not simply a modern version of Louis XIV opulence. For all the super rich who can afford to spend their lives doing nothing but trekking from one resort to another, there are thousands of ordinary people who work diligently on a year-round basis, subjected to highly stressed lifestyles. They need and are willing to pay for the rejuvenation that comes from a complete change of pace—pleasure in a special place.

This is our major market segment, our growth potential.

What does it take, in a hotel, to richly reward our travel expectations? What is required to keep it out of the cookie cutter class and assure its role as a destination of distinction?

Keeping in mind that the primary function or service provided is pleasure—although the hotel is eminently practical—attractiveness and the ambiance of the physical structure are vital to its economic success. Every hotel needs thoughtful, imaginative design. Resort hotels, which exist solely for the pleasure of their users, demand it.

But it is not simply a matter of serving up a physically beautiful hotel. We recreational travelers seeking new experiences in exotic places are looking for far more than that. We want to observe and to experience that which makes our destinations different from the places we have left. Universally, we seek that special place in a special place. That is what drives us to other parts of our own countries and to other parts of the world. We seek other cultures, other lifestyles, and the uniqueness of the region we visit.

Toward fulfilling these goals, the hotel design can be a key element. Generally, the first unhurried introduction to a new region is the hotel in which we are to stay. It becomes our temporary home base. The place where we must eat, sleep, exercise, socialize, shop, listen to music, look at art, or simply "hang out" as the younger generation would say. It should be very much a part of our escape objective, not simply where we sleep and change clothes. It is also at our hotel that we may have the closest relationship with natives of the host locale. This offers an opportunity for good social interchange between guest and host. Both benefit. The hotel provides a captive audience eager to learn. However . . .

Considering the salient and comprehensive role of the hotel in the guest's holiday experience, it naturally follows that hotel design should address the matter as creatively and effectively as possible.

There are other reasons for appropriate design. If the hotel design is sensitive to and appreciative of the culture and arts of the host area, this encourages and reinforces pride of heritage in the native resident and tends to make him or her more receptive to nonresidents. Sensitive, responsible design may also make significant contributions to the preservation and/or enhancement of a region's particular heritage. This works to the benefit of everyone.

From the developer's and operator's points of view, design appropriate to the region will quite likely result in cost savings as the facilities will be easier to construct and maintain. The design will often make use of readily available materials and technology appropriate to local construction techniques. Proper design may even eliminate the need for elevators, air conditioning and numerous other high maintenance building elements.

Designing with this kind of approach should lead to a degree of guest satisfaction that results in solid demand, excellent occupancy rates, enviable room charges, and long stays. It should also result in return visits and a generous number of referrals, each looking for a special place of escape.

Successfully meeting these goals is not a project confined to design of buildings. It is, rather, a highly complex matter encompassing the whole project continuum from master planning, design, approvals, and financing right through construction to maintenance, management, and even marketing, and in some cases periodic additions and renovations.

Meeting the challenge requires a lot of understanding—understanding by management of the challenges inherent in creating a design that fits the locality and cultural mores, and understanding by the design team of management's problems in providing services to guests and of maintaining the property in top condition. At times, it is difficult for clients, particularly in developing countries, to understand that locally inspired designs and native materials in new buildings can be as marketable as ancient temples.

Generally speaking, America has only recently begun to understand what Europe has long known—saving old landmarks and/or constructing new buildings near landmarks in such a manner as to respect and complement them is a responsibility. And a privilege.

There are many examples of this enlightened philosophy in Europe, where tourism plants are frequently integral parts of the regional cultural heritage. Ironically, many of the most successful projects are, by their very nature, difficult to find—which may be a good part of the reason for their success. They so blend into their immediate environment that they are hardly distinguishable as part of the tourist industry. Many, in fact, originally were not. Villas and houses, taverns and castles, have been converted to hotels, lodges, resorts. That they are, practically speaking, inseparable from the architecture and tapestry of life in their respective communities is a large part of their grace and appeal.

To summarize this relationship between special places and success in the pleasure travel arena: In the long run, the hotel providing the strongest possible sense of place will become the most desirable. The pleasure traveler seeks novel experiences, not a rerun of "Chicago." If the hotel patronized provides all the amenities required, while reinforcing the sense of being in an exotic location, the satisfaction quotient should be high—and this means the traveler will stay longer, return sooner, and pay more for the travel experience.

One price I paid as a traveler, I hadn't really bargained for; but with the added perspective of time, I can now treasure it as a priceless experience. Imagine a business conference in Japan with twelve stark naked men and one equally naked woman—the secretary—sitting chest deep in a steaming hot-spring bath discussing redesign of the world's largest enclosed communal "jungle bath." Also imagine being the only 6'2" blond-haired, blue-eyed Caucasian in the group. The meeting wears on; an hour later you are still sitting stark naked in that steaming bath trying to sketch design solutions before you and the paper wilts into oblivion. Making the challenge even more interesting—you are surrounded by bathers of both genders. They are curious, and slightly amused, about the way you look. Imagination is probably not vivid enough to match the reality that was.

Now, let's bring theory into focus by looking at specific projects, each with its own unique characteristics, challenges, and requirements. Ideally, there is no typical resort.

Much of what has been presented so far can be pulled together in a single case study of a small resort project that relies much less on fantasy for guest satisfaction, than on its integration with the culture of the beautiful east coast of West Malaysia. Exoticism, romance, seclusion, are key words to describe the resort. It is an unusual one, too, in that facilities are split in two sections five miles apart. They are the hotel and resort facilities at Tanjong Jara Beach and visitor center facilities at Rantau Abang.

Genesis of the design process was preparation of a tourism study in which Wimberly, Allison, Tong and Goo Architects participated. The study concluded that the economic success of a Malaysian visitor development program venture would depend in large on the country's ability to maintain and enhance Malaysia's distinctive character—its historic, cultural, and scenic attractions.

Five years later, the Malaysian Tourism Development Corporation engaged WAT&G to transform the development plan from a dream to reality, to create a hotel which would become the first step towards actualization of the master plan. The architects were charged with site selection as well as design and project development of what would become the first major tourist facility on West Malaysia's picturesque east coast.

One of the principal attractions of the area—giant sea turtles in their migration and egg laying rituals—presented both an opportunity and a responsibility. The architects felt visitors should be acquainted with the turtles' delicate life cycle and also the relationship that exists between Malaysia and the surrounding sea. On recommendation of the architects, the Malaysian government agreed to establish, as part of the overall project, a museum and visitor center near the middle of the hatching grounds, five miles from the hotel site. The two are separate yet complementary parts of an integrated whole.

Throughout concept development and the working out of details there was strong motivation to create a project so appropriate to its total environment that it would not only look and feel right but seem an inevitable outgrowth of the whole.

Before starting with the actual hotel design, extensive research took place. This involved photographs and sketches and the study of whatever documents we could obtain that dealt with the unique cultural aspects of West Malaysia's east coast.

The design team then searched the area for craftsmen whose work could be incorporated into the construction. Trengganu is fortunate in having an abundance of talent capable of doing excellent wood carving, kite making, fine weaving, and mat making plus other crafts suitable for incorporation into design plans.

Ultimately, work of these craftsmen was well utilized and integrated into the construction and interiors of the facilities. As a side effect, this involvement provided a whole new ongoing economic outlet for their production and encouraged further development of traditional crafts.

The final step in our research was into the historic architectural styles of Trengganu. We determined that the unique and handsome, 100-year-old *istanas* (Sultan's palace) were an architectural form that could be adapted for hotel use. Their design and construction was such that natural ventilation could drastically reduce the need for energy-consuming air-conditioning. Using the *istanas* as the architectural theme, we designed a resort master plan facility in the manner of a Malaysian riverside village with an existing stream as a focal point and the hotel placed on a curve of white sand beach at the foot of lush green mountains.

Architecture of the *istana*-like buildings is eminently practical in relationship to local weather conditions, makes use of materials plentiful in the area, and features traditional Malaysian art forms and craftsmanship. A salient feature of the two-story hardwood construction is that buildings are three to five feet above the ground for purposes of security, flood protection, and air circulation. Other ventilating elements are open-sided rooms, lattice soffits, steep pitched roofs with gable grilles, and locally-made bisque roof tiles left exposed "to breathe" on the inside. Buildings are constructed of native hardwood allowed to weather naturally.

Decorative motifs utilize Malaysian arts and crafts including wood carvings, woven mats, baskets, kites, shadow puppets and ceramics that are an integral part of the design and made by local artisans using traditional methods.

Rantau Abang Visitor Centre, with its sea life museum, depicts the strong traditional link between Malaysians and the sea. It serves, further, to protect the giant sea turtle during one step of its migratory life. The site is sandwiched between the coastal road and ocean with the Kabang River lying between the two.

The project consists of a complex of Malaysian-style buildings that include the museum/visitor center, a bazaar featuring Malaysian craftsmen with their wares, a Malaysian cuisine restaurant, a botanical garden featuring Malaysian plants used for food, shelter, and medicinal purposes, and a group of bungalows for overnight guests.

Structures are raised on piers above the river and sand dunes to avoid disruption of the site's natural characteristics. The height also affords a sweeping view of the turtle hatching grounds. Buildings, entirely of native hardwoods from nearby forests, are built in the centuries-old tradition of Malaysian construction by carpenters and craftsmen of the area.

Was the project well-received? Very much so. It has been critically acclaimed internationally; the client is well-pleased, Rantau Abang was awarded an American Institute of Architects Excellence in Design citation, and in 1983 Tanjong Jara/Rantau Abang captured the prestigious Aga Khan Award for Architecture. The jury commended WAT&G for having "the courage to search out and successfully adapt and develop an otherwise rapidly disappearing traditional architecture and craft, to meet the demands of contemporary architecture. The consistency and seriousness with which this approach has been pursued at all levels of design and execution has generated an architecture that is in keeping with traditional values and esthetics,

and of an excellence matching the best surviving traditional examples."

By the way, sometimes the process of learning foreign customs can be embarrassing—if somewhat humorous. A personal example happened while I was designing the project in Malaysia, where it is the usual Muslim custom in an Islamic country to wash your hands prior to partaking of food. At a business meeting, we were all served tea and each received an individual dish of delicacies. Folded neatly at the side of the dish was a thin, damp, chartreuse green sponge. I unfolded it and was diligently wiping my hands when I was shocked to see the Malaysian across from me eating his. A closer look at my ritual hand washing "sponge" revealed that it was, in fact, a coconut filled crepe.

Among WAT&G's work is a group of resort projects in several countries of the South Pacific. These projects have been extremely successful. Each is uniquely different from the others, and without exception—design for these hotels was derived from the culture of the particular host area.

Let's consider a few of them, briefly.

First, the Fijian Hotel, on Yanuca Island. The site plan of this hotel reflects the traditional Fijian village layout, with buildings clustered around a central court. Design and construction of the public rooms drew heavily on the indigenous architectural style of the Fijian *bure* (house), which is characterized by a high, steep roof and projecting ridge pole. Construction throughout was done by local natives using techniques familiar to them. The architectural firm sent a sculptor, Mick Brownlee, to work with natives in reestablishing the all but lost art of Fijian wood carving. As a result, newly trained artisans were employed to carve Fijian-motif artifacts to be used in the public rooms and established a shop on the site to sell their wares to the visitor.

One of WAT&G's most spectacularly romantic and equally as understated projects is the world renowned Hotel Bora Bora in French Polynesia. On a palm-studded promontory facing Bora Bora Lagoon are 65 beach and garden bungalows designed in the manner of the traditional Tahitian *fare* (house). Fifteen over-water luxury bungalows are perched at the reef's edge. Each unit has a view of the azure lagoon and reef, white sand beach, tropical flowers, and distant mountains. The open-air buildings, cooled by prevailing tradewinds, have bamboo walls with screened openings and roofs constructed of *lauhala* thatching. At Hotel Bora Bora, don't expect such intrusions as radios and televisions.

In almost every instance, native solutions to climatic problems—representing centuries of trial and error—are good responses to local conditions. We found this to be particularly true in American Samoa while working on design solutions for the Hotel Pago Pago Intercontinental. The Samoan *fale* (house) effectively solves the problems of building in a hot, humid climate. The traditional thatched roof protects from rain without impeding air movements; the open sides let prevailing winds pass through; palm-leaf "blinds" can be lowered to keep rain out. To base our design on this vernacular architecture and yet speak to modern requirements for comfort and sanitation, we devised a contemporary version of the *fale* combining its form and response to climate with modern materials to obtain a simple and economical structure adaptable to a variety of conditions. Our hotel *fales* were constructed by native workmen using traditional methods. Timbers were hand hewn by adzes, fitted together with wooden pegs and lashed with coconut fiber sennet. The project won a Hawaii Society American Institute of Architecture Design Award.

KEY CONCEPTS

architectural recommendations
creating infrastructure
goals of tourism development
heritage preservation
land use

obstacles to development
official tourism body
planning process
policy formulation

political aspects
preservation and environmentalism
transportation
zoning

INTERNET EXERCISES

Activity 1

Site Name: The Ecotourism Society (TES)

URL: http://www.ecotourism.org/

Background Information: The Ecotourism Society identifies key issues in the field of ecotourism that require international attention each year.

Exercise

1. What criteria does The Ecotourism Society use to determine which issues to address?

Activity 2

Site Name: Alaska Wilderness and Recreation Association

URL: http://www.alaska.net/~awrta/

Background Information: The Alaska Wilderness Recreation and Tourism Association (AWRTA) is a nonprofit trade association that promotes the recognition and protection of Alaska's wilderness.

Exercises

1. What guidelines has AWRTA established for businesses to follow when planning for tourism?

2. What planning issues are currently being addressed by AWARTA?

Activity 3

Site Name: Cyburbia—Internet resources for the built environment

URL: http://www.ap.buffalo.edu/pairc/

Background Information: Cyburbia (formerly called PAIRC—The Planning and Architecture Internet Resource Center) contains a comprehensive directory of Internet resources relevant to planning, architecture, urbanism, and other topics related to the built environment. Cyburbia also contains information regarding architecture- and planning-related mailing lists and Usenet newsgroups, and it hosts interactive message areas.

Exercise

1. Surf this web site and identify current issues facing the tourism industry. How do these issues coincide with those discussed in the textbook?

Questions for Review and Discussion

1. Basically, what is the purpose of planning?
2. Discuss the importance of transportation to tourism development.
3. Discuss the most important factors that would influence the success of a newly built resort.
4. Why is tourism developmental planning so necessary?
5. What are some of the most significant relationships between a large-sized resort development and its nearby community?
6. Referring to the previous question, if the community is a rather small one, should any input be solicited from residents of the community before major remodeling or new construction is undertaken?
7. What goals should guide the land use plan of a small lakeshore village that is popular with summer visitors?
8. Provide some descriptions of the importance of infrastructure to the following: ski resort, summer campground, fishing pier, public marina, shopping center, resort apartment condominium project.
9. From planning to completed project, name the principal individuals and organizations that would be involved.
10. Do you agree with the statement that if a community's government and business leaders are resistant or passive toward tourism, development will lag?
11. Currently, heritage preservation is a popular trend. Is it a desirable one?
12. Would you encourage tourism development if your community and area were already very prosperous ones?
13. Enumerate various kinds of environmental pollution that unwise developments can create.
14. How could greater emphasis be placed on the importance of a development process in which meticulous attention is given to the environment to create a harmonious combination of natural assets and human-made facilities?
15. Architect Gerald Allison states that he would "gladly accept a little sag in the bed for a little lift in the spirit." What does he mean by this? Do you agree? Explain.

Case Problems

1. A real estate developer, aware of a growing demand for a lakeshore resort condominium, planned for 126 apartments plus a 56-slip marina. Upon submission of his plan, the township planning board informed him that only one apartment and one boat slip would be allowed for each 100 feet of lakeshore. Because he did not own that much lakeshore, plans were redrawn to construct the planned development back from the lakeshore. Access to the lake would be provided via a canal, using one of the lakeshore lots—a "keyhole" plan. This proposal was also rejected. The developer then sued the township board to force approval. What should the court or judge decide?

2. You have accepted a United Nations Development Program assignment in tourism to a small Central American country. Your first task is to make financial calculations concerning the economic feasibility for such development. What factors do you consider when beginning this process? Assuming your findings result in a favorable conclusion, what would your next step be?

3. Hotels built in a box-like manner are cheaper to construct and maintain than those with more elaborate designs. Hotel companies normally aim to maximize profits. Thus, should all hotels be built in that manner?

Selected References

Allen, Lawrence R., Harry R. Hafer, Patrick T. Long, and Richard R. Perdue. "Rural Residents' Attitudes Toward Recreation and Tourism Development." *Journal of Travel Research*, Vol. 31, No. 4, pp. 27–33, Spring 1993.

Anderson, Don, and J.R. Brent Ritchie, eds. *Mega*

Events and Tourism Destination Development: The Challenges of International Expositions in the Third Millennium. Calgary: The Canada 2005 Exposition Corporation, 1997.

Ashworth, G., and A. Dietvorst, eds. *Tourism and Spatial Transformation.* Oxon, UK: CAB International, 1995.

Brohman, John. "New Directions in Tourism for Third World Development." *Annals of Tourism Research,* Vol. 23, No. 1, pp. 48–70, 1996.

Buhalis, Dimitrios. "Information Technology as a Strategic Tool for Economic, Social, Cultural and Environmental Benefits Enhancement of Tourism at Destination Regions." *Progress in Hospitality Research,* Vol. 3, pp. 71–93, 1997.

Butler, R. W., and L. A. Waldbrook. "A New Planning Tool: The Tourism Opportunity Spectrum." *Journal of Tourism Studies,* Vol. 2, No. 1, pp. 2–14, May 1991.

Canestrell, Elio, and Paolo Costa. "Tourist Carrying Capacity: A Fuzzy Approach." *Annals of Tourism Research,* Vol. 18, No. 2, pp. 295–311, 1991.

Cater, Erlet A. "Tourism in the Least Developed Countries." *Annals of Tourism Research,* Vol. 14, No. 2, pp. 202–226, 1987.

Conlin Michael V., and Tom Baum, eds. *Island Tourism: Management Principles and Practice.* New York: Wiley, 1995.

Cooper C., and S. Wanhill, eds. *Tourism Development: Environmental and Community Issues.* New York: Wiley, 1997.

Culpan, Refik, "International Tourism Model for Developing Economies." *Annals of Tourism Research,* Vol. 13, No. 4, pp. 541–552, 1986.

Davies, E. T., and D. C. Gilbert. "A Case Study of the Development of Farm Tourism in Wales." *Tourism Management,* Vol. 13, No. 1, pp. 56–63, March 1992.

deKadt, Emanuel. *Tourism: Passport to Development?* Washington, D.C.: Oxford University Press for UNESCO and the International Bank of Reconstruction and Development/The World Bank, 1979.

Dieke, U. C. "Policies for Tourism Development in Kenya." *Annals of Tourism Research,* Vol. 18, No. 2, pp. 269–294, 1991.

Dorwood, Sherry. *Design for Mountain Communities.* New York: Van Nostrand Reinhold, 1991.

Dowling, Ross K. "Tourism Planning: People and the Environment in Western Australia." *Journal of Travel Research,* Vol. 31, No. 4, pp. 52–58, Spring 1993.

Dredge, Dianne, and Stewart Moore. "A Methodology for the Integration of Tourism in Town Planning." *Journal of Tourism Studies,* Vol. 3, No. 1, pp. 8–21, May 1992.

Gartner, William C. *Tourism Development: Principles, Processes and Policies.* New York: Wiley, 1996.

Gee, Chuck Y. *Resort Development and Management.* East Lansing, MI: Educational Institute of the American Hotel and Motel Association, 1988.

Gill, Alison, and Rudi Hartman. *Mountain Resort Development.* Burnaby, British Columbia, Canada: Simon Fraser University, 1992.

Go, Frank M., and Carson L. Jenkins, eds. *Tourism and Economic Development in Asia and Australia.* London: Cassell, 1997.

Gunn, Clare A. *Vacationscape: Designing Tourist Regions.* Bristol, PA: Taylor and Francis, 1997.

Gunn, Clare A. *Tourism Planning.* Bristol, PA: Taylor & Francis, 1994.

Hall, Derek. *Tourism and Economic Development in Eastern Europe and the Soviet Union.* New York: Wiley, 1991.

Harrison, Lynn, and Winston Husbands. *Practicing Responsible Tourism.* New York: Wiley, 1996.

Hjalager, Anne-Metter. "Agricultural Diversification into Tourism: Evidence of a European Community Development Program." *Tourism Management,* Vol. 17, No. 2, pp. 77–86, March 1996.

Inskeep, Edward. *National and Regional Tourism Planning: Methodologies and Case Studies.* London: ITBP, 1994.

Inskeep, Edward. *Tourism Planning: An Integrated and Sustainable Development Approach.* New York: Wiley, 1997.

Lewis, James B. "A Rural Tourism Development Model." *Tourism Analysis,* Vol. 2, No. 2, pp. 91–106, 1998.

Muirhead, Desmond, and Guy L. Rando. *Golf Course Development and Real Estate.* Washington, D.C.: Urban Land Institute, 1994.

Nuckolls, Jonelle, and Patrick Long. *Organizing Resources for Tourism Development in Rural Areas.* Boulder, CO: University of Colorado, 1993.

Okrant, Mark J. *Judson's Island.* Bethlehem, NH: Wayfarer Press, 1995.

Pearce, Douglas. *Tourist Development,* 2nd edition. New York: Wiley, 1989.

Pearce, Douglas G. "Tourism Development in Paris: Public Intervention." *Annals of Tourism Research,* Vol. 25, No. 2, pp. 457–476, 1998.

Phillips, Patrick. *Developing with Recreational Amenities.*

Washington, D.C.: The Union Land Institute, 1986.

Portman, John, and Jonathan Barnett. *The Architect as Developer.* New York: McGraw-Hill, 1976.

Richter, Linda K. *Land Reform and Tourism Development.* Cambridge, Mass.: Schenkman, 1982.

Sandiford, Peter John, and John Ap. "The Role of Ethnographic Techniques in Tourism Planning." *Journal of Travel Research,* Vol. 37, No. 1, pp. 3–11, August 1998.

Smart, J. Eric. *Recreational Development Handbook.* Washington, D.C.: The Urban Land Institute, 1989.

Smith, Valene, and William Eadington. *Tourism Alternatives: Potentials and Problems in the Development of Tourism.* Philadelphia: University of Pennsylvania Press, 1992.

Teare, Richard. *Managing Projects in Hospitality Organizations.* New York: Cassell, 1992.

Tooman, L. Alex. "Tourism and Development." *Journal of Travel Research,* Vol. 35, No. 5, pp. 33–40, Winter 1997.

Tourism U.S.A. *Guidelines for Tourism Development,* Columbia, Mo.: Department of Recreation and Park Administration, University Extension, University of Missouri.

Wahab, Salah E.A. "Tourism Development in Egypt: Competitive Strategies and Implications." *Progress in Tourism and Hospitality Research,* Vol. 2, Nos. 3 and 4, pp. 351–364, September/December 1996.

Wanhill, Stephen R. C. "Evaluating the Worth of Investment Incentives for Tourism Development." *Journal of Travel Research,* Vol. 33, No. 2, pp. 33–39, Fall 1994.

Williams, Alan M., and Gareth Shaw. *Tourism and Economic Development: Western European Experiences.* London: Belhaven Press, 1988.

World Tourism Organization. *Presentation and Financing of Tourist Development Projects.* Madrid: WTO.

Yu, Lawrence. "Hotel Development and Structures in China." *International Journal of Hospitality Management,* Vol. 11, No. 2, pp. 99–110, May 1992.

TOURISM AND THE ENVIRONMENT

- Recognize the worldwide importance of natural resource conservation and sustainable tourism development.

- Learn how ecotourism can benefit local people.

- Understand the dangers and limitations of ecotourism.

- Understand tourist codes of ethics and guidelines.

- Learn current environmental practices of tourism organizations and suppliers.

- Learn how to maintain natural destinations.

◀ **LEARNING OBJECTIVES**

◀ *The cliffs that make up the Dorsey Heritage Coast are a popular natural attraction in England. (Photo courtesy of the British Tourist Authority.)*

543

INTRODUCTION

As tourism moves into the twenty-first century, the enterprise will have to make the environment a priority. Because tourism is now the world's largest industry, the environment is taking center stage in tourism development. Tourism is not only a powerful economic force but a factor in the physical environment as well. Because more attention will be paid to the environment in the future, projects that are economically feasible but not environmentally desirable will remain unbuilt. The environment is the core of the tourism product. Profitability in tourism depends on maintaining the attractiveness of the destination people want to see and experience.

Tourism has the power to enhance the environment, to provide funds for conservation, to preserve culture and history, to set sustainable use limits, and to protect natural attractions. It also has the power to destroy. If tourism is not properly planned and implemented, it can destroy vegetation, create overcrowding, litter trekking areas, pollute beaches, result in overbuilding, eliminate open space, create sewage problems, cause housing problems, and ignore the needs and structure of the host community.

It is being recognized that tourism must preserve and protect the environment and natural attractions so that people will continue to travel and to set use limits so that sites will be truly sustainable. The problem is how to do this. Concepts such as ecotourism, nature tourism, sustainable development, carrying capacity, and alternative tourism have been proposed and are examined in this chapter. Also, we look at the industry's efforts to be environmentally responsible.

DOES TOURISM THREATEN THE ENVIRONMENT?— THE WTTC POSITION

Before addressing how tourism can best respond to the negative impacts on the environment, it is useful to explore the extent to which these impacts are significant. The World Travel and Tourism Council has issued a position statement[1] in which it examines these issues and presents its case in support of tourism.

In presenting its case, the WTTC first reviews what it considers to be its certain myths and misconceptions regarding tourism. The box on the next page describes four "myths" and the WTTC views concerning them.

The very preparation of their position paper indicates the seriousness that the WTTC accords to the environmental issue. In their report, the WTTC argues that:

> The causes of environmental problems are much debated; their effects cannot yet be predicted with any certainty. There are those who doubt even the existence of some problems. Nonetheless, it is clear that the world's environment is being altered by human activity, and that, without remedial action, the results may be catastrophic.

---

[1] WTO, *Round Table on Planning for Sustainable Tourism Development*, 10th General Assembly (Bali, Indonesia: World Tourism Organization, 1993).

Myth #1: Travel & Tourism is a nonessential, "mass" activity of affluent people in developed countries.

In fact, tourism, as defined by the WTO in 1992, is an integral part of the lives of many populations, for business, social, cultural, religious, and recreational reasons as well as holidays. In some countries and many regions it is an essential economic activity; it may be the largest earner of foreign currency, providing the essential economic underpinning of the local population's employment and welfare services.

Myth #2: Tourism's major environmental impact is damage to developing countries.

In fact, over 80 percent of the world's international tourism occurs between developed countries, which also generate the bulk of domestic tourism. Package tourism to developing countries is probably under 5 percent of the world Travel & Tourism as defined by the WTO in 1992 and as measured by WTTC in the same year.

Myth #3: Ecotourism is the only logical, sustainable response to the environmental impacts of Travel & Tourism.

In fact, ecotourism—that is, tourism with the specific motive of enjoying wildlife or undeveloped natural areas—can only make a marginal, though important, contribution because of the limited nature of its market. Without careful management, it is no more sustainable than other forms of tourism development, and it may cause more problems than it solves. The true target for better performance and a globally relevant contribution must be the core 95 percent of the world's Travel & Tourism.

Myth #4: Comprehensive planning regulations and control are the only way to curb the environmental exploitation of Travel & Tourism.

In fact, there is no evidence that politicians, lawyers, sociologists, and enforcement agencies have the necessary knowledge of the complexities of the modern international business of Travel & Tourism. They are in no position to use "control and command" techniques to secure sustainable tourism development. At best, they can control supply by establishing barriers, but they cannot positively influence the future of international demand. In their position paper the WTTC attempted to show the realities of the Travel & Tourism response to environmental issues. They agree that evidence obtained from WTTERC's databases indicated that transnational companies are increasingly moving toward addressing their environmental impacts and developing programs to improve their environment performance. The report analyzes the progress made by leading companies and shows what has been achieved by a range of Travel & Tourism companies in response to the major environmental issues.

They subsequently proceed to examine the key environmental issues under five headings:

- Global warming
- Depletion of the ozone layer
- Acid rain
- Depletion and pollution of water resources
- Depletion and pollution of land resources

In examining the possible implications for tourism, the WTTC expressed particular concern with respect to the depletion and pollution of land resources. They state that:

> The long-term implications of resource depletion are obviously extremely serious. Even over the next few decades the Travel & Tourism industry could find that:
> - Political instability or increased competition for land could lead to loss of potential new tourism destinations and degradation of existing destinations.
> - Loss of landscape and wildlife could cause a decrease in customer satisfaction with tourism products and hence lower propensity to travel to some destinations.
> - Higher fuel prices could lead to operational price increases and corresponding decreases in the number of travelers in this price-sensitive market.

They further note that:

> Ultimately whole segments of tourism are threatened by the disappearance of habitats and species. The World Wide Fund for Nature estimates that of the $55 bn earned by Travel & Tourism in developing countries in 1988, some $12 bn was due to ecotourism (EIU 1992). Ecotourism—that is, tourism with the specific intention of enjoying wildlife or undeveloped natural landscapes—is a rapidly growing sector. In some destinations, such as the Galapagos Islands, the wildlife of the area is the major attraction. However, even where the tourist's primary aim is not to see wildlife, the opportunity to do so once or twice during the trip may influence the choice of destination. The ecotourism market cannot be sustained without quality environments. The industry itself can implement careful management of existing destinations, but new destinations may be destroyed by other less sustainable forms of activity, such as commercial logging, preventing this market from reaching its full capacity.

As one might realistically anticipate, the WTTC response to the question "Does the world's largest industry have the world's largest impact on the environment?" is as follows:

> The simple answer is no. However, as environmental concern becomes more and more widespread, Travel & Tourism must expect to be increasingly questioned about how it will meets its environmental obligations. Existing patterns of economic activity, and the global consumption and pollution of natural resources, are not sustainable at current rates. Travel & Tourism, at 6 percent of

GDP, is a vital component of economic activity, and must play its part in tackling environmental issues.

The effects of environmental damage will not be distributed according to any sense of justice. All regions and industries will be affected by emerging environmental problems. In addition to being the world's largest industry, Travel & Tourism has perhaps the most powerful incentive to secure a clean and healthy environment. For leisure travel, at least, visits are made by choice. There is declining consumer desire to visit polluted environments now and such preferences are predicted to be more significant over the next decade.

All industries, from agriculture and automotive to manufacturers of washing machines and refrigeration equipment, are having to respond to exactly the same environmental pressures as Travel & Tourism. Many are further along the road to improved practice. But, as the examples of good practice in the following sections illustrate, Travel & Tourism companies are increasingly developing systems and programmes to manage their environmental impact.

In addition to presenting its defense of tourism's case, the WTTC also presents a positive vision of Travel & Tourism and the environment. Their vision comprises the following elements:

- Travel & Tourism is an integral aspect of modern societies.
- Global awareness of environmental damage is developing rapidly.
- The resources of the world's largest industry can and must be harnessed to achieve environmental goals.

As travel and tourism increases, environmental concern becomes more widespread. Government agencies, international organizations, and private operators are working together to develop environmentally responsible practices. (*Photo courtesy of the Boeing Company.*)

- The industry has the potential to influence billions of customers per year and to use its leverage to achieve beneficial environmental effects.

- The customer challenge will exert a growing pressure to achieve environmental improvements.

- Environmental lobbies will add pressure to develop good environmental practice.

- Self-regulation must be developed rapidly and effectively and used to influence the development of appropriate and workable regulations.

- Corporate environmental mission statements are a vital first step toward self-regulation.

- Environmental leadership must come from the major international companies.

SUSTAINABLE DEVELOPMENT

The concept of **sustainable development** has achieved prominence and acceptance in recent years; hopefully, it will permeate all levels of economic development and tourism development, from local to global, in the future. It has become popular because it is an approach that holds out the promise of maintaining a standard of living somewhat similar to that which we possess today while recognizing that we cannot continue to exploit the global environment as we have in the past. While other sectors of the economy are undoubtedly the greatest focus of concern, tourism is increasingly being brought under the microscope regarding its role in contributing to the long-term well-being of the planet. So far, tourism has not attracted the cries of alarm that have accompanied major oil spills, the depletion of nonrenewable resources, or the destruction of the ozone layer. To date, the criticisms directed at tourism from an impact of development standpoint have tended to focus on the deterioration of natural and cultural environments that tourism can cause. Clearly, the foregoing is a much too simplistic assessment of tourism and its impacts (both positive and negative) on our total environment. Because of its pervasive and diverse nature, tourism affects, and is affected by, many factors relating to our social and economic well-being. The use of nonrenewable petroleum is perhaps the best single example; tourism depends heavily on the fuel that is burned to transport travelers both around the block and around the world. As such, any policies that affect the use of petroleum-based fuels will affect the tourism sector.

This point, the interdependency of tourism with other sectors, is being emphasized because any effort to deal with the topic in isolation would be naive and futile. Once this is recognized, however, it is also true that tourism does have major responsibility to contribute to the debate (and the subsequent action) concerning sustainable development.

We Are All Responsible

If it is to work, sustainable development must become a normal way of thinking and acting by a majority of the global community. It cannot be the exclusive purview of the enlightened segments of a society or of an industry. It cannot be something we practice on Sunday. It cannot be only the burden of the less privileged members of the local or the world community. And it cannot be only the concern of those nations and regions whose population growth is under control. In brief, if sustainable development is to be an effective model for the future, it must be a workable approach to ensuring that we can replace what we consume and that in the process of consumption we do not create by-products that pollute or destroy the ecosystem on which future generations depend.

In discussing the responsibility for sustainable development in the field of tourism, four main areas need to be addressed:

1. The premises on which sustainable development policy in tourism should be based
2. The most critical areas of sustainable development as applied to tourism
3. How responsibility for sustainable development in tourism should be allocated
4. An agenda of suggested sustainable development actions for the tourism sector

Some Premises of Sustainable Development in Tourism

The concept of sustainable development is not new. Although the words are more modern and more widely accepted, there have always been similar causes. The concepts of conservation, preservation, and environmental protection have always had as their goal the desire to prevent the destruction of desirable natural conditions and species. What is perhaps new is the insertion into the equation a recognition that the human race seeks economic, social, and cultural development—and that any attempt to prevent such development on a strictly ideological basis is unlikely to gain widespread acceptance. In parallel, there is also the recognition that demographic, economic, social, and cultural growth that is consumptive and/or destructive cannot continue unabated without serious impacts on the natural environment on which we depend for life itself.

This said, we need to enunciate several key premises on which sustainable development policy, as it applies to tourism, should be based. These premises are simply statements that need to be kept clearly in mind as we in the tourism industry attempt to wrestle with the concept of sustainable development and how it can best be applied to tourism.

The Premise of Interdependency

As implied above, tourism as a sector affects, and is affected by, a whole range of social and economic activities. We first need to identify the most important of these interdependencies. We then need to work with those individuals/groups/organizations that have responsibility for and a commitment to sustainable development in the sectors affected by these interdependencies.

The Premise of Multidisciplinarity

In seeking to implement initiatives to support sustainable development, it will be essential to draw on the ideas and experience of a broad range of disciplines. Indeed, as we have realized for some time now, a true understanding of the phenomenon of tourism is not possible using the thinking and the tools of a single discipline. Similarly, an understanding and implementation of actions to realize sustainable development in tourism will, by necessity, involve the seeking and acceptance of concepts, methodologies, and approaches of individuals from many fields.

For example, natural resource managers have developed carrying-capacity limits so that natural attractions will not be overwhelmed by visitors. Carrying capacity is defined as the maximum amount of development, use, growth, or change that a site can endure without an unacceptable alteration in the physical environment, the community's social fabric, and the local economy and without an unacceptable decline in the quality of experience by the visitor. Thus, for sustainable development, one needs to call on experts in many fields: botanists, ornithologists, zoologists, and foresters, to name a few.

The Premise of Previous Experience

It is always difficult to accept that there is nothing new under the sun, or at least not much. When it comes to sustainable development, we certainly do not know everything, but we do know a lot as to what may work and what may not work. For example, there is much useful research knowledge gained from the energy crisis of the 1970s concerning how various segments of the population reacted to a range of alternative approaches to reduce consumer energy use. Undoubtedly, there are many findings from other fields that would also be helpful. While they, of course, need to be screened and assessed for their continued relevance and significance, they should not be ignored.

The Premise That Nature Is Better

Perhaps one of the most important premises of the sustainable development movement is that the natural state is generally preferred to the developed state. This is, of course, one of the areas that provides the greatest room for both apparent agreement and mutual deception on the part of individuals and groups that have substantially different views. This important problem aside, it would seem that adherents to the sustainable development lifestyle generally believe that the natural ecosystem is preferable to artificially built environments or settlements. The compelling argument—that the balance of nature is sounder than the imbalance of civilization—has considerable merit. At the same time, the educated world is only too well aware of certain of the excesses and cruelties of nature, as well as the continuous changes that occur in nature over long periods of time. As a result, there is still room for a legitimate questioning of this premise and its universality.

The Premise of Politics and Power

This premise has been left until the last because it is both the easiest and the most difficult to deal with. As the world has evolved over the past several centuries, we have seen the growing disparity that has developed between the have and have-not nations. Today, we find ourselves in a situation where a relatively few advanced nations having small populations possess most of the world's wealth and consume most of its resources. At the other end of the spectrum, we find the poorer countries with rapidly growing populations. By any logic, a long-term projection of this situation and associ-

An Arctic fox. The world's cold regions are rich in wildlife, inducing ecotours to Alaska, northern Canada, and even regions of Antarctica. *(Photo by William Boehm; courtesy of International Expeditions, Inc.)*

ated trends would lead to the conclusion that the present equilibrium is far from being sustainable. Thus, in our discussions of sustainable development for tourism, we need to keep in mind constantly the question, Sustainable for whom?

Sustainable Development and Tourism: The Critical Areas

Now that at least some of the critical premises underlying sustainable development have been identified explicitly, it may be useful to define those areas in tourism that merit our consideration. Four such areas are presented for discussion.

Defining the Relevant Population/Community

This issue takes off directly from the last premise discussed above and focuses on the question of sustainable development for whom? As professionals in the field, we need to know if we are to take a global, macro perspective in our discussions of tourism and sustainable development or whether we should restrict our thinking to a more local focus. While recognizing that there is a need for global thinking, we also need to recognize that we may need to restrict the allocation of our energies to those jurisdictions where we have the power to act and to make a difference.

In any event, the principle being enunciated here is that, as professionals, we need to define our sphere of interest and action. If we are acting as part of the World Tourism Organization, we will have a very global sphere of concern. If we are respon-

552 Chapter 17 • Tourism and the Environment

sible for tourism in Prince Edward Island, we will have a different sphere of responsibility. In each of these cases, the impacts and populations of relevance may be quite different, and, consequently, so may our likely actions.

Defining the Time Horizon

While sustainable developments as a concept implies forever, this may be impractical to deal with and can even lead to a feeling of helplessness. There is some merit in seeking to develop programs that are sustainable in perpetuity, but such programs may require huge amounts of resources and considerable time for their implementation. It may be wiser and more effective to undertake a less demanding series of phased programs that initiate movement in desired directions rather than delaying action until longer-term programs can be put in place.

Defining the Dimensions of Sustainability

The concept of sustainability is relevant in practical terms only when we define what is to be sustained. From a tourism perspective, discussions on sustainability may pertain to the environment, cultural identity, economic well-being, or social stability. Individuals responsible for, or interested in, each of these areas taken separately may very legitimately focus on their area of concern and attempt to achieve sustainability in relation to some acceptable ongoing carrying capacity of the destination.

However, from an overall destination management perspective, the task becomes much more complex. Here the challenge becomes one of attempting to balance the sustainability of economic, cultural, social, and environmental systems. While one hopes for compatibility in the pursuit of sustainability within and across these systems, such is not always possible. Often, the reason for such incompatibility is a divergence of the values from which the goal of sustainability is being pursued.

Defining the Values That Underlie Sustainable Development

In any democratic society, at any given point in time, there is bound to be a range of values as to what is really important in life. Through time, these values become reflected in the political process and the decisions that flow from elected leaders. Unfortunately, this is a somewhat traditional view of the political process and one that is being called into question by today's movements for direct involvement of the people with regard to decisions that affect their lives. Tourism will not, and indeed should not, escape this emerging but powerful trend.

Regardless of the way in which the values of a society are determined, they will ultimately determine the policies that emerge with regard to sustainable development. Whether these policies are the result of compromise or consensus is the concern of the political entity involved. In the end, however, the political process and the power of different political units will determine the level and form that sustainability will take. Those of us in the tourism sector have traditionally ignored this reality, and we are weaker for it.

Allocating Responsibility

It should be apparent from the nature of the foregoing discussion that the allocation of responsibility for tourism-related sustainability issues and decisions will not be a

Unspoiled tropical rainforests, such as this one in southeast Asia, are of great interest to ecotourists. *(Photo by William Boehm; courtesy of International Expeditions, Inc.)*

neat and tidy exercise. The highly interdependent, multidisciplinary, multisector, and political nature of the decisions does not allow for simplistic answers. However, as long as this caveat is taken seriously, it may be possible to provide some guidelines as to how the process might be conducted and how the prime agents might be assigned to different areas of responsibility.

The Concept of Shared Responsibility

Society is no longer (if it ever was) contained in neat boxes. Rather, at best, it may be viewed as consisting of very ill-defined clusters that change shape constantly as they interface with one another. To complicate matters, a particular citizen may belong to more than one cluster (and indeed probably does) and may change his or her perspective as he or she assumes different roles in society. For example, as a wage earner we may have one perspective, as a parent another, and as a member of a particular religious group, yet another. In the end, however, each person must reach a weighted position with respect to any given issue.

From the standpoint of the tourism sector, the reality is that all questions related to the nature and extent of tourism development must be supported by the community at large. This means that whatever direction tourism development takes in a community, region, or country, it must have the support of the majority of citizens who are affected by it. This means very simply that the perceived benefits from tourism must be seen to outweigh the total costs (economic, environmental, cultural, social) associated with it.

All this said, it then becomes necessary to propose an operational allocation of re-

TABLE 17.1
Sustainable Development (SD) in Tourism: A Possible Allocation of Responsibility

Level/Organization	Responsibilities
Host community/region	Defining the tourism philosophy and vision for the community/region
	Establishing social, physical, and cultural carrying capacity for the host community/region
Destination management/ community organization	Coordination of implementation of community SD plan for tourism
	Monitoring of levels and impact of tourism in the community/region
Individual tourism firms and operators	Fair contribution to implementation of SD plan for tourism
	Observance of regulations, guidelines, and practices for SD
Host community/region	Encouragement/acceptance of tourism within parameters of SD plan
Visitors/tourists	Acceptance of responsibility for minimal self-education with respect to values of host region
	Acceptance and observance of terms and conditions of host community SD plan for tourism

sponsibility that remains true to the democratic model and the concept of resident-responsive tourism. See Table 17.1 for a proposed allocation of responsibilities.

An Agenda for Action

Once a framework for the allocation of responsibility has been agreed upon, it becomes imperative to establish an agenda and a process for implementation. While the total community bears the ultimate responsibility for this agenda, it is suggested that in practice the destination management organization should assume a leadership role in developing the action agenda and should serve as a catalyst for generating the process that brings about its implementation. Examples of the kind of activities involved in this process include:

- Coordinating the development of a tourism philosophy and vision for the community/region
- Specifying the major goals of the community/region with respect to tourism
- Obtaining consensus concerning the social, physical, and cultural carrying capacity of the community/region in question
- Identifying the specific action initiatives necessary to meet the tourism development objectives while respecting the destination's carrying capacities
- Gaining agreement on the measures to be used in monitoring the impacts of tourism in the community/region
- Gathering and disseminating information concerning the impacts of tourism on the community/region

Based on these findings, it is suggested that an action agenda to support a sustainable development program for tourism might include the following elements:

- Maximum total visitation levels to a community/region
- An obligatory tax to support tourism infrastructure planning, development, and maintenance
- Community-supported legislation to protect and preserve unique resources and heritage sites
- Community and industry consensus concerning architectural and signage standards
- Support for standards and certification programs that encourage staff development and the delivery of high-quality service

Tourism has long been touted as a "renewable industry" that is to be greatly preferred over the traditional "smokestack industries" of the manufacturing age. However, we have learned that tourism can engender its own forms of degradation to the environment and to a society unless it is carefully planned and managed.

The concept of sustainable development is an approach by which efforts are made to balance the benefits or outputs of an industry with the investments and restrictions required to ensure that the industry can continue to exist without depleting or destroying the resource base on which it depends. In the tourism sector, this implies caring for the natural and built environments in a way that will ensure their continuing viability and well-being. Although we in the tourism sector are starting to understand what this implies, there is much that remains to be learned. The industry needs to identify an action agenda and allocate responsibility for its implementation so that we can move toward the goal of a truly sustainable tourism system.

Acknowledgment and acceptance of the importance of achieving sustainable tourism has given rise to the concept of "Ecotourism." Indeed, in the tourism world the two terms tend to be used interchangeably. While they certainly are strongly related, each contains a particular nuance that many regard as significant. In our view, the concept of "ecotourism" conveys a greater concern for the fundamental obligation of all travelers to avoid harming, and indeed to protect, all sites that they visit. As such, ecotourism is highly value-laden in an intrinsic sense; that is, individual travelers must accept responsibility for their behavior and its impact. In contrast, the term "sustainable tourism" conveys a more functional societal obligation to ensure the conditions necessary to maintain the physical environment in a "preserved state" for future generations. These conditions are not simply economic and political dimensions—a recognition that desirable values and good intentions must be supported by hard cash and tough decisions.

Ecotourism: Common Terms Used

Ecotourism, nature tourism, green tourism, low-impact tourism, adventure travel, alternative tourism, environmental preservation, symbiotic development, responsible tourism, soft tourism, appropriate tourism, quality tourism, new tourism, sustainable development, and *sustainable tourism* all are monikers for similar types of tourist activities and developments. Of all the terms, **ecotourism** and **sustainability** are most frequently used. The principle of both is to sustain or even enhance the quality and attractiveness of the natural environment.

Definitions of ecotourism abound. A workable one is simply "responsible travel to natural areas that conserves the environment and sustains the well-being of local people." A more expansive definition given by International Expeditions is as follows:

> purposeful travel to natural habitats to create an understanding of the cultural and natural history pertaining to that environment, emphasizing care not to alter the integrity of the ecosystem, while producing economic benefits to local people and governments that encourage the preservation of the inherent resources of the environments there and elsewhere.

Dianne Brouse[2] defines ecotourism as responsible travel in which the visitor is aware of and takes into account the effects of his or her actions on both the host culture and the environment.

Other definitions reported in the Travel Industry Association of America's study, *Tourism and the Environment,* are as follows:

- Ecotourism is environmentally friendly travel that emphasizes seeing and saving natural habitats and archeological treasures.
- Ecotourism is a tool for conservation.
- Ecotourism is ecologically responsible tourism.
- The World Wildlife Fund, which issued a study on ecotourism in 1990, defines it in general terms: "tourism to protect natural areas, as a means of economic gain through natural resource preservation . . . any kind of tourism that involves nature . . ."
- The Ecotourism Society defines ecotourism as "purposeful travel to natural areas to understand the culture and natural history of the environment, taking care not to alter the integrity of the ecosystem, while producing economic opportunities that make the conservation of natural resources beneficial to local people."
- The Pacific Asia Travel Association (PATA) defines ecotourism as follows:

A form of tourism inspired primarily by the natural history of an area, including its indigenous cultures. The ecotourist visits relatively undeveloped areas in the spirit of appreciation, participation and sensitivity. The ecotourist practices a non-consumptive use of wildlife and natural resources and contributes to the visited area through labour or financial means aimed at directly benefiting the conservation issues in general, and to the specific needs of the locals. Ecotourism also implies a managed approach by the host country or region which commits itself to establishing and maintaining the site with the participation of local residents, marketing them appropriately, enforcing regulations, and using the proceeds of the enterprise to fund the area's land management as well as community development.

---

[2] Dianne Brouse, "Socially Responsible Travel." *Transitions Abroad* (January/February 1992), p. 23.

Adventure travel, one type of ecotourism, is a rapidly growing market. A popular adventure travel experience is white-water rafting. These rafters are on the Stanislaus River in California. *(Photo by Robert Holmes; courtesy of the California Division of Tourism.)*

In short, Travel with particular attention to Nature's wonders and leave them as you found them.

- Broadly defined, ecotourism involves more than conservation. It is a form of travel that responds to a region's ecological, social, and economic needs. It also provides an alternative to mass tourism. It encompasses all aspects of travel—from airlines to hotels to ground transportation to tour operators. That is, each component of the ecotourism product is environmentally sensitive.

- As a form of travel, ecotourism nurtures understanding of the environment's culture and natural history, fosters the ecosystem's integrity, and produces economic opportunities and conservation gains.

If the definitions above sound like a case of the best of all possible worlds for the traveler, the destination, and the locals, to a degree it is. The problem is living up to the promises of the definitions and making ecotourism a reality. Otherwise, ecotourism becomes an oxymoron bringing visitors to fragile environments and ruining them rather than preserving them. In fact, many people quarrel with the word "ecotourism." If you consider the two parts of the word *ecotourism*—"ecology" and "tourism"—the inconsistencies are apparent. *Ecology* is defined as the science of the relationships between organisms and environment. When *tourism* is connected to it, a foreign entity is introduced and nature's relationships are changed. Thus the term *ecotourism* is really an oxymoron (an epigrammatic combination of contradictory or incongruous terms). This is especially true when a magazine such as *Popular Mechanics* refers to ecotourism using high-clearance four-wheel-drive vehicles in the back country to view wildlife. Ecotourism does not work when ecotours are so popular that they destroy the very environment they seek to protect.

A number of these organizations participate in **debt for nature swaps,** which are a rather unique method of financing new or enlarging existing natural areas. The World Wildlife Fund and Conservation International arrange to pay off a country's debt, in part, and at a discount, in exchange for protecting certain areas. These areas are usually new national parks possessing superb scenic and natural history resources, or the country involved promises to enlarge existing parks, wildlife refuges, or forests. Such plans have already succeeded in Latin American and Asia. An example is an agreement between Bolivia and Conservation International. This pact provides that in return for $650,000 of Bolivia's outstanding debt purchased by Conservation International, Bolivia will provide a 3.7-million-acre expansion of the Beni Biosphere Reserve in the heart of the Amazon rainforest wilderness. Over a decade or so, the cumulative effect of this kind of imaginative program in countries rich in natural resources for ecotourism will be to possess very attractive destinations for the ecotourist. Similar programs in other parts of the world are also taking place.

Benefits and Importance of Ecotourism

1. Provides jobs and income for **local** people
2. Makes possible funds for purchasing and improving protected or natural areas to attract more ecotourists in the future
3. Provides environmental education for visitors
4. Encourages heritage and **environmental preservation** and enhancement (the creation of new or enlarged national and state parks, forest preserves, biosphere reserves, recreation areas, beaches, marine and underwater trails, and attractions.)

Third World countries host many ecotourists. The total for all types of tourism to Latin America, Africa, and Indonesia has been estimated at about $55 billion.[3] In Brazil, nature travel has become the country's largest new source of revenue. In south central Africa, Rwanda's ecotourism is the third largest source of foreign exchange earnings. Much of this is generated by visitors to the Mountain Gorilla Project begun in the 1970s. The success of this project has convinced the national government to preserve and protect the critical habitat of the gorilla. It has also brought about support for other parks and reserves in that country.

In Costa Rica, 60 percent of visitors are interested in seeing the national park system, which comprises 11 percent of the country's land area. If biological and private reserves are added, the protected areas total 23 percent of the nation.

Ecuador's Galápagos Islands in the eastern Pacific had about 50,000 ecotourists in 1990, about twice the number that the government deemed optimal.[4] Strict rules of

---

[3] Ruth Norris, "Can Ecotourism Save Natural Areas?" *National Parks* (Jan/Feb 1992), pp. 30–34.

[4] J. Molner, "Ecotourism—with Conscience as Our Guide." *The Seattle Times* (March 24, 1992), Sunday, Final Edition.

Paos Volcano National Park in Costa Rica is a popular natural attraction. In addition to the giant volcano crater, the park also possesses abundant wildlife and unusual vegetation. *(Photo by Richard Mills; courtesy of International Expeditions, Inc.)*

conduct enforced by national park trained and educated tour guides have essentially maintained the quality of the visitor experience.

Translating Idealism into Sustainable Ecotourism

The idealism of ecotourism must be translated into reality. To do so, experts in the field and practicing managers have identified a number of "indicators." These indicators focus on what managers need to know most to reduce their risk of inadvertently making decisions that may damage the natural and cultural environments on which the tourism industry depends. These include measures of:

- The general relationship between tourism and the environment
- The effects of environmental factors on tourism
- The impacts of the tourism industry on the environment

In effect, indicators seek to identify specific cause–effect relationships between tourism and the environment. Through their measurement and use, managers can more effectively do the following:

- Identify emerging issues, allowing prevention or mitigation
- Identify impacts, allowing action before they cause problems
- Support sustainable tourism development, identifying limits and opportunities

- Promote management accountability, developing responsible decisionmaking built on knowledge

There are two types of indicators that are of value to tourism managers:

- *Core indicators of sustainable tourism* which have been developed for general application to all destinations.
- *Destination-specific indicators* applicable to particular ecosystems or types of tourism. These indicators fall into two categories:
  - *Supplementary ecosystem-specific indicators* for application to particular ecosystems (e.g., coastal areas, parks and protected areas, or mountainous regions).
  - *Site-specific indicators* that are developed uniquely for the particular site. These indicators reflect important factors of the site, which may not be adequately covered by the core and supplementary ecosystem-specific indicator sets, but are nonetheless needed for management of the particular site.

Examples of indices developed by an expert task force for the World Tourism Organization are given in Table 17.2. By identifying "desirable" levels of each indicator for a particular destination or site and then working toward meeting these ideals, managers can put in place a process that will ensure sustainability to the greatest extent possible.

It should be noted in reviewing these sets of indicators that they do not address environments or ecological goals alone. There are also indicators that seek to ensure desirable levels of visitor satisfaction and local resident satisfaction as well as satisfactory levels of contributions to the local economy. The use of the indicators helps ensure the economic means to support sustainable ecotourism as well as public (and thus political) support for tourism with a destination.

A Major Commitment to Sustainable Tourism—Banff National Park

One of the most significant commitments to **sustainable tourism** is that by the Canadian Government in its efforts to protect and enhance its premiere national park as well as one of Canada's national tourism treasures.

The town of Banff, located within Banff National Park (Alberta, Canada), has long been one of Canada's (and indeed the world's) major tourism destinations. As the crown jewel in Canada's national park system, Banff also must reflect all the values of a national park; values that related to concern for both the ecological and commemorative integrity of the entire Banff–Bow Valley region in which the park is located.

Because of its growing national and international appeal, by the early 1990s, visitation levels have reached a point where many expressed concern for the ecological integrity of the park.

To respond to this concern, the Minister, commissioned a major (two-year $2.5 million CDN) study. The study's terms of reference described its purpose:

The Banff–Bow Valley Study will be a comprehensive analysis of the state of the Bow Valley watershed in Banff National Park. The study will provide a baseline for understanding the implications of existing and future develop-

TABLE 17.2
Core Indicators of Sustainable Tourism

Indicator	Specific Measures
Site protection	Category of site protection according to IUCN[a] index
Stress	Tourist numbers visiting site (per annum/peak month)
Use intensity	Intensity of use in peak period (persons/hectare)
Social impact	Ratio of tourists to locals (peak period and over time)
Development control	Existence of environmental review procedure or formal controls over development of site and use densities
Waste management	Percentage of sewage from site receiving treatment (additional indicators may include structural limits of other infrastructural capacity on site, such as water supply)
Planning process	Existence of organized regional plan for tourist destination region (including tourism component)
Critical ecosystems	Number of rare/endangered species
Consumer satisfaction	Level of satisfaction by visitors (questionnaire-based)
Local satisfaction	Level of satisfaction by locals (questionnaire-based)
Tourism contribution to local economy	Proportion of total economic activity generated by tourism only

Composite Indices[b]	Specific Measures
Carrying capacity	Composite early warning measure of key factors affecting the ability of the site to support different levels of tourism
Site stress	Composite measure of levels of impact on the site (its natural and cultural attributes due to tourism and other sector cumulative stresses)
Attractivity	Qualitative measure of those site attributes that make it attractive to tourism and can change over time

[a] IUCN, International Union for the Conservation of Nature and Natural Resources.

[b] The composite indices are largely composed of site-specific variables. Consequently, the identification and evaluation of the indicators composing these indices require on-site direction from an appropriately trained and experienced observer. In the future, based on the experiences in designing composite indicators for specific sites, it may be possible to derive these indices in a more systematic fashion. See the case studies for Villa Gesell and Peninsula Valdes for application of these indices.

Source: World Tourism Organization.

ment and human use, and the impact of such on the heritage resources. The study will integrate environmental, social and economic considerations in order to develop management and land use strategies that are sustainable and meet the objectives of the National Parks Act.

Objectives

The **Banff–Bow Valley Study** had three major objectives:

- To develop a vision and goals for the Banff–Bow Valley that will integrate ecological, social and economic values
- To complete a comprehensive analysis of existing information and to provide direction for future collection and analysis of data to achieve ongoing goals

- To provide direction on the management of human use and development in a manner that will maintain ecological values and provide sustainable tourism

The study was led by a five-person expert Task Force and involved an extensive process of public participation.[5] The Task Force's final report made a total of over 500 recommendations designed to maintain and enhance the region's ecological integrity and to consolidate and strengthen Banff's international stature as a world class tourism destination.

The great majority of the Report's recommendations dealt with the many environmental issues facing the region. At the same time, it also strongly confirmed Banff's long-term role as a premiere national and international tourism destination. This confirmation, supported in detail by a number of specific recommendations, was encapsulated through the endorsement of a **"Touchstone tourism destination model"** for the entire region (see Figure 17.1). This model recognized the primacy of ecological integrity and stressed a new emphasis on visitor education and heritage (com-

FIGURE 17.1 The Touchstone tourism destination model.

The Model Has As Its Foundation, The:

Values and Diverse Interests of Canadians and Shared, Open Decision Making

Its Goal, Above All, Is To Facilitate And Enhance:

Learning – Understanding – Appreciation Of Nature And The Rocky Mountain Culture

While Providing Visitors With:

High Quality, Authentic Experiences – A Hospitable Ambiance – Fair Value

In Doing So, It Will Maintain:

Ecological Integrity – Fair & Equitable Access

While Contributing To:

Regional Economic Vitality — National Pride & Unity

As It Respects The Rights Of :

Tourism Operators – All Canadians – Community Residents

While In Return Making:

A Fair Contribution To Park Well-Being

---

[5] R. Page, S. Bayley, et al., *Banff–Bow Valley: At The Crossroads* (Technical Report), Banff–Bow Valley Task Force. Prepared for the Honourable Sheila Copps, Minister of Canadian Heritage, Ottawa, Ontario, Canada, 1996, p. 432.

memorative) integrity, in addition to the traditional stress on recreation and the enjoyment of nature.

It is particularly important to note (see Figure 17.1) that the future role of tourism within Banff National Park has as its foundation "the values and diverse interests of Canadians" within "a process of shared, open decision making." These **values** were explicitly identified by the public participation process (see Table 17.3).

In the same vein, the final report also emphasized the importance of observing a defined set of principles when implementing the total set of recommendations to the Canadian Government (see Table 17.4). In contrast to a number of studies of this type, the recommendations of the Banff–Bow Valley Study has led to a number of significant decisions to protect the park and to enhance nature- and heritage-based tourism within its confines.

TABLE 17.3
Values Underlying Sustainable Tourism to Banff National Park

- The value of exercising restraint and self-discipline today, for the sake of future generations
- The value of nature in and of itself
- The value of nature to human experience
- The value of National Parks as protected areas
- The value of Banff National Park for all the people of the world as a World Heritage Site
- The value of the Banff Bow Valley for its essential ecological role in the context of the park and the larger ecosystem
- The value of the Banff Bow Valley, including the national transportation corridor, to the national, regional, and local economy
- The value of safe, healthy, and hospitable communities
- The value of culture and history
- The value of open, participatory decision-making
- The value of equal opportunity for a sense of wilderness and a range of quality park experiences
- The value of predictable, consistent and fair regulation
- The value of competent, accountable management
- The value of national parks to Canadians' sense of identity
- The value of wilderness preservation to Canada's image around the world
- The value of respect for others
- The value of freedom of access
- The value of education, enjoyment, and other park related benefits of the Bow Valley to visitors

CURRENT TOURISM INDUSTRY PRACTICES

It is fortunate that a concern for the environment has become a major trend that is still gathering momentum. Environmentalism is now a major international and national force with the development of the green movement and other concerned groups. Protection of the environment has been embraced by the tourism industry. Recognition is a start and progress is underway.

TABLE 17.4
Principles to Be Observed in Implementing the Touchstone Tourism Destination Model

The following principles guide all actions by government, business, communities, and the public.

- All actions, initiatives, and programs undertaken to realize the vision are implemented in full accordance with the spirit and requirements of the National Parks Act, Parks Canada's Guiding Principles and Operational Policies, and the Town of Banff Incorporation Agreement.
- Standards are defined, enforced, and reviewed so as to ensure the maintenance of ecological and commemorative integrity.
- Regulation and decisionmaking are responsive, open, participatory, consistent, and equitable.
- There is individual and shared responsibility to provide for protection and preservation of heritage resources, including buildings, within the park.
- Proactive, adaptive, and precautionary management take into account cumulative effects and limits to growth in recognition of the finite nature of the Valley.
- Services and opportunities that provide high-quality, affordable park experiences from front country to wilderness and that enhance understanding of national park values are stressed.
- Stewardship, based on sound science, is practiced through environmentally sensitive management, mitigation, and restoration.
- Education and experiences foster knowledge and understanding of the Banff Bow Valley, and they clarify its role in the larger ecosystem and also as part of a national park and a World Heritage Site.
- Educational opportunities are provided to foster understanding, appreciation, and respect for local culture.
- Integrity and common sense underlie all decisionmaking.
- Economic analyses include consideration of natural, social, and cultural assets.
- Only kinds and levels of activities, facilities, and services that are appropriate to Banff National Park are permitted.
- Marketing and communications programs are designed to develop knowledge and understanding of Banff National Park, including expectations and limitations and reach out to all.

Individual Tourists' Responsibilities

If ecologically sustainable tourism is to become a reality, it will require efforts by all the players in the tourism arena, starting with the tourists themselves. Tourists have responsibilities and must be educated as to their obligations and responsibilities to contribute to socially and environmentally responsible tourism. Tourists must first be brought into the process as clients (guests) for the tourist destination and second as persons co-responsible for maintaining the destination.

Several "codes of ethics," guidelines, and ten commandments for tourist behavior have been developed. Again, they are a start in the process of educating the tourist. Two examples are presented here. The first, and one of the most publicized, was produced by the American Society of Travel Agents (ASTA).

ASTA's Ten Commandments on Ecotourism

Whether on business or leisure travel:

1. *Respect the frailty of the earth.* Realize that unless all are willing to help in its preservation, unique and beautiful destinations may not be here for future generations to enjoy.

2. *Leave only footprints.* Take only photographs. Leave no graffiti. Do not litter. Do not take away "souvenirs" from historic sites and natural areas.

3. To make your travels more meaningful, *educate yourself about the geography, customs, manners, and cultures of the region you visit.* Take time to listen to the people. Encourage local conservation efforts.

4. *Respect the privacy and dignity of others.* Inquire before photographing people.

5. *Do not buy products made from endangered plants or animals, such as ivory, tortoise shell, animal skins, and feathers.* Read "Know Before You Go," the U.S. Customs list of products that cannot be imported.

6. *Always follow designated trials.* Do not disturb animals, plants, or their natural habitats.

7. Learn about and *support conservation-oriented programs and organizations* working to preserve the environment.

8. Whenever possible, *walk or utilize environmentally sound methods of transportation.* Encourage drivers of public vehicles to stop engines when parked.

9. *Patronize those* (hotels, airlines, resorts, cruise lines, tour operators, and suppliers) *who advance energy and environmental conservation;* water and air quality; recycling; safe management of waste and toxic materials, noise abatement; community involvement; and also patronize those who provide experienced, well-trained staff *dedicated to strong principles of conservation.*

10. Ask your ASTA travel agent to *identify those organizations that subscribe to the ASTA Environmental Guidelines* for air, land, and sea travel. ASTA has recommended that these organizations adopt their own environmental codes to cover special sites and ecosystems.

The second code is that developed by the Tourism Industry Association of Canada and the National Round Table on the Environment and the Economy of Canada.

Code of Ethics for Tourists

A high-quality tourism experience depends on the conservation of our natural resources, the protection of our environment, and the preservation of our cultural heritage. The Canadian Tourism Industry has developed and adopted a **Code of Ethics and Practices** to achieve these objectives. You can help us in our continuing efforts to

Ecotourists discover a dramatically different perspective of the world of nature when they proceed along the rainforest canopy walkway at the Amazon Center for Environmental Education and Research. *(Photo by Richard Mills; courtesy of International Expeditions, Inc.)*

provide a high-quality tourism experience for you and future guests by giving consideration to the following guidelines.

1. Enjoy our diverse natural and cultural heritage and help us to protect and preserve it.

2. Assist us in our conservation efforts through the efficient use of resources, including energy and water.

3. Experience the friendliness of our people and the welcoming spirit of our communities. Help us to preserve these attributes by respecting our traditions, customs, and local regulations.

4. Avoid activities that threaten wildlife or plant populations or that may be potentially damaging to our natural environment.

5. Select tourism products and services that demonstrate social, cultural, and environmental sensitivity.

These codes address the conduct of individual travelers and provide guidelines for responsible behavior while traveling. They emphasize travel behavior associated with natural resources, languages, host populations, cultural heritage, shopping, and social interaction. Although the codes above are illustrative of the work being done, it should be recognized that other organizations are also active. The National Audubon Society has been a leader, publishing their *Travel Ethic for Environmentally Responsible Tourism* in 1989. Save Our Planet published *Guidelines for Low-Impact Vacations* in 1990. The Center for Responsible Tourism in San Anselmo, California has also developed a *Tourist Code of Ethics.*

Codes and guidelines are fine, but the next step is making tourists aware of the codes and educating them to follow the important guidelines so they will become responsible travelers.

Travel Organization's Efforts

Efforts to increase environmental protection are being made by major tourism organizations such as the World Tourism Organization (WTO), World Travel and Tourism Council (WTTC), Pacific Asia Travel Association (PATA), Travel Industry Association of Canada (TIAC), and the Travel Industry Association of America (TIA).

As evidenced by their 1982 statement, WTO has been an advocate of protecting the environment for years: "The satisfaction of tourism requirements must not be prejudicial to the social and economic interests of the population in the tourist areas, to the environment, or above all, to natural resources which are fundamental attractions of tourism." Today, WTO has an Environmental Committee because they have recognized the need to understand and manage the link between tourism and the environment. The WTO Environmental Committee is developing a set of internationally acceptable indicators. A set of indicators will help tourism planners and managers prevent problems and protect the resource base.

Environmental concerns led the WTTC to establish the **World Travel and Tourism Research Center** (WTTERC) in September 1991 in cooperation with the Oxford Centre for Tourism and Leisure Studies. The center is a key component in WTTC's comprehensive program to achieve lasting environmental improvement. The center's aims are (1) to collect information about current corporate practice in the field of tourism and the environment, from which to establish ways that the center can contribute to practical environmental management; (2) to provide an international database designed to define and promote environmentally compatible growth in the tourism industry which enhances the experience of visitors and host communities; (3) the development of contacts with other international organizations dealing with the environment; (4) the preparation of objective analyses, evaluations, and summaries of principles of "good practice" for growth in environmentally compatible tourism, with particular reference to environmental impact assessments and audits to be carried out at the company level; (5) the identification of projects around the world relevant to enhancing and sustaining the environment through tourism; and (6) the communication to the tourism industry of current developments and practices in the field of the environment. In addition to its environmental center, the WTTC has also published a set of environmental guidelines that are based on principles established by the International Chamber of Commerce (ICC) Business Charter for Sustainable Development. These guidelines are given in Reading 17.2 at the end of the chapter.

Regional organizations such as PATA have also developed codes for environmentally responsible tourism. The PATA code lists 18 guidelines that their 2100-member organizations are to follow with respect to tourism's environmental relationships.

The PATA code urges association and chapter members and their industry partners to:

- Adopt the necessary practices to conserve the environment, including the use of renewable resources in a sustainable manner and the conservation of nonrenewable resources.

- Contribute to the conservation of any habitat of flora and fauna, and of any site, whether natural or cultural, which may be affected by tourism.

- Encourage relevant authorities to identify areas worthy of conservation and to determine the level of development, if any, which would ensure that those areas are conserved.

- Ensure that community attitudes, cultural values, and concerns, including local customs and beliefs, are taken into account in the planning of all tourism related projects.

- Ensure that environmental assessment becomes an integral step in the consideration of any site for a tourism project. Ensure that assessment procedures recognize the cumulative as well as the individual effects of all developments on the environment.

- Comply with all international conventions in relation to the environment.

- Comply with all national, state, and local laws in relation to the environment.

- Encourage those involved in tourism to comply with local, regional, and national planning policies and to participate in the planning process.

- Provide the opportunity for the wider community to take part in discussions and consultations on tourism planning issues insofar as they affect the tourism industry and the community.

- Acknowledge responsibility for the environmental impacts of all tourism-related projects and activities and undertake all necessary responsible remedial and corrective actions.

- Encourage regular environmental audits of practices throughout the tourism industry and encourage necessary changes to those practices.

- Foster environmentally responsible practices, including waste management, recycling, and energy use.

- Foster in both management and staff an awareness of environmental and conservation principles in all tourism-related projects and activities.

- Support the inclusion of professional conservation principles in tourism education, training, and planning.

- Encourage an understanding (by all those involved in tourism) of each community's customs, cultural values, beliefs, and traditions and how they relate to the environment.

- Enhance the appreciation and understanding (by tourists) of the environment through the provision of accurate information and appropriate interpretation.

- Establish detailed environmental policies and/or guidelines for the various sectors of the tourism industry.

National organization codes have also been developed, with the TIAC leading the way. The TIAC has created not just one code, but a series of ethical codes for the tourism industry as a whole, for tourists, and for specific sectors of its membership, such as accommodation, food services, tour operators, and government bodies. A particularly distinguishing feature of the TIAC codes is that they extend beyond just protection of the environment guidelines and incorporate the philosophy of sustainable development, which includes all facets of development—social, cultural, and economic. For those seeking more information or a copy of TIAC's Code of Ethics for Tourists, Code of Ethics for the Industry, or Guidelines of Tourist Industry Associations, contact the Tourism Industry Association of Canada, Suite 1016-130 Albert Street, Ottawa, Ontario, Canada K1P 5G4.

Finally, the United Nations itself, within its UNEP (United National Environment Program), has demonstrated its interest and concern in the topic. In a 1995 report,[6] the organization carried out a review of a range of environmental codes of conduct for the tourism industry. Following this review, they concluded that such codes must be positive, specific, and action-oriented. If codes are too vague, they have no bite and signatories commit themselves to very little when adopting them. Real change requires real codes, with real objectives.

Although codes must be tailored specifically to the situation they confront, most have several features in common. These are:

- The need to make an overall commitment to the physical and human environment, to accept responsibility for environmental damage and take corrective action where necessary, and to promote and reward outstanding environmental performance

- The need to develop policies and strategies that take account of land-use planning regulations and the need to protect some areas from further development

---

[6] UNEP, *Environmental Codes of Conduct for Tourism.* (Paris: United National Environment Programme, 1995).

- The need to develop management policies that enhance beneficial and minimize adverse impacts on the environment

- The need to cooperate with other firms, sectors, and countries

It is important that codes are not developed in isolation. All codes should be the result of partnerships with other businesses, with tourists themselves, or with potential host communities, as appropriate.

Secondly, codes are nothing more than words on paper if they are not implemented. It is essential to consider the implementation and monitoring of codes from the very beginning, even at the time when they are being drafted. While many organizations have already prepared codes, far fewer have given serious thought to implementation and monitoring. Those that have, however, have developed interesting packages of measures that comprise the following:

- Publicity and dissemination campaigns

- Publications of all types

- The provision of expert services to signatories of the code

- The provision of networks to improve communications between participants

- The organization of conferences and seminars for the exchange of ideas

- The provision of awards for outstanding environmental behavior

- The organization of demonstration projects to set examples for others to follow

To be most efficient, measures such as publications, seminars, and conferences must be practical in orientation and directed at specific audiences.

Yet a further effort spearheaded by the United Nations was the first World Conference on Sustainable Tourism held in Lanzarde in Spain's Canary Islands in April 1995. The conference was co-sponsored by the United Nation's Environment Program, UNESCO's Man and the Biosphere Program, the World Tourism Organization, and the Spanish and Canary Islands governments. From this conference emanated the Lanzarde Charter for Sustainable Tourism (see Table 17.5).

One of the main worries expressed by delegates to the conference was the lack of participation from private enterprise. Despite this concern, many firms have recognized the need for action on their daily operations.

Individual Firm Efforts

A third set of environmental codes focuses on individual companies. These codes tend to be quite technical and operations-oriented, covering the day-to-day management practices of businesses such as airlines, accommodations, cruise lines, theme parks, tour operators, and others. What distinguishes these codes from those discussed previously is their effort to integrate the best business practices with sound environmen-

TABLE 17.5
Main Points of the Lanzarde Charter for Sustainable Tourism

The following is a summary of some of the main points of the charter, which has been sent to the United Nations Commission on Sustainable Development:

- Tourism development shall be based on criteria of sustainability, which means that it must be ecologically sound in the long term, economically viable, as well as ethically and socially equitable for the local communities.
- The sustainable nature of tourism requires that it should integrate the natural, cultural, and human environments. It must respect the fragile balances that characterize many tourist destinations, in particular small islands and environmentally sensitive areas.
- Tourism must consider its effects on cultural heritage and traditional elements, activities and dynamics of each local community. These elements must at all times play a central role in the formulation of tourism strategies, particularly in developing countries.
- Sustainable development means the solidarity, mutual respect, and participation of all players implicated in the process, especially those indigenous to the locality. This must be based on efficient cooperation mechanisms at all levels: local, national, regional and international.
- Governments and authorities shall promote actions for integrating the planning of tourism with environmental nongovernment organizations (NGOs) and local communities.
- Measures must be developed to permit a more equitable distribution of the benefits and burdens of tourism. This implies a change in consumption patterns and the introduction of ecologically honest pricing. Governments and multilateral organizations are called on to abandon subsidies that have negative effects on the environment.
- Environmentally and culturally vulnerable spaces, both now and in the future, shall be given special priority in the matter of technical cooperation and financial aid for sustainable tourism development. Similarly, special treatment should be given to spaces that have been degraded by obsolete and high-impact tourism models.
- Government, authorities, and NGOs with responsibility for tourism and the environment shall promote and participate in the creation of open networks for information, research, dissemination, and transfer of appropriate tourism and environmental knowledge and technology.
- There is a need to support and promote feasibility studies, vigorously applied scientific field-work, tourism demonstration projects within the framework of sustainable development, the development of programs in the field of international cooperation, and the introduction of environmental management systems.
- Attention should be given to the role and environmental effects of transportation in tourism, and economic instruments should be developed and implemented in order to reduce the use of nonrenewable energy.

Source: WTO News, May 1995.

tal management. Companies such as Canadian Pacific Hotels and Resorts, ITT Sheraton, Ramada International Hotels and Resorts, Marriott International, British Airways, American Airlines, United Airlines, USAir, Avis Rent-A-Car/System, Busch Entertainment Corporation, Anheuser–Busch, Universal Studios, Walt Disney Company, and American Express have focused on recycling, reuse, energy conservation, water con-

Environmentally responsible tourism can be achieved through the combined efforts of private operators, travel organizations, and individuals. *(Photo courtesy of the Hawaii Visitors and Convention Bureau.)*

servation, community involvement, and community environmental obligations to employees and guests.[7]

Some case descriptions illustrate the activities of some firms environmental responsibility. Because actions speak louder than words, these cases represent enlightened current practice.

Inter-Continental Hotels has produced and distributed a 300-page manual for its properties worldwide with guidelines on waste management, product purchasing, air

[7] Suzanne Hawkes and Peter Williams. *The Greening of Tourism* (Burnaby, B.C.: Centre for Tourism Policy and Research, Simon Fraser University, 1993); and U.S. Travel Data Center, *Tourism and the Environment* (Washington, D.C.: Travel Industry Association of America, 1992).

quality, energy conservation, noise pollution, fuel storage, asbestos, pesticides, herbicides, and water.[8]

Ramada International Hotels and Resorts has made a company-wide commitment to environmental integrity. Many of the Ramada hotels in North America have expanded or initiated solid-waste recycling programs for items such as tin, aluminum, paper, glass, broken china, and plastics (including dry cleaning bags and empty amenity bottles in guest rooms).

The WAT&G-designed Ramada in Cairns, North Queensland, Australia was designed and built without disrupting one tree. It has been used in full-page ads to promote Ramada's commitment to the environment.[9]

As evidence that recycling has taken on an important role at the Four Seasons, the heads of design and engineering, Chris Wallace and J. Peter Buyze, are working to develop design standards for future hotels, which incorporate the increased space and power required for bailers, crushers, and containers. Looking beyond recycling, the Four Seasons will not use halon at new properties and is modifying specifications for all new hotels to eliminate CFC (chlorofluorocarbon) usage in refrigeration.[10]

Hyatt Hotels and Resorts has implemented an international recycling program that saves the organization more than $3 million annually. Hyatt's commitment is not only to recycle, but also to close, the recycling loop by establishing a market for recycled products. This is important when you consider that a typical Hyatt guest room generates 383 pounds of garbage annually, according to the consulting firm International Recycleco.

Under Hyatt's new plan, the same guest room will generate an average of only 37 pounds of nonrecyclable garbage annually, saving the company $2 million in annual waste-hauling costs. Under design is a trash container for guest rooms to encourage separation of paper, plastics, and aluminum.

With the help of their recycling consultant, the Chicago Hyatt Regency is now operating its own miniature materials recovery facility. The MRF processes nine different items, including leftover soap, and cuts the annual disposal costs in half. The program has saved the hotel money by retrieving hotel items discarded by mistake, including linens, silverware, and coffee pots.

In addition, all new Hyatt hotels in the United States will be designed with recycling centers. Hotels outside the United States will implement programs in accordance with local guidelines and availability of environmentally friendly products.[11]

A recent report by Disney to cast members on company-wide environmental activities includes these recycling statistics:

Lumber. Disney has recycled enough lumber to give everyone in the United States a popsicle stick: 768,000 pounds of lumber.

Paper. The amount of office paper recycled by the entire company to date is equivalent to the weight of a 747: 2,000,000 pounds of paper.

---

[8] Wimberly Allison Tong & Goo, *Do Not Disturb* (Newport Beach, CA: WAT&G, n.d.).

[9] Ibid.

[10] Ibid.

[11] Ibid.

Cardboard. In 1990, the company recycled enough cardboard to cover Epcot, The Magic Kingdom, and Gatorland: 2,300,000 pounds of cardboard.

Aluminum cans. Disney has recycled enough aluminum cans to produce a cola can more than 100 miles high: 26,000 pounds of aluminum.[12]

According to Ritz–Carlton President Horst Schulze, an employee asked him why the company wasn't doing more in the area of recycling. Thanks to that employee, Blake Edwards, an engineer with the Ritz–Carlton Buckhead in Atlanta, a part-time recycling effort has blossomed into a full-time environmental management program and Edwards has been named environmental recycling systems manager. Prior to initiating the recycling program, Ritz–Carlton's disposal costs in the Atlanta property were increasing 50 to 62 percent annually. By decreasing the volume and weight of waste material, costs have been reduced by 50 percent. Food that is prepared but unused is donated to organizations for the homeless. At the Ritz–Carlton Laguna Niguel, 13,000 pounds of cardboard, 5000 pounds of computer paper, and 6000 pounds of glass are being collected on a monthly basis.[13]

Sheraton has several programs. They select products such as cleaning solvents and containers for their conservation and recyclability. Their "Going Green" program invites guests at Sheraton hotels in Africa and the Indian Ocean region to add a dollar to their final bill. Sheraton then matches this amount in local currency and contributes the money to local conservation projects that the World Society for the Protection of Animals has identified.[14]

United Airlines recycles aluminum aboard its aircraft and food containers up to 30 or 40 times. It has also reduced the amount of water carried on board and is replacing its fleet with quieter, more fuel-efficient aircraft.[15]

Busch Entertainment Corporation works for an improved environment through recycling, community involvement, corporate environmental planning, and conservation education to solve critical environmental problems.[16]

Sea World of Florida operates a beached animal rescue and rehabilitation program that aids sick, injured, or orphaned manatees, dolphins, whales, otters, sea turtles, and birds.[17]

A CLOSING NOTE

This chapter concludes with a statement by Ken Brown, Chairman of Mauna Lani Resorts, Inc., in Hawaii. It epitomizes the attitude that developers need to have to be sensitive to the environment. Having orchestrated one of the most highly acclaimed destination resorts in the world, his views bear careful study. Brown states: "Developers

---

[12] Ibid.

[13] U.S. Travel Data Center, *Tourism and the Environment.*

[14] Ibid.

[15] Ibid.

[16] Ibid.

[17] Ibid.

must not act like elephants at a picnic." He reminds us: "We should not only be sensitive to the environment, we should also add something to the life of the people—something aesthetic, physically beautiful, socially and economically enriching. We need to examine our actions and ask, 'Is this really benefiting the community?' "

Public response and numerous awards attest to Mauna Lani's success as an environmentally conscious achievement in tourism development. Among other honors, the resort has received a prestigious historic preservation award for the restoration and maintenance of ancient fish ponds, creation of a 27-acre historical park, and contributions to preserve petroglyphs (ancient rock carvings) along the Hawaiian Islands' Kohala coast.

Brown's convictions about environmental responsibility run deep. "I am absolutely convinced that environmental concerns are ethical and moral issues." Acknowledging the high economic cost of environmentally responsive development, Brown expresses confidence in its long-range profitability. He has been inspired by the late Noboru Gotoh—Japanese industrialist, Tokyu Group chairman, and Mauna Lani developer—whose motto, "For the Betterment of Mankind," set exacting standards for Mauna Lani.[18]

SUMMARY

Responsible citizens of the world have cause to realize that all of humankind's activities must be increasingly examined in a very critical manner with respect to their impact or their sustainability of this planet. Tourism is only one of these activities, but it is an extremely important one. It follows that tourism must understand and accept those limitations that are essential to maintaining high quality of life for all species.

The main concept of ecotourism is responsible travel to natural areas that conserves the environment and sustains the well-being of local people. From the tourists' viewpoint, ecotourism is typically the gratification provided by a unique experience in an undisturbed natural environment viewing flora, fauna, birds, animals, land forms, scenery, and natural beauty.

Benefits of ecotourism include providing jobs, helping preserve more areas, educating, and encouraging heritage and environmental enhancement. Benefits to the local people are maximized by hiring as many locals as possible and obtaining supplies and services locally.

Carrying capacity for visitors must be determined. It is defined as the maximum number of daily visitors that the area can receive without damaging its attractive features. Enforcement of this limit, along with good management and maintenance, is essential.

Sustainable tourism development is development that has been carefully planned and managed. It is the antithesis of tourism that has developed for short-term gains. Because of the expected continuing growth of tourism, sustainable devel-

---

[18] Wimberly Allison Tong & Goo, *Do Not Disturb*. (Newport Beach, CA: WAT&G, n.d.).

opment is the approach that will be needed. Because of the pressure on the world's resources, it is the only sensible approach.

No business sector has greater reason to promote and enforce environmental and business ethics codes than tourism. The environment is the resource base for tourism; and without protection, the natural attraction that brought the tourist in the first place will be lost. As a result, a number of codes for tourists, the tourism industry, and the environment have emerged. If the codes developed by the American Society of Travel Agents, World Travel and Tourism Council, Pacific Asia Travel Association, the Travel Industry Association of Canada, and other organizations are followed, the possibility of truly sustainable tourism can be a reality.

ABOUT THE READINGS

Reading 17.1 is "Ecotourism: Nature's Ally," by Richard Ryel of International Expeditions, Inc., of Birmingham, Alabama. International Expeditions has been identified as one of the leading responsible ecotour companies. Mr. Ryel addresses ecotourism and ends with a challenge for everyone.

The World Travel and Tourism Council (WTTC) is a global coalition of Chief Executive Officers from all sectors of the industry working to promote environmentally compatible tourism growth. They have developed a set of environmental guidelines that are reproduced in Reading 17.2.

Reading 17.3 addresses the issue of translating the ideals of environmentalism into reality. It discusses how the Hyatt Regency Scottsdale has done just that. It describes an environmental program to positively impact on air and water quality.

READING 17.1

ECOTOURISM: NATURE'S ALLY

by Richard Ryel
International Expeditions, Inc.

There is a growing global concern over the rapidly deteriorating ecological state of the Earth. As we gobble up more and more of our natural resources, it becomes alarmingly obvious how finite they are. Clean waters, pristine forests, untilled moorland and unfilled swamps are becoming very rare indeed. Still, the most ecologically aware of us are hard pressed to come up with even an insignificant part of our daily lives that we would be willing to give up in order to alleviate the problem. Starving, cold and desperate folk eking out a living from eroded land don't have the luxury of even making a choice.

It is into this miserable scenario a glimmer of hope shines. The populations of richer nations seem to be more concerned than ever with conservation matters. People are traveling more, and by doing so come to realize for themselves the actuality of the world's ecological problems. Acid rain legislation, controlled timber cutting, and protection of habitats are finally coming about—and more is being done.

Ecotourism (culturally and ecologically sensitive travel) has evolved as a result of two basic facts of modern life—the struggle of poor nations to catch up by exploiting their splendid natural resources, and the concern of rich nations for the Earth's preservation.

Ecotourism operators are discovering that if governments can be persuaded to preserve their unspoiled natural habitats, the result will be a great boost to their national economies from tourism dollars. This has been demonstrated in Rwanda where the Mountain Gorillas, once poached to near extinction, are slowly making a comeback as a result of carefully controlled tourism.

Obviously, tourism to such delicate and endangered habitats can have its hazards. Extreme caution cannot be overemphasized. It is easy to see the effect of trash on a forest walkway, but what of the effects we cannot see—the effect of flashbulbs on nesting patterns of birds or the unaccustomed noise of people on animal populations and habits. It all takes a vigilance that before now was not considered vital, and therefore not encountered in the travel industry. Naturalists, biologists, anthropologists and others of similar background are needed to make these expeditions work both for the enlightenment and enjoyment of the travelers and, most importantly, for the preservation of the dwindling wild places of our Earth.

With this awareness of the state of world resources, what element or elements of your lifestyle would you be willing to give up for the sake of conservation? We welcome your comments.

READING 17.2

THE WORLD TRAVEL AND TOURISM COUNCIL ENVIRONMENTAL GUIDELINES

A clean, healthy environment is essential to future growth—it is core of the Travel & Tourism product.

The WTTC commends these guidelines to Travel & Tourism companies and to governments and asks that they be taken into account in policy formation:

- Travel & Tourism companies should state their commitment to environmentally compatible development.
- Targets for improvements should be established and monitored.
- Environmental commitment should be company-wide.
- Education and research into improved environmental programs should be encouraged.
- Travel & Tourism companies should seek to implement sound environmental principles through self-regulation, recognizing that national and international regulation may be inevitable and that preparation is vital.

Environmental improvement programs should be systematic and comprehensive. They should aim to:

- Identify and continue to reduce environmental impact, paying particular attention to new projects.
- Pay due regard to environmental concern in design, planning, construction and implementation.
- Be sensitive to conservation of environmentally protected or threatened areas, species and scenic aesthetics, achieving landscape enhancement where possible.
- Practice energy conservation.
- Reduce and recycle waste.
- Practice fresh-water management and control sewage disposal.
- Control and diminish air emissions and pollutants.
- Monitor, control and reduce noise levels.
- Control and reduce environmentally unfriendly products, such as asbestos, CFCs, pesticides and toxic, corrosive, infectious, explosive or flammable materials.
- Respect and support historic or religious objects and sites.
- Exercise due regard for the interests of local populations, including their history, traditions and culture and future development.
- Consider environmental issues as a key factor in the overall development of Travel & Tourism destinations.

READING 17.3

HYATT "GREEN TEAM" LEADS WITH ENVIRONMENTAL VISION

by Paul F. Hayes
Environmental Program Manager
Hyatt Recency Scottsdale at Gainey Ranch

Hyatt Regency Scottsdale at Gainey Ranch has taken on an environmental program that will focus our efforts on conserving natural resources through waste management, water conservation, and energy management. Hyatt recognizes its duty to protect the natural environment and its resources both locally and globally. As a result, we are striving to be an example of environmental responsibility within the community, as well as the hospitality industry. We have made a commitment to develop and maintain an efficient and effective program that will have a positive impact on our air and water quality.

Team Initiatives

Our staff is proud that our resort is doing its share in the fight to preserve the Earth and its natural resources. In fact, the line employees have generated many of the ideas and practices. Hyatt Regency Scottsdale's "Green Team" is an environmental steering committee established so that employees can help implement, promote, and maintain the property's environmental initiative. Team members are enthusiastic individuals who welcome their responsibilities, which include attending monthly meetings. Goals of the group include not only the education of our coworkers about Hyatt's program, but also the dissemination of simple steps that employees may use in their homes, if desired. Members feel it is everyone's responsibility to protect and preserve our future. It is through their involvement that we build understanding.

Energy Management

The single biggest impact on ecology is the conservation of natural resources. With an energy management commitment, our Hyatt has reduced the amount of electricity used. Before changes could be made, we had to review the way we operate the resort and judge the impact on our guests. One example is the lobby doors. The open-air ambiance of the

lobby with its picturesque view of the resort framed against the McDowell Mountains, has tremendous impact as guests arrive at the front entry. While the view is the signature sight of the resort, a hundred feet of open doors also allows hot air to flow into the building. We assessed the loss of energy vs. the visual impact lost by closing the doors and determined that the environmental impact should take precedence. As temperature extremes dictate, the lobby doors are closed.

Some of the other techniques Hyatt has implemented include the use of T-8 lights in all back-of-the-house areas. Motion sensors, which automatically turn off lights when a room is empty, have been placed in closets, meeting rooms, and banquet facilities. We calculate that by reducing our energy requirements, we have had a significant impact on the environment; the resultant decrease in the amount of coal burned equates to hundreds of tons every year.

Water Savings

Through technology and infrastructure innovations, we have created natural resource savings in several areas, particularly in water conservation. Hyatt's lagoon adds ambiance to the beauty of the resort and is now maintained naturally by aquatic life. We no longer use strong chemicals to prevent algae growth, since such chemicals might have the potential to affect ground water. We've also come up with an innovative way to deal with Arizona's notoriously warm "cold" water. Lettuce and other vegetables require *cold* water to remain fresh. We now store cold water in the resort's main kitchen and use this to supply the kitchen's sinks.

Our laundry has also developed strategies to minimize water consumption. By adding one step before rinsing, we are able to eliminate one whole rinse step. This works because the additional two-minute extraction step removes residual detergent before the final rinse. This short extraction saves hundreds of gallons of water.

Installation of water-conserving devices such as faucet aerators, toilet flow restrictors, and showers has decreased the resort's water usage. All main feeds to water features and irrigation systems were retrofitted with submeters to quickly detect leaks. Although grass requires a large amount of water, the resort limits its use to areas for on-site activities. The irrigation schedule reduces evaporation by watering the grounds at off-peak times (at night as opposed to the heat of the day). Most of our landscaping has been converted to utilize drip irrigation, which further reduces evaporation. Natural predator insects, such as ladybugs, are released on an ongoing basis to control landscape-hungry white flies and aphids. To reduce evaporation and toxic chemical use, the swimming pools' chlorine filtration systems have been replaced with calcium hypochloriate systems. Lastly, we conserve water by utilizing the Gainey Ranch Waste Water Reclamation Plant, a water treatment facility drawn from the city's main sewer line, to irrigate the twenty-seven-hole golf course.

Landscaping

As part of our landscaping strategy, we considered the physical effects of our building upon the ecosystem. For example, our Terrace Court receives full sun and heat that radiates off the building's granite block throughout the day. In the past, we had landscaped this function area with bushes and plants that continually died. We've now introduced native plants and cacti, which thrive in the area and provide an excellent educational backdrop for our guests, while emphasizing the resort's compatibility with the man-made environment.

Recycling

The resort's recycling program leads our solid waste management efforts. Three-color posters are located throughout the resort to teach and remind employees where items are to be placed. Color-coded receptacles make sorting items easier. Office paper, colored paper, chipboard, and magazines are co-mingled in green receptacles, while newspapers and their inserts are collected in yellow bins. Plastics number one and two, glass, aluminum, and tin are all collected for recycling in blue bins. In addition, corrugated cardboard is broken down and baled for recycling. Printed materials that are produced in-house are made from no less than twenty percent post-consumer materials. Office documents are double-sided to utilize half the amount of paper. Grass clippings and tree limbs get transformed into fertilizer. Our programs conserve natural resources in two ways. We choose products that require fewer raw materials to produce and we actively recycle our waste matter. Both methods yield positive benefits to air and water quality.

Innovative Use of Broken Dishes

The resort's Squash Blossom restaurant and Room Service use vibrant hand-painted Italian ceramic Caleca tableware. Hyatt's environmental program has found a way to recycle the chipped or broken pieces by donating them for mosaic art projects in art classes throughout the Valley. The glassware used in our Lobby Bar and the Squash Blossom restaurant is itself a recycled product made from soda bottles in Guadalajara, Mexico.

Merging the Natural Environment

Hyatt Regency Scottsdale seeks to merge the design of the resort with the natural environment. While the McDowell Mountains provide a brilliant backdrop with spectacular views of the surrounding areas they are also home to native plant and animal life. Because of the resort's interconnection with the local environment, several species of birds have chosen Hyatt as their home. Blue herons, green herons, great horned owls, roadrunners, cactus wren, white wing doves, Gila peckers, and native mockingbird species may be seen throughout the property.

The resorts' commitment is further evidenced by its inclusion of a full-time environmental manager on its staff. This manager, in addition to other responsibilities, participates in the orientation of new employees and attends departmental meetings to update the staff on the environmental program's procedures and new facets of the operation.

Employee Participation

Every employee is involved in and is an integral part of our environmental program. Whether it be in one of our restaurants (recycling mixed products such as aluminum and plastic) or in the sales departments (recycling office paper), employees are actively contributing to our environmental mission. What is more, their brains and hearts are involved; employees regularly develop solutions that help integrate recycling into their job areas.

The environmental program at Hyatt Regency Scottsdale at Gainey Ranch is funded through an operating budget within the resort. Our emphasis for the program is not monetary rewards, but positive benefits to the community and the future stability of tourism in the area. We know that people come to a destination to experience the beauty of the surrounding area. This beauty is closely related to a healthy environment. Air and water quality have a significant impact on the future success of our tourism industry—not just in faraway destinations, but within the scope of our own locales. Each of us can make a difference. We've already begun to.

Key Concepts

ASTA's ten commandments
Banff–Bow Valley Study
benefits of ecotourism
carrying capacity
code of ethics
debt for nature swap
ecotourism
ecotourism development
environmental preservation

land-use planning
local populations and benefits
principles for implementing sustainable tourism
PATA code for environmentally responsible tourism
sustainable development
sustainable tourism
Touchstone tourism destination model
WTTC Research Centre

Internet Sites

American Society of Travel Agents
http://www.astanet.com

Earth Pledge
http://www.earthpledge.org

Earthwatch International
http://gala.earthwatch.org

Ecotourism Society
http://www.ecotourism.org

Ecoventure
http://134.121.164.23/ecoventure.htm

Environmental Information
http://boris.qub.ac.uk/cvni/info.html

Environmental Information Resources Network
http://www.erin.gov.au/database.db/html

Gateway to Antarctica
http://www.icair.iac.org.nz

Green Net
http://www.gn.apc.org

Pacific Asia Travel Association
http://www.pata.org

United Nations Environment Program
http://www.unep.ch

World Conservation Monitoring Centre
http://www.wcmc.org.uk

World Conservation Union, Paris
http://www.icun.org

World Heritage
http://www.unesco.org/whc/welcom/htm

World Tourism Organization
www.world-tourism.org

World Travel and Tourism Council
www.wttc.org

World Wide Web Resources: Environment
http://www.uky.edu/Subject/environment.htm

Internet Exercises

Site Name: Earth Pledge Foundation
URL: http://www.earthpledge.org/
Background Information: The Earth Pledge Foundation is a nonprofit organization founded in 1991 by businessman and labor mediator Theodore W. Kheel

to promote the principles and practices of sustainable development. The foundation enjoys a broad mandate to work on projects that span the fields of art, architecture, community development, politics, agriculture, cuisine, tourism, education, technology and the media.

Exercises

1. Surf the web site and discuss what is meant by the "greening of the hotel industry."
2. Describe how the Sundance Resort struggled with their impact on the environment.

3. Discuss how AMR (parent company for American Airlines) views marketing sustainable tourism.

QUESTIONS FOR REVIEW AND DISCUSSION

1. What exactly is ecotourism? Why are there so many different terms for this idea?
2. Why has this concept become so popular?
3. Give some examples of the resources necessary for an ecotourism destination.
4. Are resources other than natural ones involved? Are these meaningful? Explain.
5. Describe the role of local people.
6. Why are preservation planning principles so important?
7. What should be the goals of ecotourism for a tour company; the ecotourist; the local popula-

tion; the local government; a conservation organization.
8. Differentiate ecotourism policy in developing and developed countries.
9. Identify the principal limitations to ecotourism.
10. Referring to question 9, state some ways that these limitations might be ameliorated.
11. Why is capacity so important?
12. Why is it important to identify the values on which tourism development is based?
13. Of what use are "principles" in implementing recommendations to achieve sustainable tourism?

CASE PROBLEMS

1. Bonnie S., CTC, is an agency travel counselor. She has decided that her agency's market area has a good potential to sell more ecotours. How should Bonnie proceed to identify prospective buyers of such tours?
2. As director of Ecuador's national park system, Ernesto B. has become increasingly concerned about the overuse of Galápagos National Park. He worries that the current popularity of the park—about 50,000 tourists each year—may actually be sowing the seeds of destruction. This situation may be inducing a disastrous future drop in visitor numbers. Outline some steps that he might take to:
   a. Ascertain the present quality of the visitor experience.
   b. Remedy some aspects of overuse of the park, to ensure future success.
3. Nathan M. is the local managing director of a tour company specializing in ecotourism. His company operates big game/bird photo safaris in Tanzania.

He has decided that his firm would be more socially responsible if his tours (by minibus) would obtain practically all needs from local sources. Give some examples of how he might do this and describe the benefits that would accrue locally. (When discussing, include both economic and social benefits.)
4. Upon graduation, you have secured a job as tourism specialist with the World Wildlife Fund. Your first assignment is to be a team member charged with helping to formulate plans for some kind of wildlife protection area in Zambia. This country is located in south central Africa. Their government is considering a new national park and has requested expert assistance from the fund. The president of the fund, has made it very clear to the team that such plans must also aim to improve living standards for the local population. These standards, at present, are grievously low. Most local people are subsistence farmers. They occasionally shoot big game animals that damage their crops, and also for meat.

After extensive field study, a particularly attractive area has been found in which the scenery is spectacular, climate very pleasant, the natural history resources outstanding, and the local people friendly and hospitable. Thus the proposed park seems to have an excellent potential for attracting substantial numbers of ecotourists. Propose some conceptual ideas as to how this challenge can be met successfully.

5. A very vocal environmental group has recently voiced harsh criticism of the state's tourism business. They claim that the industry rapidly consumes valuable natural resources, provides mostly low-paying unskilled employment, and degrades the culture of the main tourist centers. As the state's tourism director, how would you answer these charges?

6. Referring to case 5, the same environmental group has succeeded in convincing the state's attorney general that all roadside billboards be eliminated. The various state hotel, motel, restaurant, attractions, and tourist promotion organizations vehemently oppose such legislation. Can you think of some kind of compromising plan that might satisfy both of these opposing groups?

SELECTED REFERENCES

Abraham, C. "Environment Slipping as a Priority." Calgary, Alberta, Canada: *Calgary Herald*. December 12, page A3, 1997.

An Action Strategy for Sustainable Tourism Development. Globe '90 Conference, Vancouver, British Columbia, Canada: Tourism Stream Action Strategy Committee, 1990.

Anonymous. "Local Conservation Efforts Prompt Environmental Award," *Focus*, World Wildlife Fund, p. 4, July/August 1993.

Ayala, Hana. "Resort Ecotourism: A Paradigm for the 21st Century." *Cornell Quarterly*, Vol. 37, No. 5, pp. 46–53, 1996.

Ayala, Hana. "Resort Ecotourism: A Master Plan for Experience Management." *Cornell Quarterly*, Vol. 37, No. 5, pp. 54–61, 1996.

Bell, Charles A. "Bali's Example: Fragile Resort Areas and How to Maintain Them." *Cornell Hotel and Restaurant Administration Quarterly*, Vol. 33, No. 5, pp. 28–31, October 1992.

Blamey, Russell K. "Ecotourism: The Search for an Operational Definition." *Journal of Sustainable Tourism*, Vol. 5, No. 2, pp. 109–122, 1997.

Boo, Elizabeth. "Tourism and the Environment: Pitfalls and Liabilities of Ecotourism Development," *WTO News*, Vol. 9, pp. 2–4, October 1992.

Boyd, S. W., and R. W. Butler. "Managing Ecotourism: An Opportunity Spectrum Approach." *Tourism Management*, Vol. 17, No. 8, pp. 557–566, 1996.

Braithwaite, Richard. "Ecotourism in the Monsoonal Tropics." *Issues*, Vol. 23, pp. 29–35, May 1993.

Bramwell, B., and A. Fearn. "Visitor Attitudes to a Policy Instrument for Visitor Funding of Conservation in Tourist Area." *Journal of Travel Research*, Vol. 35, No. 2, pp. 29–33, Fall 1996.

Bramwell, B., and B. Lane. "Sustainable Tourism: An Evolving Global Approach." *Journal of Sustainable Tourism*, Vol. 1, No. 1, pp. 1–5, 1993.

Briguglio, L., et al., eds. *Sustainable Tourism in Islands and Small States: Case Studies*. London: Pinter, 1996.

Briguglio, L., et al., eds. *Sustainable Tourism in Island and Small States: Issues and Policies*. London: Pinter, 1996.

Cater, Erlet. "Ecotourism in the Third World: Problems for Sustainable Tourism Development." *Tourism Management*, pp. 85–90, April 1993.

Cater, E., and G. Lowman. *Ecotourism: A Sustainable Option?* New York: Wiley, 1994.

Clark, Jackie. "A Framework of Approaches to Sustainable Tourism." *Journal of Sustainable Tourism*, Vol. 5, No. 3, pp. 224–233, 1997.

Cooper, C. P., and I. Ozdil. "From Mass to "Responsible" Tourism: The Turkish Experience." *Tourism Management*, Vol. 13, No. 4, pp. 377–386, December 1991.

Cousteau, Jean-Michel. "Tread Lightly Ecotourists." *Calypso Log*, Vol. 18, No. 3, p. 3, 1991.

D'Amore, Louis J. "A Code of Ethics and Guidelines for Socially and Environmentally Responsible Tourism." *Journal of Travel Research*, Vol. 31, No. 3, pp. 64–66, Winter 1993.

Dimanche, Frederic, and Ginger Smith. "Is Ecotourism an Appropriate Answer to Tourism's Environmental Concerns? *Journal of Hospitality and Leisure Marketing*, Vol. 3, No. 4, pp. 67–76, 1995.

Ding, Peiyi, and John Pigram. "Environmental Audits: An Emerging Concept in Sustainable Tourism Development." *Journal of Tourism Studies,* Vol. 6, No. 2, pp. 2–10, December 1995.

Downs, Bob. "Study: Environment Big Issue with Travelers." *Travel Trade,* Vol. 58, No. 27, p. 7, 1992.

Eagles, Paul F. "The Travel Motivations of Canadian Ecotourists." *Journal of Travel Research,* Vol. 31, No. 2, pp. 3–7, Fall 1992.

Eagles, P. F. J., et al. *Ecotourism: An Annotated Bibliography for Planners and Managers,* The Ecotourism Society, 1993.

Farrell, Bryan H., and Dean Runyan. "Ecology and Tourism." *Annals of Tourism Research,* Vol. 18, No. 1, pp. 26–40, 1991.

FNNPE. Loving them to death?: Sustainable tourism in Europe's Nature and National Parks, Federation of Nature and National Parks of Europe.

Fuller, Kathryn S. "Balancing Tourism and Conservation." *Focus,* World Wildlife Fund, p. 2, September/October 1993.

Fuller, Kathryn S. "Local People Play Critical Role in Protecting World's Forest Resources." *Focus,* World Wildlife Fund, p. 2, March/April 1993.

Garrod, Brian, and Alan Fyall. "Beyond the Rhetoric of Sustainable Tourism?" *Tourism Management,* Vol. 19, No. 3, pp. 199–212, 1998.

Goeldner, Charles R., Gin Hayden, and Carol Krismann. *Ecotourism Bibliography: An Information Source Guide.* Lexington, KY: National Tour Foundation, 1997.

Griffin, George. "Ecotourism: The Good and the Bad of It." *Florida Living,* pp. 30–31, April 1992.

Gunn, Clare A. "Rerefining the Tourism Product, the Environmental Experience." *WTO News,* Vol. 3, pp. 2–3, March 1992.

Hall, Colin Michael, and Margaret E. Johnston. *Polar Tourism: Tourism in the Arctic and Antarctic Regions.* New York: Wiley, 1995.

Harris, R., et al. *Sustainable Tourism: A Global Perspective.* London: Butterworth Heinemann, 1998.

Hawkes, S., and Peter Williams. *The Greening of Tourism: From Principles to Practice.* Burnaby, British Columbia, Canada: Center for Tourism Policy and Research, Simon Fraser University, 1993.

Hjalager, Anne-Mette. "Environmental Regulation of Tourism: Impact on Business Innovation." *Progress in Tourism and Hospitality Research,* Vol. 4, No. 1, pp. 17–30, March 1998.

Hughes, G. "The Cultural Construction of Sustainable Tourism." *Tourism Management,* Vol. 16, No. 1, pp. 49–59, 1995.

Hunter, C. J. "On the Need to Re-Conceptualise Sustainable Tourism Development." *Journal of Sustainable Tourism,* Vol. 3, No. 3, pp. 155, 1995.

Hunter, Colin, and Howard Green. *Tourism and the Environment: A Sustainable Relationship?* New York: Routledge, 1995.

Hunter, Colin. "Sustainable Tourism as an Adaptive Paradigm." *Annals of Tourism Research,* Vol. 24, No. 4, pp. 850–867, October 1997.

Kavallinis, Ioannis, and Abraham Pizam. "The Environmental Impacts of Tourism—Whose Responsibility Is It Anyway?" *Journal of Travel Research,* Vol. 33, No. 2, pp. 26–32, Fall 1994.

Lawrence, Thomas, B., Deborah Wickins, and Nelson Phillips. "Managing Legitimacy in Ecotourism." *Tourism Management,* Vol. 18, No. 5, pp. 307–316, 1997.

Lindberg, Kreg, and Donald E. Hawkins, eds. *Ecotourism: A Guide for Planners and Managers.* North Bennington, VT: The Ecotourism Society, 1993.

Mak, James, and James E. T. Moncur. "Sustainable Tourism Development: Managing Hawaii's 'Unique' Touristic Resource—Hanauma Bay." *Journal of Travel Research,* Vol. 33, No. 4, pp. 51–57, Spring 1995.

Malloy, David Cruise, and David A. Fennel. "Ecotourism and Ethics: Moral Development and Organizational Cultures." *Journal of Travel Research,* Vol. 36, No. 4, pp. 47–56, Spring 1998.

Mason, Peter. "Tourism Codes of Conduct in the Arctic and Sub-Arctic Region." *Journal of Sustainable Tourism,* Vol. 5, No. 2, pp. 151–165, 1997.

May, Vincent. "Tourism, Environment and Development Values, Sustainability and Stewardship." *Tourism Management,* Vol. 12, No. 2, pp. 112–118, June 1991.

McIntyre, G., et al. *Sustainable Tourism Development: Guide for Local Planners.* Madrid: World Tourism Organization, 1993.

McKercher, B. "The Unrecognized Threat to Tourism: Can Tourism Survive Sustainability?" *Tourism Management,* Vol. 14, No. 2, pp. 131–136, 1993.

Moore, S., and B. Carter. "Ecotourism in the 21st century." *Tourism Management,* Vol. 14, No. 2, pp. 123–130, 1993.

Moscardo, Gianna, Alastair M. Morrison, and Philip L. Pearce. "Specialist Accommodation and Ecologically-Sustainable Tourism." *Journal of Sustainable Tourism*, Vol. 4, No. 1, pp. 29–52, 1996.

Mowforth, M. and I. Munt. *Tourism and Sustainability: New Tourism in the Third World*. London: Routledge, 1998.

Nelson, J. G., R. Butler, and G. Wall. *Tourism and Sustainable Development: Monitoring, Planning, Managing*. Waterloo, Ontario, Canada: University of Waterloo, 1993.

Orams, M. B. "Towards a more desirable form of ecotourism." *Tourism Management*, Vol. 16, No. 1, pp. 3–8, 1995.

PATA. *Green Leaf*. Vancouver: Pacific Asia Travel Association, 1995.

Patterson, C. *The Business of Ecotourism: The Complete Guide for Nature and Culture-Based Tourism Operations*. Rhinelander, WI: Explorer's Guide Publishing, 1997.

Pigram, John J. "Best Practice Environmental Management and the Tourism Industry." *Progress in Tourism and Hospitality Research*, Vol. 2, No. 3 and 4, pp. 261–271, September/December 1996.

Poirier, Robert A. "Environmental Policy and Tourism in Tunisia." *Journal of Travel Research*, Vol. 35, No. 3, pp. 57–60, Winter 1997.

Priestley, G. K., J. A. Edwards, and H. Coccossis, eds. *Sustainable Tourism? European Experiences*. New York: Oxford University Press, 1996.

Prugh, T. *Natural Capital and Human Economic Survival*. Solomons, MD: ISEE Press, 1995.

Richez, G. "Sustaining Local Cultural Identity: Social Unrest and Tourism in Corsica." in *Sustainable Tourism? European Experiences*, New York: Oxford University Press, p. 176, 1996.

Ruschmann, Doris M. "Ecological Tourism in Brazil." *Tourism Management*, Vol. 13, No. 1, pp. 125–128, March 1992.

Sawhill, John. "Using Debt to Save the Rainforest." *Nature Conservancy*, Vol. 41, No. 1, p. 3, 1991.

Singh, Tej Vir. "The Development of Tourism in the Mountain Environment: The Problem of Sustainability." *Tourism Recreation Research*, Vol. 16, No. 2, pp. 3–12, 1991.

Sirakaya, Ercan, and Robert W. McLellan. "Modeling Tour Operators' Voluntary Compliance with Ecotourism Principles: A Behavioral Approach." *Journal of Travel Research*, Vol. 36, No. 3, pp. 42–55, Winter 1998.

Sirakaya, Ercan. "Attitudinal Compliance with Eco-

tourism Guidelines." *Annals of Tourism Research*, Vol. 24, No. 4, pp. 919–950, October 1997.

Sofield, Trevor. "Sustainable Ethnic Tourism in the South Pacific: Some Principles." *Journal of Tourism Studies*, Vol. 2, No. 1, pp. 56–72, 1991.

Stabler, M. J. *Tourism and Sustainability: Principles to Practise*. Oxon, UK: CAB International, 1997.

Stankovic, Stevan. "The Protection of Life Environment and Modern Tourism." *Tourist Review*, No. 2, pp. 2–4, April/June 1991.

TIAC. *Greening the Canadian Tourism Industry*. Ottawa, Ontario, Canada: Tourism Industry Association of Canada, 1995.

Tisdell, Clem. "Investment in Ecotourism: Assessing Its Economics." *Tourism Economics*, Vol. 1, No. 4, pp. 375–387, December 1995.

Todd, Susan E., and Peter W. Williams. "From White to Green: A Proposed Environmental Management System Framework for Ski Areas." *Journal of Sustainable Tourism*, Vol. 4, No. 3, pp. 147–173, 1996.

Travel & Tourism Environment and Development. Brussels: World Travel and Tourism Council, 1992.

UNEP. *Environmental Codes of Conduct for Tourism*. Paris: United National Environment Programme, 1995.

U.S. Travel Data Center. *Tourism and the Environment*. Washington, D.C.: Travel Industry Association of America, 1992.

van den Bergh, J. C. J. M. and J. van der Straaten. *Toward Sustainable Development: Concepts, Methods, and Policy*. Covelo, CA: Island Press, 1998.

Vasanthakaalam, Hilda. "Environmental Concern for Tourism Planning in India." *Indian Journal of Tourism and Management*, Vol. 1, No. 1, pp. 1–9, January/March 1992.

Wahab, S. and J. J. Pigram, eds. *Tourism, Development and Growth: The Challenge of Sustainability*. London, UK: Routledge, 1997.

Wheatcroft, Stephen. "Airlines, Tourism and the Environment." *Tourism Management*, Vol. 12, No. 2, pp. 119–124, June 1991.

Whelan, Denise. *Nature Tourism: Managing for the Environment*. Washington, D.C.: Island Press, 1991.

Wight, Pamela A. "Ecotourism: Ethics or Eco-sell?" *Journal of Travel Research*, Vol. 31, No. 3, pp. 3–9, Winter 1993.

Wight, Pamela A. "North American Ecotourists: Market Profile and Trip Characteristics." *Journal of Travel Research*, Vol. 34, No. 4, pp. 2–10, Spring 1996.

Wight, Pamela A. "North American Ecotourism Markets: Motivations, Preferences, and Destinations." *Journal of Travel Research,* Vol. 35, No. 1, pp. 3–10, Summer 1996.

Wight, Pamela A. "Ecotourism accommodation spectrum: does supply match the demand?" *Tourism Management,* Vol. 18, No. 4, pp. 209–220, 1997.

Woodley, S., et al., eds. *Ecological Integrity and the Management of Ecosystems.* Delray Beach, FL: St. Lucie Press, 1993.

WTO. *Tourism and Environmental Protection.* Madrid: World Tourism Organization, 1996.

WTTERC. *Travel & Tourism: World Travel & Tourism Environment Review.* Oxford, UK: World Travel & Tourism Environment Research Centre, 1993.

Zeiger, Jeffrey B., and Dan McDonald. "Ecotourism: Wave of the Future." *Parks and Recreation,* Vol. 32, No. 9, pp. 84–92, September 1997.

PART 5

ESSENTIALS OF TOURISM RESEARCH AND MARKETING

◄ *Children and adults are caught up in the excitement of this roller coaster ride. (Copyright © 1999 Busch Entertainment Corp. Reproduced by permission of Busch Gardens Williamsburg. All rights reserved.)*

TRAVEL AND TOURISM RESEARCH

- Recognize the role and scope of travel research.

- Learn the travel research process.

- Study secondary data and how it can be used.

- Understand the methods of collecting primary data.

- Know who does travel research.

◀ LEARNING OBJECTIVES

◀ *The information derived from travel and tourism research helps private firms and public agencies make informed decisions on complex tourism development issues. (Photo courtesy of the Huron–Clinton Metropolitan Authority, Michigan.)*

INTRODUCTION

Information is the basis for decisionmaking, and it is the task of travel research to gather and analyze data to help travel managers make decisions. Travel research is the systematic, impartial designing and conducting of investigations to solve travel problems. Examples of travel research are:

1. United Airlines investigating consumer attitudes and behaviors to enable the airline to better serve the flying public
2. Marriott Hotels and Resorts studying the leisure travel market
3. The Aspen Skiing Company conducting a market profile study to understand its customers
4. The U.S. Travel Data Center measuring the economic impact of travel in the United States

Although travel research does not *make* decisions, it does help travel decisionmakers operate more effectively. Managers can plan, operate, and control more efficiently when they have the facts. Thus research, which reduces the risk in **decisionmaking,** can have a great impact on the success or failure of a tourism enterprise.

ILLUSTRATIVE USES OF TRAVEL RESEARCH

Some of the **uses or functions** of travel research are as follows:

1. *To delineate significant problems.* The constant pressure of day-to-day business operations leaves the travel executive with little time to focus on problem areas that handicap operations. The isolation of causes and problems that are creating inefficiency is often one of the most important single contributions that travel research makes to management.
2. *To keep an organization or a business in touch with its markets.* Travel research identifies trends, interprets markets, and tracks changes in markets so that policies can be developed that are aimed in the right direction and are based on facts rather than on hunches or opinions. Research reduces the risk of unanticipated changes in markets. In a way, research is insurance against these changes to make sure that a business does not stick with a product until it becomes obsolete. Reading 18.1 is an example. It presents highlights of the Canadian Tourism Commissions' study of the *American Tourism Market to 2010.* The United States is Canada's most important tourism market.
3. *To reduce waste.* Research has always been effective in measuring methods of operation to eliminate those methods that are inefficient and to concentrate on those that are the most effective. Automation of travel makes this use even more important. The energy crisis led to research that has produced dramatic savings in aircraft fuel requirements.
4. *To develop new sources of profit.* Research can lead to the discovery of new markets, new products, and new uses for established products. Re-

search can show the lodging industry the types of rooms and the type of lodging facilities that should be offered to meet customers' needs.

5. *To aid in sales promotion.* Many times the results of research are interesting not only to the firm but also to the public and can be used in advertising and promotion. This is particularly true of consumer attitude research, as well as research where consumers are asked to rank products and services.

6. *To create goodwill.* Consumers react favorably to travel research; they feel that the company that is involved in research really cares about them and is trying to create a product or service that will meet their needs.

THE STATE OF THE ART

Travel research today runs from the primitive to the sophisticated—from simple fact gathering to complex, mathematical models. For those who really wish to dig into the subject, there are several references worth noting. The most important is *Travel, Tourism and Hospitality Research: A Handbook for Managers and Researchers,* published by John Wiley & Sons in 1994; the second is *Tourism Analysis,* published by Longman in 1995; and the third is the *Journal of Travel Research,* published by Sage Publications.

Measurement is a critical element in research activity, and the lack of standard or precise definitions has hampered the development of travel research. Without definitions, measurement cannot be taken and data cannot be generated and compared from study to study. Economic projections or analytical findings made by sophisticated models or pure intuition must be based on some kind of data. Without a quantitative record of past experiences, only individual, isolated studies making a limited contribution to the state of the art are possible. That is basically where we stand in the area of travel research at the present time. Giant strides are being made, improving travel research by adopting techniques developed by other disciplines and utilizing new and more sophisticated techniques; however, the existing body of literature largely consists of individual isolated studies utilizing different definitions that were set up only to solve the immediate problem at hand. Fortunately, some researchers are now using an approach termed "meta-analysis," in which an attempt is made to extract the common findings from a broad range of studies on a related topic.

THE TRAVEL RESEARCH PROCESS

The key to good travel research is to define the problem and work through it in a systematic procedural manner to a final solution. The purpose of this section is to describe briefly the basic procedures that will produce a good research result.

1. *Identify the problem.* First, the problem must be defined or identified. Then you are in a position to proceed in a systematic manner.

2. *Conduct a situation analysis.* In this step you gather and digest all the information available and pertinent to the problem. The purpose is to

One of the first steps in researching a tourism problem is to review and discuss the problem with a research firm representative. *(Photo courtesy of the Travel and Tourism Research Association.)*

become familiar with all the available information to make sure that you are not repeating someone else's work or that you have not overlooked information that will provide a ready solution to the problem. The situation analysis is an exhaustive search of all the data pertinent to the company, the product, the industry, the market, the competition, advertising, customers, suppliers, technology, the economy, the political climate, and similar matters. Knowledge of this background information will help you to sort out the likely causes of the problem and will lead to more efficient productive research. The organization will get the most from the research result when you understand the organization's internal environment and its goals, strategies, desires, resources, and constraints. In addition to a trip to the library, the Internet is an ideal new tool to use in conducting the situation analysis.

3. *Conduct an informal investigation.* After having gotten background information from available sources, you will talk informally with consumers, distributors, and key people in the industry to get an even better feel for the problem. During both the situation analysis and informal investigation, you should be developing hypotheses that can be tested. The establishment of hypotheses is one of the foundations of conducting research and is a valuable step in the problem-solving process. A hypothesis is a supposition, a tentative proposal, or a possible solution to a problem. In some ways it could be likened to a diagnosis. If your au-

tomobile quit running on the interstate, you might hypothesize that (1) you were out of gas or (2) the fuel pump had failed or (3) you had filter problems. An investigation would enable you to accept or reject these hypotheses.

4. *Develop a formal research design.* Once adequate background information has been developed and the problem has been defined against this background, it is time to develop the specific procedure or design for carrying out the total investigation or research project. This step is the heart of the research process. Here you have to develop the hypotheses that will be tested and determine the types and sources of data that are to be obtained. Are secondary sources available, or will it be necessary to conduct primary research? If primary research has to be conducted, then it is necessary to develop the sample, the questionnaires, or other data collection forms and any instruction sheets and coding methods and tabulation forms. Finally, it is necessary to conduct a pilot study to test all of the foregoing elements. The results are then written up in a detailed plan that serves as a guide that any knowledgeable researcher should be able to follow and conduct the research satisfactorily.

5. *Collect the data.* If the data are available from secondary sources, then collecting the data becomes primarily desk research. However, if primary data are collected, this step involves actual fieldwork in conducting survey research, observational research, or experimental research. The success of data gathering depends on the quality of field supervision, the caliber of the interviewers or field investigators, and the training of investigators.

6. *Tabulate and analyze.* Once the data have been collected, they must be coded, tabulated, and analyzed. Both this step and the previous one must be done with great care; it is possible for a multitude of errors to creep into the research process if collection, tabulation, and analysis are not done properly. For example, if one is going to use the survey method, then interviewers must be properly selected, trained, and supervised. Obviously, if instead of following the carefully laid out sample the interviewers simply fill out questionnaires themselves, the data will not be useful. In today's environment, it is likely that tabulation will take place on the computer. A number of excellent packages are available for this purpose. One of the most used is SPSS, the Statistical Package for the Social Sciences.

7. *Interpret.* Tabulation results in stacks of computer printout, with a series of statistical conclusions. These data must now be interpreted in terms of the best action or policy for the firm or organization to follow—a series of specific recommendations of action. This reduction of the interpretation to recommendations is one of the most difficult tasks in the research process.

8. *Write the report.* Presentation of the results of the research is extremely important. Unless the data are written up in a manner that will en-

courage management to read them and act upon them, all of the labor in the research process is lost. Consequently, emphasis should be put on this step in the research process to produce a report that will be clearly understood with recommendations that will be accepted.

9. *Follow up.* Follow up means precisely that. A study sitting on the shelf gathering dust accomplishes nothing. While many people will consider the researcher's task to be done once the final report or presentation has been made, the work is not completed until the results of the survey are put into action. Research is an investment, and an ultimate test of the value of any research is the extent to which its recommendations are actually implemented and results achieved. It is the task of the researcher to follow up to make the previous investment of time and money worthwhile.

SOURCES OF INFORMATION

Primary data, secondary data, or both may be used in a research investigation. Primary data are original data gathered for the specific purpose of solving the travel re-

A library is a good source of secondary data for a situational analysis. Gin Hayden, Project Director of the Travel Reference Center, University of Colorado, is in charge of maintaining the largest collection of travel research studies in the United States. *(Photo courtesy of the Business Research Division, University of Colorado at Boulder.)*

search problem that confronts you. In contrast, secondary data have already been collected for some other purpose and are available for use by simply visiting the library or other such repositories of secondary data. When researchers conduct a survey of cruise passengers to determine their attitudes and opinions, they are collecting primary data. When they get information from the Bureau of Census on travel agents, they are using a secondary source.

The situation analysis step of the travel research process is emphasized because it focuses on the use of secondary sources; however, their use is not confined to this step. One of the biggest mistakes in travel research is to rush out and collect primary data without exhausting secondary source information. Only later do you discover that you have duplicated previous research when existing sources could have provided information to solve your problem for a fraction of the cost. Only after exhausting secondary sources and finding that you still lack sufficient data to solve your problem should you turn to primary sources.

Secondary Data

In the last 10 years there has been a virtual explosion of information related to tourism, travel, recreation, and leisure. A competent researcher must be well acquainted with these sources and how to find them. The Internet is a source that contains a wealth of information.

If you are fortunate enough to find secondary sources of information, you can save yourself a great deal of time and money. Low cost is clearly the greatest advantage of secondary data. When **secondary data** sources are available, it is not necessary to construct and print questionnaires, hire interviewers, pay transportation costs, pay coders, pay data inputers, and pay programmers; it is easy to see the cost advantage of utilizing secondary data. Secondary data can also be collected much more quickly than can primary data. With an original research project, it typically takes a minimum of 60 to 90 days or more to collect data; secondary data could be collected in a library within a few days.

Secondary data are not without disadvantages; for example, many times the information does not fit the problem for which you need information. Another problem is timeliness—many secondary sources become outdated. For example, the Census of Population and Housing is conducted every 10 years; as we get to the end of that time period, the data are not very useful.

Evaluating Secondary Data

While it is not expected that everyone will be a research expert, everyone should be able to evaluate or appraise secondary data. Any study, no matter how interesting, must be subjected to evaluation: "Is it a valid study? Can I use the results to make decisions?" On such occasions the researcher must evaluate the secondary data and determine whether they are usable.

The following criteria may be used to appraise the value of information obtained from secondary sources:

1. *The organizations supplying the data.* What amount of time went into the study? Who conducted the study? What experience did the personnel

have? What was the financial capacity of the company? What was the cost of the study? An experienced research firm will put the proper time and effort into a study to yield results, whereas a novice or inexperienced organization may not.

2. *The authority under which the data are gathered.* For example, data collected by the IRS are likely to be much better than data collected by a business firm. Data that are required by law, such as census data, are much more dependable than is information from other sources.

3. *Freedom from bias.* One should always look at the nature of the organization furnishing the data. Would you expect a study sponsored by airlines to praise the bus industry for providing the lowest-cost transportation on a per mile basis in the United States?

4. *The extent to which the rules of sampling have been rigidly upheld.* What is the adequacy of the sample? Adequacy is frequently difficult to evaluate because deficiencies in the sampling process can be hidden. One indication of adequacy is the sponsor's willingness to talk about the sample. Will the sponsor release sampling details? Are the procedures well-known, acceptable methods?

5. *The nature of the unit in which the data are expressed.* Here even simple concepts are difficult to define. In defining the term "house," how do you handle such things as duplexes, triplexes, mobile homes, and apartment houses? Make sure that good operational definitions have been used throughout the research so there will be no problems in understanding it. Research results that are full of terms such as "occasionally" and "frequently" are not likely to be useful; these terms have different meanings to different people.

6. *The accuracy of the data.* The need here is to examine the data carefully for any inconsistencies and inquire into the way in which the data were acquired, edited, and tabulated. If at all possible, check the data against known data from other sources that are accurate. For example, check the demographics in a study against known census data.

7. *Pertinency to the problem.* You must be concerned with fit. You may have a very good study; but if it does not pertain to the problem at hand, it is not worth anything to you. The relevance of secondary data pertaining to the problem must stand up; otherwise, the study cannot be used.

8. *Careful work.* Throughout your evaluation, always look for evidence of careful work. Are tables constructed properly? Do all totals add up to the right figures or 100 percent? Are conclusions supported by the data? Is there any evidence of conflicting data? Is the information presented in a well-organized, systematic manner?

Primary Data

When it is not possible to get the information you need from secondary sources, it is necessary to turn to primary sources—original, firsthand sources of information. If you need information on travelers' attitudes, you would then go to that population and sample it. As stated earlier, you should turn to collecting **primary data** only after exhausting all reasonable secondary sources of information.

Once you have determined that you are going to collect primary data, then you must choose what method of gathering primary data you are going to use. The most widely used means of collecting primary information is the survey method. Other methods are the observational method and the experimental method. It is not uncommon to find one or more of these methods used in gathering data. These basic methods are discussed in the next section.

BASIC RESEARCH METHODS

Focus Groups

It has been said the **focus group** may be the worst form of market research—except for all others. Because of this reality, focus-group interviewing is a popular form of market research in tourism. Their primary purpose is exploratory: either to establish the parameters for subsequent survey research or to delve into the motivations and behaviors of travelers.

A focus group is a form of qualitative research that brings together a small number of individuals (usually some 8 to 12) for an in-depth discussion regarding the topic of interest to the client. Typical topics include the most desirable/least desirable characteristics of a planned attraction or service, reaction to a planned advertising theme or program, or the probable public reaction to developments in an environmentally sensitive region.

Focus-group participants are chosen to represent a cross section of the population having a likely interest or stake in the area to be studied. However, because they are not selected scientifically (usually availability and willingness to participate play a major role in focus-group composition), great care must be taken in extrapolating the findings of focus-group sessions to the general population. In addition, because the session facilitator can significantly influence the nature of the discussion, it is essential that they be well trained and very familiar with the underlying goals of the focus group.

Despite these cautions and concerns, focus-group interviewing remains one of the most insightful and valuable ways of gaining a true understanding of the factors affecting complex managerial situations and decisions.

The Survey Method

If we look at the methods of collecting travel research data, we will find that the **survey method** is the most frequently used. The survey method, also frequently referred to as the questionnaire technique, gathers information by asking questions. The survey method includes factual surveys, opinion surveys, or interpretative surveys, all of which can be conducted by personal interviews, mail, or telephone techniques.

Factual Surveys

A quick look at the types of surveys will reveal that factual surveys are by far the most beneficial. "In what recreational activities did you participate last week?" is a question

An experienced tourism research firm can conduct surveys, observations, or experiments to accomplish the goals of the research project. *(Photo courtesy of the Travel and Tourism Research Association.)*

for which the respondent should be able to give accurate information. While excellent results are usually achieved with factual surveys, all findings are still subject to certain errors, such as errors of memory and ability to generalize or the desire to make a good impression. Nonetheless, factual surveys tend to produce excellent results.

Opinion Surveys

In these surveys, the respondent is asked to express an opinion or make an evaluation or appraisal. For example, a respondent could be asked whether tour package A or B was the most attractive or which travel ad is the best. This kind of opinion information can be invaluable. In studies of a ski resort conducted by the University of Colorado, vacationer respondents were asked to rate the resort's employees' performance as excellent, good, average, or needs improvement. The ratings allowed resort management to take action where necessary. Opinion surveys tend to produce excellent results if they are properly constructed.

Interpretive Surveys

On interpretive studies the respondent acts as an interpreter as well as a reporter. Subjects are asked why they chose a certain course of action—why they participated in a particular recreation activity the previous week (as well as what activity), why they flew on a particular airline, why they chose a particular vacation destination, why they chose a particular lodging establishment.

While respondents can reply accurately to "what" questions, they often have difficulty replying to "why" questions. Therefore, while interpretive research may give you a feel for consumer behavior, the results tend to be limited. It is much better to utilize motivational and psychological research techniques, which are better suited for obtaining this information.

In summary, try to get factual or opinion data via the survey method and utilize in-depth interviewing or psychological research techniques to get "reason why" data.

It was mentioned earlier that surveys can be conducted by personal interviews, telephone, or mail. The purpose of a survey is to gather data by interviewing a limited number of people (sample) who represent a larger group. Reviewing the basic survey methods, one finds the following advantages and disadvantages.

Personal Interviews

These are much more flexible than either mail or telephone surveys because the interviewer can adapt to the situation and the respondent. The interviewer can alter questions to make sure that the respondent understands them or probe if the respondent does not respond with a satisfactory answer. Typically, one can obtain much more information by personal interview than by telephone or mail surveys, which by necessity must be relatively short. Personal interviewers can observe the situation as well as ask questions. For example, an interviewer in a home can record data on the person's socioeconomic status, which would not be possible without this observation. The personal interview method permits the best sample control of all the survey techniques.

A major limitation of the personal interview method is its relatively high cost. It tends to be the most expensive of the three survey methods. It also takes a considerable amount of time to conduct, and there is always the possibility of personal interviewer bias. There is also the problem of working couples today, which means it is difficult to find respondents at home.

Telephone Surveys

Respondents are interviewed over the telephone with this approach. Telephone surveys are usually conducted much more rapidly and at less cost than are personal interviews. The shortcomings of telephone surveys are that they are less flexible than personal interviews, and of necessity they are brief. While a further limitation of phone surveys is that not everyone has a telephone, those with telephones tend to have the market potential to travel or buy tourism products. Consequently, this limitation is not very serious for travel research. Speed and low cost tend to be the primary advantages of telephone interviews. Computer-assisted telephone interviewing using random dialing is growing at a rapid pace.

This involves a survey questionnaire entered into computer memory. The interviewer reads the questions from the computer screen and records the respondent's answers into computer memory by using a keyboard and simply touching a sensitive screen. Because the data are recorded immediately, these systems tend to be faster and less expensive than traditional methods.

Although expensive, personal interviews are one of the best methods of obtaining information. Creating a successful tourism product depends on accurately identifying best markets. Research firms have the capability to do this. *(Photo courtesy of the Travel and Tourism Research Association.)*

Mail Surveys

Mail surveys have the potential of being the lowest-cost method of research. As would be expected, mail surveys involve mailing the questionnaire to carefully selected sample respondents and requesting them to return the completed questionnaires (see Figure 18.1). This survey approach has a great advantage when large geographical areas must be covered and when it would be difficult to reach respondents. Other advantages of this approach are that personal interview bias is absent and the respondent can fill out the questionnaire at his or her convenience.

The greatest problem in conducting a mail survey is having a good list and getting an adequate response. If a large percentage of the target population fails to respond, you will have to question whether those who did not respond are different from those who have replied and whether this introduces bias. Length is another consideration in mail questionnaires. While they can be longer than telephone surveys, they still must be reasonably short. Another limitation of mail surveys is that questions must be worded carefully and simply so that respondents will not be confused. While questions may be very clear to the person who wrote them, they can be very unclear to the respondent.

Electronic Devices

A relatively new way of conducting survey research is the use of computer-type electronic devices to ask the consumer questions and immediately record and tabulate the results. This equipment can be placed in a hotel lobby, mall, or other high-traffic location and attract consumers to record responses to questions. Use of these machines

CAREY AMERICAN LIMOUSINE Colorado Springs Shuttle Service

Please take a moment to respond to the following questions. This information will be used to evaluate areas of service to afford you quality service for your next trip. Thank you.

1. Was the vehicle on time? Yes _____ No _____ (Delay time: _____ Reason given   )
2. What was the condition of the equipment? Clean _____ Average _____ Unkempt _____
3. Was your driver courteous? Yes _____ No _____
4. How was your service: Excellent _____ Fair _____ Poor _____ (Why?   )
5. Was it easy to make your reservation? Yes _____ No _____ (Why:)
6. Where did you find out about our company? Travel agent _____ Advertisement _____ Referred by:
7. Was the scheduled time convenient for you? Very _____ Acceptable _____ Inconvenient
8. Were you traveling on Business _____ Pleasure _____
9. Will you recommend our service to others? Yes _____ (Name & Address   ) No _____
Comments:

Name: If you represent a company or travel agency, please include that
Address: information:
City: _____ State: _____ Zip: _____
COLORADO TRANSPORTATION GROUP   Telephone (   )

FIGURE 18.1 **A sample mail questionnaire.**

is a low-cost method of getting consumer information because the questions are self-administered, saving the cost of interviewers, and the results are tabulated automatically. A disadvantage is that children, who like to play with such machines, may distort the results. The prediction that such devices will become increasingly popular in the future has yet to materialize.

Observational Method

The **observational method** relies upon the direct observation of physical phenomena in the gathering of data. Observing some action of the respondent is obviously much more objective and accurate than is utilizing the survey method. Under the observational method, information can be gathered by either personal or mechanical observation. Mechanical recorders on highways count the number of cars that pass and the time that they pass. Automatic counters at attractions observe and count the number of visitors.

Advantages of the observational method are that it tends to be accurate and it can record consumer behavior. It also reduces interviewer bias. Disadvantages are that it is much more costly than the survey method and it is not possible to employ in many cases. Finally, the observational method shows what people are doing but does not tell you why they are doing it. It cannot delve into motives, attitudes, or opinions. If the "why" is important, this would not be a good method to use.

Experimental Method

This method of gathering primary data involves setting up a test, a model, or an experiment to simulate the real world. The essentials of the **experimental method** are the measurement of variations within one or more activities while all other conditions and variables are being controlled. The experimental method is very hard to use in tourism research because of the difficulty of holding variables constant. There is no physical laboratory in which tourism researchers can work. However, it is possible for resort areas to run advertising experiments or pricing experiments or to develop simulation models to aid in decisionmaking. Such test marketing is being conducted successfully; and as time passes, we will see the experimental method being used more and more.

WHO DOES TRAVEL RESEARCH?

Many organizations are involved in the use and conduct of travel research. The types of firms and organizations that engage in travel research include government, educational institutions, consultants, trade associations, advertising agencies, media, hotels and motels, airlines and other carriers, attractions, and food service organizations.

Government

The federal government has been a major producer of travel research over the years. Tourism Industries, U.S. Department of Commerce conducts studies on international visitors, focusing on both marketing information and economic impact. State and local governments also employ travel research to assist in making marketing and public policy decisions. Examples are studies of highway users, the value of fishing and hunting, the economic impact of tourism in various geographic areas, inventories of tourism facilities and services, tourism planning procedures, and visitor characteristics studies. In other countries, research inaugurated by the official tourism organization of a state or country often has very significant ramifications for tourism development and promotion. Research done in Mexico, England, Spain, France, Poland, and Croatia has been outstanding.

Educational Institutions

Universities conduct many travel research studies. The chief advantage is that the studies are usually conducted without bias by trained professionals. Many of the studies have contributed greatly to the improvement of travel research methods. Institutions of higher learning, particularly universities with departments of hotel and restaurant management, hospitality management, and tourism, have a vital need for such information. Such educational organizations are concerned with the teaching of tourism or related subjects and need the most current available research findings to do an effective teaching job. Research is also needed by such academic departments as geography, fisheries and wildlife, resource development, park and recreation resources, and forestry. All these departments have an interest in the effect on the environment because of the use of the natural landscape for recreation and tourism.

Many departments of universities are qualified to accomplish pure research or applied research in tourism. Bureaus of business and economic research are often active in this field. An example is the research accomplished by the Business Research Division of the University of Colorado at Boulder. This organization has published many tourism research findings, bibliographies, and ski industry studies. Departments of universities that can be helpful include psychology, sociology, economics, engineering, landscape architecture and urban planning, management, hotel and restaurant administration, theater, home economics, human ecology, forestry, botany, zoology, history, geography, and anthropology.

Consultants

Numerous organizations specialize in conducting travel research on a fee basis for airlines, hotels, restaurants, ski areas, travel agents, resorts, and others. Consultants offer the service of giving advice in the planning, design, interpretation, and application of travel research. They will also provide the service of conducting all or a part of a field investigation for their clients.

The primary advantage of consultants or consulting firms is that they are well-trained, experienced specialists who have gained their experience by making stud-

D. K. Shifflet Associates Ltd. is one of the many firms available to conduct travel and tourism research studies. They have been providing research studies to clients for over 16 years. *(Photo courtesy of the Travel and Tourism Research Association.)*

ies for many different clients. They also provide an objective outsider's point of view, and they have adequate facilities to undertake almost any job. The disadvantage of consultants is that of any outsider—the lack of intimate knowledge of the internal problems of the client's business; however, management can provide this ingredient. Many travel firms with their own research departments find it advantageous to use consultants or a combination of their own internal staff and consultants.

There are many well-known firms specializing in travel research. A few of these are Opinion Research Corporation, Davidson–Peterson Associates, Economic Research Associates, the Gallup organization, Arthur D. Little, Midwest Research Institute, Plog Research, Robinson, Yesawich & Pepperdine, SDR, Inc., Angus Reid Group, Leisure Trends, D. K. Shifflet & Associates, Longwoods International, Menlo Consulting Group, National Demographics & Lifestyles, Somerset R. Waters, and Simmons Market Research Bureau.

An example of a syndicated service is one offered by the Menlo Consulting Group in Palo Alto, California called TravelStyles, which provides research on the U.S. market for international travel. It is a source of information on travel trends, market segments, and the changing preferences of Americans who travel outside the country.

Trade Associations

Extensive travel research is conducted by trade associations. Appendix A lists trade associations that are a source of travel information. The trade association often provides facilities for carrying on a continuous research service for its members, particularly in the area of industry statistics. Many associations have excellent Internet sites and make their data available to the public.

Advertising Agencies

Today, advertising agencies typically maintain extensive research departments for both their own and their clients' needs. The agency must have basic facts if it is to develop an effective advertising campaign for its travel client in today's rapidly changing world. Advertising agencies that have been leaders in travel research are Ogilvy and Mather Worldwide; J. Walter Thompson; BBDO Worldwide; Foote, Cone and Belding; Leo Burnett; and DDB Needham Worldwide.

Media

Trade journals often conduct outstanding tourism research. *Travel Weekly*'s comprehensive study of the travel agency market is a classic example of good media research. The 1998 edition represents the publication's fourteenth in-depth probe of the travel agency industry. Consumer magazines have also been active producers of travel research. *Time, U.S. News and World Report, Newsweek, Better Homes and Gardens, National Geographic, New Yorker, Sunset, Southern Living, Sports Illustrated*, and *Travel/Holiday* are all known for their travel research.

Hotels and Motels

Hotels and motels constantly use current research findings concerning their markets, trends in transportation, new construction materials, management methods, use of electronic data processing, human relations techniques, employee management, advertising, food and beverage supplies and services, and myriad other related information.

Airlines and Other Carriers

This group offers services designed for the business and vacation traveler. Because of their needs and the importance of research to their operations, airlines and other carriers will usually have their own market research departments to conduct ongoing studies of their customers and the market. They are also frequent employers of outside consultants.

Attractions

The most ambitious private attractions in the country are the major theme parks, and research has played a major role in the success of these enterprises. That research has run the gamut from feasibility studies to management research. Walt Disney's thinking still dominates the industry. The Disney formula of immaculate grounds, clean and attractive personnel, high-quality shops, tidy rest rooms, and clean restaurants are still the consumers' preferences today. Research shows that if attractions are not clean, they are not likely to be successful.

Food Service

Much of the pioneering work in the use of research by restaurants has been done by franchises and chains because what will work in one location will typically work in others, resulting in a large payoff from funds invested in research. All travel firms, whether they are restaurants, airlines, hotels, or other hospitality enterprises, need to be in touch with their markets and find new and better ways of marketing to sell seats, increase load factors, and achieve favorable occupancy ratios.

THE U.S. TRAVEL DATA CENTER AND THE TRAVEL AND TOURISM RESEARCH ASSOCIATION

Two unique organizations serve the travel research area: the **U.S. Travel Data Center** (USTDC) and the **Travel and Tourism Research Association** (TTRA). Following is a brief description of the operations of these organizations.

The U.S. Travel Data Center is the research arm of the Travel Industry Association of America (TIA) that devotes its resources to measuring the economic impact of travel and monitoring changes in travel markets. The Data Center has become a recognized source for current data used by business and government to develop tourism

Plog Research is well known for their research in the travel and leisure fields and have been strong supporters of the *Journal of Travel Research*. *(Photo courtesy of the Travel and Tourism Research Association.)*

policies and marketing strategy. Market and economic research provided by the Data Center is utilized by all major sectors of the travel industry.

The objectives of the Data Center are to (1) develop and encourage standard, sound travel research terminology and techniques, (2) develop and encourage consistent estimates of travel activity over time and geographic areas, (3) monitor trends in travel activity and the travel industry over time, (4) measure the economic impact of travel over time and on geographic areas, (5) evaluate the impact of major government programs affecting travel and the travel industry, (6) monitor, evaluate, and help develop techniques to forecast travel supply and demand, and (7) develop techniques to measure the cost and the benefits of travel in the United States.

The Data Center carries on an active research and publications program. The majority of its publications are available for purchase by writing TIA. For more information on TIA's research, visit their web site at **http://www.tia.org.**

The Travel and Tourism Research Association is an international organization of travel research and marketing professionals devoted to improving the quality, value, scope, and acceptability of travel research and marketing information. The association is the world's largest travel research organization, and its members represent all aspects of the travel industry, including airlines, hotels, attractions, transportation companies, media, advertising agencies, government, travel agencies, consulting firms, universities, students, and so on.

TTRA's mission is to be the global leader in advocating standards and promoting the application of high-quality travel and tourism research, planning, management, and marketing information, with the following specific objectives:

- To serve as an international forum for the exchange of ideas and information among travel and tourism researchers, marketers, planners, and managers

- To encourage the professional development of travel and tourism researchers, marketers, planners, and managers

- To facilitate global cooperation between producers and users of travel and tourism research

- To promote and disseminate high-quality, credible, and effective research to the travel and tourism industry

- To foster the development of travel and tourism research and related curricula in institutes of higher education

- To advocate the effective use of research in the decisionmaking process of professionals in the travel and tourism industry

TTRA has chapters in Europe, Canada, the central states, Florida, Texas, the mountain states, the western states, the Southeast, Hawaii, the south central states, and Washington, D.C. TTRA contributes to the publication of the *Journal of Travel Research,* the TTRA newsletter, annual conference proceedings, and other special publications. TTRA has an extensive awards program that recognizes excellence and encourages professional development of researchers, marketers, planners, and students involved in the travel and tourism industry. The organization helped establish the Travel Reference Center located at the Business Research Division, University of Colorado, Boulder, Colorado 80309. This service was established to assist the travel industry in finding information sources and solving business problems. Those wishing further information on TTRA should visit the association's web site at **http://www.ttra.com.**

SUMMARY

Travel research provides the information base for effective decisionmaking by tourism managers. Availability of adequate facts allows managers to plan, operate, and control more efficiently and decreases risk in the decisionmaking process.

Useful travel research depends on precise identification of the problem; a thorough situation analysis supplemented by an informal investigation of the problem; careful research design; and meticulous collection, tabulation, and analysis of the data. The researcher must also present a readable written report with appropriate recommendations for action and then follow up to ensure that the recommendations are actually implemented so that results can be achieved.

The research itself may use secondary (preexisting) data or require collection of primary data (original research). Primary data may be gathered by survey—personal interview, mail, or telephone surveys—or by the observational and experimental methods. Numerous organizations and agencies use and conduct travel research. Two special professional organizations serve the field: the U.S. Travel Data Center, the research arm of TIA, and the Travel and Tourism Research Association.

ABOUT THE READINGS

The first reading reports the highlights of the study, The American Tourism Market Evolution to 2010 and presents data on the rich U.S. tourism market from now to 2010 and beyond. It was prepared by the Canadian Tourism Commission to assist Canadian tourism operators.

The second reading presents the results of an actual research study and the different reactions to it by the client, Resorts Ontario. The need for dialogue between researchers and users is stressed. The outcome demonstrates that when meaningful discussion takes place, analysis of data can provide good usable information for management decisions.

READING 18.1

THE AMERICAN TOURISM MARKET: EVOLUTION TO 2010: IT'S COMING FASTER THAN YOU THINK

Source: Canadian Tourism Commission.

CTC market researchers have looked at the future and like what they see. The growth markets of the next millennium are the middle-aged and the mature. A new report examines the rich opportunities in the U.S. tourism market from now to 2010 and beyond. This could be the best thing to ever happen to astute Canadian tourism operators.

Baby-Boomers are aging and heading from middle-age to retirement. Economically and demographically they are the most influential market segment in the United States. In their retirement years they will have the free time and financial independence to enjoy travel like never before. In theory, Canada is an ideal destination for this generation—it's a destination whose time has come.

It won't be a cakewalk. But the Canadian tourism industry, through concerted strategic marketing, can rise to the challenge and win. Focus, commitment, and most of all, determination are key. The potential rewards in the U.S. tourism market outweigh the risk.

The U.S. market is dynamic. The population is shifting. Growth is taking place in southern states. States like Florida, Texas and California are booming as job-seekers and retirees flock to the south and southwest. States in the north and northeast—Canada's traditional markets—are experiencing slow growth. It's time for the Canadian tourism industry to look further afield.

International competition in the U.S. market is stiff and increasing with new products coming on stream. The U.S. itself, with its wealth of travel destinations, is Canada's biggest competition. And lack of awareness remains a drag on Canada's performance in the U.S. market. The Canadian tourism industry can rise to the challenge by targeting favourably predisposed market segments and promoting Canada's competitive advantage.

The aging of the Baby-Boom generation presents tremendous opportunities. But the Canadian tourism industry's success depends on how well its stakeholders merge into a strong partnership—one that can understand the market and adopt to change.

Highlights of the Report

The report bases its conclusions on statistics and research from a variety of sources including the U.S. Bureau of the Census, American Demographics Consumer Trends, and Statistics Canada.

A prosperous tourism market requires a strong economy.

The U.S. economy has been booming for seven years. The U.S. and other G7 countries are interested in restoring confidence to the Asian economies. In the U.S. the long-term outlook for the GDP is sustained growth at the rate of 2.0–2.3%.

As the U.S. economy grows, so does consumer confidence and disposable income.

Life stage and earning power have a tremendous influence on customer demand for a wide range of goods and services, including leisure travel.

The entire Baby-Boom generation, born between

1946 and 1964, numbers about seventy-eight million. With each passing year, another four million Baby-Boomers turn 50 and enter a significant new stage of life.

At every stage of life the Baby-Boom generation has transformed the market and fuelled the economy. Consider how this generation created a demand for new maternity hospitals, schools and universities, housing, and consumer goods. The same will be true as the Baby-Boomers reach retirement: they will exert a powerful demand for travel experiences tailored to their needs and wants.

Now in middle-age, Baby-Boomers are highly educated, health-conscious, and at the height of their earning power. This is the generation that made two-income families a mainstream family unit. A significant number are independent women of means. Added to their own incomes and retirement pensions, Baby-Boomers will inherit $10.4 trillion from their parents' generation.

Throughout their lives Baby-Boomers have valued education, health and fitness, youth, individuality, and fun. During their mature years these basic values will remain.

But aging inevitably creates changes. In their retirement, Baby-Boomers are likely to expect higher levels of comfort and service when they travel. The Canadian industry will need to focus on improved and consistent service, staff training, and accommodations that are accessible to mature people with a variety of physical needs.

Even attractions will have to transform themselves to serve an aging market. Physically fit and healthy Baby-Boomers will continue to enjoy the thrill of downhill skiing, whitewater rafting, and wildlife watching. But creative resorts may want to offer a variety of activities such as workshops, gourmet cooking classes, and lectures. The demand for luxuries such as health spas will increase. And at the end of the day, it may be that parties with live rock music and restaurant menus featuring hamburgers, hotdogs, and fries are out, while jazz combos and gourmet menus are in.

To increase awareness in the U.S. market, Canada will need to differentiate its tourism products from what is available in the United States. This is a great challenge.

The best research says that Canada does not need to remake or reinvent itself to appeal to the American market. Canada's best virtues—our unspoiled wilder-

ness and great outdoors, our safe, clean and sophisticated cities, and our authentic heritage and cultural attractions—are our most distinctive and best-known qualities. After all, Canada is the country that exports elks and wolves to the United States.

To borrow a phrase from the environmental movement, sustainable development is what Canadian tourism should be planning for. While the United States sees its wilderness areas shrinking, Canada enjoys unspoiled natural areas in every region, not only in remote areas. Even major cities are an easy striking distance from pristine wilderness.

There are no neon signs lighting the Cabot Trail. Even busy destinations like the Niagara Region and the Rockies have a quality that culture can never duplicate: *authenticity*. Canadian destinations are real, natural, unspoiled, safe, uncrowded. These are qualities that give Canada a competitive advantage.

The Canadian industry needs to recognize the growing southern market because that is where the most growth will occur. The challenge is enormous because awareness of Canada is low in the southern U.S. Americans who move south to look for jobs or to retire will assist our effort by taking along their own higher awareness of Canada.

New technologies are changing the business of travel and tourism. The use of the Internet and the World Wide Web to plan and book travel is increasing in the U.S. market and is expected to grow exponentially. Baby-Boomers are enthusiastic users of these technologies.

According to a recent survey, in 1996, 3.1 million Internet users made travel reservations or plans over the Net. In 1997 6.3 million Net users made reservations and 13.4 million made plans. This is over 5 times the 1996 volume of travel related Internet use.

The increased use of the Internet could prove damaging to the retail travel industry. But while the Internet is a threat to business, it may also hold the key to new prosperity. Travel agencies need to figure out how they can participate in technological change and reap the rewards.

In the fiercely busy U.S. marketplace, Canada's real competition comes from the United States itself. Only a small fraction of U.S. travellers venture outside their borders. With its wealth of travel destinations and aggressive marketing, the United States manages to keep the overwhelming majority of travellers at home.

Lack of awareness of Canada is a persistent problem. If Canada spreads itself too thin and dilutes the marketing effort, the situation is unlikely to improve. But if Canada can maintain its presence in selected markets, chances are much better that awareness will increase. The Challenge is to choose markets where Canada has the best chances of making a difference.

Marketing and advertising will increase in the 21st century. That means the American marketplace, already competitive and noisy, will get more congested. The trick to making advertising more effective is not simply to advertise more, but to advertise better. Advertising will continue to be important in creating awareness, generating interest and motivating that first purchase, but it must be focused.

As the Market becomes more fragmented, marketers will need to focus on their best customers, instead of the *Mass* Market. Direct marketing and relationship marketing will become more sophisticated.

Three different, yet complementary, approaches to market segmentation may help marketers tailor their advertising and marketing efforts. Demographic segmentation looks at factors such as market size, age, household composition, and income. This approach identifies and describes the Baby-Boom generation as a significant growth market with economic clout.

Psychographic segmentation considers consumers' attitudes and values. Using this approach, research indicates that Americans who visit Canada have a unique set of values: they are more independent, more likely to take risks, more adventurous.

A newer approach considers *Media Literacy* as an insight to market segmentation. Media Literacy categorizes consumers into groups according to their media habits. Education and income influence media usage.

So What Will the American Tourism Market Look Like in 2010?

There is no doubt that it will be an older market where the middle-aged and mature travellers dominate. In 2010 nearly one-third of the entire U.S. population will be 50 or older. Given the favourable economic outlook, doing a considerable amount of leisure travelling.

But predictions about the future are risky. Who will win and who will lose in the brave new world of tourism in the year 2010 is not certain.

To succeed in the tourism market of 2010, operators will have to know their market and know their consumers in order to offer them distinctive products and travel experiences. High-quality service, aided by technology, and advertising will be based on sound research.

To order your copy of the full report, please contact:

CTC Distribution Centre
2574 Sheffied Road
Ottawa, Ont K1B 3V6
Canada
Attn: Debbie April

Tel: (613) 744-3786
Fax: (613) 744-8894
E-Mail: boyd@magi.com

READING 18.2

USING TOURISM RESEARCH

by Gordon D. Taylor, Judy Rogers, and Bruce Stanton
Reprinted from the *Journal of Travel Research*, Vol. 34, No. 4, Spring 1994 pp. 9–12, copyright © 1994 by Sage Publications. Reprinted by permission of Sage Publications.

The amount of research that has been developed over the years by a variety of tourism agencies has grown consistently. What has not grown has been the use of this research by the many tourism businesses which have need for the information and which are often cited by public agencies as one of the reasons for doing the research in the first place. At the TTRA Canada annual conference in Regina in October 1992, representatives of the tourism industry stated very clearly that a major gap still exists between the users and the producers of research. Representatives were equally emphatic that there is a real need to eliminate that gap. The problem that the word "gap" exemplifies is not new—it has been discussed many times in the past. It is clear that the tourism industry is not getting the most mileage possible for every research dollar spent. In order to begin to close the gap, it is equally clear that there needs to be a great deal of cooperation between researchers and users.

The impetus provided by the Regina conference led the Canada chapter to approach the Tourism Industry Association of Canada and offer to develop a workshop for their annual conference in February 1993. The offer was accepted and a case study approach was decided upon. An actual research study and the use made of the results by one of the sponsoring operators was selected. What is more important is how the process developed that allowed the operator to make critical business decisions from the research.

The Research

The research was conducted for Resorts Ontario in the early part of 1992. Resorts Ontario is a tourism sector of approximately 560 properties across the province. It consists of small, owner-operated establishments, nonunion and vigorously independent. It was a group in search of answers—answers that would give them some comfort about their futures. Where were the opportunities for growth? What changes needed to be made to make their products and marketing successful? The need for research was motivated by slumping business levels in 1991 and 1992, an oversupply of resort rooms brought on by expansion in the late 1980s, and the realization that the resort sector was being outmaneuvered by stiff competition both within and outside Ontario. Resorts Ontario needed a strategy that would be built on sound industry facts and consumer needs and wants.

Resort operators perceived early in 1991 that with consumer expectations becoming more difficult to meet, the traditional resort product would need significant improvement to remain competitive in the 1990s. The research project set out to build the foundation for this redevelopment of resort products. The purpose of the project was to develop a strategic framework (vision) for Ontario's existing resort industry, and to suggest short-, medium- and long-term priorities for improvements to products, marketing, operations, and organization of the resort sector. The project's priority objective was to analyze market conditions and consumer trends in order to determine Ontario resorts' market position and potential for attracting new customers.

The project began in December 1991 and was virtually complete by May 1992. The process was managed by a steering committee whose members included representatives from each of four resort

sectors (country inns, resort hotels, resort lodges, and housekeeping resorts), the Ontario Ministry of Tourism and Recreation, Tourism Canada, and the hospitality consulting firm of Pannell Kerr Forster (who were the prime contractors). Ruston/Tomany's role was to conduct primary consumer research that included 300 interviews with existing customers and 350 interviews with potential visitors to Ontario resorts. Care was taken to ensure that sampling for the interviews preserved the integrity of the results.

The results of the consumer research were the highlights of the project. Resorts Ontario was able to identify the strengths, weaknesses, opportunities, and threats for their sector. Resorts Ontario was in a position to take a lead in developing a long-term strategy for the sector. The individual operators could begin to position themselves within their respective class of resort rather than within a broader and less meaningful universe. The results also made clear the need for ongoing consumer and operator surveys.

The Surprise

The research results indicated that the position of Ontario resorts was somewhat different than conventional wisdom dictates. While the majority of resorts considered themselves to be "family-oriented," research results indicated the majority of the market is adults traveling without children. There are a large number of single adults and couples, younger and less affluent than existing customers, who are already predisposed to visiting Ontario resorts, but they perceive the resorts as being too expensive and not all that much fun. The resorts are meeting most of their customers' important expectations such as rest and relaxation, natural beauty but they could improve accommodation and food quality and put more emphasis on making customers feel special. In the eyes of potential visitors and existing customers, Ontario resorts stacked up better than competitors in Quebec, New York, and Michigan. New England resorts were viewed as being more attractive than those in Ontario.

The opportunity to capitalize on the strong loyalty of existing customers is clear. The resorts could improve referrals by providing incentives to existing customers for referring new business. The resorts stand to attract new customers by projecting an image that addresses the negative impressions held by potential visitors as they pertain to price and quality of service. Results of this nature seemed to give the resort sector new hope. Some thoughtful business planning and marketing could begin to steer the sector out of its current slump.

The Frustration

The enthusiasm that the research results generated in the steering committee was not shared by all of the individual operators. After looking at the final document, many said, "That's a nice piece of work for the broader industry but how can I begin to put this to use at my level?" The problem was a familiar one: research conducted for a large agency or association has relevance for the main sponsor but seems to be completely irrelevant to individual operators. During the release of the project, research operators were very up front, however, about the fact that the document did not do much for them. It needed relevance at the operator level.

At this stage of the project it was realized that the research had missed a key analytical point. A second look seemed to be needed at the consumer research in order to make the research results more relevant to the operator of housekeeping resorts, resort lodges, or hotels (i.e., to be more specific about how attracting families differed from attracting young singles). Now here was a novel idea. Let's take some existing consumer research and look at it in such a way as to find meaning and usefulness for the operator. An idea that is not so familiar in tourism was to be tested.

The Dialogue

The results of the market research that packaged customers into neat bundles of 300, or potential customers in parcels of 150 or 200, provided some important information. They gave a "big picture," but discussions with individual operators revealed very quickly that the big picture is not necessarily a practical picture. More importantly, it is not necessarily an actionable picture. The dialogue between industry and the researcher, the industry telling the researcher what they needed to know and the researcher determining whether the data can meaningfully address these information needs, was a critical but all too commonly missed step in the researcher/user process.

Industry representatives and researchers have very different areas of expertise. Researchers do not need to know how to fix leaking faucets, hire chefs, build walkways or swimming pools, or decide which radio station or newspaper should carry the advertising in order to be good at their jobs. Industry people do not need to know how to test for statistical significance, do multivariate analysis, or extract the four, five, or 10 numbers that are the main theme or story line in pages and columns of computer tabulations. What is needed is dialogue that brings the operators' particular needs to the fore and gives the researcher a way of looking at the data to see what concrete, actionable information can be provided.

The researcher then has the responsibility of keeping the process honest. Can the numbers support the information requirements once they have been disaggregated or taken apart into smaller subgroups? In this case it was agreed to look at resort subsectors, such as housekeeping cottages and resort lodges/hotels, and demographic subgroups such as the family market and the mature adult market. This information was important to the operators. The computer crunched away at the new definitions and produced thousands of new numbers; some so wobbly on their statistical feet that they would fall right over in a slight breeze, while others were firm enough to stay upright during a major New Brunswick gale.

Industry representatives should not be expected to be able to tell which numbers are solid and reliable and which are not. In fact, the researcher has an obligation to inform the ultimate user. Without this important step in the process, operators can be led right down a major garden path and wind up using the wrong numbers to develop marketing plans and promotional strategies.

The Big Picture

A key question in the study was, "How interested is the overnight traveller in visiting an Ontario resort in the next two or three years?" This question yielded three simple, clear figures that tell an important story.

(1) Since 9 in 10 current resort customers plan to return to an Ontario resort, a resort operator would be wise to provide sustained marketing support within the current customer base to ensure a high level of conversion from "intention" to "booking."

(2) Explore what resorts are doing so well that 9-in-10 customers want to return. When more is known about what customers think is being done right, it is possible to incorporate these very specific strengths into the advertising and promotional activities.

(3) If advertising budgets are limited, concentrate on the Ontario overnight travel market rather than one in the U.S. border states. It will likely be an easier and more fruitful sell.

From these total column numbers some straightforward decisions about how to market the product emerge.

The Smaller Picture

At the operator level, it is necessary to disaggregate the data in order to be able to explore market differences in greater detail. Some of the important questions that were specified as a result of the industry research dialogue were:

(1) What factors do customers take into account when selecting a specific resort?

(2) What do resorts need to tell the customers about themselves and in what order?

(3) Where should resorts put their priorities in advertising messages?

(4) Should the message or the emphasis in the message vary for different sectors of the market?

Two of the 20 factors that were considered in the research were "rest and relaxation" and "variety of services and facilities." These two factors are used for illustrative purposes. Potential customers should be told clearly about the rest and relaxation possibilities of the resort. After that they could be told about the services and facilities offered. Housekeeping cottage resorts might put less emphasis on services and facilities than would a resort lodge/hotel property. If the primary market were young singles or mature adults, less emphasis would be put on services and facilities than would be the case if the target was a family market.

Advertising Dollars

Customers learn about a resort by word of mouth. Visitors are the best ambassadors and should be used to reach the non-visitors. If a resort was trying to attract some customers from U.S. border states, would it not be better to offer an incentive to current customers to bring friends along rather than pay for newspaper ads in the border states?

The Format

Good tourism research is much more than data collection. It is more than gathering and crunching the numbers. Interpretation and presentation make the difference between the ability to use the research and the likelihood of it collecting dust on a shelf somewhere. Canada's tourism research community recognizes that it all too often creates the latter—dust collectors. In order to reduce the dust collectors a dialogue is necessary. Industry needs to tell research what it needs to know. Once researchers have a clearer idea of the information needs of industry, they will be in a much better position to supply what is really needed.

(1) Recognize that the language of industry and research are not the same. With an open dialogue, researchers will learn industry terms so that they can prepare materials in a language industry understands.

(2) Researchers will be able to present facts along with their logical, marketing-oriented implications such as those discussed here. Many different numbers contributed to the general conclusions. Like all research studies, good tourism studies tell a story, and researchers have to spend more time developing the themes and subplots as part of the analysis.

(3) Provide background or contextual information. It is not enough to say mature adults are the market of the future. It is necessary to tell much more about the market—its size, shape, and characteristics.

(4) Provide short, targeted, and, above all, accurate presentations of the findings that both respect the integrity of the research process and help with everyday business decisions.

Dollars

Good research is expensive. The current economic climate dictates that there are not a lot of extra dollars, if any, to spend on collecting data. However, tourism operators still need reliable, current market intelligence information. In fact they may need to be better informed about their potential markets than ever before if they want to stay competitive in tourism markets. It is imperative that tourism operators get the most information possible out of any research study that is done, be they ad hoc studies or ongoing ones like the Canadian Travel Survey, the International Travel Survey, provincial resident studies, and exit studies.

Adopt a researcher to help explore what further insights can be gained from intensive secondary analysis. Further analysis of most studies can yield useful, viable data at a relatively low cost. Be prepared to pay for the extra analysis. The big research money is in the primary collection of information, not in the analysis. The additional interpretation dollars are very smart ones to spend because they make you smarter about what you are selling and to whom.

The Real Questions

The dialogue that took place between research and industry revealed that there was a keen interest in and a need for information, and that the individual resort owners could not use the highly aggregated standard issue market research reports. It became clear that there was a need for the tourism research community to do a much better job of transforming what they found out into something the industry can and will use.

From the industry standpoint the issues have been defined more clearly. Two types of operators are apparent:

(1) Those who have not given the research more than a cursory glance, and

(2) Those who are using the research data and are benefiting from it.

Industry has seen that primary research can go beyond graphs and pie charts to provide useful information. The additional analysis phase would not have been reached if some of the clients had not been so up-front about the project's shortcomings in meeting their immediate business needs.

The Real Answer: Has the Process Worked?

In the view of one operator, the process did work. He has new hope that his business will have a more prosperous future than he would have thought possible a year ago. The information has cleared up the uncertainty and laid the foundation for recovery from recession. With a little luck and some good management, a healthy market is there in the medium- and long-term. He has seen firsthand how research can help and he would encourage any operator or association of tourism businesses to take an active and vigorous approach to obtaining the best tourism intelligence that they can. It is out there and with surprisingly little investment tourism operators can benefit and plan their way to prosperity in the millennium.

KEY CONCEPTS

basic research methods	measurement	Travel and Tourism Research Association
decisionmaking	observational method	travel research process
experimental method	primary data	uses of travel research
feasibility studies	secondary data	U.S. Travel Data Center
focus groups	sources of information	
information	surveys	

INTERNET SITES

The Internet sites mentioned in this chapter are repeated here for convenience plus some selected additional sites. For more information, visit these sites. Be aware that Internet addresses change frequently; so if a site cannot be accessed, use a search engine. Also use a search engine to locate many additional sites that are available.

Annals of Tourism Research
http://www.elsevier.com

CAB International
http://www.cabi.org

Canadian Tourism Commission
http://www.canadatourism.com

Journal of Travel Research
http://www.sagepub.com

NEON Web
http://library.nevada.edu/neonweb

Tourism Industries
http://tinet.ita.doc.gov

Tourism Research in Europe
http://www.wu-
wien.ac.at/inst/tourism/locale.html

Tourism Research Laboratory
http://www.tourism.uiuc.edu/trl/trl.html

Tourism Resources
http://www.vir.com/~chamonix/tourism.h
tml

Travel and Tourism Research Association
http://www.ttra.com

Travel Industry Association of America
http://www.tia.org

**World Tourism Education and Research
Centre**
http://www.ucalgary.ca/MG/tour/wterc/
index.html

World Tourism Organization
http://www.world-tourism.org

INTERNET EXERCISE

Site Name: Tourism Research Laboratory

URL: http://www.tourism.uiuc.edu/trl/trl.html

Background Information: The primary mission of the Tourism Research Laboratory is to foster quality inter- and multi-disciplinary research in the varied aspects of tourism.

Exercise

1. Discuss how the TRL supports its research mission.

QUESTIONS FOR REVIEW AND DISCUSSION

1. What does a situation analysis cover?

2. What problems can travel research solve?

3. When should you use primary data? Secondary data?

4. What are the basic research methods?

5. What are the strengths and weaknesses of focus groups?

6. Why would you choose survey research over focus groups?

7. Why are research findings so important to intelligent decisionmaking?

8. If you were director of a major city's convention and visitors bureau, how would you use travel research?

9. As a consultant, you are researching the feasibility of a new resort hotel project. What procedures would you use, step by step?

10. How would a resort developer use a consultant's report when the report is completed? Once the resort is built, does the manager need further research?

11. What methods could be used by a state tourist office to survey out-of-state visitors?

12. Should a state tourist office conduct its own research or hire an outside supplier? Why?

SELECTED REFERENCES

AIEST. *Tourism Research: Achievements, Failures, and Unresolved Puzzles.* St-Gallen, Switzerland: Association Internationale Experts Scientific de Tourism, 1994.

Baker, Kenneth G., et al. "Marketing Research and Methodology and the Tourism Industry: A Nontechnical Discussion." *Journal of Travel Research*, Vol. 32, No. 3, pp. 3–7, Winter 1994.

Bar-on, Raphael Raymond, Abraham Pizam, and John C. Crotts. "Pacific Area Tourisim: A Guide to Key Sources of Tourism Statistics." *Journal of Travel and Tourism Marketing*, Vol. 6, No. 1, pp. 93–108, 1997.

Bonfield, Rhonda L., Jiann-Min Jeng, and Daniel R. Fesenmaier. "Comparisons of Approaches for Measuring Traveler Motivations." *Tourism Analysis*, Vol. 1, pp. 39–47, 1996.

Brunt, P. *Market Research in Travel & Tourism*. Oxford, UK: Butterworth Heinemann, 1997.

Bryman, A. *Disney and his Worlds*. London: Routledge, 1995.

Callan, Roger J. "The Critical Incident Technique in Hospitality Research: An Illustration from the UK Lodge Sector." *Tourism Management*, Vol. 19, No. 1, pp. 93–98, February 1998.

Camacho, Frank E. and D. Matthew Knain. "Listening to Customers: The Market Research Function at Marriott Corporation." *Market Research: A Magazine of Management and Applications*, Vol. 1, No. 1, pp. 5–14, March 1989.

Crouch, Geoffrey I. "A Meta-Analysis of Tourism Demand." *Annals of Tourism Research*, Vol. 23, No. 1, pp. 103–118, 1996.

Dann, Graham, Dennison Nash, and Philip Pearce. "Methodology in Tourism Research." *Annals of Tourism Research*, Vol. 15, No. 1, pp. 1–28, 1988.

Fesenmaier, Daniel R. Joseph T. O'Leary, and Muzaffer Uysal, eds. *Recent Advances in Tourism Marketing Research*. Binghamton, NY: The Haworth Press, 1996.

Green, Howard, Colin Hunter, and Bruno Moore. "Application of the Delphi Technique in Tourism." *Annals of Tourism Research*, Vol. 17, No. 2, pp. 270–279, 1990.

Hinkin, Timothy R. Bruce Tracey, and Cathy A. Enz. "Scale Construction: Developing Reliable and Valid Measurement Instruments." *Journal of Hospitality and Tourism Research*, Vol. 21, No. 1, pp. 100–120, 1997.

Hughes, Julia Christensen, "Sociological Paradigms and the Use of Ethnography in Hospitality Research." *Journal of Hospitality and Tourism Research*, Vol. 21, No. 1, pp. 14–27, 1997.

Jones, Peter. "Hospitality Research—Where Have We Got to Go?" *International Journal of Hospitality Management*, Vol. 15, No. 1, pp. 5–10, March 1996.

Lickorish, L. J. "Travel Statistics—The Slow Move Forward." *Tourism Management*, Vol. 18, No. 8, pp. 491–498, December 1997.

Morgan, David L. *The Focus Group Guidebook*. Thousand Oaks, CA: Sage Publications, Inc., 1997.

Pacific Asia Travel Association. *PATA Annual Statistical Report: 1998*. San Francisco: PATA, annual.

Paxon, M. Chris. "Increasing Your Survey Response Rates: Practical Instructions from the Total-Design Method." *Cornell Hotel and Restaurant Administration Quarterly*, Vol. 36, No. 4, pp. 66–73, August 1995.

Pearce, Douglas G., and Richard Butler. *Tourism Research: Critiques and Challenges*. New York: Routledge, 1993.

Pearce, Philip L. "Recent Research in Tourist Behaviour." *Asia Pacific Journal of Tourism Research*, Vol. 1, No. 1, pp. 7–17, 1996.

Plog, Stanley C., and Anne Adams. "The Respondent Specific Method: A New Approach to Conversion Research." *Journal of Travel and Tourism Marketing*, Vol. 5, No. 3, pp. 241–252, 1996.

Pursell, Joshua R., and Richard K. Miller. *The 1997 Sports Business Market Research Handbook*. Norcross, GA: Richard K. Miller and Associates, Inc., 1997.

Ritchie, J. R. Brent, and Charles R. Goeldner, eds. *Travel, Tourism and Hospitality Research: A Handbook for Managers and Researchers*. New York: Wiley, 1994.

Rogers, Judy. "A Non-technical Perspective on Data Collection Methodologies for Travel Surveys: A Discussion Paper." *Journal of Travel Research*, Vol. 29, No. 3, pp. 43–46, Winter 1991.

Rylander, Roy G. II, Dennis B. Propst, and Terri R. McMurty. "Nonresponse and Recall Biases in a Survey of Travel Spending." *Journal of Travel Research*, Vol. 33, No. 4, pp. 39–45, Spring, 1995.

Seaton, A. V. "Unobtrusive Observational Measures as a Qualitative Extension of Visitor Surveys at Festivals and Events: Mass Observation Revisited." *Journal of Travel Research*, Vol. 35, No. 4, pp. 25–30, Spring 1997.

Schonland, Addison M., and Peter W. Williams. "Using the Internet for Travel and Tourism Survey Research: Experiences from the Net Travel Survey." *Journal of Travel Research*, Vol. 35, No. 2, pp. 81–88, Fall 1996.

Smith, Stephen L. J. *Tourism Analysis: A Handbook*, second edition. Essex, UK: Longman, 1995.

Taylor, Gordon D., Judy Rogers, and Bruce Stanton. "Bridging the Research Gap between Industry and Researchers." *Journal of Travel Research*, Vol. 32, No. 4, pp. 9–12, Spring 1994.

Taylor, Stephen, and David Edgar. "Hospitality Research: The Emperor's New Clothes?" *International Journal of Hospitality Management,* Vol. 15, No. 3, pp. 211–227, September 1996.

Testa, Mark R., John M. Williams, and Dale Pietrzak. "The Development of the Cruise Line Job Satisfaction Questionnaire." *Journal of Travel Research,* Vol. 36, No. 3, pp. 13–19, Winter 1998.

Van Hoof, Hubert B., and Marja J. Verbeeten. "Tourism Research Inquiries: The Response of the State Office of Tourism." *Journal of Travel Research,* Vol. 35, No. 4, pp. 75–76, Spring 1997.

Walker, Terry C., and Richard K. Miller. *The 1997 Casino and Gaming Business Market Research Handbook.* Norcross, GA: Richard K. Miller and Associates, Inc. 1997.

Walle, Alf. "Quantitative versus Qualitative Tourism Research." *Annals of Tourism Research,* Vol. 24, No. 3, pp. 524–536, July 1997.

Wicks, Bruce E., and Cheryl K. Baldwin. "The Cost–Accuracy Trade-Off: Testing the Utility of Nonprobability in Tourism Marketing Research." *Tourism Analysis,* Vol. 1, No. 1, pp. 1–8, 1998.

Williams, Peter W., et al. "Using the Internet for Tourism Research: 'Information Highway' or 'Dirt Road'?" *Journal of Travel Research,* Vol. 34, No. 4, pp. 63–70, Spring 1996.

WTO. *Collection of Tourism Expenditure Statistics:* Technical Manual No. 2. Madrid: World Tourism Organization, 1995.

WTO. *Collection of Domestic Tourism Statistics:* Technical Manual No. 3. Madrid: World Tourism Organization, 1995.

WTO. *Collection and Compilation of Tourism Statistics:* Technical Manual No. 4. Madrid: World Tourism Organization, 1995.

Yaman, H. Ruhi, and Robin N. Shaw. "The Conduct of Marketing Research in Tourism." *Journal of Travel Research,* Vol. 36, No. 4, pp. 25–32, Spring 1998.

Yaman, H. Ruhi, and Robin N. Shaw. "Assessing Marketing Research Use in Tourism with the USER Instrument." *Journal of Travel Research,* Vol. 36, No. 3, pp. 70–78, Winter 1998.

CHAPTER 19

TOURISM MARKETING

- Become familiar with the marketing mix and be able to formulate the best mix for a particular travel product.

- Appreciate the importance of the relationship between the marketing concept and product planning and development.

- Understand the vital relationship between pricing and marketing.

- Know about distribution systems and how this marketing principle can best be applied to a variety of travel products.

- Be able to do market segmentation to plan a marketing program for the business you are the most interested in.

- Understand the principles of branding and examine their applicability to destination branding.

- Demonstrate the linkage between tourism policy and tourism marketing.

- Provide an example of an operational marketing plan.

◀ LEARNING OBJECTIVES

◀ *The Statue of Liberty is an internationally recognized tourism "icon" that greatly enhances market awareness of New York City—and the entire United States—as a travel destination. (Photo courtesy New York Division of Tourism.)*

INTRODUCTION

Tourism marketing is:

- The State of New York creating a tourism promotion fund, developing a marketing plan, and creating an advertising campaign around the theme "I Love New York."
- Marriott International's segmenting its lodging product into many brands.
- United Airlines offering different classes of service, supersaver fares, Mileage Plus, advertising the "friendly skies," developing a logo, adding new routes and schedules, using their own reservation system and travel agents, and working with tour groups.
- Using the Internet as a new medium.

Marketing includes all of the above and much more. Marketing has been defined in a variety of ways. The American Marketing Association defines marketing as "the performance of business activities that direct the flow of goods and services from the producer to the consumer or user." Others have stated that marketing is the delivery of the standard of living to society. You are no doubt acquainted with the old adage "nothing happens until somebody sells something."

Most people have little idea what marketing is all about and would probably say that it has something to do with selling or advertising. However, marketing is a very broad concept, of which advertising and selling are only two facets. Marketing is goal-oriented, strategic, and directed. It both precedes and follows selling and advertising activities. Marketing is the total picture in getting goods and services from the producer to the user.

Unfortunately, "marketing" often conjures up unfavorable images of used car salespeople, TV furniture advertisers, high-pressure selling, and gimmicks, leading to the perception of marketing in terms of stereotypes. In fact, marketing plays a critical role in all organizations whether they are nonprofit educational institutions, tourist resorts, or manufacturers. The role of marketing is to match the right product or service with the right market or audience.

Marketing is an inevitable aspect of tourism management. Marketing can be done effectively and well, with sophistication, or it can be done poorly in a loud, crass, intrusive manner. It is the goal of this chapter to discuss the basic elements of marketing so that it can be done effectively, with style, and with a favorable economic impact.

MARKETING CONCEPT

The heart of good marketing management today is the **marketing concept,** or a **consumer orientation.** Tourism organizations that practice the marketing concept find out what the consumer wants and then produce a product that will satisfy those wants at a profit. The marketing concept requires that management thinking be directed toward profits rather than sales volume.

Assume that you are going to develop a new major resort area. This is a difficult exercise in planning that requires that the designs that are developed be based on how consumers view the product. One of the first steps is to employ the marketing concept and do research to understand the consumer's (the market's) needs, desires, and wants. Designers of products and consumers of products often perceive them differently. Architects, for example, may see a hotel in terms of such things as space utilization, engineering problems, and design lines or as a monument; consumers may see the hotel as a bundle of benefits—as being attractive, as offering full service and outstanding food, as having recreational facilities, and so on. Once consumer views are determined, the task is to formulate strategic marketing plans that match the resort and its market. In today's competitive environment where consumers have choices, firms need to employ the marketing concept.

THE MARKETING MIX

The marketing program combines a number of elements into a workable whole—a viable, strategic plan. The tourism marketing manager must constantly search for the right **marketing mix**—the right combination of elements that will produce a profit. The marketing mix is composed of every factor that influences the marketing effort:

1. *Timing.* Holidays, high season, low season, upward trend in the business cycle, and so on, must all be considered.

2. *Brands.* The consumer needs help in remembering your product. Names, trademarks, labels, logos, and other identification marks all assist the consumer in identifying and recalling information about your product.

3. *Packaging.* Although tourism services do not require a physical package, packaging is still an important factor. For example, transportation, lodging, amenities, and recreation activities can be packaged and sold together or separately. Family plans or single plans are other forms of packaging.

4. *Pricing.* Pricing affects not only sales volume but also the image of the product. A multitude of pricing options exist, ranging from discount prices to premium prices.

5. *Channels of distribution.* The product must be accessible to the consumer. Direct selling, retail travel agents, wholesale tour operators, or a combination of these methods all comprise distribution channels that must be developed.

6. *Product.* The physical attributes of the product help to determine its position against the competition and provide guidelines on how to best compete.

7. *Image.* The consumer's perception of the product depends to a great extent on the important factors of reputation and quality.

8. *Advertising.* Paid promotion is critical, and the questions of when, where, and how to promote must be carefully considered.

9. *Selling.* Internal and external selling are essential components for success, and various sales techniques must be incorporated in the marketing plan.

(a)

Tourism icons, such as the Golden Gate Bridge in San Francisco, can be used to promote travel to a given location. Not all icons are bridges or statues, however. For example, the Southern Belle of Mississippi is an enduring symbol of southern hospitality. *(Golden Gate Bridge photo by Robert Holmes; courtesy of the California Division of Tourism; Southern Belle photo courtesy of the Mississippi Department of Community Development/Division of Tourism Development.)*

10. *Public relations.* Even the most carefully drawn marketing plan will fail without good relations with the visitors, the community, suppliers, and employees.

The preceding list makes it obvious that the marketing manager's job is a complex one. Using knowledge of the consumer market and the competition, the marketing manager must come up with the proper marketing mix for the resort, attraction, or other organization. The marketing manager's job begins with planning to allow direction and control of the foregoing factors.

The many elements in the marketing mix have been defined most frequently as **"the four Ps,"** a term popularized by E. Jerome McCarthy, author of *Basic Marketing and Essentials of Marketing*.[1] While the four Ps are an oversimplification, they do pro-

---

[1] E. Jerome McCarthy and William D. Perreault, *Essentials of Marketing* (Homewood, IL: Richard D. Irwin, 1994).

(b)

vide a neat, simple framework in which to look at marketing and put together a marketing program. The four Ps are **product, place, promotion, and price.** The product includes not only actual physical attributes of the product but also product planning, product development, breadth of the line, branding, and packaging. Planning the product should consider all these aspects in order to come up with the "right" product.

Place is really concerned with distribution. What agencies, channels, and institutions can be linked together most effectively to give the consumer easy access to the purchase of your product? Where is the "right" place to market your product?

Promotion communicates the benefits of the product to the potential customers and includes not only advertising but also sales promotion, public relations, and personal selling. The "right" promotional mix will use each of these promotional techniques as needed for effective communication.

Price is a critical variable in the marketing mix. The "right" price must both satisfy customers and meet your profit objectives.

Mill and Morrison (1998) have added another "three P's" that they believe are particularly relevant to tourism. *Programming* involves special activities, events, or other types of programs to increase customer spending or to give added appeal to a package or other tourism service. As noted in Chapter 15, tourism policy views programs as a strategic consolidation of a range of different activities designed to ensure a clear focus (Ries, 1996) for development and marketing efforts.

The second of the additional three P's concerns *people*. This P is intended to stress that tourism is a "people business"—that we must not lose sight of the importance of providing travel experiences that are sensitive to the human side of the visitor as well as to the functional requirements.

The final P is defined as *partnership*. This highlights the high degree of interdependency among all destination stakeholders; as well as the need for alliances and working relationships that build a cooperation—sometimes with competitors as well as colleagues. Edgell's concepts of coopetition captures the value of partnership in a unique way.

Product Branding

A very fundamental concept in traditional marketing is that of the product brand: "a distinguishing name and/or a symbol (such as a logo, trademark, or package design) intended to identify the goods or services of one seller, or groups of sellers, and to differentiate those goods or services from competitors who would attempt to provide products that appear to be identical" (Aaker, 1991).

Recently, tourism marketers have been attempting to "brand" their destination. While the approach has considerable potential, the transference of its application from traditional products and services and to the tourism setting is not without its difficulties (see Reading 19.1 for further insights into tourism branding).

Product Planning and Development

The objective of most firms is to develop a profitable and continuing business. To achieve this objective, companies must provide products and services that satisfy consumer needs, thereby assuring themselves of repeat business. **Product planning** is an essential component in developing a profitable, continuing business and has frequently been referred to as the "five rights"—planning to have the right product, at the right place, at the right time, at the right price, in the right quantities.

A product is much more than a combination of raw materials. It is actually a bundle of satisfactions and benefits for the consumer. Product planning must therefore be approached from the consumer's point of view. Creating the right service or product is not easy: Consumer needs, wants, and desires are constantly changing, and competitive forces typically carry products through a **life cycle**, so that a product that is successful at one point declines and "dies" at a later time.

Figure 19.1 shows the phases that a new product goes through from inception to decline: (1) introduction, (2) growth, (3) maturity, (4) saturation, and (5) decline. Because of the rapidly changing consumer lifestyles and technological changes, the life cycle for products and services has become shorter, but the product life cycle remains a useful concept for strategic planning. Each stage of the product life cycle has certain marketing requirements.

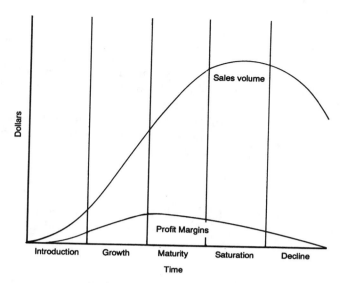

FIGURE 19.1 **Product life cycle.**

Introduction

The introductory phase of the product's life cycle requires high promotional expenditures and visibility (the most productive time to advertise a product or service is when it is new). Operations in this period are characterized by high cost, relatively low sales volume, and an advertising program aimed at stimulating primary demand; in this stage of the life cycle, there will be a high percentage of failures.

Growth

In the growth period, the product or service is being accepted by consumers. Market acceptance means that both sales and profits rise at a rapid rate, frequently making the market attractive to competitors. Promotional expenditures remain high, but the promotional emphasis is on selective buying motives by trade name rather than on primary motives to try the product. During the growth stage, the number of outlets handling the product or service usually increases. More competitors enter the marketplace, but economies of scale are realized and prices may decline some.

Maturity

The mature product is well established in the marketplace. Sales may still be increasing, but at a much slower rate; they are leveling off. At this stage of the product's life cycle, many outlets are selling the product or service; they are very competitive, especially with respect to price, and firms are trying to determine ways to hold onto their share of the market. The ski resort is an excellent example of a mature product. After years of spectacular growth, sales are now leveling off, and the resorts are looking for ways to hold market share and diversify.

Saturation

In the saturation stage, sales volume reaches its peak: The product or service has penetrated the marketplace to the greatest degree possible. Mass production and new technology have lowered the price to make it available to almost everyone.

Decline

Many products stay at the saturation stage for years. However, for most products, obsolescence sets in, and new products are introduced to replace old ones. In the decline stage, demand obviously drops, advertising expenditures are lower, and there is usually a smaller number of competitors. While it is possible for a product to do very well in this stage of the product life cycle, there is not a great deal of comfort in getting a larger share of a declining market. Hot springs resorts are a good example of a tourist product in the decline stage. These facilities, at their peak in the 1920s, are no longer the consumer's idea of an "in" place to go.

Pricing

One of the most important marketing decisions is the **pricing** decision. Price determines how consumers perceive the product and strongly affects other elements of the marketing mix.

Southwest Airlines is well known for their low airfares, but they also have a reputation for going out of their way to deliver fun service to keep customers happy.
(Photo courtesy of Southwest Airlines.)

Firms have a choice of three strategies in pricing their products. First, they may decide to sell their product at the market price, which is the same price that everyone else charges. They then compete on nonprice terms. Selling at a price equal to competitors' tends to prevent price cutting and protect margins, and customers are not driven away by price. However, because there is no price individuality, there can be no price demand stimulation.

Second, firms may decide to price below the current market price. Firms that adopt such a discount policy are trying to create the reputation of having the lowest prices and underselling all competitors. To be successful, such firms must make sure that demand is elastic; otherwise, they will gain only at the expense of their competitors and start a price war. This pricing strategy is more successful when, it is based on the elimination of services. Motel 6, Inc., for example, took its name from its original $6-a-night charge and built its network on a no-frills philosophy. Today it is one of the top budget chains in the United States.

The third approach is to charge above-market prices. Premium pricing strategy must be coupled with the best service in the industry and other features and amenities to make this higher price attractive. Such an approach emphasizes quality, which many consumers think is a function of price; provides higher margins; generates more revenue for promotion; and makes better service possible. However, premium pricing reduces volume, raises overhead costs, and encourages substitution. Nevertheless, numerous tourism firms successfully use this approach, including the Ritz–Carlton (winner of the U.S. Malcolm Baldridge National Quality Award in 1992), Fairmont, Hyatt, Marriott, and Westin hotels.

Some firms choose to employ two or three pricing strategies and develop a product to appeal to consumers in each market segment. The lodging industry has moved to employing this strategy in the last decade. Ramada, Choice, Marriott, Holiday Inn Worldwide, and others have developed products to appeal to a broad range of market segments.

The tourism marketing manager must consider the following factors that influence price policies:

1. *Product quality.* The quality of the product really determines the price–value relationship. It is common sense that a product that offers greater utility and fills more consumer needs than a competitive product can command a higher price.

2. *Product distinctiveness.* A staple or standard product with no distinctive features offers little or no opportunity for price control. However, a novel and different product may be able to command higher prices. The Hyatt Corporation, for example, features lobby atriums; this attractive novelty combined with excellent service and facilities makes it possible for the Hyatt Hotels to command higher prices.

3. *Extent of the competition.* A product that is comparable to competitors' products must be priced with the competitors' prices in mind. The product's price to some extent determines its position in the market.

4. *Method of distribution.* The price of the product must include adequate margins for tour operators, travel agents, or the company's own sales force.

5. *Character of the market.* It is necessary to consider the type and number of possible consumers. If there is a small number of consumers, then the price must be high enough to compensate for a limited market. However, one must also consider the ability of consumers to buy and their buying habits.

6. *Cost of the product and service.* It should be obvious that price must exceed cost over the long run or else the business will not survive. Both cost and market conditions should serve as guides to pricing.

7. *Cost of distribution.* Distribution costs must also be included in the pricing equation. Unfortunately, in many cases they are much more difficult to estimate than other costs.

8. *Margin of profit desired.* The profit margin built into the price of the product must be more than returns realized on more conventional investments in order to compensate for the risk involved in the enterprise.

9. *Seasonality.* Most tourism products are affected by seasonality because of school year patterns and vacation habits; consequently, the seasonal aspects must be considered in developing prices.

10. *Special promotional prices.* Many times it is good strategy to offer introductory prices and special one-time price offers to acquaint consumers with your product. However, these must be carefully planned so that they fill the proper intent and do not become a regular discount price.

11. *Psychological considerations.* Throughout our economy we see psychological pricing employed, usually using prices that are set in odd amounts such as 19¢, 99¢, $19.95, or $29.99. Consumers respond well to odd pricing, and there seems to be something particularly magical about prices that end in nine.

Price Skimming

In the pricing of a new product or service, the two pricing philosophies that prevail are called price skimming and penetration pricing. A price-skimming strategy sets the price as high as possible. No attempt is made to appeal to the entire market, but only to the top of the market; consequently, this approach is frequently called skimming the cream. The strategy is to sell the product to as many consumers as possible at this price level; then, as either buyer resistance or direct competition develops, the seller will lower prices step by step. This approach typically results in higher profits and more rapid repayment of development and promotion costs. It also tends to invite competition. Skimming is appropriate when the product or service has the following characteristics: (1) price inelasticity, (2) no close substitutes, (3) high promotion elasticity, and (4) distinct market segments based on price.

Penetration Pricing

The opposite approach to price skimming is market penetration, in which the seller attempts to establish the price of the product as low as possible to penetrate the market as completely as possible. A low price makes the product available to as many income levels as possible, and the sellers are likely to establish a large market share quickly. When penetration pricing is used, this introductory price tends to become the permanent price of the product. It results in a slower recovery of fixed costs and requires a greater volume to break even. The factors that would recommend a penetration pricing approach would be (1) high price elasticity, (2) large savings from high-volume production (economies of scale), and (3) an easy fit of the product into consumer purchasing patterns.

Place (Distribution)

Another difficult decision for the marketing manager concerns what distribution channel or channels will be used. The distribution decisions affect the other elements of the marketing mix, and in the best marketing mix all aspects will be compatible with each other. Chapter 7 contains a description of the travel distribution system.

Channels of distribution are selected by (1) analyzing the product, (2) determining the nature and extent of the market, (3) analyzing the channels by sales, costs, and profits, (4) determining the cooperation you can expect from the channel, (5) determining the assistance you will have to give to the channel, and (6) determining the number of outlets to be used. For example, if you want intensive distribution, exposing your product to maximum sale, you will use many travel agents. In contrast, with an exclusive distribution policy, you would sell your product through one or a few agents who would have the sole right to sell your product or service in a given area.

Promotion

The aim of promotion activities is to create demand for a product or service. Promotion is a broad term that includes advertising, personal selling, public relations, publicity, and sales promotion activities such as giveaways, trade shows, point of purchase, and store displays.

To sell the product, it is necessary to (1) attract attention, (2) create interest, (3) create a desire, and (4) get action. Either personal selling or advertising can carry out all of these steps in the selling process; however, the two used together tend to be much more powerful. Advertising is ideally suited to attract attention and create interest in the products and services. Personal selling is best suited to creating desire and conviction on the part of the customer and to closing the sale. Advertising and personal selling are even more effective when supplemented by publicity and sales promotion activities.

Advertising

Advertising has been defined as any nonpersonal presentation of goods, ideas, or services by an identified sponsor. In travel marketing, these paid public messages are designed to describe or present a destination area in such a way as to attract consumers. This can be done through the use of the major advertising media such as newspapers, magazines, direct mail, television, outdoor, or radio. Effective advertising gains the attention of the prospective visitor, holds the attention so the message can be communicated, and makes a lasting positive impression on the prospect's mind.

Each advertising medium has advantages and disadvantages. A key decision in developing promotional strategy is to select the right medium to maximize advertising

While not as famous as the Statue of Liberty, this photo shows the world's only monument to a pest, the Boll Weevil Monument, in Enterprise, Alabama. In 1915, the boll weevil devoured much of the area's cotton crop, which led to diversified farming. The monument serves as a reminder of the insect that helped make Enterprise a prosperous town, as well as a tourism attraction and great publicity generator. *(Photo courtesy Alabama Bureau of Tourism and Travel.)*

expenditure. To assist in media selection, turn to Standard Rate and Data Service, 1700 Higgins Road, Des Plaines, IL 60018. SRDS publications contain advertising rates and other media information required to make intelligent decisions. The advantages and disadvantages of the major media are as follows.

Newspapers

Newspapers give comprehensive coverage of a local market area, are lower in cost than other media, are published frequently, are flexible (short lead time) and timely, have a wide audience, and get a quick response. Most newspapers have travel sections. The major disadvantages are low printing quality and short life.

Direct Mail

Although mail costs have increased rapidly, direct mail is one of the most important advertising methods for tourism enterprises. It is the most personal and selective of all the media; consequently, it is the most effective medium in minimizing waste circulation. Direct mail gets the message directly to the consumers that one wishes to contact. Direct mail advertising is self-testing when it asks for a response. The critical problem with direct mail is obtaining and maintaining the right mailing lists. Many types of lists are commercially available through firms specializing in this activity. (One source of such information is Standard Rate and Data Service.)

For the tourism industry, previous visitors comprise the most important mailing list sources. However, names and addresses must be correct, and the lists must be kept in ready-to-use form, such as address plates or on a computer. Other good sources of prospects are the inquiry lists.

Web Sites

Although a relatively recent arrival on the advertising scene, web sites have very rapidly established themselves as one of the most pervasive and most powerful means of directly communicating with individuals in the marketplace. They are particularly valuable to small and medium-sized tourism operators, who in the past had difficulty conveying information regarding their products and services to their many potential customers. Care must be taken, however, to ensure a well-designed web site. Because of the ease of access to web sites, many firms assume that a simple listing of products and services is adequate. This is far from true. The growing sophistication of web site marketers means that both innovation and functionality must be carefully built into a web site for it to be successful.

Television

Television presents both an audio and visual message and comes as close to approximating personal selling as a mass medium can. Television requires minimal exertion on the part of listeners and is very versatile. However, television is not a flexible medium, commercials have a short life, and advertising on television is expensive relative to the costs of using other media. Nevertheless, despite television's expense, many destinations are using television and finding it is very cost effective.

Magazines

The major advantage of magazines is their print and graphic quality. Other advantages are secondary readership, long life, prestige, and favorable cost per 1000 circulation. Many special interest magazines reach specialized market segments effectively, making it possible to target markets. Regional editions allow further selectivity, with a minimum of waste circulation. Some of the unfavorable characteristics of magazines are that they require long lead times and that changes cannot be made readily. Magazines also reach the market less frequently than do newspapers, radio, and television.

Radio

Radio has the advantage of outstanding flexibility and relatively low cost. While the warmth of the human voice adds a personal touch to the selling message, radio has the disadvantage that it presents only an audio message. Tourists driving in their automobiles are typically radio listeners, and many attractions find radio an excellent medium.

Outdoor Advertising

Outdoor advertising has been used with great success by many tourism organizations. It is a flexible, low-cost medium that reaches virtually the whole population. It has made the Wall Drugstore in Wall, South Dakota world famous. Outdoor advertising

This outdoor sign at Ayers Rock Resort in Australia features the resort's logo, reinforcing a branded image in the consumer's mind. *(Photo by the author.)*

has the disadvantage that the message must be short; however, it does reach travelers. An additional problem is highway signing laws, which are making it more difficult to advertise tourism attractions.

Using an Advertising Agency

While promotion managers must know the fundamentals of marketing, advertising, personal selling, and public relations, the specialized skill and experience of an **advertising agency** can greatly increase business—and can do it profitably. An advertising agency will do the following:

1. Work with ideas in copy and layout. "Copy" is the term used to describe written messages; "layout" refers to the arrangement of copy, art, and pictures.

2. Advise on the choice of media to convey advertising messages, devising an organized and carefully worked-out plan using newspapers, magazines, radio, TV, guide books, posters, direct mail, postcards, folders, or other advertising media.

3. Conduct market analysis and research so that advertising efforts can be directed to the best prospects.

4. Assist in planning and carrying out a public relations program.

The advertising program must be planned objectively by setting forth specific, achievable goals. The advertising agency can help to establish such goals. When seeking the services of an advertising agency, look at the agency's experience in promoting tourism, and check the agency's past advertising campaigns and clients to determine the campaign's effectiveness.

The Advertising Budget

No magic formula exists for setting the advertising budget. How much to spend is always a perplexing question. Commonly used methods include a percentage of last year's sales, a percentage of potential sales, or the industry percentage. These methods are all flawed because advertising should create sales and cause things to happen, not react to what has happened in the past or in other companies. Consequently, the best method of setting advertising budgets is to determine the objectives to be performed and allocate the proper amount to reach these objectives.

Promoting a new tourist destination area will require more money than will promoting one with an established clientele. The specific amount to budget for advertising and sales promotion will depend on each situation. However, as a rule of thumb, most resorts spend about 3 percent of sales on media advertising and about 3 percent on other sales promotion activities.

No matter what expenditures are, efforts should be made to coordinate the promotion program so it is consistent with the product offered and consumer expectations will be met. Word of mouth is the least expensive, most convincing form of personal advertising. A friendly and capable host encourages this type of communication. Visitors who are treated as very important persons will not only come back, they will recommend the area to their friends. All facilities, services, hospitality, and pricing policies must be directed to this one goal—a happy, satisfied visitor.

Research

Successful tourism marketing depends in large part on research. Tourism promotion efforts undirected by research are largely wasted effort. Unless the following characteristics are known, advertising expenditures cannot be productive:

1. Who are the present visitors, and where do they live?
2. What do you know about their likes and dislikes?
3. Who are your potential customers, and where do they live?
4. What are their travel and vacation preferences and interests?
5. What are your visitors' travel destination preferences?
6. What are your visitors' preferences for shopping and entertainment?
7. What is your competitive situation?
8. What are the trends in competition?
9. What are the likely future trends in your share of the market?
10. What are the prospects for increasing demand for your area?
11. What kind(s) of marketing program(s) appears to be needed?
12. How will these programs be implemented?

Carefully review questions of this kind; adequate answers to them are obtained only through research.

In determining the market, research can be classified into three main categories: geographic market orientation (where present and potential visitors reside), demographic market orientation (age, sex, levels of education, income, population distribution, family status, and similar data), and psychographic market orientation (motivations, interest, hobbies, responsiveness to advertising, and propensity to travel). Guidance of the subsequent marketing program will rest largely on the results of such research and the success of the marketing upon the adequacy of the research. See Chapter 18 for methods of conducting tourism research.

Personal Selling

Personal selling is the most used and oldest method of creating demand. Because it is adaptable to the prospect, it is the most compelling and effective type of selling. In contrast to advertising, which is the impersonal component in the promotional mix, personal selling consists of individual, personal communication. The U.S. economy depends on salespeople; there are over 13 million compared to about 500,000 working in advertising. In many companies, personal selling is the largest operating expense item, ranging from about 8 to 15 percent of sales. Expenditures for salespersons' compensation, expenses, training, and supervision and the cost of operating sales offices make management of the sales force an important task.

Personal selling is so widely used because it offers maximum flexibility. Sales representatives tailor their presentation to each individual customer. They can tell which approaches are working and which are not and adjust accordingly. Prospects can be identified so target market customers are approached and efforts are not wasted.

The Hertz #1 Club is a highly successful marketing program designed to reward loyal customers by providing special services and privileges. (*Photo courtesy of the Hertz Corporation © Hertz System, Inc. Hertz is the registered service mark and trademark of Hertz System, Inc.*)

Counterbalancing these advantages is the fact that personal selling is the most expensive means of making contact with prospects, and productivity gains are unlikely. Another limitation is that it is not always possible to hire the caliber of person needed for the sales job.

Because of the importance of personal selling, all staff should be sales-minded. All salespeople must be trained to offer sales suggestions to prospects when opportunities present themselves. This includes expert selling on the telephone as well as the telephone receptionist, who can create a favorable image for a resort. Inquiries can often be the opening for a polite and skillful sales effort. Obviously, an unfriendly manner can discourage customers and sales.

Public Relations

Public relations may be defined as an attitude—a "social conscience" that places first priority on the public interest when making any decisions. Public relations permeates an entire organization, covering relations with many publics: visitors, the community, employees, and suppliers.

Acceptance of any tourist destination by the public is of utmost importance. No business is more concerned with human relations than is tourism, and all public interests must be served. Serving one group at the expense of another is not sound public relations. Furthermore, each individual business manager and the group he or she represents must be respected and have the confidence of the community. There is no difference between a personal reputation and a business reputation.

Favorable public relations within the firm emphasize respect for people. Employees must have reasonable security in their jobs and be treated with consideration. Externally, tourism employees have a powerful influence on the public as they represent the owners in the public's eye. Employees should be trained to be courteous, respectful, and helpful to guests. Little things make a big difference, and the attitude of employees can make or break a public relations effort.

Considerations for the public relations effort include being aware of public attitudes toward present policies—ask some of the visitors for feedback. Communication is the lifeblood of good relations. In publicizing the firm, first do good things and then tell the public about them. Above all, give the public factual information about your area. False information is detrimental; you must describe conditions as they exist.

MARKET SEGMENTATION

The strategy of **market segmentation** recognizes that few vacation destination areas are universally acceptable and desired. Therefore, rather than dissipate promotion resources by trying to please all travelers, you should aim the promotional efforts specifically to the wants and needs of likely prospects. One of the early steps in marketing tourism, then, is to divide the present and potential market on the basis of meaningful characteristics and concentrate promotion, product, and pricing efforts on serving the most prominent portions of the market—the target markets.

An effective market strategy will determine exactly what the target markets will be and attempt to reach only those markets. The target market is that segment of a total potential market to which the tourism attraction would be most salable. Target mar-

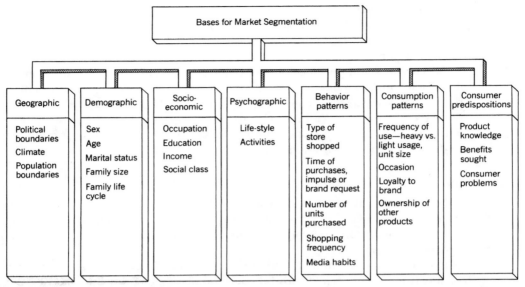

FIGURE 19.2 Typical bases for market segmentation. *(Source: W. Zikmund and M. D'Amico,* Marketing, *3rd ed., copyright © 1984, John Wiley & Sons, Inc., New York; adapted by permission of Prentice-Hall, Upper Saddle River, NJ, from Philip Kotler,* Principles of Marketing, *copyright © 1980, p. 297.)*

kets are defined geographically, demographically (age, income, education, race, nationality, family size, family life cycle, gender, religion, occupation), or psychographically (values, motivations, interests, attitudes, desires) (see Figure 19.2).

Once **target markets** have been determined, appropriate media are chosen to reach these markets. For example, if tennis players are a target market, advertising in tennis magazines would give comprehensive coverage of this market. This would be using a "rifle approach" to zero in exactly on the market in which you are interested. In contrast, a "shotgun approach" would be to advertise in *Time* magazine, which would reach only a small number of your target market and result in large waste circulation.

Market segmentation must be employed in the marketing programs if a shotgun approach is to be avoided. Every tourism attraction can appeal to a multitude of market segments, and market segments can overlap a great deal. The marketing manager must look at market segments and determine which ones offer the most promising potential for his or her services. An excellent example of target marketing to a particular segment is provided by Courtyard by Marriott. The product was designed to appeal to the business traveler with a moderate price and an attractive room. Marriott has been very successful in attracting this market segment.

Tourist resorts typically segment in a variety of ways. One of the most common is geographic. Here the segments tend to be destination visitors (those visitors traveling long distances to vacation at the resort), regional visitors (those who live within the region of the resort and can arrive within four hours' driving time), and local residents.

Proximity of the destination area to the market is an important factor. Generally, the nearer the tourist destination is to its major market, the more likely it is to attract large numbers of visitors. For example, Boblo Island is just a few miles from Detroit and may be reached by excursion boat. As might be expected, this vacation destina-

By promoting their Children's World play area, Carnival Cruise Lines seeks to capture a specific target market: families with young children. *(Photo courtesy of Carnival Cruise Lines.)*

tion receives many times the number of visitors from the greater Detroit area than does Bermuda or the Bahamas.

It follows then that the prime target area for promotion of any given tourist destination area will be that area of greatest population density nearest the vacation area. In the United States, the best concentration of markets for tourism promotion are the metropolitan statistical areas (MSAs), formerly called standard metropolitan statistical areas (SMSAs). These are defined by the U.S. Bureau of Census as a county or group of contiguous counties containing at least one city of 50,000 inhabitants or more. An authoritative source of market data concerning these areas is found in **Survey of Buying Power** published by Sales and Marketing Management, 355 Park Avenue South, New York, N.Y. 10010.

Demographics also provide good segmentation variables. Demographics are the social statistics of our society. Age groups are an excellent example.

Psychographic Market Segmentation

Several models have been developed to classify people according to **psychographic** types. One such model was developed by Stanley C. Plog, who classified the U.S. population along a psychographic continuum—ranging from the psychocentric at one extreme to the allocentric at the other.[2]

---

[2] Stanley C. Plog, "Why Destination Areas Rise and Fall in Popularity," *The Cornell Hotel and Restaurant Administration Quarterly*, Vol. 14, No. 4 (February 1974), pp. 55–58; and Stanley C. Plog, *Leisure Travel: Making It a Growth Market . . . Again!* (New York: Wiley, 1991).

The term **psychocentric** is derived from *psyche-* or *self-*centered, meaning the centering of one's thought or concerns on the small problem areas of one's life. Such a person tends to be self-inhibited and nonadventuresome. **Allocentric,** on the other hand, derives from the root word *allo,* meaning "varied in form." An allocentric person is thus one whose interest patterns are focused on varied activities. Such a person is outgoing and self-confident and is characterized by a considerable degree of adventure and a willingness to reach out and experiment with life. Travel becomes a way for the allocentric to express inquisitiveness and satisfy curiosity. Table 19.1 shows personality and travel characteristics of allocentrics and psychocentrics.

Plog found that the U.S. population was normally distributed along a continuum between these two extreme types. This is illustrated in Figure 19.3. Other groups have been identified between the allocentrics and psychocentrics. Most people fall in the midcentric classification.

A new dimension was added with the establishment of an energy vs. lethargy scale. It was determined that this dimension was not correlated, making it possible to place individuals into four quadrants based on how they scored on the two scales. The four quadrants were high-energy allocentrics, low-energy allocentrics, high-energy psychocentrics, and low-energy psychocentrics. High-energy allocentrics have an insatiable desire to be active on trips, exploring and learning what is new and exciting at a destination. Low-energy allocentrics would travel at a more leisurely pace, be more intellectual, and delve into culture, history, and local customs. At the other end of the continuum, the low-energy psychocentrics were most likely to stay at home.

Through further research, Plog identified the travel preferences of psychocentrics and allocentrics. These are summarized in Figure 19.4. In studying the population on the basis of income level, Plog discovered another interesting relationship. At the lower end of the income spectrum, he discovered a heavy loading of psychocentrics. People at the upper end of the income levels were found to be predominantly allocentric. However, for the broad spectrum in between—for most of America—interrelations are only slightly positive. This finding has several implications.

It is evident that at extremely low levels of family income, travel patterns may be determined largely by the income constraints. Regardless of the psychographic type, a person at the low end of the income spectrum may be compelled to take what Plog considers to be psychocentric-type vacations. College students are a good example of this. They may be allocentric by nature but cannot afford an allocentric-type vacation because such vacations are generally very expensive (a trip to Antarctica or a mountain climbing expedition in Nepal). They travel, instead, to nearby destinations, spend less money, and participate in familiar activities. Therefore, it may be erroneous to conclude that a person with a low income is likely to be psychocentric. The severe income constraint may distort the person's classification in terms of psychographics.

Having defined types of destinations and types of tourists, one is tempted to link these two classifications directly, as Plog has done. Plog superimposed a list of destinations on the population distribution curve, suggesting that allocentrics would travel to such destinations as Africa or the Orient. Psychocentrics, on the other hand, would vacation in nearby destinations (such as Cedar Point, Ohio, theme park for a psycho-

TABLE 19.1

Personality and Travel-Related Characteristics of Allocentrics and Psychocentrics

Psychocentrics	Allocentrics
Intellectually restricted	Intellectually curious
Low risk-taking	Moderate risk-taking
Withhold income	Use disposable income
Use well-known brands	Try new products
Territory bound	Exploring/searching
Sense of powerlessness	Feel in control
Free-floating anxiety/nervousness	Relatively anxiety-free
Nonactive lifestyle	Interested/involved
Nonadventurous	Adventurous
Lacking in confidence	Self-confident
Prefer the familiar in travel destinations	Prefer nontouristy areas
Like commonplace activities at travel destinations	Enjoy sense of discovery and delight in new experiences, before others have visited the area
Prefer sun-and-fun spots, including considerable relaxation	Prefer novel and different destinations
Low activity level	High activity level
Prefer destinations they can drive to	Prefer flying to destinations
Prefer heavy tourist development (lots of hotels, family-type restaurants, tourist shops, etc.)	Tour accommodations should include adequate-to-good hotels and food, not necessarily modern or chain-type hotels, and few "tourist-type" attractions
Prefer familiar atmosphere (hamburger stands, familiar-type entertainment, absence of foreign atmosphere)	Enjoy meeting and dealing with people from a strange or foreign culture
Complete tour packaging appropriate, with heavy scheduling of activities	Tour arrangements should include basics (transportation and hotels) and allow considerable freedom and flexibility
Travel less	Travel more frequently
Spend more of income on material goods and impulse buys	Spend more of income on travel
Little interest in events or activities in other countries	Inquisitive, curious about the world and its peoples
Naive, nondemanding, passive traveler	Demanding, sophisticated, active traveler
Wants structured, routinized travel	Wants much spontaneity in trips
Expects foreigners to speak in English	Will learn languages or foreign phrases before and during travels
Wants standard accommodations and conventional (American) meals	Seeks off-the-beaten-path, little known local hotels, restaurants
Buys souvenirs, trinkets, common items	Buys native arts/crafts
Prefers returning to same and familiar places	Wants different destination for each trip
Enjoys crowds	Prefers small numbers of people

Source: Stanley C. Plog. *Leisure Travel: Making it a Growth Market . . . Again!* (New York: Wiley, 1991).

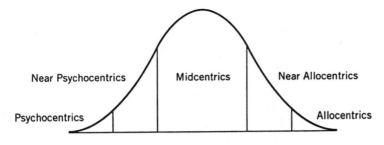

FIGURE 19.3 U.S. population distribution by psychographic type. [*Source: Stanley C. Plog, "Why Destination Areas Rise and Fall in Popularity."* Cornell Hotel and Restaurant Administration Quarterly, *Vol. 14, No. 4 (February 1974), pp. 55–58; and Stanley C. Plog, Leisure Travel: Making It a Growth Market . . . Again!, John Wiley & Sons, New York, 1991.*]

centric from Toledo). The intervening psychocentric types are similarly identified with particular destinations (refer to Figure 19.4).

Plog determined that it is possible to define the psychological character of the destinations in terms of the types of people they appeal to based on the psychographic curve presented in Figure 19.3. Figure 19.4 indicates where some world spots appeared when the concept was first presented. Figure 19.5 shows the view for the early 1990s and verifies Plog's contention that over time there is a steady movement of most destinations toward more psychocentric characteristics. What starts out as a grand exotic place loses favor and image as more tourists discover it and come.

Such a direct linkage between the classification of tourists and of destinations does not consider the important fact that people travel with different motivations on different occasions. A wealthy allocentric may indeed travel to Africa on an annual vacation, but may also take weekend trips to a typically psychocentric destination during other times of the year. Similarly, though probably not as likely, psychocentrics could conceivably vacation in essentially allocentric destinations (with the exception of people with extremely low incomes). For instance, a psychocentric may travel to a remote area under the security provided by traveling with a group of similar tourists, which, being escorted at all times, may persuade a psychocentric to travel, say, to Asia. Is Asia, then, a psychocentric or an allocentric destination? Clearly, a direct relationship between psychographic types and destinations is tenuous at best.

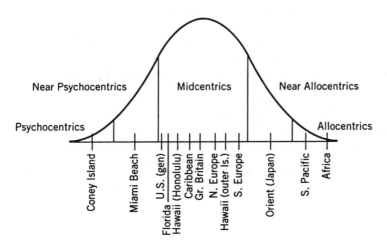

FIGURE 19.4 Psychographic positions of destinations, 1972.

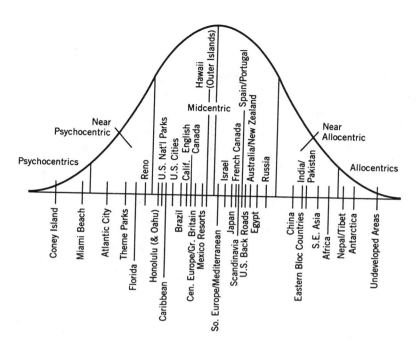

FIGURE 19.5 Psychographic positions of destinations, 1991.
(*Source: Plog Research, Inc.*)

What, then, is the link between the types of tourists and the types of destinations? To develop such a linkage, which will provide a method for predicting travel patterns, two things must be realized. First, as already pointed out, a tourist may travel for different reasons from one trip to the next. Second, a given destination can provide a variety of travel experiences, suitable to a wide range of tourists, depending on the manner in which the trip is planned. The only way in which a systematic linkage can be developed between the types of destinations and the types of tourists is to consider each trip in isolation and examine the motivations that have prompted the trip.

Figure 19.6 illustrates the relationship between types of tourists, travel motivations, and types of destinations. As indicated in the figure, travel motivations link types of tourists and types of destinations in two ways:

1. The primary link is the tourist flow and client satisfaction that will result when a customer is directed to the appropriate type of destination. Such a choice is most likely to maximize satisfactions and produce the kind of travel experience that he or she seeks. A clear understanding is needed of the client's psychological and demographic profile and hence his or her travel motivations for that particular trip. Knowing this enables the purveyor of tourism services (such as a travel counselor) to recommend the types of tour packages (escorted or unescorted, fully planned or flexible), the types of destinations, and the types of travel experiences that will best suit the client or customer's needs. Travel experiences planned in this manner will yield the highest level of client satisfaction.

2. The secondary link relates to the promotion, development, and marketing of destinations to appropriate target markets. Understanding the

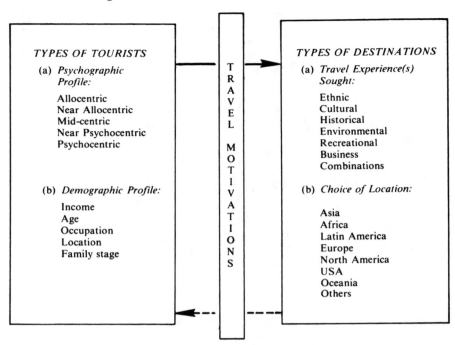

FIGURE 19.6 **Relationships among types of tourists, travel motivations, and types of destinations.**

types of tourists in the target market and the travel motivations of this market will provide a sound basis for deciding the types of environments and services that should be provided at the destination. These understandings will also govern the message content of a promotion campaign.

The following list shows many travel motivations. It should be clear from this list that some motivations are shared by a wide variety of tourists (from allocentric to psychocentric), while other motivations relate to a more narrow spectrum of psychographic types.

Allocentric Motivations

1. Education and cultural motives—learning and increased ability for appreciation, scientific or purposeful; trips with expert leaders or lecturers

2. Study of genealogy

3. Search for the exotic—Hawaii, Polynesia, Japan, Thailand, East Africa, India

4. Satisfactions and sense of power and freedom—anonymity, flying, control, sea travel, fast trains

5. Gambling—Las Vegas, Atlantic City, Monte Carlo, Bahamas, Puerto Rico

6. Development of new friendships in foreign places

7. Sharpening perspectives—awaken senses, heighten awareness

8. Political campaigns, supporting candidates, government hearings

9. Vacation or second homes and condominiums

Near-Allocentric Motivations

10. Religious pilgrimages or inspiration

11. Participation in sports events and sports activities

12. Travel as a challenge, sometimes a test of endurance such as exploring, mountain climbing, hiking, diving

13. Business travel, conferences, meetings, conventions

14. Theater tours, special entertainment

15. A chance to try a new lifestyle

Midcentric Motivations

16. Relaxation and pleasure—just plain fun and enjoyment

17. Satisfying personal contacts with friends and relatives

18. Health—change in climate, sunshine, spas, medical treatment

19. The need for a change for a period of time

20. An opportunity to escape from life's problems

21. The real or imagined glamour of the destination

22. Appreciation of beauty—national and state parks, forests, lakes, wilderness areas, canoe trips, ocean shores

23. Sensual indulgence—food, comforts, luxuries for the body, romance, sexual enjoyment, rest, relaxation

24. Shopping—souvenirs, gifts, expensive possessions like cameras, jewels, furs, cars, antiques, art

25. Joys of transportation—cruise ships, gourmet meals, buffets, comfortable trains, buses, airplanes, autos

26. Pleasure of pre- and post-travel—planning the trip, anticipation, learning, dreaming; then showing pictures and describing the trip after completion

27. Family or personal matters

Near-Psychocentric and Psychocentric Motivations

28. Ego enhancement, quest for status

29. Travel for acceptance, to be comfortable socially

30. Travel as a cultural norm—paid vacations required by law

31. Visit to places seen or read about in the news

32. Visit to amusement parks

Plog first developed his model in 1972, some 27 years ago, and it has been widely cited in tourism literature since that time. It was one of the first attempts to provide a framework within which to analyze tourist behavior. The world has changed considerably since Plog introduced his model. For example, today there are fewer countries

Couples on a honeymoon or celebrating an anniversary remain a popular target market for resorts and cruise lines, which have developed marketing campaigns promoting the romance of travel and the thrill of visiting exotic destinations. *(Photo courtesy of Commodore Cruise Lines.)*

that are considered exotic. Also, there are now other ways to look at tourists, such as through lifestyle analysis or benefit segmentation. Plog's pioneering efforts, however, should not be overlooked. His model still provides a way to examine travel and think about developments using current market conditions.

Plog has modified his model of destination preferences based on more recent research (1995). According to Plog's findings, *Dependables* prefer a life that is more structured, stable, and predictable. These individuals would rather follow a set pattern or routine in order to be able to plan their lives. *Venturers* tend to go more places more often. Leisure travel occupies a central place in their lives, and they eagerly seek out new, exotic, and/or unknown places. Venturers are more likely to fly to their destinations, and they shun guided tours in favor of exploration. *Centrics* comprise the largest group, as one would expect. It is easier to move Centrics, because they possess characteristics of both Dependable and Venturers, and they tend to react favorably to destinations, activities, and events that appeal to travelers on either end of the lifestyle continuum.

VALS

A popular segmentation system used today is **VALS,** which stands for "Values, Attitudes, and Lifestyles" and was developed by SRI International. Its use as a tool for tourism market research in Pennsylvania has been reported by David Shih of the Pennsylvania Department of Commerce.[3]

The basis of the Value and Lifestyle Program is the VALS typology. It divides Americans into nine lifestyles or types, which are grouped in four categories based on their self-images, their aspirations, their values and beliefs, and the products they use. The four categories and nine lifestyles are the following:

- Need-driven groups
  - Survivor lifestyle
  - Sustainer lifestyle
- Outer-directed groups
  - Belonger lifestyle
  - Emulator lifestyle
  - Achiever lifestyle
- Inner-directed groups
  - I-am-me lifestyle
  - Experiential lifestyle
  - Societally conscious lifestyle
- Combined outer- and inner-directed group
  - Integrated lifestyle

The VALS program can be a useful tool for tourism marketing. Lifestyle variables reveal something beyond demographics and are real, meaningful, and relevant. The key VALS segments—belongers, achievers, and the societally conscious—provide valuable information about market segmentation, advertising copy appeals, and media selection.

VALS research conducted in Pennsylvania substantiates the "friendly people" theme as an effective message for the state. Overall, no radical change is indicated in the Pennsylvania tourism campaign's creative approach. However, an objective should be to strengthen the "belonger" base traveling to Pennsylvania, while at the same time to attract more achievers and societally conscious persons. Also, in-state TV advertising should be continued, and additional print advertising in appropriate publications is warranted to attract the achievers and the societally conscious.

One thing that can be counted on in marketing is change; consequently, SRI International has come up with a new VALS 2 (Figure 19.7). The nine original VALS psy-

---

[3] David Shih, "VALS as a Tool of Tourism Market Research: The Pennsylvania Experience," *Journal of Travel Research,* Vol. 24, No. 4 (Spring 1986), pp. 2–11

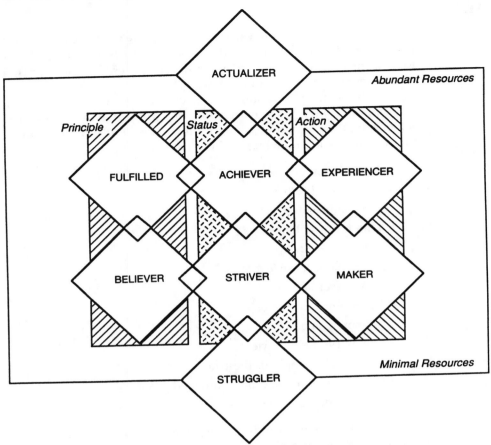

FIGURE 19.7   VALS 2 segmentation system. This system, developed by the Values and Lifestyles Program at SRI International, is a psychographic system for segmenting consumers and predicting consumer behavior. (*Source:* SRI International.)

chographic segments have been replaced by eight new psychographic groups. The eight VALS 2 groups and some of their characteristics are as follows:

- *Actualizers*: Have highest incomes, high self-esteem, abundant resources. Consumer choices are directed toward "the finer things in life."
- *Fulfilleds*: Mature, responsible, well-educated professionals, open to new ideas. High-income, practical, value-oriented consumers.
- *Achievers*: Successful, work-oriented, receive satisfaction from jobs and family. Favor established products.
- *Experiencers*: Youngest of segments, median age of 25. Seek variety and excitement. Avid consumers who spend on clothing, fast food, music, and other youthful favorites.

- *Believers*: Lives centered on family, church, community, and nation. Conservative and predictable consumers who favor American products and established brands.
- *Strivers*: Have values of achievers but few resources. Style is important as they strive to emulate the people they wish they were.
- *Makers*: Practical people who value self-sufficiency. They focus on the familiar.
- *Strugglers*: Have lowest incomes. Lives are constricted. Within means tend to be brand-loyal consumers.

MARKETING PLANNING: THE TOURISM MARKETING PLAN

To this point, the chapter has examined a broad range of fundamental marketing concepts and attempted to give selected examples of their utilization in a tourism context.

In order to make these concepts truly valuable from a tourism standpoint, they must be applied in a comprehensive, integrated manner. The process of application is known as **marketing planning**. The end result of this process is the marketing plan.

The marketing plan for a destination or firm is one of the most important working documents that exists. It serves to translate the many ideals of tourism policy into an active process for attracting visitors and providing the range of experiences they seek from a destination.

The State of California Marketing Plan

While tourism marketing plans can take different forms, one example that we regard as exemplary is that of the State of California as it existed as of March 1, 1998 (see web site **http://www.gocalif.ca.gov/tma/ctma.html**) and Reading 19.2.

The discussion which follows summarizes the State of California Marketing Plan (as of March 1, 1998) as one example of an operational marketing plan. Because marketing plans are by nature "living" documents that change over time, readers should keep this fact in mind. The example is intended to convey the principle of tourism marketing planning rather than the details of implementation of the California Plan. The authors express their appreciation to California for the innovative leadership and planning demonstrated by those responsible for developing the California plan.

Policy as a Framework for Marketing

One of the distinctive characteristics of the California Tourism Marketing Plan (CTMP) is the fact that it actually flows from a policy framework. The California Tourism Policy Act (see Reading 15.1) first provides a philosophical foundation for tourism development and marketing in one of the most significant tourism destinations in the world. It subsequently asserts the need for an effective marketing program (CTMP) to realize the ideals and goals of its philosophical foundation. Furthermore, it also sets out an organizational policy (in the form of the California Tourism Commission) to support implementation of its marketing goals. Finally, it takes the all important step of providing for a funding policy (private assessments) to support the operations of the Commission.

Joint Marketing Efforts

In the majority of cases, a tourism organization will want to market its product and services individually; however, in other cases, joint cooperative efforts will be the most profitable. Typically, these efforts are launched through associations or government agencies. Colorado Ski Country, USA and the Utah Ski Association are groups that jointly promote the services of their members, many of whom are in competition with each other. Publishing posters and directories, answering inquiries, and providing snow reports promote the industry in the most cost-effective way. In addition to these joint marketing efforts, the areas have their own individual marketing programs. They may also work with other private firms such as airlines, rental car companies, and credit card firms to stretch their marketing dollars.

Experience to date has shown that tourism promotion on a country or state basis is best accomplished by a cooperative effort of private industry and government. Joint promotion by private interests and official government tourist organizations is an effective and efficient procedure. One of the examples of the pooling of private and government funds is the Hawaii Visitors Bureau, an independent nonprofit organization that conducts tourism promotion under contract with the State Department of Planning and Economic Development. Approximately 10 percent of the funding comes from private sources and 90 percent from state sources.

In some states, specific "matching funds" are provided by a government tourism agency for tourist promotion, such as the provision of a portion of advertising costs of a private regional tourist promotion association. Various combinations of "matched" funds are possible, depending on the amount of funds available and the provisions of the legislation that authorizes such expenditures of public funds. The Pennsylvania Bureau of Travel Development operates the largest matching grants fund program in the United States.

Summary

Marketing can be defined as the performance of business activities that direct the flow of goods and services from the producer to the consumer or user. Such activities are vital to tourist businesses. The finest, most satisfying tourist facility would be unprofitable without marketing. People have to be informed about a travel destination and become interested in going there before a market can be created.

Basic to the marketing effort are the marketing concept, the marketing mix, product planning and development, pricing, branding, distribution channels, promotion, market research, personal selling, public relations, and market segmentation.

Joint marketing efforts among official tourism organizations, public carriers, and providers of accommodations or even with nearby competing destination areas are strategically sound and typically successful.

A destination and organization's marketing plan defines the approach by which prospective visitors are identified and selectively attracted through promotion and other marketing tools outlined in a destination or organization's marketing plan. This chapter reviews the basic concepts of marketing as applied to tourism and subsequently provides a summary of the marketing plans developed by the State of California for fiscal year 1998/1999.

ABOUT THE READINGS

The first reading examines how traditional branding theory and concepts can be transferred and adapted for us in tourism. It also identifies some of the potential difficulties in doing so.

The second reading provides a comprehensive summary of the marketing plan developed and used by the State of California for the fiscal year 1998/1999.

READING 19.1

THE BRANDING OF TOURISM DESTINATIONS[*]

J. R. Brent Ritchie (University of Calgary) and
Robin J.B. Ritchie (University of British Columbia)

Setting the Stage for the Use of Branding Theory and Practice in Destination Management

It was probably quite predictable, but somehow, it has rather quietly crept up and overtaken us. Despite the fact that "Destination Marketing" has been a well-established component—if not the leading component—of Tourism Destination Management (TDM), we have tended to neglect the "Branding" function of marketing in efforts to develop and implement Destination Marketing Plans.

The foregoing may be due to the fact that the promotion dimension of the marketing function has been so dominant for so long, and that many neophytes in the field tend to equate destination marketing with destination promotion. The great majority of professionals who have not fallen prey to this common "oversight," have recognized the importance of long term "product" development, carefully crafted distribution channels, astute "value pricing," and even the need for internal marketing programs that motivate and empower the highly valued front line staff who provide quality service to visitors on a day-to-day basis.

Despite this progress, we have "somehow" failed to recognize the significance of the Branding function in our efforts to increase awareness of destinations and to create the positive attitudes that are so essential to the final choice of a travel destination.

One immediate response may be that we have not really neglected the branding function; rather we have dealt with it under the alternative label of "Destination Image" (Echtner and Ritchie, 1991). To the extent that we wish to let ourselves off the hook, this may indeed be true. Conversely, to the extent that we wish to more critically assess our performance, we need to recognize that the Branding function is substantially broader in scope than simply image. As such, it can provide a more intensive and rigorous framework for managing the total reputation, or "identity" of a destination (Park, Jaworski et al., 1986) and the manner in which this reputation influences the ability of a destination to attract visitors.

The Role of Branding in Tourism Destination Management

In light of our neglect to date, the purpose of this presentation is to attempt to contribute to the process of adapting and integrating "branding" concepts from the mainstream marketing literature into the tourism management literature, and more specifically, into the literature directly addressing the concerns of Destination Management. Before proceeding, it should be noted that this process of transference and adaptation has just recently been initiated in a major way, both in theory and in practice. It is not insignificant

[*] *This reading is a revised version of a keynote address to the Annual Congress of the International Association of Scientific Experts in Tourism (AIEST) held in Marrakesh, Morocco.*

that the theme of this year's Annual Conference of the International Travel and Tourism Research Association (TTRA, 1998) focused on the theme of "Branding the Travel Market". Undoubtedly, this theme was partly chosen to reflect the western character of the Host City (Forth Worth, Texas). However, the location only served to accelerate a process that was already well under way, as evidenced by such very aggressive efforts of the state of Florida branding initiative (FLA USA, 1997), and an initiative by the province of Saskatchewan to reposition itself (1997). At the national level, both Britain (1997) and Canada (CTRI, 1996) are currently seeking to establish a clearer identity as tourism destinations through systematic "rebranding" campaigns.

Although the level of activity regarding the branding of destinations is substantial and growing, this activity does not appear to be supported by the same level of conceptual and measurement rigour that has characterized the generic field of branding: (Aaker and Keller, 1990), (Aaker, 1991), (Aaker and Biel, 1993), (Aaker, 1996), (Aaker, 1997), (Ambler, 1997), (Biel, 1997), (Blackston, 1995), (Broniarczyk and Alba, 1994), (Carpenter, Glazer et al., 1994), (Cobb-Walgren, Ruble et al., 1995), (Dacin and Smith, 1994), (Duncan and Moriarty, 1997), (Feldwick, 1996), (Fournier, 1998), (Gatignon, Weitz et al., 1990), (Gregory and Wiechmann, 1997), (Kapferer, 1994), (Keller, 1993), (Leclerc, Schmitt et al., 1994), (Park, Jaworski et al., 1986), (Park and Srinivasan, 1994), (Raj, 1985), (Shocker, Srivastava et al., 1994), (Smith and Park, 1992), (Sujan and Bettman, 1989), (Weilbacher, 1995), (Zaichkowsky, 1995).

Previous Uses of Branding in Travel and Tourism

Before launching into the primary theme of the Basic Report regarding the branding of destinations, it should be acknowledged that the overall field of travel and tourism has minimally used branding in several sub-contexts. An obvious example is the hotel sector. From a macro perspective, since 1980, 113 new hotel brands have been introduced in the United States, with twenty new brands in the past two years. From 1980 through 1995, the survival rate for new product was just over 50% (Turkel, 1997). At a strategic level, concern for the impact of branding has reportedly played a significant role in decisions on whether or not to undertake specific facility developments (Morey and Dittman, 1997). Similarly, the airlines have developed strong "brands" and associated logos and "wordmarks." Car Rental firms have also estab-

lished highly recognized international "brands". Certain attractions, most notably "Disneyland", "Sea World", "Six Flags over Texas", "Legoland", and "Dollywood", have, over time, established well recognized and well defined brands and associated images.

Fundamentals of Brand Theory and Brand Management

In examining the applicability and utility of branding for a tourism destination standpoint, we judge it essential to have a basic understanding of the fundamentals of brand theory and brand management.

The Lexicon of Branding

The conceptual terminology associated with branding is both diverse and complex. As a first step in grasping this terminology, it is useful to review a summary of definitions prepared by Upshaw (see Table 1). In particular, Upshaw distinguishes between "Brand Valuation" and "Brand Identity."

Brand Valuation refers to assessing those factors that have a direct bearing on the worth of the brand, including its financial assets and intangible "goodwill." The total accumulated value and worth of a brand is referred to as "Brand Equity"—a term that is used extensively, both in theory and practice.

Brand Identity refers to that part of the equity resulting from the perceived benefits offered by a brand that makes it attractive as the object of a possible purchase. Brand identity is considered to be a product of the melding of a brand's positioning and its personality, and is played out in the product/service performance, the brand name, its logo and graphic system, the brand's marketing communication, and in other ways in which the brand comes into contact with its constituencies (Upshaw, 1995, p. 15).

Aaker on Brand Equity

While the foregoing has introduced the concept of Brand Equity as conceptualized by Upshaw, the area has been most extensively explored and popularized by Aaker (1991). Although Aaker remains active in the field, his framework model for managing Brand Equity (Aaker, 1991) has already established him as a pioneer in the field.

Aaker defines a **Brand** as "*a distinguishing name and/or a symbol (such as a logo, trademark, or package design) intended to identify the goods or services of one seller, or group of sellers, and to differentiate those goods or service from competitors who would attempt to provide products that appear to be identical*" (Aaker 1991, p. 7).

TABLE 1
The Lexicon of Branding

In recent years, as brands and branding have commanded more attention, marketing researchers, consultants, and academicians have created a complete vocabulary to describe various aspects of a brand's makeup. Here is a brief glossary:

- *The brand "equity"*—The total accumulated value or worth of a brand; the tangible and intangible assets that the brand contributes to its corporate parent, both financially and in terms of selling leverage.
- *The brand "identity"*—Part of the brand's overall equity; the total perception of a brand in the marketplace, driven mostly by its positioning and personality.
- *The brand "positioning"*—What a brand stands for in the minds of customers and prospects, relative to its competition, in terms of benefits and promises.
- *The brand "personality"*—The outward "face" of a brand; its tonal characteristics most closely associated with human traits.
- *The brand "essence"*—The core or distillation of the brand identity.
- *The brand "character"*—Having to do with the internal constitution of the brand, how it is seen in terms of its integrity, honesty, and trustworthiness.
- *The brand "soul"*—Related to the brand character, defined as the values and emotional core of the brand.
- *The brand "culture"*—The system of values that surround a brand, much like the cultural aspects of a people or a country.
- *The brand "image"*—Generally synonymous with either the brand's strategic personality or its reputation as a whole.

Source: Upshaw (1995) p. 14.

Aaker defines **Brand Equity** as *"a set of brand assets or liabilities linked to a brand, its name and symbol, that add to or subtract from the value provided by a product or service to a firm and/or to that firm's customers"* (Aaker 1991, p. 15).

He further identifies five categories of assets and liabilities on which brand equity is based.

These include:

1. Brand Loyalty
2. Name Awareness
3. Perceived Quality
4. Brand Associations in addition to perceived quality
5. Other propriety brand assets—patents, trademarks, channel relationships, etc.

Aaker's pioneering work (1997) subsequently examined each of the foregoing assets/liabilities, and their relation to Brand Equity in considerable detail. Some of the key aspects of the examination include:

- The value of Brand Loyalty and how to create and maintain Brand Loyalty
- The nature and value of Brand Awareness
- The nature and dimensions of Perceived Quality
- The nature of brand associations, image, and positioning, and the value of these factors

- The characteristics and roles of effective names, symbols, and slogans
- The characteristics of successful brand extensions
- Strategies for brand revitalization

A Non-Traditional Perspective on "Branding"

While not intended as pejorative, it may be said that both Aaker and Upshaw provide a fairly traditional perspective on the nature and role of branding. It is highly likely that most practitioners in this field will find these approaches to be most relevant and useful. At the same time other readers may find that a recent, somewhat different perspective (referred to as "marketing aesthetics," or the "marketing of sensory experiences in corporate brand output that contributes to the organization's brand identity"), provides some rather innovative insights and some alternative approaches regarding the branding of products and services (Schmitt and Simonson, 1997).

The S&S Marketing Paradigm

Schmitt and Simonson (S&S) stress immediately that their focus is "on the experiential benefits provided by a company or a brand as a whole and the aesthetic planning that is essential to developing and implementing a corporate brand or identity." In effect, this marketing of aesthetics is about experiencing a brand/company; (e.g. Starbucks, ABSOLUT, Pepperidge Farm, Nike, UPS, Leggo, OXO, CAT) where Experiencing = Look, feel, taste, smell, touch, colour, typeface, sound, etc." (S&S, 1997, p vii).

The S&S Paradigm: Its Relevance to Tourism

One highly relevant aspect of the S&S conceptualization of branding is the almost religious call for a strong "NO" to commodilization—i.e. an avoidance of the current situation where "we are awash in high quality look-alike/me-too products and services" (S&S, 1997; p xii). This 1997 sentiment represents an aggressive, in-depth response to a major policy concern regarding the "homogenization of destinations" identified by some 100 international experts in tourism at a policy forum held nearly a decade ago (Ritchie, Hawkins et al., 1993). The S&S approach also reflects a growing recognition among strategic thinkers in tourism that rather than emphasizing only high quality of service (QOS), a greater emphasis needs to be placed on providing "high quality experiences" (QOE) (Otto and Ritchie, 1995). Under this conceptualization, a "travel experience" is viewed as a series of individual service transactions.

Keeley (1992) has expressed similar statements: "There is an overall trend away from product attributes towards lifestyle or value systems." S&S (1997) further reinforce this perspective; "The consumer of today makes choices based on whether or not a product fits into her or his lifestyle; whether it represents an exciting new concept—a desirable experience."

The S&S Marketing Paradigm— Implications for Tourism Destination Management

It is probably already evident from the discussion to this point that the S&S approach stresses the development of an Organizational (Destination) identity where value is provided by satisfying customer experiential needs—their aesthetic needs (S&S, 1997; p. 3). This shift in thinking is reflected in the evolving "Focus of Marketing Approaches" identified by the authors (S&S, 1997). This shift is from the attributes/benefits of a product/service to the sensory experiences it provides—see Figure 1.

As S&S stress "Aesthetics is not esoteric. The vital-

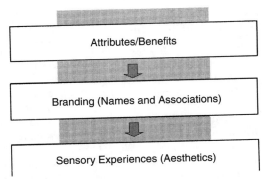

FIGURE 1 Evolving focus of marketing approaches. *[Source: S&S (1997), p. 16.]*

ity of aesthetics in customers' lives provides opportunities for organizations to appeal to customers through a variety of sensory experiences. . . ." The result is the ability to obtain a number of specific benefits that are otherwise difficult to obtain.

The TTRA Focus on Destination Branding

As mentioned earlier, it is only recently that we have seen a significant number of serious attempts at formal Destination Branding (DB). Evidence of DB's "arrival" as a recognized component of the DMO marketing "tool kit" is the previously noted fact that the 1998 annual conference of the International Travel and Tourism Research Association's (TTRA) focused exclusively on destination branding. A number of examples were presented. They included:

- the Silver Dollar City Brand (Henry, 1998)
- "Brand Oregon" (Curtis, 1998)
- the Branding of Outdoor Park Recreation Products (Mills, 1998)
- the Branding of Canada (Meis, 1998)
- the Branding of Small Destinations—the Case of Fredericksburg, Texas (Reeh, 1998)
- the Branding of Branson, Missouri—and the Importance of Research in Achieving Success (Fiveash, 1998)
- Nostalgia as a Branding Strategy for New Orleans (Vesey and Dimanche, 1998)
- the Branding of Hawaii (Okamoto, 1998)

While each of these studies is individually valuable, it is the collective focus on branding that is truly significant. This focus, within one of tourism's major conferences, clearly conveys the importance of current efforts to adopt and adapt traditional branding theory and practices to the tourism field. What is needed now, is the development of a coherent and commonly accepted framework for the use of branding theory in a tourism destination context.

Towards a Framework for Destination Branding

The discussion to this point has attempted to provide an understanding of the fundamental theoretical concepts of generic branding as applied to the traditional marketing literature. Our focus now turns to the adaptation of these concepts to tourism destination marketing. The Report concludes by identifying several theoretical and practical concerns that we believe need to be addressed as we move to include destination branding as an accepted component of destination management.

Destination "Brand": A Definition

A simple transference of the Aaker definition would infer that a "Destination Brand" is a "*distinguishing name and/or symbol (such as a logo or trademark) intended to identify the destination and to differentiate it from competitive destinations.*" Because of the importance that we attach to the concept of "experience" in tourism theory and management, we propose the following definition:

> "*A Destination Brand is a name, symbol, logo, word mark or other graphic that both identifies and differentiates the destination; furthermore, it conveys the promise of a memorable travel experience that is uniquely associated with the destination; it also serves to consolidate and reinforce the recollection of pleasurable memories of the destination experience.*"

The first part of the foregoing definition addresses the traditional **identification** and **differentiation** functions of a brand. The second part, in contrast to traditional product branding, emphasizes that it is especially important that a destination brand convey, either explicitly or implicitly, the promise of the essence of leisure travel—a memorable experience—and one that, if at all possible, is uniquely available at the destination in question. While product brands are also intended to convey a promise associated with satisfactory product usage, the promise is, usually, of a more functional nature in terms of either product performance or the quality of a particular service transaction. Exceptions might be for more pleasure

orientated products (such as perfume), or services (such as massage). In tourism, for a destination to compete and succeed, it must offer a high quality "stream of product/service transactions"—or what is referred to as a "quality experience" (Otto and Ritchie, 1995). At the same time, since anticipation and memory are significant components of a quality experience, any attempt at destination branding must attempt to reassure the individual concerning the promise or expectations of future pleasure and/or excitement. Following travel, the brand can also play an important role to consolidate, and reinforce the post travel recollections of a memorable destination experience.

Measures of Brand Effectiveness

Based on the foregoing discussions, we assert that the primary roles of a destination brand are to provide:

Pre-Experience—Selection

1. Identification
2. Differentiation
3. Anticipation } of the destination re: the destination experience
4. Expectation
5. Reassurance

Post-Experience—Recollection

a) Consolidation } of destination memories
b) Reinforcement

In this regard, Figure 2 attempts to convey the "layered" functioning of a brand as it fulfills the pre-experience roles of selection and reassurance; i.e. creating awareness (identification), image/knowledge (differentiation) anticipation (preference/choice) and finally expectation (desire). As shown, these roles are layered one on top of the other in a complementary manner. In contrast, the "Reassurance" function of the brand acts as a surrounding "cloud of comfort" that things will not go wrong and if they do, they will be appropriately corrected.

The "post-experience" role of a destination brand is captured in Figure 3. As shown, with the "Recollection" function, brands play an important role in consolidating and reinforcing the memories of the destination experience. In effect, it serves as the vehicle to bind or "chain" the many diverse "recall bits" into a holistic memory of the experience.

It follows that the effectiveness of a brand is de-

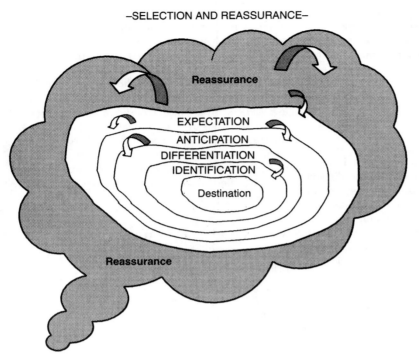

–SELECTION AND REASSURANCE–

FIGURE 2   The pre-experience structure and functioning of a destination brand. Reassurance is a "surrounding cloud of comfort."

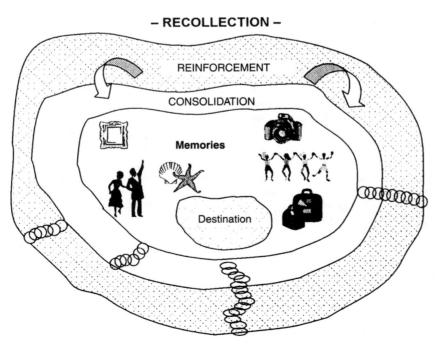

– RECOLLECTION –

FIGURE 3   The post-experience structure and functioning of a destination brand.

Table 2
Measures of Destination Brand Performance

Roles	Measure
Selection *Sub-Components*	• the extent to which the destination is chosen over others
Identification	• degree of recognition/association
Differentiation	• lack of confusion with other destinations
	• lack of confusion with other products/services
Anticipation	• the extent to which brand generates a desire to visit the destination
	• the intensity of the desire to visit that the brand generates
Expectation	• the nature and importance of the specific benefits the visitor expects to realize for the destination experience
Reassurance	• the extent to which the brand provides a "cloud of comfort" for the visitor—a feeling that all is, or will go well during the destination visit
Recollection *Sub-Components*	• the ease, frequency, and strength of recall of the destination experience
	• the extent to which the brand helps create memories of the destination and the visitor's experiences
	• the intensity or warmth of memories elicited
	• the degree of comfort provided that the future/current choice was/is a sound one
Consolidation	• the ability of the brand to serve as a catalyst to tie together the many "bits" of memory of the destination experience
Reinforcement	• the ability of the brand to "cement" the consolidated memory of the destination experience

pendent on how well it performs each of these roles. Measures of these preferences are summarized in Table 2.

Secondary Roles of a Destination Brand

The foregoing discussion has focused on the primary roles for a destination brand. Some less important, or secondary, roles that a brand may play are:

• To serve as a coordinating symbol for a broad range of community development and promotion efforts, many of which fall outside of the normal responsibility of a tourism DMO. Used in this fashion, a destination brand having tourism origins can greatly enhance the status of tourism within a community. The counter risk, of course, is that the other agencies, whose efforts are being coordinated under the destination brand umbrella, may view destination branding as an attempt by the DMO to covertly assume some of their responsibilities and to co-opt associated resources.

• To generate revenue from the sales of clothing and memorabilia bearing the destination name/logo, etc.

• To serve as a security/theft identifier for materials and equipment belonging to the destination.

From Generic Branding to Destination Branding; Some of the Challenges We Face

By its very nature, the field of tourism management is a marketing driven phenomenon. As opposed to the banking sector whose theoretical and managerial roots lie in the field of finance, tourism is a marketing based phenomenon. As such, we have borrowed and adapted many of the concepts, theories, and methodologies of the marketing field. The transference and use of branding in tourism is thus part of this larger process.

This process of borrowing/adaptation is not, however, without its own difficulties. Often the context of tourism is sufficiently different so as to raise questions as to whether marketing concepts and theories or practices are truly appropriate in a tourism setting. As such, those responsible for the marketing of a destination need to constantly question themselves as to the applicability of the traditional marketing approach to branding. Readers wishing to review these concerns are referred to the original version of this reading.

References

The Economist (1997). A new brand for Britain. 43–44.

Calgary Herald (1997). Saskatchewan 'sky high.' Calgary, Alberta.

Aaker, D. A. (1991). *Managing Brand Equity: Capitalizing on the Value of a Brand Name*. New York, The Free Press.

Aaker, D. A. (1996). *Building Strong Brands*. New York, The Free Press.

Aaker, D. A. and A. L. Biel (1993). *Brand Equity and Advertising: Advertising's Role in Building Strong Brands*. Hillsdale, N.J., Lawrence Erlbaum Associates, Inc.

Aaker, D. A. and K. L. Keller (1990). Consumer Evaluations of Brand Extensions, *Journal of Marketing*, 54 (January): 27–41.

Aaker, J. L. (1997). *Dimensions of Brand Personality*, 34(August): 347–356.

Ambler, T. (1997). Do Brands Benefit Consumers? *International Journal of Advertising*, 16: 167–198.

Biel, A. L. (1997). Discovering Brand Magic: the hardness of the softer side of branding, *International Journal of Advertising*, 16: 199–210.

Blackston, M. (1995). The Qualitative Dimension of Brand Equity, *Journal of Advertising Research (Research Currents)*, (July/August): 2–7.

Broniarczyk, S. M. and J. W. Alba (1994). The Importance of the Brand in Brand Extension, *Journal of Marketing Research*, 31(May): 214–228.

Carpenter, G. S., R. Glazer, et al. (1994). Meaningful Brands from Meaningless Differentiation: The Dependence on Irrelevant Attributes, *Journal of Marketing Research*, 31(August): 339–350.

Cobb-Walgren, C. J., C. A. Ruble, et al. (1995). Brand Equity, Brand Preference, and Purchase Intent, *Journal of Advertising*, 24(3): 25–40.

CTRI (1996). *Hot Branding Maximizes Marketing Dollars*, Canadian Tourism Research Institute of The Conference Board of Canada, Ottawa, July/August 1996.

Curtis, J. (1998). *Brand Oregon: The Evolution of a State Image*. 1998 Travel and Tourism Research Association Annual Conference, Fort Worth, Texas, TTRA.

Dacin, P. A. and D. C. Smith (1994). The Effect of Brand Portfolio Characteristics on Consumer Evaluations of Brand Extensions, *Journal of Marketing Research*, 31(May): 229–242.

Duncan, T. and S. Moriarty (1997). *Driving Brand Value: Using Integrated Marketing to Manage Profitable Stakeholder Relationships*. New York, McGraw-Hill.

Echtner, C. M. and J. R. B. Ritchie (1991). The Meaning and Measurement of Destination Image, *Journal of Tourism Studies*, 2(2): 2–12.

Feldwick, P. (1996). What is brand equity anyway, and how do you measure it? *Journal of Market Research Society*, 38(2): 85–104.

Fiveash, R. (1998). *Destination Branding Campaign—Small Budgets (Branson, Missouri)*. 1998 Travel and Tourism Research Association Annual Conference, Fort Worth, Texas, TTRA.

Fournier, S. (1998). Consumers and Their Brands: Developing Relationship Theory in Consumer Research, *Journal of Consumer Research*, 24(4): 343–373.

Gatignon, H., B. Weitz, et al. (1990). Brand Introduction Strategies and Competitive Environments, *Journal of Marketing Research*, 27(November): 390–401.

Gregory, J. R. and J. G. Wiechmann (1997). *Leveraging the Corporate Brand*. Lincolnwood, Illinois, NTC Business Books.

Henry, J. (1998). *The Silver Dollar City Brand*. 1998 Travel and Tourism Research Association Annual Conference, Fort Worth, Texas, TTRA.

Kapferer, J.-N. (1994). Strategic Brand Management: New Approaches to Creating and Evaluating Brand Equity. *Journal of Marketing*. 58: 118–119.

Keller, K. L. (1993). Conceptualizing, Measuring, and Managing Customer-Based Brand Equity, *Journal of Marketing*, 57 (January): 1–22.

Leclerc, F., B. H. Schmitt, et al. (1994). Foreign Branding and Its Effects on Product Perceptions and Attitudes, *Journal of Marketing Research*, 31(May): 263–270.

Meis, S. (1998). *Assessing the Economic Outcomes of Branding Canada: Results, Implications and Applications of the Canadian Tourism Satellite Account*. 1998 Travel and Tourism Research Association Annual Conference, Fort Worth, Texas, TTRA.

Mills, A. S. (1998). *Camper Brand Loyalty for Public Campgrounds*. 1998 Travel and Tourism Research Association Annual Conference, Fort Worth, Texas, TTRA.

Morey, R. C. and D. A. Dittman (1997). An Aid in Selecting the Brand, Size and Other Strategic Choices for a Hotel, *Journal of Hospitality & Tourism Research*, 21(1): 71–99.

Okamoto, B. (1998). *Destination Branding Campaigns (Hawaii Visitor and Conventions Bureau)*. 1998 Travel and Tourism Research Association Annual Conference, Fort Worth, Texas, TTRA.

Otto, J. E. and J. R. B. Ritchie (1995). Exploring the Quality of the Service Experience: A Theoretical and Empirical Analysis, *Advances in Services Marketing and Management* 4: 37–61.

Park, C. S. and V. Srinivasan (1994). A survey-based method for measuring and understanding brand equity and its extendibility, *Journal of Marketing Research*, 31(2): 271–288.

Park, C. W., B. J. Jaworski, et al. (1986). Strategic Brand Concept-Image Management, *Journal of Marketing*, 50(October): 135–145.

Raj, S. P. (1985). Striking a Balance Between Brand "Popularity" and Brand Loyalty, *Journal of Marketing*, 49(Winter): 53–59.

Reeh, P. C. (1998). *Destination Branding Campaigns— Small Budgets (Frederisckburg, Texas)*. 1998 Travel and Tourism Research Association Annual Conference, Forth Worth, Texas, TTRA.

Ritchie, J. R. B. (1975). Some Critical Aspects of Measurement Theory and Practice in Travel Research, *Journal of Travel Research*, 14(1): 1–10.

Ritchie, J. R. B., D. E. Hawkins, et al. (1993). *World Travel and Tourism Review: Indicators, Trends and Issues*, Oxford University Press.

Schmitt, B. and A. Simonson (1997). *Marketing Aesthetics: The Strategic Management of Brands, Identity, and Image*. New York, The Free Press.

Shocker, A. D., R. K. Srivastava, et al. (1994). Challenges and Opportunities Facing Brand Management: An Introduction to the Special Issue, *Journal of Marketing Research*, 31(May): 149–158.

Smith, D. C. and C. W. Park (1992). The Effects of Brand Extensions on Market Share and Advertising Efficiency, *Journal of Marketing Research*, 29(August): 296–313.

Sujan, M. and J. R. Bettman (1989). The Effects of Brand Positioning Strategies on Consumers' Brand and Category Perceptions: Some Insights From Schema Research, *Journal of Marketing Research*, 26(November): 454–467.

TTRA (1998). *Branding the Travel Market.* TTRA Annual Conference, Fort Worth, Texas, TTRA.

Turkel, S. (1997). Nobody Asked Me, but . . . , *World's-Eye View on Hospitality Trends*, (Fall): 23.

Vesey, C. and F. Dimanche (1998). *Let the Good Times Roll: Nostalgia as Image Maker.* 1998 Travel and Tourism Research Association Annual Conference, Fort Worth, Texas, TTRA.

Weilbacher, W. M. (1995). *Brand Marketing: Building Winning Brand Strategies That Deliver Value and Customer Satisfaction.* Lincolnwood, Illinois, NTC Business Press.

Zaichkowsky, J. L. (1995). Defending Your Brand Against Imitation: Consumer Behavior, Marketing Strategies, and Legal Issues. *Journal of Marketing*: 99–100.

READING 19.2

SUMMARY OVERVIEW OF THE CALIFORNIA MARKETING PLAN (FY 1998/99)

The following plan is still in development by the Marketing Advisory Committee. Following completion of their work, it will be submitted to state destination marketing organizations for comment and then be presented to the California Travel and Tourism Commission for final approval.

Mission

To promote California as a travel destination for the expressed purpose of increasing travel spending within the state, generating additional tax revenues from increased travel spending and sustaining and expanding travel and tourism-related employment within California.

Purpose of this Marketing Plan

The California Division of Tourism (CalTour) marketing plan:

- motivates residents of other U.S. states to travel to and within California,

- stimulates travel to and within California by residents of other countries and

- encourages Californians to travel within California.

In support of these, the plan is divided into five program areas:

- research

- collateral and fulfillment

- national marketing

- international marketing
- media relations.

Various marketing tactics are used within each of these program areas to accomplish the plan's major objectives, such as: market research, economic research, program evaluation research, advertising, publicity, promotions, direct marketing, sales missions, trade shows, press trips and trade familiarization tours, collateral, fulfillment and special events. These tactics apply to several of CalTours programs.

The California Tourism Policy Act (1984) specifies that the California Tourism Commission (CTC) or its succeeding California Travel and Tourism Commission (CTTC), in cooperation with CalTour and the Trade and Commerce Agency, adopt and annually update this plan. This was reasserted in the California Tourism Marketing Act (1995/96).

CalTour's Marketing Plan, to the extent practical and feasible, is intended to:

- Serve as a guide for effectuating the California Tourism Policy Act/California Tourism Marketing Act with available resources,
- Include an assessment of the activities and accomplishments of CalTour (in annual report),
- Outline the intended program of tourism promotion and visitor service activities for the oncoming year,
- Delineate the ways, means and programs by which tourism shall be promoted, including any cost-effective marketing methods and techniques to be employed,
- Identify resources as are reasonably necessary from all sources both public and private, to accomplish these promotion and marketing activities,
- Identify and articulate cooperative or shared cost programs, or opportunities for these ventures, with private entities,
- Identify licensing opportunities, including licensing agents (p. 47), and
- Contain other information, data or recommendations that may be germane to the marketing efforts of California pursuant to the intent of the California Tourism Policy Act and the California Tourism Marketing Act.

In effectuating these points, various industry advisory committees consisting of qualified professionals and experts in various segments of the tourism industry aid in the preparation of this plan. They include:

- Marketing (advertising, overall marketing program, promotions)
- California Countryside (rural)
- International
- California Connection (NTA)
- Fun Spots (attractions)
- Cultural Tourism
- Research
- Publications
- California Travel Market

CalTour develops program proposals then presents them to the CTTC or to one of several industry advisory committees for review, comment and refinement, prior to final approval by the CTTC. This process provides the CTTC with the input of industry experts prior to seeing a finished product. There has been significant statewide interest by travel industry individuals who would like to serve on various of these committees. Typically, this interest can be accommodated due to turnover. Interested parties are invited to send requests to serve on an industry advisory committee to CalTour. The CTTC, to the maximum extent possible, attempts to balance membership of advisory committees with representatives from small to large businesses, from all tourism regions, and from diverse industry segments.

CalTour's Role

- Serve as the official travel and tourism marketing representatives of the "destination of California."

- Serve as the marketing umbrella for California under which California destinations and businesses can gain increased attention from consumers, the trade and the media. In accomplishing this, CalTour does not replace the private sector's efforts in marketing individual destinations and businesses within the State, but complements these marketing efforts.

- Manage programs that benefit travel and tourism businesses of all sizes and segments within California.

- Serve as a catalyst in developing strong public/private partnerships to promote tourism to the State, via the execution of marketing programs designed to achieve the mutually beneficial objectives of all participants—public and private.

- Seek appropriate opportunities for cooperative marketing efforts with the private sector in order to gain maximum impact from the program.

- Stimulate California tourism industry involvement in participating in the selling of California and their businesses/destinations at selected domestic and foreign travel trade shows.

- Inform California's travel and tourism industry about opportunities to participate in CalTour's program and of information of value in advancing travel and tourism.

- Inform the media and travel trade of new developments in California travel and tourism for the purpose of stimulating their interest in California as a destination.

- Inform the traveling public (leisure) of the variety of travel opportunities available within California and serve to keep California top-of-mind when they are deciding where to travel.

- Measure and assess effectiveness and impact of Cal-Tour marketing programs. *The State does not have a "main gate" or ticket counter" at which to measure sales, so other methods, such as visitor characteristic studies, visitor impact studies, pre/post research focus groups and coupon redemption are used to assess effectiveness.*

- Generate private-sector support to assist the State in communicating California's unique offerings and attractions.

- Educate and motivate the travel trade via sales missions, familiarization tours (fam tours), educational seminars and sales calls promoting California in targeted markets.

- Encourage competing businesses and destinations to work together for the greater purpose of attracting visitors to California. *At times, CalTour's investment on a given program element is minuscule compared to the industry's. On the California Fun Spots promotion, for example, CalTour provides $180,000 in funding and participating, California attractions raise many times that amount. These attractions are competitors and it is highly unlikely that they would cooperate with one another, were it not for the fact that they want to take advantage of the leadership, vision, equity and financial contribution of the State. Similarly, the $15,000 per rural region provided as seed money for regional marketing, has stimulated additional investment by communities and businesses throughout these regions. Without CalTours involvement, the regions would quickly split into competing marketing groups, resulting in confusing messages to travelers and lowering visitation to the individual regions and California overall.*

- Utilize research to segment marketing activities by demography, sociography, geography and travel interests in order to maximize effectiveness. *CalTour utilizes market research to determine where likely visitors live, who they are and what will motivate them to visit. In the past few years, CalTour has been successful in communicating to a select number of consumer travel typologies (family travel, romantic getaways, recreation and sports, nature, and cultural experiences). Research pinpoints visitors with these interests to be the most likely to be motivated to travel to California.*

Objectives

- Stimulate positive, top-of-mind awareness of California as a "premiere" travel and vacation destination among primary target audiences in targeted areas of the United States, Canada, Mexico and overseas.

- Encourage, persuade and motivate "target audiences" to select California as their travel and/or vacation destination.

- Develop domestic and international markets for California with emphasis on markets which bring new tourists and, thus, new revenue into the State. *The State of California serves a critical role in the industry's ability to tap these lucrative and growing markets, in that it often opens relations and lines of business with new markets due to its official diplomatic stature as an element of state government. This often provides benefits not available to private companies. This can give California travel and tourism businsses a competitive advantage over businesses in less-active or effective states or destinations.*

Strategies

- Conduct travel and tourism marketing that individual businesses and destinations within the state cannot do, as effectively, on their own. *Generally, this involves promoting the concept of California as travel destination.*

- Utilize well-known California tourism icons, such as the Golden Gate Bridge, Disneyland, Half Dome, The Hollywood Sign®[1]–and others, to stimulate recognition and purchase of California vacations. *Just because a destination is successful or highly recognized does not eliminate it from being promoted within the State's marketing program. In fact, just the opposite may*

---

[1] "The Hollywood Sign" is a registered trademark of the Hollywood Chamber of Commerce and is used with permission whenever seen in CalTour communications and marketing.

be needed in order to effectively sell travel to California. Likewise, just because a destination is little-known or unrecognized does not eliminate it from being promoted within the State's marketing program, either. New destinations are just as useful in stimulating travel to California.

• Where possible, useful and or practical, promote travel to all regions, destinations and attractions within California. *CalTour is open to criticism whenever it singles out a particular destination or business for attention, but to be effective, this is often necessary. It is impossible to identify every place or business when promoting California as a travel destination. The state is just too big. However, CalTour attempts to be fair and balanced in its representation of all regions, destinations and attractions within California, but it is not always possible or productive to identify every city, region or attraction within the state. At times, it may be counterproductive to do so. The objective of this program is to effectively market travel to and within California. To best accomplish this, decisions on what to identify or what works best for the given market is left to the professional judgment of CalTour with direction, review and approval provided by the Commission.*

• When marketing within California, promote travel to California's lesser-known and under-utilized destinations.

• When marketing outside California, promote travel to all California destinations.

• Stimulate travel to lesser-known and under-utilized destinations and work with these destinations in the development of regional and related tourism marketing programs.

• Make best use of resources by applying cooperative partnership and funding techniques, where they serve California's best overall interests in attracting travel to and within California.

Primary Target Audiences

• When marketing within California: Adult travel consumers, 25-plus, with annual household income exceeding $35,000

• When marketing in North America, outside California: Adult travel consumers, 35-plus, with annual household income exceeding $50,000

• When marketing outside North America: Adult travel consumers, 35-plus with annual household income exceeding $75,000

• Tour operators, tour wholesalers, receptive operators, travel agents

• Consumer and trade travel media

Program Budget

Research	$ 392,100
Collateral and Fulfillment	1,518,000
California Countryside	410,000
National Marketing	4,682,000
International Marketing	1,426,200
Media Relations	386,000
Reserve	460,167
CalTour Operations	1,806,833
CTTC; Operations	275,400
Assessment Administration	943,3002[2]
Total	**$12,300,000[3]**

Note: Because full descriptions of previous year activities are identified in the Annual Report, the FY 1998/99 Marketing Plan does not detail every activity. It describes only major new additions of departures from the previous plan. For descriptions of undescribed activities, refer to the Annual Report.

Research

This budget proposes growth in the areas of program evaluation and communications.

Research Budget

Budget Economic Impact Analysis	$52,000
Program Evaluation/Return on Investment	85,000
Domestic Market Research	71,000
International Market Research	48,400
Reports and Communications	50,000
Data Collection	32,700
Market Analysis	45,000
Meetings/Reports	3,000
Reserve	5,000
Total Research	**$392,100**

---

[2] Includes current year costs of $550,500 and previous year reimbursable costs of $392,800.

[3] Represents a State allocation of $7.3 million and an industry contribution through assessments of $5 million.

Collateral and Fulfillment

This budget anticipates increased distribution of publications in response to increased advertising and marketing activities. It also adds distribution of publications overseas.

Collateral and Fulfillment Budget

Fulfillment	$612,000
Postage	680,000
Student Packets	35,000
Photography	10,000
Calendar of Events	115,000
Teale Data Center (Web Server)	36,000
Internet Assessed Business List	20,000
Web Site Maintenance	10,000
Total Collateral and Fulfillment	**$1,518,000**

California Countryside

Timing

Year-round
- Rural Grants

Winter
- Ski California

Strategies

- Provide financial incentives that bring together communities and businesses in rural regions to conduct regional destination marketing for the purpose of stimulating increased visitor spending.
- Assist the California ski industry in attracting midweek business from long-haul markets.

Rural Grants

This budget proposes increasing regional marketing grants from $15,000 per region to $25,000 per region . . . $20,000 for general marketing and $5,000 to participate in CalTour organized international sales missions.

California Snow

This off-season co-op program was recently recognized by the Travel Industry Association of America in 1997 as being the finest international marketing program in the United States. CalTour proposes to strengthen its cooperative support to the California Ski Industries Association in order to expand the program in the US, the UK, Brazil, Argentina, Japan and The Netherlands and Chile.

Countryside Budget

Consumer Shows	$10,000
California Grants	200,000
California Snow	200,000
Total Countryside	**$410,000**

National Marketing

Target Audiences

Because advertising is intended to stimulate vacation travel, a high standard is applied to the advertising program's target audiences:

- Adults who took a trip of 100 miles or more away from home during the past 12 months.
- Parents, 35 plus years of age (skewed female) with household incomes in excess of $50,000 per year.
- New visitors.
- Repeat visitors.

Timing

Winter/Spring
- National Advertising
- California Conference on Tourism

Summer/Fall
- TV Pilot Development

Year-round
- California Fun Spots
- California Counselor
- Cultural Tourism
- "California" IMAX Film
- Marketing Consultants

Situational
- Marketing Alliances

Strategies

- Heighten positive top-of-mind awareness of California's diversity and increase the desire to visit California as a tourism destination, throughout the U.S.
- Generate in excess of $5 million in co-operative funds from the private sector to join the State in communicating California's unique offerings and attractions.

- Educate and motivate the travel trade with special promotions, familiarization trips, and sales calls promoting California in targeted markets.

- Generate 500,000 telephone and reader service inquiries from prospective vacationers and, as a result, stimulate potential visitors to travel to California via widespread distribution of the consumer fulfillment guide.

- Support the domestic advertising effort with a strong, positive publicity campaign on California and its 12 regions.

- Create broad-based promotions which complement the goals and objectives of the overall domestic marketing campaign and motivate private sector participation.

- Stimulate economic activity in support of arts, heritage and cultural tourism particularly where the community or cultural facility is financially disadvantaged.

- Provide California hotels, motels and inns, of all sizes, with the promotional benefit of electronic brochures on the world wide web and a direct connection between California marketing efforts and measurement of sales, through the use of a lodging reservation service.

- Improve visitor information available to travelers with disabilities.

Advertising

In 1996, the last year in which state tourism advertising was conducted, very positive returns for California were measured. A study by Dr. Patrick Tierney of San Francisco State University established that CalTour's $2.2 million campaign attracted 785,000 incremental visitors to California, generated $729 million in new travel spending statewide, stimulated $27.7 million in new State tax revenues and $13.3 million in local tax revenues and supported approximately 8,700 new jobs.

This produced a return on investment of 327 to one in increased travel spending and 112 to one in new state tax revenues. Approximately $243 million of the incremental spending occurred in lesser-known and under-utilized parts of California.

However in 1997, the state had to stop advertising in order to finance the implementation of the California Tourism Marketing Act. This resulted in a 52% decline in calls to CalTours 800 number and a significant drop in consideration of California as a travel destination compared to its competitors. In order to respond to this, a new $2.5 million advertising campaign was developed and will be seen during the spring of 1998. It is designed to boost calls and awareness levels. Additionally, the new funds generated by the California Tourism Marketing Act will double the amount available to advertise California as a travel destination in the coming fiscal year.

The national advertising campaign proposed for FY 1998/99 will total $4 million and include a combination of print and television commercials with an entirely new advertising approach. Mering & Associates, the incumbent advertising agency, will be tasked with conducting the advertising program in the coming fiscal year. It has an outstanding reputation for creative work and has teamed with Western Media to provide California with powerful media buying capabilities. Mering was selected on the basis of its creative and account management strengths, after competitive bidding to coordinate California's tourism advertising. It is located in Sacramento.

Prior to 1992, California used the advertising theme "Discover the Californias." This approach emphasized California's diversity by promoting each of the state's 12 tourism regions, individually. In 1992, CalTour recommended a shift in strategy from promoting California as 12 places to promoting the diverse experiences within one place . . . California. In 1994, J. Walter Thompson advertising proposed focusing on the types of vacations taken by California visitors: family, romance, nature and sports.

The four vacation "typologies" of family vacations, romantic getaways, nature outings and recreation-based trips have proven to work well. So, Mering has proposed continuing the approach while also communicating the emotional reasons to vacation in California. The theme recommended for this campaign is "California. Find Yourself Here."

The 1998 Mering TV ads will convey the emotions connected to a California family, romance, nature or sports vacation. Two 30-second television ads for spot market airing were produced in winter, 1998: family and romance. It is anticipated that two others: nature and sports will be produced in fall of 1998, completing a package of ads to run through spring of 1999.

Magazine ads are designed to provide a national supporting presence, though the FY 1998/99 media plan has not been finalized. The magazine ads are full-page, four-color, depicting humorous headlines with dramatic photos. Icons and lesser-known images of California form an impression of our state as an entertaining, satisfying and interesting place to vacation.

Advertising Strategies

- Motivate first-time and repeat domestic visitors to consider California for their vacation;
- Provide a presence for California in major national magazines and on network and spot TV during the critical travel planning season;
- Complement the target marketing program with an advertising program;
- Generate interest and inquiries for vacation planning information from the Division of Tourism;
- Stop the decline of market share experienced in major western out-of-state leisure travel market;
- Boost travel trade inquiries;
- Stimulate use of the State's new reservation service;
- Primarily direct advertising in support of spring/ summer visitation; and
- Secondarily direct advertising in support of fall/ winter visitation and
- Promote State's cultural diversity and lifestyle

Fun Spots

The Fun Spots promotion has added a major new element utilizing the Fun Spots Card. In cooperation with Safeway Select branded products. The Fun Spots will conduct a major point of sale promotion in Safeway Stores throughout Western states and Western Canada. This promotion will multiply the investment made by the state many fold in increased advertising exposure and place California attractions in a non-competitive environment reaching millions of consumers each week through the extent of the promotion.

Shop California

CalTour will coordinate the development of a new cooperative marketing program designed to entice travelers to California's retail centers and shopping districts.

Cultural Tourism

CalTour is working with the California Arts Council, California Office of Historic Preservation and California Council for the Humanities, as well as with the convention and visitors bureaus of San Francisco, Los Angeles, and San Diego in promoting California's cultural riches. This program creatively packages vacation concepts for travel agents, tour operators, the media and consumers and features arts tourism (performing arts, visual arts), heritage tourism (historic sites, structures, districts) and cultural tourism (ethnic communities, festivals). This year's program builds upon this start by expanding materials available to travel agents, tour operators and consumers in promoting cultural tourism.

A 22-minute video produced in early 1998 and highlighting Latin, Asian, African and Native-American communities and festivals will be marketed to various cable television channels for viewer broadcast.

National Marketing Budget

Advertising	$4,000,000
California Fun Spots	180,000
Shop California	100,000
California Counselor	50,000
Cultural Tourism	75,000
"California" IMAX Film	158,000
Marketing Consultant (Jay Key)	85,000
Marketing Alliances (TIA, PATA, NTA, JATA, ACTA, ASTA)	10,000
California Conference on Tourism	5,000
NTA	9,000
Video Duplication	10,000
Total National Marketing	**$4,682,000**

International Marketing

Approximately 290 million visitor trips occur in California annually, of which international visitation accounts for 3 percent or roughly 9 million person-trips. Although the numbers of international travelers to the state falls far below that of the domestic traveler, the sector is still highly profitable and worth all of the attention California can provide and California is the world's eighth most visited destination.

Typical characteristics of the international traveler such as a longer length of stay and higher daily expenditure justify the effort and expense to attract them. Because they plan their trips so far in advance, they have also proven to be more dependable than domestic travelers who may be dissuaded by short-range changes in weather or disaster. And, due to alternate seasons in some markets (it's summer in Australia when we are wintering), they can be relied upon to fill seasons when U.S. travelers aren't traveling.

International markets continue to represent the

fastest growing segments today and California is ideally positioned to benefit from the spectacular growth in international tourism due to its allure and its geographic location. Yet, despite California's positive international image and allure, our state has strong competition for the international traveler, not only from other states, but from other countries.

In previous years, CalTours international marketing efforts were strategically designed to maximize cost effectiveness by leveraging its dollars with key private sector partners, such as selected airlines. This has proven to be very successful. Further strengthening these efforts has been the cooperation from the state's travel industry such as: convention and visitor bureaus, hotels, associations, attractions, motorcoach companies, etc. With the tremendous involvement and support of all of these partners, the effectiveness of California's efforts to identify our state as a special destination and thus influence the international traveler through the travel trade and media, has been bolstered.

Pursuing the international traveler is certainly worth the chase for all the reasons stated above and many others, but it is also expensive. The cost of attending trade shows, developing literature in foreign languages, implementing creative promotions, the need for extensive educational programs and an extended time period for results all provide expensive challenges. Often, the cost for providing developing components is born solely by the state, especially in emerging markets where the industry relies on CalTour to "test" the market. If positive results are seen and demand is evident, CalTour is then able to attract the interest of more California businesses and destinations and build a larger presence marketing in these countires, allowing the industry to participate at lower costs than if they tried to open these markets on their own.

Approval of the Marketing Act provides California to compete more effectively with other states and destinations overseas. An increase in funding of nearly twice what the program had before will allow it to dramatically increase its marketing efforts abroad. This is a very positive step in helping California exceed its competitors in pursuing the coveted foreign traveler.

Target Markets

The target markets CalTour will focus on will be composed of a mixture of California's primary and secondary markets. Based on resources, potential emerging markets such as eastern block European regions and non-traditional South American and Asian nations may also be included, but on an exploratory market development basis only.

Canada
- Western Provinces consisting of Alberta and British Columbia
- Main population centers in Eastern Provinces consisting of Montreal and Toronto

Western Europe
- Austria
- Benelux Countries (Belgium, Luxembourg)
- France
- Germany
- Italy
- The Netherlands
- Scandinavia (Sweden, Finland, Norway, Denmark)
- Switzerland
- United Kingdom

Pacific Rim
- Australia/New Zealand
- Japan
- Korea
- People's Republic of China (Taiwan)

Latin America
- Argentina
- Brazil
- Chile
- Mexico

Emerging Markets
- China (Mainland)
- India
- Russia
- Singapore/Malaysia

Goals

The goals for the international program are many and varied. Priority will be given to maintaining the highest communication and service possible to those within the industry who rely on CalTour's services to maximize their selling efforts.

- Improve overall response time to travel trade inquiries for information and publication requests from all markets
- Maintain high visibility to the consumer and travel trade in Western Canada
- Increase awareness among the consumer in Eastern Canada markets

- Increase product awareness among travel trade across Canada
- Improve awareness and delivery of information to the consumer in the UK and Germany markets
- Increase efforts to reach buyers directly through sales calls in all markets
- Expand efforts to educate the travel trade in all markets
- Strengthen relationship with United Airlines regional sales offices in selected markets
- Expand efforts to assist rural regions in promoting their areas to international markets
- Expand efforts to reach consumers directly in appropriate markets through leveraged special promotions
- Strengthen relationships with the travel trade in selected markets through establishing official representation services
- Increase awareness among Japanese travelers as to potential vacation destinations beyond traditional gateways
- Improve awareness and convenience for consumer to access information in selected markets
- Improve awareness among travel trade in all markets regarding CalTour and services available
- Maintain high level of communication with travel industry partners

Travel Trade Development

The fundamental tool necessary to stimulate international travel is salesmanship. This occurs by meeting with, educating and motivating tour packagers, tour operators and travel agents (buyers). The most efficient and effective method of doing this is still by attending trade shows. Trade shows provide a cost-effective way of meeting a country's most influential buyers, answer their questions, determine their needs and establish lines of communication and supply of consumer and trade information. CalTour, as discussed in the Annual Report, has been moving its international travel trade development efforts away from organizing and conducting expensive sales missions to increasingly conducting specific educational efforts for travel agents. Good examples of how Cal-Tour does this is seen in the educational seminars proposed for Canada, though similar efforts are apparent throughout the following calendar.

Fall (September–November)
- Western Canada Travel Agent Educational Seminars
- World Travel Market—London
- Association of Canadian Travel Agencies British Columbia/Yukon Travel Exchange (ACTA BC/Yukon)
- VUSAMART (Asia)
- La Cumbre (Latin America)
- Visit USA Fair–Korea
- Travel Trade Workshop—Switzerland
- Association of Brazilian Agencias Viajes (ABAV) Brazil

Winter (December–March)
- Expo Vacaciones—Mexico
- Australia/New Zealand Destination Seminars
- International Tourism Exchange, Bourse (ITB)—Germany
- Visit USA Workshops—Switzerland, Austria and France
- Visit USA Workshops—Belgium and The Netherlands
- Visit USA Seminars—Sweden and Finland
- Destination Seminars—Canada (Quebec and Ontario)
- California Travel Market (Anaheim)

Spring (April–June)
- Visit USA Travel Trade Shows—Argentina, Brazil, Chile
- Travel Industry Association of America—Discover America Pow Wow
- European Incentive Business Travel Market, Switzerland
- Associacion De Representantes De Lineas Aereas En Guadalajara, Guadalajara-Mexico

Foreign Representation

California's contracted representatives in the UK, Germany and Japan have been a significant factor in increasing California's presence in these markets, as evidenced by the growing number of UK tour operators that have added California to their tour packages. When the UK contractor was established, only 79 packages featured California. Today, 132 packages feature California. Similar successes have been achieved in Germany and Japan.

The amount spent in the State's top three markets has not increased for several years, while travel trade and consumer interest in California has grown significantly. To respond to this increased need for service and information, CalTour proposes increasing the financial support to its three international contractors.

Additionally, CalTour proposes either hiring contractors to represent California in several important developing markets or adding a California tourism employee to the Trade and Commerce Agency staff, where representative firms are not as effective. In the coming year, CalTour proposes adding a tourism employee in the TCA office in Mexico City. If market conditions are favorable a similar position should be considered for TCA's Taiwan office to support development of Chinese tourism from Taiwan and Hong Kong.

The need for an increased California presence is also needed in Australia/New Zealand and Brazil/Argentina/Chile/Uruguay, where tourism is of present significance or growing quickly. Since the closure of USTTA, California has suffered a major lapse in reaching the travel trade in the Australia and New Zealand markets. At this time, CalTour is not prepared to pursue establishing a representation office there, but we recommend that a visitor information distribution service be retained for the travel trade, there. Brazil represents a market with a proven demand for the west coast and is ripe for an introductory California presence to bolster its twice a year attendance at travel trade exhibitions.

Visit USA Information Centers

As the result of USTTA's demise, the State of California's role in providing travel planning information and education to the international trade and airlines has become increasingly important. Emerging as replacing USTTA are privately financed Visit USA Information Centers. CalTour plans to place California information in several of these centers in countries where the State does not have its own visitor information center or travel trade representation. At a nominal fee for $750–$1,200 per each center annually, these facilities provide a cost-effective option to maintain constant delivery of California's message to the trade.

Promotions

California businesses and destinations have benefited from various types of consumer and trade promotional programs conducted by CalTour. For example, the *California Dream Days* campaign in Canada has gained substantial recognition over its fourteen years. Similarly, cooperative ventures (with Virgin Atlantic in the UK in support of California Ski Industry Association marketing and with United Airlines in Japan dur-

ing the *California Dream* promotion) have proven to be highly beneficial in stimulating increased visitation.

The primary cooperative venture between CalTour and United Airlines for 1998–99 is the new *My California* campaign targeted at the Japanese traveler. United plans to support this campaign with $2 million in advertising and promotional investment, and CalTour is coordinating the support and involvement of several California companies and destinations.

Miscellaneous

Other elements also play a major role in effectively promoting a product or service to the international market. CalTour will continue to use familiarization tours to provide a personal experience that will better enable buyers to know aspects of California and effectively package them. In addition, CalTour believes a stronger and more consistent communication should be established with the international travel trade and the development of a quarterly or half-yearly newsletter will assist in California maintaining top-of-mind presence.

The existing foreign language brochure developed by CalTour for use in selected markets is long overdue for an update and will be redesigned and printed in eight languages. As well, the use of the 10-minute video is needed to assist in CalTour's educational efforts and additional copies will be made.

Finally, due to the wide range of publications produced by CalTour and the expense of shipping bulk quantities overseas, a consolidated trade show piece will be distributed at exhibitions. The piece will provide information regarding CalTour's services, web site details, valuable contact information for major tourism entities and new tourism developments as well as reduce waste and shipping expenses.

International Marketing Budget

WTM	$75,000
CTM	40,000
Trade Shows	$50,000
Foreign Representation/Offices	
Germany/UK (Theresa Carey,	
Martin Walter)	$180,000
Japan (Ko Ueno)	$175,000
New Foreign Representatives/Offices	$200,000
Mexico City (TCA/ITI)	
Australia/New Zealand	
Brazil/Argentina/Chile/Uruguay	
Taiwan/Hong Kong (TCA/ITI—	
conditional on Asian financial situation)	

Visit USA Centers

Belgium	$1,200
Canada (Vancouver, Montreal, Toronto)	$3,000
Chile	$1,000
Colombia	$750
Costa Rica	$750
Ireland	$800
Italy	$900
Korea	$1,000
Netherlands	$1,300
New Zealand	$500
Switzerland	$500

Promotions

California Dream Days (Canada)	$90,000
United Airlines Co-op	$20,000
Exhibition Networking/ International Co-op Promotions	$25,000

Miscellaneous

Foreign Language Brochure	$200,000
International Consumer Fulfillment	189,000
International Fulfillment—Schotte	11,000
Familiarization Tours	$15,000
Video Duplication	$10,000
Trade Show Piece	$7,500
International Travel Trade Newsletter	$12,000
Miscellaneous Expense	15,000
Travel Trade Consultant (Lisa Kruttschnift)	$100,000
Total International Marketing	**$1,426,200**

Media Relations

Media Outreach and Editorial visits will be expanded and added to key international markets. Domestic and international press trips will be increased substantially in response to media outreach efforts and in support of larger advertising and cooperative marketing activities.

CalTour will develop monthly feature stories and photography for distribution nationally, and for placement in weekly and community newspapers through matte and syndicate services.

A new quarterly newsletter directed to domestic tour operators and travel agents (California Counselors) will stimulate their interest in adding new aspects of California to their packages. In addition, Insights will be sent via e-mail on an intranet, allowing for immediate and ongoing communications with all assessed businesses and marketing partners. And, a media relations crisis communications reserve will be retained specifically to respond to disasters.

Media Relations Budget

Media Outreach (Domestic) New York, Los Angeles, San Francisco	$75,000
Media Outreach (International) Canada, Germany, Japan, United Kingdom	60,000
Publicity	
Press and Feature Releases	40,000
Matte Service	20,000
What's New in California (quarterly)	10,000
Press Trips	20,000
Evaluation	
Newsclipping Service & Analysis	25,000
Newsletters	
Insights (quarterly)	51,000
Intranet	30,000
Trade Newsletter	30,000
Technical Assistance	
Crisis Communications	25,000
Total Media Relations	**$386,000**

[*Note:* An expanded media relations program is predicted on the hiring of a full-time publicist and/or retaining the services of a public relations firm.]

Licensing Opportunities and Agents

No licensing opportunities or agents are detailed at this time for 1997/98. The decision whether or not to investigate licensing opportunities will be left to the CTTC.

Reserve

Total Reserve	**$450,167**[4]

Caltour Operations

Salaries & Benefits	$883,817
General Expense	85,357
Printing	35,000
Communications	65,000
Postage	98,390
Travel, In-State	62,000

---

[4] includes potential industry campaign reimbursement costs.

Travel, Out-of-State	98,583
Training	5,375
Facilities Operations	101,167
Contracts—Internal (DF&A)	15,000
Central Administrative System	1,029
Equipment	7,140
Distributed Administration	223,975
Interns	75,000
Data Processing/Laptop Computers	20,000
Memberships	20,000
Conference Fees	10,000
Total CalTour Operations	**$1,806,833**

CTTC Operations

Total CTTC Operations	**$275,4005**[5]

[5] This is a ballpark figure inserted for budget development purposes only. The CTTC will determine its ongoing operational costs.

Assessment Administration[6]

Personnel Services	$253,900
General Operating Expense	109,400
Data Processing Services	14,400
Assessment Printing & Postage	21,300
Consultant Services	151,500
FY 1997/98 Assessment/Operations	$392,800
Total Assessment Administration	**$943,3007**[7]

[6] Annual recurring assessment costs are projected to be $392,800.

[7] Includes partial year set-up costs and one-time hardware/software costs of $550,500.

KEY CONCEPTS

advertising
advertising agency
allocentric
branding
channels of distribution
consumer orientation
four Ps
marketing
joint marketing efforts
market research

market segmentation
marketing concept
marketing plan
marketing planning
marketing mix
place
pricing
product
product life cycle

product planning and development
promotion
psychocentric
psychographics
public relations
selling
Survey of Buying Power
target market
VALS

INTERNET SITES

The Internet sites mentioned in this chapter are repeated here for convenience plus some selected additional sites. For more information, visit these sites. Be aware that Internet addresses change frequently, so if a site cannot be accessed, use a search engine. Also use a search engine to locate many additional sites that are available.

Advertising Age
http://www.adage.com

American Marketing Association
http://www.ama.org

INTERNET EXERCISES

Site Name: Switzerland Tourism

URL: http://www.schweizferien.ch/shadwelcome.html

Background Information: Information regarding tourism in Switzerland

Site Name: Welcome to Lago di Garda

URL: http://gardalake.it/

Background Information: Tourism information on Lake Garda, Italy

Site Name: Visit China

URL: http://visit-china.com/

Background Information: A comprehensive, up-to-date guide of China's tourism, international trade and investment opportunities. Visit China provides you with the information on China's tourist sites and travel services as well as China's market and products.

Site Name: New Zealand Guest Information Services

URL: http://www.gisnz.com/

Background Information: NZ Guest Information Services is a company in its fifth year of operation. This information service company promotes tourism in New Zealand.

Site Name: Egypt's TourismNet

URL: http://www.idsc.gov.eg/tourism/

Background Information: Egypt's TourismNet provides searchable directories of Egypt's hotels, restaurants, cruise lines, travel agents, transportation companies, and tourist attractions.

Site Name: Queen Victoria Market, Australia

URL: http://www.qvm.com.au/

Background Information: The Queen Victoria Market is more than just Melbourne's shopping mecca—it is an historic landmark, a tourist attraction and an institution for Melbournians.

Site Name: Travel Alaska Online

URL: http://www.travelalaska.com/intro/indexintro2.html

Background Information: Travel Alaska Online provides vacation-planning information.

Site Name: Kentucky Network Services

URL: http://www.uky.edu/kentucky-network-services.html

Background Information: Provides travel and tourism information for Kentucky.

Site Name: Genuine Nebraska

URL: http://visitnebraska.org/

Background Information: This web site offers extensive, database-driven information about places to go and things to see and do in Nebraska.

Site Name: Vermont/New Hampshire WWW Resources

URL: http://www.destek.net/Maps/VT-NH.html

Background Information: Provides links to people, places and industries in both Vermont and New Hampshire.

Site Name: Guide to Shooting Film in Wyoming

URL: http://www.wyomingfilm.org/

Background Information: This Guide has been created with one goal: to help you find information about Wyoming quickly and efficiently.

Site Name: State of Delaware

URL: http://prodhp.state.de.us/

Background Information: The information shown in this tourism section of the State of Delaware's web site was prepared by the Delaware Tourism Office with the assistance of the University of Delaware's Small Businesses Development Center which provides counseling and business planning assistance to small businesses throughout the state.

Exercises

Choose three state and three international tourism sites from the list above.

1. Which sites have the most powerful marketing concept in each category?

2. What characterizes the sites you have chosen?

3. What marketing concepts do these sites employ?

4. What is your opinion of using the Internet as a channel of distribution for advertising? Why?

5. How do the U.S. sites compare with the international sites?

QUESTIONS FOR REVIEW AND DISCUSSION

1. What is the marketing concept?

2. Do you regard the concept of consumer-oriented marketing as a step forward? Why or why not?

3. What are the stages in the product life cycle? What are the marketing implications of each stage?

4. What are the key factors a tourism marketing manager must consider in setting price?

5. Discuss the conditions when penetration pricing should be used. Price skimming?

6. Discuss how a tourism firm's pricing strategy may influence the promotional program.

7. How are channels of distribution selected? Using an example, explain.

8. How does the branding of a tourism destination differ from the branding of (a) a tube of toothpaste, (b) an automobile, (c) a computer, (d) a fast food restaurant, (e) a hotel?

9. What does "branding" a tourism destination really mean?

10. How would you go about identifying a "brand" for (a) a city, (b) a state, (c) a country? What difficulties do you think you will encounter?

11. What might be an effective brand/logo/symbol/icon for Switzerland? Poland? Miami? Boise, Idaho? Moose Jaw, Saskatchewan? Moscow?

12. The cost of running an ad on the back cover of *Time* magazine is more expensive than is hiring a salesperson for a year. As the marketing manager for a leading hotel chain, you have just been told by the president of the company to eliminate ads and hire more salespersons. You feel that this would be a serious mistake. What would you do to change the president's mind?

13. What are some examples of realistic objectives of a tourism marketing program? Use a resort hotel, a motorcoach, and a tour company.

14. Explain the statement "tourism promotion efforts undirected by research are largely a waste of effort." Do you agree?

15. What are the advantages of marketing vacation packages?

16. Give an example of a vacation package that might be marketed in your area. How would you market it? To whom?

17. Why is marketing planning so important?

18. Why should a state's market plan be related to its tourism planning?

19. Would marketing planning for Montana be different from that for California? How? Why?

20. What value do you see in market segmentation? Give an example.

21. As the planner of a new wing on your resort hotel, how does product planning and development in a marketing context apply?

22. You are a restaurant manager in a popular year-round resort area. How do you decide on the price levels of your meals?

23. What kind of advertising program is best for a cruise company?

24. As president of your local convention and visitors bureau, propose a joint marketing scheme that would have surefire results.

25. As a resort hotel manager, would you always advertise your destination area along with your individual resort property? Explain why or why not.

CASE PROBLEM

A Midwest lakeshore community is economically depressed. By 1999, industrial employment had fallen to 50 percent of its 1970 level. Tourism seems to be a logical industry to expand. The county has 25 miles of beautiful Lake Michigan sandy beaches and is adjacent to a 1.5 million-acre national forest. The forest has many fine rivers and inland lakes, offering bountiful year-round recreation. This area is only about a five hours' drive from Chicago or Detroit and has thrice-daily air service from Chicago.

The chamber of commerce has virtually no budget for tourism promotion. State law authorizes an added

2 percent local tourism promotion tax to the 4 percent state rooms tax. However, enacting the added tax must be approved by local lodging establishments. Vote is apportioned by number of rooms owned. Managers of the two larger motels are in favor of the tax, but they suspect that the smaller motel owners will not collect all or part of the tax, lowering their room rates proportionally and creating a price advantage over the honest larger motels. Added tourism is greatly needed to stimulate the local economy. How can this impasse be resolved?

SELECTED REFERENCES

Aaker, D. A. *Managing Brand Equity: Capitalizing on the Value of a Brand Name.* New York: The Free Press, 1991.

Abbey, James R. *Hospitality Sales and Advertising,* 3rd edition. East Lansing, MI: Educational Institute of the American Hotel and Motel Association, 1998.

Ananth, Mangala, et. al. "Marketplace Lodging Needs of Mature Travelers." *Cornell Hotel and Restaurant Administration Quarterly,* Vol. 33, No. 4, pp. 12–24, August 1992.

Augustyn, Marcjanna, and Samuel K. Ho. "Service Quality and Tourism." *Journal of Travel Research,* Vol. 37, No. 1, pp. 71–75, August 1998.

Barskey, Jonathan D. "Building a Program for World-Class Service." *Cornell Quarterly,* Vol. 37, No. 1, pp. 17–27, February 1996.

Berry Leonard L. *Great Service: A Framework for Action.* New York: The Free Press, 1995.

Bonn, Mark A., and Richard R. Brand. "Identifying Market Potential: The Application of Brand Development Indexing to Pleasure Travel." *Journal of Travel Research,* Vol. 34, No. 2, pp. 31–35, Fall 1995.

Bowen, John, James Makens, and Stowe Shoemaker. *Casino Marketing.* New York: Wiley, 1999.

Briggs, S. *Successful Tourism Marketing.* London: Kogan Page, 1997.

Burke, James E., and Barry P. Resnick. *Marketing and Selling the Travel Product.* Cincinnati, OH: South-Western Publishing Company, 1991.

Butterfield, David W., Kenneth R. Deal, and Atif A. Kubursi. "Measuring the Returns to Tourism Advertising." *Journal of Travel Research,* Vol. 37, No. 1, pp. 12–20, August 1998.

Chiames, Christopher. *How to Write a Public Relations Plan.* New York: Travel Industry Association of America, 1995.

Chon, Kye-Sung, and William P. Whelihan III. "Changing Guest Preferences and Marketing Challenges in the Resort Industry." *FIU Hospitality Review,* Vol. 10, No. 2, pp. 9–16, Fall 1992.

Crotts, John C., and Chris A. Ryan. *Marketing Issues in Pacific Area Tourism.* Binghamton, NY: The Haworth Hospitality Press, 1997.

Davidoff, Philip G., and Doris S. Davidoff. *Sales and Marketing for Travel and Tourism.* Englewood Cliffs, NJ: Prentice-Hall, 1994.

Dev, Chekitan S., Saul Klein, and Reed A. Fisher. "A Market-Based Approach for Partner Selection in Marketing Alliances." *Journal of Travel Research,* Vol. 35, No. 1, pp. 11–17, Summer 1996.

Faulkner, Bill, and Robin Shaw. *Evaluation of Tourism Marketing.* Canberra, Australia: Bureau of Tourism Research, no date.

Fodness, Dale, and Brian Murray. "A Typology of Tourist Information Search Strategies." *Journal of Travel Research,* Vol. 37, No. 2, pp. 108–119, November 1998.

Gartrell, Richard B. *Destination Marketing for Convention and Visitor Bureaus.* Dubuque, IA: Kendall/Hunt, 1988.

Hanna, J. R. P., and R. J. Millar. "Promoting Tourism in the Internet." *Tourism Management,* Vol. 18, No. 7, pp. 469–470, November 1997.

Harris, Kimberley J. "International Hospitality Marketing on the Internet: Project "Interweave." *International Journal of Hospitality Management,* Vol. 15, No. 2, pp. 155–163, June 1996.

Health, Ernie, and Geoffrey Wall. *Marketing Tourism Destinations: A Strategic Approach.* New York: Wiley, 1992.

Holloway, C. J., and C. Robinson. *Marketing for Tourism,* 3rd edition. Essex, UK: Longman, 1995.

Horner, S., and J. Swarbrooke. *Marketing Tourism Hospitality and Leisure in Europe.* London, UK: ITBP, 1996.

Kotler, Philip, Donald H. Haider, and Irving Rein. *Marketing Places.* New York: The Free Press, 1993.

Kotler, Philip, John Bowen and James Maken. *Marketing for Hospitality and Tourism.* London: Prentice-Hall, 1998.

Laws, Eric. *Tourism Marketing: Service and Quality a Management Perspective.* Leckhampton, England: Stanley Thornes, 1991.

Lewis, Robert C. *Cases in Hospitality Marketing and Management.* New York: Wiley, 1997.

Lewis, Robert C., and Richard E. Chambers. *Marketing Leadership in Hospitality: Foundations and Practices.* New York: Wiley, 1995.

Lickorish, Leonard, and Alan Jefferson. *Marketing Tourism: A Practical Guide.* Essex, UK: Longman, 1991.

Lumsdon, I. *Tourism Marketing.* London, UK: ITBP, 1997.

Mancini, Marc. *Selling Destinations: Geography for the Travel Professional.* Cincinnati, OH: South-Western Publishing Company, 1992.

Messmer, Donald J., and Robert R. Johnson. "Inquiry Conversion and Travel Advertising Effectiveness." *Journal of Travel Research,* Vol. 31, No. 4, pp. 14–21, Spring 1993.

Middleton, Victor T. C. *Marketing in Travel and Tourism.* Oxford, England: Butterworth Heinemann, 1994.

Mill, R. C., and A. M. Morrison. *The Tourism System: An Introductory Text.* Dubuque, IA: Kendall/Hunt Publishing Company, 1998.

Morgan, Nigel, and Annette Pritchard. *Tourism, Promotion, and Power.* New York: Wiley, 1998.

Morrison, Alastair M. *Hospitality and Travel Marketing,* 2nd edition. Albany, NY: Delmar, 1996.

Nykiel, Ronal A. *Marketing in the Hospitality Industry.* East Lansing, MI: Educational Institute of the American Hotel and Motel Association, 1997.

O'Neill, John W. "Effective Municipal Tourism and Convention Operations and Marketing Strategies: The Cases of Boston, San Antonio, and San Francisco." *Journal of Travel and Tourism Marketing,* Vol. 7, No. 3, pp. 95–125, 1998.

Otto, Julie E., and J. R. Brent Ritchie. "The Service Experience in Tourism." *Tourism Management,* Vol. 17, No. 3, pp. 165–174, May 1996.

Perdue, Richard R. "Target Market Selection and Marketing Strategy: The Colorado Downhill Skiing Industry." *Journal of Travel Research,* Vol. 34, No. 4, pp. 39–46, Spring 1996.

Plog, Stanley C. *Leisure Travel: Making It a Growth Market . . . Again!* New York: Wiley, 1991.

Plog, Stanley C. *Vacation Places Rated.* Redondo Beach, CA: Fielding Worldwide, Inc., 1995.

Powers, Tom. *Marketing Hospitality.* New York: Wiley, 1997.

Pritchard, Annette, et al. "Reaching Out to the Gay Tourist: Opportunities and Threats in an Emerging Market Segment." *Tourism Management,* Vol. 19, No. 3, pp. 272–282, 1998.

Reich, Allen Z. *Marketing Management for the Hospitality Industry: A Strategic Approach.* New York: Wiley, 1997.

Reid, Robert D. *Hospitality Marketing Management.* New York: Van Nostrand Reinhold, 1989.

Richardson, John I. *Marketing Australian Travel and Tourism: Principles and Practice.* Victoria: Australia: Hospitality Press, 1996.

Ries, A. *Focus: The Future of Your Company Depends on it.* New York: Harper Business, 1996.

Ryan, Chris, "Tourism and Marketing: A Symbiotic Relationship?" *Tourism Management,* Vol. 12, No. 2, pp. 101–111, June 1991.

Selin, Steven W., and Nancy A. Myers. "Tourism Marketing Alliances: Member Satisfaction and Effectiveness Attributed of a Regional Initiative." *Journal of Travel and Tourism Marketing,* Vol. 7, No. 3, pp. 79–94, 1998.

Shaw, Margaret. "Positioning and Price: Merging Theory, Strategy and Tactics." *Hospitality Research Journal,* Vol. 15, No. 2, pp. 21–30, 1992.

Shoemaker, Stowe. "Scripts: Precursor of Consumer Expectations." *Cornell Quarterly,* Vol. 37, No. 1, pp. 42–53, February 1996.

Stamatis, D. H. *Total Quality Service: Principles, Practices, and Implementation.* Delray Beach, FL: St. Lucie Press, 1996.

Stevens, Blair. "Price Value Perceptions of Travelers." *Journal of Travel Research,* Vol. 31, No. 2, pp. 44–48, Fall 1992.

Timm, Paul R. *Customer Service: Career Success Through Customer Satisfaction.* Upper Saddle River, N.J.: Prentice-Hall, 1998.

USTDC. *The Minority Traveler.* Washington, D.C.: U.S. Travel Data Centre, July 1996.

Walle, A. H. "Tourism and the Internet: Opportunities for Direct Marketing." *Journal of Travel Research,* Vol. 35, No. 1, pp. 72–77, Summer 1996.

Williams, Anna Graf, and Jennifer Adams Aldrick. *Hospitality Cases in Marketing and Operations.* Upper Saddle River, NJ: Prentice-Hall, 1997.

Witt, S. F., and L. Moutinho, eds. *Tourism Marketing and Management Handbook,* Student Edition. London, UK: Prentice-Hall, 1995.

Woodside, Arch G. "Measuring Advertising Effectiveness in Destination Marketing Strategies." *Journal of Travel Research,* Vol. 29, No. 2, pp. 3–8, Fall 1990.

WTO. *Shining in the Media Spotlight: A Communications Handbook for Tourism Professionals.* Madrid: World Tourism Organization, 1997.

WTO. *Tourism Market Trends: The World.* Madrid: World Tourism Organization, 1997.

PART 6

TOURISM PROSPECTS

◄ *A mariachi band entertains visitors to Mexico City. (Photo courtesy of the Mexican Government Tourism Office)*

TOURISM'S FUTURE

- **Examine forecasts concerning the growth of international tourism.**

- **Identify the major global forces that are shaping the tourism of tomorrow.**

- **Understand the impacts, both positive and negative, which these forces are likely to have on tourism markets and on the ability of destinations to re-**

spond to the demands of these markets.

- **Highlight the powerful and positive impact that the environmental movement has had, and will increasingly have, on tourism development.**

◀ **LEARNING OBJECTIVES**

◀ *New technology has brought high-speed trains that move passengers efficiently, helping to solve transportation and environmental problems. Shown here is Japan Railway's Shinkansen super express. (Photo courtesy of the Japan Information Center.)*

INTRODUCTION

According to most forecasts, the future of tourism is full of promise. Projections concerning the levels of arrivals, receipts, and growth in employment for most destinations have all painted a fairly rosy picture. For the most part, the contents of this chapter reflect the general optimism that pervades the travel industry.

Over and above this optimism, what is especially important about this chapter is its attempt to first define some of the more specific dimensions of future opportunities. In addition, it seeks to indicate how the travel product may need to evolve in response to these opportunities.

Finally, we also wish to sound a cautious note. As the "Asian Flu" crisis of 1998 has shown, even the most dynamic of economies can turn sour. While we continue to be optimistic that long-term stability and growth will return to these regions, the lessons of history are that we must learn to manage effectively in bad times as well as good. So while readers should prepare for the optimistic future trends this chapter presents, they should also ask themselves, "What if?" How might the travel industry take advantage of periods of lower economic growth? How might the travel industry be a catalyst for other sectors of the economy? As we said at the beginning of this text—Bon voyage!

TOURISM IN THE THIRD MILLENNIUM

The purpose of this book has been to provide the student with a basic understanding of the principles, practices, and philosophies of tourism as they relate to the industry of today. To understand the present, it has, of course, been necessary to review the evolution and historical development of the field. Clearly, the tourism industry of today is the product of many forces that have shaped both its structure and the manner in which it functions. As has been pointed out on several occasions, the growth and development of tourism has been particularly rapid over the past half century. As noted by the World Tourism Organization[1]:

- Since 1950, when international travel started to become accessible to the general public, tourist activity has risen each year at an average rate of 7.1 percent, from 25 million to 625 million arrivals in 1998, and by 12.2 percent based on international tourism receipts (at current prices and excluding spending on international transport) from U.S. $2.1 billion to U.S. $445 billion.

- International tourism receipts grew faster than world trade in the 1980s and now constitute a higher proportion of the value of world exports than all sectors other than crude petroleum/petroleum products and motor vehicles/parts/accessories.

The result is that tourism in the late-1990s is a very large and dynamic sector of the economy. Because of the rapid growth and change of the past, one might be in-

---

[1] World Tourism Organization, *Tourism 2020 Vision: A New Forecast from the World Tourism Organization* (Madrid: WTO, 1997).

The concierge at the Sheraton Hotel in Casablanca, Morocco offers important information and service to make the customer's travel experience more rewarding. The continued growth of international travel will add more than 100 million new jobs around the world over the next decade. *(Photo by the author.)*

clined to believe that tourism has now reached a mature phase of its development in which the rate of change and expansion will decrease.

On the other hand, a realistic assessment of the probable future suggests that tourism is likely to continue to grow and develop much more rapidly and more dynamically than many other sectors for many years to come.

THE WORLD OF TOURISM IN 2020

Forecasts 1995–2020

As shown in Table 20.1, international tourist arrivals are forecast to rise to 692 million in 2000, top 1 billion in 2010, and reach 1.6 billion in 2020. These volumes represent an overall average annual rate of growth between 1995 and 2020 of 4.3 percent, with no slackening of growth over the period (i.e., 1995–2000 4.2 percent per annum (p.a.); 2000–2010 4.2 percent p.a.; 2010–2020 4.4 percent (p.a.).

TABLE 20.1
Forecasts of International Tourist Arrivals (millions) Worldwide and by Region 1995–2020

Regions	Tourist Arrivals (million)			
	1995	2000	2010	2020
Europe	335	390	527	717
East Asia/Pacific	80	116	231	438
Americas	111	134	195	284
Africa	20	27	46	75
Middle East	14	19	37	69
South Asia	4	6	11	19
World	**564**	**692**	**1047**	**1602**

Source: World Tourism Organization.

- Europe will remain the largest receiving region, though its below global average rate of increase between 1995 and 2020 (3.1 percent p.a.) will result in a decline in market share from 59 percent to 45 percent. East Asia and the Pacific, increasing at 7.0. percent p.a., will pass the Americas (up 3.8 percent p.a.) as the second largest receiving region, holding a 27 percent market share in 2020 against 18 percent by the Americas. The respective shares of Africa, the Middle East, and South Asia will all record some increase to 5 percent, 4 percent, and 1 percent by 2020.

- Most significantly, WTTC research shows that some 328 million people around the globe—will be employed in jobs that exist because of demand generated by Travel & Tourism by 2010.

Over the next decade, this impact will grow by some 46% in real terms, adding more than 100 million new jobs across the world economy. Among the OECD nations, which amount to more than 70% of the travel-related GDP, the most significant employment producers are the United States with 13.4 million travel-related jobs, Japan with 6.1 million, and Germany with 3.6 million.

The bottom line is that Travel & Tourism is driving, directly and indirectly, more than 10 percent of employment today, globally, regionally, and nationally.

THE NATURE OF FUTURE GROWTH

As we have seen, tourism is expected to continue to grow. However, the nature of this growth and development will in many ways be quite different from that of the previous five decades. As has become abundantly clear over the past several years, the period of the 1990s is proving itself to be dramatically different from that of the previous three decades. As a global community we are living through widespread changes whose scope and significance are barely perceptible at this point in time. Yet somehow, we know that what has come to be known as the "New World Order" of the post–cold war era is evolving in some very fundamental ways as we rush toward the magical year 2000 and the third millennium of Western history (see Table 20.2).

TABLE 20.2
Tourist Directional Flow Growth Prospects, by Origin/Destination Region, 1990–2000

Region Outbound	Region Inbound						
	Europe	Americas	East Asia/The Pacific	South Asia	Middle East	Africa	Overall
Europe	✈	✈✈✈	✈✈✈	✈✈✈	✈✈	✈✈	✈
Americas	✈	✈	✈✈	✈✈	✈✈	✈✈✈	✈✈
East Asia/ The Pacific	✈✈	✈✈✈	✈✈✈	✈✈✈	✈✈	✈✈✈	✈✈✈
South Asia	✈✈	✈✈	✈✈✈	✈✈✈	✈✈✈	✈✈	✈✈✈
Middle East	✈	✈✈✈	✈✈✈	✈✈✈	✈✈✈	✈✈✈	✈✈
Africa	✈✈	✈✈	✈✈✈	✈✈	✈✈	✈✈✈	✈✈✈
Overall	✈	✈✈	✈✈✈	✈✈✈	✈✈	✈✈	✈✈

Key: ✈ below average   ✈✈ average   ✈✈✈ above average

Source: Based on WTO presentation at Seminar on *Tourism Trends to the Year 2000 and Beyond,* Seville, September 1992, and amended in the light of WTO analysis undertaken between October 1992 and July 1993.

Some of the dimensions of this evolution are already recognizable; and indeed, some are even predictable. Others are but as yet stirrings of anxiety or discontent. These stirrings are possibly the most disconcerting for the mature adults of the so-called "developed" nations, whose well-being and prosperity has improved constantly over their lifetime. For perhaps the first time, the fundamental changes occurring around them threaten to leap out of control and to undermine the foundations of their secure and attractive lifestyles. Others, in less fortunate circumstances, see these same changes as possibly the only glimmer of hope for what they view as a more equitable distribution of all the opportunities that life has to offer. Ironically, they may see these same changes as irrevocably condemning themselves to a life of endless poverty.

LEISURE, TOURISM, AND SOCIETY IN THE THIRD MILLENNIUM

A significant component of the high-quality lifestyle that has characterized the last half of the twentieth century has been access to, as well as the use of, increasing amounts of leisure time. Although the extent of this increase in leisure time has been questioned for decades,[2] there is little doubt that in aggregate terms the populations of the developed Western nations have had greater and more broadly based access to recreation and travel opportunities than has any previous society. As a result, tourism has grown to the point where it can now claim to be the "world's largest industry."[3] While

---

[2] Juliet B. Schor, *The Overworked American: The Unexpected Decline of Leisure* (New York: Basic Books, 1991).

[3] World Travel and Tourism Council, *Travel and Tourism: A New Economic Perspective* (Brussels: WTTC, 1993).

traditionally those in the tourism sector have lamented the lack of recognition received by the industry from both governments and the public, this situation is changing dramatically—in many cases, to the chagrin of the tourism establishment. Suddenly, tourism is being blamed for the destruction of cultures, degradation of the environment, and homogenization of lifestyles. In brief, because of its growing economic and social importance, tourism has suddenly found itself thrust into the mainstream of societal concerns—this at a time when all aspects of society are being questioned as to their value, their continued relevance, and, perhaps above all, their sustainability over the long term.

It is against this background of global societal change that several leading organizations and individuals having a strong interest in the future of tourism have attempted to understand the important forces of change in the world and their likely implications for the future of tourism. A review and analysis of the conclusions of these efforts indicates that the tourism of tomorrow will face a number of constraints and limitations that cannot be ignored. These "new realities" will force tourism policymakers and the tourism industry to alter dramatically the way it both develops and operates. They will also require that tourists themselves alter their demands and their behaviors. These changes that are now imposing themselves are, however, by no means entirely negative. Many can be viewed as corrections to the bad judgments and excesses of the past. Others represent opportunities for innovative and exciting new products and experiences. These "new horizons" in tourism may well prove more rewarding, and certainly more sustainable, than those of the past.

THE FUTURE SHAPE OF TOURISM

Three reviews of the future shape of tourism are those carried out by the World Tourism Organization,[4] by the firm Economic Research Associates,[5] and by the International Tourism Policy Forum (ITPF).[6] While there are a number of other valuable sources of information in this regard (see the Selected References at the end of this chapter), ITPF, the WTO, and ERA reports provide the most comprehensive and perhaps most insightful assessments of the forces that are affecting tourism and their probable implications for its future.

The WTO study involved a review and analysis of an extensive range and volume of existing research reports, papers, and articles produced by various authoritative institutions, tourism operators, and experts. In contrast, the ERA perspective reflects the collective experience of the members of a leading consulting firm in the field of tourism. Finally, the ITPF analysis used as its initial input the views of over 90 industry experts from 21 countries that were brought together for three days under the direction of the International Tourism Institute at the George Washington University.

---

[4] World Tourism Organization, *Global Tourism Forecasts to the Year 2000 and Beyond* (Madrid: WTO, 1993).

[5] Clive B. Jones, *The New Tourism and Leisure Environment* (San Francisco: Economic Research Associates, 1993).

[6] J. R. Brent Ritchie, "Global Tourism Policy Issues: An Agenda for the 1990s," *World Travel and Tourism Review*, Vol. 1 (Wallingford, England: C.A.B. International, 1991).

"Space tourism" has in some ways already arrived. While interplanetary travel is not yet a reality, it is reported that some agencies are taking deposits for trips into space. Until such trips become a reality, however, visits to land-based space attractions such as the U.S. Space and Rocket Center will continue to be a big draw. *(Photo courtesy Alabama Bureau of Tourism and Travel.)*

These experts were given the task of identifying those global forces which it was felt will most highly shape the entire spectrum of human activities in the coming years, and they were also asked to examine how these forces are likely to affect tourism in the 1990s and beyond.

ITPF: The Global Forces of Change

One of the first reports to extensively explore the factors shaping the future of tourism was issued by the International Tourism Policy Forum (ITPF).

The ITPF identified some 19 major forces that it felt should be the focus of leaders and decision makers in the field in the coming decade (Ritchie, 1991):

- The **physical environment** is taking "center stage" in tourism development and management.

- There is a recognition that there are finite limitations to tourism development, in terms of both physical and social carrying capacity of destinations.

- **Residents responsive tourism** is the watchword for tomorrow: community demands for active participation in the setting of the tourism agenda and its priorities for tourism development and management cannot be ignored.

- Tourism must strive to develop as a socially responsible industry; more specifically, it must move proactively rather than simply responding to various pressures as they arise.

- **Cultural diversity** should be recognized within the context of a global society.
- **Demographic shifts** are occurring which will dramatically influence the level and nature of tourism.
- The human resource problem: there is a continuing and growing need to increase the supply of personnel and to enhance their professionalism.
- Patterns of tourism are being transformed by increasingly **diverse lifestyles**.
- The political shift to market-driven economies is bringing about a global restructuring in which market forces rather than ideology are used to guide decisions and develop policy.
- The trend to **market economies** and shrinking government budgets is creating strong pressures for privatization and deregulation of tourism facilities and services.
- Regional, political, and economic integration/cooperation will predominate.
- The growing demands of the high cost of capital for development of the tourism infrastructure and rising taxation/fees will maintain and increase financial pressures on the tourism industry.
- The rise in influence of the global transnational firm will accelerate.
- The widening gap between the **north/south** (developed/developing) nations continues to cause frictions and to be a constant source of concern for harmonious tourism development.
- Continued regional conflicts and terrorist activities are impediments to the development and prosperity of tourism.
- Health and security concerns could become a major deterrent to tourism travel.
- Technological advances are giving rise to both opportunities and pressures for improved productivity, human resource development, and restructuring of the tourism industry.
- Despite recent progress, recognition by governments of the tourism industry and its importance to social and economic development and well-being of regions is still far from satisfactory: one part of the reason is a lack of credibility of tourism data.
- Growing dissatisfaction with governing systems and processes may lead to a new framework (paradigm) for tourism.

There is little doubt that these forces and the associated policy issues do represent very significant and very powerful pressures that will reshape the tourism of tomorrow. However, two important questions that beg to be asked when reviewing such conclusions are (1) whether or not the forces represent strong but merely temporary winds of change or whether they represent a more fundamental, more powerful metamorphosis of our society which is likely to harden with time and (2) whether or not the list, which has been generated in a tourism context, has truly identified all the societal forces that are likely to alter the shape of tourism, even if in a more indirect manner.

With respect to the first question, a reexamination of the 19 forces leads one to conclude that they do in fact reflect some very real and very fundamental forces for lasting societal change. Such a reexamination also reveals the possibility of reducing this set of forces to a more limited set of major themes. Seven such themes are proposed:

Environmentalism

As noted by the Tourism Policy Forum, concern for the environment has now taken "center stage" in tourism. This tourism reality is, however, a reflection of a much broader societal realization that it is now time that the world's population—all of it—must get serious about the health of our planet. At this stage, it is abundantly clear that spaceship earth has a limited capacity to sustain life as we know it.

As the Tourism Policy Forum noted explicitly: "Development must, in the future, be compatible with the environment." The Forum also pointed out, however, ". . . that tourism is among the better alternatives for land use." While such compatibility is laudable, it must also be stressed that there are other areas where compatibility between tourism and the environment is perhaps not so obvious. It was noted by the Forum that the use of fossil fuels for transportation and their polluting effect cannot be denied.[7] As a consequence, the sustainability of tourism in the long term is in doubt unless alternative nonpolluting energy sources become available.

The Spread of Democracy

Historians will long debate exactly why the period 1989–1991 was the specific point in time that saw such a dramatic spread of the democratic movement. The record will show that very few individuals (experts or ordinary people) foresaw the very rapid transformations of the political systems that occurred in Eastern and Central Europe during this period. Of course, all is not as simple as it seems. Many other forces were at work that allowed this rather focused eruption of democracy to occur. Indeed, as will be argued later, this very visible political shift was only symptomatic of a much more fundamental and underlying desire by people all over the world to participate more directly in the governing processes that affect their lives. From a tourism perspective, these forces have led to the very powerful concept of **resident responsive tourism**. No longer can it be assumed that the residents of a tourism destination/region will automatically accept all (or any) forms of tourism development that the industry proposes or attempts to impose. Tourism development in the third millennium will actively have to seek the support of the communities it affects most directly. To do this, those responsible for tourism will have to seek to involve destination region residents on an ongoing basis in the assessments of the costs and benefits associated with all forms of proposed (and even existing) facilities and activities. Unless a consensus is reached that the net benefits to the community are positive, it is questionable that tourism development in the year 2000 will have the support necessary to proceed.

---

[7] Ibid.

Demographic Shifts

Although very little in the social sciences is truly predictable, there is one notable exception: the demographics of the world's present population. In this regard, the forces of change that will drive and shape the face of the next generation are already evident. The populations of the developed Western world are aging and will decline in relative size. At the same time, the populations of the developing world continue to explode. While, in the short term, such changes may present opportunities for the tourism industry, they also raise some very fundamental long-term questions. These questions concern not only the distribution of the income and wealth on which travel depends, but also the geographic distribution of the world's population.

The Economic Imperative

While history may very well prove us wrong in the longer term, the foreseeable future indicates that economic forces will continue to triumph over ideologies. Over the past decade, throughout the world, we have seen the emergence of what appear to be overpowering pressures to adopt the model of the market economy. As part of this model, we have seen movements to deregulation, to privatization, to regional economic integration, and to a greater role for the transnational corporation. Whether or not, these movements represent winds of change or a lasting restructuring of our economic system remains to be seen. However, for the moment, the direction of the tide is unquestionable.

Diversity Within a Homogeneous World

One of the more insightful observations of the Tourism Policy Forum was that despite the trend to "sameness" around the world, there are strong counterpressures to maintain individual and cultural distinctiveness. A visit to any major city in the world demonstrates how information, economic pressures, and the tendency to imitate has left the world "less different" than it was a century, even decades, ago. It seems, however, that the human entity, while recognizing the pragmatic value of sameness, is determined at the same time to make every effort to preserve and enhance his or her unique identity. Whether or not the culture that spawned the Bolshoi Ballet is threatened by the arrival of McDonald's restaurants remains to be seen. However, if the determination of those who are facing this issue is any indication, the existence of cultural diversity within a global society is a reality whose time has come.

The Technology–Human Resource Dilemma

While tourism has traditionally been characterized as a "people industry," it is now coming face to face with the realities of the massive advances in technology that have occurred over the past several decades. During this period, industries which are less dependent on the human interactions that characterize the tourism sector have adapted labor-saving technology with a vengeance. As a consequence, these industries have been able to improve wage levels and enhance career opportunities for employees while keeping costs under control.

On the other hand, the travel industry (or should we call it the "hospitality industry" in this context?) has generally preferred to keep wages low, thus avoiding the need for technological innovation, particularly in the actual delivery of its services. Although technology has been used extensively in a supporting role to enhance performance and effectiveness (e.g., computer reservation system, air control technology), there has been a great reluctance to replace human service providers with technologically driven alternatives (such as the banks did when replacing human tellers with automatic teller machines). Similarly, aside from fast-food restaurants, there has been relatively little focused effort to undertake a major rethinking or redesign of travel-related facilities and support systems so as to substantially reduce personnel requirements or to enhance the productivity of employees. While some "tinkering" has occurred in selected areas and sectors, we have not yet seen the benefits from technology that are possible. Until technology is adapted more widely, it will be difficult for the travel industry to make new travel experiences available to a mass audience and to do so at prices that are affordable by much of the population.

On the other side of the coin—and this is the dilemma—the introduction of technology is viewed as a "job killer." Indeed, the conclusion of the Policy Forum was that both skilled and not-so-skilled personnel in the labor force could be replaced by various forms of technology. While some argue that the increased use of capital and technology will require highly skilled labor, others argue that technology (particularly computer technology) may, in fact, increase the demand for a less skilled labor force.

Addressing the "North–South Gap"

Despite the recognition that economic and social disparities are a destabilizing influence on global affairs, and despite efforts to reduce such disparities, the problem grows worse instead of better. As the summary report of the Tourism Policy Forum stated:

> While . . . this issue needs to be addressed on a very broad scale by all sectors of the economy, tourism must also do its part. In this regard . . . there is a growing demand for specialized tourism research facilities particularly focused on developing countries . . . a need for . . . greater assistance to third world tourism enterprises. In particular, they must be given the benefits of appropriate technology and human resource development programs to enhance their international competitiveness. In addition, they must be supported by policies that minimize the leakage from tourism development so as to ensure a fair and equitable return from tourism development to the host nations.

Little else needs to be said.

Other Forces of Change

In addition to the foregoing, there are several other less evident yet equally powerful forces at work which will less directly but no less significantly shape the global society of tomorrow. Some are logical consequences of the forces described above, while others are much less obvious. Some are already evident and their impact fairly predictable, others are only emerging. As such, their potential for change, as well as the nature of the changes they may bring about, is still very uncertain.

Shifting Value Systems

Consistent with the increasing concern for the environment (which runs somewhat counter to the movement to a market economy model) is the emergence of what appears to be a shift in the value system which drives human behavior. Although difficult to characterize, it would seem to reflect a certain rejection of hedonism and materialism and a return to simpler human values. In certain societies, this shift contains strong elements of religious fundamentalism. In others, it reflects a tendency to turn inward to family and friends—in more popular terminology, a "cocooning" behavior.[8] One must take care not to imply that the human race is suddenly and dramatically about to change the way it lives from day to day. However, there would seem to be some discomfort—a certain malaise—concerning the pace of life and the level of consumption of resources necessary to feed that pace of life. Taken to the extreme, this malaise and the accompanying shift of values could position tourism as "socially undesirable," due to its heavy use of nonrenewable resources. This view of tourism could lead to a widespread movement to limit all "nonessential" travel. While the parallel is by no means perfect, the similarity with the impact that the animal protection movement has had on the sale and consumption of fur products should not be ignored.

The Quest for Stability and Security

Although it should perhaps be obvious, the cocooning phenomenon referred to above is but one example of the efforts of many members of Western society to deny or escape from what has suddenly become a somewhat frightening world. After literally decades of economic growth and relative stability, many highly successful and valued persons are suddenly facing the prospect of decreasing economic well-being—and in many cases, even unemployment. This was not how it was suppose to turn out. In response to this threat, we have seen a strong reluctance to spend, even by those who have the resources. Although the resulting increase in saving rates may provide the investments necessary for modernization and long-term economic growth, the more immediate impacts on leisure and tourism spending are already being felt.

In the area of physical (as opposed to economic) security, we have known for some time that risk of physical danger is certain to diminish the prospects of a given tourism destination or travel-related firm. War in the Middle East has affected tourism both locally and worldwide. Terrorism aimed at U.S. air carriers has diverted traffic to competitors. Concern for health is of increasing importance, particularly for older travelers. In a different but related vein, the growing threat of AIDS has added yet another dimension of concern—only this time for younger segments of the population. Without exaggeration, the wise tourist visiting certain regions of the world now seeks a traveling companion having a compatible blood type in case a blood transfusion is required. Such concern and attention to detail with respect to health care while traveling should not be dismissed as an aberration of the few.

Emergence of the Knowledge-Based Society

Certain of the developed nations have already entered the era where one of their greatest competitive advantages is the information or knowledge they possess rather

---

[8] Faith Popcorn, *The Popcorn Report* (New York: Doubleday, 1991).

than their ownership of natural resources or their access to cheap labor. Assuming that such a trend continues and expands to other countries, it behooves the tourism industry to examine how the travel behavior of people in a knowledge-based society might differ from that of people in a manufacturing or more traditional service-based setting.

If the world's leading economies are any indication of trends in this regard, we can expect travelers from knowledge-based economies to be more experienced, more discerning, and more demanding. In particular, we can expect that they will be seeking more individualized experiences, often characterized as **special-interest travel**. Such travelers ". . . are more interested in enriching their lives with experience rather than hands-off entertainment. They seek interactive, highly involved, quality travel experiences, focusing on in-depth coverage of the special interest topic or destination at hand."[9]

Pushing the limits even further, certain individuals and groups are now espousing the potential of **virtual reality** as a replacement for travel.[10] This technology represents perhaps the outer limits of the knowledge-based industries in that it purports to provide simulated experiences which conceptually are equivalent to the real thing. By merely strapping on the necessary technology, it is asserted that some day (supposedly not too far away), people will be able to "experience" a destination without actually visiting it. While it is easy for the traveler of today to dismiss such an idea as sheer fantasy, it does seem logical that such an approach would (if truly feasible) find ready acceptance among members of a knowledge-based society. It goes without saying that (if successful), "virtual reality tourism" would have profound impacts on the travel industry as we know it.

A Decline in the Meganation—The Rise of the City-State

Participants in the International Tourism Policy Forum very appropriately noted the increasing importance of regional trading blocs. The new "borderless Europe" is almost a reality. The North American Free Trade Agreement has created another bloc. In response to these two initiatives, the Asian nations are starting to reflect on the need for an equivalent arrangement.

Although it is too early yet to reach firm conclusions regarding the changes that free movement of labor will bring to the social fabric of Europe, it does seem reasonable to anticipate that the importance of each existing nation state will decline. Indeed, one of the major goals of European integration is to arrive at common standards, a common currency, and a more common political system. At first glance, one might argue that the creation of the new Europe will result in another meganation. In strictly pragmatic terms, this may be the case. Certainly, the effective elimination of borders will greatly facilitate travel flows. At the same time, it will, over time, greatly reduce national distinctiveness and thus the appeal of a particular country as a unique travel destination.

Although speculative at this point, there is some evidence that as a reaction to the

---

[9] Robert J. Forbes and Maree S. Forbes, "Special Interest Travel," *World Travel and Tourism Review,* Vol. 2 (Wallingford, England: C.A.B. International, 1992).

[10] Travel and Tourism Research Association, "Examining the Dynamics of New Partnerships, Strategies and Products," *Newsletter,* Boise, ID: TTRA, 1992).

decline of national identities, there will be a reactive rise in the importance of major metropolitan centers—or city-states. These city-states, it is argued, may become the focal point for both economic development and for individual identity. Of direct relevance to tourism is the possibility that the new city-states may also become the primary basis for destination development and promotion.

Pressures for Mass Migration

As fading borders increasingly facilitate population movements within trading blocs, there will be those who will first request, and then demand, the right for such freedom of movement to be extended. The day is not far off when freedom of movement of all peoples of the world may be termed a "basic human right." Although this certainly does not mean that this right will be granted, it will undoubtedly be asserted. Clearly, the implications of this still weak but emerging pressure go far beyond the concerns of those in the leisure and tourism field. This said, however, it is very clear that should such pressures succeed in even a modest way, the entire landscape of leisure and tourism planning and development will change dramatically.

ERA: The New Tourism and Leisure Environment

A second approach to examining the future shape of tourism is the thinking of the firm Economics Research Associates (see Reading 20.1). The author of this paper, Clive Jones, examines a number of dimensions along which tourism and leisure behavior patterns appear to be changing. His analysis then proceeds to identify some of the specific shifts that he believes are likely to occur along each of these dimensions.

WTO: Tourism to the Year 2020

The World Tourism Organization study was undertaken to provide an overview of the factors affecting the long-term development of tourism worldwide. The intent of the project was to provide policymakers in the travel and tourism sector with a series of probable scenarios contemplating future development patterns and alternative strategies to cope with them. A particular emphasis of the WTO strongly was to identify and understand the qualitative aspects or factors that combine to "shape" the way in which tourism will grow. Table 20.3 summarizes what the WTO study identified as the "principal influences" on tourism for the period in question. They argue that these many factors in combination will produce a polarization of tourist tastes and supply. As a consequence, individualized tourism will grow in importance for both large mass markets and for smaller niche markets. In particular, the *Vision 2020* report emphasized the following:

> The world in the year 2020 will be characterized by the penetration of technology into all aspects of life. It will become possible to live one's life without exposure to other people, with automated service the norm and full access to, and exchange of, information on everything possible from one's own home. Even the emergent space tourism of that time will be by definition an activity that is undertaken largely in isolation. In consequence, people will crave the human touch; and tourism will be a principal means through which they seek to achieve this.

TABLE 20.3
Principal Influences on Tourism (1995–2020 Period)

The principal determinants of, and influences on, international tourism activity taken over the duration of the 1995 and 2020 period are identified as being:

Economic

- Continued moderate-to-good rates of global economic growth
- Above-average economic performance of the Asian tiger economies
- Emerging importance of new tiger economies (i.e., China, India, Brazil, Indonesia, Russia)
- Widening gap between rich and poor countries
- Spread of harmonization of currencies

Technology

- Information technology development
- Transport technology advances

Political

- Removal of barriers to international travel
- Transport and other forms of deregulation

Demographic

- Aging population and contracting workforces in industrialized countries leading to south → north migration
- Erosion of the traditional Western household

Globalization

- Growing power of international economic and market forces and consequent reduced control of individual states and nonglobal corporations

Localization

- Conflict in developing countries between identity and modernity
- Demand from groups defined on ethnicity, religion and social structures to be recognized in their own rights

Socioenvironmental Awareness

- Boosted public awareness of socio-cultural and environmental issues
- Greater media reporting on major global problems (e.g., reducing water supplies)

Living and Working Environments

- Growing urban congestion both in the industrialized and (especially) developing worlds

Change from "Service" to "Experience" Economy

- Focus switching to delivering unique experiences that personally engage the customer

Marketing

- Use of electronic technology to identify and communicate with market segments and niches

Technology will continue to penetrate all sectors of the tourism industry. These Internet kiosks, which are being placed in airports around New York City, allow airline passengers to access the Internet, or their own email, while traveling. *(Photo courtesy of the Get2Net Corporation.)*

New Realities, New Horizons

It is an interesting exercise to identify the global forces that are likely to affect societal behavior and well-being in the coming millennium, but the exercise does not serve much purpose unless it can provide some insight into the possible implications of these forces. As indicated at the beginning, an important goal of this essay is to assist in providing these insights. Toward this end, Table 20.4 attempts to provide an assessment of some of the most significant realities that must be addressed by the tourism sector in relation to each of the global forces identified by the International Tourism Policy Forum. The table seeks, as well, to identify some important initial insights into the realities that must be faced by the tourism sector as we proceed toward the year 2000 and beyond. Finally, they furnish some ideas concerning the opportunities that are likely to emerge as evolving global forces shape the nature of leisure and tourism in the third millennium.

Some Deeper Forces Loom Large on the Horizon

The discussion of the future of tourism has to this point been conducted at two levels:

- First, a mechanical one in which the qualitative measure of trends in visitations and the measures of performance have been put forth and examined. These trends have very significant economic implications and cannot be ignored. However, they are the end result of many other factors that have

TABLE 20.4

Tourism in the Third Millennium: New Realities and New Horizons Resulting from Emerging Global Forces

New Horizons	New Realities
Environment on Center Stage	
• Virtually all future tourism development will be constrained by the need for environmental sensitivity.	• Conservation, preservation, and restoration present new themes for the design of tourism experiences. Regions that are presently undeveloped or in a natural state have a unique opportunity to provide an attractive experience to visitors.
• The noneconomic costs of tourism will need to be factored into development decisions. The cost of development, using nontraditional accounting frameworks, will increase, thus forcing higher prices on the travel experience.	• Emphasis on the quality of the tourism experience will reduce growth in the number of travelers but enhance net financial and nonfinancial impacts on tourism destinations.
The Spread of Democracy	
• The tourism planning and development process will be increasingly constrained and slowed by the need for meaningful public involvement and input.	• Implementation of approved development plans will be easier as "surprises" will be minimized and as broader agreement results from public involvement.
• It will be more difficult for individual operators to proceed with nonconforming developments—sometimes at the risk of inhibiting innovation.	• The formulation of "resident responsive visions" of local/regional tourism will provide more commitment to tourism and greater coherency in the tourism product/experience provided by a destination.
Demographic Shifts	
• The aging of travelers from traditional tourism-generating countries will cause demands for new experiences and new facilities. As a consequence, existing tourism plant may become economically obsolete.	• For the next 20 years, residents of developed nations in the 45–65 age category will increase substantially. These individuals will have the time, the discretionary income, and the desire to travel.
• Increasingly diverse lifestyles will make market segmentation increasingly important. However, the tailoring of "designer vacations" will make it harder to standardize the tourism product and, thus, to control costs.	• Firms that can read, anticipate, and respond to the specific needs/desires of high quality niche or "special interest" markets in innovative ways will have great opportunities for success.
Shifts to The Market Economy	
• Many high-quality public facilities and attractions that have traditionally been supported and/or subsidized by governments will come under serious funding pressures.	• Market competition will prove a powerful force in keeping the costs of travel under control, thus keep tourism accessible to a large percentage of the population.
• It will become more difficult to justify and to publicly finance large-scale "megaprojects" or "megamonuments," some of which have become	• There will be new opportunities for innovative financing approaches for megaprojects and megadevelopments that enjoy the support

TABLE 20.4 (*Continued*)

New Horizons	New Realities
major, symbolic tourism attractions. As well, supporting infrastructure, such as roads and airports, will be more difficult to finance.	of the residents of a destination (e.g., community bonds).

Cultural Diversity in a Homogeneous World

• The power and success of global brand names and franchises will increasingly put pressure on small, independent travel and tourism operators. • The integrity of truly unique and interesting cultural events and attractions will be threatened as they attempt to respond to visitor demands in regard to access and frequency.	• Traditional cultural events and activities that no longer are economically feasible may be preserved through tourism. • Increasing acceptance of the value of other cultures will greatly broaden the range of facilities, events, and attractions which are of potential interest to tourists.

The Technology–Human Resource Dilemma

• The human resource base of the tourism industry is ill-equipped and thus ill-disposed toward the widespread adoption of technology. At least passive resistance can be expected at all levels. • Introducing technology without losing the warmth of the human experience will be difficult. Choosing the appropriate balance of high-tech/high-touch will require insight and good judgment.	• Because of the present low level of penetration of technology on tourism, there is much potential for significant gains on performance and productivity in terms of both facility design and service delivery. • Education and training levels will have to increase if managers and staff are to select and implement technology-based improvements in an effective manner.

Addressing the "North–South Gap"

• The tourism infrastructure in developing countries (in both quantitative and qualitative terms) is in many cases totally inadequate at the present time. • The disparity in the wealth and well-being that exists between developing-world residents and developed-world tourists frequently creates unhealthy tensions between hosts and guests as well as distortions of local lifestyles.	• Many developing countries have extremely rich cultures and histories that have not been experienced by many segments of the traditional tourism markets. • The relatively low level of visitation to many developing countries provides an alternative to take the pressure off heavily visited sites in traditional tourism destinations.

Shifting Value Systems

• Leisure/vacation travel could be viewed as frivolous, wasteful, and harmful in a world where economies are stagnant, renewable resources are declining, and toxic emissions threaten the health of the planet. • The developing mood to "look inward" may lead to greater economic protectionism (at the macro level) and more home/family oriented uses of leisure time (at the micro level). Both would reduce the demand for travel.	• An increased emphasis on special interest tourism—such as cultural, educational, and professional development travel—may greatly strengthen and enrich the meaning of the travel experience. • An increased emphasis on "human relationships" may encourage new forms of tourism in which contact between hosts and guests is less superficial, leading to more intensive and enduring relationships.

TABLE **20.4** (*Continued*)

New Horizons	New Realities
Quest for Stability and Security	
• Increasing levels of crime in tourist destinations is a major deterrent to both leisure and conference travel.	• Organized travel and/or receptive visitor services that shelter and protect the traveler from crime will be welcomed; destinations that eliminate or control crime will be preferred.
• Aging populations, underfunded medical systems, and the growth of AIDS have heightened concerns about the cost, availability, and safety of health care services when traveling.	• Firms that offer specialized products and services that protect the health of the traveler and/or facilitate access to reliable and reassuring medical services while in foreign environments will have a strong competitive edge.
The Knowledge-Based Society	
• Modern technology is increasingly attempting to provide alternatives to physical travel. Teleconferencing is finally gaining wider acceptance; virtual interface technology purports to provide the travel experience without travel.	• Travelers will increasingly want to truly experience and understand a destination. As a result, they will be interested in spending more time in a region and interfacing with residents in more meaningful ways.
• Knowledge-based employees tend to work in sanitized, controlled environments. As such, they may shun travel experiences that are physically challenging, moderately uncomfortable, or culturally threatening.	• Travelers of the future will be increasingly receptive to technologies and services that facilitate travel while reducing costs and minimizing the need for menial and/or demeaning labor.
Rise of the City State	
• Large countries will find it less desirable and less productive to undertake general awareness-type promotion; budgets for such promotions will decline.	• Those highly focused destinations that have high visibility, good access, and an attractive product and which can develop a distinctive image will dominate the market.
• Smaller destinations having no particularly unique characteristics will find it even more difficult to complete with higher-profile centers.	• Strategic alliances and reciprocal agreements between city-states that complement one another will grow in importance.
• Nations/economic communities may become much more demanding in terms of visitor entry requirements as they perceive that "tourists" risk transforming themselves into refugees or defacto immigrants.	• Diverse, multicultural societies brought about through immigration will create increased demand for travel as people exchange visits with families and friends.
• Destination residents may become increasingly less tolerant of "visibly" or "linguistically" different visitors whom they see as posing a threat as a potential immigrant.	• Ethnic groups in tourism generating countries will have the opportunity to develop educational/cultural travel experiences for their compatriots. Such experiences could involve both pre-travel and travel experiences.

While technology often takes the spotlight when talking about the future, it is equally important to take action that protects our environment, our heritage, and our animals for future generations. *(Photo courtesy of the San Diego Zoo.)*

been at work for some time; namely the **"global forces"** which have been examined earlier in some depth.

- These global forces represent a very significant set of factors that, as we have seen, can profoundly effect the resultant trends just discussed. Because these forces are being increasingly understood, it is largely a question of adaptation to them so as to maximize current performance levels.

- There is also a third set of factors, some deeper emerging forces looming on the horizon, a set that we do not yet understand, or even know exists. Many of today's "global forces" were once in that category. Now they are more evident and better understood. The challenge we currently face is to search out this emerging set of forces and to determine their impact on the tourism of tomorrow.

How we do this is not so obvious. Their identity still hides in the minds and works of the many "Thinkers of Tomorrow." They may include *Boom, Bust, and Echo: How to Profit from the Coming Demographic Shift* (Foot, 1996). This reference has probably already passed to the category of recognized global forces. It starts from the very basic premise that "with every passing year, each human and each population becomes one year older; and with every passing year comes a change in the needs and behaviours of individuals—and these changes are often quite observable and quite predictable." Furthermore, they result in similarly predictable changes in the types of travel experiences that are being sought and travel products/services that are bought. Somehow, even though we all knew demographics was important, it has taken an unusually long time for managers, particularly those in the travel industry, to realize the true depth and scope of the impact the systematic aging of large segments of the population. Now we know, but we still need to explore and understand better.

In *The World in 2000: Power, Culture, and Prosperity,* a treatise by McRae (1994) of the Harvard Business School, McRae identifies several areas that may have profound emerging implications for tourism. McRae reminds us of a lesson that should be obvious, but one we have chosen to ignore, namely, that the underlying goal of economic growth should be to increase the well-being and happiness of citizens rather than simply to increase the traditional GDP. This lesson states that, in economists' jargon, the "welfare" of citizens must also take into account social and environmental concerns." McRae strongly asserts that "the quest for growth alone can lead to catastrophe." At the same time, he further asserts that "even if growth itself does not solve all problems, the absence of growth makes the problems more infinitely difficult to tackle."

In a world where many have started to view growth in primarily negative terms, this assertion raises profound concerns. If, in fact, we do need growth to improve living standards, the issue becomes growth "measured by what standards?" How can we integrate environmental and social accounting into the traditional financial accounting models of the chartered accountants? The task of attaching an economic value to the scenery of a destination and the culture of a unique destination, or to the ecological integrity of a pristine waterway, has been undertaken by a very few. Prugh (1995) is one of the few. Those in the tourism industry should start to reflect on the approaches he proposes—even though others claim it to be an impossible task.

McRae also points out the future need to focus on the fundamental task of improving productivity in the services sector. He notes that we are all aware of the extent to which most areas of manufacturing in the 1980s and 1990s retreated from the search for efficiency through mass production. He discusses the enormous changes made in the use of labor in rich countries—where instead of large numbers of people performing repetitive tasks, a much smaller number are performing more highly skilled jobs.

Outside of the McDonaldization of the food sector, tourism and hospitality is only beginning to awaken to the pressure for enhanced productivity so as to raise margins and be able to pay better wages. Unless tourism finds ways to enhance productivity (via education and training), it will be marginalized within a well-to-do-society.

Diversity as a weakness is a politically incorrect position that McRae asserts we must confront. He argues that the "babble of many tongues" has weakened the performance of many societies and has forced Europe toward a common economy. Underlying the European move to the integration of diverse cultures is the powerful underlying pressure for intense specialization. This specialization and standardization has led to wealth. It is argued that in economic terms, it has been the culture of America and the flexibility of thought that the culture encourages that has given the culture its unique and enviable role in the world.

Despite the foregoing, the tourism sector needs to question itself as to whether or not it can manage diversity without creating a society of have's and have-not's, a process that is already well-advanced. Can tourism, which depends on an atmosphere of safety, security, and relaxation, continue to flourish in an ambience of inequality and conflict?

Finally, the *500 Year Delta* identifies further underlying challenges facing all of society today—and thus tourism. Taylor and Wacker (1997) have raised the specter of a society based on rational theory that has been replaced by a society based on chaos theory—a society in which you cannot do, you cannot plan, you cannot reason to an end point. In chaos, you can only be.

Even more threatening in a "chaos theory world" is the dismissal of previous assumptions that we all hold to be unerringly true—for example, that experience was the best teacher, that experience is valuable. In a chaos-based world, change moves too fast, and time is too compressed to draw any link with experience. Ironically, the more successful you have been in a reason-based world, the harder it will be for you to succeed in a chaos-based world; past success breeds failure. The knowledge of value in a national world is a liability in a chaos-based world. "Loyalty," an asset of the past (either to a company or to a spouse), becomes a questionable asset. In this context, the rationality of experiences becomes replaced by "the rise of intuition." The excess of information forces one to make choices purely on arbitrary basics—because they "feel right."

In this type of world, what is the logic of tourism planning? Will it only result in the wrong answers, in products or services that are passé by the time they hit the street? Sound familiar?

Similarly, in a "chaos-based world" we observe a dramatic reversal of desired behavior; conspicuous consumption, the very foundation of status in the past world, is a large black Mercedes. Today is the death knell of status. Rather, inconspicuous consumption by the wealthy (the Timex instead of the Rolex) becomes the desired mode of consumption. "Functionality rather than flash"—at least at the level of public consumption. "Quiet quality" becomes the watchword of the day.

For those of us in the tourism sector we must "pay attention." The choice in packaging of travel packages takes on a whole new understanding. Educational travel, heritage travel, and ecotourism—practiced in a sincere manner—start to take on a new significance.

SUMMARY

Social and economic trends in developed countries seem to favor long-term growth in both domestic and international travel demand. More long-term leisure, increased disposable income, higher levels of education, and more awareness of other countries and peoples are significant factors influencing a growing market for travel.

Technological trends are also favorable. Transportation equipment is now more efficient and more comfortable; hotel and motel accommodations have become more complete, attractive, convenient, and comfortable; and new developments have given much more attention to environmental considerations.

Tourism is believed to have a positive effect on world peace. As people travel from place to place with a sincere desire to learn more about their global neighbors, knowledge and understanding grow. Then at least a start has been made in improving world communication, which seems so important in building bridges of mutual appreciation, respect, and friendship.

We trust that you are now ready to contribute your part toward making this world a bit more prosperous and peaceful through tourism.

ABOUT THE READING

This reading takes yet another look at how major shifts in the leisure and tourism environment will change not only tourist behavior and travel patterns, but indeed the very nature of tourism itself. The implications for the way we travel and the way in which the industry must adapt both its products and its marketing efforts are profound.

READING 20.1

THE NEW TOURISM AND LEISURE ENVIRONMENT

by Clive B. Jones, Senior Vice President
Economics Research Associates (ERA)

The tourism and recreation industry is increasingly recognized as an important economic, environmental and social force which can bring both benefit and adversity. The financial community (and governments) also know that the industry has had spectacular successes and colossal failures. We have found that a key element of successful development is the ability to recognize and deal with change across a wide range of behavioral and technological factors and the way they interact. In ERA, we annually discuss the fundamental changes in our industry. For the Nineties, we see major shifts in the leisure and tourism environment reflecting changing consumer values, political forces, and the explosive growth of information technology. No aspect of the industry will remain untouched.

Means Turning Away From *Old Travel Patterns* →	And Turning Towards *New Travel Patterns*
• East–West flows	• North–South flows
• Atlantic dominance	• Asia-Pacific dominance
• Long trips	• Short breaks
• Travel barriers	• Free trade

New travel patterns reflect changes in consumer behavior, economic strength of source markets, new destinations, and political realignments. Shifts to North–South flow are occurring in Asia (towards Australia and Pacific Islands), in North America (towards Mexico, Central and South America) and in Europe (towards North and South Africa). Along with the growth in North–South travel is the shift in travel to within the Asia-Pacific region. This region represented 25% of worldwide air travel in 1985 and is forecast to represent 40% by 2000.

The shift from long trips to short breaks will increase the demands for leisure facilities close to source markets. This has been reflected in the success of the close-in Centerparc type resorts in Europe (95% ± occupancy) while long haul resort

products are failing. These close-in "artificial environments experiences will spread to North America and Asia." Disney is reportedly developing a similar product.

Artificial barriers to travel will continue to come down with the deregulation of international air travel and the decline in use of bilateral agreements. Political realignments in the EC and North America free trade zone will encourage travel to and within each region. Reduction in differential on branded goods as well as duties and tariffs will encourage many forms of travel but reduce the importance of shopping as a trip generator. (As the price differential for branded goods in Japan drops below 20%, both shopping trips and expenditures will decline.)

Countering this trend are destructive efforts to increase direct and indirect industry taxes (through departure fees; air fuel surcharges and tourist business taxes).

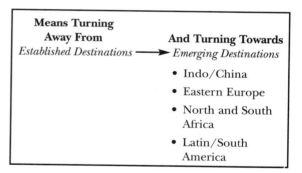

Means Turning Away From *Established Destinations* →	And Turning Towards *Emerging Destinations*
	• Indo/China
	• Eastern Europe
	• North and South Africa
	• Latin/South America

New destinations will provide the traveler with greater choice and lower cost alternatives to established destinations. Principal new destinations include Indochina (Vietnam is the newest member of the Pacific Asia Travel Association), Eastern Europe (the EC is funding massive tourism infrastructure and development programs), North Africa (primarily financed by World Bank and UNDP) and Latin America.

There are also emerging markets, including the new economic powerhouses of Asia (Korea, Taiwan, Hong Kong, Singapore) and the increasing number of potential travelers in large population countries (India, China, Indonesia, Brazil, Argentina, Mexico and, to some extent, the Eastern European countries). Existing markets, however, will continue to dominate leisure development.

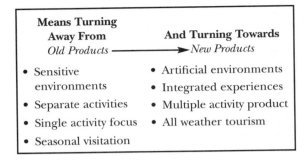

Means Turning Away From *Old Products* ———▶	And Turning Towards *New Products*
• Sensitive environments	• Artificial environments
• Separate activities	• Integrated experiences
• Single activity focus	• Multiple activity product
• Seasonal visitation	• All weather tourism

New leisure products will move away from environmentally and culturally sensitive environments and use new technology to create artificial environments close to origin markets. The Centerparcs "Tropical Paradise" waterparks represent a first stage of this but other environments will follow. Simulation and virtual reality experience being developed in California and elsewhere will revolutionize the design of resorts, attractions, retail and education/interpretive facilities. Virtual reality body suits will be able to simulate any human experience.

Multi-dimensional development will move further to the true integration of shopping and recreation, entertainment and education, and culture and meetings/business center development. Leisure destinations will also have to provide a greater menu of activities to accommodate the increasingly wide range of activities and interests of the individual consumer and the family. Destinations and products will also seek to become both weather independent (through artificial environments) as well as attractive to markets that are less weather dependent (conventions; specialty markets—ecotourism, culture/heritage, education and training).

Means Turning Away From *Fragmented Tourism Industry* ———▶	And Turning Towards *Economic Development Tool!*
• Number of visitors	• Economic and social benefit per visitor
• Regional competition	• Intelligent cooperation
• Product dominance	• Customer orientation

Governments are slowly realizing that tourism is not fun and games, but serious business with far reaching community consequences. In ERA's recent study of the impact of the L.A. riots, we found a 25% drop in tourism accounting for a loss of thousands of jobs in the most affected areas and a fiscal hit of over $10 million in lost transient occupancy and sales taxes.

Destinations will increasingly measure leisure and tourism success not by number of visitors but by total benefit and, particularly, net benefit per visitor. The old 'numbers game' inevitably means greater mass marketing and eventually into giving away product for no net benefit. The emphasis on net benefit will mean targeted marketing to consumers who spend more and interact well with social and environmental resources.

Means Turning Away From *Developer Control* ———▶	And Turning Towards *Community Control*
• Political lobbying	• Approvals via referendum
• Economic impact	• Jobs and small businesses
• Environmental protection	• Environmental improvement
• Cultural intrusion	• Heritage protection

This greater realization of the business of tourism will lead to more intelligent cooperation among destinations and regions in marketing, promotion, and product development.

The host community is becoming increasingly sophisticated and demanding in terms of leisure development. Entitlements are increasingly difficult to obtain and maintain if the developer cannot demonstrate a range of economic, social, and environmental benefits.

Community interest and tourism must work together for any chance of long term success. The most rewarding forms of tourism are those that involve both residents and tourists. "Rewarding" means both in terms of the visitor and resident experiences and the economic viability to the developer. In ERA's experience, the reasonably safe range of participation must be a balance between 30% and 70% for either resident or tourist attendance. Being outside this range generally leads to alienation and an inefficient operating environment.

Small business development opportunities, not just jobs, will be an increasingly important element of the community benefit package (ERA recently conducted a national policy study in this area for the U.S. Congress).

Means Turning Away From *Financial Illusion* →	**And Turning Towards** *Financial Reality*
• Mega attractions	• Franchise opportunities
• Meeting everyone's needs	• Needs of the investors
• Exit scenarios	• Operating discipline
• Ego architecture	• Economic simulation
• New investment	• Revenue enhancement
• Price inflation	• Price resistance

The last four years have not been kind to the schemes and dreams of many recreation promoters and investors. The sad state of the hotel industry is well known (some new mega resorts are reportedly losing up to $3 million per month) and major theme parks have had to reduce effective prices to maintain attendance. Economic reality brings a renewed discipline to the planning, development and financial community to first improve the performance of existing assets; and second, acquire strategic undervalued assets before considering major new investments. Experienced market analysis and economic simulation models will guide future development.

Major leisure operators are also looking to capitalize on their brand equity by franchising smaller scale, specialty recreation opportunities.

Means Turning Away From *Mass Markets* →	**And Turning Towards** *Specialty Markets*
• Mega attractions	• Ecotourism
• Meeting everyone's needs	• Adventure tourism
• Exit scenarios	• MICE
• Ego architecture	• Any specialty you can think of

At first segmenting markets seems a more difficult task and a more expensive way to reach consumers. In reality it is a great opportunity—since each of the markets usually has a sophisticated information system and network distribution to reach its members. These are of-

ten represented by reasonably accessible databases for direct customer communication. Examples include:

- 140 ecotourism and adventure tourism operators in USA that control market factors and set standards/expectations for product delivery.
- 6,000 meeting planners control the vast majority of meeting business—about 10,000 room nights each and total visitor expenditures of around $12 billion.

Targeted communication to specialty markets is extremely cost effective given this type of leverage.

Means Turning Away From *Passive Consumers* →	**And Turning Towards** *Involved Participants*
• Inexperienced tourist	• Value conscious traveler
• Self-destruction	• Self improvement
• Fully packed tours	• Menu of optional experience
• Theme parks	• Individual experience centers

Leisure participants, like anyone else, need to be treated as individuals and feel an interaction with their environment. As travelers become more experienced, they are no longer satisfied to be processed through an impersonal, non-interactive system. It is the "old tourism" to see rows and rows of deck chairs surrounding some Californian's idea of a rockwork/waterfall tropical paradise. This style reflects an attitude of "processing the numbers" rather than providing a rewarding customer experience. The new consumers want to be involved—to learn new experiences, to interact with the community, and to learn about and appreciate the destination at more than a superficial level.

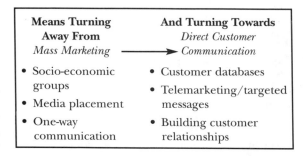

Means Turning Away From *Mass Marketing* →	**And Turning Towards** *Direct Customer Communication*
• Socio-economic groups	• Customer databases
• Media placement	• Telemarketing/targeted messages
• One-way communication	• Building customer relationships

Possibly the most powerful tool in marketing, customer databases are poorly utilized by visitor industry associations and the public sector. Database marketing programs of certain airlines and hotels are renowned for their effectiveness. However, National Tourism Organizations, local Visitors Bureaus and many recreation operators are reluctant to apply this technology. They prefer to place expensive (and generally ineffective) media rather than pursue direct customer contact. Exceptions include the Hi-Line booking and reservation system (Scotland), ATLAS (Queensland), and the Club France frequent visitor program. At least six U.S. states are looking at developing such systems.

The conventional ways of looking at consumer behavior—especially in tourism and leisure—have become outdated. No longer (if they ever were) are the purchasing habits of the leisure customer predictable by labeling a group as a segment of the market and describing it with average characteristics. More and more, marketers are turning to tailored and targeted marketing to individuals. This is now possible through new technology with sophisticated database management systems and immense amounts of historical and purchased information (lists) on individual preferences and consumption patterns. This trend is particularly appropriate for tourism marketing since there is a world of paradoxes in leisure behavior. Sameness and diversity and security and risk taking seem side by side. Some accountants sky dive; people eat at McDonalds for lunch and a four-star restaurant for dinner; take luxury BMW's to the self service petrol pump; trade a large investment portfolio through a discount broker; visit Hawaii and never go in the ocean. Leisure lifestyles, in particular, are inconsistent and contradictory.

This multi-profile customer is difficult to motivate by traditional institutional means. The 1990s and beyond belong to the individual. Destination marketing and leisure product development must adjust to this new environment.

KEY CONCEPTS

city-state
concern for safety
cultural diversity
demographic changes
environmental sensitivity
global forces of change

high-tech/high-touch interface
knowledge-based society
lifestyle diversity
market economy
need for stability
"north–south gap"

population migration
resident responsive tourism
special-interest tourism
spread of democracy
value-system changes
virtual reality

 ## INTERNET SITES

World Tourism Organization
http://www.world-tourism.org

World Travel and Tourism Council
http://www.wttc.org

 ## INTERNET EXERCISES

Activity 1
Site Name: High Tech is Our Future, Not Tourism

URL: http://www.amcity.com/pacific/stories/081296/editorial 2.html

Background Information: This article by Richard Moody (the founder and president of Aloha Conferencing) appeared in Pacific Business News. The article discusses the tourism industry and the high-technology industry in Hawaii.

Exercise

1. In the article, Richard Moody writes in favor of developing other industries in Hawaii in addition to tourism. What is his motivation for expressing this view?

Activity 2

Site Name: The Euro—Europe's New Currency

URL: http://pacific.commerce.ubc.ca/xr/euro/

Background Information: On January 1, 1999, eleven European countries replaced their national currencies and introduced a single European currency, the euro. As of this date, the euro is the official currency in the eleven participating countries.

Site Name: The Euro Currency Countdown

URL: http://www.ibec.ie/euro/menu.htm

Background Information: Within this site you will find practical information on managing the changeover to the euro plus the latest news on preparations for Economic and Monetary Union.

Site Name: The Association of Chambers of Commerce and Industry

URL: http://www.eurochambres.be/

Background Information: Eurochambres is an Association of more than 1200 Chambers of Commerce and Industry and represents 14 million businesses at the European institutions in Brussels.

Site Name: The Euro—One Currency for Europe

URL: http://europa.eu.int/euro/html/home5.html? lang=5

Background Information: This is the European Commission's Internet site dedicated exclusively to the euro—one currency for Europe. This site has useful and interesting information in all eleven official languages of the European Union.

Site Name: U.S. Business & Economic Policy for the New Europe

URL: http://www.nsinc.com/euroimpact_program.htm

Background Information: A Conference on the Implications of the European Monetary Union for the United States.

Site Name: Tourism to Benefit from Single European Currency

URL: http://www.world-tourism.org/ows-doc/press-rel/euro-a.htm

Background Information: Comments from World Tourism Organization Secretary-General Francesco Frangialli at a news conference held during the ITB tourism fair in Berlin.

Site Name: International Effects of the Euro

URL: http://www.brook,edu/comm/PolicyBriefs/pb042/pb42.htm

Background Information: This policy brief discusses the beneficial economic effects that a single European currency will have on commerce and trade.

Exercises

Explore several of the euro sites listed above.

1. What impact do you think the new euro will have on tourism in Europe?

2. What impact might the euro have on tourism in the United States and U.S. citizens traveling to Europe?

QUESTIONS FOR REVIEW AND DISCUSSION

1. As a travel counselor, what questions might you ask of a prospective tourist to determine his or her interest in a life-seeing or local hosting program?

2. What might be an obstacle to the optimistic projections of increased international tourism forecast in this chapter?

3. Intelligent, creative, sensitive tourism developments can actually improve the environment and heighten the appeal of an area. Give examples of how this might happen.

4. Can tourism enhance and improve a destination area's cultural and hospitality resources? Provide actual or hypothetical examples.

5. What is the expected trend in health-oriented accommodations and programs? Food services?

6. Can tourism really contribute to a narrowing of the "north-south gap"? What specific initiatives or programs do you think would help to make this happen?

7. What are the realistic prospects for a four-day workweek?

8. Does early retirement appeal to most workers?

9. How can tourism interests obtain a growing share of leisure market expenditures?

10. Specifically, in what way can world peace be enhanced by tourism?

SELECTED REFERENCES

Archdale, G. "Computer Reservation Systems and Public Tourist Office." *Tourism Management,* Vol. 14, No. 1, pp. 3–14, 1993.

Ashford, D. M. "Prospects for Space Tourism." *Tourism Management,* Vol. 11, No. 2, pp. 99–104, June 1990.

Chervenak, Larry. "Hotel Technology at the Start of the New Millennium." *Hospitality Research Journal* (The Futures Issue), Vol. 17, No. 1, pp. 113–120, 1993.

Christensen, Julia. "The Diversity Dynamic: Implications for Organizations in 2005." *Hospitality Research Journal* (The Futures Issue), Vol. 17, No. 1, pp. 69–86, 1993.

Collins, Galen R. *Hospitality Information Technology: Learning How to Use It.* Dubuque, IA: Kendall/ Hunt, 1992.

D'Amore, L. J., and Jafar Jafari. *Tourism: A Vital Force for Peace.* Montreal: First Global Conference, 1988.

Durocher, Joseph F., and Neil B. Niman. "Information Technology: Management Effectiveness and Guest Services." *Hospitality Research Journal* (The Futures Issue), Vol. 17, No. 1, pp. 113–120, 1993.

Edgell, David L. *World Tourism at the Millennium.* Washington, D.C.: U.S. Travel and Tourism Administration, 1993.

Edgell, David L., and Ginger Smith. "Tourism Milestones for the Millennium: Projections and Implications of International Tourism for the United States Through the Year 2000." *Journal of Travel Research,* Vol. 32, No. 1, pp. 42–46, Summer 1993.

Enz, Cathy A. "Organizational Architectures for the 21st Century: The Redesign of Hospitality Firms." *Hospitality Research Journal* (The Futures Issue), Vol. 17, No. 1, pp. 103–112, 1993.

Forbes, Robert J., and Maree S. Forbes. "Special Interest Travel," in *World Travel and Tourism Review,* Vol. 2, J. R. Brent Ritchie and Donald E. Hawkins, eds. Oxon, UK: C.A.B. International, 1992, pp. 141–144.

Foot, David K. *Boom, Bust and Echo: How to Profit from the Coming Demographic Shift.* Toronto: Macfarlane Walter & Ross.

Go, F. "The Role of Computerized Reservation Systems in the Hospitality Industry." *Tourism Management,* Vol. 14, No. 1, pp. 15–21, 1992.

Godbey, Geoffrey. "Time, Work, and Leisure: Trends That Will Shape the Hospitality Industry." *Hospi-tality Research Journal* (The Futures Issues), Vol. 17, No. 1, pp. 49–58, 1993.

Goeldner, Charles R. "Trends in North American Tourism." *American Behavioral Scientist,* Vol. 36, No. 2, pp. 144–154, November 1992.

Haywood, K. M. "A Strategic Approach to Managing Technology." *Cornell Quarterly,* Vol. 30, No. 1, pp. 39–45, 1990.

Hitchins, Fred. "The Influence of Technology on U.K. Travel Agents." *Travel and Tourism Analyst,* No. 3, pp. 88–105, 1991.

Hobson, Perry, and Muzaffer Uysal. "Infrastructure: The Silent Crisis Facing the Future of Tourism." *Hospitality Research Journal* (The Futures Issues), Vol. 17, No. 1, pp. 209–218, 1993.

Lago, Dan, and James Poffley. "The Aging Population and the Hospitality Industry in 2010: Important Trends and Probable Services." *Hospitality Research Journal* (The Futures Issue), Vol. 17, No. 1, pp. 29–48, 1993.

McRae, H. *The World in 2020: Power, Culture and Prosperity.* Boston: Harvard Business School Press, 1994.

Mieczkowski, Zbigniew. *World Trends in Tourism and Recreation.* Frankfurt: Peter Lang, 1990.

Mills, Susan F., and Hudson Riehle. "Food Service Manager 2000." *Hospitality Research Journal* (The Futures Issue), Vol. 17, No. 1 (1993), pp. 147–160.

Moore, Richard, and Scott Wilkinson. "Communications Technology." *Hospitality Research Journal* (The Futures Issue), Vol. 17, No. 1, pp. 133–146, 1993.

Mowlana, H., and G. Smith. "Tourism, Telecommunications, and Transnational Banking." *Tourism Management,* Vol. 11, No. 4, pp. 315–324, 1990.

Mueller, Hansruedi. "Long-Haul Tourism 2005—Delphi Study." *Journal of Vacation Marketing,* Vol. 4, No. 2, pp. 193–201, April 1998.

Nykiel, Ronald A. "Ten Trends to the Millennium." *Journal of Hospitality and Leisure Marketing,* Vol. 4, No. 2, pp. 25–48, 1997.

Parsa, H. G., and Mahmood A. Khan. "Quick Service Restaurants of the 21st Century: An Analytical Review of Macro Factors." *Hospitality Research Journal* (The Futures Issue), Vol. 17, No. 1, pp. 161–174, 1993.

Poon, A. "Tourism and Information Technologies." *Annals of Tourism Research,* Vol. 13, No. 4, pp. 531–549, 1988.

Poon, A. *Tourism, Technology and Competitive Strategies.* Oxon, UK: C.A.B. International, 1993.

Popcorn, Faith. *The Popcorn Report*. New York: Doubleday, 1991.

Powers, Thomas F. "The Standard World of 2005: A Surprise-Free Scenario." *Hospitality Research Journal*, Vol. 16, No. 1, pp. 1–19, 1992.

Prugh, Thomas. *Natural Capital and Human Economic Survival*. Solomons, MD: ISEE Press, 1995.

Reid, R. Dan, and Melvin Sandler. "The Use of Technology to Improve Service Quality." *Cornell Quarterly*, Vol. 33, No. 3, pp. 68–73, June 1992.

Ritchie, J. R. Brent. "Global Tourism Policy Issues: An Agenda for the 1990's." *World Travel and Tourism Review*, Vol. 1: Oxon, England: C.A.B. International, 1991.

Schor, Juliet B. *The Overworked American: The Unexpected Decline of Leisure*. New York: Basic Books, 1991.

Shafer, E. L. "Future Encounters with Science and Technology." *Journal of Travel Research*, Vol. 27, No. 4, pp. 2–7, Spring 1989.

Shanklin, Carol W. "Ecology Age: Implications for the Hospitality and Tourism Industry." *Hospitality Research Journal* (The Futures Issue), Vol. 17, No. 1, pp. 219–230, 1993.

Stipanuk, D. M. "Tourism and Technology: Interactions and Implications." *Tourism Management*, Vol. 14, No. 4, pp. 267–278, 1993.

Taylor, J., and W. Wacker. *The 500 Year Delta: What Happens After What Comes Next*. New York: HarperCollins, 1997.

WTO. *Tourism 2020 Vision: A New Forecast from the World Tourism Organization*. Madrid: World Tourism Organization, 1997.

Associations and Organizations

Adventure Travel Society
6551 S. Revere Parkway
Suite 160
Englewood, Colorado 80111

Air Transport Association of America
1301 Pennsylvania Avenue N.W.
Suite 1100
Washington, D.C. 20004

American Association of Museums
1575 Eye Street N.W.
Suite 400
Washington, D.C. 20005

American Association of Retired Persons
601 E. Street N.W.
Washington, D.C. 20049

American Automobile Association
1000 AAA Drive
Heathrow, Florida 32746

American Bus Association
1100 New York Avenue
Suite 1050
Washington, D.C. 20005

American Car Rental Association
1225 Eye Street N.W.
Suite 500
Washington, D.C. 20005

American Hotel and Motel Association
1201 New York Avenue N.W.
Washington, D.C. 20005

American Recreation Coalition
1225 New York Avenue N.W.
Suite 450
Washington, D.C. 20005

American Resort and Development Association
1220 L Street N.W.
Suite 510
Washington, D.C. 20005

American Society of Travel Agents
1101 King Street
Suite 200
Alexandria, Virginia 22314

American Youth Hostels
733 15th Street N.W.
Washington, D.C. 20005

Association of Retail Travel Agents
501 Darby Creek Road
Suite 47
Lexington, Kentucky 40509

Association of Travel Marketing Executives
P.O. Box 109
Riverdale, New Jersey 07457

Australian Tourist Commission
GPO Box 1545
Canberra, Australia 2601

Bureau of Economic Analysis
U.S. Department of Commerce
Washington, D.C. 20230

Bureau of the Census
Demographic Surveys Division
U.S. Department of Commerce
Washington, D.C. 20233

Canadian Tourism Commission
235 Queen Street
8th Floor, West Tower
Ottawa, Ontario K1A 0H6 Canada

Caribbean Tourism Association
20 East 46th Street
New York, New York 10017

Cruise Lines International Association
500 Fifth Avenue
Suite 1407
New York, New York 10110

Ecotourism Society
P.O. Box 755
North Bennington, Vermont 05257

European Travel Commission
1 Rockefeller Plaza
New York, New York 10020

Federal Aviation Administration
800 Independence Avenue S.W.
Washington, D.C. 20591

Gray Line Worldwide
Building C, Suite 300
2460 W. 26th Avenue
Denver, Colorado 80211

Hospitality Sales and Marketing Association
   International
1300 L Street N.W.
Suite 800
Washington, D.C. 20005

Institute of Certified Travel Agents
148 Linden Street
Wellesley, Massachusetts 02181

International Academy for the Study of Tourism
WTO Building
Capitan Haya, 42
28020 Madrid, Spain

International Airline Passengers Association
P.O. Box 700188
Dallas, Texas 75370

International Air Transport Association (IATA)
IATA Building
2000 Peel Street
Montreal, Quebec
Canada H3A 2R4

International Association of Amusement Parks and
   Attractions
1448 Duke Street
Alexandria, Virginia 22314

International Association of Convention and Visitors
   Bureaus
2000 L Street N.W.
Suite 702
Washington, D.C. 20036

International Association of Scientific Experts in
   Tourism (AIEST)
Varnbuelstrasse 19
CH-9000 St. Gallen
Switzerland

International Bureau of Social Tourism (BITS)
63, rue de la Loi
B-1040 Brussels, Belgium

International Federation of Women's Travel
   Organizations
13901 North 73rd Street
#210 B
Scottsdale, Arizona 85260

International Society of Meeting Planners
1224 North Nokomis, NE
Alexandria, Minnesota 56308

National Air Carrier Association
1730 M Street N.W.
Suite 806
Washington, D.C. 20036

National Association of Railroad Passengers
900 2nd Street, N.E.
Suite 308
Washington, D.C. 20002

National Association of RV Parks & Campgrounds
8605 Westwood Center Drive
Suite 201
Vienna, Virginia 22182

National Caves Association
4138 Dark Hollow Road
McMinnville, Tennessee 37110

National Park Service
Socio-Economic Studies Division
P.O. Box 25287
Denver, Colorado 80225

National Recreation and Park Association
22377 Belmont Ridge Road
Asburn, Virginia 20148

National Restaurant Association
1200 Seventeenth Street N.W.
Washington, D.C. 20036

National Ski Areas Association
133 S. Van Gordon Street
Lakewood, Colorado 80228

National Tour Association
546 East Main Street
P.O. Box 3071
Lexington, Kentucky 40596

National Trust for Historic Preservation
1785 Massachusetts Avenue N.W.
Washington, D.C. 20036

Pacific Asia Travel Association (PATA)
One Montgomery Street
Telesis Tower, Suite 10
San Francisco, California 94104

Recreation Vehicle Industry Association
P.O. Box 2999
1896 Preston White Drive
Reston, Virginia 20195

Society of American Travel Writers
4101 Lake Boone Trail
Suite 201
Raleigh, North Carolina 27607

Society of Incentive Travel Executives, Inc.
21 West 38th Street
10th Floor
New York, New York 10018

Tourism Industry Association of Canada
130 Albert Street
Ottawa, Ontario
Canada K1P 5G4

Tourist Railway Association
P.O. Box 1022
Madison, WI 53701-1022

Travel & Tourism Research Association
P.O. Box 2133
Boise, Idaho 83701

Travel Industry Association of America
1100 New York Avenue N.W.
Suite 450
Washington, D.C. 20005

United Motorcoach Association
113 South West Street
4th Floor
Alexandria, Virginia 22314

United States Tour Operators Association
342 Madison Avenue
Suite 1522
New York, New York 10173

Tourism Industries
International Trade Administration
U.S. Department of Commerce
Washington, D.C. 20230

United States Travel Data Center
1100 New York Avenue N.W.
Suite 450
Washington, D.C. 20005

Universal Federation of Travel Agents' Associations
  (UFTAA)
1 Avenue des Castelons
Entrée H
Monaco, Monaco MC-98000

World Tourism Organization
Calle Capitan Haya 42
Madrid, Spain E-28020

World Travel & Tourism Council
20 Grosvenor Place
London, SW1X 7TT
United Kingdom

U.S. State and Territory Contacts

Alabama
Alabama Bureau of Tourism and Travel
401 Adams Avenue
Montgomery, Alabama 36103

Alaska State Division of Tourism
333 Willoughby Avenue, 9th Floor
State Office Building
P.O. Box 110801
Juneau, Alaska 99811-0801

American Samoa Office of Tourism
P.O. Box 1147
Pago Pago AS 96799

Arizona Office of Tourism
2702 N. 3rd Street
Suite 4015
Phoenix, Arizona 85004

Arkansas Department of Parks and Tourism
One Capitol Mall
Little Rock, Arkansas 72201

California Division of Tourism
801 K. Street, Suite 1600
P.O. Box 1499
Sacramento, California 95814

Colorado Travel & Tourism Authority
1127 Pennsylvania Avenue
Denver, Colorado 80203

Connecticut Office of Tourism
505 Hudson Street
Hartford, Connecticut 06106

Delaware Tourism Office
99 Kings Highway
Box 1401
Dover, Delaware 19903

Visit Florida
661 East Jefferson Street
Suite 300
Tallahassee, Florida 32301

Georgia Department of Industry, Trade and Tourism
285 Peachtree Center Avenue
Marquis Tower Two, 10th Floor
P.O. Box 1776, Department TIA
Atlanta, Georgia 30303

Guam Visitors Bureau
401 Pale San Vitores Road
P.O. Box 3520
Tumon Guam 96911

Hawaii Tourism Office
250 South Hotel Street, 4th Floor
P.O. Box 2359
Honolulu, Hawaii 96813

Idaho Division of Tourism Development
700 West State Street
Boise, Idaho 83720

Illinois Bureau of Tourism
State of Illinois Center
100 West Randolph, Suite 3-400
Chicago, Illinois 60601

Indiana Tourism Division
One North Capitol
Suite 700
Indianapolis, Indiana 46204-2288

Iowa Division of Tourism
200 East Grand Avenue
Des Moines, Iowa 50309

Kansas Travel & Tourism Division
700 S.W. Harrison Street
Suite 1300
Topeka, Kansas 66603-3957

Kentucky Department of Travel Development
500 Mero Street #22
Frankfort, Kentucky 40601-1968

Louisiana Office of Tourism
P.O. Box 94291
Baton Rouge, Louisiana 70804-9291

Maine Office of Tourism
33 Stone Street
59 State House Station
Augusta, Maine 04333-0059

Marianas Visitors Bureau
P.O. Box 861
Saipan MP 96950

Maryland Office of Tourism Development
217 East Redwood, 9th Floor
Baltimore, Maryland 21202

Massachusetts Office of Travel & Tourism
100 Cambridge Street, 13th Floor
Boston, Massachusetts 02202

Travel Michigan
105 West Allegan, 3rd Floor
P.O. Box 30226
Lansing, Michigan 48933

Minnesota Office of Tourism
100 Metro Square
121 Seventh Place East
St. Paul, Minnesota 55101-2112

Mississippi Tourism Development Division
520 George Street
P.O. Box 849
Jackson, Mississippi 39201

Travel Montana
1424 Ninth Avenue
P.O. Box 200533
Helena, Montana 59620-0533

Nebraska Division of Travel & Tourism
301 Centennial Mall South
P.O. Box 94666
Lincoln, Nebraska 68509

Nevada Commission on Tourism
Capitol Complex
5151 South Carson Street
Carson City, Nevada 89710

New Hampshire Office of Travel and Tourism
Development
172 Pembroke Road
P.O. Box 1856
Concord, New Hampshire 03302-1856

New Jersey Division of Travel & Tourism
20 West State Street, CN826
Trenton, New Jersey 08625-0826

New Mexico Department of Tourism
491 Old Santa Fe Trail
Santa Fe, New Mexico 87503

New York State Division of Tourism
One Commerce Plaza
Albany, New York 12245

North Carolina Division of Tourism, Film, and Sports
 Development
301 North Wilmington
Raleigh, North Carolina 27601-2825

North Dakota Tourism Department
Liberty Memorial Building
604 East Boulevard
Bismarck, North Dakota 58505

Ohio Division of Travel & Tourism
7 South High Street
P.O. Box 1001
Columbus, Ohio 53215

Oklahoma Travel and Tourism Division
15 North Robinson, Suite 801
Oklahoma City, Oklahoma 73102

Oregon Tourism Commission
775 Summer Street N.E.
Salem, Oregon 97310

Pennsylvania Office of Travel, Tourism and Film
 Promotion
453 Forum Building
Harrisburg, Pennsylvania 17120

Puerto Rico Tourism Company
575 5th Avenue, 23rd Floor
New York, New York 10017

Rhode Island Economic Development Corporation
One West Exchange Street
Providence, Rhode Island 02903

South Carolina Department of Parks, Recreation &
 Tourism
1205 Pendleton Street, Suite 106
Edgar A. Brown Building
Columbia, South Carolina 29201

South Dakota Department of Tourism
Capitol Lake Plaza
711 East Wells Avenue
Pierre, South Dakota 57501-3369

Tennessee Department of Tourist Development
320 Sixth Avenue North
P.O. Box 23170
Nashville, Tennessee 37202-3170

Texas Tourism Division
1700 North Congress, Suite 200
P.O. Box 12728
Austin, Texas 78701

U.S. Virgin Islands Division of Tourism
78-123 Estate Contant
P.O. Box 6400
Charlotte Amalie, USVI 00802

Utah Travel Council
Council Hall
Salt Lake City, Utah 84114

Vermont Department of Tourism and Marketing
134 State Street
P.O. Box 1471
Montpelier, Vermont 05602

Virginia Tourism Corporation
901 East Byrd Street, 19th Floor
Richmond, Virginia 23219

Washington State Tourism Development Division
101 G.A. Building
P.O. Box 42500
Olympia, Washington 98504-2500

Washington, D.C. Convention and
 Visitors Association
1212 New York Avenue N.W.
Suite 600
Washington, D.C. 20005

West Virginia Division of Tourism and Parks
2101 Washington Street East
Charleston, West Virginia 25305

Wisconsin Department of Tourism
201 West Washington Avenue
Madison, Wisconsin 53702

Wyoming Division of Tourism
Frank Norris Jr. Travel Center
I-25 & College Drive
Cheyenne, Wyoming 82002-0660

America's Heartland
Station 8207
12755 State Highway 55
P.O. Box 59159
Minneapolis, Minnesota 55441

Capital Region USA, Inc.
c/o Maryland Office of Tourism Development
217 East Redwood Street
Baltimore, Maryland 21202

Discover New England
Unit C-3A, Heritage Place,
205 Worcester Court
East Falmouth, Massachusetts 02540

Foremost West
770 East South Temple, Suite B
Salt Lake City, Utah 84102

Great Lakes of North America
35 East Wacker Drive #1850
Chicago, Illinois 60601

Mississippi River Country
Station 8207
12755 State Highway 55
P.O. Box 59159
Minneapolis, Minnesota 55441

Rocky Mountain International
1815 Evans Avenue
P.O. Box 5031
Cheyenne, Wyoming 82003

Travel South USA
3400 Peachtree Road N.E.
Atlanta, Georgia 30326

Canadian Provincial Contacts

Alberta
Travel Alberta
Suite 300, 10155-102 Street
Edmonton, Alberta
Canada T5J 4G8
Phone: 1-800-661-8888
Web site: www.explorealberta.com

British Columbia
Tourism British Columbia
Ministry of Small Business, Tourism and Culture
Parliament Buildings
Victoria, B.C.
Canada V8V 1X4
Phone: 1-800-663-6000
Web site:
    www.tbc.gov.bc.ca/tourism/tourismhome.html

Manitoba
Travel Manitoba
155 Carlton Street, 7th Floor
Winnipeg, Manitoba
Canada R3C 3H8
Phone: 1-800-665-0040
Web site: www.gov.mb.ca/Travel-Manitoba

New Brunswick
Department of Economic Development, Tourism
   and Culture
P.O. Box 6000
Fredericton, New Brunswick
Canada E3B 5H1
Phone: 1-800-561-0123
Web site: www.gov.nb.ca/tourism

Newfoundland
Department of Tourism, Culture, and Recreation
4th Floor, Confederation Building Complex
P.O. Box 8700
St. John's, Newfoundland
Canada A1B 4K2
Phone: 1-800-563-6353
Web site: www.gov.nf.ca/tourism

Northwest Territories
NWT Arctic Tourism
PO Box 610
Yellowknife, Northwest Territories
Canada X1A 2N5
Phone: 1-800-661-0788
Web site: www.nwttravel.nt.ca

Nova Scotia
Nova Scotia Economic Development and Tourism
P.O. Box 519
5151 Terminal Road
Halifax, Nova Scotia
Canada B3J 2R7
Phone: 1-800-565-0000
Web site: http://explore.gov.ns.ca

Ontario
Ontario Ministry of Economic Development, Trade
   and Tourism
9th Floor, 77 Bloor Street West
Toronto, Ontario
Canada M7A 2R9
Phone: 1-800-668-2746
Web site: www.ontario-canada.com

Prince Edward Island
Department of Economic Development and Tourism
Shaw Building, 5th Floor
105 Rochford Street
P.O. Box 2000
Charlottetown, Prince Edward Island
Canada C1A 7N8
Phone: 1-800-463-4734
Web site: www.gov.pe.ca/development//index.asp

Québec
Tourisme Quebec
C.P. 979
Montreal, Québéc
Canada H3C 2W3
Phone: 1-800-363-7777
Web site:
http://www.tourisme.gouv.qc.ca

Saskatchewan
Saskatchewan Tourism Authority
5th Floor, 1919 Saskatchewan Drive
Regina, Saskatchewan

Canada S4P 3V7
Phone: 1-800-667-7191
Web site:
http://www.gov.sk.ca/econdev/investment/sixsctrs/
tourism

Yukon
Yukon Tourism
P.O. Box 2703
Whitehouse, Yukon
Canada Y1A 2C6
Phone: 1-800-661-0494
Web site: http://www.touryukon.com

APPENDIX B

SOME SUGGESTED INFORMATION SOURCES

Introduction

In this day and age of information technology, the first recommendation is to seek information using the Internet and locating useful web sites. A number of web sites have been listed at the end of most chapters in this book, and hopefully you have already explored many of them. The travel industry is well represented on the Web. In fact, travel is the Internet's second largest commerce area after computer technology. Destinations, airlines, accommodations, car rentals, attractions, tour operators, cruises, and travel agencies from all over the world have pages on the Web. Government tourism offices, tourism associations, and visitor and convention bureaus have home pages and in addition to their own information the majority provide links to other sites. There are also the generic engines such as Yahoo, InfoSeek, Magellan, Lycos, or Excite that can be used.

The second recommendation is don't forget other sources. There are still many valuable information sources in addition to the Internet. Make sure you include the library and print services in your information search. Following are some information source suggestions.

Information Centers and Libraries

Centre Des Hautes Études Touristiques, 8 Perspective Mozart, Parc Mozart, 13100 Aix-en-Provence, France.

Cornell Hotel School Library, Cornell University, Statler Hall, Ithaca, New York 14853.

Information Center, American Hotel and Motel Association, 1201 New York Avenue, Washington, D.C. 20005.

Tourism Research and Documentation Centre (TRDC), 235 Queen Street, Ottawa, Ontario K1A 0H6, Canada.

Travel Reference Center, Business Research Division, Campus Box 420, University of Colorado, Boulder, Colorado 80309.

William F. Harrah College of Hotel Administration Library, University of Nevada, Las Vegas, 4505 Maryland Parkway, Box 456039, Las Vegas, Nevada 89154.

Yearbooks, Annuals, and Other Sources

Air Transport. Air Transport Association of America, 1301 Pennsylvania Avenue, N.W., Washington D.C. 20004. Annual.

Civil Aviation Statistics of the World. International Civil Aviation Organization, 1000 Sherbrooke Street West, Montreal, Quebec, Canada H3A 2R2. Annual.

Compendium of Tourism Statistics. World Tourism Organization, Capitán Haya, 42 28020 Madrid, Spain. Annual

Impact of Travel on State Economies. Travel Industry Association of America, 1100 New York Avenue, N.W., Washington, D.C. 20005. Annual.

Leisure, Recreation and Tourism Abstracts. CAB International, Wallingford, Oxon OX10 8DE, United Kingdom. Quarterly.

1998 Meetings Market Report. Cahners Travel Group, 500 Plaza Drive, Secaucus, New Jersey 07094. Biennial.

1998 Outlook for Travel and Tourism. Travel Industry Association of America, 1100 New York Avenue, N.W., Washington, D.C. 20005. Annual.

1997–98 Survey of State Tourism Offices. Travel Industry Association of America, 1100 New York Avenue, N.W., Washington, D.C. 20005. Annual.

1998 Travel Agency Survey. Cahners Travel Group, 500 Plaza Drive, Secaucus, New Jersey 07094. Biennial.

PATA Annual Statistical Report. Pacific Asia Travel Association, 1 Montgomery Street, Telesis Tower, San Francisco, California 94104. Annual.

Tourism's Top Twenty. Travel Industry Association of America, 1100 New York Avenue, N. W., Washington, D.C. 20005. Quadrennial.

Tourism Works for America. National Travel and Tourism Awareness Council, Travel Industry Association of America, 1100 New York Avenue, N.W., Washington, D.C. 20005. Annual.

Travel Industry World Yearbook: The Big Picture. Child and Waters Inc., P.O. Box 610, Rye, New York 10580. Annual.

Trends in Travel and Tourism Advertising in United States Measured Media. Ogilvy and Mather, 9th Floor, 309 West 49th Street, New York, New York 10019. Annual.

World Air Transport Statistics. International Air Transport Association, 2000 Peel Street, Montreal, Quebec, Canada H3 A2 R4. Annual.

Academic Journals

ANATOLIA: An International Journal of Tourism and Hospitality. Anatolia, P.K. 589-06445, Yenisehir, Ankara, Turkey.

Annals of Tourism Research. Elsevier Science Ltd. Pergamon, Langford Lane, Kidlington, Oxford OX5 1GB United Kingdom.

Asia Pacific Journal of Tourism Research. Department of Tourism, Dong-A-University, 840, Hadan-Dong, Saha-gu, Pusan 604-714 Korea.

Cornell Hotel and Restaurant Administration Quarterly. Elsevier Science Inc., Box 945, New York, New York 10010.

Current Issues in Tourism. Channel View Books/Multilingual Matters Ltd., Frankfurt Lodge, Clevedon Hall, Victoria Road, Clevedon B521 7HH, United Kingdom.

Festival Management & Event Tourism. Cognizant Communication Corporation, 3 Hartsdale Road, Elmsford, New York 10523.

FIU Hospitality Review. Florida International University, North Miami Campus, 151 1st St. and Biscayne Blvd., N. Miami, Florida 33181.

Hospitality and Tourism Research Journal. Council on Hotel, Restaurant and Institutional Education, 1200 17th St., Washington, D.C. 20036.

Hospitality and Tourism Educator. Council on Hotel, Restaurant and Institutional Education, 1200 17th St., Washington, D.C. 20036.

International Journal of Contemporary Hospitality Management. MCB University Press Limited, 60/62 Toller Lane, Bradford, West Yorkshire, BD8 8BY, United Kingdom.

International Journal of Hospitality Management. Elsevier Science Ltd., Bampfyble, Exeter, EX1 2AH, United Kingdom.

The International Journal of Hospitality and Tourism Technology. Department of Hotel, Restaurant and Travel Administration, University of Massachusetts, Amherst, Massachusetts 01003.

Journal of Applied Recreation Research. Wilfrid Laurier University Press, Waterloo, Ontario, Canada N2L 3C5.

Journal of Convention & Exhibition Management. Haworth Press Inc., 10 Alice St., Binghamton, New York 13904.

Journal of Hospitality and Leisure Marketing. Haworth Press Inc., 10 Alice Street, Binghamton, New York 13904.

Journal of International Hospitality & Leisure and Tourism Management. Haworth Press Inc., 10 Alice St., Binghamton, New York 13904.

Journal of Leisure Research. National Recreation and Parks Association, 22377 Belmont Ridge Road, Ashburn, Virginia 20148.

Journal of Park and Recreation Administration. Sagamore Publishing, P.O. Box 647, Champaign, Illinois 61824-0647.

Journal of Restaurant & Foodservice Marketing. Haworth Press Inc., 10 Alice Street, Binghamton, New York 13904.

Journal of Sports Tourism. Sports Tourism International Council, International Headquarters, P.O. Box 5580-Station F, Ottawa, Canada K2C 3M1.

Journal of Sustainable Tourism. Channel View Books/Multilingual Matters, Ltd., Frankfurt Lodge, Clevedon Hall, Victoria Road, Clevedon BS21 7SJ, United Kingdom

Journal of Tourism Studies. Department of Tourism, James Cook University, Townsville, Queensland, Australia 4811.

Journal of Travel Research. Sage Publications, Inc., 2455 Teller Road, Thousand Oaks, California 91320.

Journal of Travel & Tourism Marketing. Haworth Press Inc., 10 Alice St., Binghamton, New York 13904.

Journal of Vacation Marketing. Henry Stewart Publications, Russell House, 28-30 Little Russell St., London WC1A 2HN, England.

Leisure Sciences. Taylor and Francis Ltd., Pankine Rd., Basingstoke, Hants RG2 48PR, United Kingdom.

Leisure Studies. Chapman & Hall Journals, Dept. 2-6, Boundary Row, London, SE1 8HN, United Kingdom.

Managing Leisure. Chapman & Hall, ITPS Ltd., Cheriton House, North Way, Andover, SP10 5BE, United Kingdom.

Pacific Tourism Review. Cognizant Communication Corporation, 3 Hartsdale Road, Elmsford, New York 10523-3701.

Praxis—The Journal of Applied Hospitality Management. Cecil Day School of Hospitality Management, Georgia State University, Atlanta, Georgia 30303.

International Journal of Tourism Research. John Wiley and Sons Ltd. Baffins Lane, Chichester, West Sussex, PO19 1UD, United Kingdom.

The Tourist Review. AIEST, Varnbuelstrasse 19, CH-9000, St. Gallen, Switzerland.

Tourism Analysis. Cognizant Communication Corporation, 3 Hartsdale Road, Elmsford, New York 10523.

Tourism, Culture & Communication. Victoria University of Technology, Department of Hospitality and Tourism Management, P.O. Box 14428, MCMC, Melbourne, Victoria 8001, Australia.

Tourism Economics. In Print Publishing Ltd., Coleridge House, 4-5 Coleridge Gardens, London NW6 3QH, United Kingdom.

Tourism Geographies. Routledge Journals Department, 29 West 35th Street, New York 10001-2299.

Tourism Management. Elsevier Science Ltd., Bampfylde Street, Exeter EK1 2AH Devon, United Kingdom.

Tourism Recreation Review. Centre for Tourism Research and Development, A-965/6 Indira Nagar, Lucknow 226016 India.

Travel & Tourism Analyst. The Economist Intelligence Unit Ltd., 40 Duke Street, London, W1A 1DW, United Kingdom.

Visions in Leisure and Business. Appalachian Associates, 615 Pasteur Avenue, Bowling Green, Ohio 43402.

Trade Publications

Air Transport World. Penton Publishing, Inc., 1350 Connecticut Avenue N. W., Washington, D.C. 20036.

Courier. National Tour Association, 546 East Main Street, Lexington, Kentucky 40508.

Hotels: The Magazine of the Worldwide Hotel Industry. Cahners, 1350 East Touhy Avenue, Des Plaines, Illinois 60018.

Lodging. American Hotel and Motel Association, 1201 New York Avenue N. W., Washington, D.C. 20005.

Meetings and Conventions. Cahners Travel Group, 500 Plaza Drive, Secaucus, New Jersey 07094.

Meeting News. Miller Freeman, One Penn Plaza, New York, New York 10119.

OAG Travel Magazines. OAG, 1775 Broadway, New York, New York 10019.

Successful Meetings. Bill Communications, 355 Park Avenue South, New York, New York 10010.

Tour and Travel News. Miller Freeman, One Penn Plaza, New York, New York 10019.

Travel Agent Magazine. Advanstar. Communications, Inc., 131 West First Street, Duluth, Minnesota 55802.

Travel Industry Indicators. James V. Cammisa, Jr., Inc., PO Box 6616, Miami, Florida 33154.

Travel Trade. Travel Trade, 15 West 44th Street, New York, New York 10036.

Travel Weekly. Cahners Travel Group, 500 Plaza Drive, Secaucus, New Jersey 07094.

Books

Bowen, John, James Makens, and Steve Shoemaker. *Casino Marketing.* New York: John Wiley and Sons, 1999.

Davidson, Rob, and Robert Maitland. *Tourism Destinations.* London: Hodder and Stoughton, 1997.

Dickenson, Robert, and Andrew Vladmir. *Selling the Sea.* New York: John Wiley and Sons, 1996.

Eade, Vincent, and Raymond Eade. *Introduction to the Casino Entertainment Industry.* Upper Saddle River, NJ: Prentice-Hall, 1997.

Fridgen, Joseph D. *Dimensions of Tourism.* East Lansing, Michigan: Educational Institute of the American Hotel and Motel Association, 1991.

Friedheim, Eric. *Travel Agents.* New York: Universal Media, Inc., 1992.

Gartner, William. *Tourism Development: Principles, Processes, Policies.* New York: John Wiley and Sons, 1996.

Gartrell, Richard. *Destination Marketing: For Convention and Visitor Bureaus.* Dubuque, Iowa: Kendall/Hunt, 1996.

Gee, Chuck, James Makens, and Dexter Choy. *The Travel Industry.* New York: John Wiley and Sons, 1997.

Getz, Donald. *Event Management and Event Tourism.* Elmsford, New York: Cognizant Communication Corporation, 1997.

Goldblatt, Joe. *Special Events.* New York: John Wiley and Sons, 1996.

Goldblatt, Joe. *The Dictionary of Event Management.* New York: John Wiley and Sons, 1996.

Gunn, Clare A. *Tourism Planning.* New York: Taylor and Francis, 1994.

Harrison, Lynn, and Winston Husbands. *Practicing Responsible Tourism.* New York: John Wiley and Sons, 1996.

Holloway, J. Christopher. *The Business of Tourism.* London: Longman, 1998.

Inkpen, G. *Information Technology for Travel and Tourism.* Essex: Longman, 1998.

Inskeep, Edward. *Tourism Planning.* New York: John Wiley and Sons, 1991.

Jackson, Ian. *An Introduction to Tourism.* Victoria, Australia: Hospitality Press, 1997.

Kahn, Mahmood, Michael Olsen, and Turgut Var. *VNR's Encyclopedia of Hospitality and Tourism.* New York: Van Nostrand Reinhold, 1993.

Krippendorf, Jost. *The Holiday Makers.* London: Butterworth-Heinemann, 1989.

Kotler, Philip, John Bowen, and James Makens. *Marketing for Hospitality and Tourism.* Upper Saddle River, New Jersey: Prentice-Hall, 1999.

Lavery, Patrick. *Travel and Tourism.* Huntingdon, England: Elm Publications, 1996.

Lickorish, Leonard J., and Carson L. Jenkins. *An Introduction to Tourism.* Oxford, UK: Butterworth-Heinemann, 1997.

Medlik, S. *Dictionary of Travel, Tourism and Hospitality.* Oxford, England: Butterworth-Heinemann, 1996.

Medlik, S. *Understanding Tourism.* Oxford, England: Butterworth-Heinemann, 1997.

Mill, Robert Christie, and Alastair M. Morrison. *The Tourism System.* Dubuque, Iowa: Kendall/Hunt, 1998.

Morgan, Nigel, and Annette Pritchard. *Tourism, Promotion and Power.* New York: John Wiley and Sons, 1998.

Morrison, Alastair. *Hospitality and Travel Marketing.* Albany, New York: Delmar Publishers, 1996.

Nash, Dennison. *Anthropology of Tourism.* Oxford, UK: Pergamon, 1996.

Nickerson, Norma P. *Foundations of Tourism.* Upper Saddle River, New Jersey: Prentice-Hall, 1996.

Oppermann, Martin. *Sex Tourism and Prostitution.* Elmsford, New York: Cognizant Communications Corporation, 1998.

Pearce, Philip, Gianna Moscardo, and Glenn Ross. *Tourism Community Relationships.* Oxford, UK: Pergamon, 1996.

Powers, Tom, and Claytan Barrows. *Introduction to Management in the Hospitality Industry.* 6th ed. New York: John Wiley and Sons, 1999.

Ritchie, J. R. Brent, and Charles Goeldner. *Travel, Tourism, and Hospitality Research: A Handbook for Managers and Researchers.* New York: John Wiley and Sons, 1994.

Starr, Nona. *Viewpoint: An Introduction to Travel, Tourism and Hospitality.* Upper Saddle River, New Jersey: Prentice-Hall, 1997.

Sheldon, Pauline. *Tourism Information Technology.* Oxon, UK: CAB International, 1997.

Stowkowski, Patricia A. *Riches and Regrets: Betting on Gambling in Two Mountain Towns.* Niwot, Colorado: University Press of Colorado, 1996.

Superintendent of Documents. *Outdoor Recreation: A Reader for Congress.* Washington, D.C.: U.S. Government Printing Office, 1998.

Swarbrooke, John. *The Development and Management of Visitor Attractions.* Woburn, Massachusetts: Butterworth-Heinemann, 1995.

Theobald, William, ed. *Global Tourism: The Next Decade.* Oxford, UK: Butterworth-Heinemann, 1994.

Turner, Louis, and John Ash. *The Golden Hordes.* London: Constable, 1975.

Van Harssel, Jan. *Tourism: An Exploration.* Upper Saddle River, New Jersey: Prentice-Hall, 1994.

Vukonic, Boris. *Tourism and Religion.* Oxford, UK: Pergamon, 1996.

Walker, John. *Introduction to Hospitality.* Upper Saddle River, New Jersey: Prentice-Hall, 1999.

Witt, Stephen F., and Luiz Moutinho. *Tourism Marketing and Management Handbook.* London: Prentice-Hall, 1994.

GLOSSARY

A

Accommodation Facilities for the lodging of visitors to a destination. The most common forms are hotels, motels, campgrounds, bed & breakfasts (B&Bs), dormitories, hostels, and the homes of friends and relatives.

Adventure travel A form of travel in which the perception (and often the reality) of heightened risk creates a special appeal to certain segments of the travel market. Examples include white-water rafting and mountaineering.

Affinity group A group bound together by a common interest or affinity. Where charters are concerned, this common bond makes them eligible for charter flights. Persons must have been members of the group for six months or longer. Where a group configuration on a flight is concerned, the minimum number of persons to which the term would apply may be any number determined by a carrier rule-making body. They must travel together, on the departure and return flight, but they can travel independently where ground arrangements are concerned.

Agreement, bilateral An agreement regulating commercial air services between two countries.

Agreement, multilateral An agreement regulating commercial air services between three or more countries.

Airline Reporting Corporation (ARC) A corporation set up by the domestic airlines that is concerned with travel agent appointments and operations.

Air Transport Association of America (ATA or ATAA) The authoritative trade association maintained by domestic airlines.

Alliance An association to further the common interests of the parties involved.

American plan A room rate that includes breakfast, lunch, and dinner.

Attractions Facilities developed especially to provide residents and visitors with entertainment, activity, learning, socializing, and other forms of stimulation that make a region or destination a desirable and enjoyable place.

B

Balance of payments or trade Practical definition of an economic concept. Each nation is assumed to be one tremendous business doing business with other big businesses. When a business (country) sells (exports) more than it buys (imports), there is a positive balance of payments. When a country buys (imports) more than it sells (exports), there is a negative balance of trade. Tourism is a part of balance of trade classified under Services.

Built environment The components or activities within a tourism destination that have been created by humans. These include the infrastructure and superstructure of the destination, as well as the culture of its people, the information, and technology they use, the culture they have developed, and the system of governance that regulates their behaviors.

C

Cabotage The ability of an air carrier to carry passengers exclusively between two points in a foreign country.

Capacity The number of flights multiplied by the number of aircraft seats flown.

Carrier A public transportation company, such as air or steamship line, railroad, truck, bus, monorail, and so on.

Carrier—participating A carrier over whose routes one or more sections of carriage under the air waybill or ticket is undertaken or performed.

Carrying capacity The amount of tourism a destination can handle.

Charter The bulk purchase of any carrier's equipment (or part thereof) or passengers or freight. Legally, charter transportation is arranged for time, voyage, or mileage.

Charter flight A flight booked exclusively for the use of a specific group of people who generally belong to the same organization or who are being "treated" to the flight by a single host. Charter flights are generally much cheaper than regularly scheduled line services. They may be carried out by scheduled or supplemental carriers.

Clients Those persons who patronize travel agencies.

Climate The meteorological conditions, including temperature, precipitation, and wind that prevail at, or within, a tourism region.

Code sharing An agreement between two airlines which allows the first carrier to use the airline designation code on a flight operated by the second carrier.

Concierge This is a wonderful European invention. Depending on the hotel, the concierge is a superintendent of service, source of information, and link between the guest and city or area.

Conservation Management of human use of the environment to yield the greatest sustainable benefit to present generations while maintaining its potential to meet the needs and aspirations of future generations.

Consolidator A travel firm that makes available airplane tickets, cruise tickets, and sometimes other travel products at discount prices. These are usually sold to retail travel agencies but are also sometimes sold directly to the public.

Consortium A privately owned firm (not owned by its members as is a cooperative) that maintains a list of preferred suppliers. This list is made available to members, resulting in superior commissions earned.

Continental breakfast A beverage, roll, and jam. Sometimes a fruit juice is added. In Spain, Holland, and Norway, cheese, meat, or fish is sometimes included.

Continental plan A hotel rate that includes continental breakfast.

Cooperative A membership group of retail travel agencies that offers advantages to each agency member, such as lower prices on wholesale tour offerings, educational opportunities, problem solving, and other aids.

Coupon flight The portion of the passenger ticket and baggage check or excess baggage ticket that indicates particular places between which the coupon is good for carriage.

Culture The totality of socially transmitted behavior patterns, arts, beliefs, institutions, and all other products of human work and thought that are characteristic of the destination population.

D

Destination The ultimate stopping place according to the contract of carriage. Can also be defined as a place offering at least 1500 rooms to tourists.

Development Modification of the environment to whatever degree and the application of human, financial, living, and nonliving resources to satisfy human needs and improve the quality of human life.

Domestic independent travel (DIT) A tour constructed to meet the specific desire of a client within a single country.

E

E-commerce The transaction of commercial dealings (advertising and promotion, sales, billing, payment, and customer servicing) by electronic means rather than through traditional "paper" channels.

Entertainment Performances, shows, or activities that attract and hold the attention of visitors. A successful destination will seek to integrate the travel, hospitality, and entertainment dimensions of tourism.

Environment All aspects of the surroundings of human beings both cultural, natural, and man-made, whether affecting human beings as individuals or in social groupings.

Eurailpass A special pass sold overseas for unlimited first-class rail travel in 15 European countries. Youth and children's passes are also available. They are sold for varying numbers of days.

European plan A hotel rate that includes only lodging, no food.

Events Includes a broad range of "occurrences," "happenings," and "activities" that are designed around various themes, with a view to creating or enhancing interest in the destination. Local festivals and mega-events (such as the Olympic Games and world expositions) have proven to be most effective.

Excursionist A traveler who spends less than 24 hours at a destination.

F

Familiarization tour Free or reduced rate arrangements for travel agents or public carrier employees that is intended to stimulate them to sell travel or tours as experienced on the "fam" tour.

Federal Aviation Administration (U.S.) A governmental regulatory agency concerned with airport operation, air safety, licensing of flight personnel, and other aviation matters.

Flag carrier An international airline often owned and/or operated by the government of its home country.

Flight, connecting A flight that requires a change of aircraft and flight number en route to a destination.

Flight, direct A flight that may make intermediary stops en route to a destination.

Flight, nonstop A flight that travels to a destination without any intermediary stops.

Food services Facilities that provide food and meals to visitors to a destination. The most common forms are restaurants, fast-food outlets, snack bars, cafeterias, food fairs, and the homes of friends and relatives.

Foreign independent travel (FIT) An international prepaid tour for an individual or family planned for them by a travel agent or tour operator. It is individually designed.

Frequent flyer plan Program where bonuses are offered by the airlines to passengers who accumulate travel mileage.

G

Governance The system that defines the organizations, the processes, and the complex of political institutions, laws, and customs through which power and authority within a destination are exercised.

Ground arrangements All those services provided by a tour operator after reaching the first destination. Also referred to as land arrangements.

Group inclusive tour (GIT) A tour that includes group air and ground arrangements for a minimum of 15 persons. They may or may not stay together as a group for both the land and air portions of the trip.

H

Hub and spoke A system that feeds connecting passengers into major gateway airports from short-haul or point-to-point downline routes.

I

Incentive tour A tour arranged especially for employees or agents of a company as a reward for achievement, usually sales. Spouses are typically included on the trip.

Inclusive tour A travel plan for which prearranged transportation, wholly by air or partly by air and partly by surface, together with ground facilities (such as meals, hotels, etc.) are sold for a total price.

Infrastructure The facilities, equipment, and installations needed for the basic functioning and daily lives of the residents of a region. These include communication systems, water and sewage facilities, public protection, health, transportation, and education systems.

Information Knowledge obtained from investigation, study, or instruction.

International Air Transport Association (IATA) The authoritative trade association maintained by international and overseas airlines.

Internet service providers Companies that provide domain space for others on computer servers they own, companies that provide travel information that they develop, and companies that provide a combination of the two.

M

Modified American plan A room rate that includes a full American breakfast and lunch or dinner, usually dinner.

O

Open jaw A pairing of two or more nearby destinations which allows a passenger to arrive at one airport and depart from a second.

Open skies An agreement between two or more nations which allows its air carriers to fly unrestricted within each others' borders; the United States and the Netherlands recently signed an open skies pact.

P

Package A prepaid tour that includes transportation, lodging, and other ingredients, usually meals, transfers, sightseeing, or car rentals. May be varied, but typically includes at least three ingredients sold at a fixed price.

Passport Issued by national governments to their own citizens as verification of their citizenship. It is also a permit to leave one's own country and return.

Pension A French word widely used throughout Europe meaning guest house or boarding house.

People Those humans who reside in, or visit, a tourism destination.

Physiography The physical geography of a tourism destination.

R

Reception agency A tour operator or travel agency specializing in foreign visitors. American Adventure Tours is such a company.

Retail travel agency Mostly in the United States. Travel agents sell carriers' tickets and wholesalers' or operators' tours. In perspective, retail agents are commissioned or subagents. Usually, all or most of the gross revenue is from commissions.

Revalidation The authorized stamping or writing on the passenger ticket showing that it has been officially altered by the carrier.

Run-of-the-house A hotel term to guarantee a firm price that applies to any room in the house. Often a hotel will provide a superior room, if available, in an effort to please the guest and the tour operator.

S

Spa A hotel or resort providing hot springs or baths and other health-enhancing facilities and services.

Superstructure The facilities, equipment, and facilities needed to meet the particular needs of the visitors to a region. These include accommodation and food services, visitor information and services, tourism attractions, special events, supplementary transportation, and special education and training programs for front-line staff and industry managers.

Supplier An industry term meaning any form of transportation, accommodations, and other travel services used by a travel agency or tour operator to fulfill the needs of travelers.

T

Tariffs The published fares, rates, charges, and/or related conditions of carriage of a carrier.

Technology The entire body of methods and materials used to achieve commercial, industrial, or societal objectives.

Time share Concept of dividing the ownership and use of a lodging property among investors.

Tour-basing fare A reduced, round-trip fare available on specified dates, and between specified times, only to passengers who purchase preplanned, prepaid tour arrangements prior to their departure to specified areas.

Tourism (1) The entire world industry of travel, hotels, transportation, and all other components, including promotion, that serves the needs and wants of travelers. Tourism today has been given new meaning and is primarily a term of economics referring to an industry. (2) Within a nation (political subdivision or transportation-centered economic area of contiguous nations), the sum total of tourist expenditures within their borders is referred to as the nation's tourism or tourist industry and is thus ranked with other national industries. More important than just the total monetary product value of tourism is its role in the balance of trade. Here tourism earnings from foreigners truly represents an export industry. Tourism is an "invisible" export.

Tourist A person who travels from place to place for nonwork reasons. By U.N. definition, a tourist is someone who stays for more than one night and less than a year. Business and convention travel is included. This thinking is dominated by balance-of-trade concepts. Military personnel, diplomats, immigrants, and resident students are not tourists.

Tour operator A company that specializes in the planning and operation of prepaid, preplanned vacations and makes these available to the public, usually through travel agents.

Tour organizer An individual, usually not professionally connected with the travel industry, who organizes tours for special groups of people, such as teachers, church leaders, farmers, and the like.

Tour package A travel plan that includes several elements of a vacation, such as transportation, accommodations, and sightseeing.

Tour wholesaler A company that plans, markets, and (usually) operates tours. Marketing is always through intermediaries such as retail travel agents, an association, a club, or a tour organizer—never directly to the public as is sometimes done by tour operators. The wholesaler would not operate the tour if, for example, it was functioning as a wholesaler in the United States for tours operated by a foreign firm. In industry jargon, tour operator and tour wholesaler are synonymous.

Transportation The act or process of carrying or moving people or goods, or both, from one location to another.

Travel (*see* **Tourism**) Often interchangeable with tourism. Actually, this term should represent all direct elements of travel. Included in the term travel are transportation, vacations, resorts, and any other direct passenger elements, including but not limited to national parks, attractions and auto use for any of the above purposes. To make a journey from one place to another.

Travel industry services Includes those organizations, firms, and individuals that provide a diverse range of services that enable and facilitate travel, as well as make it more convenient and less risky. Examples include computer support services, financial services, insurance, information, and interpretation.

Travel trade Includes those organizations, firms, and individuals that provide various elements of the total travel experience.

V

Vacation ownership A term often used to describe resort timesharing.

Visa Document issued by a foreign government permitting nationals of another country to visit or travel. The visa is usually stamped on pages provided in one's passport but may also be a document fastened to the passport.

Y

Yield management The use of pricing and inventory controls, based upon historical data, to maximize profits by offering varying fares over time for the same product.

SELECTED TOURISM ABBREVIATIONS

▼

AAA	**American Automobile Association**
ABA	**American Bus Association**
ABC	**Advanced Booking Charter**
ACTO	**Association of Caribbean Tour Operators**
AHMA	**American Hotel and Motel Association**
AIEST	**International Association of Scientific Experts in Tourism**
AIT	**Academie Internationale du Tourisme**
ATME	**Association of Travel Marketing Executives**
Amtrak	**National Railroad Passenger Corporation**
AP	**American Plan**
APEX	**Advance Purchase Excursion Fare**
ARC	**Airlines Reporting Corporation**
ARDA	**American Resort and Development Association**

ARTA	**Association of Retail Travel Agents**
ASTA	**American Society of Travel Agents**
ATA	**Air Transport Association of America**
ATC	**Air Transport Committee (Canada)**
BIT	**Bulk Inclusive Tour**
BTA	**British Tourist Authority**
CHRIE	**Council on Hotel, Restaurant and Institutional Education**
CITC	**Canadian Institute of Travel Counselors**
CLIA	**Cruise Lines International Association**
COTAL	**Conference of Tourist Organizations of Latin America**
CRS	**Computerized Reservations System**
CTA	**Caribbean Travel Association**
CTC	**Canadian Tourism Commission**
CTC	**Certified Travel Counselor**

CTO	Caribbean Tourism Organization
DIT	Domestic Independent Tours
DMO	Destination Management Organization
DOT	U.S. Government Department of Transportation
ECOSOC	Economic and Social Council of the United Nations
EP	European Plan
ETC	European Travel Commission
FAA(U.S.)	Federal Aviation Administration
FHA	Federal Highway Administration
FIT	Foreign Independent Tour
GIT	Group Inclusive Tour
HSMAI	Hotel Sales Management Association International
IAAPA	International Association of Amusement Parks and Attractions
IACVB	International Association of Convention and Visitors Bureaus
IAF	International Automobile Federation
IAST	International Academy for the Study of Tourism
IATA	International Air Transport Association
IATAN	International Airlines Travel Agent Network
ICAO	International Civil Aviation Organization
ICC	Interstate Commerce Commission
ICCL	International Council of Cruise Lines
ICSC	International Council of Shopping Centers
ICTA	Institute of Certified Travel Agents
IFWTO	International Federation of Women's Travel Organizations
IHA	International Hotel Association
IIPT	International Institute for Peace Through Tourism
IIT	Inclusive Independent Tour
ILO	International Labor Organization

ISMP	International Society of Meeting Planners
ISTTE	International Society of Travel and Tourism Educators
IT	Inclusive Tour
ITC	Inclusive Tour Charter
IYHF	International Youth Hostel Federation
MAP	Modified American Plan
MCO	Miscellaneous Charges Order
MPI	Meeting Professionals International
NACOA	National Association of Cruise Only Agents
NAPVO	National Association of Passenger Vessel Owners
NARVPC	National Association of RV Parks and Campgrounds
NCTA	National Council of Travel Attractions
NCUTO	National Council of Urban Tourism Organizations
NRA	National Restaurant Association
NRPA	National Recreation Parks Association
NTA	National Tour Association
OAG	Official Airline Guide
OAS	Organization of American States
OECD	Organization for Economic Cooperation and Development
PAII	Professional Association of Innkeepers International
PATA	Pacific Asia Travel Association
RAA	Regional Airline Association
RPM	Revenue Passenger Miles
RTF	Rural Tourism Foundation
RVIA	Recreational Vehicle Industry Association
SATW	Society of American Travel Writers
SITE	Society of Incentive Travel Executives
S&R	Sell and Report
TI	Tourism Industries (U.S.)
TIA	Travel Industry Association of America
TIAC	Tourism Industry Association of Canada

TTRA	Travel and Tourism Research Association
UFTAA	Universal Federation of Travel Agents Association
UNDP	United Nations Development Program
UNESCO	United Nations Educational, Scientific and Cultural Organization
USTDC	United States Travel Data Center
USTOA	United States Tour Operators Association

WATA	World Association of Travel Agents
WHO	World Health Organization
WTAO	World Tourism and Automobile Organization
WTO	World Tourism Organization
WTTC	World Travel and Tourism Council
WWW	World Wide Web
XO	Exchange Order

INDEX